Ex
Libris

Lowell R. Kantzer

POLITICAL
THOUGHT

from Plato
to the present

McGRAW-HILL SERIES IN POLITICAL SCIENCE

JOSEPH P. HARRIS, CONSULTING EDITOR

POLITICAL THOUGHT

from Plato to the present

M. JUDD HARMON

DEPARTMENT OF POLITICAL SCIENCE
UTAH STATE UNIVERSITY

McGRAW-HILL BOOK COMPANY
NEW YORK   SAN FRANCISCO   TORONTO   LONDON

POLITICAL THOUGHT: From Plato to the Present

Copyright © 1964 by McGraw-Hill, Inc. All Rights Reserved.
Printed in the United States of America. This book, or parts thereof,
may not be reproduced in any form without permission
of the publishers.
Library of Congress Catalog Card Number 63-20724

26625
5 6 7 8 9 – M P – 9 8

PREFACE

Most academicians and probably all college teachers experience, at some point in their lives, the urge to write a book. The majority are able to resist the temptation; I am one of those who could not. This is the most compelling reason for the appearance of yet another history of political thought. The world could undoubtedly muddle along without the contribution. I trust that colleagues and students will not feel that the world is a poorer place because of it.

I make no claims for a revolutionary approach. The book deals with the men and the developments that I have come to regard as indispensable in my own teaching of an introductory course in political thought. Aside from a presentation of the fundamental ideas of the major political philosophers, I have attempted to do two things. First, I have supplied some historical background for the men and their ideas. Second, I have tried to show the significance of the ideas in terms of the present. It seems to me that without an understanding of these references to past and present the study of political thought is largely useless.

I have made an effort to be fair-minded in presenting and appraising the political ideas with which the book is concerned. Surprisingly, I found this impartiality less difficult than I had anticipated. Gunnar Myrdal has said that objectivity for the writer in the social sciences requires that he state his preconceptions. The point is well taken, and I shall comply by admitting that I am a democrat. This has not precluded an appreciation of the views of such philosopher aristocrats as Plato or Burke or Hobbes. Whether or not one agrees, in whole or in part, with what they had to say, one must admit that these great exponents of political thought are important—and they wrote magnificently. It is only in the last chapter of the book, in which fascism and national socialism are discussed, that I admit to any considerable departure from an impartial attitude. I cannot regard these ideas as anything but villainous. An ideology that justifies the cold-blooded extermination of millions of human beings cannot be considered dispassionately—at any rate not by me.

I have not had help from a great many persons in writing this book.

But those who have given assistance have given so much that I am embarrassed not to have their names appear with my own on the cover. Two friends have read every word of the manuscript. Milton R. Merrill of Utah State University often disputed my historical facts and interpretations and criticized my composition. As it turned out he was right on every occasion. Francis D. Wormuth of the University of Utah took valuable time from his own scholarly efforts to give me the benefit of his encyclopedic knowledge of political thought. I also wish to acknowledge the help given by Moyle Q. Rice and Milton C. Abrams of Utah State University. Finally a word of thanks to my secretary, Miss Kathleen Hansen, whose efficiency has been exceeded only by her cheerful cooperativeness.

I wish that in addition to giving these good people credit for whatever may be praiseworthy in this work I could hold them responsible for its shortcomings. Justice demands, however, that I assume this burden myself.

M. JUDD HARMON

CONTENTS

one

INTRODUCTION

This book deals with the history of political thought. The subject is highly important, and no one avoids its impact; yet certainly only a few are informed on it. The bulk of the political opinion men freely express is formulated without knowledge of or reference to the long history of the ideas that have had such great influence upon the political climate and institutions existing today. We shall be concerned here with the major phases of that development. Many writers have explained the distinctions between political theory, political philosophy, political science, ideology, and other branches of the subject. Such discussion, in spite of its value, is not essential to our purposes. Our attention will be generally directed to the study of political thought as it has involved attempts to explain, justify, or criticize the various aspects of political relationships, that is, the relationships between those who govern and those who are governed. As we shall see, a great many subjects are subsumed under this heading. Every member of society is affected by these relationships; he always has been and he always will be. He may give the matter much of his attention or very little of it, but he cannot escape the fact that what he is and what he does are determined to a considerable degree by the political system of which he is a part. And underlying the political system is political thought.

It may be argued that while political relationships and political acts have significance for the individual, political thought does not. Action may be taken and institutions may be established; but although political theories are formulated to justify them, those actions and institutions are not in fact any different from what they would be in the absence of the theories. According to this argument, political theory is merely ex post facto and has no causative effect. Karl Marx substantially agreed. Ideas, he held, are determined by material conditions; they cannot alter those conditions—unless, it might be added, the ideas are created by a Marx. The point has some merit. Political theories are often rationalizations of actions or positions already taken or of institutions previously established. Many illustrations come to mind, one of the most recent being the formulation of a pseudo-Hegelian theory by the Fascists of Italy to support a regime which had long been established.

The ex post facto position, however, is an oversimplification. Ideas do influence action. A theory that has been developed to justify an existing situation almost invariably affects subsequent events. The theory of separation of powers was enunciated by Montesquieu after his (somewhat faulty) observations of the operation of the English government had convinced him of the correctness of the theory. But in later years that theory strongly influenced the constitutional form taken by a number of governments, especially the government of the United States. As a consequence, the lives of millions have been affected. The theories of the past, including those that have been largely discarded, such as the divine right of kings, form a part of our heritage of thought. They influence us in a multitude of ways. They lead to the development of personal conceptions, on the basis of which we make judgments on matters of public policy. If the ideas that go into the formulation of these conceptions are false, our judgments may be bad. If they are true, the judgments may be good. A study of political thought should lead the student to an appraisal of his own views. It should also be helpful in the creation and elaboration of a set of political ideas through which intelligent judgments may be made.

We shall consider shortly some of the ways in which men use political thought when they defend or attack political acts or institutions. First, however, we shall give some thought to a few general "rules" that should be borne in mind in any appraisal of a particular political idea. To a great extent the validity of a political theory is relative to the circumstances in which it is formulated. The relationship of governor and governed, manifested in the establishment of a special kind of political institution with its underlying ideals may be entirely appropriate to a given set of conditions and completely inappropriate under different circumstances. It would be naïve today to speak of the direct democracy of the New England town meeting or the Greek city-state as if all its principles were applicable to the large and impersonal nation state of the present. Similarly the theoretical premises which underlay the constitutional operation of the simple agrarian states of the eighteenth century can hardly be deemed adequate to the functioning of the complex industrial states of the twentieth century. Yet we have a tendency to continue to adhere to anachronistic ideas and institutions. For reasons to be explored further in the course of this work, people cling to political forms and the ideals underlying them in the face of conditions that make the forms unsuitable to their needs. They are frequently so strongly conditioned by the prevalent pattern of the ideas of the community that they rarely think of questioning them. People generally need a major catastrophe, such as war or economic depression, to jolt them into a significant shift in their ideological leanings.

Men are of a predominantly conservative temper. They prefer the familiar difficulties to the possible benefits of the unknown. Unless they face overwhelming problems they would rather try to solve them within the framework of the known society than confront a new way of life, which would be the concomitant of the adoption of new institutions and ideals. This proclivity is challenged by the inexorability of historical change. Nothing is more certain than that the world changes. There are many causes of change—war, technological progress, discovery of new lands, improved education, to name only a few. Although many of these changes are beneficial, opening new vistas of opportunity for many people, they are also feared, resented, and opposed because they upset the status quo—because they alter or eliminate the familiar. Problems arise when the popular reaction takes the form of opposition to any alterations of political institutions.

Governmental forms must be adapted to meet the needs of its citizens; the essential purpose of government, at least in democratic polities, is to serve those needs. And as needs change, so too must government. This does not mean that a new constitution and governmental structure will be required every few years, but it does imply that alterations must occur almost continuously; new laws must be enacted, new agencies must be established, and new services must be provided. It is extraordinary that the same person who witnesses with approval the revolutionary changes of the scientific-industrial age will often at the same time strenuously oppose all efforts to adapt government to the new circumstances. As has been said many times, eighteenth-century government is not adequate to the demands of the space age. The inadequacy ought to be thoroughly understood. History demonstrates clearly that in the long run either governments will alter peacefully to accord with the necessities of changing times, or they will be thrown out and new ones installed. In the struggle between the advocates of change and the defenders of the status quo, political thought always plays a significant role.

Another "rule" is that political thought deals with moral postulates and that wide differences of opinion in ethical matters are possible. Most of the political thinkers with whom we shall be concerned seek to develop a theory that will lead to the good life for the individual. Yet political theorists differ widely in describing the good life. A theorist's conclusions will depend largely upon his view of human nature. Is man naturally selfish, or is he altruistic? Is he intelligent or stupid? Is he aggressive or cowardly or timid? More important, are men equal or unequal? If they are equal, in what way or ways is their equality evidenced? These are the most significant questions for the political theorist, and indeed, for anyone who is attempting to arrive at some intelligent conclusions on the subject of political theory. Because political thought deals with moral postulates, it is difficult to approach the subject objectively. If fascism, with the moral premises involved in that ideology, were accepted as a desirable system, the means to its achievement could be considered objectively. The problem is that because people differ strongly in their moral preferences, and because, therefore, a great many persons do not want to pursue the goal of fascism, a consensus on any such matter is impossible to attain. The student of political thought may well formulate a political theory perfectly satisfactory to himself, a theory that may indeed set all his doubts at rest, but he will find it much more difficult to come to an agreement with his neighbor on the subject. The natural scientist has few problems of this kind. The medical researcher attempts to develop a cure for cancer without first having to debate with his colleagues whether or not cancer is bad and should be cured. The engineer may argue with his fellows over the best procedure to build a dam; but the building of the dam generally does not involve a debate over moral principles, or if it does, the debate becomes a moral or political, rather than an engineering, argument.

We now direct our attention to some of the problems with which political thought is concerned. Many are perennial, and no permanent solutions to them have yet been discovered. The purpose of this work is not to provide solutions but merely to point out the problems and consider a few of the answers that have been suggested by some of the political thinkers in history who are generally recognized as authorities. The student is entitled to his own conclusions with respect to the validity of the theories discussed. Many may prove to be attractive, many repulsive, but in any case they have all been important and have had their impact not only upon the development of ideas but also upon the establishment and functioning of political institutions.

If we grant that men require a government, we meet an initial question: Who shall govern? One man, a few, or many, or a combination of all these? What should be the governmental form? Men have long distinguished among three governmental functions—the making of the law, the enforcement of law, and the judging of disputes concerning the meaning and application of law. Should power to perform these functions be vested in the hands of a single person or agency, or should the power be divided and allotted to several persons or agencies? Does it make any difference which of these alternatives is selected, and if so, why? What are the possible advantages of one form as compared with another?

Closely related to this question of who shall govern is the basis on which the governor shall be chosen. That he should be a "good" man all will agree, but substantial disagreement is certain to arise over the meaning of "good." To the Italian patriot, Machiavelli, the good ruler is the strong and unscrupulous despot who can achieve and maintain national unity. To Plato the good ruler is the wise man, the philosopher-king, who knows better than others what ought to be done and how to do it. To the Church in the Middle Ages the good ruler is the godly man, and his selection must be made or at least approved by the Church. To the German Nazi he is the natural leader who has survived and forged his way to the top in the competitive struggle to which all men are subjected. To the democrat the good governor is one who best serves the interest of the majority of the people to whom he is also responsible.

How should the governor be selected? Should he be the man who has the strength to impose himself upon the people irrespective of their wishes in the matter? Does might, in this instance, mean right? Should he be selected or approved by the Church? If devoutness is a necessary attribute of rulership, what better way can be conceived than Church appointment of the sovereign? Should selection of the governor be in the hands of the owners of property? Property qualifications for voting were widespread in Europe and the United States during the eighteenth and nineteenth centuries, and the use of property as a measure of political ability is very old in political history. Should the right to choose the governor be in the hands of those who are educated? If so, what kind of education and how much should be required?

Or should all persons have an equal right to choose those who govern them? In the matter of suffrage, at least, can it properly be said that all men are equal? The problem has plagued men through the centuries. In the strict sense, obviously many differences exist among human beings—distinctions of mentality, of physical strength, of sex, of age, and of race. All of them have been used to justify restrictions upon the principle of political (as well as social and economic) equality. The trend of democratic communities has been gradually to abandon such distinctions and to insist that whatever be the differences among humans, all men are entitled to an equal voice in the selection of those who are to govern them. In these communities, age (aside from citizenship and residency) is the principal barrier that separates those who may from those who may not vote and hold public office. The other side of the coin is represented by those communities, such as Nazi Germany, which have expanded rather than limited the restrictions upon political equality. A hierarchical view of society evolved in Germany in the thirties, which culminated in the grotesque theory of the "master race" and the too nearly successful attempt to destroy the "subhumans."

Closely associated with the disputes over equality has been the problem of majority rule. The matter, which is far too complex to be considered in detail here, will be given considerable attention in subsequent chapters. The problem, however, troubles even democratic polities. Although people generally believe that most issues ought to be resolved according to the will of the majority, they also recognize some limitations of the principle. In the constitutions of free countries these limitations are specified in "bills of rights," which preserve the liberty of the individual in matters relating to speech, press, assembly, petition, religion, and others, even in the face of majority opposition. Why the individual should need such protection and how far it should be carried are matters that have intrigued generations of interested thinkers. Their opinions on these important questions will be explored at length.

Assuming the possibility of obtaining a consensus with regard to the important problem of the selection of governors, we still must consider the question of what those governors may legitimately do. What are the proper limits of state power? What areas of human activity should be regarded as beyond the scope of governmental regulatory authority? Here again wide differences of opinion prevail, and each opinion is supported by a body of political thought. In recent times the doctrines of fascism and national socialism have asserted that individual freedom is a false value and that the only true "freedom" consists in the complete subjection of the individual to the state. In this view no human activity should be considered exempt from the pervasive authority of the state. Diametrically opposed to the fascist-Nazi doctrine, which exalts the state, is the doctrine of anarchism, which holds that the state is a barrier to human progress and perfection. According to the anarchists, the state and all political authority should be abolished. Without the imposition of authority, they contend, the human spirit will flower and develop its full potential. Men are innately good, and if they were not corrupted by evil institutions they could live in peace with their fellows, the only restrictions necessary being those that naturally flow from the dictates of their consciences. These doctrines, of fascism and national socialism on the one hand, and anarchism on the other, assume completely different views of human nature. The first is extremely pessimistic about the ability of man to govern himself; the second is inordinately optimistic in its assumption that human nature is so good, so altruistic, that no governmental organization whatsoever is required.

Somewhere in between these two extremes lie the many opinions concerning the desirable balance of individual liberty and authority to be maintained. Most political thinkers, indeed most persons, agree that both authority and freedom are necessary to the good life. They believe that men, collectively, are neither all good nor all bad. Therefore, while a government must regulate conduct in some aspects of life, such regulation need not be imposed upon all human activity. As the complexities of life have multiplied in consequence of the accelerating scientific-industrial revolution, less attention has been paid, in the development of political thought, to the matter of the "goodness" or "badness" of human nature. Life in modern civilization is so involved and so difficult that even a band of angels would obviously need some kind of government to accomplish their purposes.

The "in-between" position is sensible and has long been espoused by the peoples of the democracies of the West. But merely to accept the idea that the good life calls for a judicious balance of freedom and authority is far from solving the political problems of the community. Honest and conscientious men can and do disagree, often bitterly, over what constitutes a "judicious balance." It has been justly said that democracy is the most difficult of all systems of government. The difficulty is incurred because democracy cannot draw a hard and fast line between the respective realms of liberty and authority; those who live in democracies are constantly engaged in disputes over where the line should be drawn at any given moment. Should government permit Communists openly to advocate the overthrow of free government? If so, the Communists may succeed, and free government may disappear. But if government proscribes such advocacy, it thereby curbs freedom of speech, and as a result free government is less free. Here is a genuine dilemma over a question that is by no means merely hypothetical. Should government establish a system of medical insurance for its people? To do so may improve health but will also impose limits upon individual action in areas where freedom formerly prevailed. Should government prohibit the private exploitation of natural resources in certain sections of the public domain in order to provide additional recreation facilities for the public? To do so may be highly desirable in many respects, but the prohibition will limit the liberties of some people.

Almost all important public issues involve controversy over the respective limits of authority and freedom. It is impossible to evolve a formula for the solution of these problems that will satisfy everyone. Many have tried and failed. Constitutions may serve as guides, but experience has demonstrated that in order to be successful, in order to maintain their viability, constitutions must be flexible enough to accommodate differences of opinion and changes of interpretation. For changing circumstances necessitate alterations in the line between liberty and authority. An industrial society, it is generally conceded, demands a greater degree of governmental regulation of the economy than does a primitive agrarian society. But an industrial society may also witness a considerable expansion of civil liberties. The problem is very complex and not likely to become simpler. Indeed the search for simple solutions has proved to be highly dangerous. As we shall see when we consider the doctrines of fascism and national socialism (Chapter 21), perhaps the greatest appeal of the emerging dictatorships of the 1920s and 1930s lay in their promise to relieve the people's anxieties engendered by the problems of a complex industrial civilization. The solution, though couched in mystical terms, involved the forfeiture of individual liberty. The people were told that they must trade liberty (which, it was contended, was valueless anyway) for the security assured to them by a leader who would solve their problems. The exchange proved to be a poor bargain for the people. Even if the promised security had been forthcoming, the people would probably have found the cost too great. But security was illusory; death and devastation were the result of the agreement.

If we are to live with our fellows and enjoy the advantages of communal life, some sacrifice of personal interest must be made to the community interest. This point is understood even by the democratic communities with the strongest tradition of individualism, and it is a corollary of the problem of achieving the proper balance of freedom and authority. No one person can be permitted to seek his own interest, to pursue his own goals, without consideration of the effect his actions may have upon others. For centuries the individual pursuit of self-interest was rigidly restricted by kings, emperors, and feudal lords. When the authoritarian power of governments was broken in the revolutions of the seventeenth and eighteenth centuries, the tendency was to supplant the theories of absolutism with those of individualism and *laissez faire,* which demanded limitations upon governmental power and supported the idea that the unrestricted (or at least the little-restricted) pursuit of individual interest would benefit the community as a whole. The reaction to absolutism, however, created troublesome problems. A particularism, often akin to anarchy, led to dissension within free communities and threatened to tear them apart. Probably it is normal for each person to think that what benefits him will benefit everyone, but experience has amply demonstrated the fallacy of the belief. There is a public as well as a private good. Each must on occasion give way to the other. The problem is to arrive at agreement on the matter of when one or the other should prevail and to do so peacefully, without destroying the social fabric. The solution of this difficult problem has sometimes been sought, unfortunately, in the total sacrifice of individualism to some kind of totalitarian system.

What are the criteria by which the actions of government may be judged? A great many have been suggested. Plato maintained that a good political system will provide justice for all; and his *Republic* is, in part, a definition of justice and a statement of the manner in which it can be secured. The Christian Fathers believed that good government helps man to live so that he will be enabled to enter the kingdom of God, and its principles must accord with God's law. To the Stoics and others the natural law appeared to incorporate the principles of good government and to impose restrictions upon the authority of rulers. There were, as we shall see, differences of opinion with regard to the content of the natural law, but for many centuries hardly anyone doubted the existence of such a law. For Machiavelli the excellence of government was to be gauged by the degree of success it enjoyed in achieving and maintaining national unity. Thomas Hobbes's judgment was based upon the ability of government to safeguard the lives of citizens. John Locke and other members of the "natural-rights" school held that men were naturally endowed with the rights of life, liberty, and property, and that governments which inadequately protected those rights should forfeit their authority. Jeremy Bentham and the utilitarians argued that the function of government was to secure the "greatest happiness of the greatest number," and Bentham developed a "felicific calculus" by which the success of government in accomplishing this énd could be measured. The foregoing opinions constitute a sample of the proposals made rather than a comprehensive summary of those we shall later consider. They are sufficient to indicate the nature and the scope of the problem. The matter merits our attention. As individuals and as members of interest groups we may be too prone to judge the actions of government solely in material terms. We are, we may assert, taxed too much; we are underpaid; our business or farm is overregulated; too much is spent for foreign aid. These are all real and important matters, but if we could appraise them in terms of some underlying principle other than that of their personal and material effect, we should have a more valuable criterion.

We live in a world dominated as never before by considerations of foreign policy. We speak in terms of the "free world," the "Communist world," and the "uncommited or neutral nations." One of the major elements of world struggle since the close of World War II has involved the contest between communism and the West for influence among the neutral countries. Almost every conceivable strategy has been employed —force, propaganda, threats, foreign aid, military assistance, and ideology. The last-named is by no means the least significant. Communism has a highly developed and flexible ideology with which it attempts to woo the uncommitted nations to its side. That much of the ideology is without foundation in fact and is unsupported by historical evidence does not mean that it lacks appeal. It promises a vastly improved life, particularly to the poverty-ridden and depressed peoples who comprise a substantial majority within the countries to which the appeals are directed. It attributes the miserable condition of the masses in the underdeveloped countries to the imperialist colonial policies of the Western nations, and there is enough truth in the charges to make them persuasive. Communism's own variety of imperialism is often not recognized, and its dangers are too often deprecated. Communists argue that the democratic ideology of the West is merely camouflage for exploitation; their own system, they say, will bring material and aesthetic progress.

The appeal of communism might be countered more effectively by emphasizing democratic ideas in a more positive manner. Too often this alternative has been rejected in favor of a confused and sometimes hysterical anticommunism. Too much attention has been given to calling the Communists liars and blaming all the troubles of the world upon them. We venture here the opinion that this is an ineffective tactic which will not persuade those to whom the appeal is made. Ideas alone will not succeed in winning the friendship and support of the uncommitted peoples for either of the contending parties. Nevertheless, the people who have not made up their minds warrant a great deal of attention. The need is for effective ideas, constructive rather than reactionary. But democratic ideas, if they are to be effective, cannot merely be put together by experts and exported ready-made for the consumption of those toward whom they are directed; they must be representative of the people of a democracy and incorporate their fundamental views. In the West considerable confusion exists as to precisely what the people's views are. A great deal is said in support of the democratic ideals of liberty, equality, majority rule, minority rights, voting privileges, and all the rest, but the ambiguity of the statements shows little understanding of the complications and contradictions involved in such ideas. It is not unusual to hear a speaker enthusiastically endorse two mutually contradictory democratic principles. Democracy can draw upon a substantial tradition of political thought, but to do so sensibly requires some study of that tradition. Supporters of democracy will also want to know the equally long tradition of antidemocratic ideas and to understand why those ideas can be attractive. A wise military commander needs not only to know the strength of his own troops but as much as he can of the enemy's resources. Any contestant should make his appraisals as objective as possible, always granting, of course, that he wants his own side to win.

two

THE GREEK
CITY-STATE

Men are to a great extent products of their institutional environment. Probably Marx exaggerated the importance of this generalization; yet we cannot deny that it has considerable validity. It justifies us in prefacing a consideration of the political ideas of the great philosophers, Plato and Aristotle, with a discussion of the Greek city-state, its inhabitants and its institutions. The brilliance of the personalities who occupied the stage of the city-state sometimes obscures the stage itself. We shall do well to bear in mind not only that the men molded the institutions, but that they were also molded by the institutions. Socrates, Plato, and Aristotle might have been regarded as outstanding thinkers had they spoken and written in some environment other than that of the city-state; but the fact remains that they and others did speak in this environmental context, and that what they spoke and wrote was conditioned by the society within which they functioned. Even when they attacked the society the premises of their assault were supplied by the city-state.

The personal and intimate city-state of Greece was far different from the leviathan nation-state of the twentieth century. And although much of the vocabulary of modern politics derives from city-state sources, we must, in using that vocabulary, understand that its meanings have altered substantially in the course of more than two thousand years. Some political or economic device that worked well for the Greeks and was admired by them might be worthless in a large and modern democratic

11

republic. The lessons of city-state politics must be deduced from a proper understanding of their institutional environment. No one could interpret the rationale of United States foreign policy without a knowledge of those isolating factors that were so important in determining policy in the first years of the Republic. No one can gain a proper perspective of the philosophies of Plato and Aristotle without some understanding of the world in which they lived.

It is impossible to discuss *the* city-state as if all city-states were the same. Among the many city-states in Greece were vast social and political differences. Despite the common ties of language and religion, wars were commonplace. The differences stimulated interest in political thought and its development. For the purposes of this study, it is the city-state of Athens that merits attention, and for compelling reasons. Athenian experiments in democratic government and in the pursuit of the good life have intrigued generations of scholars. Athens was the center of culture and education in the ancient world, and her influence was so great that she retained her unique position for many years subsequent to her defeat and decline as an economic and military power. Men of good will are interested in living with their fellows in a spirit of equality and comradeship; they resent and reject autocracy. Athens, which for a brief period in history was able to enjoy the fruits of better living in a democracy, is a more rewarding subject of study than Sparta, which scorned the laxity of Athenian society and lived the cold and comfortless life of the barracks. Sparta's power declined as did that of Athens, but when Sparta's military power was lost, all was lost. The cultural heritage that sustained the Athenians could not console Spartans in their period of decline. Athens lives on in the contributions she has made. Sparta is dead.

Yet, while Athens is cited here as an example of democracy, we must understand that Athenian democracy did not emerge full-blown, but was a stage in a long political development. The transition from a simple pastoral society into one of landowners and tenants and ultimately into a commercial economy was accompanied by a succession of governmental forms, from monarchy to aristocracy, from aristocracy to tyranny, and from tyranny to democracy. Each change involved a serious struggle between those who held and those who sought political power. When it came, democracy did not stand unchallenged. It had to fight to maintain itself against the demands of the rich and well born. The latter asserted their claims in the name of property rights and social distinction. The majority sought a philosophic answer, and the issue was joined.

> Political theory owed its existence in Greece to the need of correcting a theory already in vogue, and political thought began as soon as the Many attempted to answer by argument the claims of aristocratic prestige. From

the beginning of the sixth century to the close of the fourth—from Solon and Theognis to Plato and Aristotle—the weighing of the claims of the wise and virtuous Few against those of the Many is a constant staple of Greek speculation.[1]

Even when democracy was most popular, many still ridiculed its underlying assumptions and attacked its institutions. Indeed, such attacks and the defenses of democracy against them occupy a great deal of the Greek thinkers' attention. That little of an original nature has been proposed by way of argument, pro or con, since that time is evidence of the far-reaching nature of political speculation of the ancient Greeks. Nor must we await the arrival on the scene of Socrates, Plato, and Aristotle, to see the beginnings of interest in political philosophy. As early as Homer's time, Greeks were concerned with ideas relating to an ethical basis of politics. The ideas may not have been consciously democratic, but men were already debating such subjects as government by consent and the rule of law. And long before Plato, Hesiod was pleading the cause of the agricultural worker and demonstrating the role of the economy in the establishment of social justice.

Development of the City-state Form

Geography was a determining factor in the development of the city-state. Mountains and sea divided Greece into a number of narrow valleys, and each provided the means of support for a limited population. Since access to other valleys was discouraged by the topography, communities developed in comparative isolation. The Greek did not consciously create the city-state form; he grew into it and developed with it.[2] It was as natural to him as is the nation-state to the twentieth-century citizen. The city-state was eventually to become an anachronism. Alone it could not withstand the onslaught of the empires that attacked it. Although the Greeks strove to form effective federations, they were never long successful, for the city-state mentality was an effective bar to unification just as nationalism is currently a bar to world unity.

Within the valleys the Greeks tilled their fields and developed a unique civilization. At a strategic point in the valley they built a city. This was the defense center of the valley community to which the inhabitants could repair in case of attack; the acropolis provided the heaviest fortification and was the focal point of the defense system. Defense, however, was not the only reason for the city's growth. The Greeks were gregarious, and the city was a social and recreational center. It was the

[1] Ernest Barker, *Greek Political Theory: Plato and His Predecessors*, 4th ed., Barnes & Noble, Inc., New York, 1951, p. 4.

[2] Gustave Glotz, *The Greek City and Its Institutions*, Alfred A. Knopf, Inc., New York, 1930, p. 1.

political hub of the valley, and in a community in which politics was everybody's business, the gathering place of the discussants was a highly important spot.

The city-state was, above all, a unified community. Although some citizens lived in the city and some in the country, there was no urban-rural conflict, that distinguishing feature of contemporary American civilization which has strong political, economic, and social ramifications. To the Greek the city was a center of community activity. It belonged to all and was not the exclusive possession of the city dweller. The latter spent much time in the country and took pride in the cultivated valley of the city-state even as the inhabitants of the country enjoyed the city, visited it often, and gloried in the magnificence of its buildings and the greatness of its civic institutions.

Social Classes in the Athenian City-state

The city-state was small in territory and population. At the time of its greatest expansion, Athens occupied only a little more than a thousand square miles of land. Widely divergent estimates of population have been made, and the subject is highly speculative. It is also impossible accurately to ascertain the ratios of the three principal classes that composed the city-state. Roughly, however, we may place the total population at between two hundred thousand and four hundred thousand, although some estimates are much higher. Of this total the citizen class formed approximately one-third; the slave class was probably somewhat larger; and the metic or resident-foreigner group was about half the size of the citizen class. Population pressure was a real problem for the Athenian, for although the overall population was not large, the territory to which it had to adjust was small. Agriculture was a significant factor in the economy, and the number who might be supported by the land was limited.

The existence of the metic class demonstrates some of the peculiarities of city-state citizenship and its value in the mind of the Athenian. The metic was a free man who was generally active in the commercial life of the community. Often he accumulated great wealth. But wealth or even long residence availed him little in the achievement of the coveted citizenship that was the right of the citizen by birth. Citizenship might be granted the metic in individual cases by special legislative action, but by no standard legal procedure might he become a naturalized citizen. His actions were more circumscribed by law than were those of the citizen. He was also compelled to pay special taxes from which the citizen was exempt, and he had to pay an extra fee for military protection.

The influence of slavery upon the Athenian civilization is the subject of conflicting opinion. Unquestionably the influence has been both minimized and exaggerated. Certainly Athenian culture would have been different without slavery. There were more slaves than citizens, and the duties they performed freed the citizen for more active participation in civic affairs. Still the point should not be unduly stressed. The ordinary Athenian did not live a life of luxury with slaves performing all menial duties while the master devoted full time to political and philosophical discussion. In general the slave worked with the master, and neither had a high standard of living. The citizen was perhaps more interested in the performance of civic functions than in a probably unattainable life of luxury. The Southern particularist in the United States prior to the Civil War, who argued that democracy is dependent upon a leisure class supported by slaves, and that the Athenian society offers convincing proof of this, had no valid argument.[3]

The institution of slavery in Athens was far different from that which existed in nineteenth-century America. Although the slave was a kind of property, he was protected by law and had a large measure of freedom, both of speech and of action. No master could put a slave to death, and an owner might be required to sell a slave whom he had mistreated. Physical assault on a slave by a person other than the master was punishable under the criminal law. The state might intervene to ensure the bond servant's protection. The social and economic position of the Athenian slave also was not only unlike the slave's position in the United States, but was, in fact, far better than his status in other Greek city-states. Many Athenian slaves were owned by the state and were employed as miners and mariners of the merchant fleet. Privately owned slaves were often tenant farmers and sharecroppers, and many were artisans and shopkeepers. Domicile separate from that of the master was common, and in many instances the city slave conducted his own business, paying a share of his earnings or income to the master. Stranger still, slaves occupied many positions of a governmental nature. The Athenian "bureaucracy" on the lower levels was largely made up of state slaves who, over the years, acquired some real power by virtue of their knowledge of the functioning of the governmental agencies to which they were attached. Since elective positions held by the citizens were of short tenure, generally one year, the slave civil servant was able to guide and direct the citizen official who was not so well instructed in the intricacies of public administration. There were also public slaves who held offices considered beneath the dignity of the citizen to occupy. Slaves were policemen, executioners, jailers, maintenance men, and construction workers on public projects.[4]

While slavery was accepted by the citizen as an integral part of community life, certain factions strongly opposed it. The arguments later

[3] George H. Sabine, *A History of Political Theory*, 3d ed., Holt, Rinehart and Winston, Inc., New York, 1961, p. 4.
[4] Glotz, *op. cit.*, p. 260.

employed by the American abolitionists were common in the Athenian democracy. The opponents of slavery held that it created artificial distinctions between man and man, in opposition to the spirit of democracy and detrimental to the community. The idea of equality has always been an essential ingredient of the democratic faith. The average Athenian accepted this fundamental tenet but applied it only to the relationships existing among members of the citizen class. There were, however, those who insisted that such an interpretation was excessively narrow and who demanded the abolition of slavery in the interest of a broader application of the democratic principle. The abolitionist movement never gained popular support, but the moral issues raised remained to plague subsequent generations confronted with similar problems.

Despite the existence of large and active noncitizen classes, it was the citizens who were important and whose activities and ideas are the subject of study and speculation. We must distinguish between the Athenian and the current connotations of citizenship. To the citizen of the modern democratic nation, citizenship is largely an impersonal thing implying the existence of certain rights with which the state may not interfere or which may be protected by the state against interference by private groups or governmental agents. The contemporary citizen is often a loyal member of many organizations whose activities bear no direct relationship to the state. Few citizens actively participate in governmental affairs aside from the occasional casting of a ballot. Government, especially the national government, is a thing apart. It may be admired or reviled but only as an agency that operates at a distance and has only occasionally a direct, personal, and apparent influence upon the lives of the citizens. Although the impact of modern government upon the activities of the citizenry is great, most persons make their decisions, perform their daily tasks, and seek their entertainment without any undue concern with government or any interference from it. The ties that bind together the inhabitants of the nation-state include common citizenship, but many more of their relationships have little or nothing to do with the state or politics.

Democracy and Citizenship in the Athenian City-state

Citizenship had a unique meaning for the Athenian citizen. His relations with his fellow citizens and with the state were, because the state was small, far more personal and intimate than they could be in the modern state. If any key expressions can unlock the meaning of the democracy of Athens, the phrases "spirit of equality" and "sense of belonging" might do so. The citizen did not think in terms of rights held *against* the encroachments of the state any more than he would have thought of rights held against himself. He was a part of the state, and the state was part of him. It is significant that Plato, who indicted Athenian democracy in his *Republic,* was deeply concerned with working out a plan of community organization which, while it was not democratic and left little in the way of political action for the citizen to perform, was based upon the ideal of *belonging.*

To the Athenian most questions were political questions. Every act affecting the welfare of others was a political act and subject to regulation. Professor McIlwain has expressed the concept in these words:

> The state absorbed and included the entire collective activity of its citizens, a whole outside of which its members could not even be thought of, much less exist. Hence all social life is political life, possibly because in the city-state the political life was in fact so much more "social" than with us.[5]

The Athenian citizen did not resent the pervasiveness of the state's regulatory power since he was not only subject to the power but also an agent of it. He could accept the edicts of the state in the same spirit that he could accept self-discipline. The authority of the state, though great and far-reaching, was also democratic because of the widespread citizen participation in state affairs. The feeling of separation that exists today between the people and their officials was absent in Athenian society. Men did not regard state interests as somehow antagonistic to their private interests.

Perhaps a contrast between current and Athenian views on the subject of church and state will demonstrate clearly the unity, the wholeness of Greek life. Modern democracy, as it is practiced in the United States, attempts to maintain as rigid a separation as possible between religion and state activity. Man's relationship to God is mainly a private matter. The individual may have a loyalty here which is not a matter of state concern so long as his actions do not detrimentally affect the lives and fortunes of others. A man may be a good citizen irrespective of his religious inclinations, since the two matters, religion and politics, are generally separate. In the occasional event of a conflict between individual religious activity and the welfare of the state, the courts, which may have to decide the issue, are often willing to concede that man's loyalty to his concept of God is of a higher nature than the allegiance he owes to the state. Unless some serious damage is threatened to the community through the exercise of religious freedom, that freedom must not be curbed by the state.

Here, again, we meet the ideas of separateness of loyalties and of rights held by the person *against* the state which were alien to the Athenian mind. Religion to the citizen of Athens had no implication of a division of loyalty. His gods were state gods, and they were concerned with his political affairs just as they were with his spiritual affairs—if, indeed,

[5] Charles Howard McIlwain, *The Growth of Political Thought in the West,* The Macmillan Company, New York, 1932, p. 5.

such a distinction could have been made.[6] The citizen did not have to separate his religious from his political activities; the two went hand in hand. Religion to the Greek was, in large part, a ceremonial affirmation of his membership in the group that constituted the state. His gods were the gods of state protection. Yet the state never rigorously regulated religious belief, and differences of religious opinion were not uncommon. The Greek had a too high respect for reason to be deeply religious on the basis of faith alone; he was more inclined to respect the conclusions that resulted from the application of logic than to accept any ex-cathedra pronouncement

Thus the sense of unity, of belonging, was an integral feature of Greek thought. The city-state was the focal point of Athenian loyalty because it was the agency that facilitated the desired unity. Another and larger unit of political organization would have made impossible the characteristic intimacy of Greek life in the city-state. Modern man centers his activities around his home and his place of business. The state is, to him, an abstraction in the distance. But to the Athenian the town was important, not the home or office; and only in the town, where he could discuss and play the role of citizen, did he obtain fulfillment of his desire to be a part of the group. The Greeks were aware that the city-state form gave them the advantages of unity and personal government. When Plato and Aristotle planned their ideal states, they were concerned with limitations on territory and population. Like most Greeks, both were aware that the state might easily grow beyond that point where unity through intimacy was possible. The Greeks knew that other and larger states, indeed great empires, existed beyond their shores, but these were inhabited by "barbarians" who lacked the cultural advantages of the city-state and were, therefore, inferior.

The democracy of Athens, which had been established by the middle of the fifth century, also incorporated a real spirit of equalitarianism. Unity, cohesion, and a sense of belonging may have been achieved without equality, but equality supplemented and strengthened the unity. There were, in the city-state, social distinctions and a class structure, but they were unimportant in the day-to-day relationships of citizens and in the conduct of social, economic, and political affairs. Noble and commoner worked for a living, and a man was more likely to achieve fame and win the respect of his fellow citizens because of his wisdom and his contribution to the public service than because of the wealth of his family.

The equality in Athenian thought had a meaning different from that which prevails in the modern democracy. It connoted, of course, political equality but also much more—the equality of fellowship, the equality

[6] Sabine, *op. cit.*, p. 13.

of the market place as well as of the political forum. Equality was an intimate and personal relation, without which the pervasiveness of state regulation would have been autocratic and intolerable; with it, government was democratic and admirable. Imbued as he was with the ideals of unity, intimacy, and equality, the Greek could utilize his freedom of speech to the greatest advantage in discussing the multitudinous affairs of state. Low economic standing was not a serious bar to participation in civic affairs. There was no economic equality, but public compensation for all who performed their civic duties made possible a widespread political activity that has since been unmatched.

Not all citizens of Athens took an active part in civic affairs. Even in the limited territory of the city-state, distance from the city proper was a real deterrent. Some were occupied with their business affairs. Some, like many today, were not interested. Nevertheless a relatively high percentage of citizens were directly involved in the work of government. Duty, both military and civil, engaged perhaps one in every three or four citizens, a far larger proportion than in the modern democratic nation. To the Greek, democracy would have been impossible without a great deal of popular participation. The modern citizen may be satisfied with a democratic constitution implemented by a handful of elected representatives; the Athenian demanded that implementation be by the many.

High-level participation in government implies that the Athenian had leisure time to devote to community activity. This was indeed true. The political- and social-minded Greek worked in order to exist, and a vocation to him was a bothersome business at best. His heart belonged to the public forum, for he was a political, not an economic man. The Greek word for unemployment is *schole*, or leisure; the word for business is *ascholia*, or absence of leisure.[7] Unemployment, in this sense, was preferable to employment. The Athenian judged his standard of living not by his level of consumption but by the amount of his participation and contribution in social and political affairs. The judgment again illustrates the importance which the Athenian attached to participation. To him democracy never meant majority rule quite so much as it meant the right of all men to be represented in public life and to participate in the construction of the constitution and the administration of the laws.

It has often been said that in a democracy there must be a clear, direct, and compelling relationship between public opinion and governmental action. This being so, Athenian democracy was far advanced over that prevalent today. The city-state form was conducive to the principle. In a community such as the city-state public affairs were everybody's business, everything was discussed, and as a result, public opinion was bound

[7] Alfred Zimmern, *The Greek Commonwealth*, 5th rev. ed., Oxford University Press, Fair Lawn, N.J., 1931, p. 59.

to have great force. And the size of the body politic in the city-state made the determination of public opinion an easier task than it is in the large and diversified modern democracy.

We might suppose that the Greeks who carried the concept of popular sovereignty to such great lengths would have suffered from lack of authority. We should be mistaken. The Greek was free but free only under the law; he was not an anarchist; he did not live without control. Certainty and predictability of existence were his under democracy far more than had been his lot under the preceding oligarchy. For generations the Athenian had suffered from law by caprice as pronounced by the aristocratically dominated magistracies. When the mass of citizens came to power and established popular government, reform of the law to establish its constancy was given first priority. Publication of the old laws and posting of the new were demanded and obtained.

The democrats of Athens were deeply concerned about the possibility of abuse of the lawmaking power. Although statutes were enacted and decrees issued even as in the modern legislature, stability was maintained in the underlying principle upon which the structure of government and the welfare of the people rested. The constitution provided for an indictment, called the *graphe paranomon,* against the proposing of illegal measures. A distinction was made between two kinds of law, *nomoi* and *psephismata,* which is roughly comparable to the distinction made in the United States between the Constitution and ordinary statutes. Changes in the *nomoi* could be made only by approval of a special body called the *Nomothetai.* A *nomos* was invalid if it conflicted with an earlier *nomos* without specifically repealing it. A *psephismata* was always void if it conflicted with a *nomos.* One who proposed such illegal measures was subject to the *graphe paranomon* and could be punished accordingly. It was also assumed that the principle of generality, or general applicability, of the law should prevail. A *nomos* of Athens required that, except in extraordinary cases such as those dealing with ostracism, no decree bearing upon an individual should be enacted.[8]

The great problem facing political theorists is to determine the proper balance, in the relationship of state and citizen, between freedom and authority. The Greek believed he had found this balance in his conception of the law and the role of the citizen in its making and execution. He found authority in the law and freedom in framing and administering it. There was no conflict between freedom and authority because the authority was democratically formulated and executed, and there could be no tyranny in a self-imposed discipline. Despite the pervasiveness of authority in the Athenian community, the state was not totalitarian in the modern sense. While power was great, it was citizen-made and citizen-

[8] Francis D. Wormuth, *The Origins of Modern Constitutionalism,* Harper & Row, Publishers, Incorporated, New York, 1949, pp. 6–10.

administered. There was no cult of the state. The state existed for the citizen, not the citizen for the state. Whereas modern totalitarianism repudiates the assertion of man's abilities to reason and to govern himself, the Athenian believed he had these abilities and in great abundance.

The Athenian state employed public works, defense projects, relief for the indigent, pensions for disabled veterans, business and price regulation, sharing of tribute and the spoils of war, religious festivals, and other devices to ensure a minimum standard of living for its people.[9] Such programs were considered representative of the best in democratic practice just as were the political guarantees of participation and free speech. State instrumentalism went hand in hand with the "service state." Under the leadership of Pericles, the state underwrote a minimum of economic welfare for its citizens. This was neither the "dole" nor a policy of "bread and circuses" designed to placate an unruly proletariat. It was a general acknowledgment that while economic equality was unnecessary, some measure of economic amelioration for the poorer citizens was required in the interests of political democracy. The citizen who had to spend each waking hour digging for a livelihood would have neither the time nor the inclination to share in the governing of community affairs. A small payment for all those who thus participated was only a part of a more comprehensive welfare system that benefited a substantial segment of the citizenry.

Political Institutions of the City-state

The democratic political and social ideals of Athenian citizenship found organizational expression in a unique formation of governmental institutions, the foundation of which was the Assembly or Ecclesia. This body consisted, theoretically, of all male citizens over the age of twenty years. In practice, only a minority attended its sessions. Still the number was substantial, and the Assembly was regarded as representative of the sovereign will of the people. The Assembly scheduled ten regular meetings during the year. The calling of special sessions, however, necessitated more frequent gatherings, and at times the Assembly convened as often as once in every ten days. In the Assembly were constitutionally lodged most of the supreme powers of the state—legislative authority, control of foreign policy, control of the executive. The efficient exercise of these powers, however, was handicapped by the large size of the body. Here is a problem well known to legislators and students of government today. If the interests of the entire community are to be represented and served, a legislative body needs to be large. On the other hand, open and unlimited debate by such a body precludes efficiency of operation. The Athenian saw the difficulties involved as clearly as have his political successors. The solution, then as now, was found in the creation of

[9] Zimmern, *op. cit.*, pp. 413–414.

smaller, more efficient governmental agencies to guide and direct the larger legislative group, with the latter relegated to the role of a ratifying body.

The permanent governing agency that operated between sessions of the Assembly and directed the activities of that body when it convened was the Council of Five Hundred. This organization consisted of five hundred citizens, fifty from each of the ten tribes, originally kinship groups but at this time essentially electoral units, which composed the Athenian citizen population. The five hundred were selected by the drawing of lots and were proportionally representative of the hundred or so demes (comparable to our electoral districts or local governmental units). Each deme elected a panel of candidates for the Council, the size of the panel being roughly determined by the size of the deme. The actual selection of members of the Council was made through a process of drawing lots among elected candidates of the deme's panel. The same procedure was employed for the selection of magistrates and members of the large popular juries, governmental institutions whose functions will shortly be discussed.

Terms of office in Athenian government were generally limited to one year, and holding the same office two years in succession was prohibited. The annual selection of the Council was a key event, since the political composition of the Council was influential in determining the policies of the city-state for the ensuing year. Moreover, since five hundred proved to be an unwieldy number for the functions it performed, the Council evolved a system of rotation of office which made for efficiency and still retained the desired element of tribal representation. The Council was divided into ten committees of fifty, each fifty representing one of the ten Athenian tribal organizations. A committee, along with one member from each of the remaining nine tribes, held office and represented the Council for a tenth part of the year. Each day the committee selected by lot one member who acted as president of the Council and who was in effect for one day head of the state. No person in his lifetime could serve more than one day in this position, the holding of which was regarded as the greatest honor an Athenian might achieve. All members of the committee were required to be present at meetings of the Council; other members were entitled to be present, but their attendance was not compulsory.

The powers of the Council were substantial. This body acted as a policy framer and steering committee for the Assembly. It prepared the agenda for Assembly action, and Assembly consideration was ordinarily limited to subjects presented by the Council, although the Assembly could itself initiate proposals and take direct legislative action. In addition, the Council itself might issue decrees and fill in details of legislation enacted by the Assembly. The Council supervised the performance

of functions of all executive officials, levied taxes, managed the finances of the city-state, supervised elections, and handled negotiations with foreign emissaries. The Council could, if it chose, act as a court of law, determine guilt, and assess punishment. It combined executive, legislative, and judicial powers and used them vigorously.

Still, the Council was subject to the control of the Assembly. Proposals of the Council could be rejected. All important legislative, executive, and judicial matters were brought before the Assembly, and the decree power of the Council was rarely abused. It is true that the Assembly could refer matters to the Council. Moreover there was nothing to prevent the Assembly from amending suggested enactments submitted to it or from adding provisions to the original proposals. At times the "rider" possibilities were strongly exploited. The Council was expected to exert power and it did, but there was ample protection against possible abuses.

The great popular courts of Athens were also a focal point of city-state democracy. Any Athenian thirty years of age and otherwise qualified by the possession of full civil rights was eligible to become a member of the court. The entire court panel numbered some six thousand, six hundred from each tribe chosen by lot from elected panels. The general court was divided into a number of tribunals on which each tribe was entitled to equal representation, and the members of which were assigned from the general panel. In order to minimize the possibilities of bribery and coercion, personnel were shifted so that no member could know in advance what case he was to hear.[10]

The courts, like the Assembly, were considered representative of the full sovereignty of the people. There were no appellate courts, and a decision of one court, in effect being a decision of the whole citizenry, was final. Members of the court were both judge and jury. There were no public prosecutors; an aggrieved individual pleaded his own case as did the defendant. The court first voted on the question of guilt and then, again by vote, assessed a penalty by choosing one of the alternatives suggested by the litigants. Members of the court were paid a small fee for their activity. The amount was insufficient to attract a majority of qualified citizens, and herein lay one of the serious weaknesses of the system. Since service was not compulsory but voluntary, citizens who lived any great distance from the city could not afford to serve, nor could many able-bodied city dwellers who had to devote time to earning a living. As a result the popular juries were dominated by older and less active, perhaps more shiftless, townsmen.

A vast amount of litigation was carried to the popular courts, and here the size of the body and its amateur character raised real problems. Mob psychology was sometimes employed by skilled speakers to sway the large juries. The courts heard cases in both criminal and civil law. Very often

[10] Sabine, *op. cit.*, p. 10.

important leaders were haled before a court on charges obviously politically inspired. Even Pericles was not immune from such procedure; nor, of course, was Socrates, who was condemned to death by such a court. In these instances, political inclination rather than law provided a basis of judgment. Passion and prejudice were likely to play a powerful part in the decision-making process. Although we can easily find fault with details of the system, we must bear in mind that the seeds of democracy were only beginning to sprout, and if the processes of justice were not as well developed then as they now are, Athens was at least fumbling with the elements of a peaceful judicial system and led the rest of the world at the time.

The courts also held power, in the name of the people, to control public officials. The qualifications of magistrates chosen by lot were reviewed by the courts, and they might declare the ineligibility of any official so selected. Upon conclusion of a term of office, the actions of an official were similarly scrutinized. Malfeasance was punishable by court action. The court might further direct a special audit of an official's accounts where public money was involved. These processes of screening and review minimized the possibility that the selection of officials by lot would clothe a group of rascals or incompetents with the robes of public office.

A unique and powerful group of offices were filled by ten generals, whose positions were theoretically military but who, in practice, were potent political figures as well. The generals were among the few public officials of Athens who were directly elected, without resort to the procedure of the lot, and who were eligible for reelection. The powers of the generals were legally equal, and the functions of office were divided in order to avoid duplication. One of the generals, however, was often regarded as a kind of unofficial leader, and he often dominated the group. The generals' activities, although they were primarily in the fields of foreign and military policy, extended also into finance and often were concerned with policies of a peculiarly domestic nature. The extent of the power exerted depended upon the personality of the leader and upon the existing state of affairs, emergency justifying a greater exercise of power than might ordinarily have been tolerated. For a generation Pericles, first among the generals of his time, dominated Athenian policy. The generals were thus political figures, but they were at all times responsible to the Assembly and could accomplish little without the confidence of that body. The position of the group, especially of the dominant figure, was somewhat analogous to that of prime minister in a cabinet system of government. They, as he, could convoke meetings of the Assembly and place proposals before it. Retention of power, however, was contingent upon support of the Assembly, and an adverse vote might prove fatal to a leader's tenure or even his life.

While on its face the popular election of a military leader might appear to be carrying democracy to ludicrous lengths, the accountability of the generals to the Assembly was so zealously enforced by the latter that the untrained, fearful of the consequences of ineptness or failure, did not aspire to the office.

Political Philosophy in Pre-Platonic Greece

It should be obvious from the foregoing description that the institutions of Athens were conducive to free and intense political discussion. The Athenian, proud of his own city-state, was still curious with respect to the governments, customs, and traditions of other states. Political speculation was stimulated too by the defeat of democratic Athens by autocratic Sparta in the Peloponnesian War and later by the conquests of Philip of Macedon. Was democracy to blame? Could citizens incorporate some of the virtues of Spartan discipline into democratic practice while retaining the advantages of the latter? Were monarchic or aristocratic forms of government preferable to democracy? Was democracy merely a device whereby the poor who constituted a majority exploited the wealthy and more ambitious minority? How could differences between rich and poor be reconciled? These and other significant questions were debated with vigor.

Certain intellectual concepts underlay discussions of the more or less specific political and economic problems. A feature of Greek philosophical speculation was the attempt to discover the harmonizing element in social life. The search for such a factor in community life was preceded by a similar search in physical nature. The Greek was impressed by the apparent harmony in the physical world. What regulated the seasons of the year? What explained the beneficent division of day and night? The earlier Greek philosophers, like Anaximander, sought an explanation in the discovery of some element, whose presence would account for the apparent harmony of the whole. By the middle of the fifth century philosophical interest had shifted to problems of a political and social nature. An Athens of wealth and of political democracy increased its interest in the humanities. It became apparent that the path to prestige in a democracy of the Athenian type would be more easily negotiated with the assistance of education and training for public service.

The Sophists were, in large part, the instruments of change. They were teachers who taught students who could afford to pay for instruction. Although they were not a band of philosophers who advocated a particular creed of social action and although differences of opinion divided the Sophists, yet they were agreed in the humanistic bent of their teachings. They proposed less concern with the physical world and more with a philosophical speculation that centered its interest in mankind. The Sophists advanced the cause of individualism, and they encouraged a skepticism indispensable to intellectual pursuits. Although they could not completely destroy an older mode of thought, they were successful in modifying it. The search for a harmonizing and unifying element went on, but now it was sought in the context of society and not in the physical world. The Athenians of the fifth century looked for that principle, obedience to which would bring peace, unity, and harmony to civilization despite differences of opinion among Greek thinkers. The Greek had considered his own political and social organizations evidences of his own natural superiority over the "barbarians." The new school told him that goodness and morality were more fundamental and were not to be discovered in mere evidences of a particular kind of community life.

Socrates

Socrates, the first in point of time of that great triumvirate of Athenian philosophers which included Plato and Aristotle, was appalled by the intellectual ferment of his time and by the plethora of ideas expressed, so many of which he believed contributed to the disintegration of the community. He too sought some universal principle that might bring order from chaos and provide harmony based upon intelligence and reason.

Socrates is perhaps too often thought of as a gadfly, a skeptic more interested in attacking the ideas of others than in offering a constructive philosophy of his own. This is an inaccurate appraisal. Professor A. E. Taylor has credited Socrates with establishing the tradition of morality which has prevailed in the West. That tradition holds that man possesses a *soul*, that the soul is nourished by the moral life, and that man's actions ought to accord with the nature of the soul. It is an error to assume that this view originated with Christianity; in fact Socrates' philosophy prepared the way for the Christian belief. Plato's account of his master makes clear that Socrates regarded the soul as immortal. Man in this life should minister to its needs. He must, if he is to do this, live a moral life, irrespective of what it may cost him in material terms. A moral life consists of living according to the dictates of rationality. The proper care of the soul thus demands that thought and action be judged according to the standard of rationality.[11]

From this premise Socrates proceeded to the principle which he developed and upon which he insisted—that *virtue is knowledge, that it is discoverable, and that it can be taught and learned.*[12] The Socratic method, which we know from the writings of Socrates' greatest pupil,

[11] A. E. Taylor, *Socrates: The Man and His Thought*, Anchor Books, Doubleday & Company, Inc., Garden City, N.Y., 1954, pp. 132–138.

[12] Sabine, *op. cit.*, p. 33.

Plato, was designed to pinpoint truth through a procedure of obtaining precise definition. The method involved the proposing of a question by Socrates, the answer to which he professed not to know—"Socratic irony" —in an attempt to elicit answers from other discussants. The opinions expressed were then questioned by Socrates, who pretended to possess less sophistication than he actually had. Out of the arguments would ultimately emerge an acceptable answer to the original question.

Through this method and by application of his maxim that virtue is knowledge, Socrates attacked some of the basic precepts of the Athenian democracy. Surely in any society there is a minority with greater intelligence and knowledge—consequently with more virtue—than is found in the majority. Government by the many is therefore government by the nonvirtuous and is obviously unjust. Such in brief was the argument of Socrates, if Plato accurately presents Socrates' views in the *Republic*. Socrates developed no philosophy of individual rights against the state. He may have opposed the particular governmental form employed at the time, but he knew that man was nonetheless a political animal, and his development, what he was, he owed to the state. Though Socrates was condemned to death by one of the popular juries he abhorred, he refused to take advantage of his opportunities to flee. In the *Crito* Socrates explains his position by saying that his obligations to the state are too great, that the advantages he has received as a citizen are too many for him to repudiate the authority of the state on the one occasion when it was not beneficial to him.

Still, escape was not the only alternative to execution. Socrates' freedom was assured if only he would promise to abandon his attacks upon Athenian democracy. What then? If it were the state from which all blessings flowed, surely a mere guarantee not to attack it was no price at all to pay for one's life. On the contrary, would this not be an ordinary and accepted duty of citizenship? Not so to Socrates. A man had a higher obligation, to conscience, to truth, to the seeking of virtue, which is knowledge. He must press on toward these things. If man's duty to the state conflicts with his duty to these higher ideals, he may forfeit his life to the state, but he cannot compromise his conscience. He must speak out on matters of truth irrespective of the personal cost.

Conclusions

From the upheavals in Athens that accompanied war and defeat came the great philosophies of Socrates, Plato, and Aristotle. The questions then raised with respect to the nature of man, of society, and of government have ever since been debated. The attacks upon democracy in Athens were as powerful as any that have since been proposed. Yet Athenian democracy lived to influence its conquerors and subsequent generations. The influence of Athens was greater in the era of her decline than it had been at the height of her military glory.

SELECTED BIBLIOGRAPHY

Barker, Ernest: *Greek Political Theory: Plato and His Predecessors,* 4th ed., Barnes & Noble, Inc., New York, 1951, chap. 3.

Catlin, George: *The Story of the Political Philosophers,* McGraw-Hill Book Company, Inc., New York, 1939, chap. 1.

Cook, Thomas I.: *History of Political Philosophy from Plato to Burke,* Prentice-Hall, Inc., Englewood Cliffs, N.J., 1936, chap. 2.

Dunning, William A.: *A History of Political Theories, Ancient and Medieval,* The Macmillan Company, New York, 1905.

Edman, Irwin (ed.): *The Works of Plato* (Benjamin Jowett translation), Modern Library, Inc., New York, 1928.

Glotz, Gustave: *The Greek City and Its Institutions,* Alfred A. Knopf, Inc., New York, 1930.

Greenidge, A. H. J.: *A Handbook of Greek Constitutional History,* The Macmillan Company, New York, 1896.

McIlwain, Charles H.: *The Growth of Political Thought in the West,* The Macmillan Company, New York, 1932, chap. 1.

Sabine, George H.: *A History of Political Theory,* 3d ed., Holt, Rinehart and Winston, Inc., New York, 1961, chaps. 1, 2.

Taylor, A. E.: *Socrates: The Man and His Thought,* Anchor Books, Doubleday & Company, Inc., Garden City, N.Y., 1954.

Wormuth, Francis D.: *The Origins of Modern Constitutionalism,* Harper & Row, Publishers, Incorporated, New York, 1949, chaps. 1, 2.

Zimmern, Alfred: *The Greek Commonwealth,* 5th rev. ed., Oxford University Press, Fair Lawn, N.J., 1931.

three

PLATO

Plato (427?–347 B.C.), who was born of aristocratic Athenian parents, prepared as a young man for a career in the public service. The early military successes of Athens in the Peloponnesian campaign had made it appear that such a career would be rewarding. The disastrous outcome of the war, however, coupled with the subsequent rule of the Thirty Tyrants, shook Plato's earlier resolution. A more complete disenchantment ensued with the condemnation and execution of his mentor Socrates. No other event could more greatly have strengthened Plato's belief that Socrates' attacks upon democracy had been justified. A system that could so witlessly destroy the best within it was worthy of neither loyalty nor respect. For Plato the following few years constituted a period of soul searching and intellectual development. Plato abandoned Athens to travel and to learn, but he carried with him always the basic tenet of Socratic thought, *virtue is knowledge*. Upon this foundation Plato was to build a philosophy that would hold the interest of scholars and statesmen through the ages.

Plato's wanderings carried him far from his native Athens. In the Greek cities of southern Italy he studied the doctrines of the mystic Pythagorean society, which stressed the class structure and the mathematics that were later to occupy an important position in the curriculum of Plato's Athenian academy. It is likely that Plato received instruction in mathematics in Egypt too and that he was impressed by the caste

29

system of the conservative Egyptian society. In Syracuse Plato incurred the anger of Dionysius I by lecturing that monarch on the proper methods of rulership. Dionysius had Plato enslaved, but he was soon ransomed by friends and returned to Athens to found the academy that was to be his forum until his death. Plato's Academy was the first of the great schools of philosophy, and in it Plato conducted an educational center for the training of statesmen. Through his students the Academy was to have an impact upon the political systems of Athens and of other city-states. In the Academy Plato wrote and taught. It is unfortunate that the lectures of Plato have been lost and with them, unquestionably, a considerable portion of his total contribution. Enough remains, however, of his written works to outline and assess the fundamentals of his thought; in them we find the origin of European political thought.

Plato's earlier dialogues constitute a foundation for his later great work. Many of the ideas that subsequently appear in his *Republic, Statesman,* and *Laws* were expressed by Plato in the *Apology, Crito, Protagoras, Phaedo,* and other dialogues. But these latter are essentially negative in form, constituting, for the most part, attacks upon the Athenian system. Plato's positive and constructive effort begins with his *Republic,* easily the best known of all his works and the one upon which we shall concentrate our attention here.

The Republic *of Plato*

The *Republic* is a product of the years of Plato's early maturity and speculative vigor. It is a major contribution to political philosophy, but it is more than that. In the *Republic* are considered education,[1] economics, moral philosophy, history, metaphysics and, indeed, most of the human preoccupations that are significant in the development of social life. That all these subjects are discussed within the context of the state should not be surprising if the all-encompassing nature of the city-state and its authority are kept in mind. A contemporary effort directed toward a similar end and using the same technique would be far less meaningful precisely because the relationship of the modern state to such things as religion and morals has altered so greatly. To Plato it was inconceivable that a treatise on the good life could be developed outside of the framework of the state. The good life and good citizenship meant very much the same thing; at any rate one would hardly be possible without the other.

To the casual student the *Republic* may appear on occasion to stray far from reality. But despite its utopian qualities, Plato seriously intended the *Republic* to be a scientific approach to the discovery of truth. He sought to create a system within which the good life would be

[1] Rousseau said that the *Republic* is the greatest treatise on education ever written.

assured. Plato assumed that there *is* a good, that there *are* truths which, if discovered and implemented, will create and preserve the good life in the good state. Thus Plato attempted to formulate a science of politics or society. Just as the work of the physician should proceed upon the basis of knowledge, so too must the government of the state. Plato was aware that no ideal state such as his Republic existed, but he was convinced that it should.

Always present in the philosophy of the *Republic* is Plato's idea that politics is an art and that, as with all arts, its successful practice demands expert knowledge. Thus Plato attacked the democratic system of Athens with its reliance upon the Periclean principle of "happy versatility"— the principle that government by the civic-minded amateur is best. The politics-art equation is the basis of the many analogies that Plato employs throughout the *Republic*. Plato compared the statesman's art to that of the physician. The ability to govern depends upon a knowledge of principles which must be apprehended by intelligent men through rational processes. The statesman can no more gain such knowledge through intuition than the medical student can learn anatomy by divine revelation. It follows that Plato regarded public opinion as incompetent and quite incapable of directing policy for the state. Virtue is knowledge. Men have different capacities for learning, and only a few may develop the amount of virtue required for rulership. A major function of the state of the *Republic* is to arrange matters so as to facilitate this rule by the virtuous elite. Plato had only scorn for the politicians who maintained their hold on public office by truckling to the masses, who in turn were unfit both to govern themselves and to select efficient governors.

The *Republic* represents Plato's search for justice, its definition and full content. Plato employs his favorite literary device, the dialogue form, with Socrates playing the major role in the drama of the search for truth. The setting of the *Republic* is the home of Cephalus, an old and wealthy man who has turned to religion and philosophy to comfort his old age. In a brief conversation with Cephalus Socrates elicits the former's view that justice consists of speaking the truth and paying one's debts. Thus the stage is set for the unfolding of the dialogue which discloses both Plato's view of justice and his plan for the ideal state.

Polemarchus, the son of Cephalus, generally agrees with his father. Justice, he says, is giving to every man his due. But Socrates (Plato) demurs. What does Polemarchus mean? Does he intend to say, for example, that justice consists in doing good to one's friends and harm to one's enemies? Polemarchus accepts this interpretation of his statement, and Socrates proceeds to demolish it. Is it not true, asks Socrates, that doing harm to an enemy may make that enemy worse than he was? Polemarchus sees the point and agrees that justice cannot condone the injuring of others. At this point Socrates encounters a more re-doubtable foe in Thrasymachus, a character placed in the *Republic* by Plato to represent the school of radical Sophist thought which he ab-horred. Thrasymachus states that justice is the interest of the stronger. Might is right. In any society those who have power use it for their own benefit. Not only rulers but all men, says Thrasymachus, will act alike. If given the opportunity they will serve their own interest at the expense of others. Thus justice consists of doing good for oneself but doing injustice to everyone else.

> And that is what I mean when I say that in all states there is the same principle of justice, which is the interest of the government; and as the government must be supposed to have power, the only reasonable con-clusion is, that everywhere there is one principle of justice which is the in-terest of the stronger.[2]

The strongly individualistic nature of Thrasymachus' view is protested by Socrates. The individual serves himself best not by imagining that he has interests apart from those of the whole community and that he must help himself only at a cost to others, but by adopting the view that the self is a part of the whole and is affected by what happens to the whole. Good is to the one as it is to the many, and the same can be said of evil. The just ruler does not pursue individual self-interest but the interest of all, knowing that his own welfare is inextricable from that of his people. The just ruler cares for neither money nor power. To him it is enough that through the self-sacrifice he makes as a ruler he has avoided being ruled by lesser men.

> He who refuses to rule is liable to be ruled by one who is worse than him-self. And the fear of this as I conceive, induces the good to take office, not because they would, but because they cannot help—not under the idea that they are going to have any benefit or enjoyment themselves, but as a neces-sity, and because they are not able to commit the task of ruling to any one who is better than themselves, or indeed as good.[3]

A more subtle element in the argument is introduced at this point by Glaucon, one of the discussants. Thrasymachus is wrong, Glaucon says, not in his estimate of the force of self-interest but in his conclusion as to how men react to this force. Men would certainly prefer to exploit others for their own advantage, but they fear the consequences of doing so. An ideal situation would be one in which a person could do injustice without experiencing it. But under such circumstances life would be too precarious, since we would always be apprehensive about the harm

---

[2] *The Republic of Plato* (Benjamin Jowett translation), 4th ed., Oxford University Press, Fair Lawn, N.J., 1953, bk. I, p. 20. Subsequent quotations from and references to *The Republic* are from this edition.
[3] *Ibid.*, p. 32.

others might be planning for us. Justice, then, results from fear. Men enact laws and agree to obey them because while they are selfish, they are also prudent. Centuries later Thomas Hobbes was to incorporate these views into his great treatise, the *Leviathan*.

Glaucon's views are more challenging than others that have been presented, and Socrates, who has thus far been content mainly to rebut the proposals of others, now must be more constructive. What is justice if it is not speaking truth, paying debts, rendering to each man his due, the interest of the stronger, or an agreement to obey laws? Socrates cannot accept such explanations because they are in many cases wrong, in all cases too particularistic and superficial, and because they view justice as something apart from man's soul. Justice is an integral part of the soul; thus to define and analyze it requires, in a sense, a dissection of the soul of man. This is a difficult problem, but Socrates has the solution. He gains ready assent to his proposition that the state is the individual "writ large." An analysis of the nature of the state will also be an analysis of human nature. Thus Plato arrives at the point of his real task, the construction of the just state and so the discovery of the principles of justice in the individual. The true meaning of the *Republic* would be lost if that work were to be regarded merely as a plan for the ideal state. Plato was searching for justice, and to seek it in the context of the state was typically Greek. In effect Plato equates moral with political philosophy.

Three basic forces, Plato contends, motivate men. They are the forces of desire or appetite, spirit or courage, and reason. Each is present in every man in varying amounts, but one is always predominant. Society may be divided into three classes according to the relative amount of each force present in the individuals who comprise the community. Any one class will play the role for which it is best qualified by virtue of its dominant motivating force. The men who are motivated largely by appetite or desire, will constitute the largest class. Fewer will be motivated by spirit or courage than were impelled by desire, but they will still be more numerous than those dominated by reason. Thus from the standpoint of numbers, the reasoning class will be smallest, and the courageous and spirited persons will occupy the middle position.

The state arises in the first place in answer to the demand for the satisfaction of reciprocal needs; a community organization is obviously best fitted to accomplish that end. For example, goods are needed for consumption, and certain essential tasks must be performed. Since some men perform a particular task better than others, they should perform only that task. Each person works at what he does best and through association, not only satisfies his own needs but also the needs of others for that service. The lowest of the three classes that constitute the state is the artisan class, whose function is to supply the community with the material necessities of life. The principle of specialization must be applied so as to prevent artisans from acting in any other field of state activity and to guarantee that the upper classes are not compelled to perform tasks which are the proper function of the artisans. However, a community that exists merely to gratify the appetite is no state at all but only a slightly exalted pigsty. Other components are necessary for the creation of a state. A refined civilization requires a large population and territory to contain it. Since people and land must be defended, the state must establish a military guardian class consisting of those in the community in whom the instinct for courage or spirit is dominant. Again the service is specialized; only those who are qualified will be permitted to perform the specific function of military guardianship.

From a select handful of the soldier guardians will be chosen the ruling class of the state. These few will be endowed with reason and motivated by their willingness to serve as rulers. They will not only have the greatest capacity to think philosophically and to search diligently for true principles, but they will also realize that their welfare is inextricably bound up with the welfare of the whole. These qualities, when placed in the ideal environment of the *Republic,* will flourish and permit a kind of rulership never before seen, a rulership absolutely devoted to community interest and completely lacking in the desire of a ruling class to serve its own interest at the expense of the citizenry.

But Plato is searching for justice. What have class structure and specialization to do with justice? The answer is, everything. The balance of the discussion of the *Republic* will be easier to understand if we assume initially that, to Plato, *justice is a product of class division and specialization of function.* Plato defines justice as "giving to every man his due." And his due is to be assigned the particular task which he is best qualified by aptitude and training to perform. Such a definition of justice is unusual in that it has no legal or juristic connotation. It is not concerned with the rights of an individual against the state. It has nothing to do with judicial procedures.[4] Instead, justice is the development of internal harmony both in the individual and in the state, and this harmony can be achieved only when external conditions are properly ordered. If the state arises in answer to the demand for an exchange of services, the state which satisfies this need best will be the best state, and the state which satisfies the need perfectly will be a perfect state. To Plato it is obvious that the state which arranges matters so that each person—ruler, soldier-guardian, artisan—is doing precisely what he ought to be doing is the superior state.

A duality of meaning is to be inferred from Plato's definition of justice. One relates to justice as it is found in the state, the other as it

[4] George H. Sabine, *A History of Political Theory,* 3d ed., Holt, Rinehart and Winston, Inc., New York, 1961, p. 55.

applies to the individual. The virtues of the state of the *Republic* are wisdom, courage, and self-control. Wisdom is to be found in the ruling class of philosopher-kings; courage is an attribute of the soldier-guardians; self-control is exercised by both the soldier-guardians and by the artisans when they recognize their limitations and do not attempt to interfere with the work of the rulers. The latter, too, exercise self-control when they do not abuse the position they hold. Justice in the state results from the fact that all the other virtues are made possible, and it is organization that makes them possible. The whole state is perfect because each individual part of it operates as it should.

Justice for the individual results from temperance. If each person is dominated by one of the three basic impulses—appetite, spirit, and reason—justice will be served if he lives a life in which his primary impulse is made to serve the community and the lesser impulses are strictly curbed, since permitting them free play would disrupt the state. As justice in the state results from an harmonious balance achieved through specialization, so justice in the individual is achieved when each person performs only the role for which he is qualified. The composition of the good state reflects the harmonious soul of the individual. The highest form of humanity is the person in whom appetite and spirit are dominated by reason. The highest form of state is one in which those who *know* control the affairs of state.

In the light of modern knowledge of psychology it is apparent that Plato's threefold categorization of man's instincts and capacities is naïve. The attributes, aptitudes, and capacities of men cannot be so neatly distinguished, and differences, particularly in mental capacity, are not so great as Plato imagined. As Aristotle was later to point out, experience is also important as a guide to human behavior, and it would be difficult to determine the relative values of the contributions to society of education and experience. Plato's arbitrary assignment of men to one or another of the three classes, depending upon their individual aptitudes, also destroys freedom. The "natural-born" shoemaker, if indeed any such exists, might resent devoting his life to the trade and would probably find it intolerable to be excluded entirely from any kind of activity involving the management of community affairs. Men may be happier with smaller material rewards if they are permitted the freedom to draw their own conclusions, even though the conclusions may be wrong. Democracy does not assume that the contributions of all men to the formulation of public policy are equal; it only proposes that most men have something to contribute. Plato scorned the proposition.

Education in the Republic

While criticisms of Plato's outline for the perfect state come readily to mind, it must be acknowledged that his argument is powerful and persuasive. The principle that the state should be ruled by those who know is not easily refuted, and it has had its supporters through the ages. Indeed, if the premises of Plato's thought are granted, the conclusions logically follow. There is, however, far more to the *Republic* than we have yet seen. For example, Plato considers the problem of determining capacity and developing it and the problem of maintaining the equilibrium of the society once it has been established. The answers to these problems involve two of the most significant features of Plato's plan; they are *education* and *communism*.

In proposing his own plan of education, Plato attacks the Athenian system. In Athens, even though education was compulsory it was privately administered. To Plato, the welfare of the state depended upon the educational training of its citizens; the state, therefore, was guilty of gross negligence in permitting private agencies to control the system. Moreover, Athens required only an elementary education, which was in Plato's view quite inadequate to train statesmen properly. The root of Athens' problem, he believed, was the inefficiency of Athenian education, which resulted in government by incompetents. And the Athenian women were not subject even to the modest educational requirements of the state. Plato paid particular attention to the education of women. Failure to do so, he believed, resulted in the loss of a considerable potential, which might otherwise be devoted to the welfare of the state.

The educational plan of the *Republic* has two phases. The first consists of elementary training for citizens up to the age of eighteen and is followed by a two-year period of military training. It is not clear whether members of the artisan class are to be admitted to this phase of training, but since Plato intended capacity to be the sole criterion in determining a citizen's station, we may assume that elementary education was to be open to all and that a person's degree of fitness was to be ascertained during this period. At any rate education is given to both men and women.

During the first phase citizens are to study gymnastics and music. These terms must be construed broadly. Gymnastics is to include not only exercise but all training in bodily care including diet. An essential purpose of physical education is the development of a sound physique, but since Plato was aware that mental and physical fitness are related, he probably regarded training of the body as a means of the education of the mind. This training is, moreover, designed to develop spirit and courage in those who are to become auxiliaries, or members of the military class. Training in music is to be directed less toward singing and instrumental music than to the study of poetry and literature in general. A rigid system of censorship is proposed to assure that training in "music" will conduce to the desirable social and political character of the state. All existing literature is to be revised to conform to the accepted standard, and new contributions are to be scrutinized carefully by the philosopher-kings. Dictatorship and censorship generally go hand in hand. One is reminded, by Plato's strictures, of the concern of the Soviet rulers with a similar subject in their own culture. Plato's plan was contrary to the accepted Athenian way. Free inquiry and speculation were considered valuable and necessary parts of democratic life, and it was precisely this that Plato attacked.

The second phase of education in the *Republic* involved a plan of advanced study for those who survived the selective screening process of elementary education. This group begins the program at the age of twenty and remains in it for fifteen years, if its members prove fit. Since only a few are involved in the advanced stage of education, a more individualized technique of instruction may be employed. The first ten of the fifteen years are devoted to the study of mathematics, from its basic to its higher forms, and astronomy. The final five years are spent in a study of dialectic or philosophy. This last is the ultimate in formal instruction. Here first principles are explored, and the search for the "good"—for "truth"—is launched.

At the age of thirty-five those who have successfully completed their advanced education are assigned to civil and military administrative positions in order that the state may benefit from their education and training. Even during this period, however, the screening process goes on, for the ultimate stage of state service has not yet been attained. For fifteen years more the training continues, now in the form of concrete and practical application of principles that heretofore have been principally theoretical. At the age of fifty those who have demonstrated real ability and served with genuine distinction reach the pinnacle of the state order. They join the group of guardians, whose time is divided between matters of administration on the highest level and periods of pure speculation. The guardian class labors always for the state, for the preservation of the just community. Their task is essentially one of "holding the line," of ensuring that the next generation will, in all circumstances, live as does the present generation.

The guardians, unlike the rulers of other polities, do not frame legislation. A discussion of law in its traditional sense is omitted entirely from the *Republic*, not through inadvertence but because the plan of rule by intelligence leads Plato directly to the conclusion that legislation is not only unnecessary but harmful. Law in its customary form is a framework of rules and regulations governing human behavior and having general applicability. By its very nature, law is unable to consider the many extenuating and shifting circumstances of individual cases and is rarely adjusted rapidly enough to account for those circumstances. Thus it is not just, or at any rate not as just as is a government dominated by the quality of intelligence available in the perfect state. Plato here applies his favorite analogy of doctor and patient. A first-quality physician, well versed in science and the latest techniques, a physician who is himself the master of medical craft, should not be compelled in his treatment of patients to follow the dictates of an out-moded and inferior textbook. In like manner, statesmen of the ability found among the philosopher-kings should rule according to the con-clusions reached through their own intelligence and training and must not be compelled to conform to a set of outdated and inferior laws.

Education is thus a chief concern in the *Republic*. Justice, Plato contends, consists in the creation of a community in which each indi-vidual is located in that particular niche in society where he belongs and does the work for which he is suited by aptitude and training. The educational system of Plato's *Republic* accomplishes this ordering of society. Through it specialization is facilitated and justice is achieved. Education in the *Republic* is also devoted to maintenance of the society as it has been originally conceived and planned. To this end it employs censorship and the absolute authority of the rulers. The liberal mind may repudiate the censorship and the authoritarian undemocratic as-pects of Plato's plan of education. Modern education is closely associ-ated with a democratic society. Plato, on the other hand, in the *Republic* makes an attack upon democracy. His proposal is that education shall be so planned and directed as to prevent democracy with its amateurism and inefficiency from corrupting a proper society. Not all members of the state but only the guardians have the time and facilities and indeed the right and authority to speculate freely. If Plato's premise is correct, only this class has the ability to rule. For the guardians, of course, the republic is ideally constituted. Within it the intellectual rules without having to consider law, custom, or public opinion; reason and knowledge, exercised by those who possess those attributes in the greatest measure, are supreme.

Communism in the Republic

One of the most novel features of the *Republic* is Plato's plan for communism in the upper classes. This, like education, is designed essentially to maintain the status quo. Plato's communism is, in its purpose, unlike that formulated by Marx and other modern socialists. It is not designed to improve a standard of living; it does not apply to the entire community; and it is more comprehensive where it does apply because it extends to family as well as to property. Plato's com-munism has a political or moral rather than an economic end.[5] Plato understood the disruptive force in society of disagreements over prop-

---

[5] *Ibid.*, p. 58. See also Ernest Barker, *Greek Political Theory: Plato and His Predeces-sors,* 4th ed., Barnes & Noble, Inc., New York, 1951, pp. 213–214.

erty holdings. The struggle for political power (which might be used for economic advantage) between the haves and the have-nots was well known to him. If wrangles over property were to be permitted in the perfect state, they would unquestionably upset the delicate balance that Plato was so careful to create. Such a danger could be forestalled by the elimination of private property. It could not be completely abolished or even eliminated among the majority of citizens. The artisan class, by far the most numerous, would be permitted to hold property because they, dominated by appetitive urges, were incapable of doing without it. But for the upper classes, in whom appetite was subordinated to the forces of reason and spirit, communism was both possible and necessary. For them the dangers of excessive individualism, encouraged by disparity in property holdings, would be lessened. There would be no competition for political power among the members of the ruling and military classes attributable to the desire to use such power for economic aggrandizement. The many distractions to rulers, due in one way or another to private property, would be absent in the harmonious republic.

The scheme of communism in the *Republic*, however, was not confined to private property. It extended as well to family relationships in the upper classes. Neither marriages nor any form of monogamous union were to be allowed among men and women in the ruling and military classes. Breeding was to be regulated so as to produce offspring from the best possible stock, and the regulation had as its purpose always the welfare of the state. The offspring of these controlled unions were to be reared by the state. No individual parent-child relationship was to be recognized, for parents were parents of all, and children were the children of all. The state was to be maintained at an optimum size and populated by the best of the offspring produced by men and women in their prime. Abortion, infanticide, and neglect of the chronically ill and unfit are devices recommended by Plato to maintain the size and quality of the community.

The eugenic and the communistic aspects of family life are related but not identical. Plato sought eugenic ends through state control of breeding; but the idea of a community of wives and children was devoted to the same end as that involved in the communism of private property. Family implies and is traditionally associated with the property required for its maintenance, and Plato feels that one cannot be eliminated without the other. More important, concern with marital relationships and with children would detract from the interest of the ruling class in the affairs of state and the pursuit of knowledge. Both marriage and property are distracting influences and cannot be countenanced in the ideal state.

Plato's attitude on the emancipation of women was unique. It was his view that aside from the physical distinctions, there was little difference between men and women. Women should therefore not only be permitted but compelled to perform to the best of their ability the role of citizen. Women in the state would share the military and rulership duties with men on a plane of equality with them. Women in the upper classes had a duty to bear children, but they were not to be further concerned with the care of a child after its birth. The freedom for women in which Plato was interested involved duties rather than rights. Plato, having defined justice, was intent upon its complete implementation. Women, like men, were to do those tasks for which they were best suited, and though presumably the tasks might involve household duties, often they might consist in other occupations. It was his concept of justice and not a crusading zeal for the rights of women, that led Plato to adopt the view expressed in the *Republic*. The relegation of the Athenian female to the role of childbearer and housekeeper and her complete absence from the field of civic activity Plato considered a flagrant waste of a valuable resource rather than a transgression on women's rights.[6]

In his plan of communism both in matters of property and family the ascetic quality of Plato's nature is apparent. He objected to the Athenian society in part because it had become too complicated and luxurious. In his view men needed to return to the simpler life of the past and to reject the gluttony, sensuality, and conviviality that had caused a departure from first principles. Preoccupation with the satisfaction of appetitive urges had, Plato believed, weakened the resolution of the Athenian citizenry and resulted in military and moral collapse. Not reform but renovation of the kind urged in the *Republic* was necessary if society was to be saved.

The Republic *Concluded*

One further subject in the *Republic* requires brief mention. Plato discusses states less perfect than his ideal republic in order to contrast justice with injustice as they are evidenced in state forms. The ideal state may undergo four progressive stages of degenerative corruption: from the ideal republic to timocracy or military rule, to oligarchy, to democracy, and finally to tyranny. In a timocracy, spirit is the dominating force in the state. Spirit is less desirable than reason but better than its subsequent corruptions. All the other forms of rule—oligarchy, democracy, and tyranny—are dominated by appetite. Some appetites or desires are, however, more destructive than others. Oligarchies occur when rulers are turned from the proper path by their love of wealth. Democracy represents the corruption of oligarchy and results from the revolution of poor against rich after a period of dissatisfaction and after their discovery that wealth is not true evidence of moral superi-

[6] Barker, *op. cit.,* p. 219.

ority. Democracy is anarchy; issuing from the lust for freedom, it is worse than oligarchy. By its very nature democracy cannot long remain moderate. Political demagogues exploit the orderly middle class for the benefit of a shiftless proletariat, and when the middle class objects, the demagogue becomes a tyrant. This categorization of states is particularly significant in the light of Plato's conclusions on the same subject in his later works.

Plato's relegation of democracy to the inferior place it occupies in this classification of states is simply a reiteration of the theme of the *Republic*. Plato does not hate the common man; he only believes him to be utterly incapable of governing himself. The *Republic* is based upon this assumption and is designed to offer the alternative of good, that is, expert, government. Inexpert government permits the individual appetite to run wild. Education and communism are devices employed to curb the excessive individualism that disrupts the state and is ultimately destructive of individual morality and justice.

But Plato in his zeal goes too far. In his proclaimed effort to save and improve individual morality Plato destroys individualism. The citizen loses his freedom. The fact that he is qualified to follow only one calling (if indeed we may assume that such a determination can be made) does not mitigate the harshness of the deprivation of freedom to which he is subjected. Plato recognizes the importance of the community to the individual. He is correct in his assumption that what man is he owes largely to the community and that therefore the community has an undeniable claim upon him. But again the extremity of Plato's conclusion is unwarranted. The individual's value does not lie solely in his relationship to the state, and in stressing society's claim upon him, Plato was forgetting the great moral lesson learned from the death of Socrates. A measure of freedom is probably more conducive to the harmony and unity of society than Plato supposed. The good society depends for its existence upon the ability of its members to find the proper balance of freedom and authority, and the problem cannot be solved by throwing all the weight to either side of the fulcrum. Unity in society may be purchased at too high a price. The price Plato demands is exorbitant.

The communism in property and family which Plato proposes for the upper classes is also designed to maintain the desired harmony. Plato implies that private property and family relationships are evidences of man's lower nature that must be shunned by rulers if they are to devote their energies to the welfare of the community. But the elimination of private property would hardly be so efficacious in destroying selfish tendencies. The drive for personal power, property considerations aside, is a potent one. Moreover the destruction of family life might just as easily disrupt the harmony of the community as it would promote it. Nevertheless, if Plato's knowledge of psychology is inadequate, if his planning is sometimes loose, and if many of his conclusions are faulty, we must still acknowledge that the *Republic* is a great work, provocative and supremely challenging. Plato attacks democracy at its most vulnerable point, and it still remains to be seen whether that salient can be held. With the increasing complexity of issues and the mounting difficulty experienced by men in their efforts to understand affairs in the modern world, Plato's challenge becomes more pertinent than ever. Can democracy, as it is understood to mean some kind of participation by the general public in the decision-making process, survive? Or is Plato's solution the best after all? Should the complete direction of public affairs be turned over to those who know, even at the cost of the loss of freedom? The latter solution, which has been accepted by millions in modern as well as ancient times, may be more attractive today than it has been in the past.

The Statesman

Both the *Statesman* and the *Laws* are products of a later period of Plato's life. The *Statesman* generally represents an attitude toward democracy slightly less antagonistic than was demonstrated in the *Republic,* though not yet as moderate as the view expressed in the early books of the *Laws;* and the *Statesman* probably preceded the *Laws*.[7] The *Republic* is better literature than either of the later works, but it would be incorrect to assume that the *Statesman* and the *Laws* give evidence of Plato's declining mental powers.[8] In one sense Plato has become more conservative with his advancing years. Never does he repudiate his contention that the *Republic* would be the ideal state, but he acknowledges that the ideal may not be possible and that practicality is, after all, important.

The *Statesman* continues the attack upon amateurism launched in the *Republic*. The good statesman, like the guardian ruler, should be an expert. He rules because he knows how to rule; his capacities constitute his right. Political demagogues may claim to understand the problems of statecraft, but the statesman actually knows. He is an artist. He exercises his superior talents according to his own knowledge and discretion, and they are not to be hedged about by the restrictive barriers of codified law. If the subject peoples of his realm may be improved by the ministrations of this artist statesman, whether or not they consent to the improvement is beside the point. In his arbitrary rule the statesman may use law or not as he sees fit. He is above the law even when he uses it.

We find here an obvious repetition of some of the basic principles of the *Republic*. Plato rejects democracy in favor of the rule of an able and talented guardian. The task of the ruler is to develop a virtuous

[7] *Ibid.,* p. 271.

[8] Sabine, *op. cit.,* p. 67.

people. Education is an important function of government. Law is inferior to knowledge. We may give to the later book the same criticisms and praise we gave to the *Republic,* noting, however, that the *Statesman* lacks the powerful sweep of the earlier work. The book was not intended to be a similar venture, and in so far as it repeats the principles of the *Republic* it is not perhaps of overwhelming significance.

When Plato goes on to a discussion of law and governmental problems in the real world, the *Statesman* contributes something new. Neither the ideal statesman nor the philosopher-king is to be found in this world. Yet life must go on and must follow the best direction possible under the circumstances. The law, previously ignored, shunned, or attacked, is now considered a necessity. Law is imperfect, containing as it does the collected foolishness of the people as well as their wisdom, but it has value since it does promote stability. The security and stability that result from a rigid observance of the law are not so desirable as the harmony and unity to be found in the ideal state, but stability at least prevents further degeneration. If the ignorant (and therefore the unjust) are to control government, they will do less harm if they are restrained by law.

Plato's concern with the law as a device used in imperfect, existing states leads him to a new classification of states different from that he set forth in the *Republic.* In the latter work Plato arranged five kinds of states in the order of their virtue, each inferior step constituting a degeneration of the preceding state. These ranged from the ideal state of the Republic at the top through timocracy, oligarchy, and democracy to tyranny at the bottom. In the *Statesman* Plato in effect puts the ideal state aside as desirable but impractical and proceeds to a two-fold classification of lawful and unlawful states in the following manner:

THE IDEAL STATE OF THE REPUBLIC
(Perfect but Impractical)

Lawful States	Unlawful States
Knowledge expressed by law is the directing force.	The directing force is arbitrary and is not restrained by law.
I. Monarchy—the lawful rule of one is the best state.	I. Tyranny—the unlawful rule of one is the worst of all states.
II. Aristocracy—the lawful rule of a few is the second-best state.	II. Oligarchy—the unlawful rule of a few is next to the worst of states.
III. Constitutional Democracy—the lawful and moderate rule of many is the worst of the lawful states but is better than any unlawful state.	III. Unconstitutional Democracy—the arbitrary and extreme rule of many is unlawful and thus bad but less dangerous than tyranny or oligarchy.

This new classification represents a modification of Plato's earlier views. Democracy as a governmental type occupies an improved position. It is now designated the worst of the lawful states but the best (or least dangerous) of the unlawful states. This alteration does not reflect any view of Plato that democracy is inherently virtuous. It is his opinion that the greater the concentration of authority the more capacity is found for either good or evil, depending upon whether the state is lawful or unlawful. Thus lawful rule by one man is the best, but unlawful rule by one is the worst possible government. At any rate, constitutional or lawful democracy now is regarded by Plato as better than tyranny, oligarchy, and unconstitutional democracy. More significant still is his assumption that in existing conditions, where, we must acknowledge, men are far from perfect, law is the indispensable ingredient without which the forces of brutality and greed rule unrestrained.[9] Plato's loyalty to the principle of rule by the intelligent is still apparent in the *Statesman,* but the passion of the *Republic* has been restrained, and Plato has approached the stage of moderation that is generally evidenced in his *Laws.*

The Laws

The *Laws* is a product of Plato's old age and may have been published posthumously by one of his pupils. As in the *Statesman* there is evidence in the *Laws* of Plato's declining literary talent, but in many places the powerful intellect gleams as of old. The tendency to discursiveness, the concern with religion, the conservatism, and the lack of artistry all attest to Plato's advanced age; but the *Laws* remains a great political treatise, and is, in some respects at least, more impressive than the *Republic.*

In the *Laws* Plato proposes that law shall be substituted for the philosopher-king. True, the wise ruler is preferable, and the ideal state would be best if it were a practical possibility; but it is not. Thus, since only the second-best state is possible, it should follow as closely as it can the postulates of the ideal. In the perfect state reason rules; in the best practicable state law rules. Law and reason are not identical. Some law is foolish and unwise, but since law generally derives from reason, it is substantially sound. At any rate law is a force that holds man to a sane and predictable course. Supplemented and reinforced by custom, law holds together the vast and complicated fabric of civilized life. Law, therefore, must be sovereign rather than men, since men are selfish, and if they are not restrained by law their pursuit of self-interest will disrupt the community. Moreover law must be general rather than particular. Its generality, though a defect, is better than the biased action which would result from an imperfect ruler practicing free decision. Law must be for the whole people and in the interest of the stability of society. In the *Republic* the status quo was maintained by the class

⁹ *Ibid.,* pp. 74–75.

of philosopher-guardians who used the educational system and communism to that end. Now it is the law, rigid and difficult to alter, that performs the task.

Plato abandons, in the *Laws*, the principles of division of classes and specialization that he had embraced in the *Republic*, in favor of moderation and self-control, which he hopes will conduce to the desired unity and harmony of the community. What kind of state will be most likely to develop these necessary qualities in its citizens? The answer is, a mixed constitution, which secures the desired moderation through a balance of oligarchical and democratic principles. The powers of the oligarchy must be restrained by a measure of popular control. The change in approach is a significant and startling one for Plato. For the first time in his writings he grants the principle of consent. To be sure, his is an incomplete and grudging admission, but the monolithic structure of government resting upon a foundation of absolute rule by the able, erected so carefully in the *Republic* and the *Statesman*, is now cracked.

The Model State of the Laws

In the *Laws*, as in the *Republic*, Plato's technique involves the construction of a model state. This state, he proposes, should be located inland and far enough from the sea to prevent naval militarism and to discourage commercialism. To Plato naval military power was inferior to that of land armies and tended to corrupt the nation that relied upon it. He objected to commercial traffic on the ground that it filled the city with those whose primary concern was profit rather than civic duties. The community is to be agricultural and self-supporting, but no more. A state that raises either insufficient produce or a surplus will inevitably turn to commerce, and commerce in turn will bring an invasion of the desired privacy and isolation. Agriculture as the basic means of livelihood also has another advantage: unlike commerce, it can hardly produce the great wealth that diverts the minds and energies of the citizens from civic affairs. Plato wants a body of citizens not so poor that they must spend full time grubbing for a living but not so wealthy that they think only of money.

The number of citizens in the state Plato believes should be set at 5,040. The figure is not arbitrarily chosen but demonstrates the Pythagorean influence upon Plato's thought. The figure 5,040 is capable of being divided by every number up to 10 and also by 12; thus it is a convenient figure for purposes of community organization. The state is to be divided into twelve tribes and governed by a State Council consisting of twelve committees, each of which serves an equal part of the year. The currency system and that of weights and measures are also to be based upon the numerical system selected by Plato. In proposing a uniform numerical system, Plato has in mind more than mere convenience. It will also be advantageous from an educational viewpoint, since the study of mathematics is basic, and is stimulating to the youth.

Property in the Laws

In his property arrangements for the state of the *Laws* Plato departs from the principles of the *Republic* but attempts to retain something of their spirit. The state is divided into 5,040 equal lots, one for each citizen. Though the land is privately owned, each citizen is admonished to bear in mind the social purpose of the property. There are common tables at which citizens consume the produce of the land. The land cannot be transferred except through inheritance, and it cannot be divided. Thus the number of citizens must remain constant. If a citizen has no heir he must assign ownership to the son of another; if the population increases beyond the desired point, birth control or colonization may be used to diminish it. If, as Plato believed more likely, population decreases, a system of incentives and penalties must be invoked to restore it to the ideal number. Land holdings, in all events, must be maintained on a basis of equality.

Property other than land is not so equalized. Although Plato suggests that a universal equality in property might be desirable, he recognizes that, men being what they are, it is not practicable. Nevertheless, the state exercises substantial control over other forms of property. Each citizen is permitted to hold private property up to four times the value of his land. Thus though inequality in personal property exists, it is a limited and regulated inequality. The limitation is even more significant than is initially apparent. It is designed not exclusively to prevent an excessive concern with wealth but also to determine qualifications for the franchise and the exercise of political power in the state. Active participation in government is based upon the division of the citizens into four classes, each class representing a different amount of property ownership. One class will own the least amount of private property and the others will own, respectively, two, three, and four times the value of their land in private property. The amount of political power wielded by a class is to be proportionate to the amount of private property owned.

Other methods of regulating property are utilized. All wealth gained by a citizen in excess of four times the value of his landed property must be turned over to the state. Commercial activities will be handled only by aliens who, however, will also be carefully regulated. Currency systems are to be based entirely upon local usage, and no citizen is to be permitted to own gold or silver. Plato's citizens derive their sustenance from the land. Their labor is not excessive, since the soil is tilled

by slaves, and the citizen is concerned only with maintaining his existence on a moderate level that will neither excite his desire for luxury
nor deprive him of time to devote to civic matters. Plato attempts to
combine the institution of private property with comprehensive regulation and thus produce much the same situation that existed for his
ruling classes under communism in the *Republic*. The underlying
assumption is the same; preoccupation with property matters is a disruptive influence and must be coped with one way or another. In the
Republic Plato's solution was the abolition of private property; in
the *Laws* he substitutes regulation. All citizens in the model state of the
Laws constitute a kind of ruling class. They draw their living from the
land, but their major interest is government.[10]

Marriage and the Family

In the *Laws* Plato reiterates many of the opinions expressed in the
Republic about marriage and the family. Again he deprecates the loss
to the community of half of the available citizens when women are
barred from contributing their share of civic effort. As in the *Republic,*
Plato contends that women should share the same educational advantages as men and should be free to work in the same fields. Through
a system of common tables Plato draws women into public discussions.
He does not insist that they share a table with men but recommends
that they should be seated in near proximity to them. In all phases of
training women must be treated equally with men. Education is compulsory for both sexes. Both are similarly trained in gymnastics. Women
are to serve in the military forces and must, like men, train in the
militia. The one activity which Plato neglects, as far as women are
concerned, is that of office holding and voting. It is not clear whether
the lapse is intentional or an oversight. The *Laws* is marked by inconsistencies of which this omission may be an example.

Plato does not propose a community of wives and children in the
Laws as he does in the *Republic*. Such an institution is only for the
perfect state, and the model state of the *Laws* presumably accepts members of the human race as they are. Nevertheless, certain precautions
are to be taken to assure that the welfare of the state will be safeguarded. Since this state looks for moderation in all things, the extremes in human nature should be modified by the union in marriage
of opposites. Rich should marry poor, strong should marry weak, the
hotheaded should marry the phlegmatic. There should be no legal compulsion in these arrangements, but citizens should be taught that
marriage has a public as well as a private end.

[10] Barker, *op. cit.*, p. 326.

Government in the Model State of the Laws

In his plan of government Plato seeks the quality of moderation and, even as in his recommendations concerning marriage, attempts to achieve it through a combination of extremes. The opposing governmental forms are oligarchy and democracy, and the best practicable state will be a combination of the two. Plato is evidently trying to find a balance of wisdom and numbers. That he should make the effort is indicative of the change of attitude Plato has experienced since the *Republic*. In that work it was assumed that no balance was possible and that the problem must be resolved by throwing all weight to the side of an intellectual authority. But the fact that Plato in the *Laws* permits a small measure of democracy should not lead us to assume that he does so because he has come to believe in the virtue and capacity of the average man. He advises that ample precautions be taken to prevent the direct exercise of authority by the ordinary citizen. Plato's concession results from his acknowledgement of the fact that the achievement of peace and harmony in the state is difficult if the citizens are denied some kind of voice in the governing process. Even so, Plato's plan of government in the *Laws* is so heavily weighted in favor of the authority of an oligarchy that it is difficult to distinguish any substantial element of democracy in it.

Plato's constitution for the model state is an elaborate one. The familiar organizations of assembly, council, and magistrates are present but differ from the Athenian form in their method of selection and in their scope of power. All citizens capable of bearing arms are entitled to membership in the assembly, but the election of magistrates and council constitutes practically the only power exerted by the body of citizens. Moreover, the selection of officials by the assembly employs the system of election, which was considered an aristocratic device by Athenians, rather than the drawing of lots, which was the accepted democratic way. The most interesting aspect of the electoral system is that concerned with the election of the Council of 360. Here the class structure based upon the distinctions in the holding of personal property comes into play. The entire body of citizens is divided into four classes; the class designation is dependent upon whether a citizen owns personal property equivalent to, or two, three, or four times the value of his property in land, which, it will be recalled, is equal for all. It may be assumed that the relative size of each class will be inversely proportionate to the amount of property owned; yet each class is entitled to one-fourth of the membership in the Council. Consequently the wealthier classes are far more adequately represented in this powerful body than are the poorer classes. Also in the elections, members of the fourth, or lowest, property class may vote or not as they choose, but increasingly severe penalties are levied for nonvoting on each of the successively higher levels.

Plato seemingly equates wealth with virtue, although on other occasions he refutes this point of view. Plato faces a dilemma in the *Laws*. In his *Republic* he clearly states that the virtuous should rule, and since knowledge is virtue it is only necessary to find and train the most knowledgeable in order to establish a just system of rulership. The educational system that performs this function in the *Republic* thus achieves its significance. But in the *Laws* Plato has abandoned the ideal as impractical. Still, someone must govern, and it must not be the mass of citizens. Surely sufficient concession has been made to democracy in granting permission to all citizens to hold membership in the Assembly and to cast a vote. This power, unless restricted, could bring about the ruin of the state. A check must be imposed upon the masses by the more able in the community, and Plato finds this ability among those who have managed to accumulate most property. Citizens of the first two classes are consequently granted substantial advantages in matters of elective power and holding public office. The wealth-virtue equation has many flaws, of which Plato must have been aware. Yet he could see no alternative. If we grant that the "best people" should have a dominant share of public power, and if no educational system exists whereby this elite may be chosen, then, Plato thinks, wealth is the next best (most practicable) method of determining ability. Other things being equal (and they seldom are), the person who has more shrewdness than his fellows in gathering worldly goods may also have more political ability. The assumption, whether correct or not, has had its share of illustrious advocates. Coming from Plato, however, it is mildly disappointing. Even the second-best offering of the author of the *Republic*, one feels, ought to be more original and provocative.

Plato's treatment of the operation of the state of the *Laws* is broader than that employed in the *Republic;* the state, as described in the earlier book, was essentially an educational institution. Still there are many similarities. Considerable attention is given to education. The curriculum outlined in the *Laws* parallels that of the *Republic.* Both "gymnastics" and "music" are taught. Women have opportunities equally with men. Literature is carefully censored. Education is compulsory. The minister of education is the highest of all state officers, and is in fact a kind of prime minister elected by secret ballot in a meeting of the magistrates of the state. Plato remains in the *Laws,* as in the *Republic,* vitally interested in education and insists upon the correlation between the good state and an educated citizenry.

In his concern with religion in the *Laws* Plato departs radically from the theme of the *Republic*. In the latter work religion receives only passing reference, but in the *Laws* it is given considerable attention.

Plato advocates a rigorous system of state control over religious practice. He anticipates the view of Christian rulers of the Middle Ages in assuming that loyalty to the state and religious conformity go hand in hand. It is a duty of the state to enforce obedience to religious law. Above all, the existence of the gods is not to be denied. The penalties for heresy are grim indeed and include even death.

The Reversion to Authoritarianism

Plato's avowed purpose in the *Laws* was to outline the form of a second-best but practicable state. In this community law was to replace the authoritarianism of the philosopher-kings of the *Republic*, and his persuasive eulogies on the law in the earlier sections of his work, coupled with his advocacy of a framework of government which permits a degree of democracy, make it appear that Plato is well on his way to completion of his task. As the discussion develops, however, more and more barriers are placed in the way of popular control, and it becomes clear that Plato has created only an illusion of democracy. The illusion itself tends to disappear in the twelfth book of the *Laws* with Plato's introduction of the Nocturnal Council. This unusual body consists of the most important state officials, including the ten oldest guardians of the law, the high-ranking minister of education, a number of priests, and others. The minimum age represented is fifty years, the assumption being that the conservative dedication to the status quo will be assured by such a requirement. To avoid absolute rule by the aged, Plato provides that younger men between the ages of thirty and forty may become members of the Nocturnal Council if they are acceptable to the older officeholders.[11]

This body forms a kind of supercabinet operating outside the framework of the law to direct the destiny of the state. Its membership is predominantly ex officio; yet it has power to control the elective offices of government. The men assigned to the Nocturnal Council must study astronomy, since a knowledge of the heavens brings one closer to God, and an understanding of God is necessary to the rulers if they are to bring about and maintain the goodness and unity of the state. Thus Plato returns to the authoritarianism of the *Republic*. The political institutions of the model state of the *Laws*, aside from the Nocturnal Council, are relegated to an inferior position. If Plato had concluded the *Laws* before adding the twelfth book, his state would not have offended the conservative sensitivities of a Burke; but with the superimposing of the Nocturnal Council, even the qualified approval of a limited degree of popular control and the rule of law are absent. The

---

[11] The composition of the council is not satisfactorily explained by Plato and there is some confusion on the point among various commentators. The interpretation given here is that of Barker, *op. cit.*, pp. 346–347.

members of the Nocturnal Council are the philosopher-rulers of the state of the *Laws*. They constitute an elite whose knowledge makes them supreme. It might well be argued that their knowledge, which stresses religion and mathematical mysticism, is inferior to that possessed by the guardians of the *Republic*. Plato ends up with a semitheocracy, a government at least partially composed of priests, who have a principal duty of maintaining religious conformity along with that of supervising state affairs.[12]

Conclusions

Plato was incapable of basically altering his views. From Socrates he had learned his lesson and perhaps too well. *Virtue is knowledge*. Men are *not* created equal; they vary in many respects, not the least of which is in their capacity to gain knowledge. This inequality does not signify that those with less capacity should be ignored; rather it means that they should be disciplined by those who know how to govern. These premises led Plato inevitably to his conclusion that the state must be directed by a knowledgeable (and thus a virtuous) elite. Herein lies the political essence of the *Laws,* the *Statesman,* and the *Republic*. But the *Republic* is more than a political treatise; it is an analysis of society and its problems in which the principle of the satisfaction of reciprocal needs is carried to its logical conclusion. If the psychological information upon which Plato posits his thesis of society was faulty, as it unquestionably was, the thesis itself is a powerful one. If the authority provided in the *Republic* was absolute, it was always dedicated to individual and social improvement. If Plato neglected individual liberty in his concern for the community, it is also true that society has often been neglected and abused in the name of individual liberty. If Plato rejected tradition and *stare decisis* in favor of policy direction by intelligence, it is the fact that intelligence does not often enough hold sway and that we are perhaps too much the slaves of custom.

If Plato is wrong, wherein lies his error? Perhaps he errs mainly in his analysis of human nature. Unquestionably security is desired by most people, but it may not be as attractive as Plato supposed. Freedom too is important, and considering the long struggle of humankind to achieve it (a struggle with which Plato was certainly not unacquainted), we may find Plato's comparative neglect of freedom a weakness in his philosophy. The grudging recognition he accords to the drive for freedom in his *Laws* and his apparent admission that the stability of the state depends in part upon at least a restricted principle of consent are both abandoned with the introduction of the Nocturnal Council. The fact probably is that the majority of people are neither as greedy and inept as Plato believed, nor as good as Marx presumed them to be. Men

[12] *Ibid.*, p. 351.

cannot live without both authority *and* freedom. The problem is to discover and establish the proper amount of each, and that problem cannot be solved for all time by the devising of a single formula, even though it is as complex as Plato's.

Nevertheless, Plato's criticism of democracy cannot be lightly dismissed. Democracy is a difficult system of government to maintain, perhaps especially because the freedom which must be an integral part of it is, as Plato saw, also a disruptive power. Freedom means diversity, and diversity can become a force powerful enough to break the rather fragile bonds of agreement that hold together the democratic fabric. The disruption has happened only too often in our own time. Moreover, even democracies must be led, and the omnipresent demagogic politician in a democracy is forever trying, and sometimes successfully, to supplant as leader the wise and civic-minded statesman. But the solution to the problems raised by the difficulties inherent in democracy is not to be found in discarding the democratic form. Democracy is well worth saving, and in his magnificent tribute to education, as well as in other ways, Plato provides us with a few proposals that may be helpful in saving it.

SELECTED BIBLIOGRAPHY

Barker, Ernest: *Greek Political Theory: Plato and His Predecessors,* 4th ed., Barnes & Noble, Inc., New York, 1951, chaps. 6–17.

Catlin, George: *The Story of the Political Philosophers,* McGraw-Hill Book Company, Inc., New York, 1939, chap. 2.

Edman, Irwin (ed.): *The Works of Plato* (Benjamin Jowett translation), Modern Library, Inc., New York, 1928.

Levinson, Ronald B.: *In Defense of Plato,* Harvard University Press, Cambridge, Mass., 1953.

McIlwain, Charles Howard: *The Growth of Political Thought in the West,* The Macmillan Company, New York, 1932, chap. 2.

Sabine, George H.: *A History of Political Theory,* 3d ed., Holt, Rinehart and Winston, Inc., New York, 1961, chaps. 3, 4.

The Republic of Plato (F. M. Cornford translation), Oxford University Press, Fair Lawn, N.J., 1945, introduction.

The Republic of Plato (Benjamin Jowett translation), 4th ed., Oxford University Press, Fair Lawn, N.J., 1953.

four

ARISTOTLE

In Athens Plato, the head of the Academy, was compiling material for his last major work, the *Laws,* and he was also engaged in other enterprises. In addition to administering the affairs of the school he was deeply involved in the affairs of Syracuse and Dionysius II—an involvement which was to lead to disappointment and frustration. Preoccupied as he was, Plato probably paid little attention to the enrollment in his Academy of a seventeen-year-old colonial who had recently arrived in Athens. Nevertheless, it was a significant event. When the young Aristotle attached himself to Plato's Academy rather than to the school of Isocrates (a move he had apparently considered), the train of events that closely linked the lives and philosophies of three of the greatest thinkers the world has ever known was complete. Aristotle (384–322 B.C.), chronologically the last of the distinguished triumvirate, was to disagree openly on many points with Socrates and Plato, but the area of agreement was larger than has sometimes been realized, and Aristotle was more profoundly affected by the ideas of his predecessors than perhaps even he knew.

Aristotle developed a political philosophy which, emphasizing constitutionalism and the rule of law, was closer to the Athenian democratic ideal than were those of either Plato or Socrates. Yet they were native Athenians and Aristotle was not. Aristotle was born in Stagira on the borders of Macedonia to parents of Ionian origin. His father was a physician of note and was ultimately appointed to the Macedonian court. His father's occupation influenced Aristotle early to direct his interest to the biological sciences and thus ultimately to develop the scientific method, involving the techniques of classification and comparison, which was evident in Aristotle's philosophical writings.

Aristotle came to Athens at a time more propitious to the development of democratic ideas than that in which Plato's philosophy had matured. The Athenian city-state was rapidly recovering its vitality and spirit after a period of depression following its defeat by Sparta in the Peloponnesian War and was entering upon a time of prosperity. The Spartan military state, which had appeared attractive to Plato because of its earlier successes, was not similarly appealing to Aristotle. The more liberal climate had a salutary effect on the views of even the master of the Academy; Plato was engaged in writing the *Laws*, the work in which he came nearest to an approval of democracy and the rule of law.[1] Aristotle was certainly influenced by this phase of his teacher's interest, though to what degree we do not know. At any rate the neophyte must have found the relationship with Plato satisfactory. He remained at the Academy for a period of twenty years, first as a student and then as an assistant to Plato until the old aristocrat died.

Aristotle was thirty-seven when he left Plato's Academy, but he continued his educational efforts in company with other ex-members of the Academy at Assus, and later he studied marine biology at Lesbos. At the age of forty Aristotle married the niece of Hermias, the ruler of Atarneus, after having acted as an unofficial adviser of Hermias for several years. Soon after this, Aristotle was summoned by Philip of Macedon to tutor the young prince Alexander. Thus began an association that endured for many years.

In the year 335 B.C., Aristotle returned to Athens to establish his own school, the Lyceum. The city-state had become a Macedonian protectorate, and the presence of an associate of Alexander was regarded with suspicion in many quarters, even after Aristotle and his former pupil had a well-publicized falling out. Still the school flourished, and Aristotle was immensely popular as a teacher. In the summer of 323 B.C. came the news of Alexander's death, and throughout the vast empire built by the great Macedonian, repercussions were felt. There were uprisings in Greece. In Athens much bitterness was immediately directed toward Aristotle because of his connection with Alexander. Aristotle, more prudent than Socrates and uninhibited, as the old philosopher had been, by a matter of principle, regarded flight as the better part of valor and left immediately for Chalcis, where he awaited the cooling of Athenian tempers or the restoration of Macedonian control. He was to witness neither. Within the year Antipater, Alexander's lieutenant

---

[1] This, of course, was a qualified approval. See our discussion of Plato's *Laws* in Chap. 3, pp. 44–51.

in Athens, defeated the rebellious Greeks in a great sea victory at Amorgos. But Aristotle died before the event, while still being excoriated vigorously by his enemies in Athens and elsewhere in Greece.

Aristotle's Method

No account of the political ideas of Aristotle would be complete without some reference to his method. Aristotle may properly be termed the first-known political *scientist*. He agreed with Plato that the statesman should be able to construct the ideal state. The rules, the principles, the laws that help to achieve the ideal are important. But since man, being what he is, will never be able to incorporate all the components of justice into his own community, the principal objective of the scholar of politics and the statesman is to establish the *best practicable state*, one which does not presume more virtue and ability than men actually possess. In fact the concern will be more probably with the modest reformation of an existing state than with the construction of a new state, perfect or imperfect. Aristotle and Plato agreed that the state is indispensable to man. Only within its environs can he live a wholesome life and find it possible to reach the fulfillment of his potentialities. The perfect state would develop men perfectly, but failing a perfect state, the task must be done as well as possible. Any state is better than none at all. Anarchy, involving a complete lack of community, would drag men down to an animallike existence. Aristotle anticipated Machiavelli's advice to tyrants,[2] not because he admired tyranny, but because he thought even the tyrannous state preferable to chaos.

In both the natural and social sciences Aristotle favored the evolutionary view of scientific investigation. The student must examine the process; in studying states he must consider the historic process. From his interest in the history of states Aristotle developed a healthy respect for tradition and custom. Though this respect never became a slavish devotion to old-established ways, Aristotle was convinced that something could be said for a practice long favored among a people. In this, too, his stand was opposite to that taken by Plato, who ignored the forces of tradition in his *Republic*. To Aristotle, tradition and custom had merit mainly because they functioned. Possibly they might not seem to be supported by logic, but, Aristotle contended, if there were no reason behind custom and tradition they would not have evolved initially. They ought not to be abandoned lightly.

The State: Origin and Purpose in Aristotle's Philosophy

Because he is a sociable creature, man would form a state even if he foresaw no advantages beyond the knitting together of human relations. But there are other advantages. The state is a community that makes

[2] George H. Sabine, *A History of Political Theory*, 3d ed., Holt, Rinehart and Winston, Inc., New York, 1961, chap. 5.

possible a better, fuller life than could be attained without it. Although the material benefits alone are many and important, they are less significant than the moral advantages. Man always seeks the good. That he strives for justice, for moral perfection cannot be doubted, even though he has thus far fallen short of his ultimate goal. Man is the only animal endowed with the ability to reason and to communicate. Nature is not capricious; she does nothing without a purpose. Man has been granted these marvelous gifts to enable him to think and to express himself with regard to such matters as justice and injustice, good and evil. The possession of these capabilities alone, however, does not suffice to enable man to pursue the ends of justice and moral perfection. If he lives alone and is compelled to devote each waking moment to the satisfaction of physical needs, he will be denied all possibility of progress. Man living in this manner is a beast with little to distinguish him from the lowest orders of life. In fact, no truly human life exists outside the state. The path of progress leading to human improvement—even perfection—can be negotiated only with the assistance of organization. Both instinct and reason have joined in enabling man to develop progressively more complex organizations, from the family to the village and ultimately to the state, in his struggle for self-improvement. The state, or *polis,* is the highest organization of the community through which man strives for moral perfection.

Although the state is an organization created by man for his own benefit, it is also a natural institution. The state represents the *culmination* of institutional development, but it is *prior* to the individual and to all other (and subsidiary) organizations because outside the state man is a meaningless fragment. In the interest of clarification of this essential ingredient of his philosophy, Aristotle uses the analogy of the flower seed. The seed is less representative of the true nature of the species than is the flower in full bloom; yet it precedes the flower. Thus the state is more natural than the precedent individual, family, or village. The state represents the pinnacle which man, as a social animal, has achieved after a long period of development and experience with lesser levels of organization. The state is the natural home that the individual has found in the culminating phase of his drive toward moral perfection.

Much in Aristotle's theory of development is typically Greek. Aristotle proposed a moderately organic theory of the state, one that saw the individual as a part of the state, drawing from it those benefits which give him dignity and stature as a human being. The state was not a mere instrument, even if a highly useful one; it was a *community.* It required rules of order, laws, to manage its citizens; but the people were held together by the bonds of community and fellowship more tightly than by laws. The validity of this view was easier to understand

and accept within the more intimate confines of the city-state than it possibly could be in the modern nation-state. Modern democratic thought still favors a state that leaves considerable freedom for the individual; but in recent decades liberal democratic thinkers have become increasingly conscious that the emphasis on individualism has often resulted in the abuse of the community by an unscrupulous few who have successfully pleaded immunity from responsibility in the name of individual freedom. And the state has once again been recognized, in degree and in some countries at least, as a higher form of organization indispensable to the improvement of individual and community alike and devoted to that double end.

The Various Forms of States

The state may assume an infinite variety of forms. Aristotle discusses the ideal state, the state that perfectly accomplishes the task of achieving moral perfection in its citizens. But he recognizes that to devote full time to the consideration of such a utopia would be a waste of effort. A state may be good without being perfect, and man probably must do the best he can with a bad state. The measure of the goodness or justness of a state is its capacity to serve the general interest. It is bad or unjust to the degree that it serves only the interest of its ruler or rulers. "Those constitutions which consider the common interest are *right* constitutions, judged by the standard of absolute justice. Those constitutions which consider only the personal interest of the rulers are all *wrong* constitutions, or *perversions* of the right forms." [3]

Not all the just forms of the state require the same kind of constitution. A constitution is the basic law determining the allocation of power within the state as well as the distribution of rights and rewards. The type of constitution will, in turn, depend upon the kind and quality of citizens in the state. The success of the state will depend upon how well the constitutional allocation reflects the composition of the citizen body. Justice, the end sought by the art of politics, will be achieved if rewards are distributed and if power is exerted on the basis of contributions made to the community. Since men do not contribute equally, the exercise of power and the receipt of rewards will also be unequally distributed. The division will not be as unequal as Plato believed necessary in the *Republic,* but neither will it be as equal as the radical democrats advocate. This is Aristotle's principle of *distributive justice.*

All classes of men err in making judgments on this matter. Democrats err in assuming that because men are born equally free, each man is entitled to exercise an amount of political power similar to his neigh-

---

[3] *The Politics of Aristotle* (Ernest Barker translation), Oxford University Press, Fair Lawn, N.J., 1946, III, vi, p. 112. Subsequent quotations from and references to the *Politics* are from this edition.

bor's. The oligarchs mistake superiority of wealth for virtue in all other respects. But justice, Aristotle contends, does not consist in an enforced equality in the holding of public office, nor does it mean that office shall go to those who possess wealth. Rather, "Claims to political rights must be based on the ground of contribution to the elements which constitute the being of the state." [4]

Like Plato in the *Statesman*, Aristotle classifies states according to their ability to achieve justice. There are three "right" kinds of constitutions—"right" because each one assumes that those who rule do so in the common interest and are chosen on the basis of their ability. These forms are, in order of desirability, monarchy, aristocracy, and polity (or moderate democracy). Each of these three has its corresponding perversion: tyranny, oligarchy, and extreme democracy. Monarchy (rule by the virtuous man) is the best of the good constitutions; tyranny (rule by the selfish man) is the worst of the perverted forms. Aristocracy (rule by the virtuous few) is the second-best of the good forms; oligarchy (rule by a few selfish wealthy) is the second-worst of the perversions. Polity (government *by* the people and *for* the people) is the poorest of the good; extreme democracy (mob rule) is the best of the worst. The classification is the same as that employed by Plato in his *Statesman*. Aristotle is quick to point out, however, that this classification embraces a multitude of forms. Constitutions vary with the composition of the class structure, in which is great variety.

Aristotle recognizes that the monarchical and aristocratic forms are, in fact, ideal states ruled by an omniscient and omnipotent one (or few). He has little to say concerning aristocracies, although he discusses in some detail the possibilities of monarchy, perhaps because of his association with Hermias and Alexander. If the perfect ruler or family could be found, a person or persons of such great talent and ability "as to surpass that of all the rest," it would obviously be unjust to compel him or them to accept a position of equality with other citizens. But Aristotle merely pays his respects to the demands of logical argument. There is, in fact, no perfect man or men, and even if there were, Aristotle's later emphasis upon constitutionalism and the rule of law makes it quite clear that he would be uneasy if compelled to deny the principle (although somewhat modified) of equality of citizens under the law. He quickly disposes of Plato's philosopher-king–physician analogy (that the ruler should no more be restricted by law than a physician by an outmoded text) by indicating the obvious fact that a physician is not, after all, a politician and that the motives of the two are different. "Physicians never act in defiance of reason from motives of partiality: they cure their patients and earn their fee. Politicians in office have a habit of doing

[4] *Ibid.*, III, xii, p. 131.

a number of things in order to spite their enemies or favour their friends." [5]

There are no perfect men and thus no philosopher-kings. If one investigates existing monarchical systems he realizes more clearly that rule by one man is too often selfish and unrestrained by law. Who, then, is entitled to rule? This raises the question of the validity of various claims to power in the state. Plato in the *Republic* had said that the virtuous should rule; Aristotle does not dispute this principle in theory but asks how it may be approximated in practice. That is, how may the virtuous be discovered? Virtue, he admits, may even mean equality. But what kind of equality is representative of virtue? Is it just to give all men an equal vote irrespective of birth, education, or property? In point of fact there are two important claims to power, one based upon the rights of property and one upon the claims of the people generally that their welfare be considered. Property or the demands of the masses, which is the valid claim? It would surely be inconsistent to answer that virtue has the best claim and at the same time to say that political power ought to be equated with property ownership. Yet it cannot be denied that property is entitled to protection and that those who own it thus require a share of political power. Moreover, while the claims of the radical democrats that all men are entitled to an equal share of power are wrong simply because men have different capacities and make different contributions, there is something to be said for the claim of numbers.

Thus no single class or person has a totally valid claim to power, but each has a claim that cannot be ignored. The conclusion at which Aristotle arrives is that since no class has a right to be sovereign, the position of sovereignty must be accorded to the law. The law to which Aristotle refers is that of general rules. He reviews the arguments for this kind of law as opposed to Plato's arguments for monarchy, in which discretionary decisions are made by an absolute ruler, and admits that there are advantages on both sides. Generality means impersonality, and while it cannot, as Plato said, "provide for circumstances," it forestalls bias, discrimination, and favoritism. Aristotle proposes that general rules should be mainly used, but that *psephisma,* or special legislation, equity (which is better than law since it represents what the lawmaker would have done if he could have anticipated a special circumstance), and arbitration, which follows equity, should all be employed in the interests of justice. [6]

Those who prefer their philosophy tied up in neat packages and their problems solved once and for all will find Aristotle's answer to the ques-

[5] *Ibid.,* III, xvi, p. 147.

[6] Francis D. Wormuth, "Aristotle on Law," in Milton R. Konvitz and Arthur E. Murphy (eds.), *Essays in Political Theory, Presented to George H. Sabine,* Cornell University Press, Ithaca, N.Y., 1948, pp. 45–61.

tion of who should exercise political power less attractive than that given by Plato in his *Republic*. Plato states that virtue should rule and, when confronted by the same actualities that Aristotle faced, ignores them. Property should *not* have a claim to power; the masses should *not* be considered in the power equation. We must begin again, this time to create a community in which these pestiferous problems will be absent, a community in which the ideal—rule by an intelligent, selfless, virtuous elite—will be achieved. Mission accomplished. But Aristotle, the practical man, the political *scientist,* could not take refuge in what he regarded as wishful thinking. Whether property or numbers *should* have a claim to political power was beside the point. The fact was that they *did,* that they always had, and that, most likely, they always would have. This was a condition not of Aristotle's own choosing but one that the wise and practical man must face.

We must at this point insert a brief comment on Aristotle's view of slavery and the relationship that should exist between master and slave. Aristotle contends that slavery as an institution is justified in a situation in which the slave is naturally inferior to the master. The master should, first, be superior to his slave in his capacity to employ reason. Aristotle concludes that some men differ from one another "as much as the body differs from the soul" or as much as man differs from the lower animals (and these are obvious differences between those whose natural ability limits them to service and those whose ability entitles them to such service). Those who serve are natural slaves; it is beneficial to them to be ruled. A man is a slave by nature if he is "capable of becoming the property of another," and this, in fact, is why he becomes another's property. Such a person lacks the capacity to reason sufficiently to govern himself, although he may recognize such capacity in others.[7] Physical distinctions also separate master and slave. The latter is capable of performing only the "menial duties of life"; the former can serve in the military and hold public office.

Aristotle admits that the distinctions are not always easily perceived and that the ideal is sometimes not achieved. There is such a thing as legal yet wrongful slavery, which occurs when a person whose mental and physical attributes are such as to warrant his being a free man is nonetheless held in slavery. And it is true also that a master should always be kind to his slave; for the good of both he should treat the slave as a living instrument. Nevertheless, if the above conditions are met, Aristotle considers slavery a justifiable, just, and natural institution. As Aristotle puts it: "It is thus clear that, just as some are by nature free, so others are by nature slaves, and for these latter the condition of slavery is both beneficial and just."[8]

[7] *Politics*, I, v, p. 13.
[8] *Ibid.,* I, v, p. 14.

The Area of Practicability

The task of the practicing statesman and political scientist is fourfold. He must, as Plato did and as Aristotle does, study the ideal constitution. He must know what kind of constitution is practicable in a given set of circumstances, recognizing that the situation is not going to be ideal; he must study a constitution which is neither ideal nor even the best practicable and understand how to preserve it; and he must determine the components of the best practicable average constitution for all states. It is difficult to persuade citizens to accept a new constitution, and almost equally difficult to obtain consent for the reform of an existing constitution. The good statesman must know how to help along reform—a tedious and often frustrating task that requires the qualities of a practical man. The student of politics must also know what kind of laws are appropriate to each of the various kinds of constitutions. Laws must accord with the constitution, and the variety of existing constitutions attests to the fact that all states cannot utilize the same kind of laws.

In the first three books of the *Politics* Aristotle interweaves the concepts of politics and ethics in his constitutional discussions. A constitution was presumed to be not only the basic law determining governmental structure and the allocation of powers but also a reflection of the way of life of the citizen. When, in Book IV, Aristotle directs his attention to political actualities, his constitution becomes primarily a legal and political document defining the arrangement of offices and the distribution of power. Economics is treated as a related but separate subject. Even law and the social structure become separate entities in Book IV. The treatment is in line with Aristotle's scientific bent and his devotion to analysis based upon careful classification. In making the separation of law from economics and social structure he moved far outside the customary bounds of typical Greek thought which regarded all such factors as social, religious, legal, and economic forces within the broad definition of politics. To Aristotle a combination of ethics and politics is possible only in the ideal state, which is itself an impossibility. Aristotle has become now fully the practical man and scientist, quite willing to deal with affairs as they are ("without disgust") even if his realism leads to the necessity of telling tyrants how to maintain their tyrannies. He also shrewdly warns (an admonition which should be easily understood by Americans) that the way a constitution is supposed to operate and the way it actually does may well be two different things.

In practice, in the world of the nonideal, states are predominantly either oligarchic or democratic, and the statesman must deal with these two forms. A number of factors, mainly social, political, and economic, predispose a state toward one or another or a combination of these forms. *How* oligarchic or *how* democratic a state may be will depend upon the distribution of wealth, the size, relative strength, and disposition of the classes, and other such circumstances. The large number of possible combinations complicates the task of classification and thus makes more difficult the solution to governmental problems. Unfortunately, however, this is the way things are, and the statesman or scholar must accustom himself to dealing with complicated problems.

For instance, there are many kinds of democracies, from moderate to extreme. The form taken depends upon the relative number of the populace who hold power, and this proportion, in turn, is determined by the kind of property qualification employed. The worst democracy is one in which not only is the property qualification entirely absent but the people are paid for their participation, as in the popular courts of Athens. This type of democracy lodges power in the hands of an urban proletariat who use that power in an unrestrained manner to benefit themselves at the expense of the moderate, intelligent, and industrious citizens. The best practicable democracy is composed mainly of farmers who are occupied on their land and permit trained administrators to conduct public affairs in the general interest. Here, although the ultimate power resides with the people, they will not use it unless malpractice on the part of the administrators makes such action necessary. What Aristotle has in mind is a representative, rather than a direct, democracy. The basic problem in any democracy, says Aristotle, is that of combining popular sovereignty with good administration. Aristotle indeed places a discerning finger upon the perennial problem of democracies.

There are also many types of oligarchies. Governments are more or less oligarchical, depending upon the degree of concentration of property and the consequent restrictiveness of the property qualification required for voting and holding public office. If property ownership, and thus political power, is not too concentrated—that is to say, if a fairly large number of property owners hold political power—and if the oligarchy does not abuse its privileges, a law-abiding state is a possibility. The danger of the oligarchic form is that it may become *too* oligarchic, that the concentration of power, becoming progressively greater until only a few control, will create dissatisfaction among the masses of people. In short the possibility of failure of either the democratic or oligarchic form stems from the danger of either form being too much itself, from carrying either principle to an extreme.

The Polity

Aristotle's analysis of the democratic and oligarchic states leads him to an important conclusion. The best *practicable* state must be based upon a balance of democratic and oligarchic principles. Such a state, the polity or constitutional state, will not be ideal. As we have seen, Aristotle is here concerned not with the unattainable ideal but with what may practicably be expected by ordinary men who must accept circumstances as they are and do their best with them. "We shall only be concerned with the sort of life which most men are able to share and the sort of constitution which it is possible for most states to enjoy." [9]

There are two contending forces in any society—quantity and quality. By quality is understood wealth, birth, social position, education, in fact, the oligarchic factors of the community. By quantity is understood numbers, the claims of the mass of the people—the democratic force. A state dominated completely by either force alone would be a bad state, unlawful, unstable, and selfish. The two forces can neither be removed nor ignored. The best procedure, practically, is to balance each against the other so as to negate the worst features of each and achieve the stability that is a concomitant of balance. In practice the state may arrive at this stability by lodging power in a middle class which, if it is sufficiently large, will hold in check the disruptive forces of extreme oligarchy and extreme democracy.

The polity represents the principle of the mean, of moderation. Every state has its rich, its poor, and its middle class, the latter comprising the mean in the class structure. This class is the logical receptacle of power. The rich have too many advantages and are unwilling to accept discipline. The poor have too few advantages and lack spirit. The rich know only how to command; the poor understand only obedience. The rich are preoccupied with thoughts of property, and their covetousness of the possessions of others creates faction. The poor are jealous of the property of the few, and they listen to demagogues who promise redistribution of the wealth and lead them to revolution which, in the end, brings not relief but tyranny. The middle class is more inclined to reason. They are not so poor as to be degraded; neither are they so rich as to become factious. Since the well-being of the state depends upon a friendly community spirit, these are matters of the greatest importance. Both Plato and Aristotle recognized the disruptive potential of the property question. Plato's solution, it will be recalled, was to abolish private property for the ruling class. Aristotle says, in effect, that *property must be distributed equitably enough* (and this is the true significance of the middle-class state) *so that contention over its possession will be greatly minimized.*

The polity is also representative of Aristotle's concept of the mixed state or mixed constitution. The mixture is one of oligarchy and democracy; that is, the polity not only balances these forces, but it also mixes them. Aristotle does not assume that the middle class will interfere with administration. Presumably this class consists of sober, industrious folk whose primary concern is with the ordinary pursuits of life but who, nevertheless, keep a wary eye on those who administer the affairs of state.

Ibid., IV, xi, p. 180.

Aristotle accepts the necessity of a modest property qualification for voting in order to restrict the number of those in whom power resides, although the power is exercised by a representative group. Aristotle's polity, his best practicable state, is thus the state of the mixed constitution, resting upon the principle of balance of the forces of oligarchy and democracy, and representative of the mean of the conflicting elements of society. It is the middle-class state, and its stability is commensurate with the size of that class.

Aristotle's equating of stability in the state with a predominant middle class is highly perceptive political thinking. Governments through the ages to their sorrowful regret have permitted the development of a gross imbalance of the economic forces. Political democracy cannot survive such a great concentration of economic wealth that the only freedom of which the citizenry is aware is the dubious freedom to starve to death. To carry Aristotle's point further than he intended, we may also say that the democratic structure is not the only thing so threatened. Successful despots have also learned that their support cannot safely be entrusted to a handful of avaricious robber barons. In modern times the great democracies are middle-class democracies. The Fascists, Hitler and Mussolini, unwise in many things, were both shrewd enough politicians to appeal to, and base their dictatorships upon, the bourgeoisie. And the Soviet Union, dedicated theoretically to the destruction of the bourgeoisie, rapidly developed its own middle class, consisting of military officers, professional people, and civil servants; thus they could prop up a structure which otherwise must necessarily have been based, in large part at least, upon the unreliable foundation of force. Stability in the state derives from the good will of a sizable (and potentially powerful) group of citizens who have a vested interest in the conduct of government and who are doing well enough to be generally immune to the appeals of those who demand change. It does not require genius to create such a state. Men are sufficiently conservative to accept a situation of considerable hardship before they demand a change of the status quo. A moderate governmental concern is generally all that is required to guarantee the support of the middle class. The lesson is difficult to learn, as history amply demonstrates, but Aristotle well understood the principle and stated it with great clarity.

Maintaining Constitutional Stability

Aristotle's consideration of the causes of revolution and the precautions to be taken to ensure stability of the state, in Book V of the *Politics*, is closely related to and logically follows the discussion of the best practicable state in Book IV. Aristotle states the general proposition thus: If we know how to destroy constitutions, we also know how to preserve them. The ensuing investigation and the recommendations based upon it range widely through the field of political speculation and give evidence of Aristotle's knowledge and versatility. He is not solely concerned with maintaining the stability of the polity or best practicable state. Indeed in a sense the polity is a solution in itself. To the degree that any constitution approximates the polity, its constancy will be that much assured. That is not the problem. As Aristotle has already pointed out, in practice states will tend to be oligarchic or democratic. They may also, of course, be tyrannical, and regrettable as this eventuality would be, it is nevertheless to be anticipated. Such states should be taught how they may improve themselves by working toward the principles of the polity. But if in fact they do not do so, what then? Is man to desert the state and become a hermit? Never. Poor as the state may be, it is better than anarchy because only within its matrix may progress occur, and morality and the good life be achieved. It follows, therefore, that the state must be preserved, that the stability of the constitution must be assured.

If it were not for Aristotle's insistence upon the state as the *sine qua non* for a human existence, some of his advice on the subject of constitutional stability would be distinctly unpalatable. To the democrat he appears coldly calculating. In his defense we must plead again that Aristotle is a practical man. Aristotle admonishes tyrants to degrade, humiliate, and enslave their subjects, to create distrust among them, to impose extremely heavy taxes—in short to prevent the possibility of a unity that may lead to revolution. He suggests that they may also be well advised to maintain a feeling in their subjects of imminent danger, since fear of something unknown makes men more desirous of retaining what they have. The tyrant should quickly dispose of anyone who, in his opinion, constitutes a threat to his rule. Many other equally menacing expedients are suggested.

All this, however, is less relevant than Aristotle's point that the principal cause of instability in oligarchies and democracies is that they are too much themselves. The maintenance of an approximate *mean* is most desirable.

> Both oligarchy and democracy may be tolerable forms of government even though they deviate from the ideal. But if you push either of them further still in the direction to which it tends, you will begin by making it a worse constitution, and you may end by turning it into something which is not a constitution at all.[10]

Certain general principles must be safeguarded in either form of government. A careful guard against lawlessness, especially in its petty forms, must be observed. Each element of the civic body must be protected in those benefits, honors, and privileges to which it is entitled by virtue of the contribution it makes to the community.

No element of the citizenry should be permitted to predominate to the

[10] *Ibid.*, V, ix, p. 232.

degree that others become dangerously resentful. Balance must be maintained. Rulers of oligarchies and democracies must not be permitted to use office for their own profit. The avoidance of venality is particularly important in oligarchies. The masses are less offended at being excluded from public office than they are by the knowledge that their representatives are embezzling public funds. In democracies the property of the rich must be carefully guarded; in oligarchies the welfare of the poor should be protected. In all cases administrators must be efficient and law-abiding. Aristotle wisely says that the state cannot be better than its people. Therefore everything must be done to produce a wise, temperate, and moral body of citizens. A prudent citizenry will not only obey the laws but will also conduct their lives in such a way as to preserve the constitution. This admonition is more significant than it appears at first glance. There is often a conflict between individual desire and public good. Although the laws themselves may not stand in the way of serving the selfish interest at the expense of the whole public, a people who abuse such freedom will, in the long run, destroy their constitution and themselves.

Aristotle's Criticism of Ideal States

Widely separated books of the *Politics* deal with Aristotle's criticism of ideal states (in Book II) on the one hand and his own proposals for an ideal state (in Book VII) on the other. The two subjects, however, are related and will be so considered here. Aristotle's criticism of the writings of Hippodamus of Miletus, Phaleas of Chalcedon, and especially Plato, should be studied for its positive rather than its negative aspects, for when Aristotle condemns, the condemnation contains constructive recommendations which constitute an important segment of his political thought. Indeed the criticism itself, particularly that directed at the *Republic* of Plato, is often superficial and sometimes inconsistent, too often attacking minor features of Plato's plan and ignoring the essence. Nevertheless Book II constitutes a not inconsiderable portion of the *Politics* and should not be ignored.

Aristotle is highly critical of Plato's proposals for communism in his ideal state. Plato adopts communism in order to achieve unity because, in his opinion, unity in the *polis* is productive of the highest good. This, Aristotle charges, is a complete misinterpretation of the nature of the *polis*. Unity of the kind advocated by Plato is applicable to a household rather than to a *polis*, and thus the end which Plato seeks is wrong. So too are the means employed. Communism will not produce that unity which Plato values so highly. A community of wives and children (if it could be formed) will not constitute an improvement over traditional family ties. Instead of all men feeling a responsibility for all children under such a system no man would feel responsible for any child.

Aristotle also finds fault with Plato's scheme for communism of property. The arguments were for the most part as familiar when Aristotle uttered them as they are now. The denial to men of the right to own property, he said, is opposed to human nature. It is sufficiently difficult for men to work together in almost any kind of mutual endeavor, and doubly difficult where mutuality of property is involved. Some men would surely produce more than others and would demand a reward commensurate with effort. Thus factions would arise. How could unity be maintained? The existence of private property makes possible demonstrations of liberality and permits expression of the best in human nature. A man feels, also, a natural satisfaction in regarding something as his own. These are persuasive arguments, but they should not lead one to assume that Aristotle is preoccupied with the property issue or believes in the sanctity of private property. He believes that property is a natural perquisite of man in that each citizen is entitled to enough, so that the necessity of eking out a living does not make his existence sheer drudgery. But neither should he have so much property that its accumulation becomes an obsession. It is an error, Aristotle asserts, to attribute the troubles of the world to the institution of private property; they are rather the results of the evils of human nature, and communism will not correct them. Property should, however, be regarded as a means and not an end. Property, correctly used, can make possible that vitally necessary leisure which the citizen must have if he is to live the good life. Aristotle is neither socialist nor capitalist. While he defends the existence of private property, he insists that it is justified only on the basis of its social and political function, of its facilitating the achievement of a better life. Aristotle soundly condemns usury. Money, being inanimate, should not beget money, and such a practice is highly immoral. Phaleas of Chalcedon, a contemporary of Plato, charged that the major difficulties of society stemmed from the unequal distribution of land. Aristotle rejects the argument as incomplete. Many things cause unrest in the community. If it is true that the masses are discontented when property is unequally distributed, it is also true that the more able few become revolutionary when public offices are democratically or equally distributed. And crime does not result only from the unequal distribution of property but also from greed. "Men do not become tyrants in order to avoid exposure to cold." [11] Making a point equally applicable to the proposals of Plato and Phaleas, Aristotle says that it is wiser to "equalize men's desires" than to provide for an equal distribution of property and that such a moral change requires training under good laws.[12] Thus it would be better to educate men to use their property in the public interest than to attempt equalization.

[11] *Ibid.*, II, vii, p. 66.
[12] *Ibid.*, II, vii, p. 64.

Aristotle is also critical of Plato's advocacy of the rule of the elite and his abandonment of the rule of law. Despotism means the loss to the citizen of individual freedom and dignity. Where the law is supreme, men can be ruled by their own consent. Where the despot rules, men lose that vitally important moral and natural equality that must exist between man and man and between ruler and citizen in the good state. The rule of law permits the experience of the ages and the wisdom of the people to play a role. Men in the mass produce a knowledge superior to that of a single lawgiver, even though he be of the wisest variety. Plato ignored custom, an integral part of the law as construed by Aristotle. Aristotle protests:

> We are bound to pay some regard to the long past and the passage of the years, in which these things would not have gone unnoticed if they had been really good. Almost everything has been discovered already; though some of the things discovered have not been co-ordinated, and some, though known, are not put into practice." [13]

Stability and predictability are also components of the rule of law. Plato's substitution of the whim of the philosopher-king for the sovereignty of law and Hippodamus's advocacy of innovation in the law are both regarded as frivolous by Aristotle. Neither proposal offers much chance of improvement. Defects in law and government will always be found, but they had best be left alone if correcting them involves too much tampering. "The benefit of change will be less than the loss which is likely to result if men fall into the habit of disobeying the government." [14]

Plato and Aristotle, teacher and pupil, disagreed on many points, but not on all. The pupil was quite willing to concede to the teacher a greater originality of mind than his own, but protested his lack of practicality. Yet both philosophers decried the influence of the demagogue and the hack. Both believed that the state was the sole agency through which the good life could be found, and both assumed that intelligence and science were the proper tools for the statesman to use in developing the state. Both men sought justice, although each found it in a different place. This is the essential difference between the two: Plato found justice in the rule of men (presumably perfect); Aristotle found justice (less than perfect, but attainable) in the rule of law.

Aristotle's Ideal State

Aristotle's consideration of the ideal state differs from Plato's study in the *Republic*. Convinced that the ideal cannot be attained, Aristotle appears more concerned with the ideals of the good state than with the

[13] *Ibid.*, II, v, p. 52.
[14] *Ibid.*, II, viii, p. 73.

elaborate formulation of a hypothetical but unrealizable perfect structure. His work, therefore, to a greater extent than Plato's, deals with political science in general.

The aspirations of the state should conform to those of the citizen; consequently the form of the constitution ideally must reflect the good life of the individual. The ingredients of the good life are threefold—"external goods; goods of the body; and goods of the soul." The happy and well-balanced person requires all three, but he must give due consideration to the question of priority and relative importance. Excessive concern with external goods, by which Aristotle means material possessions, distorts the soul. The same may be said of "goods of the body," or preoccupation with physical condition. It is the "goods of the soul" that are truly important, that constitute the true end of human concern; all else is useful or not depending upon how well it contributes to that end. By this standard constitutions may be judged. The good state establishes priority for the inculcation of morality among its citizens and subordinates material things to that end. The good state is never aggressive or imperialist, but solely concerned with peace and internal improvement, although it will maintain sufficient military strength for defense, the state will not use its power to annoy its neighbors.

There is an optimum size for ideal states. Largeness in itself cannot be equated with goodness; virtue is rather to be determined by how well the state performs its task and attains its goal. A too large state will find it difficult to enforce the law, and a good state must be well ordered. If it is too small, the state will not have the virtue of self-sufficiency. Aristotle thinks exclusively in terms of the city-state form, a fact evidenced by his assertion that civic functions can be performed properly only if citizens know one another personally. In terms of territory, too, the principle of moderation must be maintained. The state should be large enough to allow its citizens to extract a livelihood from their work and to permit them sufficient leisure time to reflect and to perform their civic duties. But it should be no larger and no more prosperous than that. Leisure, in the constructive sense in which it was considered by the Greeks, was the goal, not luxury.

As to location, both military and commercial advantage must be considered. The state must be strategically situated for defense, and for naval and trading purposes it must have access to the sea. But precautions are necessary here. It is possible for the state to become preoccupied with naval power and with the wealth that flows from maritime commerce. The naval forces must be adequate for defense, but naval personnel must be excluded from the body politic or their numbers (and Aristotle refers to the many oarsmen required to man the ships of the time) would enable them to overpower the balance of the citizenry.

Commercially, the state should import its necessities and export its surpluses, but it should not act as broker or shipper for other states, and the goal should be self-sufficiency, not profit.

Six distinct services must be performed in the state—agriculture, arts and crafts, defense, land ownership, religion, and government service. Two kinds of people, generally, inhabit the state—the full citizens and those whose function it is to perform services which free the citizens to seek and enjoy the good life. Thus the problem arises of how the above services may properly be distributed. The functions of agriculture and arts and crafts are too demanding of time and effort to be undertaken by citizens who, if they were to perform them, would be unable to devote sufficient time to higher duties. Farming and the mechanic and commercial pursuits must be the work of a separate and lower social class. Three higher functions—defense, religion, and civil service—must be performed by citizens, but not all three by the same citizens since not all men are capable of doing well in each function. The best arrangement will allocate defense to the younger citizens, governing to those of middle age, and the religious function to the aged. In this manner each citizen will perform all functions, but only at that period of his life when he is best qualified for his duty by training and temperament.

The service of land ownership is shared by all citizens but involves a more complex arrangement. Aristotle proposes that some land be communally owned, enough to provide the produce to supply a system of common tables for the citizens and to support the institutions of public worship. This system will help to create harmony and a measure of unity in the state. The balance of the land will be privately owned; each owner will hold two plots of land, one near the city and one in the frontier area. The purpose of this arrangement is to achieve unity of purpose in case of border warfare by equalizing risk for all. Also, though citizens own the land, slaves or serfs do the actual work.

Again, the best state is the one which has the greatest ability to help its citizens achieve the good life. There are three means by which citizens may gain such goodness—"natural endowment," "proper habits," and "rational principle" or the capacity to reason. The first, natural endowment, is substantially, although not entirely, beyond the control of the state. Men are born with certain capacities, and the state is generally powerless to increase them. But the other two, proper habits and the power of reason, can be affected and improved by education. The most important function of the legislator is so to improve these qualities in the citizen as to give each one the greatest possibility of achieving the good life. At this point Aristotle's discussion of plans for the ideal state are transformed primarily into a treatise on education. The good state educates to achieve goodness. The main problem thus concerns the kind of educational system that should be established. Aristotle does not complete his outline of a proper educational system, but some of the features are sufficiently provocative to warrant consideration.

The educational system must be common to all citizens, and it must be a publicly supported, not a private system. In the good state the young will be governed by their elders, but the young, in being educated to obey a free government, will also be educated to govern. A good system of education is designed to produce the good man. Here two distinctions must be made: First, the different parts of the soul must be distinguished. There is a rational or reasoning part and an obeying part, which takes direction from the rational. Second, the different aspects of life must be distinguished: There is action, including warlike action, and there is leisure, or the peaceful and reflective aspect. All these factors are present and necessary in life, and the proper educational system will take each into account, but it must exercise care not to overemphasize any one of them. Sparta fell because her educational system stressed only the obeying part of the soul and the warlike activities of life. These things should have been regarded as means to, rather than ends of, the good life.

Obedience must, of course, be taught. From this training comes the development of proper habits. In point of time the training in good habits comes first, and with the child this must precede training in rational principle. In the interest of providing the best possible material for the good state Aristotle at this point takes a brief excursion into eugenics. The marriage of citizens should be regulated in some respects by the state. The best ages for marriage, in terms of the quality of children to be produced, are thirty-seven for the male and eighteen for the female. A too large family is to be avoided through the exposure of deformed children and the induction of miscarriage. Procreation should not be permitted to begin prior to the attainment of the ages indicated above, and it should cease before senility. Aristotle also advises exercise during pregnancy for the prospective mother. And he does not avoid giving advice on the care of children. Infants, he says, should be given much milk and little wine. They should be compelled to exercise a great deal and should become accustomed to cold. Association with slaves should be restricted, and careful supervision must prevent the use of bad language or the accessibility of pornography. Thus early training is primarily directed toward the development of a strong physique and good habits. Once these have been established, training of the rational element may begin, but at this point physical training should cease. Study and physical training should not be undertaken simultaneously since one hampers the other.

A proper course of study, following the elementary stage of physical development and habit forming, will consist of reading, writing, drawing, and music. Some of these studies—reading, writing, and drawing—

may have a predominantly utilitarian value. They do not constitute an end in themselves but enable the citizen to carry on the ordinary activities of life. They may also have a higher end in that their study may contribute to material welfare. Music (including literature and related arts) is different from the other disciplines in that it has an intrinsic rather than a merely utilitarian value. It is good in and of itself, leading as it does to the higher life and occupying that leisure time which is the most valuable part of a person's life. Aristotle develops the discussion in greater detail, but for practical purposes he thus concludes the *Politics*. Neither his plan for the ideal state nor his consideration of the educational system has been completed, and the termination is abrupt. Much the same can be said of other discussions throughout the *Politics*.

Conclusions

A great deal of the exposition in the *Politics* does not concern the modern student of politics. Much of Aristotle's thought is anachronistic, applies too specifically to the city-state, or for other reasons lacks pertinency. Nevertheless, Aristotle teaches us some of our greatest lessons. Perhaps we should more appropriately say that he has attempted to teach us, since obviously the lessons have not always been well learned. Aristotle's insistence upon the scientific method, the use of reason, and his practical approach to problems had a great impact upon scholars of the Middle Ages, who found inspiration in the works of the great master. Man and society may be improved, not by speculating on what might be if man were only perfect but by employing the tools at hand. This was Aristotle's not inconsiderable contribution. He also reemphasized Plato's idea of the indispensability of the state, that highest level of community organization which man may employ in his struggle toward moral perfection. This too was a challenging concept to scholars in later ages who had become accustomed to thinking that the massive and powerful medieval Church structure could alone control man's moral destiny. The intelligence with which Aristotle developed his theory of the middle-class state has perhaps received sufficient attention here. The wisdom of Aristotle's position has been attested by the actions of many astute political manipulators, both democratic and undemocratic. Moreover, the clamor of disparate factions of the state for recognition may often appear unjustified if logic alone is our criterion; but, as Aristotle clearly understood, stability cannot be achieved unless all such demands are considered. Stability is by no means an end in itself, despite Aristotle's apparent preoccupation with the problem. But stability is a highly necessary means to an end, the end of moral improvement and the good life to which Aristotle was devoted. Like James Madison, many centuries later, Aristotle repudiated destruction as the solution to the problem of conflicting factions. Factions in a free society (and there must be freedom) are bound to exist. The correction of their evil is to be found in controlling their effects, not in destroying the factions themselves. To Plato the annoyances and the disruptive tendencies of free factions could be mitigated only by providing the absolutely unified state—at the cost of personal freedom. Aristotle was unwilling to pay such a price. Unity is desirable, but it can too easily become the goal, and complete unity can only be gained at the cost of individual liberty.

The cohesiveness and harmony demanded by Plato produced a despotic extreme. The despotism was perhaps benevolent, but it was despotism nonetheless. Despotisms are extreme governments, and Aristotle was the apostle of moderation. The best practicable government is one that finds a working balance of liberty and authority. Such a government is likely to permit a number of injustices. No one will be completely satisfied with it; it does not place each person in his particular and appropriate social niche as does Plato's *Republic*. But Aristotle believed that such perfect justice did not exist, and if it did, the manipulation would rob man of that "natural equality" which was an indispensable component of the good life. Aristotle believed that no man and no class could practically be entrusted with unrestricted governmental power. It is true that men should not share equally in all aspects of state operation. Intelligence, birth, education, even wealth, should count for something, and those who possess these advantages should be considered accordingly in the distribution of government office. But they should not be permitted to rule arbitrarily; they must follow the dictates of the law. No one but a fool would expect the law to be perfect; it is nevertheless better than rule without law. Custom and tradition should particularly be observed as regulatory devices and as a part of the law, for while legislators will often err, custom and tradition represent the accumulated wisdom of the people. It might also be argued that custom and tradition contain the accumulated errors of the people as well as their wisdom, and Aristotle would not deny the contention; but he would undoubtedly argue that, balancing the wisdom and error of tradition, we shall find that wisdom is the greater force. At least it is predictable and not capricious as is the rule of the despot, and a great deal may be hoped for from law which is predictable and constant even if it lacks perfection.

Aristotle's greatest legacy, a valuable one indeed, is constitutionalism. The rule of law and not of force should govern men. Governments must in some way be responsible to those they govern. True freedom in society can be achieved only if men participate in making the laws which they are compelled to obey. Men are not equal in all respects, not even in many; but in a good society they must be entitled to equal standing under the law. This standard may not be attained, but the rule of law demands that it be approximated and that men keep on striving to achieve its full realization. Such a society may lack the security of the community proposed by Plato, but a great many champions of freedom prefer it.

SELECTED BIBLIOGRAPHY

Barker, Ernest: *The Political Thought of Plato and Aristotle,* G. P. Putnam's Sons, New York, 1906, chaps. 5–11.

Catlin, George: *The Story of the Political Philosophers,* McGraw-Hill Book Company, Inc., New York, 1939, chap. 3.

McIlwain, Charles H.: *The Growth of Political Thought in the West,* The Macmillan Company, New York, 1932, chap. 3.

The Politics of Aristotle (Ernest Barker translation), Oxford University Press, Fair Lawn, N.J., 1946.

Sabine, George H.: *A History of Political Theory,* 3d ed., Holt, Rinehart and Winston, Inc., New York, 1961, chap. 5.

Taylor, A. E.: *Aristotle,* rev. ed., Dover Publications, Inc., New York, 1955.

Wormuth, Francis D.: "Aristotle on Law," in Milton R. Konvitz and Arthur E. Murray (eds.), *Essays in Political Theory, Presented to George H. Sabine,* Cornell University Press, Ithaca, N.Y., 1948, pp. 45–61.

five

ROMAN
POLITICAL THOUGHT

The contributions of the Greeks to the development of political thought do not end with Aristotle. But Aristotle is the last of the great Greek philosophers to think exclusively in terms of the city-state. As we have seen, political life in the Athens of Aristotle, Plato, and Socrates was marked by widespread citizen participation in the various functions of government. This principle could be worked out in the city-state but was inapplicable to the large and impersonal empire that followed it. Why Aristotle should have failed to realize the significance to his own philosophy of the conquests of Philip and Alexander is hard to understand. The city-state was obsolete; it was incapable of providing solutions to the problems with which its citizens were confronted. The city-states were unable to develop and hold together a federation that could withstand the pressure of Macedonian imperialism. As a consequence they were defeated and became dependent fractions of the empire.

Many of the principles developed by Plato and Aristotle would have been continuously pertinent, although in all probability neither man would have so contended. It was generally assumed that philosophies so closely associated with the city-state form would have no validity outside it. When Athens fell to Alexander, the Greek lost not only his independence but also much of the whole structure of beliefs which had given meaning and purpose to his life. Defeat was a shattering experience, and it had an enormous impact upon the Greek world.

The intellectual preparation for a new concept of society had begun long before Alexander's incorporation of Athens into the Macedonian empire. Some thinkers of ability had rejected the principles of the city-state at the same time that Plato and Aristotle assumed their indispensability. The voice of protest against the city-state form was faint in the beginning, but as the centuries passed it developed a mightier volume and ultimately became the foundation of a new and different way of life. Though ultimately several different schools were voicing a variety of protests against the city-state and its ideals, they largely agreed that a new standard of values would have to find acceptance—a standard that would enhance the importance of the individual and lessen that of the political community. The new thought was embraced by those who suffered disappointment and frustration from the failure of the city-state, but even before this it had attracted many dissidents, especially of the metic or resident-foreigner class, who had long been denied the benefits of citizenship in the city-state and who consequently had no compelling reason for admiring its institutions. We may sample the doctrine of protest of this period by investigating two of the schools that expressed it, the Epicureans and the Cynics.

The Epicureans

The Epicurean school was established in Athens in 306 B.C. by Epicurus (342–270 B.C.), who instructed his followers in the hedonistic doctrine that the main goal of man is the attainment of his own individual pleasure. This could best be achieved, Epicurus argued, by avoiding the worrisome or painful aspects of life, and he included in these categories any kind of participation in public affairs or in religion. The Epicureans did not believe that there was a life after death and held that the gods had no interest in human affairs. All men are by nature selfish, they maintained; selfishness, indeed, is the only natural law. But since the pursuit of individual self-interest is likely to produce conflict, government and laws are necessary to security, and men agree among themselves to submit to authority in order to avoid the anxiety and pain that must attend anarchy.

The Epicureans rejected the Aristotelian principle that man is a political animal as they opposed the idea that man is born for justice. Man has gradually developed a civilized society because his experience has taught him that such a society is more conducive to pleasure than is a more primitive state. He obeys the law because he fears the consequences of disobedience. He is not concerned with the type of government but only with its ability to provide him with the desired security. A monarchy will probably be best, not because the king is divinely ordained to rule or because monarchy can boast any kind of moral superiority but because that form of government can more probably exercise the necessary degree of authority. In any event the wise man will have nothing to do with government and politics. Political participation will only bring trouble and occupy time that could better be devoted to the pursuit of pleasure. We note immediately the striking contrast between the Epicurean philosophy of withdrawal and the emphasis placed by Aristotle and Plato on participation.

The Epicureans were, and are, sometimes incorrectly understood to have embraced a doctrine of "Eat, drink, and be merry." But this summary does injustice to the philosophy. The pleasure that Epicurus advised the individual to seek was not sensual. Epicurus himself was careful to avoid such an identification.

> When we say that pleasure is the purpose of life, we do not mean the pleasures of the sensually self-indulgent, as some assert, but rather freedom from bodily pain and mental disturbance. The life of pleasure does not come from drinking or revels, or other sensual pleasures. It comes from sober thinking, the sensible investigation of what to choose and to avoid, and getting rid of ideas which agitate the soul. Common sense is our best guide. It tells us that we cannot live happily unless we live wisely, nobly, and justly; nor can we live wisely, nobly, and justly without being happy. The virtues are inseparably linked with pleasure.[1]

Still, Epicureanism was a philosophy of negativism. It retreated in the face of adversity instead of going forward. It advised man to avoid his troubles rather than to face and solve them. Its assumption that man is wholly selfish led inevitably to authoritarianism, for authority alone can check the evil tendencies prevalent in human beings. The doctrine may have brought a measure of solace to some people, but it did not answer the many problems confronting the city-state and its citizens.

The Cynics

A more bitter protest against the principles of the city-state was voiced by the Cynics, a rather ill-defined group of scholars found mainly among the foreign element in Athens. The Cynics made their appeal to the poor and the disfranchised, who had little reason to be enthusiastic about the advantages of life in the city-state. Theirs was a class appeal but of a peculiar nature, for it did not propose overthrow of the government and seizure of power by the proletariat. Instead it urged the individual to withdraw and to become so self-sufficient that the troubles which beset him in civilization would no longer be of consequence. Cynicism proposed that the distinction between men is the distinction between the wise man and the fool. The wise man is self-sufficient; the fool requires the institutions and conventions of political society.

[1] Epicurus, *Golden Maxims*, in Walter R. Agard, *The Greek Mind*, D. Van Nostrand Company, Inc., Princeton, N.J., 1957, pp. 161–162.

The Cynic taught that the city-state and the whole structure of ideas, institutions, and conventions associated with it were of no value and constituted an insurmountable barrier to human development. They must all be shunted aside in order to develop moral character. This development provides no place for the amenities of civilized living. Simplicity is the key to the good life. Those things are important that are achievable by the individual alone and that conduce to his self-improvement. A person should have no interest in social, economic, or political status. The slave has equal opportunity with the freeman to live the good life; all men are equal in this respect. The Cynic was not an abolitionist; he merely argued that the condition of slavery was unimportant since it did not prevent the slave from developing his moral character. Not all men could succeed in the attainment of this goal, but the wise could do so, and when they did they became citizens of a greater community than the city-state. They became citizens of the world, apart from and above the petty conventions of the law, customs, and government of the traditional political community.

Cynicism was too negative in its approach and its advocates too crude in their actions for the doctrine to be generally appealing. At any rate, the Athenian had not yet become disillusioned with his city-state. Plato and Aristotle were speaking for the majority of their fellows in asserting the superiority of the city-state form. The time had not yet arrived when an attack so fundamental in nature as that made by the Cynics would be taken seriously by a considerable number of people. Certain elements of Cynic doctrine were to become important later, but not until basic changes were made, and not until the crudities had been eliminated from the philosophy. Then out of Cynicism would grow Stoicism—a highly significant development in the history of political thought.

The Stoics

When Zeno came from Citium to Athens, about 320 B.C., to found the Stoic school, the conditions were auspicious for a general acceptance of a new philosophy. Now not only the lower economic classes and the disfranchised criticized the city-state but also many who formerly had believed implicitly in the eternal validity of that form. By 320 B.C. Athens was under the control of Alexander. The city-state was more generally regarded as an anachronism, and disillusionment was widespread. The Greek sought a new *raison d'être*, which obviously would have to represent a departure from, even a negation of, the old ways. The new philosophy would have to accord with life as it was. It would have to recognize, first of all, a new and larger community and a new view of the individual that would make his life meaningful outside the context of the city-state.

There was much in Cynic thought to satisfy the demands of the new philosophy, but Cynicism was too harsh and unrefined as well as too negative to appeal to Zeno. Zeno, and later Chrysippus, developed an eclectic Cynicism which came to be known as Stoicism, the term stemming from the fact that Zeno and his followers lectured from a *stoa* or porch in Athens. The Stoics rejected the idea that *who* one is has importance. Rather it is *what* one is that matters. If one is good, it makes no difference whether one is Greek or barbarian, slave or free, rich or poor. A man is not to be judged by his standing relative to others, but by what he is as an individual. And in this, man is master of his own fate.

The Stoic philosophy raised the question of the meaning of goodness in man. How can a man be *good?* The answer is that goodness is conformance with nature. Nature is a force that seeks perfection through growth. It is a law that acts upon and governs all living things. Nature is absolute and inexorable, and it is always beneficent. To resist the natural law will always be harmful; to submit by acting according to its demands will always be beneficial. The early Stoics accepted the Cynic distinction between the wise man and the fool. Wise men, they said, can understand the law through their reason, and in their wisdom they are joined in a universal brotherhood. The Stoic contended that the fact of mutual citizenship neither held men together nor provided a measure of equality. Instead, the common tie among wise men was that they recognized the universality of nature and the necessity of their own submission to it.

Life to the Stoic was real and earnest. He had a task to perform. Doing his duty might not bring pleasure in the Epicurean sense, but personal pleasure was a luxury he could not afford. His own role might be great or small, but this too mattered not at all. As long as he performed his duty he was living a good life, in accordance with nature and God. He might be called upon to perform some public service in the pursuance of his calling, and if so, the Stoic was required to accomplish his task as well as he could. The service itself was valuable only insofar as it advanced the course of nature's progress and improved the character and goodness of the person who performed it. In this sense, early Stoicism represented the tendency toward withdrawal that was so marked in Epicureanism and Cynicism. The duties of citizenship did not weigh heavily upon the early Stoics. To them the experience of Athens had demonstrated that the glories of political participation were only illusory. It was as an individual, not as a citizen, that man achieved dignity. The wise man acknowledged his obligations to God, to nature, and to himself; he had none to the state. He was not concerned with material things. He was not trying to "win" anything, not even immortality, since the Stoic's religious views did not include such a belief. The good man lived and acted as he did because it was the "right" thing to do, because there was a law and it had to be obeyed, and because from such a life a person received satisfaction, although probably at the cost of comfort.

Stoicism and Roman Thought

By 167 B.C. Rome had defeated Macedon and supplanted the latter as the controlling force in Greece. But if Rome dominated the Greeks militarily, she was herself strongly influenced by Greek philosophy. Rome contributed little originality to political thought; the Roman bent was mainly administrative and legal. Roman thinkers, however, intensively cultivated the fertile field of Greek learning, seeking knowledge and a philosophy to support the public spiritedness of Roman citizens and the imperialistic tendencies of Roman foreign policy.

The teachings of Plato and Aristotle were well known to the Romans, and they were greatly admired. Much of the older Greek philosophy, however, was not germane to the Roman situation. The insistence upon the desirability of the city-state form was unrealistic in the face of the actualities of the Roman Empire. The Roman could believe that man was a political animal and had a responsibility to the state but not that state and society are one and that they completely absorb the individual.

Nor did the Epicurean philosophy have much to offer. The Epicurean repudiation of public service as a worthwhile ideal was directly contrary to both Roman thought and to Roman necessity. The Epicurean assumption that the state is, at best, a necessary evil and that the wise man will seek his own pleasure with as little reference as possible to the state was completely unacceptable. Moreover, the Epicurean's lack of concern with religion, based upon the belief that the gods had no interest in the welfare of man, was contrary to the religion of Rome.

Only in the now well-established and highly developed doctrines of Stoicism did the Romans find a suitable philosophy. Significant alterations had to be made, but certain of the fundamental features of Stoicism were admirably suited to meet Roman needs. For one thing, Stoicism permitted a devout man to attend to his religious duties; for another, it rejected the idea that the individual enjoyment of pleasure was a proper goal of humankind. Above all, the Roman was attracted to the Stoic principle that life is a stern calling, to be devoted to duty and to be lived in accordance with nature. Service to imperial Rome was not ordinarily undertaken by those who lacked a sense of duty and of purpose. Conquest was a serious business and demanded the single-minded attention of those who could subject their own desires to the needs of the state. Stoic doctrine could underwrite these views.

The Stoicism of Zeno and Chrysippus was, for several reasons, inadequate to the needs of Rome. It emphasized self-sufficiency rather than public service, and it was too exclusive, confining, as it did, the applicability of its doctrine only to the "wise men," who, presumably, were few in number. Also, early Stoicism was too lacking in humaneness to attract widespread support. It was Panaetius of Rhodes, a Stoic leader of the late second century B.C., who adapted Stoic philosophy to Roman needs. In so doing he altered the character of Stoic doctrine, but he vastly expanded its appeal and, consequently, its importance. Panaetius softened the harshness of Stoicism and made it applicable to all men, not merely to the wise. All men, he held, are endowed with the ability to understand nature and conform to its laws, and in this sense all men are equal, even though there are considerable differences among them in other respects. Furthermore the good man will not devote himself to the service of self, even though that service be the high-minded struggle for moral development demanded by the early Stoics.[2] Instead, his ideal should be public service, a dedicated and energetic helping of his fellows through the institutions of the state. The influence of Panaetius's Stoicism upon Roman thought was great and will become more apparent when we later consider Cicero and the Roman law.

Polybius

Any account of the influence of Greek political thought upon Rome must include a reference to Polybius (204–122 B.C.), a contemporary and friend of Panaetius. Polybius was a citizen of Arcadia, an important member of the Achaean League. He was one of a thousand leading Achaeans who were arrested and carried to Rome as hostages as a result of charges made by the radical pro-Rome element of the League. The Achaeans were never brought to trial although they were detained for seventeen years. The years of captivity, however, went swiftly for Polybius, who was regarded more as a guest than as a prisoner. He became a close friend of Scipio (Scipio Africanus the Younger), and this friendship opened the way to the highest political circles of Rome. Polybius studied diligently the history and institutions of Rome, becoming, in the process, an ardent admirer of the Roman state. Scipio's generosity enabled Polybius to conduct lengthy and expensive historical investigations, and the result was a work of forty books, of which only the first five exist in their entirety, together with fragments of the remaining thirty-five. Polybius's purpose was to discover the reasons for Rome's greatness. He found what he considered to be the answer in the excellence of the Roman constitution, which had avoided the dangers that always confront the unmixed form of state, a state wholly a monarchy, an oligarchy, or a democracy. Polybius, relying mainly upon an application of Aristotle's theory of the mixed constitution, asserted that a state employing solely a monarchical, or aristocratic, or democratic form is

[2] George H. Sabine, *A History of Political Theory*, 3d ed., Holt, Rinehart and Winston, Inc., New York, 1961, pp. 152–153.

bound to deteriorate into its corruption—monarchy into despotism, aristocracy into oligarchy, and democracy into mob rule.

Rome, Polybius held, had been able to check the natural tendency to decay through the use of a mixed constitution. In a mixed constitution elements of the simple governmental forms are present but in equal force. Each checks the other and prevents it from being too much itself. In this best of all possible situations, tyranny cannot be so great as to provoke revolt, oligarchy so powerful as to stimulate popular resentment, or democracy so uncontrolled as to become anarchy. Such a system permits movement and progress but does not permit it to get out of hand.

The idea of a mixed constitution was not new. As we have seen, Aristotle had thought along similar lines, but he had proposed that all social elements be infused into each institution and function. Polybius was the first to apply the principles to governmental institutions and to create a system of checks and balances, as it is known today. His analysis and conclusions were as superficial as those of Montesquieu centuries later. Like Montesquieu's, they were, nevertheless, important. The idea came to fruition in the Constitution of the United States, a document which places great emphasis upon separation of powers and checks and balances. Critics of the doctrine argue that the division of governmental power results in stalemate, but Polybius, though aware of this criticism, was convinced that unity would be achieved and action would result when necessary. It might fairly be said that checks and balances have conduced to the preservation of individual freedom, but that on the other hand they have not been an unmitigated blessing and that the charge that they *can* lead to divisiveness and frustration is not entirely unfounded.

Legal Theory of Rome

Rome's greatest and most enduring contribution to the Western world was its development of law. The period of growth, culminating in the Code of Justinian of the sixth century A.D., covered more than a thousand years and is so complex that only the major features can be considered here. Still, the basic principles of the law and its development must be understood since the Roman law had a great impact upon the Church Fathers, the whole structure of medieval political theory, and the ultimate establishment of the law throughout Europe.

The earliest Roman law was essentially custom and tradition. There was no feeling that it could be *made*. It had, it was assumed, always been in existence and always would be. It came from the gods and was unalterable and divine. Such a view of the law, however, could apply only under the most primitive conditions, and as the community grew, the need for new regulations and for some kind of codification gave rise to the idea that the law, in large part, came from the governmental organs of the state. The concept of law as legislation and the inclusion of the principle of popular consent was predominant from the early days of the republic down to the middle of the third century before Christ.

This early law applied only to Roman citizens. It was *jus civile,* and in theory foreigners had no access to it and were not protected by it. In law, a foreigner in Rome had no rights that a citizen was bound to respect. His person and property were at the mercy of the citizens. Our knowledge of this period is so incomplete that we can only speculate as to the possible discrepancies between theory and practice on this matter. At any rate, as the affairs of Rome brought a closer involvement of her citizens with other peoples of the world, particularly as Rome extended her rule and influence over others, the demands of commerce, to say nothing of justice, resulted in significant alterations of the legal process.

One of the changes involved the appointment of an official called the *praetor peregrinus,* whose function it was to settle legal disputes involving foreigners. In arriving at decisions the *praetor peregrinus* sought those elements of justice that were common among citizens of different states. He relied heavily upon reason, and the rules enunciated were an admixture of a type of informal Roman law together with ideas of other peoples, especially the Greeks.[3] It became customary for a *praetor* to publish the edicts he had proclaimed during his term of office at the close of that term. The system of law thus established was assumed to represent principles of justice having universal applicability, and it came to be known as *jus gentium,* a law common to all peoples. *Jus gentium* represented a different approach to the law than *jus civile,* since the latter was legislative in form, applied only to Romans, and represented the idea of will, whereas *jus gentium* was judge-declared (although not precisely judge-made) law, applicable to all persons, and represented the idea of justice.

The most important period of development of the law came in the classical period of the second century and the first half of the third century after Christ.[4] During this time the emperor was the chief source of the law. It was he who directed the work of the jurists and legal scholars toward defining and classifying the great mass of diverse principles which had accumulated over the years, in order to provide a systematic instrument for use in the control of an empire. The reign of Justinian (A.D. 527–565) brought the great code of Roman law which bears the emperor's name and which so largely determined the form and content of the legal systems of the modern world.

[3] H. F. Jolowicz, *Historical Introduction to the Study of Roman Law,* Cambridge University Press, New York, 1939, p. 102.

[4] *Ibid.,* p. 6.

Cicero

The pages of Roman history are liberally sprinkled with the names of great jurists, statesmen, and military leaders, but not with the names of great political philosophers. Cicero (106–43 B.C.) was a lawyer and a very good one. He was a statesman of the highest quality and order; indeed he rose to the post of consul during his distinguished career. But we find little originality in the writings for which he is best known, his *Republic* and *Laws*. Both the style and the substance of these works are Greek. Cicero used the dialogue form as did Plato, but far less skillfully. The philosophy is Stoicism, another Greek invention. Nevertheless, the works of Cicero have been widely read, and most of what we know of Stoicism, as it was developed by Panaetius, we learn from Cicero's exposition.

Cicero's statement of Stoic philosophy is clear and compelling. There is, he says, a law of nature which is the constitution of the world. It is the same for everyone everywhere. On the basis of its dictates the rules of governments and the actions of rulers will be judged.

> True law is right reason in agreement with nature; it is of universal application, unchanging and everlasting; it summons to duty by its commands, and averts from wrongdoing by its prohibitions. And it does not lay its commands or prohibitions upon good men in vain, though neither have any effect upon the wicked. It is a sin to try to alter this law, nor is it allowable to attempt to repeal any part of it, and it is impossible to abolish it entirely. We cannot be freed from its obligations by senate or people, and we need not look outside ourselves for an expounder or interpreter of it. And there will not be different laws at Rome and at Athens, or different laws now and in the future, but one eternal and unchangeable law will be valid for all nations and all times, and there will be one master and ruler, that is, God, over us all, for he is the author of this law, its promulgator, and its enforcing judge. Whoever is disobedient is fleeing from himself and denying his human nature, and by reason of this very fact he will suffer the worst penalties, even if he escapes what is commonly considered punishment.[5]

Under this law all men are equal. It is properly binding on all because all men, endowed as they are with the capacity to reason, can understand it.

> Reason, which alone raises us above the level of the beasts and enables us to draw inferences, to prove and disprove, to discuss and solve problems, and to come to conclusions, is certainly common to us all, and, though varying in what it learns, at least in the capacity to learn it is invariable.[6]

[5] *The Republic*, III, 22, in Cicero, *De Re Publica, De Legibus* (with an English translation by Clinton Walker Keyes), the Loeb Classical Library, Harvard University Press, Cambridge, Mass., 1928. Subsequent references to Cicero's *Republic* and *Laws* are to this edition.

[6] *Laws*, I, 10, 30.

Men share the same characteristics everywhere, though there are differences among them. "But what nation does not love courtesy, kindliness, gratitude, and remembrance of favours bestowed? What people does not hate and despise the naughty, the wicked, the cruel, and the ungrateful?" [7]

Men may be corrupted by bad habits, and justice is not always done, but men have received right reason and *they are all equal under the law*. Not merely citizens are equal, but all men. Cicero is considerably more cosmopolitan than Aristotle, who thought of equality only as applicable to the relationships among citizens of the city-state. Even the slave, in Cicero's view of the natural law, is entitled to a measure of equality. Slavery need not be abolished, but the slave is nevertheless a human being with the capacity to reason, and he has rights that must be respected. His owner should treat him as he would a hired laborer. The state, too, must rest upon these principles. It has an inescapable obligation to act according to the principles of the natural law. The laws of the state must be judged on the basis of how well they accord with the laws of nature. A law does not represent justice merely because it has utility—because it "works." Nor is a law necessarily just because it has the consent of the people to give it force. A law may "work" injustice, and the people may be unjust, as indeed they are when they will wrongful actions and laws.

Cicero's apparently unqualified endorsement of the Stoic theory of natural law can be misleading. One would be justified in assuming that Cicero was wholeheartedly endorsing a democratic system of government; but the assumption would not be entirely warranted. Cicero lived in the waning years of the Roman republic, and the venerable republican structure was undergoing great stress in attempting to cope with the imperialist problems with which it was confronted. There was a powerful movement toward dictatorship as a solution, and Cicero was a leader of the forces who opposed such a denouement. He believed that a reassertion of the republican principles under which Rome had achieved its greatness was the answer to Rome's problems. In his *Republic* Cicero outlined the structure of what he believed to be a perfect state and attempted to show how Rome had evolved toward that ideal. His efforts were essentially a restatement of Polybius's doctrine of the mixed state, and they share the weaknesses and fallacies of that theory.

If the application of the theory of the mixed state was faulty, Cicero's objective was praiseworthy. He was strongly opposed to despotism of any kind. In his view democracy could easily degenerate into mob rule just as monarchy could turn into tyranny or aristocracy into oligarchy. Cicero's firm advocacy of the doctrine of natural law never led him to propose a democratic governmental form. Only a government repre-

[7] *Ibid.*, I, 10, 32.

sented by all three of the possible governing elements, monarchy, aristocracy, and democracy, could provide the necessary degree of stability that would prevent despotism. And even though the best government is always of the mixed kind, the commonwealth itself is the affair of the people and exists to secure the common good and justice; at least this universal beneficence is its only moral justification for existence. Since all men can reason and can understand the natural law, they are entitled to a share in the exercise of political power. Though Cicero was not a democrat, he endorsed such principles as human equality, the natural law, governmental responsibility, and public participation. The man himself was a conservative and a moderate, who chose to return to the past rather than to offer progressive solutions to his country's problems. Nevertheless, praise must be accorded Cicero's courageous stand against dictatorship, a stand which led to his murder by members of the Mark Antony group a year after the assassination of Julius Caesar.

Seneca

From Cicero, who was representative of Stoic thought in the last years of the republic, we turn to Seneca (4? B.C.–A.D. 65), who expresses the Stoic doctrine of the opening years of the Roman Empire. There are both similarities and differences in the ideas expressed by these two men. Both believed that nature provides the standard by which men should live. Both accepted the validity of the principle of human equality; Seneca was more explicit in his defense of the principle than was Cicero. Seneca was careful to point out that the difference between master and slave is only a matter of legal convention and that as a human being the slave has the same origin as does the master and is fully as capable of achieving virtue. Bad luck alone makes a man a slave. Seneca, like Cicero and the earlier Stoics, thus sharply repudiated Aristotle's assumption that men are naturally unequal.[8]

Seneca's Stoicism appears melancholy when compared with that of Cicero. Cicero had been optimistic that the splendor of Rome could be recovered if reforms were adopted to restore the vigor and integrity of the republic. Seneca too believed that the republic was superior to the Empire, although he had little hope that the spirit of the old days could be recovered. Conditions were such that only a powerful monarch could keep order. The degradation of the mass of men made democracy an impossibility. Seneca was far less concerned than was Cicero with a comparison and appraisal of governmental forms since Seneca was convinced that government could not be considered in terms of good and bad but only in terms of utility. Order had to be main-

[8] R. W. Carlyle and A. J. Carlyle, *A History of Mediaeval Political Theory in the West,* Barnes & Noble, Inc., New York, 1953, vol. I, p. 21.

tained, and that government was best which could exercise most efficient control.

With such a view of the nature and function of government, Seneca naturally repudiated to some extent Cicero's view and that of the earlier Stoics generally that the good and wise man will offer his services to the state. Seneca did not consider service to the state particularly objectionable, but neither did he think it a major contribution. Wise men could perform a more valuable service. They could and should serve that other commonwealth, that greater society than the state, the one that encompasses all mankind.[9] Seneca reasserted a principle common to those earlier thinkers, forerunners of Stoicism, who held the tie of human brotherhood to be superior to that of citizenship. In doing so he made a considerable departure from the Stoicism of Cicero, who had held that the main moral obligation of man was to serve his country. Seneca also believed that man had a moral obligation, but it was an obligation to the greater society of mankind, not merely to one's fellow citizens. He believed in the worth of the man who does not actively serve his fellows in any capacity but who devotes himself to the contemplation of virtue, nature, and God.[10] Such a man is at least innocent of wrongdoing, and he is preparing himself for future service. It is important to contrast Seneca's Stoicism with the idea of Plato and Aristotle (and even Cicero) that citizenship is the most valuable function man can perform. To Plato and Aristotle the state was indispensable to the development of virtue and the good life. To Seneca the state is a reflection of man's evil nature. In his elaboration of this thesis Seneca formulated his idea of the "golden age" or state of nature, which has ever since played such a significant role in the history of political ideas.

According to Seneca, man once lived happily and innocently, though ignorantly, in a primitive state. Private property did not exist, all goods being held and consumed in common. There were rulers (although "leaders" is here a more descriptive term), but no laws and no agencies of enforcement. Men, directed by wise and just rulers, followed the rules of nature and found all others unnecessary. Because nature's dictates are always just, man did not need to be coerced into obedience. Man in this state was not morally perfect; he was virtuous because he had no knowledge of evil. But this happy state of affairs was disrupted

[9] The early Stoics had suggested that men are members of two communities—the civil state and the greater community to which men belong by virtue of their capacity to reason. To Seneca the larger community is society; its ties are "moral or religious" rather than "legal and political." See Sabine, *op. cit.*, pp. 175–176.

[10] Seneca here anticipates the religious bent of the Stoic philosopher, the Emperor Marcus Aurelius, a hundred years later. By this time Stoicism had assumed religious overtones similar in many respects to Christianity.

by the institution of private property. Men were then no longer satisfied to share their possessions, but each wished title to his own. Avarice became a powerful force among both rulers and ruled. Rulers became tyrants, and men struggled greedily against one another for additional property. Now there was a necessity for laws, coercive government, and the institutionalization of private property. Seneca found nothing inherently good in these additions; neither did he consider them evil. They were simply necessitated by man's degeneracy. If man were virtuous, government, law, and private property would be unnecessary; they are the badges of his lost innocence.

The parallels between Seneca's views and Christian doctrine are striking. The Garden of Eden and Seneca's "golden age" both represent the stage of man's carefree existence. Private property is Seneca's version of the serpent. This interpretation circulated among early Christians and sometimes resulted in the establishment of primitive communistic communities. The belief that law and government are necessitated by private property and that they might successfully be dispensed with if property were held in common has never lost its fascination for reformers through the ages. Both Christian and Communist have been intrigued by it. The golden age of liberty and the absence of property is one of the meanings of the *jus naturale* (natural law). In some Roman law texts this is superseded by the *jus gentium* which brought in government and slavery. These ideas, and these uses of the terms, became commonplace in the Middle Ages.

Conclusions

As we have seen, enormous changes in political thought occurred after Alexander's conquest of Athens in 320 B.C. and the resulting decline of the city-state. In the beginning of this period the philosophy of withdrawal expressed by the Epicureans, the Cynics, and the early Stoics constituted a repudiation of the city-state doctrine of Aristotle and Plato. Plato and Aristotle had always assumed the city-state to be a necessary precondition of man's moral development and the good life. The later schools of thought taught that political association might bring security but little or nothing more. Panaetius, and later Cicero, reconstructed Stoic philosophy and made it acceptable to the Romans, who were attracted by most of its features and demanded only that it be altered to justify the ideal of public service. Seneca did not wholly reject the concept of service but there is considerable difference between Cicero's Stoicism with its emphasis on the value of good government and Seneca's proposition that government is only necessary because man is evil. The chasm between Seneca and the philosophers of the city-state, Plato and Aristotle, is unbridgeable.

Of equal importance is the transformation in political thought of the concept of human equality. For this new and strongly democratic view the development of the doctrine of natural law is responsible. Aristotle had written of equality but had considered it a valid principle only insofar as it applied to the relationship between citizens. Under the natural law of Stoic philosophy, however, *all* men were brothers. Man's ability to reason enabled him to comprehend the immutable rules of nature and to act accordingly—although, of course, he did not always act properly. Though, as has been shown, a general acceptance of the ideals of human equality and universal brotherhood did not lead immediately to the creation of democratic governments, at least some of the bases for democracy were established; and while men continued for centuries to live under a great variety of tyrannies they had the tools with which to work and they ultimately achieved some success in their use.

SELECTED BIBLIOGRAPHY

Agard, Walter R.: *The Greek Mind,* D. Van Nostrand Company, Inc., Anvil Books, Princeton, N.J., 1957, part 2, readings 18, 19, 20.

Buckland, W. W., and Arnold D. McNair: *Roman Law and Common Law,* Cambridge University Press, New York, 1936, chap. 1.

Carlyle, R. W., and A. J. Carlyle: *A History of Mediaeval Political Theory in the West,* Barnes & Noble, Inc., New York, 1953, vol. I, part 1.

Coker, Francis William: *Readings in Political Philosophy,* rev. ed., The Macmillan Company, New York, 1938, chap. 4.

Cook, Thomas I.: *History of Political Philosophy from Plato to Burke,* Prentice-Hall, Inc., Englewood Cliffs, N.J., 1936, chap. 5.

Coulanges, Fustel de: *The Ancient City,* Anchor Books, Doubleday & Company, Inc., Garden City, N.Y., 1956, bk. I, chap. 1.

Ebenstein, William: *Political Thought in Perspective,* McGraw-Hill Book Company, Inc., New York, 1957, chap. 4.

Jolowicz, H. F.: *Historical Introduction to the Study of Roman Law,* Cambridge University Press, New York, 1939, chaps. 4, 6.

Sabine, George H.: *A History of Political Theory,* 3d ed., Holt, Rinehart and Winston, Inc., New York, 1961, chaps. 7–10.

Wanlass, Lawrence C.: *Gettell's History of Political Thought,* 2d ed., Appleton-Century-Crofts, Inc., New York, 1953, chap. 6.

six

THE POLITICAL THEORY OF THE EARLY FATHERS

Jesus and the Apostles

It may seem superfluous to point out that Christianity was a religious rather than a political movement. Yet considering the vast body of political writing Christianity produced and the tangled web of political controversy in which it became involved, the student of politics sometimes needs to remind himself of its original concern with man's relation to God. Jesus apparently had little interest in politics. His doctrine was designed to save souls, not to create states and governments or to provide instruction in how those secular institutions should function. His few scattered statements on politics were evoked by situations (such as his appearance before Pontius Pilate) not of his own choosing, and those statements demonstrated a willingness to leave temporal affairs in the hands of the constituted authorities. As Professor Dunning has properly said, it required considerable ingenuity on the part of later writers to attribute great political significance to those few remarks of Jesus which he made on the subject of government.[1] We shall consider shortly the circumstances which necessitated this development, but we may state here that the Christian political doctrines of a later age often seem to make more of the matter than did Jesus. The statements, "Render therefore unto Caesar the things which are Caesar's; and unto

[1] William Archibald Dunning, *A History of Political Theories, Ancient and Medieval,* The Macmillan Company, New York, 1905, p. 153.

God the things that are God's" [2] and "My kingdom is not of this world" [3] are not those of a man with a deep and abiding interest in things political.

We find more of political significance to consider in the teachings of Christ's apostles than in the words of the Master. Here too we may suppose that the apostles were not concerned with the development of a political theory beyond that necessitated by circumstances. The very nature of Christian doctrine, which subordinated the temporal to the spiritual, made some political involvement unavoidable. Christ had clearly stated that the next world was far more important than this. The hereafter lasted forever; this life is only a temporary interlude, significant mainly because a person's conduct on earth determines his fate hereafter. The Christian, of course, was bound by such a doctrine to regard temporal affairs, including government, as less important than spiritual, and also to judge the acts of secular government by the measuring rod of Christian dogma. Many early Christians interpreted the doctrine of a divine government under the fatherhood of God to mean that secular government was both unnecessary and undesirable. That the imperial government of Rome should have regarded such an attitude with suspicion and persecuted the Christians accordingly may be deprecated, but their action is understandable. The apostles were certainly aware of this problem, and their statements on occasion demonstrated that they did not construe the teachings of Jesus to justify anarchism among members of the Church. The most concise injunction, in this respect, is found in St. Paul's letter to the Romans.

> Let every soul be subject unto the higher powers. For there is no power but of God: the powers that be are ordained of God. Whosoever therefore resisteth the power, resisteth the ordinance of God: and they that resist shall receive to themselves damnation. For rulers are not a terror to good works but to the evil. Wilt thou then not be afraid of the power? Do that which is good, and thou shalt have praise of the same: For he is the minister of God to thee for good. But if thou do that which is evil, be afraid; for he beareth not the sword in vain: For he is the minister of God, a revenger to execute wrath upon him that doeth evil. Wherefore ye must needs be subject, not only for wrath, but also for conscience sake. For for this cause pay ye tribute also: for they are God's ministers, attending continually upon this very thing. Render therefore to all their dues: tribute to whom tribute is due; custom to whom custom; fear to whom fear; honor to whom honor. [4]

A more unequivocal endorsement of the principle of the divine right of government can scarcely be imagined, and so it was construed by

[2] Matthew xxii:21. All references are to the King James version.
[3] John xviii:36.
[4] Romans xiii:1-7.

the early Fathers of the Church, at least until the power of the Church enabled it to take exception to actions of the secular authorities. But aside from this matter, other issues require mention. The Christians accepted, perhaps unconsciously, a number of tenets of Stoic philosophy concerning natural law, the equality of man, the role of government, and property. Certain changes were necessitated by the demands of doctrine, but the similarities of Christian social and political ideas to those of Stoicism outweigh the differences between them.

St. Paul again provides us with the early Christian view on the natural law.

> For when the Gentiles, which have not the law, do by nature the things contained in the law, these, having not the law, are a law unto themselves: which shew the work of the law written in their hearts, their conscience also bearing witness, and their thoughts the meanwhile accusing or else excusing one another.[5]

In this statement Paul assumes that there is a natural law which is neither the written law of the state nor the revealed word of God but which may be apprehended by the reason of Christian and gentile alike. Four hundred years later the early Fathers accepted this interpretation and through them it was passed on into the medieval period.[6] Although the application is Christian and some Christian writers equated natural law with God's law, the idea is essentially Stoic and shows no practical departure from the ideas of Cicero on the same subject.

There is also a similarity in the Stoic and Christian views of the equality of man. A commonsense interpretation of the teachings of Christ would seem to be that all men, being the children of God, are equal in his sight. The idea is like that of the Stoics not only in its assumption of man's equality but also in the universality of its application. St. Paul reinforced the doctrine of his Master. "There is neither Jew nor Greek, there is neither bond nor free, there is neither male nor female: for ye are all one in Christ Jesus." [7] And Paul said to the Romans: "For there is no difference between the Jew and the Greek: for the same Lord over all is rich unto all that call upon him." [8] Such expressions on human equality were commonplace in Stoic thought, especially that of Cicero and Seneca. But we must guard against attaching too much significance to them, in Christian as in Stoic writings. We should not be justified in holding, on the basis of what has been cited above, that Paul was an abolitionist. The early Christian may

---

[5] Romans ii:14, 15.
[6] Lawrence C. Wanlass, *Gettell's History of Political Thought*, 2d ed., Appleton-Century-Crofts, Inc., New York, 1953, p. 98.
[7] Galatians iii:28.
[8] Romans x:12.

have believed that all men were equal, but he meant that they were equal only in the eyes of God. He did not propose legal abolition of slavery. God does not care less for one of his children who is a slave. Slavery is an earthly institution; it does not exist in heaven. The good man who is a slave will go to heaven sooner than the bad master. Thus slavery as an institution is unimportant in that it has no bearing on the salvation of the soul. The parallel with Stoicism again is apparent. At most it can be claimed that Christianity had a humanizing influence on the institution of slavery. Paul taught that the relationship of master and slave ought to be marked by a spirit of mutual respect. The master should remember that God is master of all and the slave should perform his duty. Paul here continues the Stoic belief in a moral and spiritual equality, and like the Stoics, advocates humane treatment of the slave by his master.

The references to property in the New Testament are abundant enough, but they are insufficiently clear and many interpretations have been attached to them. Jesus was certainly concerned lest preoccupation with the gathering of material wealth should interfere with the infinitely more valuable goal of saving one's soul. To the rich young man who had obeyed all the Ten Commandments, Jesus said: "If thou wilt be perfect, go and sell that thou hast, and give to the poor, and thou shalt have treasure in heaven." [9] The price was too great, and the young man departed, whereupon Jesus told his disciples: "Verily I say unto you, that a rich man shall hardly enter into the kingdom of heaven. And again I say unto you, It is easier for a camel to go through the eye of a needle, than for a rich man to enter into the kingdom of God." [10] The Acts of the Apostles further relates that those who were inspired by the word of God were impelled to divest themselves of material wealth.

> And the multitude of them that believed were of one heart and one soul: neither said any of them that aught of the things which he possessed was his own; but they had all things in common. . . . Neither was there any among them that lacked: for as many as were possessors of lands or houses sold them, and brought the prices of the things that were sold, and laid them down at the apostles' feet: and distribution was made unto every man according as he had need.[11]

It may be tempting to construe such statements as an endorsement of communism. The parallel between the extract from Acts and Marx's utopia, in which each man is to contribute according to his ability and receive according to his need, is particularly obvious. The inter-

[9] Matthew xix:21.
[10] Matthew xix:23, 24.
[11] Acts v:32, 34, 35.

pretations have been many. Professor Carlyle, who considered the matter at length, concluded that no well-defined theory of property can be found in the New Testament. Both Jesus and his apostles admonished their followers to be generous and not to love material things better than God.[12] The quotations cited above seem to indicate that poverty is, in God's view, a more blessed state than affluence. But this acceptance of poverty did not mean that Jesus or his apostles advocated the abolition of the institution of private property itself.

The Rise of Christianity

The period of Christianity's development from the time of Christ and his apostles until the reign of Galerius some three hundred years later, was one of hardship for the Christian. His refusal to worship the gods of the state and his insistence upon according the kingdom of God a higher respect than he could show the Empire were regarded and punished as treason. Christians were deprived of property and citizenship, and their churches were destroyed. But Christianity flourished despite, and perhaps because of, persecution. In 311 Emperor Galerius issued his edict of toleration which permitted the Christians finally to worship in peace. A few years later another Roman emperor, Constantine, was himself converted to Christianity, and the prestige of the Church increased enormously. Before the century had closed the Emperor Theodosius, who reigned from 379 to 395, made Christianity the official religion of the Empire.

The reasons underlying Theodosius's action may have been less theological than political. The Empire needed the Church, which had grown large and powerful, to help it hold together its far-flung and increasingly restive domains. Zealous Christian missionaries had carried the gospel to the many subject peoples of the Empire, and the Church had developed considerable strength and prestige among such people outside of Italy. As imperial administrators found it increasingly difficult to maintain cohesion in the dominions, they sought for some unifying force capable of offsetting the steadily developing particularism. A common religion seemed to be the answer, and Christianity with its tradition of civil obedience seemed to be the appropriate religion. There would be a partnership. The Church could use its great influence not only to bring about a new harmony but also to warn against the evil of revolution. The state could, on the other hand, do much to stimulate growth of the Church's membership. Such a natural partnership, caring for the temporal and spiritual requirements of the people, would provide great benefits for all concerned. As is so often the case with grandiose plans, this one did not develop as anticipated.

[12] R. W. Carlyle and A. J. Carlyle, *A History of Mediaeval Political Theory in the West*, Barnes & Noble, Inc., New York, 1953, vol. I, pp. 98–101.

Membership in the Church did in fact grow by leaps and bounds, but the rapid increase of itself created annoying problems. It was increasingly difficult to maintain the purity of the doctrine against the heresies carried in by the hordes of new Christians, who were not always willing converts. Church leaders were compelled to rely more than they would have preferred to upon secular assistance. The Church, often against its wishes, was soon deeply involved in politics. In the early years of the new association the dominant partner was the state. Only its secular organization and power were capable of solving the pressing problems the Church confronted.

Circumstances soon conspired to alter this situation. From the time of Constantine until the fall of Rome, a period of some one hundred and fifty years, the power of the Church increased while that of the state declined. There were several reasons for the trend. In the first place, a series of emperors lacked administrative capacity and the qualities of leadership. Second, a line of Church leaders possessed these attributes in considerable degree. Third, Christianity offered solace and hope to a generation that sorely needed them. An era of social and political disintegration and decay had produced among the citizens of the Empire a spirit of pessimism and withdrawal comparable to that which had accompanied the collapse of the city-state. A disillusionment with secular things, however, prompted a search for a substitute, and Christianity with its promise of otherworldly glories to follow the miseries of this world seemed to be the answer for many. Fourth, the invading barbarians, who brought Rome to her knees and devastated her secular institutions, spared the Church as well as its property.[13]

The organization of the Church, too, was developing in size and in the effectiveness of its administration. The early Church had been a decentralized structure democratically controlled by the localities. When Christianity became an official adjunct of the state there was a strong trend toward centralization. The Bishop of Rome had since an early day received deference from the whole Church as the successor of Peter, whose authority was thought to have descended to him. In the fourth century two emperors conferred upon him a kind of appellate jurisdiction in Church matters. For these and other reasons, which need not be considered here, Rome became the center of a new and powerful empire, more ecclesiastical than secular but no less important because of that. If the intention of Rome had been to use the Church largely for its own purposes, to enjoy the advantages of acquisition while still retaining power in its own hands, that intention was frustrated.

Most important, the rise of Christianity raised for large numbers of individuals for the first time the issue of divided loyalty. Government serves a valuable purpose, and it ought to be obeyed when it acts within

[13] Dunning, *op. cit.*, pp. 133–134.

its proper jurisdictional sphere. For most Christians, and for most of the time, the problem of conflicting Church-state loyalty did not arise. It was generally not too difficult to separate the things due to Caesar from the things due to God, but situations were bound to arise in which the jurisdictional lines between Church and state were hazy. Indeed it sometimes appeared to the conscientious Christian that the secular authority had invaded sacred territory. When this happened, the Christian, if he were worth his salt and especially if he were concerned about everlasting life in a state of blessedness, had to obey that authority, obviously the Church, which was more consequential. The problems were present from the beginning, and they multiplied as the Church grew stronger. Political thought in the medieval period centers in great measure on the Church-state problem. We shall next consider what some of the early Fathers of the Church said and did about that problem.

The Early Fathers of the Church

To the student of American federalism a review of the Church-state conflict that began in the fourth century raises familiar issues. The political scientist knows, for example, that the problem of the division of power between state and national governments finds no definitive solution in the words of the Constitution, no matter how clear those words appear to be. Circumstances also have necessitated a never-ending series of changes in the doctrines which have been developed to provide solutions. The conflict between the protagonists on each side of this controversy is of greater or lesser magnitude depending upon the particular issue that may be involved at any given time. On one occasion a long and costly civil war resulted from the inability of Americans to reach a peaceful settlement of the matter. In short, the Connecticut Compromise probably created as many difficulties as it eliminated.

The steadily increasing complexity of the Church-state relationship was stimulated by conditions and gave rise to consequences somewhat similar to those mentioned above. From the standpoint of doctrine the whole issue appeared settled. From Jesus's injunction to "render unto Caesar" and from the apostolic teachings which sanctioned secular government and at least partially defined its role, the idea grew that both Church and state were necessary to the good life and that each should contribute to that end in its appropriate manner. Between the two a generous spirit of cooperation should exist, but it was assumed that the spheres of jurisdiction were well defined. Reality, however, proved to be more complicated than theory. An organization as large and powerful as the Church could not escape involvement in strongly secular affairs. There was, for example, the problem of Church property and the debated right of the state to use or to tax it. Many similar ques-tions arose. The simple response of Jesus to Pilate's interrogation now only raised a further dilemma. What properly *was* Caesar's? What *was* God's?

The early Fathers of the Church did not produce a well-developed theory that could be relied upon to answer all the questions raised. Circumstances largely determined the stand that an official of the Church might take. It was far easier for the Church to be courageous when its own strength was great than when it was a small organization struggling for survival. Then, too, the Church might feel that a specific issue was not sufficiently important to warrant a test of power. By the time of the reign of Theodosius and the Empire's adoption of Chris-tianity as its official religion, the Church was in a position, occasionally at least, to assert itself. St. Ambrose (340?–397), Bishop of Milan and a stalwart defender of the Church's position, attempted to supply a reasonably consistent theory, setting out what he conceived to be the proper role of both Church and state and the relationship to be desired between them.

Ambrose held that the state is divinely ordained and that the civil ruler must be obeyed, although he may very possibly rule unjustly, not following God's will. The civil ruler should by no means interfere in ecclesiastical matters, for these are entirely under the jurisdiction of the Church, and in spiritual affairs the secular ruler is only a Church member like all others. He is subject to the rules and discipline im-posed by Church authorities. Ambrose did not hesitate to admonish and discipline the emperor when he thought it necessary. Ambrose's refusal to permit Theodosius to participate in the celebration of the Eucharist because, the crusty Bishop charged, he was responsible for a massacre, is a familiar story in early Church history. It is the duty of the Church authority, he said, to remonstrate with the emperor when it deems that he has overstepped his jurisdiction, although force is the weapon of the secular authority alone. The Church can rely only upon spiritual discipline.[14]

The most influential of the early Fathers was St. Augustine, a student of St. Ambrose. Augustine was born in Tagaste in North Africa in 354. His mother was a Christian, his father a pagan, and it appears, in view of the abandoned life that Augustine says he led as a young man, that the maternal influence was inconsiderable, at least during Augustine's early years. As he matured Augustine developed philosophical interests. He dabbled in the ideas of a number of sects and was ultimately, at the age of thirty-five, converted to Christianity. Soon after, Augustine

[14] George H. Sabine, *A History of Political Theory*, 3d ed., Holt, Rinehart and Win-ston, Inc., New York, 1961, p. 188.

joined the priesthood and rose rapidly in its ranks. At forty-two he was appointed Bishop of Hippo, in Africa. He retained the post until his death in 430.

Augustine was a prolific writer. In addition to his celebrated *Confessions,* he wrote treatises on philosophical questions, criticisms of other religions and defenses of his own, and a number of interpretations of, and commentaries on, Christian teachings. Augustine's views are not altogether consistent. His philosophy was borrowed from Plato—immediately from the neo-Platonism of Plotinus. But he was also strongly influenced by Judeo-Christian theology. In some respects these two elements agreed, but on some questions they were incompatible, and Augustine's writings evidence the resulting confusion. The most important of his works was his *City of God,* on which he spent more than twelve years and which was of enormous influence in the later medieval period. *The City of God* was designed by Augustine to defend the Church against the charge leveled against it by its enemies that Christianity was responsible for the fall of Rome to Alaric and the Visigoths. The first ten books of *The City of God* are devoted to a refutation of this charge. But in the other twelve books Augustine discusses generally his views of man and the society in which he lives. Much of the content of the work is directly in line with well-established Christian thought; but also many unique and significant contributions deserve detailed consideration.

Augustine's most distinctive contribution lay in his development of the theory of the two communities, the heavenly and the earthly cities. There is a similarity between Augustine's idea that each human being is a citizen of two communities and the Stoic idea that each person is a member of the secular community in which he lives and of the greater society of humankind in which all men are brothers. But Augustine provided a religious interpretation of the latter view. Whereas to the Stoic reason was the common tie which enabled men to understand the universal natural law and to live together in peace, to Augustine the force for mutuality was belief in and obedience to God.

Augustine's words may be easily misinterpreted. The two cities are not heaven and earth, nor are they Church and state. Rather they are the forces of good and evil that have contended from time immemorial for the possession of men's souls. They are the kingdoms of God and of Satan. Augustine's philosophy of history, which strongly influenced thinking in the Middle Ages and beyond, saw history as the struggle between the forces of the earthly city and those of the heavenly city, a struggle which would eventually culminate in the establishment of a Christian commonwealth. The earthly city is dominated by the principle of self-love to the point where God is held in contempt. Its devotees are those to whom material interests are more important than spiritual.

The heavenly city is dominated by the principle of love of God. Its inhabitants are those to whom spiritual things are paramount. Agencies are provided by God to help man achieve salvation and eternal life in God's city. These are the Church and the state. The former is by far the more important; indeed the state may even be a hindrance to men's salvation if it is not a Christian state. The Church is the great institution that represents God on earth. From the time of its establishment the forces of good on earth have had all that was required to defeat Satan. All men are born in sin but they may, Augustine says, be "grafted into Christ by regeneration" and saved, and the Church makes this regeneration possible. The very nature of its mission places it on a higher level than that occupied by the state; for it acts for God on earth in the great struggle to achieve final victory through the establishment of the city of God inhabited by a union of all saved souls.

Despite Augustine's unmistakable relegation of the state to an inferior position, he does not propose that it become a mere appendage of the Church, placed under its moral and spiritual control. Augustine's position with regard to the Church-state relationship was approximately the same as that of his predecessors. Each institution had its appropriate function, and each should be sovereign in its own area. In Augustine's time the Church was still too reliant upon the state to deprecate its value too much. But granted that the state must exist and function, it must do so in a proper manner. One of Augustine's major contributions lay in his clear and forceful definition of the good commonwealth.

What is a commonwealth? It is, Augustine says, "an assemblage of reasonable beings bound together by a common agreement as to the objects of their love." [15] This, however, is a description of any commonwealth; whether it is good or bad depends upon the object of the people's love. The good commonwealth must bring justice to its people, and justice is found in the word of God. The true commonwealth must be a Christian commonwealth which provides all the necessary conditions that the state can provide for the advancement of God's cause. There were commonwealths before Christianity, but none brought justice to its people. Cicero was right in terming his beloved Rome a republic, but he was wrong in holding that it was bound together by a "compact of justice." Justice was impossible because its people did not know the true God and worshipped the wrong gods. The same may be said of all past states.

> But what I say of this people and of this republic I must be understood to think and say of the Athenians or any Greek state, of the Egyptians, of the

<hr>

[15] St. Augustine, *The City of God* (English translation by Marcus Dods), Hafner Publishing Company, Inc., New York, 1948, xix, 24. Subsequent quotations from and references to *The City of God* are to this edition.

early Assyrian Babylon, and of every other nation, great or small, which had a public government. For, in general, the city of the ungodly, which did not obey the command of God that it should offer no sacrifice save to Him alone, and which, therefore, could not give to the soul its proper command over the body, nor to the reason its just authority over the vices, is void of true justice.[16]

It is understandable that the states of the past lacked justice, for they did not have the Church and Christian doctrine. There is no excuse for any state since Christ to be without justice. The precise relationship which should exist between the secular and the spiritual institutions may be debatable, but no argument is possible on the necessity for them to be associates in a Christian cause if they are to be just. Augustine's view became a fundamental principle of Western thought and remained so for more than a thousand years. In modern times, when the proliferation of religions has made practically impossible a legal basis for the doctrine, to say nothing of legal enforcement, it has lived on as a powerful force in the minds of a great part of the people.

Augustine considered the primary function of the state to be the maintenance of peace and order. This is as true of the non-Christian as of the Christian state. Those of the earthly city wish peace in order that they may better enjoy the objects of their love, that is material things, the goods of this world. The people of the heavenly city desire peace so that they may devote themselves to the worship of God and so that this poor life will be more endurable. The peace sought by the Christian is the only valuable peace because it makes possible an earthly service to God.[17] We must bear in mind Augustine's original purpose in writing his *City of God* if we are correctly to understand much of his commentary on the state. Essentially, Augustine contends that Rome, before it became Christian, was not a true commonwealth. The peace it established was not a proper peace since it was not directed to Chris-

---

[16] *Ibid.*

[17] Whether or not Augustine believed that justice was a necessary ingredient of the commonwealth has been a matter of controversy and the advocates on either side have been formidable. Prof. A. J. Carlyle and J. N. Figgis have taken the position that Augustine did in fact eliminate justice as a requirement for a commonwealth. The position here is that taken by Prof. C. H. McIlwain, endorsed by Prof. George H. Sabine, and expressed by Professor McIlwain in these words: "Justice and justice alone is the only possible bond which can unite men as a true *populus* in a real *res publica*. The great states before Christianity were *regna* but they were not true commonwealths because there was no recognition in them of what was due to the one true God, and without such recognition there could be no real justice, for justice is to render to *each* his due. They were, however, *regna* and their undoubted merits in many ways entitle them to great admiration and respect." (From Charles H. McIlwain, *The Growth of Political Thought in the West: From the Greeks to the End of the Middle Ages*, The Macmillan Company, New York, 1932, p. 158.)

tian ends. Roman wars were as unjust as the peace they brought since the cause of God was not served in them.

> Now, when victory remains with the party which had the juster cause, who hesitates to congratulate the victor, and style it a desirable peace? These things, then, are good things, and without doubt the gifts of God. But if they neglect the better things of the heavenly city, which are secured by eternal victory and peace never-ending, and so inordinately covet these present good things that they believe them to be the only desirable things, or love them better than those things which are believed to be better—if this be so, then it is necessary that misery follow and ever increase.[18]

The heavenly city must be established. All pagan empires must fall in the course of history; such is the will of God. What is truly important is to learn how to live in the ways prescribed by God through his church in order that *true* citizenship, that found only in the city of God, may be achieved. Existence is hard, but one should not expect it to be otherwise. Man is born in sin, and life is not supposed to be easy. Nor will perfection ever be found on earth. The political problems man faces can never be solved because the human mentality is limited. Only God is all-wise; upon him we must rely. If he is obeyed perfection *will* be achieved, and it will last forever.[19]

The concept of man's sinfulness is central to much of the political thought of Augustine and the early Fathers. Augustine particularly charges the state to keep order. But if man were not sinful he would not be disorderly. Thus government is necessitated by man's sinfulness. God did not intend it thus, for in the beginning man was to have "dominion over the fish of the sea, and over the fowl of the air, and over every creeping thing which creepeth on the earth." [20] But one man was not to be subject to another. Man's sin, however, led to an inequality manifested by slavery, government, and private property. These are not necessarily evil institutions. God himself gave them to man to enable him to live in a world in which equality was no longer possible and peace no longer normal. The citizens of the state may not establish themselves as judges of the ruler, for the ruler received his authority from God, and the manner in which he employs it is not to be criticized by the people. God gives his people what they deserve. An evil and brutal king is imposed upon the people as punishment for their sins, and he must be obeyed even as is a kindly and good king. Augustine speaks of Nero whose crimes against humankind in general and against Christians in particular are historic; but Augustine still holds that such a monarch is to be obeyed.

[18] *City of God*, xv, 4.
[19] Andrew Hacker, *Political Theory: Philosophy, Ideology, Science,* The Macmillan Company, New York, 1961, p. 121.
[20] I Timothy v:8.

> Nevertheless power and domination are not given even to such men save by the providence of the most high God, when he judges that the state of human affairs is worthy of such lords. The divine utterance is clear on this matter....[21]

Augustine does not, in short, construe Christian doctrine to be a foundation for political democracy; it is certainly not a justification for revolution.

It is not clear how far Augustine would go in advocating passive obedience of the Church to edicts of the emperor which might contravene Church doctrine; unfortunately he does not consider this matter at length. As we have seen, St. Ambrose was quick to defend the Church against what he considered to be secular trespassing, but we need not attribute to Augustine the same point of view. In fact, if we look ahead to the sixth century, we find that Gregory the Great (540–604), whose reliance on Augustine's writings was considerable, frankly proclaims a doctrine of passive obedience of Church to state. Gregory's position is somewhat difficult to understand, considering the fact that he was in a better position than his predecessors to dispute the claims to power of the state.

Carlyle gives four reasons for the development of the passive-obedience theory in Christian writings. First, there was a need to combat the tendencies to anarchism among early Christians. Second, the New Testament writings clearly state the principle that all powers come from God. Third, the Old Testament represents the king as the anointed of God. Fourth, and finally, the new Christian Church was anxious to allay the fears which the Empire had developed concerning the Church as a subversive organization.[22] Whatever may have been the differences among the early Fathers with regard to their views on the scope of secular authority, they were all agreed that the power came from God. A monarch ruled because God planned it that way. The responsibility of the ruler was to God, not to the people. The question of the source of secular power, whether it came from the people or from God, was a perennial matter of discussion throughout the medieval period. As we shall see, the position of Church leaders was not consistent.

For Augustine the function of government is not the securing and preservation of rights; it is the enforcement of order. A stable tyranny is better than a disorderly democracy. Equality, justice, and freedom are goals to be attained only in the heavenly city. Sinful human beings (and that means all of us in this world) must be subjected to an authority over which they have no control. Man must be subjected to man. Thus government is a necessity, and so is slavery. In the interest of maintaining order society is and must be based upon the authoritarian principle.

---

[21] *City of God*, v, 19.
[22] Carlyle, *op. cit.*, vol. I, p. 157.

Some must rule, and more must obey. The latter must accept their lowly existence. They may derive some comfort from the fact that if they resign themselves to their fate they will further the cause of peace and order, and these blessings they must have if they are to devote themselves to the worship of God and the attainment of salvation. God in his wisdom has seen fit to provide slavery as a punishment for sin. Augustine's view here is unmistakable. "The prime cause, then, of slavery is sin, which brings man under the domination of his fellow,—that which does not happen save by the judgment of God, with whom is no unrighteousness, and who knows how to award fit punishments to every variety of offense." [23] An appropriate objection to this view is that it would be difficult to demonstrate that all slaves are sinners. Augustine appears to anticipate the objection. It is true, he says, that "wicked masters" often have "religious men" as slaves. In such a case the slave is actually better off than the master for "beyond question it is a happier thing to be the slave of a man than of a lust." [24] This, it might be observed, provides small consolation to the slave, and of course Augustine does not meet the problem squarely at all if he is genuinely attempting to justify slavery as a necessary punishment in *individual* cases. It is more likely that Augustine's meaning is that slavery as an *institution* is necessitated by the sinfulness of all men. If injustices are evident in individual cases where the slave is a better man than his master, then although the slave's position of servitude may be unfortunate, he must console himself with the thought that his present deplorable condition is no bar to his entering the kingdom of God. He must make the best of a bad situation, do his work, and find solace and comfort in contemplating his future permanent and otherworldly existence. This appears at least to be a commonsense interpretation of the following passage, which indeed contains most of the essential elements of Augustine's thought as it pertains to slavery.

> Moreover, when men are subjected to one another in a peaceful order, the lowly position does as much good to the servant as the proud position does harm to the master. But by nature, as God first created us, no one is the slave either of man or of sin. This servitude is, however, penal, and is appointed by that law which enjoins the preservation of the natural order and forbids its disturbance; for if nothing had been done in violation of that law, there would have been nothing to restrain by penal servitude. And therefore the apostle admonishes slaves to be subject to their masters, and to serve them heartily and with good-will, so that, if they cannot be freed by their masters, they may themselves make their slavery in some sort free, by serving not in crafty fear, but in faithful love, until all unrighteousness pass away, and all principality and every human power be brought to nothing, and God be all in all.[25]

[23] *City of God*, xix, 15.
[24] *Ibid.*
[25] *Ibid.*

The view of the early Fathers is that slavery, like government, is necessitated by human sinfulness. In a state of innocence neither was necessary and neither existed. The same principle underlies the teachings relating to private property. Ambrose is clearer on the point than is Augustine, but there seems to be no substantial difference in their views. Ambrose says that God had originally meant all property to be held in common but that sinfulness in the form of avarice made fulfillment of the ideal impossible. Private property was then necessary. It is neither unlawful nor responsible for man's sinfulness; rather private property is quite in accord both with human law and the law provided by God for the governing of men on earth. Though in the state of innocence and in the heavenly city private property would be irrelevant, it is indispensable here and now. Augustine adds to this the corollary that one does not sin in owning property so long as he does not attach to it a greater value than to honor, truth, or any of the truly Christian virtues. Augustine also posits the principle of the relativity of property rights, that is, that no person may use his property in any way he sees fit but rather that his claim is limited by his obligation to use his property rightly. By "rightly" Augustine probably means in the interest of his fellow man. At any rate Gregory, a thorough student of Augustine, strongly makes this point. Contributions to the poor, Gregory asserted, are required by justice and cannot be considered as mere charity.[26]

In general, the views of the early Fathers are strikingly similar to Seneca's Stoic ideas as they relate to slavery, property, and government. Both Seneca and the Fathers regarded these institutions as legal and necessary. Nevertheless both deprecated their necessity, because to admit it was also to admit the evil nature of man. In effect both said: "It is true that we must have these things—government, slavery, property. But is it not regrettable!" The Christians, of course, could look forward to the next world, in which government under God would not require force to compel obedience, and in which neither slavery nor private property would exist. This view differs considerably from that which came to predominate centuries later, that property, far from being an evidence of man's evil nature, is a natural right which man carries with him from a state of nature into organized society.

Of the three great Fathers, Ambrose, Augustine, and Gregory, the last-named goes furthest in developing the idea of the sacred nature of government. Like Augustine he regards the bad ruler as one of God's methods of punishing sin and insists that the people have no more right to resist a bad ruler than they have to resist a good ruler. To oppose a ruler of any kind is to oppose God. It is not permissible even to *speak* against the acts of a ruler, let alone to rebel against him. Gregory himself was a vigorous administrator, who sought an extension of the power of the Church he headed. When the emperor trespassed upon what was con-

[26] Carlyle, *op. cit.*, vol. I, p. 138.

ceived to be the rightful authority of the Church, Gregory protested (although even this was apparently forbidden by Gregory to the people), but submitted.

Gelasius I

Augustine's *The City of God* was not intended as a treatise on politics, although its political significance has been considerable. The same is true of the works of Ambrose and Gregory. The fact was, as has been stated above, that the rise of Christianity raised problems with which authorities, Church and state, had to deal. The arguments and decisions that grew out of these problems became precedents upon the basis of which attempts were made to solve subsequent problems. From all this there began to emerge a fairly well-defined body of doctrine dealing with Church-state relationships, a doctrine that was generally acceptable, at least in principle if not always in application, to secular and spiritual authorities alike. This doctrine nowhere received a more definitive expression than in the writings of Pope Gelasius I in the last part of the fifth century. It is, therefore, to Gelasius that we shall look for a statement of the theory of Church-state relationship which in part provides a summary of the doctrine as it was understood in the fifth century and which also established the basis for the development of later political thought.

Gelasius's central idea was that of a great Christian society governed by two authorities, spiritual and temporal, and represented by two institutions, Church and state. The goal of both is the same—the management of affairs on earth in such a manner as to make possible the salvation of every soul. In the implementation of this goal each authority has a different responsibility. The state must keep peace and order through the proper conduct of civil government. The Church must teach the true doctrine and care for the spiritual interests of the people. Although each authority has a distinct task for which it is responsible, it must provide assistance to the other where necessary. In certain cases the proper division of authority may be difficult to determine, but dedicated leaders can solve these problems. Church leaders such as Gelasius seemed to imply that the responsibility of the Church, which was more directly concerned with the matter of salvation, was greater than that of the state; therefore if any question arose as to whether an issue was under the jurisdiction of the spiritual or temporal authority, the Church ought to make the decision. Gelasius further insisted that ecclesiastical officials should come under the jurisdiction of ecclesiastical rather than secular courts in any case involving a spiritual issue.[27] The emperor, though ruler of the state, is merely a *member* of the Church. Although God has

---

[27] It is quite possible that Gelasius, in considering the matter, argued that ecclesiastics should be tried in ecclesiastical courts regardless of the issue involved, but this is not certain.

given him the absolute power to govern that state, he must take direction in spiritual matters from those to whom God has entrusted spiritual authority. Moreover, Gelasius asserts the power of the Church to discipline an emperor who resists its authority within its proper jurisdiction, and Gelasius fortifies his position by citing a series of precedents in which Church authorities have properly taken disciplinary action against emperors.[28]

The division of authority, or the "doctrine of the two swords" as it is often called, represents the method by which God wishes people to be governed. Since Christ, no ruler can combine in his own hands the powers of church and state; the temptations to abuse such power are too great and the weaknesses of human flesh are too many. It was Christ who provided for the separation of powers in the first place, and it is incumbent upon his followers to maintain the system. Such an arrangement is as perfect as anything on earth can be. For the people life will be hard, as indeed it should be, since man is a sinful creature. But life can still be good in the sense that it can be lived so as to ensure the soul's salvation, and that is all that is truly important.

Conclusions

The theory of the two swords may serve as a summary of the development of political thought in the period extending from Christ and the Apostolic Fathers to the sixth century. We shall see in subsequent chapters that this theory became the traditional doctrine of the early Middle Ages. Although emperors and popes disagreed over the interpretation of the theory, the consensus was that the doctrine itself was right and that conflict resulted from the inability or refusal of human beings to construe it properly. Emperors and popes as well as the people agreed that the commonwealth should be Christian and that all in authority, whether representing Church or state, should work for the advancement of Christian principles.

After the doctrine of the two swords was established, if spiritual and temporal authorities had always been able to agree upon what constituted a Christian existence, and if it had been possible to avoid disputes over jurisdiction, life would probably have been more placid. Of course this outcome was impossible. The disagreements were many and often bitter. And if the outcome was sometimes disagreeable for Pope or emperor, it was also difficult for the average person, who was not infrequently caught in the middle of the struggle. Christianity as a great organized religion provided consolation and hope for the oppressed, but it also added a new dimension to the multitudinous worries of mankind. For Christianity brought with it the problem of conflicting demands on the citizen's loyalty. It was all very well to tell the Christian citizen that he

[28] Carlyle, *op. cit.*, vol I, pp. 188–189.

owed allegiance to God and to Caesar and should perform his duties to both, but what was he to do if obedience to one authority meant disobedience to another? If the choice were between suffering imprisonment or death and burning in an everlasting hell, the horns of the dilemma upon which the unhappy person found himself were sharp indeed. The obvious solution was to demand that the state grant the individual freedom to comply with his religious obligations. This in fact the state did. But demand and fulfillment were centuries apart, and between them lay the rocks and shoals of the Reformation, during which time the difficulties were greatly magnified. The problem of the correct relationship of church and state is not yet solved, although a considerable advance has been made through the gradual separation of the two institutions. The struggle for religious freedom is one of the great dramas in man's attempt to build a better world, and it has had a profound effect upon his efforts to achieve other important personal freedoms.

SELECTED BIBLIOGRAPHY

St. Augustine, *The City of God* (English translation by Marcus Dods), Hafner Publishing Company, Inc., New York, 1948.

Carlyle, R. W., and A. J. Carlyle: *A History of Mediaeval Political Theory in the West,* Barnes & Noble, Inc., New York, 1953, vol. I.

Dunning, William A.: *A History of Political Theories, Ancient and Medieval,* The Macmillan Company, New York, 1905, chap. 6.

Hacker, Andrew: *Political Theory: Philosophy, Ideology, Science,* The Macmillan Company, New York, 1961, chap. 4.

McIlwain, Charles H.: *The Growth of Political Thought in the West: From the Greeks to the End of the Middle Ages,* The Macmillan Company, New York, 1932, chap. 5.

Sabine, George H.: *A History of Political Theory,* 3d ed., Holt, Rinehart and Winston, Inc., New York, 1961, chap. 10.

Wanlass, Lawrence C.: *Gettell's History of Political Thought,* 2d ed., Appleton-Century-Crofts, Inc., New York, 1953, chap. 7.

seven

MEDIEVAL POLITICAL THOUGHT AND ST. THOMAS AQUINAS

The political philosophy of the Christian Fathers was essentially Greek and Roman. They made only two significant modifications. These were, first, that government is an instrument divinely provided, and, second, that Church and state should work cooperatively for the salvation of men's souls. The Fathers were not, by intent, political philosophers, although, as we have seen, they were often compelled by circumstances to deal with political problems. Sturdy defenders of the faith though they were, the Fathers were also Romans, citizens of the Empire, and they expressed themselves in political terms that would have been understood by Seneca and Cicero. When political problems intruded upon matters of faith, the tendency was to try to fit them into the framework of a long-established political theory.[1] A continuation of this state of affairs was contingent upon the survival of the Empire, but from the sixth to the ninth century Western Europe fell completely under the control of the Germanic invaders, and the Empire, as it had been known, was no more. The Teutons were capable warriors, but they were not philosophers, and there was little philosophical speculation from the sixth to the eleventh century. The chaos which attended the invasions made difficult, where it did not entirely preclude, an orderly study of political, social, economic, and religious institutions. In 800, Charlemagne, who

[1] R. W. Carlyle and A. J. Carlyle, *A History of Mediaeval Political Theory in the West*, Barnes & Noble, Inc., New York, 1953, vol. I, pp. 195–196.

108

believed he was restoring the Roman Empire in the West, donned the crown of emperor and restored a degree of order, but his reign was a brief interlude. His successors were unable to hold together the structure which he had built, and new invasions of Huns and Norsemen in the tenth and eleventh centuries dealt a tremendous blow to the few remaining forces for unity in the West.

The conditions under which the political ideas of the ancient period had developed underwent a drastic change after the sixth century. Yet the ideas survived. Men continued to think in terms of the natural law, equality, and the doctrine of the two swords, although with certain differences of approach. The barbarians' ideas were not so sophisticated as were the philosophies of those whom they had conquered. But the barbarians *had* ideas and customs which, interacting with those of the Romans, were to affect as well as be affected by them.

The Political Ideas of the Teutons

The Germanic (Teutonic) invaders brought with them a concept of the law very different from that of the Romans. The Teuton had no understanding of statutory law. His law was the custom of the tribe to which he belonged, and the tribe carried its law with it wherever it went. It was not territorial law, nor at first written law, although, owing to the Roman influence, it was given considerable codification from the sixth to the eighth century. It was not felt that this law had been "made" by anyone. It had existed from time immemorial, had always belonged to the people of the tribe, and could not be changed since its principles were immutable. A law was not to be judged good or bad on the basis of whether or not the people approved of it. For the people of the tribe the fact that the law was what it had always been was proof enough of its validity. If, on some undoubtedly rare occasion, the law did not provide justice to individuals in a given case, the feeling was that it was somehow being misunderstood. The authorities could then consult together and, as reasonable men, agree upon the proper interpretation and promulgate it for the benefit of the tribe. This view presumes a kind of mutuality of interest in the law. The law was not merely an edict of a king or other governing body, responsible to the people or otherwise, nor did anyone possess the authority to make it. It was there, and it had to be obeyed by all. We shall consider shortly the position of the king in regard to the law.

This concept of the law met the needs of nomadic tribes but was difficult to apply to a different set of circumstances. What, for example, was to be done when two or more tribes occupied the same territory? In such a situation confusion was bound to arise. For some three hundred years, from the sixth to the ninth century, the principle of "personality of law" was applied. This principle was that a tribe retained its own tribal law when living in association with other tribes. In specific cases a determination had to be made with regard to what law (of what tribe) was to be used. In spite of the resulting confusion, the principle of personality was highly important to the subsequent development of the legal systems of the Western world. It permitted Romans, for example, to maintain their own great legal structure in the midst of a world dominated by barbarians whose own institutions were, by comparison, far more primitive.

> For these reasons the obscure period of the personality of law must be considered one of the most critical in the whole history of political thought, for if the continuity of Roman law had been broken at this time it is safe to say that the entire subsequent development of political thought in the West would have been far other than it has been. And that continuity was in the greatest danger of being broken. Our knowledge of the full text of Justinian's Digest hangs by a single thread, the precious manuscript of it preserved at Florence. But for the effects of the principle of personality, there might well have been no Irnerius, no Bartolus, no Cujas, no Bodin.[2]

By the ninth century another step had been taken in the development of the law in the West. The nomadic habits of the Teutons had changed, and as they settled down the idea prevailed that the law was that of the territory rather than of the tribe. As Professor McIlwain has put it, "tribal customs have become *local* customs." Certain factors aside from the increased domesticity of the Teuton advanced the territorial principle. It was advantageous for a king, and the degree to which this concept was developed depended in large part upon the ability of a ruler to extend his power over the territory. The ecclesiastics also favored territorial law, especially where legal matters of concern to the Church, such as marriage, had to be settled. As the territorial view took root, the diversity of laws declined, and a more stable community was formed. Throughout the long process of development, however, the original Germanic idea that the law was the people's law was retained. We do not mean to say that the relationship of people to law at this time was similar to that in a modern democracy. Citizens today hold an indirect authority over the law because it is made by their representatives; in this sense it is the "people's law." The people of the Middle Ages did not possess their law in the sense that they could control it. Indeed they were controlled by it, but it was theirs in perhaps the same manner that God was theirs. At any rate the law was not the property of a despot to be used arbitrarily against the people's interest. The idea is hardly that of twentieth-century democracy, but the seeds of modern democratic law are there nonetheless.

[2] Charles H. McIlwain, *The Growth of Political Thought in the West: From the Greeks to the End of the Middle Ages*, The Macmillan Company, New York, 1932, pp. 169–170.

The concept of the law described above also had a significant bearing on the relationship of the king to his subjects. The Germanic peoples had no feeling that their king made the law and was therefore above it. The earlier Roman jurists had held that although the emperor received his power from the people, he was still the sole source of the law. But in early medieval times the power of the king was assumed to be inherent in the position he held. He merely promulgated the law. This must not be construed to mean that king and subjects were equal under the law. The king had more rights and immunities and greater powers than his subjects. The law did not apply equally to all, but it did apply in some measure to all, and all were obliged to conform to its dictates in the appropriate manner. By the ninth century it had become impractical to assume that no new laws were necessary. The consolidation of territory and the circumstances which attended this development created the necessity of making new laws to supplement the old. Professor Carlyle states that at this time there were three recognized forms of law—the tribal law of custom and tradition, the remnants of the Roman law, and the new laws which had to be made from time to time.[3] These latter the king might himself proclaim, but when he did so it was assumed that the action was based upon the consent of all or part of his subjects. The consent may have been mainly implied, although in many cases the king found it necessary to call his council to discuss a proposed law. The king's actual authority in such matters depended upon his own strength as compared with that of his subjects. His people could often compel him to assume a responsibility for the laws he enforced which he would not otherwise have acknowledged.

The power of the Germanic king was not equal to the former power of the Roman emperor. The principle of the absolute authority of the king was a modern, not a medieval, development. The source of kingly authority was never clearly conceived. Three separate and distinct sources were customarily cited, and with respect to the same ruler. The king ruled by right of succession, as legitimate heir to the throne; at the same time he ruled by sanction of God's divine will; and finally, he ruled with the consent of his subjects. Moreover, when a king took office he swore to rule justly, thus acknowledging an obligation to his subjects, an obligation which they often demanded be taken seriously. There was, as Professor Carlyle has said, "something like a compact" between king and subjects. The corollary to such a compact is the right of subjects to depose a ruler who, in their opinion, has violated the agreement. This was a step to be taken only after serious consideration, but Louis the Pious, emperor of the West and king of France, who was forced from his throne in 833, could attest to the fact that the right to take the step was not merely hypothetical.[4]

[3] Carlyle, *op. cit.*, vol. I, p. 235.
[4] *Ibid.*, pp. 240–250.

Among those who exhorted the king to rule according to law, the ecclesiastics played an important role. In theory it would appear that they could not have done so. There were, after all, the admonitions of Gregory, who had taught that since government was the divinely provided instrument, necessitated by man's sinfulness, a ruler should govern absolutely and subjects should passively submit. Many ninth-century writers carried the idea of the divine authority of the king to great lengths, asserting that the king stood in the place of God on earth, and strongly condemning revolt against secular authorities. But these writers who advocated the Christian doctrine of divine right were also Teutons and as such were opposed, by custom and tradition, to absolutism and irresponsibility. Churchmen who were convinced by the simple logic and religious aura of Gregory's writings that the authority of the king should be unrestricted were nevertheless repelled by the idea of absolute authority. However appealing the phrases of Gregory, the warning of St. Isidore of Seville (560?–636) was also to be heeded; a tyrant, he said, is not a true king. Too much had happened since the sixth century for the writers of the ninth to cling to the tradition of Gregory. Too many bitter disputes had erupted between emperors and bishops of Rome, and between Teutonic kings and officials of the Church. Moreover it was difficult in the extreme for an educated ecclesiastic to regard a semibarbaric, uncouth, and unlettered warrior-king as a divinely appointed instrument to whom the people owed unlimited and passive obedience. The logic of Gregory's theory may have been flawless, but the gap between theory and practice widened.

Feudalism

The collapse of Roman power in the West created a power vacuum into which rushed the forces of particularism and chaos. The centralized system of law and order, which had been maintained for centuries by Roman administrators, gave way to a control exercised by a vast number of barbarian tribal chiefs, each of whom sought to serve his own ends and those of his people. The vast, intricate, and efficient system of communications constructed by the Romans disintegrated rapidly. Courier service ceased, and the superb network of highways that connected the important parts of the Empire fell into a state of decay. Political institutions quickly followed the trend. The pattern of life in the Dark Ages was rural and local. The Greeks and the Romans had been city men; their successors, the Germans and the Slavs, were farmers and village dwellers.

Efforts were made to restore the unity and centralization of the past. In 732 Charles Martel (690?–741) defeated the Saracens at Tours and prevented the Mohammedans from overrunning Europe. His son, Pepin the Short (?–768), was able to consolidate the Frankish kingdom. The

Pope anointed Pepin, who ruled as King of the Franks from 752 to 768. The greatest gains for unification, however, were made by Charlemagne (742–814), the son of Pepin. This vigorous and ambitious king of the Franks was largely responsible for the establishment of the Holy Roman Empire and was rewarded for his efforts by the Pope, who placed the crown of empire upon the head of Charlemagne in 800. But the foundation of empire was not as solid as Charlemagne believed. His authority was severely limited by the power of the aristocrats of his realm, who were unwilling to contribute the money and manpower required to hold the Empire together. Charlemagne needed money, and in general he lacked the resources required to maintain an efficient administration. He could have learned a great deal from the Church, which had, at the time, an administrative organization far superior to that created by Charlemagne.[5]

The disunity in feudalism was so great that even Charlemagne could not conquer completely. A semblance of order was maintained under his son, Louis the Pious (788–840), but a major blow was delivered to the Empire by its threefold division among Louis's sons in the Treaty of Verdun in 843. The patchwork structure was held together by the efforts of the Pope and the Church. The unity of the Church was unimpaired by political divisions in the Empire. The Pope's position was more powerful than ever, and his authority soon outstripped that of the emperor. Nevertheless, wise popes knew that their power and prestige required, in the long run, the maintenance of a degree of secular unity, and the possibilities for this were fading rapidly. Charles the Bald (840–877) was the last emperor of the Holy Roman Empire to wield any significant power. By the close of the ninth century the authority of the emperor had practically disappeared, and that of the Pope had been seriously undermined.[6]

The proclivity of the Frankish kings to subdivide their kingdoms in proportion to the number of sons and heirs they produced conduced to the decentralization of political power and, consequently, to the weakening of kingly authority. The king's position declined, while, by comparison, that of the feudal lords improved. The feudal system was strengthening its hold in the West. It is remarkable that the monarchy survived at all, but it did, and for two principal reasons. First, the great feudal lords, who collectively exercised far more power than did the king, had some need for a central power, finding it convenient to have an arbiter of the numerous quarrels engendered by the fragmented political system. Second, the Church strongly supported the king as a

[5] Henri Pirenne, *A History of Europe,* vol. I, *From the End of the Roman World in the West to the Beginnings of the Western States* (translated by Bernard Miall), Anchor Books, Doubleday & Company, Inc., Garden City, N.Y., 1958, pp. 91–92.
[6] *Ibid.,* p. 100.

symbol of the desired Christian unity. So the king remained, but his authority was mainly theoretical; he reigned but did not rule.[7]

Aside from bringing decentralization, other features of feudalism had a bearing upon the subsequent development of political thought. In feudalism political power was concentrated in the lord who owned the land of his domain. The great landowner's main goal was to preserve his holdings and to add to them if possible. To this end there was constructed a highly complex political, social, and economic organization, capable of defending and maintaining the community against the attacks of neighboring feudal lords. The feudal period, particularly the tenth century, was one of violence. The lust for land was expressed by a policy of blood, iron, and treachery. The situation was similar to that which came to prevail in the fifteenth century, and it was probably more brutal. Survival for all classes depended upon the closest kind of co-operation, and this was secured by the gradual formulation of a system based upon the principle of the reciprocal exchange of services. The system was hierarchical, and included within it all those classes whose proper functioning was necessary for the preservation of the community. Throughout the hierarchy those who occupied a lower position gave their loyalty and service to those of higher station. In return they received the protection, mainly military, which their superiors could provide. The feudal relationships were sealed by ceremonies wherein vassals pledged themselves to obedience, in return for which the lord promised his protection. It is important to note the mutuality of the obligation. A vassal's allegiance may often have been only in theory contingent upon the proper performance of the lord's duties; but the principle of the contractual relationship between ruler and ruled was there, and it survived feudalism. The principle of contract in government implies, where it does not state clearly, the idea of consent, and consent implies the right of withdrawing agreement, or else of enforcing the terms of the contract upon a party who has violated its provisions. Again, the "right" was, in most cases, undoubtedly theoretical and its implementation contingent upon the strength of the injured person or persons. Nevertheless, the story of the Magna Charta illustrates the fact that a king could not, with impunity, transgress upon the privileges of nobles. In theory, under feudalism, each class had its own rights and was entitled to protection in them. Its safeguard, in principle if not in practice, was the prerogative of withdrawing consent and support from a contractual agreement which had been abridged.

The late Professor Pirenne has said that the concept of modern patriotism was born in the feudal principalities.[8] The "civic sentiment of antiquity" was supplanted by a new spirit that grew out of the peculiar

[7] *Ibid.*, p. 129.
[8] *Ibid.*, p. 134.

conditions of the feudal community. The feudal lord was the protector of his people, and he handed his authority down to his heir who maintained the tradition. The feudal oaths inspired a bond of loyalty and service and a kind of family relationship different from anything that had gone before. A long road connects the community sentiment of the feudal principality with the patriotic fervor of the citizen of the modern nation-state, but the route can be traced.

The Church-State Controversy

As we have seen, the decline of the Empire in the ninth century was accompanied by a deterioration of the position of the Pope. Throughout most of the tenth century the papacy was a pawn in the hands of intriguing political factions. An appalling procession of incompetents, creatures of the factions that used them, marched to the papal see. Brief tenure was the rule, and terms of office were often ended abruptly by assassination or forceful removal. The bishops also were having difficulties with the kings and magnates of the principalities of which they were inhabitants. Most of the trouble stemmed from the feudal system itself and from the position occupied by church authorities in the feudal governmental system. Many bishops, for example, were feudal lords and administrators in their own right. As such they had to take oaths of allegiance, supply men-at-arms, and attend feudal courts and councils aside from performing their churchly duties.[9] In addition, secular authorities were obliged to rely extensively upon the clergy, the only literate group in a predominantly illiterate society, for assistance in the task of administering the affairs of state. It is understandable, if not laudable, that kings should seek out for these positions those members of the clergy whose sympathy and loyalty were secularly oriented. In a period in which the power and prestige of the Church were at a low ebb this was not an impossible task. Church authorities of the feudalities were often more interested in their worldly holdings and duties than they were in serving God's cause. It was dangerous to act otherwise. Those who insisted upon promoting the interest of the Church and who in the process defied the feudal authorities were driven out or assassinated.[10]

Still, in the total picture, the position of the Church was not greatly weakened. The organization was intact, and the doctrines were influenced little, if at all. And faith and piety increased. The Pope in Rome was too weak, too much the prisoner of political forces to help his beleaguered subordinates. If help were to be provided it would have to come from below, from the lay members of the Church and from those

[9] Marshall W. Baldwin, *The Medieval Church*, Cornell University Press, Ithaca, N.Y., 1953, p. 19.
[10] Pirenne, *op. cit.*, p. 149.

who were a part of the Church organization but who were not so heavily involved in secular affairs that they could not be entrusted with the responsibilities of effecting a true reform. The Cluniac reforms became the vehicle for a movement which was to sweep Western Europe and have long-lasting consequences.[11]

The Monastery of Cluny was founded in 910 by William the Pious, Count of Auvergne. Under the direction of a succession of able and dedicated abbots, the Cluny monastery became the center and directing force of a great organization within the Church. By the middle of the twelfth century there were more than three hundred associated monasteries in the system. By about 950 the prestige of Cluny, built upon a foundation of piety and asceticism, enabled it to lead a reform movement which was to have an enormous impact upon Church-state relationships in the feudal society. The influence of the Cluny order was directed specifically against the practice of simony (the buying and selling of ecclesiastical office) and the marriage of priests. But more importantly, the Clunians fought against what they believed to be the whole corrupt alliance of Church and state, an alliance directed by the state for its own benefit. Salvation of the soul was the only true work for the Church. Its officials could not, therefore, divide their loyalty or their work.

The reform movement spread, sometimes aided by popular demonstrations and abetted by the religious fervor instilled in the hearts of secular authorities. The results were significant. Church prestige rose to heights unequaled in its history, and its strength, in relation to that of the state, was greater than it had ever been. In addition, and as an outgrowth of the reforms, the wealth of the Church increased enormously. These developments were by no means directed from Rome. The Pope had been too immersed in petty politics, willingly or otherwise, to interest himself in reform movements. Yet the Pope was to reap rich rewards from the new wave of religious enthusiasm that was spreading over the Empire. He was about to be carried to a new position of eminence from which he could do battle on far more equal terms than

[11] Mention should be made here of the so-called False Decretals which, along with the Cluniac reforms, were important later in assisting the Church to free itself from secular domination. The Decretals consisted of a body of more than a hundred forged letters purporting to emanate from popes and councils of the early Church, which provided ninth-century Church authorities with a supply of arguments in their debate with secular officials. The main intent of the Decretals was to increase the power of the bishops, to lessen that of the archbishops, who were considered to be too close to the secular authorities, and, finally, to strengthen the position of the Pope, who was to have supreme authority of judgment in all ecclesiastical cases. In the bitter controversy between Pope and emperor in the eleventh century, the False Decretals, then thought by everyone to be genuine, were of great value to the Pope and his supporters. (For a clear and concise consideration of the content and role of the False Decretals, see George H. Sabine, *A History of Political Theory*, 3d ed., Holt, Rinehart and Winston, Inc., New York, 1961, pp. 228–229.)

formerly with the secular power that had dominated him for so long. As Professor Pirenne has put it:

> The whole movement evolved outside Rome and apart from the Papacy. But it was bound to reach Rome, suddenly giving to St. Peter's successor—degraded by feudal intrigues and party conflicts, the impotent protégé of the Emperor—the control over this enormous force, which was working for him and awaiting the moment when it should act in obedience to his command.[12]

The stage was now set for a controversy between Pope and emperor, between Church and state, which was to influence vitally political thought in the eleventh and twelfth centuries. Most political writing of the period stemmed from this debate, and a large quantity of such writing was produced. Church-state differences were not reconciled by the close of the twelfth century. But as we shall see, new conditions in the thirteenth century substantially altered the content of the arguments.

The controversy was acrimonious; yet both sides based their cases upon the Gelasian or two-swords theory. Each assumed the validity of the theory; each believed that there was a single society under God and that God uses two agents, Church and state, to accomplish his purpose, which is to provide whatever man requires on earth to save his soul. This had been a controlling theory for many hundreds of years, and the protagonists found no reason to disagree over the principle involved. Each side, however, accused the other of having overstepped the proper and long-established lines of jurisdiction. All could acknowledge that Church and state were both engaged in serving the holy cause, but they wanted each to serve in its own way, confining its activities to its appropriate and designated sphere of responsibility. The difficulty was, however, to determine in specific cases precisely how to divide responsibilities and their correlative powers. The problem had always been troublesome, and feudalism had complicated it by involving churchmen more and more deeply in secular affairs. Up to this time, secular authorities had been able to dominate the Church-state relationship, while Church authorities, including the Pope, had been too weak effectively to assert a substantial degree of autonomy, to say nothing of superiority. By the eleventh century, the Church was ready to do battle on more equal terms.

In 1073 Gregory VII became Pope. He held the office for twelve years. Gregory began the codification of ecclesiastical law, enforced the principle of celibacy upon the clergy, powerfully asserted the predominance of the Pope in Church affairs, and fought vigorously and successfully to increase the power and prestige of the Church vis-à-vis that of the state. In 1075 Gregory issued a proclamation prohibiting the lay

---

[12] Pirenne, *op. cit.*, pp. 154–155.

investiture of bishops, the appointment of higher Church officials by secular authorities. Since lay investiture had for centuries been a common practice, there was an immediate reaction to Gregory's directive. In 1076, the youthful German king, Henry IV, attempted to remove Gregory from the papacy. In retaliation, Gregory excommunicated the king and absolved his subjects from the oaths they had taken to support him. And Gregory was not yet finished. In 1078 he stated that lay investiture was in all cases punishable by excommunication. This edict was followed by another which provided that secular authorities should restore to the Church all lands owned by the Church and held as fiefs from either clerics or princes. Failure to comply was, again, to result in excommunication. Although Gregory claimed that his actions were authorized by scripture and by the teachings of the Fathers, no previous Pope had gone so far. The embattled Henry fought back by supporting an antipope, but he was plagued by opposition from his own rebellious nobles and was unable at the time to gather the strength necessary to defeat Gregory. The nobles sponsored a new candidate for kingship, one Rudolph of Swabia, and after some procrastination Gregory also supported him. Rudolph died, and before support could be rallied for an effective substitute, Gregory's own power had been undermined by the desertion of thirteen of his cardinals, and Henry was crowned emperor by Gregory's rival, Clement III. A more detailed historical consideration need not detain us here. It is sufficient to note that the problem of lay investiture, together with its many corollaries as developed by Gregory, was not solved in the struggle between Gregory and Henry IV. Some years after Gregory's death, a compromise agreement was reached in the Concordat of Worms in 1122. The pact, similar to an arrangement made earlier in England, provided for the formal abolition of lay investiture but permitted the emperor to retain a voice in the matter of the election of bishops so that he was still able to exercise influence.[13] The controversy continued throughout the twelfth century.

The significance, for political thought, of the bitter exchanges between Gregory VII and Henry IV lies in the development by each side of its position on the matter of Church-state relationship. Never before had a Pope taken such a strong stand, and never before had the two forces, Church and state, been so equal in terms of the power they wielded. This situation contributed to the formulation of a large body of theory with which interested scholars were concerned throughout the twelfth, thirteenth, and fourteenth centuries. The key to the understanding of this theory lies in an appraisal of the arguments proposed by Gregory and Henry and their supporters.

[13] Baldwin, *op. cit.*, p. 41.

Gregory's position was that he, as Pope, had inherited the authority which had been vested in Peter, the first Bishop of Rome. His authority, therefore, extended over the entire church, and included the right to appoint and dismiss other authorities, to convoke councils, and to enforce the dictates which he enunciated. The Pope, in short, was an absolute monarch of the Church, responsible only to God for his actions. Although this view came subsequently to prevail, it was not generally accepted at the time, not even by most members of the Church, and was sharply repudiated by secular authorities. In theory Gregory's case was strong. The Church, Gregory claimed, must have overriding authority in all matters relating to morals. The Church's main concern was with the salvation of the soul; unless it could exercise control in situations where a moral issue was involved it could not properly do its work. As a general statement, there was little here with which a Christian state could disagree. The difficulty stemmed from Gregory's insistence that the Church was to be the sole judge of what was or was not a moral issue.

Gregory carried the argument even further. Excommunication was the sword of enforcement held over the heads of the emperor and all secular rulers. This was, in itself, a powerful disciplinary weapon, but it had been used by popes before Gregory. His threats to employ it were not unprecedented and therefore not so frightening as they might otherwise have been. Thus far, at any rate, an excommunicated king was still a king. But Gregory took a giant step from this point when he absolved the subjects of an excommunicated king from their feudal oaths. It appeared to Henry that this was tantamount to an attempt to destroy the power of the monarch. It was, he thought, an invasion by the Church of the jurisdiction of the state and a violation of the two-swords theory. Gregory dismissed the charge. It was the duty of the Church to discipline the morals of its members; the king was a member, and one who had a special responsibility to his subjects. The king himself, through the actions which had led to his excommunication, had violated the contract that held his subjects to him. The oaths previously taken were legally void. To Gregory this was neither a temporal action nor an improper invasion of temporal authority. He did not believe that he was undermining the foundation of the two-swords theory. Nor did Gregory suppose, in taking his firm position, that he was contending for such a degree of churchly superiority that henceforth the Church would claim that its authority was interposed between the state and God. It was not, however, very far from Gregory's claim to that made by some twelfth-century ecclesiastics, that secular authority is in fact derived from the Church. Only a few, among them Honorius of Augsburg and John of Salisbury, took such a stand, and it is not entirely clear that they were aware of its significance. In the twelfth century the matter was of no great importance and was seldom an issue. Nevertheless, Gregory's interpretation of the Church's position under the Gelasian theory constituted a substantial departure from the view that had prevailed until the eleventh century.

Gregory's arguments were designed to strengthen the Church's position in order to free it from the secular domination to which it had long been subjected. Perhaps, like a lawyer, Gregory was overstating his case in the hope that he would win less than he demanded but more than he had. However this may be, Henry and his supporters opposed any change and sought to maintain the status quo. This furnished strength for the emperor's position. Change may be easily supported by logical argument, but custom, precedent, and tradition are powerful forces resisting change. Henry had all these on his side, for Gregory, despite his citing of authorities, was demanding an entirely new set of conditions.

Henry, too, could argue, and he did. God, he pointed out, did not grant power to the king through the Pope as intermediary. Rather, he gave it to the monarch directly, and the latter was responsible for its exercise only to God. The ancient tradition of the two swords recognized that the secular and spiritual powers could never properly be wielded by the same person. Gregory, in absolving subjects of their feudal oaths, was guilty of wielding temporal powers and thus of flying in the face of the tradition which had long been understood to prohibit any such action. Henry's defenders also cited the hereditary rights involved. He was the legitimate heir to the throne, and Gregory's attacks constituted an interference with Henry's private property. The argument was legal rather than religious but significant in indicating a new trend. There were other theological arguments. Henry was on solid ground in citing the principle of passive obedience proclaimed by Gregory the Great so many centuries before, and the principle, in theory at least, still had validity.

John of Salisbury

Reference must be made at this point to John of Salisbury (c. 1120–1180), one of the less polemical and more learned political writers of the later Middle Ages. In his *Policraticus*,[14] completed in 1159, John attempted systematically to sum up political philosophy as it was understood in his time. Within a few years the recovery of a large body of works from ancient times, including a great deal from Aristotle, was to alter substantially the course of medieval thought. The *Policraticus* is important because it represents the medieval tradition as it stood before it was

---

[14] The precise meaning of the term is not certain; it is likely that John coined it, and it is generally translated "Statesman's Book."

affected by the new studies in classical writings, particularly those of Aristotle.[15]

The works of John of Salisbury are peculiarly nonfeudal in nature. John does not, for example, write in terms of the theory of contract, which was so vital a part of feudal political relationships. Instead, he follows the model, considered by Cicero, of a commonwealth governed by a public authority and in accordance with the law.[16] Although this view was not consonant with reality at the time, it was the theory favored by the Church throughout the feudal period. The particularistic qualities of feudalism were resented by an ecclesiastical organization which upheld the idea of monarchy; monarchy was more compatible with the universalism of the Christian religion. The theory had broken down in practice, but the determination of the Church to cling to it nonetheless was significant. It helped to sustain at least the idea of a unified commonwealth in the face of the intense localism of the feudal period. It was the doctrine of unification that ultimately prevailed when national monarchies supplanted the feudal communities as the dominant political and social form.[17]

Much of John's theory in the *Policraticus* is typical of the prevailing thought in the Middle Ages, but he also contributed ideas that were influential in later medieval writings. John is probably the first medieval theorist to use the "organic analogy" in describing the political community.[18] He saw the commonwealth as a body endowed with a life of its own, with the king as its head, the Church its soul, and all other members of the body politic performing some lesser function. The commonwealth, like the human body, can flourish only when all its parts are healthy. The ruler, as directing authority of the commonwealth, has the paramount obligation in this regard. He must rule justly, that is, in accordance with the law, if he is to maintain the well-being of the commonwealth. Authority to rule comes to the prince from God and from the Church, which is God's representative organization on earth. If the law is followed, the prince must be obeyed, patiently and "with pleasure." An attack upon a just ruler is an attack upon God, who endowed him with his rulership. But a prince who flouts the law and who rules by force alone is an abomination in the eyes of God. When tyranny oppresses men, the commonwealth is ill in the same sense in which the human body is ill when the brain is diseased.

[15] *The Statesman's Book of John of Salisbury: Being the Fourth, Fifth, and Sixth Books, and Selections from the Seventh and Eighth Books of the Policraticus* (translated with an introduction by John Dickinson), Alfred A. Knopf, Inc., New York, 1927, p. xvii. All subsequent quotations from and references to the *Policraticus* are from this edition.

[16] Sabine, *op. cit.*, p. 246.

[17] *Ibid.*, p. xix.

[18] Francis William Coker, *Readings in Political Philosophy*, rev. ed., The Macmillan Company, New York, 1938, p. 180.

The distinction between a just ruler and a tyrant lies in whether or not the commonwealth is governed according to law.

> Between a tyrant and a prince there is this single or chief difference, that the latter obeys the law and rules the people by its dictates, accounting himself as but their servant. It is by virtue of the law that he makes good his claim to the foremost and chief place in the management of the affairs of the commonwealth and in the bearing of its burdens.[19]

The community has no obligation patiently and passively to submit to the rule of a tyrant. A cancer should be cut out. John is the first medieval writer to develop a defense of tyrannicide, and he does so in clear and forceful terms. The tyrant is punished by God; it is only a matter of God's deciding whether the act of retribution shall be by his own or by human hands.

> Thus wickedness is always punished by the Lord; but sometimes it is His own, and at others it is a human hand, which He employs as a weapon wherewith to administer punishment to the unrighteous. . . .[20]

John of Salisbury was also probably the first writer clearly to state the doctrine of ecclesiastical supremacy over the secular authority. If we are to interpret his words literally, we are led to the conclusion that for John both the secular and spiritual swords are given to the Church, which in turn endows the prince with his power. All authority is of religious origin, but the secular is of an inferior, though necessary, kind.

> This sword, then, the prince receives from the hand of the Church, although she herself has no sword of blood at all. Nevertheless she has this sword, but she uses it by the hand of the prince, upon whom she confers the power of bodily coercion, retaining to herself authority over spiritual things in the person of the pontiffs. The Prince is, then, as it were, a minister of the priestly power, and one who exercises that side of the sacred offices which seems unworthy of the hands of the priesthood. For every office existing under, and concerned with the execution of, the sacred laws is really a religious office, but that is inferior which consists in punishing crimes, and which therefore seems to be typified in the person of the hangman.[21]

Unequivocal as this statement appears, if it is considered in the context of John's entire work it is somewhat ambiguous. Moreover, it must not be assumed that it represented a position generally accepted at the time, though the opinion was undoubtedly sufficiently widespread to elicit contrary views from the supporters of temporal power.

Most important, however, in John's theory, is his insistence that the ruler has an obligation to his subjects. The prince is not justified in

---

[19] *Policraticus*, IV, i.
[20] *Ibid.*, VIII, xxi.
[21] *Ibid.*, IV, iii.

seeking his own ends. He is the steward of God, and his responsibility is to ensure that the affairs of the community are conducted in such a way that the souls of the people are saved. The ruler must, in short, develop and maintain a Christian state. It is not enough that he should preserve peace and order; he must create the conditions of well-being for his people which are necessary to their moral welfare. The power of the ruler is, therefore, conditional. If he performs his duties properly, he must be obeyed, for he is complying with the law and with the will of God. If he acts contrary to law and divine will, the people have not only a right but a duty to remove him and even, if necessary, to kill him.

St. Thomas Aquinas

The content of medieval scholasticism was a combination of Christian dogma and the philosophy of the ancients, especially of Plato and the Stoics. Apart from specific matters of doctrine there was little conflict between these two sources. It was not difficult to reconcile much of Plato's thought with Christianity; in fact this had long since been accomplished by St. Augustine. Plato was not only an authoritarian but an idealist and mystic whose ideas were, in large part, adaptable to Christian theology. The insights of mysticism were particularly helpful during that earlier period of Christian development which preceded a later concentration of Church interest on institutional, organizational, and political affairs. But in the latter part of the twelfth century events occurred that necessitated a reappraisal of the philosophical foundations of Christianity and profoundly influenced the future formulation of political philosophy.

Of transcendent importance was the rediscovery of the major works of Aristotle, only a few of whose writings had, until this time, been known to the medieval world of the West. These works came to Christian Europe from Arabic and Jewish sources and were accompanied by a large body of commentary. The magnitude of their impact can scarcely be exaggerated. For one thing, a vast body of knowledge was presented to medieval scholars; for another, to facilitate understanding it was already neatly divided into disciplines—biology, psychology, physics, ethics, politics, metaphysics. And, what was even more important, if Aristotle contributed information he also challenged. It was bad enough, from the Church's viewpoint, that "the Philosopher," as he came to be known, should have been introduced to Christian society by infidels. It was, at first sight, worse that he should have insisted that reason was the key with which to unlock the door leading to truth and the good life. The medieval Christian could acknowledge the value, within limits, of reason. He believed, however, that truth could only be found through faith and that the genuinely good life was always a Christian life about which the Philosopher had known nothing.

Nevertheless some skeptics believed that these answers were super-ficial. They argued that the ancient Greeks, relying on reason rather than faith and living in their godless (un-Christian) society, had accomplished a great deal, and that much in that civilization was worthy of emulation. The danger of these thoughts was recognized by Church authorities, whose initial reaction was to ban the study of Aristotle as a precautionary measure. But it is difficult, perhaps impossible, to prohibit ideas; at any rate this specific prohibition was not successful. The study and translation of Aristotle's works continued, and the tactics of the Church shifted accordingly. If Aristotle's ideas were so persistently attractive, perhaps they were not so contradictory to Christian doctrine after all. The solution was not to proscribe but to accommodate. Aristotelianism was to be converted from an enemy to a pillar of support for Christian Catholic dogma. Some of the ablest of the medieval scholars, Robert Grosseteste, William of Auvergne, and Albert the Great, set about the task. The greatest of them all was St. Thomas Aquinas.

Thomas Aquinas (1227–1274), born in Calabria, was the scion of a noble family. As a child he studied under the Benedictine monks from the age of five to ten. At ten he entered the University of Naples. Later, and against strong opposition from his family, Thomas joined the Dominican order. He was taught by Albert the Great and joined with his master in the work of reconciling Aristotelianism and Christianity. Thomas was a prolific writer. In his relatively brief life (he lived only forty-seven years) a great number of commentaries on speculative theological problems flowed from his pen. The most important of his works was the *Summa Theologica,* which he intended to be a summary of man's knowledge to that time. He did not live to complete the project, and he also left unfinished a political treatise of considerable significance, his *Rule of Princes (De Regimine Principum),* although both works were completed by other writers. Only St. Augustine, perhaps, among theologians, has had as great an influence as St. Thomas Aquinas upon religious philosophy. Although there was powerful opposition in Church circles, he was canonized in 1323 by Pope John XXII. Pope Leo XIII, in an encyclical of 1879, directed that St. Thomas's teachings be regarded as a basis of Roman Catholic theology.

St. Thomas's goal was the development of a philosophy that would relate the universe, in all its aspects, to God. He had to find room for all those phases of Aristotle's works which might, superficially of course, seem to be contradictory to, or outside the scope of, Christian theology. He had to demonstrate that what appeared to be conflicting elements in Christianity and Aristotelianism were such in appearance only, and that a correct understanding and interpretation would demonstrate that there is, in fact, an all-encompassing wisdom in God and nature within which complete unity may be found if only it is sought. It may *seem,* for example, St. Thomas said, that the scientific knowledge which Aristotle gained through the use of unaided reason, and consequently without the aid of Christian faith, constitutes a refutation of the assumption that God is the fount of all knowledge. Such a conclusion, however, is unwarranted. There is a kind of knowledge, ascertainable by man through his reason, of which the various sciences are examples. Another kind is philosophy, which, through reason, attempts to discover the principles that make the specialized sciences meaningful. But there is a knowledge above these; though not unreasonable, it is above man's capacity to reason and is the source of greater truths than Aristotle, pagan as he was, could ever discover. This knowledge is Christian theology, made known to man only through revelation and at God's discretion. It is the Higher Reason, and it can be given only to Christian men.

St. Thomas's political philosophy is contingent upon his view of nature. Much the same principle applies here that applied to his view of knowledge. Nature is all-inclusive and purposive. A picture of nature is that of a triangle, a hierarchical structure with God at the apex and the lowest beings at the base. Within this system the higher dominates the lower. Responsibilities, rights, and duties for each being are determined by his place in the hierarchy, and each has a purpose—the attainment of the perfection of his kind. Man ranks high in the structure, subordinate only to God, to whom he is akin because he has a soul and the ability to reason.[22] Man's ultimate goal is the salvation of his soul, and he must create the kind of life in this world which will secure that end.

On this foundation rests St. Thomas's philosophy of government and society in general. The elaboration of the philosophy required that Thomas repudiate the Christian view of secular government which had been expressed in the writings of St. Augustine and flourished until the reappearance of Aristotle. This was the proposition that government and political authority, the subordination of man to man, including slavery, were necessitated by man's Fall and his sinful existence. The idea that truly good men could and should live without government was so far from Aristotle's statements on the problem that a reconciliation on the point was impossible. Thomas rejected Augustine rather than Aristotle. He adopted the Aristotelian view that man is a political animal whose very nature leads him into an association with others. The good life can be lived only in such association; man's requirements for the good life, being more complex than those of the lower animals, cannot be fulfilled in isolation. Fortunately his reason shows him the way to the cooperation that helps him to solve his problem.

[22] Sabine, *op. cit.*, pp. 248–249.

It is not possible for one man to arrive at a knowledge of all these things by his own individual reason. It is therefore necessary for man to live in a multitude so that each one may assist his fellows, and different men may be occupied in seeking, by their reason, to make different discoveries—one, for example, in medicine, one in this and another in that.[23]

St. Thomas accepted the fundamentals of Aristotle's political thought, but the Christianizing of the philosophy demanded that he go further than did the Philosopher and that he embellish Aristotle's theory with some decidedly un-Aristotelian additions. St. Thomas could not agree that the city-state of ancient Greece represented the most perfect form of political organization. A much larger and more populous community is needed, he said, to satisfy the demand for the varied skills and accomplishments which make the good life possible. For this purpose a kingdom is preferable. Moreover, while Aristotle was correct in urging that the state's function was to help its inhabitants live the good life, he could not, of course, be aware that the highest purpose of all was the salvation of the soul and that the good life always meant living in such a manner as to make salvation possible. Men could live rightly only in the presence of a religious organization, a church, which could minister to spiritual affairs, these being of greater value than any secular concerns. To serve the higher purpose, the good state must be a Christian state. It must be subject to direction by the Christian Church, which alone is capable of showing the way to salvation.

Aristotle's philosophy, Thomas contended, was unassailable as far as it went. The trouble was that to Aristotle the good life of the community was an end in itself, whereas any Christian knew that right living was only a means to a higher end. It was a very important means to be sure, and St. Thomas went further than his theological predecessors in outlining the requirements for a good secular community. He was fully aware that the individual who has to spend every waking moment trying to support himself and his family and who is compelled to live in the most abject poverty is not going to devote much time to the contemplation of God's great truths. St. Thomas proposed, therefore, a welfare state which would intervene directly in the lives and activities of its citizens in order to improve their condition. Though the soul's salvation is of highest importance, it requires a favorable material environment. To this end St. Thomas suggested the securing of economic justice through currency control, price regulation, care for the poor, and such other measures as might be required.[24] He was quite clear in his

[23] St. Thomas Aquinas, *De Regimine Principum*, i, 6 (the Phelan-Eschmann translation), in Dino Bigongiari (ed.), *The Political Ideas of St. Thomas Aquinas*, Hafner Publishing Company, Inc., New York, 1953, p. viii. Subsequent quotations from and references to *De Regimine Principum* and *Summa Theologica* are from this edition.

[24] Thomas I. Cook, *History of Political Philosophy from Plato to Burke*, Prentice-Hall, Inc., Englewood Cliffs, N.J., 1936, p. 224.

assertion that the state's role is much greater and more positive than that of merely keeping the peace.

Although men are reasonable creatures, they cannot rely on reason alone to guide their conduct within the community. The isolated individual may govern himself by reason, but when he enters society he does not always act rationally. He has interests that conflict with those of his fellows, and, unless controlled, discord will tear society apart. A high degree of unity is necessary if the community is going to be a good one, and this means that government is required. The question is, what kind shall it be? St. Thomas was not optimistic with respect to the possibilities of democracy, not even the moderate democracy proposed by Aristotle. It is true that all men are equal and that all can reason, but according to St. Thomas, these two propositions are separate and substantially unrelated. All men are *equal before God;* they are not equal in their capacity to reason. St. Thomas's hierarchical view of nature led him straight to the advocacy of monarchy. In all nature, the rulership principle is apparent. Nature requires that those with superior intelligence and ability shall rule. It is important again to note that St. Thomas rejected the traditional Christian notion that authority is necessitated by man's Fall. He believed, rather, that authority, including that of the monarchy, was natural and was present when man lived in a state of innocence. There was a difference, however, in the use of authority then, since in the state of innocence no coercion would have been necessary. Because of the Fall, noncoercive authority is not possible; a power must be recognized both to make and to enforce laws.

The power to govern is not absolute but conditional. It is authorized by God and may legitimately be exercised only for the purpose of creating those conditions, outlined above, which make a good community possible. Rulership is a trust, and St. Thomas recognized that kings are not always responsible to it. The problem of what to do about a monarch who serves his own interest and neglects that of his subjects was a troublesome one for St. Thomas, and his solutions are not entirely satisfactory, not even, one suspects, to St. Thomas himself. He was faced with the serious dilemma which confronts any political theorist. Unity is a necessity in any community, and a degree of authority is required to achieve it. But the authority, once granted, can be abused. It is surely possible to pay too high a price for unity. St. Thomas attempted to avoid the pitfalls of an extreme position. He was convinced that a ruler could not achieve the requisite unity unless he possessed considerable authority, but nonetheless certain precautions could be taken. Great care should be observed in the selection of a monarch in the first place, and to this end the principle of election, rather than that of heredity, should be applied. Then, too, the ruler's authority should be limited or "tempered." St. Thomas was not clear on precisely how the tempering was to be accomplished. He suggested, however, that it would be wise to give all the people "some share in the government."

Despite these precautions, a king may rule tyrannically, and the question is, what shall then be done? St. Thomas emphatically rejected the solution offered by John of Salisbury. Tyrannicide is likely to create more problems than it solves. Those who would commit such an act are not to be trusted since they would probably not act selflessly in the matter. Moreover, a dangerous precedent might be established that would open the way to the murder of good monarchs. Tyrannicide would also disrupt the unity which is so vitally necessary to the community. Legal means must be employed to remove the tyrant. If he has been elected by the people, the people have a right to depose him on the ground that the tyrant is guilty of breach of contract. If, on the other hand, the tyrant has been appointed by some superior authority, it is the responsibility of that authority to remove him. Yet St. Thomas was obviously fearful that resistance to authority might become a habit. It is better, he contended, to suffer some tyranny than to risk disunity in the state. And the tyrannical rule may possibly be inflicted by God upon the people as a punishment for their wickedness. At any rate, if legal measures do not bring relief, the people should turn to prayer. Prayer is both a safer and a wiser means to use, for if God so chooses, he can soften the heart of a tyrant or he can remove him. If God does not act, it may well be because he does not choose to do so. St. Thomas is closer to Burke than he is to Locke in this regard. He wants a king to rule justly and according to laws which are neither arbitrarily conceived nor enforced, and he wants the people to have some recourse against unjust and arbitrary action. Yet opposition to the ruler is justified only when the dangers flowing from tyranny are unquestionably clear, present, and continuing. The right of revolution is so hedged about with qualifications and restrictions as to be inconspicuous.

Thomas's major effort was directed toward the development of a theory of law, and it is for this work that he is best known politically. If he did not satisfactorily answer the question of what to do about a tyrannical ruler, he was at least clear in his statement that a good ruler follows the law. As with other aspects of the problem of accommodating Aristotelianism and Christianity, Aquinas, in formulating the theory of law, attempted to show that what appeared to be diversification was in fact harmonious. There are, he said, four categories of law. The first and highest is Eternal Law, which is, essentially, the great principle of divine wisdom by which God rules the universe. It is capable of being understood by God alone, and though not contrary to reason is beyond the capacity of a human being to comprehend. The second kind of law is Natural Law, which represents that portion of the Eternal Law in which man, as a rational creature, participates. It consists of the forces that impel all beings to necessary and proper conduct. With regard to man, the Natural Law provides those instinctive urges which he shares with the lower animals, to eat, drink, seek shelter, and procreate. Because he is a higher animal, the Natural Law also prompts man to live in society, to seek truth, to improve himself, and otherwise to develop a truly human society. The principles of the Natural Law are ascertainable by the reason of all men, whether pagan or Christian, and therefore a good secular life is possible outside of Christianity. The third category of law is Divine Law, which can be described as those codes of conduct which God has laid down in the Old and New Testaments for governing his people. They are revealed to man, and while they are by no means contrary to reason, they are not always discoverable by man on that basis. The fourth and last kind of law is Human Law. This comprises that part of the Natural Law which is applied, in codes or in custom, through human reason to the conditions man faces on earth. All four categories of the law are part of an inclusive system that governs the entire universe in a harmonious fashion.

Of particular interest to the student of political theory is Aquinas's conception of the relationship between Natural and Human Law. There is little the individual can do with regard to the Eternal or the Divine Law except to obey each in the manner indicated by the theologians who are qualified to understand it. Faith alone can point the way to proper conduct. But insofar as the good secular life is concerned, Human and Natural Law are of prime importance. Embedded in the Natural Law are those governing principles according to which secular conduct must be regulated if the good life is to be achieved. These principles are discoverable through the use of human reason, and when they are applied, institutionally or by laws or custom, they constitute the Human Law. In order to be just, the Human Law must accord with and never contravene the Natural Law. It is the function of the ruler always to govern in accordance with this principle. It may, in certain circumstances, be difficult to determine whether or not a specific Human Law is in harmony with Natural Law, but certain tests can be applied to that end. A just human law must accord with reason; it must be for the common good; it must be legitimate in the sense of being derived from the people or from an agent selected by them; and, finally, it must be promulgated.

Thomas, in considering the Human Law, leaves plenty of room "for the joints to work." The particular institutions, laws, and customs of a community may vary from time to time and from those of another community; only the requirements outlined in the preceding paragraph need be met. Thus political and economic systems may differ from one state to another, yet each may be following the dictates of the Natural Law. St. Thomas is here compelled to take issue with some of the doctrines of the early Fathers. They, for example, had agreed that a community of property was natural, but that the sinfulness of man had necessitated the establishment of private property. Thomas makes the answer to the problem hinge on another issue, that of whether circumstances make private or collective ownership more appropriate to the citizens of a particular community. Custom provides a fairly adequate guide to decision. If a people have long lived with a system of collective ownership, that system is probably right for them and in line with Natural Law.

> Community of goods is ascribed to the natural law, not that the natural law dictates that all things should be possessed in common and that nothing should be possessed as one's own, but because the division of possessions is not according to the natural law, but rather arose from human agreement, which belongs to positive law, as stated above. Hence the ownership of possessions is not contrary to the natural law, but an addition thereto devised by human reason.[25]

Aquinas, it appears, states that the only question with regard to property is whether or not it is being used in the proper manner. He argues that property should be regulated in the public interest. The Natural Law does not endow property with an aura of sanctity that places it beyond the power of the state to control under the Human Law.

The ruler is given considerable leeway within the broad principles of Natural Law. St. Thomas, however, emphasized that the authority of the king extends only to secular affairs. The king cannot direct his subjects in matters relating to salvation, since this is the duty of the Church and especially of the Pope. In fact, in all that temporal rulers do, they follow a general course outlined by the spiritual authorities. Salvation is the supreme goal of this life, and only the Church knows how it is achieved. Therefore kings are vassals of the Church. The Pope is the supreme ruler, holding both the spiritual and secular swords in his hands and granting to his subordinates in the ecclesiastical organization an indirect but important control over secular power. If the Church defines and controls the end, it must also control the means. As St. Thomas stated it: "Secular power is subject to the spiritual power as the body is subject to the soul, and therefore it is not a usurpation of authority if the spiritual prelate interferes in temporal things *concerning those matters in which the secular power is subject to him.*"[26] Nevertheless, the state is autonomous in its own affairs, and the Church may interfere only when the ruler ignores the dictates of the Natural Law. Even though the ruler is an infidel, as long as he follows the Natural Law he must be obeyed, by his Christian subjects as well as by pagans. The injunction to "render unto Caesar" has not been forgotten.

---

[25] St. Thomas Aquinas, *Summa Theologica*, II, II, q. 66, art. 2 (the Fathers of the English Dominican Province translation), in Bigongiari (ed.), *op. cit.*, p. 130.

[26] *Ibid.*, II, II, q. 60, art. 6. Italics supplied.

"Infidelity in itself does not destroy the justness of power, because power was instituted by *jus gentium,* or human law, and the distinction between believers and infidels exists by virtue of divine law, which does not destroy human law." [27] A heretical ruler is, of course, to be exceptionally treated. The Church may excommunicate him, and when it does, his subjects are absolved from their allegiance.

Conclusions

For St. Thomas, the spiritual superiority of the Church did not mean its legal superiority. The work of the Church was so important that Thomas had to assign it a general authority over the state, as well as the right to check secular authority when it overstepped the limits imposed by the Natural Law. Although Thomas assumed that his philosophy was well within the Gelasian tradition, in fact it was not. For Gelasius the secular power was derivative, conferred by God; for St. Thomas, as with Aristotle, it was natural. His views were far more moderate than those of many of his contemporaries who were asserting the legal dominance of church over state. Thomas contributed greatly to the clarification of political philosophy. This process had begun much earlier in medieval times, indeed at the very inception of Church-state controversy. The arguments against Church domination restored interest in political theory and tended to free that theory from its involvement with theology. Thomas, relying heavily upon Aristotle, did much to advance this cause.[28]

SELECTED BIBLIOGRAPHY

Baldwin, Marshall W.: *The Medieval Church,* Cornell University Press, Ithaca, N.Y., 1953, chap. 1.
Bigongiari, Dino (ed.): *The Political Ideas of St. Thomas Aquinas,* Hafner Publishing Company, Inc., New York, 1953, introduction.
Carlyle, R. W., and A. J. Carlyle: *A History of Mediaeval Political Theory in the West,* Barnes & Noble, Inc., New York, 1953, vol. I.
Cook, Thomas I.: *History of Political Philosophy from Plato to Burke,* Prentice-Hall, Inc., Englewood Cliffs, N.J., 1936, chap. 7.
Dunning, William: *A History of Political Theories, Ancient and Medieval,* The Macmillan Company, New York, 1905, chaps. 7, 8.
Hacker, Andrew: *Political Theory: Philosophy, Ideology, Science,* The Macmillan Company, New York, 1961, chap. 4.
McIlwain, Charles H.: *The Growth of Political Thought in the West: From the Greeks to the End of the Middle Ages,* The Macmillan Company, New York, 1932, chap. 5.

[27] *Ibid.,* II, II, q. 12, art. 2.
[28] Sheldon S. Wolin, *Politics and Vision: Continuity and Innovation in Western Political Thought,* Little, Brown and Company, Boston, 1960, p. 139.

Pirenne, Henri: *A History of Europe,* vol. I, *From the End of the Roman World in the West to the Beginnings of the Western States* (translated by Bernard Miall), Anchor Books, Doubleday & Company, Inc., Garden City, N.Y., 1958, bk. III.

Sabine, George H.: *A History of Political Theory,* 3d ed., Holt, Rinehart and Winston, Inc., New York, 1961, chaps. 11–13.

The Statesman's Book of John of Salisbury: Being the Fourth, Fifth, and Sixth Books, and Selections from the Seventh and Eighth Books of the Policraticus (translated with an introduction by John Dickinson), Alfred A. Knopf, Inc., New York, 1927, introduction.

Wanlass, Lawrence C.: *Gettell's History of Political Thought,* 2d ed., Appleton-Century-Crofts, Inc., New York, 1953, chap. 6.

Wolin, Sheldon S.: *Politics and Vision: Continuity and Innovation in Western Political Thought,* Little, Brown and Company, Boston, 1960, chap. 4.

eight

MARSILIO OF PADUA
AND
WILLIAM OF OCCAM

The Decline of Papal Power

Throughout the medieval period men thought in terms of a universal Christian empire controlled jointly and cooperatively by the two authorities, Church and state. Together these two were to create an ideal community within which men could lead the kind of moral life that would result in the salvation of their souls. As we have seen, the Gelasian theory of the two swords outlined the general course to be followed in establishing the division of powers between the secular and the temporal authorities. No responsible leader denied the validity of the theory. All found it difficult to obtain any kind of consensus with regard to its application. Medieval political theory stems in large part from disagreements over the question of the proper allocation of power between Church and state. In the forefront of the struggle were the Pope and the emperor. Each, in the course of the centuries, experienced both success and failure.

Early in the thirteenth century the papacy achieved what appeared to be permanent victory. The Empire had so declined in strength that it could no longer offer an effective challenge to the papacy. The Pope, assuming that his ancient antagonist had been brought to his knees once and for all, set about consolidating his victory. Innocent III (1161–1216) became Pope in 1198 and held the office for eighteen momentous years. He put into practice the powers of papal supremacy that had been claimed but unsuccessfully applied by Gregory VII. Since the Empire was unable to act, the Church, with the Pope at its head, would have to provide the unity that the medieval community had traditionally desired. To attain this end the Pope would have to wield supreme authority, both temporal and spiritual. Awesome though the responsibility was, Innocent III was eager to assume it. With his great ability he came very near to establishing a truly international order based upon the principles of Roman, canon, and feudal law.[1] To succeed, however, in the long run required the kind of secular unity which only the Empire could have made possible. The popes themselves contributed greatly to the dissolution of that unity and consequently to the creation of a new force that would ultimately crush all papal pretensions to temporal power. This new force was the national monarchy.

The popes, who had often relied upon the support of the kings in their struggles with the emperors, had had to give the kings support in turn. It seemed never to occur to them that the power of an individual king might become greater than that of the emperor. Nor could the popes conceive that the people of the Empire, disillusioned perhaps with a political organization which never achieved unity or secured peace, could give allegiance to a lesser entity than that of the Empire. But they did, and their defection was what in the final analysis defeated the Pope. A system of modern states was not quickly established, nor was the citizen's feeling toward his nation much like the patriotism of modern times. Nevertheless, in the thirteenth century, which in so many respects differed vitally from the twelfth, a solid foundation was laid for later developments.

Few could see what was happening. The intelligent and informed Dante (1255–1321) still believed that the only chance for unity and peace lay in the restoration of the Roman Empire. Dante was appalled by the turbulent conditions of the Italy of his time. Bitter local rivalries kept the country in a turmoil, and for this situation Dante assigned the Pope full responsibility. In 1311 Dante published his *De Monarchia,* in which he proposed the reestablishment of unity in the Empire, under Christianity but not under the control of the Pope. The Pope and Church, Dante argued, should confine their activities to prayer and moral exhortation and stop interfering in secular affairs. They had, in fact, no right to do otherwise, since God had granted power to govern in temporal matters directly to the emperor, not through the Pope. Dante agreed with St. Thomas that Church and state should work together toward a common goal, but he was convinced that the Church had usurped the secular powers necessary to the peace and unity of the Empire. Dante was not a nationalist. The secular powers to be employed should be lodged in the

[1] Marshall W. Baldwin, *The Medieval Church,* Cornell University Press, Ithaca, N.Y., 1953, p. 89.

emperor, who could use them to settle disagreements among the princes.

The fact that Dante was an Italian is important. Had he been French, for example, he probably would have placed his faith in the ability of the king to keep the peace. Without the model of a powerful monarch before him, however, Dante's inclination was to look to the past, to the irrecoverable Roman Empire which, by contrast with the fragmented and quarrelsome Italian world known to Dante, looked so attractive. Yet even a hundred years earlier, Dante's idea would still have been impractical. During his own lifetime events occurred that made the proposal impossible. The defeat of the Pope by the kingdoms of France and England in the last years of the thirteenth and the opening years of the fourteenth century demonstrated the inability of the papacy to compete in temporal matters with the national monarchs.

In 1294 Boniface VIII became Pope. An ambitious and arrogant man, Boniface would be content with no less power than the great Innocent III had wielded. He was, perhaps, no less able than his distinguished predecessor, but his problem was different and considerably more difficult. In England and in France the kings were working to liquidate feudalism and develop a centralized system of administration. This was an expensive process, and the temptation to hasten it by drawing heavily on the accumulated wealth of the Church was not resisted by Edward I of England or Philip IV (the Fair) of France. Boniface, however, had expensive ambitions of his own, and he moved to halt the drain of ecclesiastical revenues to secular monarchs. In 1296 Boniface issued the bull *Clericis Laicos* by which taxation of the clergy without papal consent was prohibited. Transgressors were to be excommunicated. The reaction of the French and English kings was swift and, to Boniface, startling. Edward threatened to deny protection to the clergy by placing its members outside of the king's peace. Philip counterattacked with financial reprisals designed to cut off the flow of money from France to the papal see. Boniface surrendered, explaining somewhat lamely that he had never intended the interpretation which Edward and Philip had placed upon his bull.

Soon afterward, in 1300, the first Christian Jubilee was held in Rome. Hundreds of thousands of the faithful attended and in a spirit of religious fervor proclaimed their devotion to Church and Pope. Boniface's assurance was restored. Surely the event proved the loyalty of Church members. He appeared before the throng wearing the two swords symbolic of temporal and spiritual authority and pronounced himself Pope and emperor of Christendom. In 1302 the claim was reasserted in the famous bull *Unam Sanctam,* in which Boniface restated the principle of the dependence of temporal upon spiritual authority. A key sentence of the proclamation stated: "One sword, moreover, ought to be under the other, and the temporal authority to be subjected to the spiritual." Philip repudiated the bull, whereupon Boniface excommunicated him and absolved his subjects of their allegiance. The papal action was ineffective. Philip convened his royal council, which included the higher clergy of France, and the council supported the king. Philip and the council prepared a list of twenty-nine charges, including simony, immorality, and murder, against the Pope and proposed, on the basis of this bill of particulars, the deposition of Boniface by a general council of the Church. Rather, however, than take the time to act through formal channels, Philip decided upon direct action. A group of men, acting under his agent, Nogaret, kidnapped the Pope at Anagni near Rome. The local populace intervened and freed Boniface; but the Pope died a few weeks later. Boniface's successor, Benedict XI, lived only a few months after taking office. He was followed by Clement V, a Frenchman who was far more tractable than Boniface and who shifted papal headquarters from Rome to Avignon in France. Thus began the period of the "Babylonian captivity" in which, for some seventy-five years, the papacy remained at Avignon and was dominated by the French monarchy.

The struggle between Boniface and Philip had stimulated an outpouring of arguments on either side. All the old positions were restated, and nothing really new was added. Egidius Colonna firmly supported the Pope in his *De ecclesiastica potestate,* written about 1302, with a summary of arguments drawn from Aristotelian and Augustinian sources. It is according to nature, Colonna wrote, that the lower serves the higher. Consequently, the temporal must always be governed by the spiritual. The only true state is a Christian state. With regard to property, certainly a key issue at the time, it is, Colonna said, a means to an end, that end being salvation. If the Church controls the end (and this can hardly be doubted) it is reasonable and proper to assume that it controls the means. Other arguments were advanced; they are all familiar.

Of great value to the king in this contest was the fact that for the first time he could rely upon the assistance and support of a number of professionally trained laymen of the commoner class who had worked vigorously to help the king bring the unruly nobility under control and who now directed their energies toward an attack upon the Pope. Lawyers such as Pierre Dubois (c. 1250–1312?) urged a major reform of the Church that would have seriously curbed its authority, as well as a general secularizing of society including state control of education.

The French clergy also gave support to Philip's cause. John of Paris, a Frenchman who had joined the Dominican order, presented a strong case for the state, which showed the Aristotelian influence in its philosophical content. The formation of the state, John wrote, is a natural process which has nothing to do with religion. Secular authority existed long before a Christian spiritual authority was known on earth, and therefore, could not be said to depend upon the later creation. It is quite possible to have and enjoy a good secular life without the presence of a church. On the matter of property, John stated that while the Church required some property to do its work, this limited ownership did not mean that the Church had control over *all* property. It is true that the Pope may excommunicate a king, but the action has no secular consequences; that is, excommunication has nothing legally to do with the relationship of a king to his subjects. Moreover, the Pope should exercise less power within the Church itself. The Pope is the administrative head of the Church, but his spiritual authority is no greater than that of any other bishop. And the Pope is responsible to a general council in the same manner in which a king is responsible to his parliament.[2]

The argumentation probably made no significant difference to the outcome of the controversy. What really counted was the fact that times had changed. The monarchy, with its centralized administration that could keep the peace on a widespread basis and contribute to the development of a higher degree of prosperity, was popular with the people. The people responded by supporting the king as they had never supported the emperor. Their loyalty, more than anything else, enabled Philip and Edward to win. As Professor Pirenne put it:

> If Philip and Edward had been abandoned by their subjects, as the result of religious scruples, or of mere indifference, they could have done nothing but humbly make their submission. What enabled them to triumph was the consciousness that they were supported by the assent of their peoples; that is, they had moral strength on their side, the only thing that could give them the victory in a conflict of this nature.[3]

Marsilio of Padua

The death of the emperor Henry VII in 1313 resulted in a struggle between two candidates for the crown. Imperial electors had divided their votes between Frederic of Austria and Lewis the Bavarian, and when negotiations failed to convince either aspirant that he should withdraw, an eight years' war ensued which ended with the defeat of Frederic. In this conflict, John XXII, a Pope of Avignon, vigorously supported Frederic and asserted the authority of the Pope to play a decisive role in the election of emperors. The basis for another bitter controversy between Pope and temporal authority was established. The Pope was defeated again, by a combination of forces generally like those that had overwhelmed Boniface. Yet one new and significant element was present. A radical wing of the Franciscan order, insisting upon a policy of clerical poverty, became embroiled in a dispute with the Pope over this issue. The Pope issued a

[2] George H. Sabine, *A History of Political Theory*, 3d ed., Holt, Rinehart and Winston, Inc., New York, 1961, pp. 281–283.

[3] Henri Pirenne, *A History of Europe*, vol. II, *From the Thirteenth Century to the Renaissance and Reformation* (translated by Bernard Miall), Anchor Books, Doubleday & Company, Inc., Garden City, N.Y., 1958, p. 83.

decree of heresy against the spiritual Franciscans, who promptly retaliated with the same charge against the Pope and gave their support to Lewis the Bavarian. The alliance between the Franciscans and the secular supporters of the emperor proved formidable.

Of all those who devoted their scholastic energies to the cause of the emperor, the two most important were an Italian, Marsilio of Padua (1270–1342) and an English contemporary, William of Occam. Each was more concerned with a matter of interest to himself than with the specific issue between John XXII and Lewis. William of Occam was a prominent figure among those Franciscans who were engaged in controversy with the Pope, and his primary interest lay in the curbing of papal power within the Church itself. Marsilio was a patriotic Italian who, like Dante, deprecated the disunity of Italy, to which he assigned the same cause as had his fellow countryman, that is, interference of the Pope in secular affairs. For Marsilio and William, the debate between Pope and emperor provided a convenient outlet for the expression of their philosophies. Lewis was pleased to offer protection in return for their support, although he later discarded Marsilio when the Italian had served his purpose.

Marsilio was a man of many talents. He had been trained in theology, although he had declined service in the Church. He had studied medicine and had been a soldier. He served as rector of the University of Paris and was later appointed canon of the Church of Padua by John XXII, a move which the Pope undoubtedly came to regret. Both Paris and Padua were centers of Averroism, a movement which rejected the reconciliation of faith and reason, of spiritual and temporal, evidenced in St. Thomas Aquinas's reconstruction of Aristotelianism. The Averroists accepted Christian doctrine as truth but insisted that its sole basis was revelation and that it was thus not supportable by reason. There are, it was claimed, two kinds or standards of truth, and each is apprehended in a different manner. The Averroists also maintained, with Aristotle, that the secular state can provide everything necessary to the living of a moral and happy life. They repudiated the medieval idea that the only good state is a Christian state. Marsilio's precise relationship with the Averroist movement is not known, but he was obviously influenced by it.

Marsilio's major literary effort was the *Defensor Pacis* (*Defender of the Peace*), which he probably wrote with John of Jandun, a leader of the Averroists in Paris. The book is divided into three parts. The first deals with Marsilio's theory of the state, the second with the Church, and the third consists of a series of conclusions based upon the first two parts. Marsilio's purpose was to destroy the idea of papal imperialism, the Pope's power in temporal affairs. He relied heavily upon Aristotle in the development of a purely secular justification of the state. Referring to Aristotle's discussion of the causes of revolution, Marsilio said that it omitted mention of one cause which Aristotle, living when he did, could not have known; that was the unwarranted interference in secular matters by the Pope. Such meddling could not be justified on the ground that it was necessary to the development of a good secular state. The state is a self-sufficient community, both physically and morally. The Church has, therefore, no right to interfere, and the Pope should recognize the irrelevance of his claims. The functions of Church and state are distinctly different, and so are the foundations upon which they are established. The Church's responsibility is to save souls by teaching the religious truths revealed to man by God. The state's responsibility is to provide a good life, a life in which man has sufficient leisure to pursue knowledge and culture. The creation of the proper kind of state is dependent upon a judgment based upon reason. Both state and Church are concerned with making the good life possible, but the Church should consider only life in the next world; the state's interest is with life on earth. The two should be kept entirely separate.

Marsilio follows Aristotle in comparing the state to a living organism consisting of many parts, each of which must perform its role satisfactorily if the whole is to benefit. The malfunctioning of any part is injurious to the entire organism. The main difficulty, Marsilio said, results from the fact that the clergy, who should devote their time to spiritual affairs only, interfere in temporal affairs. Faced with similar problems, St. Thomas had evolved a solution which harmonized reason and faith, Church and state, secular and canon law. Marsilio tears apart this fabric to a great extent by insisting that reason and faith are incapable of reconciliation and demanding their separation. It is possible, he said, to construct a good state in which men may live a good life without clerical interference in secular affairs. He outlines its structure.

The basis of good government is popular sovereignty. Ultimate political authority must be lodged in the people, whom Marsilio terms, collectively, the "legislator." The legislative process is vital. If the laws do not meet with the approval of the people strife and disunity will certainly ensue. The people themselves do not *formulate* the specific legislative measures; this is the function of a small number of experts who are qualified, on the basis of their superior knowledge, to formulate laws. These experts "discover" the laws through study and careful consideration; they then make their recommendations to the people, who make whatever disposition of them they choose. The people as a whole, more than any one person or group, are capable of judging the proposals and making a choice because they live under the laws and are affected by them. A traditional argument against popular participation in the political process is that each person has selfish desires which often set him against his fellows and that it is therefore impractical as well as dangerous to entrust the masses with power. Marsilio does not deny that individuals are selfish, but he contends that the people assembled in judgment are wise and responsible and that they are more likely to act in the general interest than would one man or a few. For the few are also human beings who have selfish interests.

> Indeed it would be insecure, as we have already shown, to entrust the [complete] making of the law to the discretion of the few. For they would perhaps consult therein their own private benefit, as individuals or as a group, rather than the common benefit. By this means the way would be opened to oligarchy, just as when the power to make the laws is given to one man alone the opportunity is afforded for tyranny. . . .[4]

Nor is the power of the people as legislator hedged about by the limitations imposed by a natural law. The people are genuinely sovereign. Not being infallible, they may make bad judgments, but the laws they decide upon are nonetheless binding. Marsilio believes that the people's judgment is superior to that of a tyrant or an oligarchy. But more is involved than efficiency and good judgment. There is also the matter of freedom. Even if one man or a few could demonstrably do a better job, it would still be preferable to permit the people to hold power, since only in this manner can they be free. Man can be free in society only when he obeys the laws that he helps to make.[5]

It is unrealistic, Marsilio urged, to think in terms of a possible alternative between government by the many on the one hand, and government by a benevolent king or aristocracy on the other. Good rule by one or a few just men is impossible in the long run. It soon degenerates into tyranny or oligarchy.[6] Trust must be placed in the majority. All men, if they are normal, will seek a good life and consequently the kind of laws which will assure the good life.

> The authority to make laws belongs only to the whole body of citizens . . . or else it belongs to one or a few men. But it cannot belong to one man alone . . . for through ignorance or malice or both, this one man could make a bad law, looking more to his own private benefit than to that of the community, so that the law would be tyrannical. For the same reason, the authority to make laws cannot belong to a few; for they too could sin, as above, in making the law for the benefit of a certain few and not for the common benefit, as can be seen in oligarchies. The authority to make the laws belongs, therefore, to the whole body of citizens or to the weightier part thereof, for precisely the opposite reason. For since all the citizens must

---

[4] *Defensor Pacis*, I, xiii, 5, in Alan Gewirth (ed.), *Marsilius of Padua: The Defender of the Peace*, vol. II, *The* Defensor Pacis (translated with an introduction), Columbia University Press, New York, 1956, p. 53.

[5] *Ibid.*, I, xii, 6, in vol. II, p. 47.

[6] Alan Gewirth, *Marsilius of Padua: The Defender of the Peace*, vol. I, *Marsilius of Padua and Medieval Political Philosophy,* Columbia University Press, New York, 1951, p. 206.

be measured by the law according to due proportion, and no one knowingly harms or wishes injustice to himself, it follows that all or most wish a law conducing to the common benefit of the citizens.[7]

Marsilio's use of the term "weightier part" (*pars valentior*) has given rise to considerable difference of opinion over its interpretation. The protagonists fall generally into two camps. One group argues that Marsilio was a majority-rule democrat, that the term "weightier part" simply refers to the majority of all the people, and that Marsilio would have votes counted rather than weighed. Others say that Marsilio's "weightier part" refers to an elite group whose members are distinguished by ability or position and that these make decisions in the name of the people. In short, Marsilio would, under this latter interpretation, weigh votes rather than count them. It is important in any case to understand precisely what Marsilio intended.

A consideration of the matter leads to the conclusion that Marsilio was at least more democratic than aristocratic; the whole tenor of his writings points in this direction. Still, it would be easy to carry the point too far. As we have seen, Marsilio did not believe that all men were endowed with equal political ability. He merely said that all men assembled for the legislative purpose are better judges of policy and are more likely to act in the general interest than are one man or a few. Those who have great intelligence and the leisure to study do exist, and they should surely play a more important role than the great mass of men who are well intentioned but not so capable. Professor Gewirth has considered the problem in detail and has arrived at the following conclusions which seem amply substantiated by the evidence: First, when Marsilio speaks of the "people" he is thinking in terms of functional groups or classes rather than of individuals. Second, no one group or class is to dominate the others; each must participate, and each has its rights. Third, in determining the amount of authority to be exercised by each class or group, both numbers and quality should be considered so that neither factor may dominate completely. Fourth, all people are included in the political community so that although some have more weight than others, the state itself is a "corporate whole."[8]

We have considered thus far only that phase of governmental action which relates to the finding and acceptance of the law. This is the legislative process as conceived by Marsilio, who is still enough of a medievalist not to think in terms of "making" legislation in the modern sense of the term. There still remain the executive and judicial functions. Marsilio does not really distinguish between the two; both powers are placed in the hands of a king whose function it is to apply the law, which

---

[7] *Defensor Pacis*, I, xiii, 8, in vol. II, pp. 48–49.
[8] Gewirth, *op. cit.*, vol. I, p. 199.

comes from the people, to the specific cases at hand. His is a significant task, although not so important as that of the "legislator." The ruler is bound by the laws that he enforces. He cannot make the laws, nor is it within his power to interpret them. Only the legislator has such power. The ruler is elected by the people. He is responsible to them, and they may discipline or remove him at their pleasure. The king (and Marsilio favors the single ruler) need not worry about how well his actions accord with the natural law. His main concern must be to rule according to the laws of his people, for they, not the natural law, are sovereign.

Marsilio proposed the fundamental outlines of a republican system of government. Its underlying principles are not materially different from those which prevail in the democratic republics of modern times. Marsilio assumes that even though all men are not equal in ability, all must be given a share in the political process. Better government will probably result from this democracy, but even if it does not, the people should still be trusted with a share in their government. Otherwise that "competent state of freedom" will be destroyed which is possible only when even the most lowly have some small voice in determining the laws by which they live. Marsilio also insists that a ruler should be elected by the people and be responsible to them. His authority is limited by the laws made by those who elect him. The power of the people themselves is unlimited, and in this belief Marsilio differs greatly from many of the democratic theorists who preceded and followed him. Finally, Marsilio holds that the government formed on the basis of the principles he enunciates is the only legitimate kind of government.[9]

Marsilio on Church and Clergy

Many of Marsilio's political ideas are repeated in his consideration of the proper form of Church organization. Marsilio's political principles, however, were designed to apply to a single state, probably a city-state, while the religious community was universal. Marsilio also recognized that the functioning of the Church should be regulated by the Divine Law, which differs in important respects from the law by which the state is governed. Its source is God rather than man, and its understanding and acceptance are on the basis of faith rather than reason. Violation of the Divine Law involves no earthly penalty imposed by the Church, this being a matter between God and the individual alone. The Church itself has no coercive power. The state, in the interest of peace, may possibly wish to attach a penalty to an infraction of the Divine Law, and it may legitimately do so. If, on occasion, it permits the Church to punish such violations, the coercive authority originates in the secular, not the spiritual, organization. The function of the clergy in such cases is to

[9] *Ibid.*, p. 240.

advise and inform temporal authorities; they cannot act in their own right. Even the power of excommunication is in the hands of the civil government.

Marsilio states that the Church, properly speaking, consists of the "whole body of the faithful." Within this body, all are equal in the eyes of God. The clergy enjoy no advantages here, although Marsilio recognizes that a priest has a spiritual character not conferred upon him by the state which gives him a special insight into spiritual truths. The offices of the clergy, however, are worldly offices which are made necessary by the fact that God has provided for an earthly organization of his Church. Since the offices are worldly, it is in the temporal power to assign them and to take them away. The clergy require some property to accomplish their purposes, but this property is under the control of civil authorities. Any privileges or immunities the clergy enjoy in matters involving property or taxation are granted by the temporal power. The Pope's relation to civil authority is no different from that of the lowest of the clergy. The papacy itself is a worldly office. The demands of administrative efficiency make the office necessary, but spiritually the Pope is not superior to any priest, or for that matter, to any layman. He is certainly not the successor to Peter, and Marsilio doubts the authenticity of the historical record that gave rise to the Petrine theory. In fact, he says, Paul has a better claim than Peter to the position of Bishop of Rome, since Paul preached in Rome for two years, while no evidence exists to prove that Peter was ever there.[10]

One of the causes of disunity in the state is difference of opinion over matters of scriptural interpretation. Decisions in these cases cannot safely be left to the clergy any more than policy in secular affairs may be entrusted to an oligarchy. In spiritual affairs as in secular, wisdom will more probably emanate from the whole people than from a small number. There is also a democratic principle involved in the fact that since the Church is the "whole body of the faithful" all members have a right to a voice. But the universal nature of Church organization makes mass participation in its affairs a much more difficult problem practically than it is in secular matters. Marsilio's solution is the establishment of a general council including both clergy and laymen, to be elected by the whole people of the various nations and territories of Christendom on a proportional basis reflecting both quantitative and qualitative factors. The general council should be composed of persons qualified by training and ability to perform their tasks. The council's functions include election of the Pope and making decisions involving scriptural interpretation. Decisions of the council are binding on all, although the

[10] Ephraim Emerton, *The Defensor Pacis of Marsiglio of Padua*, Peter Smith Publisher, Gloucester, Mass., 1951, p. 45. Copyright by Harvard University Press, Cambridge, Mass., 1920.

council itself has no coercive authority. To the extent that the temporal authorities deem it necessary to enforce council decisions they must so provide by secular law.

Marsilio's theory does not provide for a separation of Church and state. Marsilio does make religion a private affair in its purely spiritual phase. Man's relationship to God is the concern only of God and the individual person. Not even the Pope, Marsilio contends, can forgive sins; only God can absolve. The state cannot take cognizance of a man's beliefs and inner spiritual cogitations, although it can interfere when religious activity affects secular affairs. The clergy are, as we have seen, subject to secular control just as are other citizens. Marsilio distrusted the clergy more than he distrusted any other group, and the Pope more than any other person, because he felt that clerical ambition, greed, and meddling in secular affairs were disruptive of the peace and order of the state. The medieval tradition was too strong for Marsilio to propose separation as a solution. Even separation would have left two spheres of authority and tended to destroy the desired unity. Since events had proved that the clergy could not achieve unity through the exercise of power, there was no alternative to vesting power in the civil authorities. Individual secular freedom was carefully protected by the arrangements Marsilio made for civil government based on popular sovereignty. Religious freedom does not seem to have been so well guarded. Marsilio strongly favored freedom of religious belief and argued for toleration, but the control of the clergy by the state, which Marsilio regarded as an absolute prerequisite to peace, tended greatly to diminish the autonomy necessary to religious liberty.

William of Occam

William of Occam (c. 1280–1349) was a more prolific writer than Marsilio. The modern reader finds his ideas more difficult to understand and explain, partly because of the great volume of his writings and partly because of the form in which his views were presented. But his ideas should not be neglected, for they were significant at the time and were often referred to by subsequent writers.[11] William was associated with Marsilio on the side of Lewis in the struggle against John XXII. His interest, however, was less secular than that of Marsilio, as might be expected considering the fact that William was a member of that part of the Franciscan order which had been excommunicated by the Pope for its insistence upon the principle of clerical poverty. William was led to defend the rights of Church members against a heretical Pope. His assertion of papal heresy was based in large part upon the traditional medieval objection to despotic and abusive authority irrespective of its source.

Marsilio's answer to the challenge posed by a too powerful Pope and

[11] Occam's major political views were stated in his *Octo Quaestiones* and the *Dialogus*.

Church was to transfer the bulk of churchly authority to the state, particularly where such authority had secular manifestations. William, on the other hand, was distrustful of any kind of power, whether it was wielded by Pope, emperor, king, or people. Secular power can be abused as easily as can spiritual. Neither state nor Church should be permitted to dominate the other. Each should perform its necessary function. Each should be independent in its own field, although each should also help the other and, when necessary, check its improper action. For William it was not too late to return to the ideal of the two-swords theory. In the present situation he believed that the Pope had usurped authority properly belonging to the secular branch. More important, the Pope had also betrayed his trust by improperly interfering, in the matter of clerical poverty, with the rights of members of the Church. In both cases reform was necessary.

In general, William accepted the monarchic theory in both Church and state. Direction by one person, he thought, conduces to unity and to the fulfillment of those purposes for which man is placed on earth. The Church exists to supply the organization necessary to the salvation of souls. Christ had granted authority to Peter and his successors to direct the organization to the proper end. Although William, unlike Marsilio, is willing to grant the validity of this thesis about the derivation of papal authority, it does not lead him to the conclusion that the papal power is absolute. The power is always limited by the end which it is designed to achieve.[12] The Pope, therefore, should stay clear of secular involvement. He cannot justify interference in temporal affairs by pointing to actions taken by past popes who had exercised secular power, since such actions were themselves illegal and usurpatory. In spiritual matters, too, the papal power is limited. The Pope is charged with the responsibility for saving souls. He should do whatever is necessary to accomplish this purpose, and no rigid restrictions on papal power can be set up in advance. Circumstances may require the Pope to depart, on occasion, from what are generally regarded as normal practices. William was wise enough to recognize the dangers of an inflexible constitution and to acknowledge that an unusual exertion of power might be justified by contingency; but he required the Pope to accept responsibility for his action—an action that must always be justified by the purpose for which it was taken.

The problem remained of how and by whom this responsibility was to be enforced. The heresy of John XXII had made it clear that the problem was more than theoretical and that some device was required whereby papal absolutism could be systematically curbed. William's solution was generally the same as that proposed by Marsilio. The Church, he said, is more than the organization of the clergy; it consists of the

[12] Ewart Lewis, *Medieval Political Ideas,* Alfred A. Knopf, Inc., New York, 1954, vol. II, p. 547.

whole body of believers. Here William goes further than Marsilio, for he specifically includes women as members of the body. In matters of faith, the laity is the equal of the clergy and has the right to judge and even to depose a Pope who is deemed guilty of heresy. All Christians, of course, cannot act directly in making decisions; administratively such action would be infeasible. Moreover, some questions arise that are too technical to be understood by the rank and file. The difficulty can be remedied by the creation of a general council, representative of the whole body of believers and including laymen as well as clergy. This council should have the power to judge, to check, and to depose a Pope. William was too practical and too imbued with the medieval distrust of authority to assume that the council would always judge correctly and act properly. If the council errs, he said, an appeal should be made to the men of the Church; if they err, women and children should be brought in; finally, appeal may be made to the whole Church, the dead and the unborn, as well as the living.

If the authority of the Pope is limited by the purpose he is to serve, that is, the saving of men's souls, the power of the emperor is also restricted. His responsibility is to provide good government and to help his people live better lives. The power of any secular ruler rests upon the consent of his subjects, who have chosen him through the action of the magnates of the realm. It does not derive from the Pope. Secular power must not be arbitrary; it is limited by the principles of the law. There are different kinds of law, and each imposes restrictions upon the authority of the ruler. Above his edicts, for example, stand the Divine Law, which comes through revelation from God, and the natural law, which is given by God to all men who can understand it through their use of reason. No human edict that contravenes either of these laws may be considered just or binding.[13]

A higher human law also operates to limit secular authority. This is the *jus gentium*. Though really a part of the natural law, it is distinguished by the fact that circumstances may make it subject to change. *Jus gentium* is less perfect than pure natural law, but is as good law as can be expected to develop among men who are themselves less than perfect. It would be better if all men were to live and all governments were to be conducted according to the natural law, but since the practical world will not permit this utopian arrangement, *jus gentium,* which provides somewhat greater leeway, must be followed. Yet even though the *jus gentium* is not perfect law, its purpose is to secure, in the best manner possible, the good of the community. If the way to achieve the general welfare changes from time to time, so too may the *jus gentium*. By the term William essentially means custom. He cites it because he

[13] Max A. Shepard, "William of Occam and the Higher Law," *American Political Science Review*, vol. 26, pp. 1008–1009, December, 1932.

wants to be certain that rulers will be as bound by the traditions and customs of their subjects as they are by the commandments of God and the dictates of the natural law, since both of the latter, we may presume, are capable of being interpreted in various ways. William grants that a ruler may occasionally depart from the *jus gentium,* but his deviation is justifiable only insofar as his action serves the general welfare.[14]

Although the people, in William's theory, are sovereign, they too are limited by the force of the *jus gentium.* William wants the people to be the ultimate source of authority, but he recognizes the fact that they can abuse power just as can a single ruler. The will of the people, though important, may also represent mere whim and caprice. Stability and continuity are necessary in any well-managed state. This being so, the majority may have to be restrained in its own interest by the law. Once the people have selected a ruler they should give him the opportunity to rule. The mutual obligation that exists between ruler and ruled to act in the general interest is governed by the law, the *jus gentium,* which defines rights and duties and is binding upon both parties. The people need not tolerate a ruler who ignores the demands of the law. On the other hand, a ruler is entitled to the respect and obedience of his subjects as long as he governs according to the law.

The Conciliar Movement

The attack by Marsilio and William upon papal absolutism anticipated by only a few years a popular movement directed to the same end. The papal see had finally been returned to Italy, but the problem of papal interference in secular affairs had by no means been solved. Popes became enmeshed in Italian political struggles, and their ambitions led them to compete with secular rulers for the wealth they needed to advance their causes. There was bitter competition between the two authorities. The unseemly struggle that resulted degraded the papal office and affected the entire clerical hierarchy. A bad situation was worsened by the Great Schism (1378 to 1417) in which rival popes, fighting for supreme spiritual and political power, often were pawns in the hands of competing monarchs, who used the highest office of the Church in their own interest. The prestige of the Pope and the clergy generally declined dangerously.

A demand for reform was inevitable. Marsilio and William had laid down principles that were to prove of inestimable value to those who followed them. Wycliffe (c. 1320–1384) in England and Hus (c. 1373–1415) in Bohemia carried the battle for reform into the public arena, attracting the interest and stirring the emotions of thousands of common people by their talk about the equality of men before God and the right

[14] Thomas I. Cook, *History of Political Philosophy from Plato to Burke,* Prentice-Hall, Inc., Englewood Cliffs, N.J., 1936, p. 245.

of the body of Christian believers to discipline a rapacious and errant clergy. The ideas were essentially those of Marsilio and William, but now for the first time these ideas became the subject of a widespread debate which was vitally to interest Christians in the fourteenth and fifteenth centuries. Since, in the controversy, the reformers had to rely heavily upon secular rulers for protection, they were obligated, in return, to support those rulers. As did Luther after him, Wycliffe justified the alliance by proclaiming the doctrine of divine right of kings and by holding that the king's authority extended so far as to permit him to undertake church reform.[15]

The ideas of Wycliffe and Hus, and particularly the dangerous proclivity of those radicals to carry their case to the people, did not attract the support of a larger body of Christians who were also searching for a method and pattern of reform. These were the conciliarists, who were desperately afraid that unless the Church were reformed from within it would be reformed from without, with a resultant further loss of prestige and power and the shattering of the ancient ideal of Christian unity. The immediate problem was the healing of the schism, although action was also evidently necessary to correct papal financial abuses and to wipe out corruption at the papal court. Moreover, it would be desirable to revamp the Church organization to provide some kind of body which could, by established constitutional processes, check the power of the Pope and keep a watchful eye on developments in order to forestall future abuses. The consensus of the conciliarists was that the solution advocated by Marsilio and William, that is, the establishment of a general council, was the only correct one. It was assumed that such a council should act as a legislative body, making the policies which the Pope, as a constitutional and responsible monarch, would execute.[16]

In support of their proposal, the conciliarists offered the principle which had previously been expounded by Marsilio and William and elaborated by Wycliffe and Hus, that is, that the power of the Church is vested in all its members, that the clergy are in no way superior spiritually to the rank-and-file members, that clerics are indeed mere servants of the members, and that the Pope is similarly to be regarded as the servant, not the master, of the people. In short, the government of the Church rests upon the consent of its members. For practical purposes, because the whole body of members cannot congregate as a governing body, a council which represents and speaks for the members should be established. Neither council nor Pope should be regarded as the possessor of inherent powers. Both receive power from the body of the faithful, and each uses the power granted to it to check any arbitrary tendencies on the part of the other.

[15] Sabine, *op. cit.*, pp. 314–315.
[16] Cook, *op. cit.*, pp. 256–257.

The conciliar movement failed to reform the papacy by making the Pope into a constitutional monarch. Meetings of the council were held, in Pisa in 1409, in Constance from 1414 to 1418, and in Basel from 1431 to 1449. There were no spectacular results. The major immediate accomplishment was the settlement of the schism in the Council of Constance, but this, in a sense, proved to be a handicap to the solution of other and more deep-rooted problems, because the restoration of unity in the papacy made it appear, at least, as if the most pressing difficulty were solved. Little more could be done, aside from issuing impressive-sounding manifestoes to which few paid attention. The success of the council required a degree of unity which did not exist among its component delegations. The forces of national particularism were rampant among delegates to the council meetings, and the Pope was able, through his agents, to set one faction against another and thus to prevent the formation of a solid front which otherwise could have defeated him. Church members everywhere lost faith in the council, and popular confidence was further seriously weakened when John Hus, who had been invited under a guarantee of safe conduct to present his views to the council, was charged with heresy and executed. The resulting reaction to the conciliar movement was favorable to the Pope and so strengthened his position within the Church that it was never again successfully attacked. The movement for constitutionalization of Church government was finished. The Pope was absolute monarch of his realm. But his realm was soon to be diminished. The failure of the conciliarists to carry through a thoroughgoing program of reform left the Church with most of the same abuses from which it had long suffered, and the foundation for the Reformation was more firmly established.

The conciliarists were unable to attain their objectives, but their program was, nonetheless, significant. As we have seen, conciliarism strengthened the Pope but prepared the way for Luther and the Reformation. From the standpoint of political theory, the conciliarist movement further developed doctrines of popular sovereignty and of the rights of subjects against their rulers. In conciliarism, where the Church provided the arena in which these issues were fought out, democracy lost. But when secular rulers proclaimed a divine right to govern absolutely, their argument could be transferred without difficulty from the spiritual to the secular realm. The argument that God has vested spiritual authority in the whole body of the faithful is merely the theological counterpart of the assumption that the citizens of the state are politically sovereign. There was no immediate victory for democracy or for the people. This was a time in which power, secular and spiritual, was being concentrated. The rise of the Pope to a position of supreme authority within the Church was paralleled in the kingdoms by the ascent of the monarchs who repudiated the principle of consent of the governed. The democratic ideas implicit in conciliarism were too powerful, however, to be permanently denied. In the revolutionary movements of the seventeenth and eighteenth centuries they were back again, stronger than before.

Conclusions

The humiliating defeat of Boniface VIII in the last years of the thirteenth and the beginning of the fourteenth century by the forces of national monarchy presaged the close of one era and the beginning of another. The overweening ambitions of the papacy clashed with the aspirations of nationalistic kings. The final result was the destruction of Christian unity under the Gelasian theory. The Pope began by asserting complete authority, both temporal and spiritual; he ended by losing not only nearly all his secular power but also, in the Reformation, his spiritual authority over a significant segment of Christendom. His efforts to fortify his position by citing the works of the Fathers and the precedents of the past were fruitless. Thanks to the theory of Aristotle and to the efficiency of kingly governments, it was impossible for the Pope and his supporters successfully to argue that the only good state is dominated by a Christian Pope and clergy. In his struggle with nationalism, the Pope could not count upon the support even of his own clergy, many of whom were stirred by patriotic fervor, angered by the excesses of papal power, and revolted by the degradation of the papal court. Thus the Pope was attacked on two flanks. On the one hand he attempted to defend himself against the kings; on the other he fought against the dissident members of his own organization. He won the latter battle but lost the former.

The period produced a rich outpouring of ideas which, designed to influence the immediate course of events, vitally affected the subsequent development of political thought. Partisans of papal supremacy were prone merely to repeat the theories that had for so long been used to justify their position. Their opponents, although relying heavily upon Aristotle's concept of the self-sufficient secular community, were more original. In spite of noticeable differences in the theories propounded by William of Occam, Marsilio, Wycliffe, Hus, and the rest, they agreed upon certain fundamentals. One of the most significant was the insistence that both temporal and spiritual authority justly reside in the people (or in God who exercises it through the people). The people's power is effected mainly through a representative body whose legitimacy rests upon the fact that it speaks for the people and is responsible to them. The necessary executive authority is represented by the Pope for the Church and the king for the state, but that authority is limited and must also be responsible. Officials of both Church and state are servants of the sovereign people from whom their power is derived.

Applied to specific events and by the many theorists involved, the above statement is somewhat oversimplified. Certainly the fifteenth century did not bring with it models of modern democracy in either Church or state. In the Church, indeed, democratic reform failed, both at the time and subsequently. Nor were the monarchs of the nations then just emerging from feudalism much impressed; in their opinion, the times demanded a consolidation rather than a relaxation of personal authority. Still, the ideas with their strongly revolutionary implications were there. So long as most of the citizens felt that political authoritarianism was serving them well, they would not carry their resentment of it to the point of physical resistance. Later, when national despots through the abuse of their powers exposed themselves to charges similar to those formerly made against a too powerful Pope, the ideas of Marsilio, William, Wycliffe, and Hus would again play a prominent role. In the fifteenth century, the struggle to limit the absolute power of the Pope was lost; opposition to secular absolutism was making a new beginning.

SELECTED BIBLIOGRAPHY

Baldwin, Marshall W.: *The Medieval Church,* Cornell University Press, Ithaca, N.Y., 1953, chap. 4.

Cook, Thomas I.: *History of Political Philosophy from Plato to Burke,* Prentice-Hall, Inc., Englewood Cliffs, N.J., 1936, chaps. 7–9.

D'Entrèves, Alexander P.: *The Medieval Contribution to Political Thought: Thomas Aquinas, Marsilius of Padua, Richard Hooker,* Humanities Press, New York, 1959, chaps. 3, 4.

Emerton, Ephraim: *The* Defensor Pacis *of Marsiglio of Padua: A Critical Study,* Peter Smith Publisher, Gloucester, Mass., 1951. Copyright, 1920, Harvard University Press, Cambridge, Mass.

Gewirth, Alan: *Marsilius of Padua, The Defender of the Peace,* vol. I, *Marsilius of Padua and Medieval Political Philosophy,* Columbia University Press, New York, 1951.

——— (ed.): vol. II, *The* Defensor Pacis (translated with an introduction), Columbia University Press, New York, 1956.

Lewis, Ewart: *Medieval Political Ideas,* vol. II, Alfred A. Knopf, Inc., New York, 1954, chaps. 6–8.

McIlwain, Charles H.: *The Growth of Political Thought in the West, from the Greeks to the End of the Middle Ages,* The Macmillan Company, New York, 1932, chap. 6.

Pirenne, Henri: *A History of Europe,* vol. II, *From the Thirteenth Century to the Renaissance and Reformation* (translated by Bernard Miall), Anchor Books, Doubleday & Company, Inc., Garden City, N.Y., 1958, bk. I, chap. 4.

Sabine, George H.: *A History of Political Theory,* 3d ed., Holt, Rinehart and Winston, Inc., New York, 1961, chaps. 13–16.

nine

MACHIAVELLI

The Renaissance broke with the past and inaugurated a new and intensely interesting era, whose inspiration was the classical culture of the pre-Christian period. It was humanistic, artistic, optimistic, scientific, individualistic, and paganistic. Those who participated in the great adventure sought to break the grip of medievalism on the world. Artists abandoned the Gothic style, and thinkers repudiated Scholasticism. Philosophers of the Renaissance rejected the view of medieval theology that man was a depraved animal, marked with sin at birth, and having no better than a fair chance of being saved. The man of the Middle Ages had been ideally an ascetic; morality had meant self-restraint, the abjuration of physical pleasures. The man of the Renaissance took quite another view; essentially a pagan, he was less fearful of the Devil than was his medieval progenitor. His art returned to the classical form. Everything was changing. Before the fifteenth century was out, the New World would be discovered, and the science of the Renaissance would contribute greatly to that event. But another kind of new world was being discovered half a century prior to Columbus's voyage.

The transformation of the intellectual world was paralleled by that of the economic. During the Middle Ages commercial profit had been regarded as sinful. The merchant had been entitled to a fair price, but its fairness was gauged by the amount he needed to support himself and his family on a minimum scale. Some, of course, had always taken more, but society generally had regarded such a practice with repugnance. In the fifteenth century a new economic class was emerging. In England, France, Flanders, and southern Germany, merchant adventurers grew impatient with the restrictive local regulations imposed by a feudal economy and sought to break them.[1] For centuries commerce had centered in the cities and had been dominated by powerful producers' guilds which had been able to maintain an economic stranglehold upon the medieval economy. The difficulty of communication had contributed greatly to the perpetuation of the restrictions; but as the interchange of ideas was facilitated and able and ambitious men were ready to take advantage of every opportunity, the changes already in motion were speeded. The new economic man had no qualms about making a profit. Self-interest was a legitimate motive, in fact it was the economic expression of the individualistic spirit of the Renaissance. Capitalism was being born.

It had a difficult delivery. The forces against capitalism were strong. The new and dynamic middle class had to struggle not only against the guild system on the economic front but also against the nobility on the political. The nobles had long been able, through the imposition of local regulations and in conjunction with the guilds, to control economic enterprise within the feudality. If the rising capitalism were to survive, it had to defeat localism, the very essence of the feudal system. The movement found a powerful friend in the king, who had been struggling with the same enemy for centuries. The alliance of king and middle class was a natural one; the capitalists wanted money; the king wanted power. A strong national monarch, subsidized heavily by merchant princes, could impose his own regulations upon trade to supplant those of the local nobility, thus enhancing his own authority at their expense. National economic regulations, with the attendant destruction of local barriers, enlarged the operational area of the merchant. The cost, in terms of financial support for the king, was high, but the rewards were great. The king was delighted with his bargain. He found it far easier to obtain money from this new source than to try to wring it from a reluctant parliament which represented, in large part, the very forces he was attempting to destroy. The partnership of king and capitalist, as it turned out, was temporary. In the end the capitalist was bound to resent the regulations imposed by the monarch who, in any case, was likely to make those regulations too restrictive. The king was helping to create the power that would destroy him, but this contingency was far in the future and could not be anticipated. The combination of capitalism and the national monarchy was to have a profound influence upon the future course of history.

[1] Henri Pirenne, *A History of Europe,* Anchor Books, Doubleday & Company, Inc., Garden City, N.Y., 1958, vol. II, pp. 236–238.

The latter part of the fifteenth century was a period of advancement for the principle of absolutism in both Church and state. In the Church the Pope successfully resisted demands for that decentralization or dispersal of power that had been voiced in the conciliar movement. Although his secular authority had almost disappeared, his power to rule the Church organization as a kind of divine-right monarch was more generally acknowledged than it had been for a hundred years. The rise of monarchical power was still more spectacular. Kings gathered into their own hands the authority which they had formerly been compelled to share with the emperor, the Pope, the nobility, and parliaments. Throughout Europe kings, with the support of the middle class, raised the forces necessary to destroy their internal enemies. The long and sanguinary struggle was successful for the king. When it was over, medieval institutions had been wrecked beyond recovery. Kings took control of cities and overcame the resistance of the feudal nobility. They relieved the monasteries of their great wealth and used the money to build the power of the middle class which was supporting monarchical ambitions.[2] And they controlled the Church within their own kingdoms, making it, to a considerable degree, an instrument of national policy.

In no part of Europe were the forces for change more active than they were in Italy. So far as religion was concerned, Italians were closer to the scene than were other Europeans and consequently more repelled by the conduct of profligate popes and the scandalous operation of the papal office. Reaction was evidenced by the growth of a neopaganism that affected many aspects of Italian life. The establishment of academies of learning devoted to secular studies demonstrated Italian interest in the new learning which, with its emphasis on rationalism and empiricism, was definitely opposed to Scholasticism. Art and intellectual creativity of all kinds flourished in the new climate. Commercial pursuits were highly rewarding to those engaged in them, and the wealth so gained subsidized artistic accomplishments unequaled in world history.

In Italy, although nearly all the conditions were present which in other parts of Europe had led to national unity and progress, these forces were effectively checked by a complex set of circumstances and counterforces. The centralizing trend of governmental absolutism was frustrated by political divisions in the peninsula. Italy, at the time, consisted mainly of five states of roughly equal power: Naples, Milan, Florence, Venice, and the Papal State. If Italy were to follow the mainstream of historical development toward national unity, these five would, in some manner, have to be unified. It was generally recognized that this unification could be accomplished only by force. The greatest stumbling block was the Papal State, ruled by the Pope, who had made this geographically insignificant

[2] George H. Sabine, *A History of Political Theory*, 3d ed., Holt, Rinehart and Winston, Inc., New York, 1961, p. 333.

entity the strongest and best-administered state in Italy. The Pope would undoubtedly have been willing to extend his control over the whole of Italy, had not the Italians refused to countenance such a move. But if the Pope was not strong enough to unite Italy by force, he was capable of preventing others from doing so. There the matter stood.[3] The divisions were extremely frustrating, particularly to those who understood clearly what was happening, and they were very damaging to the morals and the morale of the people of Italy. The old institutions of Church and Empire were no longer able to evoke, as formerly, a spirit of unity and to stimulate an interest in morals, both private and public. In Spain, in England, and in France, the monarch was able to enforce unity and compel a degree of moral behavior, but Italy had no national monarch. As a result, morality declined precipitously.

> Cruelty and murder had become normal agencies of government; good faith and truthfulness had become childish scruples to which an enlightened man would hardly give lip-service; force and craft had become too frequent to need comment; and selfishness, naked and unadorned, need only succeed in order to supply its own justification. It was a period truly called the age of "bastards and adventurers," a society created as if to illustrate Aristotle's saying that "man, when separated from law and justice, is the worst of all animals." [4]

As Italy broke with the past she fell under the control of tyrants in the various states, who ruled solely on the basis of force and guile. These despots lacked, to an even greater degree than did the people, a sense of moral obligation. Their object was power, its establishment and its maintenance, and they resorted to any tactic to secure their end. Their efforts were often self-defeating. A ruler desperate to retain his throne, or an ambitious adventurer anxious to obtain one, sometimes sought the assistance of a foreign monarch. The latter, in furnishing troops, often found himself in a position to control the situation completely, whereupon the unhappy Italian became a mere pawn of his powerful ally. Or mercenary soldiers might be used who, at a crucial time, sold out to the opposition or deserted the field, in either case leaving their employer in an embarrassing predicament.

Machiavelli: The Man and His Work

Niccolò Machiavelli understood clearly the forces that barred Italy's path to unity and power. No one wished more ardently than he to clear the path or offered more definite solutions to Italy's problems. Machiavelli's purpose can be fully comprehended only in the light of the prevailing conditions. Corruption in public and private life was all about

[3] *Ibid.*, pp. 336–337.
[4] *Ibid.*, pp. 337–338.

him; he deprecated the fact and longed for the healthy public spirit which he knew must be attended by an improvement of private morals. As a diplomatic agent he had traveled abroad, observed the administration of foreign governments, and noted the spirit of the citizenry in the consolidated nations. As a patriotic Italian he hated these foreigners who so often in his own lifetime had trespassed upon his native soil and contributed to the turbulence of Italian politics. As a wise and practical politician he was convinced that Italians would have to emulate their examples. Competition among the families of the Italian nobility and among the *condottieri* had so weakened the political structure that it had easily fallen prey to the machinations of foreign monarchs. Machiavelli's efforts were dedicated to the correction of this evil. The only possible solution was Italian unification, which could be achieved solely through the leadership of a prince whose single-minded devotion to this cause would not be mitigated by any considerations of humaneness, morality, religion, or altruism. Machiavelli's ideas become more clear once this essential point is understood.

Machiavelli was born in Florence in 1469. His family claimed a relationship to the nobility but was never a part of it. Little is known about Machiavelli's early years or about his education. He appears to have been widely read in the Italian and Latin classics, but the free, vigorous, and uncomplicated style of his writings seems to denote a lack of formal scholastic training. The Florence that Machiavelli knew as a young man was ruled by the Medici family. In 1494, however, the Medicis were driven from the city, and Florence became a republic. That same year Machiavelli first entered public life as a chancery clerk. His progress, owing, no doubt, to his love of public life, was rapid. In 1498 Machiavelli became second chancellor and secretary of the Council of Ten, a body which had responsibility for war and interior affairs, and he held the post for fourteen years. He was a vigorous and intelligent man. On many occasions his services as a diplomatic observer were required, and this task carried him to the courts of Louis XII of France, Maximilian of Germany, Cesare Borgia in Romagna, and others. Machiavelli had bitterly protested his assignment to the camp of Cesare Borgia, but the longer he watched the maneuvering of that cold-blooded schemer the more impressed he became. Before he returned to Florence, Machiavelli was certain that only Borgia, or someone possessed of his qualities, could supply Italy's need for a leader who would unify and strengthen the country and enable it to throw out the foreign oppressors. Cesare Borgia became the model for *The Prince,* Machiavelli's best-known work.

In 1506 Machiavelli persuaded the Council to adopt his plan for the formation of a citizen army. His studies of Roman history, together with his observations of the practices of the national monarchs of Western Europe, convinced him that the security of the republic was contingent

upon such a move. Machiavelli himself assumed responsibility for trai-
ing the militia. In 1512 the constant state of flux of Italian politics presented an opportunity for the Medici to reestablish their control over
Florence. The citizen soldiers, upon whom Machiavelli had lavished so
much care and in whom he had great confidence, fled ignominiously at the
first contact with the Medici forces. The republic was overthrown; the
the Medici were in command; and Machiavelli was unemployed. He unquestionably preferred the republic; but whatever repugnance he may
have had toward the new tyranny was more than balanced by his desire
for public life, and Machiavelli made overtures to the new masters of
Florence. It was a vain gesture. The Medici exiled him to his country
home and forbade his presence in Florence. Soon afterward Machiavelli,
having been wrongly accused of implication in the Boscoli conspiracy
against the Medici, was imprisoned and tortured. He was eventually
freed and permitted to return to his family and to the bucolic existence
which he thoroughly detested.

Leisure was repugnant to the ambitious Florentine, and at any rate the
vagaries of Italian politics were such that the possibility of reemployment
could hardly be discounted. Machiavelli, who had previously written a
few things in his spare time, set about a literary career in greater earnest.
He began to write his *Discourses on the First Ten Books of Titus Livius*
but abandoned it in favor of *The Prince,* which he completed in 1513
before returning to the *Discourses.* In 1520 he produced his treatise on
The Art of War and his *Life of Castruccio.* In the same year he began a
history of Florence, which he did not live to complete but which was
published in part. Other efforts included a translation of the *Andria,*
three comedies, among which was *Mandragola,* one of the most highly
praised of Italian plays, and *Belfagor,* a short and satirical novel. It is
possible that Machiavelli undertook a few missions for the Medici in his
later life, but they were almost certainly unimportant. His public life
had ended in 1512, although he is known to history for what he accomplished between that date and the time of his death in Florence in
1527.

For the student of political thought, Machiavelli's *The Prince* and the
Discourses are of major importance. The relationship between the two
has been the subject of controversy. *The Prince* is by far the better known.
It is briefer than the *Discourses,* and its unqualified advocacy of an all-
powerful ruler whose actions are to be unrestricted by moral considerations has made its author famous through the ages. Many who have never
read *The Prince* or even heard of Machiavelli understand the meaning
of the adjective "Machiavellian." Some of those who have contributed
analyses of Machiavelli and his political ideas have warned against judging the man entirely by *The Prince* and have proposed that the *Discourses* more truly represents Machiavelli's ideas. Some indeed have

argued that *The Prince* was never intended for publication and general consumption and that it was written by Machiavelli for presentation to the Medici in the hope that such a gesture would cause them to look favorably upon his aspirations for employment.[5] One interesting conjecture is that the ideas contained in *The Prince* constitute such a radical departure from the tenor of Machiavelli's other writings and from his demonstrated enthusiasm for republicanism that the book can only be understood as a brilliant satire, and that Machiavelli in fact believed and advocated precisely the opposite of what he urged in *The Prince*.[6] The whole truth concerning Machiavelli's meaning and intent was probably interred with his bones, but despite conflicting opinions on the matter, certain conclusions seem warranted.

In the first place, both *The Prince* and the *Discourses* resulted from Machiavelli's overriding concern with the development and maintenance of Italian unity. In *The Prince* he deals with this problem from the viewpoint of its solution through the agency of an absolute government; in the *Discourses* Machiavelli uses the Roman republic as a model to demonstrate the superiority of a republic, providing the character of the populace will permit that form of government. The two works, however, are of a piece. That characteristic subordination of means to ends which is the hallmark of "Machiavellianism" is present in each. Chapters might be moved from one work to the other without any noticeable disruption of content. The argument that the treatises are representative of two completely disparate points of view seems to rest upon a rather strained interpretation. In the second place, it would be difficult to prove that *The Prince* was written by Machiavelli solely for the purpose of ingratiating himself with the Medici, and harder still to demonstrate that the work was intended for the eyes of the Medici alone and that Machiavelli meant to keep it from public scrutiny. In Book III, Chapter 42 of the *Discourses,* Machiavelli discussed the question of whether or not a prince should consider himself bound by pledges that had been exacted from him by force. In practice, he says, a prince does not consider himself so bound, and Machiavelli concludes the discussion with the following remark: "Whether such conduct be praiseworthy or not on the part of princes, has been so fully discussed in our treatise of 'The Prince,' that we will not touch upon that question any further here." [7] It is difficult to explain this reference if we assume that Machiavelli intended the *Dis-*

[5] See F. J. C. Hearnshaw (ed.), *The Social and Political Ideas of Some Great Thinkers of the Renaissance and the Reformation,* Barnes & Noble, Inc., 1949, p. 108.

[6] See Garrett Mattingly, "Machiavelli's *Prince:* Political Science or Political Satire?" *American Scholar,* vol. 27, pp. 482–491, Fall, 1958.

[7] Machiavelli, *The Prince* (translated by Luigi Ricci and revised by E. R. P. Vincent), Oxford University Press, Fair Lawn, N.J., 1935. All subsequent quotations from and references to *The Prince* are from this edition.

courses, but not *The Prince,* for publication and general consumption. In the third place, if *The Prince* is pure satire it is conveyed with such subtlety that its implication has escaped the notice of an overwhelming majority of distinguished scholars.

It has been said that Machiavelli developed a new political science, just as Galileo founded a new science of nature.[8] The judgment is valid for several reasons. Machiavelli's approach is purely temporal. Religion and the Church are considered, but only insofar as they relate to the matter of secular unity. Machiavelli rejects all those theological foundations for government that had been part and parcel of medieval thought. He ignores the natural law, and he is unconcerned with the matter of the responsibility of a ruler to his people. Unlike the Scholastics he does not attempt to prove his point by citing authorities. In the *Discourses,* the history of the Roman republic provides him with examples which he employs to support his argument, but this aspect of his work is weak and unconvincing; many other incidents of Roman history might easily be found that would damage Machiavelli's case. His conclusions are based upon empiricism and common sense rather than upon historical evidence. He merely cites the events of history that support conclusions at which he had long since arrived on the basis of his experience. He was a practical and practicing politician, and he wrote like one.

Machiavelli understood the cause of his country's troubles, and he was willing to pay any price to correct them. This being the case, the judgment of history has been on occasion unduly severe. Seventeenth-century writers found him a convenient whipping boy, and the literature of the Elizabethan period abounds with characters (such as Iago in Shakespeare's *Othello*) based upon the author's conception of Machiavelli. The term "Old Nick" itself derives from Machiavelli's first name. On the other hand, Machiavelli has been highly praised. Francis Bacon lauded his empiricism. "We are much beholden to Machiavelli and other writers of that class who openly and unfeignedly declare or describe what men do, and not what they ought to do." [9] Hegel and Fichte, both of whom, like Machiavelli, experienced the anguish and frustration of nationalists without a nation, profoundly admired the Italian's work. Each person may judge for himself whether Machiavelli was a patriot or a fiend, but intelligent appraisal must be based both upon a reading of his pertinent works and a consideration of the circumstances that inspired them.

The student of political philosophy will find that Machiavelli's ideas appear "modern." This is largely because Machiavelli took political theory out of the religious context in which it had been mired for a thousand years. Such independence was possible in Italy, since intellec-

---

[8] Ernst Cassirer, *The Myth of the State,* Doubleday & Company, Inc., Garden City, N.Y., 1955, p. 163.

[9] Quoted in *ibid.,* p. 148.

tuals were freer from religious influence there than elsewhere in Europe. The Church in Italy was too deeply involved in local politics to attempt to control philosophical speculation or even to interest itself greatly in spiritual matters. These and other circumstances which we have already considered contributed to make Machiavelli the first modern political theorist.[10] Unlike most of his predecessors, Machiavelli did not occupy himself with framing plans for an ideal state. He was too realistic for such speculation, and indeed he would have been happy to have a state of any kind. He was also too realistic to be much interested in what men said. He knew that men do not always, or in politics even often, act as they profess to act. He understood the drive for power because he had experienced it himself, and he believed that men were self-seeking. But he was convinced that these planks formed the platform upon which a state may and *must* be built.

Machiavelli's The Prince

The first eleven chapters of *The Prince* deal with Machiavelli's classification of despotisms and their methods of establishment. The matter of hereditary monarchies is very briefly considered, for Machiavelli's main concern is with Italy, and it is apparent to him that no hereditary monarch is going to supply that country's need for a ruler. A monarch who inherits his realm has a much easier career than a newly established ruler. He should avoid a serious breach with tradition and be reasonably intelligent in caring for his problems, but his path is not difficult to follow since he has the well-established on his side.

It is much harder for a new monarch to consolidate his control. Much depends upon the particular conditions in the country and upon the method by which the new ruler came to power. For example, a conquering prince can establish his position more easily when the people of the country he has won share the language and traditions of his own subjects. The conquered are not, in these circumstances, so aware of the change of sovereignty. A despot issuing his commands in a foreign tongue and fundamentally altering the mores of the country would quickly provoke resentment and jeopardize his position. A conqueror is bound to stimulate some antagonism, irrespective of the course he follows, and he must be quick to suppress opposition where it occurs. Malcontents must be eliminated with complete ruthlessness. Halfway measures for this purpose merely increase resentment and do not sufficiently curb the power of the opposition. The new ruler should seek out and cultivate the minority groups that were oppressed under the preceding administration, for they may provide some foundation of support in cases where the majority of the people resent the imposition of a new tyranny. The

[10] Sheldon S. Wolin, *Politics and Vision*, Little, Brown and Company, Boston, 1960, p. 198.

prince must be careful, however, that he does not go too far in this regard, for he can really trust no one, and it is a cardinal rule that the despot must never consciously add to the power of anyone who might later threaten his position.

The conqueror who imposes his rule upon a republic faces unique and painful problems. Those accustomed to tyranny may resent a new tyrant, but since their basic pattern of life does not change significantly they will find it easy to adjust to the new situation. But the people of a republic are resentful of their loss of freedom. They will not easily give it up, and they will fight for its restoration at the slightest provocation. As Machiavelli puts it: "But in republics there is greater life, greater hatred, and more desire for vengeance; they do not and cannot cast aside the memory of their ancient liberty. . . ." [11] The only recourse for the ruler is to destroy completely the customs and institutions of a free people. He must "lay them waste" in order that he may begin again to create a new community not infected with the virus of freedom. "Reform" is a troublesome business. The people are naturally conservative, resisting change of any kind. The successful ruler must persevere, and he must be tough in order to alter any society. The change can be made, however, as the careers of Moses, Cyrus, Theseus, and Romulus amply demonstrate. And when the ruler has attained his goal, he will be honored for having done so.

Some rulers reach their high positions by sheer treachery and brutality. But harsh and perfidious methods do not create a solid foundation upon which to build, and the long-run success of the prince who has come to power in such a manner depends upon the skill which he subsequently demonstrates. For one thing, brutality, though it may be necessary, should be intelligently, not senselessly, applied—used thoroughly but briefly. A continuous reign of terror will defeat the purposes of the ruler.

> Whence it is to be noted, that in taking a state the conqueror must arrange to commit all his cruelties at once, so as not to have to recur to them every day, and so as to be able, by not making fresh changes, to reassure people and win them over by benefiting them. Whoever acts otherwise, either through timidity or bad counsels, is always obliged to stand with knife in hand, and can never depend upon his subjects, because they, owing to continually fresh injuries, are unable to depend upon him. For injuries should be done all together, so that being less tasted, they will give less offence. Benefits should be granted little by little, so that they may be better enjoyed. And above all, a prince must live with his subjects in such a way that no accident of good or evil fortune can deflect him from his course; for necessity arising in adverse times, you are not in time with severity, and the good that you do does not profit, as it is judged to be forced upon you, and you will derive no benefit whatever from it. [12]

[11] *The Prince*, chap. 5.
[12] *Ibid.*, chap. 8.

A prince may be carried to power as a result of class conflict. The nobility may fear the people and support a ruler who, they hope, will suppress the majority. The people, on the other hand, may support a prince who presumably will give them relief from an oppressive nobility. In the first case the wise ruler will seek to obtain the support of the people; in the second he will endeavor to maintain their support. For while a tyrant may not require popular acclaim to achieve power he must know that only the people can provide him with the solid foundation which is a prerequisite of governmental stability. The people are more dependable than the nobility; all they ask is freedom from oppression, while the nobility will compete for power with the prince himself.

Certain principalities are governed by ecclesiastical authorities. Such dominions may be acquired by ability or good fortune, but they require less effort in their maintenance than do other types of governments. In these states a built-in stability rests upon the fact that they are held together by "ancient religious customs." Even though the princes are corrupt and lack capacity, they may enjoy success because their citizens will follow the dictates of a religion that acts as a powerful political cement. It is easily possible to detect a strong note of irony in Machiavelli's statement that "These [ecclesiastical] princes alone have states without defending them, have subjects without governing them, and their states, not being defended, are not taken from them; their subjects not being governed do not resent it, and neither think nor are capable of alienating themselves from them." [13]

In Chapters 12 through 14 of *The Prince,* Machiavelli discusses the use of military power. Regardless of the method employed by a ruler to gain power and irrespective of the type of governmental system established, two things are necessary to the maintenance of the state—good laws and the strength required to enforce them. "The chief foundations of all states, whether new, old, or mixed, are good laws and good arms." [14] What is the basis of an effective military force? Here Machiavelli introduces the theme to which he returns again and again in his writings. The subject interests him to the point of obsession. The armed forces must consist of citizen-soldiers. Despite his disappointing experience with the Florentine militia, Machiavelli places his trust in this kind of military force. Mercenary troops are not to be trusted; they who fight for money alone are without honor; only those who fight to defend their homes, their honor, and the virtue of their women will lay down their lives in battle, and soldiers who will not risk death will fail. Auxiliaries are not much better. The troops of another sovereign give their primary loyalty to him. Even if a prince wins his battle by employing the armed forces of another, he generally ends as the prisoner of the one who has supplied

[13] *Ibid.,* chap. 11.
[14] *Ibid.,* chap. 12.

the soldiers. The foremost duty of a ruler is to create an efficient army. His soldiers must have both practical, that is to say, military, and psychological training. They must, moreover, receive training in time of peace that will prepare them for war when it comes. The ruler who waits for the emergency before he prepares for it will surely lose.

In Chapters 15 through 18 Machiavelli expresses the advice to princes that is largely responsible for his unenviable reputation through the centuries. Rulers are admonished to secure their power by employing whatever tactics may be necessary. They will only waste time and court danger if they try to plan perfect commonwealths and ideal lives. Human nature, dominated by the egoistic drive, provides no realistic basis for such endeavor.

> It now remains to be seen what are the methods and rules for a prince as regards his subjects and friends. And as I know that many have written of this, I fear that my writing about it may be deemed presumptuous, differing as I do, especially in this matter, from the opinions of others. But my intention being to write something of use to those who understand, it appears to me more proper to go to the real truth of the matter than to its imagination; and many have imagined republics and principalities which have never been seen or known to exist in reality; for how we live is so far removed from how we ought to live, that he who abandons what is done for what ought to be done, will rather learn to bring about his own ruin than his preservation. A man who wishes to make a profession of goodness in everything must necessarily come to grief among so many who are not good. Therefore it is necessary for a prince, who wishes to maintain himself, to learn how not to be good, and to use this knowledge and not use it, according to the necessity of the case.[15]

The wise prince will avoid excessive liberality. Generosity, in the final analysis, is less advantageous than parsimony. A ruler who is lavish with his favors must advertise that fact, and the people will soon resent a policy of prodigality, for they will realize that they themselves are paying for it. The ruler who is parsimonious will discover that while the people may at first resent his attitude they will, upon consideration, appreciate the fact that the prince is being cautious with their own property. This economy will be appreciated, and the stability of the state will be strengthened.

The ruler's relationship to his people is much like that of a father to his son. If a father wants unity in the family and obedience to his commands, he must rule firmly. A prince must not be too kind, for kindness will be construed as laxity, and anarchy will be the result. He must constantly bear in mind that his greatest responsibility is to hold the state together. This responsibility may often necessitate measures which are not as cruel in fact as they appear to be, or which are at least preferable to the greater cruelty that attends the disintegration of the body politic.

---

[15] *Ibid.*, chap. 15.

> A prince, therefore, must not mind incurring the charge of cruelty for the purpose of keeping his subjects united and faithful, for, with a very few examples, he will be more merciful than those who, from excess of tenderness, allow disorders to arise, from whence spring bloodshed and rapine; for these as a rule injure the whole community, while the executions carried out by the prince injure only individuals.[16]

The ruler, of course, would prefer to have both the affection and respect of his subjects. Of the two, respect is more important. The same people who pledge their undying devotion to a prince will abandon him as soon as they feel that a danger to themselves may be mitigated by their desertion. If the ruler is feared and respected, however, subjects will not dare to do other than support him. The prince must nonetheless take care that he does not become hated, for hatred would weaken the foundation of support upon which his authority must rest. To avoid this malevolence he must respect the property and the women of his subjects. He may have to execute some of his people, and if he does he should do so with dispatch, "but above all he must abstain from taking the property of others, for men forget more easily the death of their father than the loss of their patrimony." [17]

There are two methods of settling conflict; the one is by law, and the other is by force. Law is the way of men; force is the way of beasts. Unfortunately there is a great deal of the beast in man, and the ruler must understand his nature and act accordingly. When the prince is compelled to act as a beast he should combine the cunning of the fox with the strength of the lion. The ruler must learn to play the game as it will assuredly be played by his opponents.

> A prince being thus obliged to know well how to act as a beast must imitate the fox and the lion, for the lion cannot protect himself from traps, and the fox cannot defend himself from wolves. One must therefore be a fox to recognize traps, and a lion to frighten wolves. Those that wish to be only lions do not understand this. Therefore a prudent ruler ought not to keep faith when by so doing it would be against his interest, and when the reasons which made him bind himself no longer exist. If men were all good, this precept would not be a good one; but as they are bad, and would not observe their faith with you, so you are not bound to keep faith with them.[18]

A cunning prince can always find an acceptable pretext for breaking his promises. Machiavelli states that "an infinite number of modern examples" could be cited to prove this point—scarcely an exaggeration. A faithless prince then is by no means a bad one if his object is maintenance

---

[16] *Ibid.*, chap. 17.

[17] *Ibid.*

[18] *Ibid.*, chap. 18.

of the state. Nevertheless he ought not openly to break his word. He ought to be "a great feigner and dissembler." He need not be too concerned about the people for they are easy to deceive, particularly if the deceiver does not have the appearance of a rogue.

Chapters 19 through 25 deal with Machiavelli's advice to a prince on the consolidation of his power. Machiavelli is prone to repeat himself on many occasions throughout *The Prince* and the *Discourses,* and much of what is said in these chapters merely reproduces portions of the previous section. The prince, for example, is again admonished with regard to the property and wives of his subjects, and he is warned concerning the importance of his armed forces. In addition, the prince must create a favorable image of himself in the minds of his people. He must appear to possess integrity, courage, determination, and strength of will. The citizenry must feel that they may rely upon their ruler in any emergency. Machiavelli stresses often the absolute necessity of popular support in the interest of the stability of the state.

In the event of war between two of his neighbors, the prince must take a stand with one or the other. If possible, he should play the balance-of-power game by supporting the weaker of the two. He should at any rate avoid neutrality, for both countries will hate him if he stands aloof, and he will probably be at the mercy of the victor when the war is over. Lack of resolution in taking sides, as in so many other matters, is the most dangerous course for the prince. What he does he must do quickly. A bold stroke may win the battle.

One of the ruler's chief problems is the selection of his officials and advisers. He must bear in mind that they will advance their own cause rather than his own if they are permitted to do so. The prince, therefore, must be ruthless in purging his official ranks of those who do not serve him well. He should be equally assiduous in rewarding those who do. A prince who is feared must also guard against sycophancy among the members of his official family. Advisers may tell him what they think he wishes to hear rather than what he ought to hear, knowing that the bearer of bad news is rarely popular. A prudent monarch must seek trustworthiness above all other virtues in a council, and he should demonstrate that no person need fear the giving of sound advice, no matter how unpalatable it may be.

A fatalistic (although not a pessimistic) quality is evidenced in the twenty-fifth chapter of *The Prince*. Machiavelli, perhaps in the light of his own experience, knows that the best-laid plans often go awry. Even the wisest and most prudent prince cannot anticipate events controlled by God or by fortune. Yet he warns against the assumption that there is no room for the exercise of free will. "I think it may be true," he says, "that fortune is the ruler of half our actions, but that she allows the other half or thereabouts to be governed by us." [19] Fortune is like a river which occasionally floods its banks and destroys the work of men. Its effects can be controlled if people are wise enough in advance to build the dikes that may contain the flood or the canals that may divert its flow. Some damage may still be done, but it is nothing compared to what might have been. A far-seeing ruler will do what he can to control the effects of fortune in order that a possibly fatal combination of circumstances may be only damaging. Only a prince of the kind Machiavelli favors can erect bulwarks against destruction. The lack of such a person in Italy has left that country unprotected against the floods which in such countries as France, England, and Spain have been adequately controlled.

The twenty-sixth and final chapter of *The Prince* consists of an appeal to the Medici to set about the task of unifying Italy and driving out the foreign invaders. Critics differ in their opinions regarding the place which this section occupies in the general pattern of the book, some contending that it is an integral part of the whole and some that it is an appendage designed by Machiavelli to flatter the ruling family of Florence. The motive is unimportant. The final chapter serves the purpose of clarifying the goal which Machiavelli has had in mind throughout *The Prince*. It is a passionate appeal for national unity by a patriot. It is the end which justifies, for Machiavelli at least, the means to which the balance of *The Prince* is devoted. *The Prince* may certainly be read as a handbook of advice to tyrants and without reference to the situation that prompted its writing. To do so, however, would be less than fair to Machiavelli.

The Discourses

Machiavelli's *Discourses on the First Ten Books of Titus Livius* is a longer work than *The Prince*. It is also more discursive. Rambling from one subject to another and back again, it lacks the impact of the shorter book. It represents, however, another and integral phase of Machiavelli's general theory, and its content is closely related to that of *The Prince*. The latter, as we have seen, deals mainly with the problem of establishing a state where one did not previously exist and creating some kind of basis for its survival. In the *Discourses,* Machiavelli reasserts the validity of his contention that this phase of the task must be undertaken by a single individual. A ruthless prince, combining the qualities of the lion and the fox, must establish a state and reform its institutions. To accomplish this purpose, any and every action is justifiable.

> It is well that, when the act accuses him, the result should excuse him; and when the result is good, as in the case of Romulus [who killed his brother], it will always absolve him from blame. For he is to be reprehended who

[19] *Ibid.,* chap. 25.

commits violence for the purpose of destroying, and not he who employs it for beneficent purposes.[20]

Still, the long-term survival of the state depends upon the support of the many; for this support a republic is required, for "although one man alone should organize a government, yet it will not endure long if the administration of it remains on the shoulders of a single individual; it is well, then, to confide this to the charge of many...."[21] The point is demonstrable, to Machiavelli's satisfaction, by reference to the history of the Roman republic. From that history we can learn the lessons necessary to instruct us in how best to solve current problems. Human nature is now as it was then, and the circumstances are either the same or so similar that the past provides a reliable guide to the present.

In the great work of establishing and maintaining a state, a ruler must understand human nature. The people constitute the raw material with which the architect of government must work. A realistic attitude is vital here, for a misunderstanding will result in collapse of the community. Men, Machiavelli observes, are selfish and evil by nature. They act properly "only upon compulsion."

> Nature has created men so that they desire everything, but are unable to attain it; desire being thus always greater than the faculty of acquiring, discontent with what they have and dissatisfaction with themselves result from it. This causes the changes in their fortunes; for as some men desire to have more, whilst others fear to lose what they have, enmities and war are the consequences; and this brings about the ruin of one province and the elevation of another.[22]

Men's selfishness does not, however, make unity impossible. A powerful ruler may achieve unity through coercion, as is amply demonstrated in France and Spain where human nature is certainly no better than it is in Italy. But a stable society cannot long rest upon a corrupt populace. Reform is necessary, and it is possible, without altering human nature, to create the kind of institutions that will develop public-spiritedness and make a republic both possible and necessary. The people may be selfish and greedy, but they also demand security in their lives and possessions, and they can learn, through the ministrations of a wise prince, that security can be enjoyed only when the laws are good, when they are obeyed, and when that support which is a prerequisite of unity is given to the ruler. We must understand that when Machiavelli uses the term "republic," he does not have in mind a political community

[20] Machiavelli, *Discourses on the First Ten Books of Titus Livius* (translated by C. E. Detmold), in *The Historical, Political, and Diplomatic Writings of Niccolò Machiavelli*, J. R. Osgood and Company, Boston, 1882, I, 9. Subsequent quotations from and references to the *Discourses* are from this translation.

[21] *Ibid.*

[22] *Ibid.*, I, 37.

in which the people play an important role in government. A republic to Machiavelli is a state in which a ruler is voluntarily supported by the people. Moreover the "liberty" which Machiavelli advocates for the people of a republic should be understood first, as security, and second, as freedom from oppression, rather than as any system of rights which the individual possesses within the control of the state.

When corruption has been eliminated and the republic is firmly established, it will be found that the people can be trusted to do the right thing and to deliver wise judgments. The ability of the public to make decisions is limited. They are not wise enough to formulate high-level policy, but on those issues which they are capable of understanding they will be superior to princes.

> I believe also that we may conclude . . . that no wise man should ever disregard the popular judgment upon particular matters, such as the distribution of honors and dignities; for in these things the people never deceive themselves, or, if they do, it is much less frequently than a small body would do, who had been especially charged with such distributions.[23]

The people are wiser, too, in those things which conduce to the preservation of the state, and "if princes show themselves superior in the making of laws, and in the forming of civil institutions and new statutes and ordinances, the people are superior in maintaining those institutions, laws, and ordinances, which certainly places them on a par with those who established them." [24] Thus Machiavelli takes his stand for a republic, of a kind. He next explores the causes of disunity in republics and recommends the appropriate countermeasures. In this discussion Machiavelli is as thoroughly "Machiavellian" as he is in *The Prince.*

A major source of disunity is the class of idle rich, the nobility, who parasitically feed upon the work of others and thrive upon the political chaos which they do so much to perpetuate. Only a powerful monarch can control these "gentlemen." Their very existence makes a republic impossible, for the basis of a republic is equality, just as the foundation of a monarchy is inequality.

> If any one should wish to establish a republic in a country where there are many gentlemen, he will not succeed until he has destroyed them all; and whoever desires to establish a kingdom or principality where liberty and equality prevail, will equally fail, unless he withdraws from that general equality a number of the boldest and most ambitious spirits, and makes gentlemen of them. . . . Let republics, then, be established where equality exists, and, on the contrary principalities where great inequality prevails; otherwise the government will lack proper proportions and have but little durability.[25]

[23] *Ibid.,* I, 47.
[24] *Ibid.,* I, 58.
[25] *Ibid.,* I, 55.

Another disruptive force is, or can be, religion. The right kind of religion can be of great value in creating stability in the state. Religion provides a sanction without which oaths may be useless, and it may increase loyalty and unity. Machiavelli's judgment of religion is strictly utilitarian. He is unconcerned with "truth" and with the salvation of souls. A religion is "good" if it supports the state and contributes to state ends. Christianity in its original form, Machiavelli holds, might well have been a good religion from this viewpoint, but it no longer has this virtue. It is a tragic paradox, Machiavelli asserts, that Christians who are nearest the seat of Church government (he refers, of course, to the Italians) are the least religious of all. Machiavelli's resentment of Church and Pope is extreme. "We Italians," he writes, "then owe to the Church of Rome and to her priests our having become irreligious and bad; but we owe her a still greater debt, and one that will be the cause of our ruin, namely that the Church has kept and still keeps our country divided." [26] A country can be united and happy only if it is ruled by a single government, and the Church prevents this unity.

> The Church, then, not having been powerful enough to be able to master all Italy, nor having permitted any other power to do so, has been the cause why Italy has never been able to unite under one head, but has always remained under a number of princes and lords, which occasioned her so many dissensions and so much weakness that she became a prey not only to the powerful barbarians, but of whoever chose to assail her.[27]

One great advantage enjoyed by the citizens of the Roman republic was the superiority of their religion. The pagans attached great importance to honor and material possessions, and they fought to secure them. Christianity teaches the superiority of spiritual values and esteems humility. It exalts the contemplative man rather than the warrior. "These principles," Machiavelli laments, "seem to me to have made men feeble, and caused them to become an easy prey to evil-minded men, who can control them more securely, seeing that the great body of men, for the sake of gaining Paradise, are more disposed to endure injuries than to avenge them." [28]

A stable republic requires an effective military establishment. Machiavelli returns again to the theme of the citizen-soldier and his superiority to the mercenary which he had considered at length in *The Prince*. A great deal of the *Discourses* is devoted to the discussion of a variety of military matters, most of which need not concern us here. There are, however, some points of a politico-military nature which may briefly be cited. Machiavelli states that the prince with a good army should fight his battles on his own territory. A republic is no more immune to war

[20] *Ibid.*, I, 12.
[27] *Ibid.*
[28] *Ibid.*, II, 2.

than is a kingdom; it must be at least as well prepared. A prudent ruler will never rely upon the internal divisions in the enemy's country as a factor in his own favor; an attack upon a divided country will quickly unite its people. Threats and insults hurled at a prospective foe serve no useful purpose; they merely strengthen his resolution. A victorious ruler should not grind down his enemy more than is necessary; the worse conquered people are treated, the more difficult they are to control. When a country inhabited by a strong and free people is conquered, however, the people must either be annihilated or appeased; halfway measures are dangerous, for the conquered will not forget either their humiliation or their lost state of freedom. A good tactician will place his own troops in a position which compels them to fight but which leaves the enemy a choice of combat or retreat. Military forces must be always under a single commander; division of responsibility here can be catastrophic. Deceit may be wrong in all things except in the conduct of war; here it is "laudable and honorable." This brief summary will suffice to indicate the general nature of Machiavelli's thought on military matters. It should also be enough to explain the acknowledged enthusiasm of Napoleon I for the works of the brilliant Florentine.

Conclusions

Machiavelli was the apostle of power politics. In this he differed not at all from many of his contemporaries. He was not the first to advocate the use of force to attain national objectives; he was a good student of Cesare Borgia, Ferdinand of Spain, Henry VII of England, or any one of a number of other ambitious rulers and would-be rulers of the period. His reputation is less attributable to his uniqueness than it is to the fact that he spelled out for his own and for subsequent generations the tactics which he and they thought necessary to the fulfillment of their goal.

That goal was the achievement of national unity. To this end Machiavelli was willing to subordinate every means. *Raison d'état* was always enough for Machiavelli. There is no substantial evidence in either *The Prince* or the *Discourses* that he was concerned with the welfare of the people. If it is argued that Machiavelli sought national unity for the people's sake, the counterargument must be that he did not say so, and we are entitled to draw conclusions only on the basis of what he said. A superficial examination of his writings, especially of the *Discourses,* might lead one to assume that Machiavelli really was a compassionate man. After all, did he not admonish princes in a republic to safeguard the property of their subjects, to protect their women, to increase their wealth, and to rule gently and justly wherever possible? Did he not state that a republic was better than a principality and that the people of a republic, having some wisdom, should be given a voice in those matters which they were capable of understanding? It is true that Machiavelli said all this and more. But his goal is never the good, or the free, or the democratic life for citizens. The goal is unity. Machiavelli did not seek unity because he believed it would bring these advantages; he advocated the good things of democracy because, under certain conditions, they would contribute to unity. Such a view may be deprecated, but it is fair to say that twentieth-century citizens of the nation-state can at least understand it. Many would sympathize.

There is considerable wisdom in Machiavelli's writings. He compels us, as Bacon commented, to see things as they are rather than as we would like them to be. And we must not construe this lesson solely in terms of Machiavelli's subordination of means to ends. For example, he showed great astuteness in his warning to rulers and republics that changing circumstances will necessitate institutional reform.

> The ruin of states is caused in like manner, as we have fully shown above, because they do not modify their institutions to suit the changes of the times. And such changes are more difficult and tardy in republics; for necessarily circumstances will occur that will unsettle the whole state, and when the change of proceeding of one man will not suffice for the occasion.[29]

Another piece of advice that demonstrates Machiavelli's perspicacity and his pertinency for the modern political observer is his warning to officials not to be overly credulous when taking the testimony of exiles for use in the formulation of policy or strategy.

> We see, then, how vain the faith and promises of men are who are exiles from their own country. As to their faith, we have to bear in mind that, whenever they can return to their own country by other means than your assistance, they will abandon you and look to their vain hopes and promises, such is their extreme desire to return to their homes that they naturally believe many things that are not true, and add many others on purpose; so that, with what they really believe and what they say they believe, they will fill you with hopes to that degree that if you attempt to act upon them you will incur a fruitless expense, or engage in an undertaking that will involve you in ruin.[30]

Many intelligence officers and higher officials of the present day have probably discovered adequate reasons, on the basis of their own experience, to acknowledge the wisdom of this observation. In short, it is not only despots, incumbent or merely aspiring, who may profit from a reading of Machiavelli. He possessed a shrewd understanding of politics, of the causes of weakness and disunity in the state, and of the measures that might be taken to correct them. Machiavelli probably believed that in *The Prince* and the *Discourses* he was writing more than a tract for

[29] *Ibid.*, III, 9.
[30] *Ibid.*, II, 31.

the times, as indeed he was. Much of what he said would lack validity today simply because conditions have so drastically changed. His prognosis was by no means always correct even for his own period. As Professor Sabine has pointed out, Machiavelli overestimated the changes that are wrought by statesmen, no matter how skilled or ruthless they may be. Moreover, although modern political thought is marked by the secularism that was so typical of Machiavelli, the Protestant Reformation began only a few years following the publication of *The Prince.* More than two centuries were to elapse before political philosophers would again consider their subject with the degree of detachment, where religious truth was concerned, displayed by Machiavelli.[31]

The Prince and the *Discourses* are still modern. They still raise the problems with which men in a nationalistic world must contend. It is likely to be a long time before the majority of the people of the world will genuinely disagree with Machiavelli when he says:

> For where the very safety of the country depends upon the resolution to be taken, no considerations of justice or injustice, humanity or cruelty, nor of glory or of shame, should be allowed to prevail. But putting all other considerations aside, the only question should be, What course will save the life and liberty of the country?[32]

SELECTED BIBLIOGRAPHY

Allen, J. W.: *A History of Political Thought in the Sixteenth Century* (reprinted with revised bibliographical notes), Methuen & Co., Ltd., London, 1957, part 4, chap. 2.

Butterfield, H.: *The Statecraft of Machiavelli,* The Macmillan Company, New York, 1956.

Cassirer, Ernst: *The Myth of the State,* Doubleday & Company, Inc., Garden City, N.Y., 1955, chaps. 10, 11.

Cook, Thomas I.: *History of Political Philosophy from Plato to Burke,* Prentice-Hall, Inc., Englewood Cliffs, N.J., 1926, chap. 10.

Dunning, William A.: *A History of Political Theories, Ancient and Medieval,* The Macmillan Company, New York, 1905, chap. 11.

Hacker, Andrew: *Political Theory: Philosophy, Ideology, Science,* The Macmillan Company, New York, 1961, chap. 5.

Hearnshaw, F. J. C. (ed.): *The Social and Political Ideas of Some Great Thinkers of the Renaissance and the Reformation,* Barnes & Noble, Inc., New York, 1949, chap. 4.

Machiavelli: *The Prince* and the *Discourses* (with an introduction by Max Lerner), Modern Library, Inc., New York, 1950, introduction.

Mattingly, Garrett: "Machiavelli's *Prince:* Political Science or Political Satire?" *American Scholar,* vol. 27, pp. 482–491, Fall, 1958.

[31] Sabine, *op. cit.,* p. 352.
[32] *Discourses,* III, 41.

Pirenne, Henri: *A History of Europe,* Anchor Books, Doubleday & Company, Inc., Garden City, N.Y., 1958, vol. II, bk. III, chap. 1.

The Ruler: A Modern Translation of Il Principe (translated by Peter Rodd; introduction by A. Robert Caponigri), Gateway Editions, Henry Regnery Company, Chicago, 1955, introduction.

Sabine, George H.: *A History of Political Theory,* 3d ed., Holt, Rinehart and Winston, Inc., New York, 1961, chap. 17.

Strauss, Leo: *Thoughts on Machiavelli,* The Free Press of Glencoe, New York, 1958.

Wolin, Sheldon S.: *Politics and Vision,* Little, Brown and Company, Boston, 1960, chap. 7.

ten

LUTHER AND CALVIN

The Reformation

Political writing in the sixteenth century was strongly influenced by the ideas and events that accompanied the Protestant Reformation. The Reformation did not spring full-blown from the doctrines of Martin Luther. The stage had been set long before by Marsilio of Padua, William of Occam, and their contemporaries as well as by the conciliar movement. The Reformation was in part a continuation of conciliarism with its demand for a curbing of papal authority and for a system of representation in Church government reflective of nationalist sentiment. In the thought of Luther and Calvin are many ideas that had been made familiar by earlier reformers. The Reformation was also a culmination of the failing effort of the Church to contain the dissent developed during the long history of sectarianism. In 1517 that dissent broke through and permanently altered the structure of the Church.

The Reformation differed from the preceding reform movements partly because its leaders insisted upon doctrinal as well as organizational reconstruction. Luther was no more appalled by the corruption in the papal court, no more antagonistic to the draining of ecclesiastical revenues to Rome, no more opposed to Church interference in secular affairs than were many of the conciliarists. Indeed, much of the doctrine enunciated by both Luther and Calvin is clearly traceable to Marsilio and William. The pre-Reformation agitators, dedicated as they were and convinced of the rightness of their position, were reformers, not revolutionaries, and they did not advocate secession and the consequent disruption of Christian unity as a solution to the Church's problems. Luther and Calvin, on the contrary, were revolutionaries, willing to wreck the monolithic structure of the Roman Church in the interest of the salvation of their followers.

The failure of conciliarism accounts in part for the success of the Reformation. For in that controversy the Pope won, but the Church lost. The immorality of the papal court infected Church officialdom. In turn, the Church lost the respect of its members. Religion became a habit, a mere formality, rather than a way of life. The more exalted the position in the hierarchy, the less likely were its members to inspire faith and confidence. The true believer visiting Rome toward the end of the fifteenth century was likely to suffer serious disillusionment when he saw that the Pope and his cardinals "consorted publicly with their mistresses, acknowledged their bastards, and enriched them at the cost of the Church." [1] It is understandable that Luther and Calvin both challenged the whole concept of Church hierarchy, repudiated Scholasticism as the corrupt product of that hierarchy, and urged a return to those first principles which might be ascertained from a sincere study of the Scriptures.

Luther: The Man and His Work

All the forces, religious and political, necessary for a reaction against the abuses of the Pope and the Church hierarchy were present in the opening years of the sixteenth century. Only a catalyst was necessary to set them in motion, and that was provided in the form of a young German priest with a passionate and unrelenting zeal for reform. His name was Martin Luther. He was born in Eisleben in 1483, the son of free peasants, who maintained a devout and highly disciplined home. Hans Luther, Martin's father, was a miner, who ultimately achieved a modest degree of prosperity as the lessee of several smelting furnaces. But the Luther family was very poor during Martin's early youth, and after attending the Latin school in his home town, young Martin was compelled to support himself at Magdeburg, where he went to continue his education. From Magdeburg Luther went to Eisenach, where he attracted the attention of a prosperous family and was enabled to study by the generosity of their support. In 1501 Luther entered the University of Erfurt, at the time the most famous of German educational institutions. He was an excellent student, and Erfurt offered a stimulating intellectual climate. It was here that Luther became a follower of those

[1] Henri Pirenne, *A History of Europe,* Anchor Books, Doubleday & Company, Inc., Garden City, N.Y., 1958, vol. II, p. 272.

instructors who taught the ideas of William of Occam. Luther remained at Erfurt for four years. In 1505 his father, who had had some success in the smelting industry and had been appointed to the town council, persuaded Martin to begin the study of law. His flirtation with the law, however, was a brief one. After two months Luther, to the consternation of his parents, left law school and entered a monastery. He had received a call, and the Erfurt Augustinians, whose ranks he joined, tested it fully. For two years Luther submitted to the drudgery and the rigors of training preparatory to becoming a priest. He was ordained in 1507 and assigned to continue the theological studies for which he had demonstrated great aptitude at Erfurt. In 1508 he was appointed lecturer on Aristotle's *Ethics* at the University of Wittenberg, a position he held until 1511. In 1512 he took his degree as doctor of philosophy and became a professor of philosophy at Wittenberg.

In 1510 Luther paid a brief visit to Rome. As a young and devout priest and pilgrim he was deeply shaken by the experience. He had, of course, been aware of the scandals of the Roman court, and as a student of the ideas of William of Occam he was surely cognizant of the many reforms of the papal office which had long been urged. The visual evidence, however, was more impressive than any academic discussion. Luther returned to Wittenberg disillusioned but firmly resolved to do something to achieve the necessary reform. It was not until the winter of 1512–1513 that Luther decided upon a course of action. Until then he apparently had gone no further than to review the proposals for reform that had been made by others and to strengthen his own resolve to live a pure life in line with the strictures of the monastic order to which he belonged. But he became convinced that the most rigid observance of the rules, including living a life of the strictest asceticism, was failing to give him a satisfactory inner assurance that he was in that rapport with God which would ensure his own salvation. It appeared doubtful, too, that any intercession with God by his superiors could be efficacious in view of the widespread corruption of the clerical hierarchy. This doubt was the nub of the matter; and it was his disillusionment that led Luther to take issue with the Roman Church on a matter of doctrine rather than merely to recommend a change of organization in the form of a more representative system.

Still Luther did not make a sudden break with the Church. Even four years later, in 1517, when he posted his famous "Ninety-five Theses" attacking the abuse of indulgences, he believed that reform from within was possible. This event, however, set off a controversy, during the course of which Luther moved still further from the orthodoxy demanded by Rome. In 1519 he repudiated the divine right of the Pope and asserted the supremacy of the Scriptures. It was the final step. The following year the Pope issued a bull condemning Luther's position and giving him sixty days in which to recant. Luther's response was a public burning of the edict. The Pope ordered the emperor, Charles V, to execute a decree of excommunication. At the Diet of Worms, called by the emperor in 1521 to investigate the matter, Luther refused to retract his views and was subsequently condemned. But he had by this time gathered considerable support, both from the people and from the nobility. He was saved when he was taken into the protective custody of his benefactor, Frederick the Wise, elector of Saxony, at his castle in Wartburg. In these friendly surroundings Luther continued to assail his antagonists. The emperor's Edict of Worms formally placed Luther and his followers under the ban of the Empire and forbade the publication of their works. The move was ineffective. Luther had become enormously popular and influential with the German people. More important, the emperor could not control the princes of Germany. As long as Luther was protected by them he had no fear for his life.

Among Luther's denunciations of Roman Church practices was an attack upon the principle of clerical continence. Marriage, he said in his *Vindication of Married Life*, is a natural and divine institution. He found it so himself after having married Catherine von Bora, a former nun who had renounced her vows. Catherine bore five children, two daughters and three sons, and lived happily with her husband during the remaining twenty years of his life. It was an eventful twenty years. Luther's prestige with the German people was at its height in the early 1520s. No previous reformer had had so wide an audience. Luther had consciously set about building his public support. He was an able speaker, and he spoke often and to many. His writings reached an even larger audience; he wrote in the vernacular and made use of that great new force, the printing press.

But the road of reform and revolution is not smooth, and Luther encountered difficulties. Late in 1524 the German peasants, stimulated by Luther's evangelism and attaching an interpretation to his religious doctrine that Luther had never intended, rose in rebellion against the princes. Luther, himself of peasant stock and personally acquainted with the abject misery of peasant life, could sympathize. He admonished the princes for their mismanagement, but he could not countenance rebellion, and he urged the princes to put it down, bloodily where necessary. His stand undoubtedly cost Luther popular support. Other difficulties arose among the members of his movement over issues of doctrinal interpretation. Luther sorrowfully viewed the splintering of his organization and sought secular intervention in his own behalf. The princes helped, but only for a price; that price was an increasing secular control over the church. Luther devoted the last ten years of his life to his work of vindicating and consolidating the Reformation. He died in 1546 at Eisleben, the place of his birth.

Luther's Religious Ideas

Our primary interest is in Luther's political, rather than his religious, thought; but since his ideas on civil reform stem from his conviction about the central concern of religion, we must consider Luther's position on spiritual doctrine if we are to have a clear idea of his political theory. Certainly Luther regarded theology as infinitely more important than politics, and probably never thought of himself as a political philosopher. He was not uninterested in political affairs. Whether he liked it or not he was compelled to think politically because what he taught and what he did had political implications from which he could not escape. One of Luther's main objections to the Roman Church was that it had become too political. It had become irretrievably enmeshed in secular affairs and had attempted to justify its involvement and extend its temporal influence through the elaboration of its organization, the enactment of ordinances, and the proliferation of the mass of treatises and essays produced by the Scholastics. All this increased influence, Luther contended, was achieved at the expense of the spiritual aspects of Christianity. What men needed was a return to a pure, simple, and more primitive religion, one that they could all comprehend and adhere to without having to be subjected to the tortuous doctrinal interpretations of an ecclesiastical hierarchy.[2]

The central idea of Luther's theology is that faith, rather than works, leads to salvation. By this Luther meant that the true Christian has a personal, intimate, and direct relationship with God that enables him to understand God's word through a contemplation of the Scriptures. Luther followed the conciliarists in asserting that the true church is a community of all believers. All men are equal in the eyes of God and in their ability to understand God's word. The clergy as intermediaries between God and the individual are not only unnecessary but they also constitute a positive hindrance to the development of the proper spiritual relationship. Between man and God the clergy have constructed an impenetrable barrier of organization, misconstrued doctrine, and canon law. All this must be eliminated before the individual may once again experience that inner feeling of faith which is necessary to his salvation. It is true that all men are not religious and many never will be, but the Church, far from helping them, prevents a genuine religious awakening. The Church has forgotten its mission. It is concerned with worldly things and has neglected the spiritual. The Church should not be rich, for material wealth precludes a concentration on spiritual affairs. The sale of indulgences exemplifies the preoccupation of the Church with wealth that has led to its corruption and degradation and the consequent loss of faith by its members.

[2] Sheldon S. Wolin, *Politics and Vision*, Little, Brown and Company, Boston, 1960, pp. 143, 145.

Luther's first major assault on the Church was directed toward this specific abuse. Designed originally as part of the penitential system which included contrition and confession, indulgences involved a money payment to the clergy for the purpose of mitigating, in part, the discipline imposed upon a member as punishment for sin. In course of time the sale of indulgences became a lucrative source of income for the clergy, and especially for the Pope. The practice was bitterly resented by the rank-and-file members, who regarded it as a travesty of God's justice and also as a social abuse since its practical effect was to permit only the rich to purchase exemption from punishment for sins. In the Ninety-five Theses Luther stated that papal authority to remit penalties applied only to those which the Pope himself had imposed or those resulting from a transgression against the canon law. Only God, he said, could remit the *guilt* of sin, and this was a matter of concern only to God and the sinner. Luther, who had not yet broken with the Church, did not deny that the Pope and clergy had a role in the process, but he insisted that their function was only declaratory.

For Luther the true church was a community of believers whose only superiors were God and Christ. The function of the ministry was to explain and administer the word of God, but members of the clergy ranked no higher with God than did lay members. Their office was a worldly one. They were, if they were true believers (and this did not necessarily follow), merely members of the Christian community and could be removed by the community. The democratic implications of this doctrine are apparent. Luther rejected the Platonism of the Catholic view that only a select few are capable of understanding the truth and that it is their responsibility to impose it on others. He also repudiated the medieval assumption that any society required a head to give direction to the members and that the hierarchical principle, in which the lower must be subjected to the higher, is indispensable.[3] Luther would have preferred to take his stand on this ground, but annoying questions compelled him to adjust his defenses. As a consequence he was led into the political involvement that plagued and distracted him the rest of his life.

Luther's Political Thought

Luther acknowledged that many persons were not true Christians. They bore the name Christian, attended services, and proclaimed themselves members of the faith, but they were in fact nonbelievers. It was their presence that created the problems for the community; if all were true believers there would be no need for authority of any kind. Genuine Christians would obey God's law as outlined in the Scriptures and would not even need a Church organization. But the presence of nonbelievers made such a utopia impossible.

[3] *Ibid.*, pp. 153–155.

Mere baptism does not make a Christian. Among the baptized are some who would take advantage of the name of Christian to destroy their fellows. Thus the community cannot be ruled by the Gospel alone. Secular government based upon force is a necessity. Those who argue that such government is not required because Christian communities need only God's law and the fear of the consequences of breaking it are not to be trusted.

Luther distinguished between the invisible church, which consists of the whole body of believers, and the visible church, which comprises all members of the community, including nonbelievers. After his break with the Catholic Church, Luther conceded that because there are non-believers secular authority is indispensable. The clergy cannot properly exercise any kind of coercive authority. That power rests, therefore, entirely in the hands of the secular government, which has sole responsibility for keeping the peace. The princes were not reluctant to assume the burden. The withdrawal of ecclesiastical authority removed their only real competitor. They could enrich themselves through the confiscation of ecclesiastical property, and they no longer felt hedged about by the restraining influences of the canon law. As a result, their power expanded greatly.

It was Luther's antagonism to clerical involvement in secular matters, rather than any personal admiration for temporal government, that led him to assign great power to the secular authorities. But he was not at a loss to provide justification for the step once it had been taken. Like St. Augustine, Luther held that government was necessitated by the Fall and by man's consequent sinfulness. For Luther, secular government was not a human device growing out of man's reason and resting upon the consent of the governed; rather it was an instrument provided by God in his wisdom and goodness for the purpose of maintaining the peace and order that men require if they are to live according to God's word in this world and find salvation in the next. Christians are equal in the eyes of God, but they are not equal in their capacity to govern. Democracy, therefore, is impossible, and power must be concentrated in the hands of the prince. Each person has the right to interpret the word of God according to the dictates of his own conscience. In his *Concerning Secular Authority: To What Extent It Should Be Obeyed,* Luther insisted that men are responsible for their own faith. No one can believe for anyone else, just as no one can be rewarded or punished for the acts of another. The beliefs of men are solely a matter of conscience. They cannot be forced. It follows that secular governments should assume no responsibility in those things that deal with belief. What men believe neither strengthens nor lessens the secular power. But this faith must be an inner experience and produce no outward and unpeaceful manifestations. When Luther first propounded this doctrine of the individuality and freedom of religious experience he failed to anticipate the diversity of opinion that would result from it. He was shocked by the socialism and anarchism of the Anabaptists as he was by the Peasant Revolt of 1524. Yet in both instances the sins of the radicals stemmed from their insistence upon acting in accordance with what their consciences told them was the word of God.

Anarchy, Luther said in his *An Open Letter to the Christian Nobility*, was the work of the Devil. Order must be maintained at all costs. The function of the prince is to rule; that of the subjects is to obey. Subjects have no right actively to resist the ruler; they have the duty of passive obedience to him. To think in any other terms is to invite disaster. The clergy are subject in precisely the same manner as are other members of the community, and their position is a worldly one which entitles them to no special considerations. Why, Luther asks, should the canon law be so concerned with lives, liberties, and properties of the clergy and ignore so completely those aspects of the lives of the laity? The latter are also Christians and "as good Christians" as the clergy. The life of the cleric is worth no more than that of the layman, providing the latter obeys the laws of God. The same protections ought to be offered to both and the same punishments assessed. All men are alike in the sight of God.

Since the visible church is a temporal organization and since the ruler controls all secular affairs, the prince has jurisdiction over the church just as he does over the state. He may not coerce belief, and he may not command anything against God. If he should attempt either form of coercion, his subjects must refuse to obey him. They must, however, not rebel against him; their only recourse is to a policy of passive disobedience. Nor may the prince define faith, this being a matter of individual determination; but the interference of an evil ruler in religious belief may again be met only with the passive disobedience of his subjects. Luther suggests that in meeting such transgressions the people should pray for help from God, who alone can punish an evil ruler.

Luther was not a systematic thinker, but he was an enthusiastic advocate of his views. His passion for whatever view he was expounding at the time often led him to overstate his case; consequently he was sometimes inconsistent and even self-contradictory. He was a mystic, and his deepest convictions stemmed from his mysticism, but he was compelled, frequently, by practical necessity to act contrary to his convictions.[4] Although Luther's nature led him to accord respect to civil authority, he had not intended to go so far in assigning it power. He had clearly stated on many occasions his belief that it was the secular office, and not the man,

[4] J. W. Allen, *A History of Political Thought in the Sixteenth Century* (reprinted with revised bibliographical notes), Methuen & Co., Ltd., London, 1957, p. 15.

to which loyalty and respect were due. In his *Concerning Secular Author-ity*, Luther admitted that there had been few wise or pious princes in the history of the world. They are generally "fools" or "knaves," and one can expect little from them, especially in matters of religion. Yet God needs them to act as his "jailers and hangmen," as his instruments for the pun-ishment of the wicked, and as the means by which he keeps the peace on earth. These are not the words of a sycophant, but Luther had himself built the trap into which he fell. He had denied temporal power to any church organization; the only circumstance, therefore, which could lead him to deny its use to the prince would be the prevalence of a state of perfect peace. This was obviously impossible to achieve, and any mani-festation of disorder would have to be controlled by secular power. Lu-ther's religious doctrine stating the right of individuals freely to interpret God's word had loosed the forces that made for disorder, and Luther had to call upon the princes to control them. He sincerely wanted man's re-lationship to God to be personal and private and removed from the juris-diction of any earthly authority, clerical or temporal. But he had been frightened by the radicalism of the Anabaptists and by the resort to force of the peasants in 1524. It seemed to Luther in 1525 that his movement was endangered. From this point Luther moved further in the direction of the support of secular power. In 1523 he had insisted that "heresy can never be kept off by force." Now he called upon the state to suppress un-orthodoxy.[5] And what was unorthodox? Luther denied that the state could define the true faith. It was beyond its competence to determine what was either heretical or orthodox. But when Luther gave the state the power to *enforce* orthodoxy in order to maintain peace, for all prac-tical purposes he gave it the right to *determine* what was orthodox.[6] The power that enforces also defines, and in the end the state not only defined faith, but also compelled membership in the visible church. Luther's intent had not been to establish a state church, but a state church was established and on the basis of a logical development of Luther's own ideas.

Reformation: The Calvinist Phase

Luther ignited the flame of the Reformation, but he was unable to keep it burning. Circumstances conspired to limit the spread of the movement. Luther was so closely allied with the German princes and so dependent upon them that the German environment stamped its own impression upon Lutheranism. As a consequence, the religion became nationalistic rather than truly international. It was established in the Scandinavian

[5] William Montgomery McGovern, *From Luther to Hitler: The History of Fascist-Nazi Political Philosophy*, Houghton Mifflin Company, Boston, 1941, p. 33.

[6] George H. Sabine, *A History of Political Theory*, 3d ed., Holt, Rinehart and Winston, Inc., New York, 1961, p. 360.

countries and throughout much of Germany by kingly decree rather than through voluntary conversion. Religious conviction was less responsible for the expansion of Lutheranism than was the mandate of secular rulers. Conversion followed, but slowly. The Peace of Augsburg of 1555 had acknowledged the right of princes to embrace Protestantism and to determine the official religion of their countries. It had also required that subjects profess the faith of their rulers.

Calvinism was plagued with few of these difficulties, and it enjoyed some real advantages. In Geneva, a republic, Calvin was protected from the political currents which had forced Luther constantly to adjust his views, and could afford to be more consistent than Luther in his development of a body of doctrine. His legalistic training and the logic of his presentation also conduced to that end. Luther's ideas, and particularly his political principles, were considerably less systematic because of his attempts to adapt theory to circumstances and to reconcile his rational conclusions with the more mystical and emotional nature of his thought. Luther's theology, too, was quietist, while Calvin's was activist. Luther stressed faith and the personal and individual relationship of man to God as an inner experience; Calvin asserted that the only way a person could demonstrate that he was one of God's elect was to work briskly in God's vineyard. Calvin could not rely upon princes forcefully to expand his congregation. He and his followers had to work for conversions. Theirs was a more difficult task than Luther's, but it produced more valuable results in the form of an enthusiastic following. Calvin also received the support of a vigorous bourgeoisie which was intrigued by a theology that did not condemn the lending of money at interest. Luther's physiocratic predilections led him to attack the sharp practices of the new money economy; yet as it turned out, the rising capitalist class proved to be a more valuable ally than the princes. Calvin's position was more open to competition than was Luther's. The latter had taken his enemies by surprise and had been able to consolidate his position before the ponderous machinery of the Roman Church could react effectively. But by Calvin's time it had not only reacted but was on the attack in an attempt to prevent further depredations and to recover lost ground.[7] That Calvinism, in the face of the forces pitted against it, was able to organize a dynamic and rapidly growing movement, resulted in no small part from the enormous ability and vitality of its founder.

Calvin: The Man and His Work

John Calvin, the second son of Gerard Calvin and Jeanne le Franc, was born at Noyon, in Picardy, on July 10, 1509. His father was a lawyer and a notary-apostolic of the ecclesiastical court at Noyon. The family intended that John should become a priest, and his earliest studies were

---

[7] Pirenne, *op. cit.*, vol. II, pp. 294–305.

designed to support that ambition. When he was eighteen, however, his father decided that the talents displayed by his son were better suited to a legal than to a theological career. John read law at the University of Orleans and at the University of Bourges. At the same time Calvin studied the classics, and the combination of legal and classical education led him seriously to question the validity of medieval Scholastic writings. In later years Calvin spoke of his "sudden conversion," which he attributed to divine intervention, as having taken place in about 1532 or 1533. There is no doubt that a considerable change in his thinking occurred at this time, but the real beginnings of the development of his reformist temperament evidently coincided with his studies at Bourges and Orleans. This was a period when Luther's revolt was making itself felt in France, and although no open rebellion broke out in that country, there was a great deal of sympathy for the German reformer's cause. Calvin's associates during this time were mainly representative of the humanist school, and the young Calvin was undoubtedly impressed by them.

During the years at Orleans and Bourges Calvin formulated the fundamentals of his doctrine. He had been moving in the direction of Protestantism for several years, perhaps without being fully aware of the fact. But by 1533 the process was complete, and he became more outspoken in his attack upon the conservative theology. In that same year he was compelled to flee Orleans to avoid persecution. The charges against him were dropped, however, and Calvin went to Angoulême as the guest of Louis du Tillet. It was in du Tillet's library that Calvin began the writing of his famous *Institutes of the Christian Religion*. In 1534 he formally broke with the Roman Church. He was arrested and imprisoned, and although he was soon released, he decided that it would be prudent to leave France. In the company of his friend du Tillet, Calvin went to Basel, where he was warmly welcomed. In Basel he completed the first draft of the *Institutes,* which was published in Latin. Calvin's translation of the work into French was published in 1540. The early editions were brief, consisting of only six chapters. Intended merely as a statement of the faith of Protestants, they contained the essentials of Calvin's theology from which he did not depart during the course of his life.

In 1536 Calvin went to Geneva at the request of Guillaume Farel, a reformer who sought Calvin's aid in the establishment of a Protestant organization in that city. Calvin was twenty-eight at the time, but he was already well known and influential. He found Farel's proposition attractive and agreed to lend assistance to the work. For three years Calvin labored strenuously in the cause. Indeed he was too assiduous for many; his stern and uncompromising attitude provoked rebellion, and Calvin was driven out. He accepted a position as professor of theology at Strasbourg, but his sojourn there was short. When the Geneva movement began to collapse, Calvin was strongly urged to return, and in 1541, after an absence of two years, he reentered Geneva. Not all opposition had disappeared, but what remained offered no practical problem. By 1555 he had consolidated his position to the point where he was, for all practical purposes, the ruler of Geneva. During the remaining nine years of his life he wasted no time. It was his purpose in Geneva to build a theocratic regime in which all secular and clerical authority was devoted to the service and glorification of God. Geneva became the model for a new system of life. From the city reformers went forth to preach the new doctrine with a zeal that produced a large number of followers throughout Western Europe.

Calvin was interested in every phase of Genevan life; no aspect of it was exempt from his passion for regulation. Law enforcement, trade, manufacturing, and education were all of vital concern to him. He founded a university, stimulated trade to make the city wealthy, and introduced and enforced a sanitation code which made Geneva the envy of Europe. Every moment he could spare from his administrative duties Calvin devoted to the writing of a great number of exegetical works, including an elaboration of the *Institutes*. It was a heavy strain on a man who had never been strong. When he realized that his strength was failing, he made his plans carefully. His affairs were in good order when he died quietly on May 27, 1564.

The Theological Foundations of Calvin's Political Thought

The central idea of Calvin's theology is the sovereignty of God. The things of this world have importance only insofar as they relate to God's power and to man's salvation. The state, therefore, has significance only in the sense that it conduces to these higher ends. Knowing God should be man's main purpose, and only a few will ever succeed in fulfilling that purpose. God is the fount of all that is good. Man, since Adam's transgression, is evil and corrupt, born in sin, and afflicted with the curse placed upon Adam. His redemption has been made possible through Christ's sacrifice, but his salvation is dependent upon his becoming united with Christ through the Holy Spirit, who operates in the faithful to make them partakers of Christ's death and resurrection. The faithful may repent, have their sins forgiven, and thus be accepted by God.

Thus far there is nothing particularly new about Calvin's doctrine. It is the deterministic aspect of his thought that sets it apart from the traditional theory. For Calvin, life is a drama staged by God. God has written the script for his people, who are actors playing a predetermined role, but who do not know in advance what that role is. Only God knows. We cannot, like God, understand the true meaning of the drama in which we participate. But if we are saved, we shall make this great discovery after death. God has predestined some for salvation and others for eternal damnation. Nothing one can do will alter the course of this destiny; works have nothing to do with the matter. No injustice is involved in damnation, for God's decision, incomprehensible though it may be, is always just.

> Predestination we call the eternal decree of God, by which he has determined in himself, what he would have to become of every individual of mankind. For they are not all created with a similar destiny; but eternal life is fore-ordained for some, and eternal damnation for others. Every man, therefore, being created for one or the other of these ends, we say, he is predestinated either to life or to death.... In conformity, therefore, to the clear doctrine of the Scripture, we assert, that by an eternal and immutable counsel, God has once for all determined, both whom he would admit to salvation, and whom he would condemn to destruction. We affirm that this counsel, as far as concerns the elect, is founded on his gratuitous mercy, totally irrespective of human merit; but that to those whom he devotes to condemnation, the gate of life is closed by a just and irreprehensible, but incomprehensible, judgment.[8]

The fact that man's fate is predetermined does not relieve him, however, from the obligation to conform to God's moral law, which is based upon the Decalogue. Sin must be extirpated and the community purified. This is the function of the elect. But who are the elect? Those whom God has favored will know of their state of blessedness through the inward call they will receive, through their compulsion toward service to God, and through the position they attain in this world. If a person enjoys worldly success through proper actions it is likely that God has numbered him among the elect.

Like Luther, Calvin distinguishes between the visible and the invisible church. For him, as for Augustine, the true church is a community of true believers, separated in time and place but a true community and church all the same. The visible church, or the worldly organization of the church, includes both believers and nonbelievers. All must be members, and the elect must exercise a rigid discipline over themselves and over the nonbelievers in their midst. The rules of behavior for every aspect of life on earth are prescribed in the Scriptures. Carrying out these rules meant, in practice, observance of those ordinances prescribed by Calvin through his interpretations, which were based mainly on the Old Testament. To assist in the great work, God has provided the church on earth, its laws and its sacraments. All true believers are equal before

---

[8] From John Calvin, *The Institutes of the Christian Religion,* 7th Amer. ed. (translated by John Allen), The Presbyterian Board of Christian Education, Philadelphia, 1936, II, iii, 21, pp. 176, 181. Used by permission. Subsequent quotations from and references to Calvin's *Institutes* are from this edition.

God, but some are endowed with special talents that enable them to act as pastors and teachers, and their duty is to expound the laws and administer the sacraments to the end that God's glory will be enhanced and his will be done.

Calvin's Political Theory

Luther had at first thought that it was only necessary for the faithful to escape from the control of the top-heavy and corrupt administration of the Roman Church in order for men to live properly and according to God's will in a free and voluntary association of true believers in Christ. His doctrine led him to deny to church organization every coercive form of disciplinary authority. When he discovered that the "visible church," with its nonbelievers mixing with the faithful, required direction, he was obliged to grant power to the secular government. In turn, that government proceeded to dominate both church organization and doctrine. Calvin was too practical-minded ever to believe in the possibility of an undirected society. He saw that sinful men living in association with one another could never avoid the difficulties which necessitated political authority. Yet he knew that authority could be abused. The dilemma could be resolved only if the secular and religious organizations were linked together in a corporate community that would provide all the necessary control.[9] Where Calvin's views found organizational expression, Calvinism typically developed into a theocracy, in which a formal separation of church and state was maintained but in which secular affairs were dominated by the clergy.

If God's will is to be served, Calvin taught, there must be order and unity in human society. Both secular and religious discipline must be wielded. Both are devoted to the same end, but each acts in a different way. Both are divinely provided.

> But as we have just suggested that this kind of government is distinct from that spiritual and internal reign of Christ, so it ought to be known that they are in no respect at variance with each other. For that spiritual reign, even now upon earth, commences within us some preludes of the heavenly kingdom, and in this mortal and transitory life affords us some prelibations of immortal and incorruptible blessedness; but this civil government is designed, as long as we live in this world, to cherish and support the external worship of God, to preserve the pure doctrine of religion, to defend the constitution of the Church, to regulate our lives in a manner requisite for the society of men, to form our manners to civil justice, to promote our concord with each other, and to establish general peace and tranquility; all which I confess to be superfluous, if the kingdom of God, as it now exists in us, extinguishes the present life. But if it is the will of God, that while we are aspiring towards our true country, we be pilgrims on the

[9] Wolin, *op. cit.*, p. 168.

earth, and if such aids are necessary to our pilgrimage, they who take them from man deprive him of his human nature.[10]

Temporal government is not a necessary evil. If this world were peopled only by the elect, government would not be needed. But since men are born in sin they must be restrained, and God has given us government as an instrument with which to restrain them. Political authority is thus exalted authority. It preserves life, but more important, it enforces the rules necessary to maintain the holiness of life.

Since earthly government is a divine instrument, civil rulers occupy a divine office. They are to be obeyed even as God is obeyed. "The first duty of subjects toward their magistrates is to entertain the most honourable sentiments of their function, which they know to be a jurisdiction delegated to them from God, and on that account to esteem and reverence them as God's ministers and vicegerents." [11] Calvin is not much concerned with the matter of governmental forms. He prefers a plural magistracy but does not deny that there have been some admirable monarchs, particularly in ancient Israel. At any rate, God provides the kind of government which he deems best, and it is not the privilege of man to question what God has done. Whatever form exists must be respected. And whatever kind of ruler holds office must be obeyed. All power comes from God, and the power must never be resisted. If the people are oppressed, they may make their representations to the ruler, but they must still obey. Bad rulers are entitled to obedience just as are good rulers. God does nothing without a purpose; thus it is clear that evil rulers are placed over us by God as punishment for our sins.

> But, if we direct our attention to the word of God, it will carry us much further; even to submit to the government, not only of those princes who discharge their duty to us with becoming integrity and fidelity, but of all who possess the sovereignty, even though they perform none of the duties of their function. For, though the Lord testifies that the magistrate is an eminent gift of his liberality to preserve the safety of men, and prescribes to magistrates themselves the extent of their duty, yet he at the same time declares, that whatever be their characters, they have their government only from him; that those who govern for the public good are true specimens and mirrors of his beneficence; and those who rule in an unjust and tyrannical manner are raised up by him to punish the iniquity of the people; that all equally possess that sacred majesty with which he has invested legitimate authority.[12]

Calvin, like Luther, provides an exception to the principle of passive obedience. If a ruler commands anything against God, he is not to be obeyed.

[10] *Institutes*, II, iv, 20, p. 772.
[11] *Ibid.*, p. 795.
[12] *Ibid.*, p. 798.

The Lord, therefore, is the King of kings; who, when he has opened his sacred mouth, is to be heard alone, above all, for all, and before all; in the next place, we are subject to those men who preside over us; but no other wise than in him. If they command anything against him, it ought not to have the least attention; nor, in this case, ought we to pay any regard to all that dignity attached to magistrates; to which no injury is done when it is subjected to the unrivalled and supreme power of God.[13]

Yet even a ruler's command against God does not constitute a justification for active revolt. We may passively refuse to obey an order that contravenes God's will, but we cannot take up arms against the prince. Some constitutions provide that lesser magistrates may resist an unjust ruler. Such a provision, Calvin said, may be made in France, where all the estates are entitled to wield authority; but the people have no such right. Calvin was no apostle of the right of revolution.

Yet if God has seen fit to give his people a form of government in which they have the privilege of selecting their rulers, they should treasure their good fortune. For there is no question but that such a government is to be preferred to a tyrannous one.

When ... God gave such a privilege [of electing their rulers] to the Jews, he ratified thereby his adoption and gave proof that he had chosen them for his inheritance, and that he desired that their condition should be better and more excellent than that of their neighbors, where there were kings and princes but no liberty.... If we have the liberty to choose judges and magistrates, since this is an excellent gift let it be preserved and let us use it in good conscience.... If we argue about human governments we can say that to be in a free state is much better than to be under a prince. It is much more endurable to have rulers who are chosen and elected ... and who acknowledge themselves subject to the laws, than to have a prince who gives utterance without reason. Let those to whom God has given liberty and freedom (*franchise*) use it ... as a singular benefit and a treasure that cannot be prized enough.[14]

The pattern of government, as it developed under Calvin in Geneva, reveals the theocratic nature of the Calvinist society. There were, formally at least, two separate governing bodies. The Supreme Civic Council was the leading secular agency; the Consistory was the ruling body for the church. In theory the functions of each were separate, but in practice the agencies cooperated closely. In Calvin's theory there should be no antagonism between the temporal and religious authorities. Their goal is the same—to rule society according to the word of God. They are both

[13] *Ibid.*, p. 805.

[14] Quoted in *John Calvin on God and Political Duty* (edited with an introduction by John T. McNeill), copyright 1950, 1956 by the Liberal Arts Press, Inc., and reprinted by permission of the Liberal Arts Press Division of the Bobbs-Merrill Company, Inc., pp. xxiii–xxiv.

devoted to the maintenance of order; both are provided by God for this purpose, and each must support the other. Officials of the church in Geneva were also public officials. Prospective ministers were examined and "recommended" by a body of pastors; the "recommendations" were invariably accepted by the Supreme Civic Council, which formally made the appointment after presentation of the candidates to the congregation for ratification. Ministers were required to take an oath of allegiance to the government of Geneva. The Consistory included ministers and a somewhat larger body of lay elders who were also nominally appointed by the Civic Council, but whose appointments were in fact dominated by the ministers. Since the government was in all cases to function in accordance with the word of God, and since the ministers were presumed to be best qualified to determine what that word was, the Consistory, or better, perhaps, the ministerial minority of the Consistory, was the true governing body of Geneva. It dominated the Civic Council. The latter enjoyed a theoretical right to appoint and remove ministers, but in fact it never refused a nomination of the pastors and it never removed a member of the ministry unless prompted to do so by the ministerial body.[15] In Calvin's belief, no phase of human life was too unimportant to be of interest to God. In the social life of the community the practical consequence of this principle was a detailed regulation of, and interference in, the personal affairs of the people by the Consistory. That body exercised an enormous and pervasive authority. It had the right of entry into private households. It enforced church attendance, controlled education, regulated business transactions, punished the taking of excessive interest, decided marriage suits, and excommunicated. Anyone so unfortunate as to be expelled from the church was also deprived of his citizenship and of any secular office he might hold, and was banished.

There was little democracy in Calvin's political theory or in the Genevan state. Calvinism, as we shall see, later provided a stimulus to democratic development, but Calvin did not so intend it. Much has been made of the principle of participation by the congregation as "proof" of the democracy inherent in the Calvinist theology. Eventually this development had genuine significance, but in Calvin's time congregational participation was limited. The congregation in Geneva had the authority to ratify, or refuse to ratify, candidates for the Consistory who had been nominated by the pastors and accepted by the Civic Council. But the congregation did not nominate, and we have surely seen in the twentieth century too many examples of political systems based upon the Calvinist assumption, that is, that the people have only the ability to approve or disapprove of a single slate of candidates presented to them, to account such a procedure democratic. Calvin, with his view of man as a sinful and corrupt creature, could not go further. His was the doctrine of the

[15] Allen, *op. cit.*, p. 64.

elect. There was *a truth* which was expounded by the few and which governed all men, even those who were consigned to hell, irrespective of their compliance with the truth. The machinery of government was designed to enforce conformity. Crimes against the church were punished by the state, which permitted no religious unorthodoxy. Heresy, idolatry, blasphemy, as defined by the church, were to be eradicated by the secular arm of government. It was a grim and authoritarian society.

Calvinist Economics [16]

Calvinism broke with the venerable Christian tradition which frowned upon profit making and advocated economic endeavor for subsistence only. Calvinist teachings were directed mainly to the commercial classes, and Calvinist leaders, operating in an urban environment, took for granted the necessity of a business economy. Calvin stated that he could not see "why the income from business should not be larger than that from landowning." [17] Calvin and his followers were not laissez-faire economists, and they did not equate wealth with virtue. Their attitude, however, departed considerably from that of Catholics and Lutherans alike.

> Early Calvinism . . . has its own rule, and a rigorous rule, for the conduct of economic affairs. But it no longer suspects the whole world of economic motives as alien to the life of the spirit, or distrusts the capitalist as one who has necessarily grown rich on the misfortunes of his neighbor, or regards poverty as in itself meritorious, and it is perhaps the first systematic body of religious teaching which can be said to recognize and applaud the economic virtues. Its enemy is not the accumulation of riches, but their misuse for purposes of self-indulgence or ostentation. Its ideal is a society which seeks wealth with the sober gravity of men who are conscious at once of disciplining their own characters by patient labor, and of devoting themselves to a service acceptable to God.[18]

Calvin's strictures on usury typify the early Calvinist economic point of view. Moneylending at interest, he held, is not an immoral and irreligious act, providing that it is hedged about by restrictions that protect all the parties involved. First, the rate of interest must not exceed a fair maximum, and it is the right and duty of the state to regulate rates. Second, no interest should be charged on loans to the poor. Third, the borrower must benefit equally with the lender. Fourth, the lender must not demand excessive security. Such stipulations were scarcely designed to gladden the hearts of financiers.

In Calvinism the goal of man is the glorification of God rather than the salvation of his own soul, since his salvation has been predetermined

---

[16] The best single source on this subject is still R. H. Tawney, *Religion and the Rise of Capitalism*, Harcourt, Brace & World, Inc., New York, 1926.

[17] Quoted in *ibid.*, p. 105.

[18] *Ibid.*

by God, and nothing can be done to alter the divine plan. This does not mean, however, that one should sit idly by and accept his fate. He who works for the glorification of God is one who has been saved; his works are proof of his salvation. Calvinism taught that religious reform and the regeneration of mankind could be achieved by exercising those virtues—thrift, sobriety, hard work—upon the basis of which economic success could be achieved. That these were precisely the virtues required for the accumulation of the surplus funds that made capitalism possible was incidental but important. The doctrine came, too, at a most opportune time. The Western world was preparing for an era of great prosperity, but it lacked a philosophy to sanction an emphasis on material values. Calvinism filled that need. Members of the bourgeoisie could now exercise their talents much more freely. Although Calvin had not intended it, his doctrine provided justification for the subsequent revolutions of the middle class. As Professor Tawney has correctly said, in a sense Calvin was to the middle class of the sixteenth century what Marx was to the nineteenth-century proletariat.[19]

But if Calvinism proposed a more favorable attitude toward a commercial economy and toward the holding of wealth, it did not in any sense establish or propose a free-enterprise society. The powerful Geneva Consistory, acting on the principle that no human activity was immune from church regulation, ordered the functioning of the economy. Surely the word of God had to prevail here as elsewhere. Who else, then, was competent to interpret and apply that word? Their duty, as they conceived it, was to establish an economic order worthy of God's kingdom. Its excellence implied many things besides wealth; and while the ministry endorsed profit taking and a comfortable material life, it did not do so without qualification. For the Calvinist, every economic enterprise was vested with a public interest and was subject to regulation. The poor were instructed to work diligently and to live morally; the rich were warned that they had an obligation to the poor that could be discharged only by conformance with the regulations, designed to benefit the public, imposed upon them. The prosperous members of the middle class approved wholeheartedly of the injunctions directed to the poor; they were less than enthusiastic about the regulations imposed upon themselves. In the decade or two following Calvin's death, nothing contributed more persistently to the disturbance of the domestic tranquility than the arguments which arose over this matter between the clergy, who complained bitterly of exploitation, and the magistrates, who were members of or represented the bourgeoisie. Although Calvinism contributed indirectly to the building of the foundation upon which capitalism ultimately rested, that later development was not in accordance with the strictly regulated society planned by Calvin and his ministerial entourage.

[19] *Ibid.*, p. 122.

Conclusions

There were elements of democracy in Luther's religious doctrine. The equality of all men before God, their right to interpret the Bible in accordance with the dictates of their own consciences and to establish their own personal relationship with him—all these indicated that Luther's inclination to religious liberality was stronger than Calvin's. In the end this liberal spirit was to have an influence upon political thought. If men are equal before God, they may logically contend that they should be so regarded in the eyes of men. If they may interpret the Scriptures according to their consciences and establish their own relationship to God, the cause of individual freedom in the state may also be served. It could properly be asked whether man should not enjoy a political status and civil rights equal to those he was acknowledged to have in his religion. These were to be future developments however; Luther himself did not argue for political freedom. He opposed the absolutism of the Roman Church, and the principles of equality and freedom he enunciated were applicable only to that body and had, for him, no secular connotation. If the arguments he employed against a despotic church were later used by others against a tyrannical state, Luther himself never assumed that the cases were comparable. The immediate result of Luther's doctrine was the increase of secular power. Princes who had formerly shared power with the church organization suddenly found themselves in possession of all power within the state. Then, believing that secular unity required religious conformity, they used their power to deny those rights of the individual which had constituted the heart of Luther's theology. Luther went along, justifying this perversion of his movement by claiming (and perhaps he believed it) that secular rulers could only *enforce* the truth; they could not *define* it. What he failed to understand is that where there are no competitors in the field, truth is whatever the dictator says it is.

In Geneva Calvin avoided the road that Luther had taken in Germany. His ability to do so depended more upon the favorable circumstances he enjoyed than upon anything else, although probably Calvin was a more practical man than Luther and a better organizer and administrator. Calvin did not make the mistake of allowing the church organization so to deteriorate that it could offer no resistance to secular authority. In effect Calvin restated the two-swords theory; two directing forces were needed, each of which should perform a different function. Each had the same essential purpose, that is, to create a society dedicated to the glorification of God, and a close cooperation between church and state should exist to achieve that great end. But Calvin followed the lead of the medieval Popes in placing, for all practical purposes, both swords in the hands of the spiritual leaders. The ministers of the Genevan Consistory were no less authoritarian than the German princes to whom Luther had surrendered. From his own point of view, Calvin was more successful than Luther, but whether the Genevan community was to be preferred to the Germany of Luther is a matter of opinion. From the democratic standpoint, neither was desirable.

A central point of Calvin's political theory is the principle of passive obedience. Men are always to obey the temporal authority placed over them, except when a command is given in direct contravention of God's will. Even in this situation the people can only refuse, again passively, to obey. They have no right to resist that authority which has, according to the Scriptures, been provided by God himself. But an inner contradiction in Calvin's thought led to a divergency of political attitude, once Calvinism was established outside of Geneva. That contradiction stemmed from the fact that the church was given the power to define doctrine and that the exercise of this power often brought it into direct conflict with the state, which was granted supreme secular authority and was not to be resisted. In Geneva the virtual amalgamation of church and state precluded any serious conflict. The same was true in the Puritan settlement at Massachusetts Bay. Wherever Calvinists were in control, church and state ruled cooperatively and with an iron hand in a theocratic society.

The contradiction was most likely to be evident in a society in which Calvinists were under the jurisdiction of a non-Calvinist ruler. Scotland in the sixteenth century typified that situation. John Knox, leader of the Scottish Calvinists, led the opposition to Mary, Queen of Scots, who was a Catholic. If Knox had followed Calvin's theology, he could only have admonished his people not to obey the queen when she ordered something against what the Calvinists conceived to be God's word. Knox went much further and in fact substantially altered Calvin's political theory. He stated that in cases where a ruler contravenes the true religion he should be resisted. Knox called upon the nobility and the magistrates to resist the queen, and he urged the people to follow their lead, thus repudiating Calvin's doctrine of passive obedience. Knox hinted that the authority of the ruler derives from the people and that he is responsible to them, but the idea was somewhat obscurely stated, and Knox can hardly be placed in the democratic camp on the basis of his ambiguous reference. A clearer statement of the principle was expressed in the course of the religious wars in France, where Calvinists again opposed a Catholic monarchy.[20] The point to note here is that Calvinism was capable of being construed in support of either passive obedience or the right to resist. The construction depended largely upon the circumstances in which Calvinists found themselves at any particular time.

[20] Sabine, *op. cit.*, p. 370.

SELECTED BIBLIOGRAPHY

Allen, J. W.: *A History of Political Thought in the Sixteenth Century* (reprinted with revised bibliographical notes), Methuen & Co., Ltd., London, 1957, part 1, chaps. 2–4.

Calvin, John: *The Institutes of the Christian Religion*, 7th Amer. ed., (translated by John Allen), Presbyterian Board of Christian Education, Philadelphia, 1936, vol. II, bk. iii, chap. 21; bk. iv, chap. 20.

Coker, Francis William: *Readings in Political Philosophy*, rev. ed., The Macmillan Company, New York, 1938, chap. 12.

Cook, Thomas I.: *History of Political Philosophy from Plato to Burke*, Prentice-Hall, Inc., Englewood Cliffs, N.J., 1936, chaps. 11, 12.

Hearnshaw, F. J. C. (ed.): *The Social and Political Ideas of Some Great Thinkers of the Renaissance and the Reformation*, Barnes & Noble, Inc., New York, 1949, chaps. 7, 8.

MacKinnon, James: *Calvin and the Reformation*, David McKay Company, Inc., New York, 1936.

McGovern, William Montgomery: *From Luther to Hitler: The History of Fascist-Nazi Philosophy*, Houghton Mifflin Company, Boston, 1941, chap. 2.

McNeill, John T. (ed.): *John Calvin on God and Political Duty*, Bobbs-Merrill Company, Inc., Indianapolis, 1950.

Pirenne, Henri: *A History of Europe*, Anchor Books, Doubleday & Company, Inc., Garden City, N.Y., 1958, vol. II, bk. 3, chap. 2.

Sabine, George H.: *A History of Political Theory*, 3d ed., Holt, Rinehart and Winston, Inc., New York, 1961, chap. 18.

Tawney, R. H.: *Religion and the Rise of Capitalism: A Historical Study*, Harcourt, Brace & World, Inc., New York, 1926, chap. 2.

Wolin, Sheldon S.: *Politics and Vision*, Little, Brown and Company, Boston, 1960, chaps. 5, 6.

eleven

MONARCHOMACHS, DIVINE RIGHT, AND THE THEORY OF JEAN BODIN

The Monarchomachs

The Calvinist creed had been widely disseminated before the death of its founder, and the movement increased in momentum following that event. Its missionaries were zealous and courageous and as intolerant as their Catholic enemies, who, now awakened to the fact that Calvinism was not merely another minor heresy to be put down by proclamation, drew the line of battle. There was no chance for a compromise. Even if the religious issue had been the only one in question, it is doubtful, given the long-standing bitterness against the abuses of the Roman Church, that a reconciliation could have been effected. The whole issue, however, was much more complicated. Social, economic, and political problems were inextricably bound up with the theological argument. An accommodation in all these areas would be required for a final settlement in any one of them. The struggle took a number of different forms. In Germany the princes fought against one another. In the Netherlands the Dutch revolted against the Catholic Spanish tyranny and made their country a haven for the persecuted Protestants of Western Europe. In Spain and in England the national monarchies were powerful enough to prevent rebellion. In Scotland and in France there were civil wars. It is to France that we must turn to investigate the development of political theory in the latter part of the sixteenth century.

In the sixteenth century France was under the most powerful monarchy in Europe, but the monarchical structure was not as solid as French kings wanted it to be. A powerful and contentious nobility was resentful of the royal power and sought to undermine it. The interests, customs, and traditions of the southern and western provinces set them apart from the nation and led them to oppose the establishment of a unifying parliamentary body. This was an era of national consolidation. Everywhere the king was a moving force in the process. In England, however, he shared the centralizing power with the Parliament. The question in England was not whether there should be a nation but rather by whom, king or Parliament, it should be directed. In France the contest was between the monarch, who stood for centralization, and the forces of provincial rulers and the nobility, who represented feudal particularism. The struggle would have been bitter in any case. The religious ingredient made civil war a certainty.

The French Calvinists, generally called Huguenots, although a minority in France were aggressive and militant, and they numbered among their members some of the most powerful figures of the feudal nobility. Their enemy, however, was more powerful than they. The Catholics constituted a majority of the people; more important, the monarchy was opposed to Protestantism. In France there was no contest between king and Pope which might split the alliance of monarchy and Catholic Church. Since the Concordat of Bologna of 1516, the king had appointed the higher clergy and largely controlled papal taxation. The conditions which had driven secular rulers into the arms of Protestantism in Germany were absent in France. The monarchy threw its weight against the Huguenots; they refused to give ground; and the stage was set for the religious wars that were to scourge the French nation for more than thirty years. Probably no wars in history are more cruel than those fought in God's name, and France suffered their ravages in the last third of the sixteenth century. Atrocities were common on both sides, the most spectacular being the St. Bartholomew's Day Massacre of 1572, which began in Paris on August 24, spread to other cities, and did not end until September 17. Estimates as to the number of Protestants killed range from ten thousand to fifty thousand. Even this, however, did not settle the issue. In 1589 the Huguenot, Henry of Navarre, succeeded to the throne as Henry IV, following the assassination of Henry III. He was unable, however, to consolidate his reign until he renounced his faith and became a Catholic. Henry IV extended a measure of freedom to the Protestants in the Edict of Nantes of 1598, in which for the first time official recognition was given to the principle that two religions could coexist within the same nation. The edict was a compromise and ideologically unsatisfactory to both sides, but it was supported by a great many Frenchmen who were heartily sick of civil war.

The Massacre of St. Bartholomew's Day broke the back of Huguenot physical resistance, but the controversy raged on in the form of a war of words between the protagonists on both sides. There were two conflicting points of view. On the one hand, the defenders of royal absolutism ultimately took their stand for the divine-right theory and insisted upon the duty of passive obedience of subjects to their king, who, they held, was responsible only to God for his actions. Opposing them were the so-called monarchomachs, who repudiated the theory of divine right, declared that the authority of the king derives from the people to whom he is responsible, and maintained that a monarch may, in certain situations, be resisted and even removed by his subjects.

In France the antiroyalist theory was highly developed by the Huguenots. As we saw in the preceding chapter, such an attitude was contrary to the doctrine of passive obedience taught by John Calvin. But the revolt of French Protestants against a Catholic monarch illustrates the point made previously—that Calvinists were likely to obey passively only those secular governments which they controlled. At any rate, the controversial literature of this period was not identifiable on the basis of religious affiliation. The premises of the arguments changed with the situation, and there were Catholics among those who developed theories attacking the idea of royal absolutism. Many in France who were opposed to the Huguenots might nevertheless have been willing to extend religious toleration to them. That they did not do so was attributable less to the theological views of Calvinists than to their political posture.

Allied as the Huguenots were with the nobility, they were placed in the unenviable position of attempting to stem the tide of national centralization. The king in France was the prime mover of this centripetal force, and its strength made him irresistible. On his side was the middle class, which was rapidly increasing in size and wealth. The bourgeoisie had, in the sixteenth century, witnessed many abuses of the royal power and they were often apprehensive of monarchy, but they had no real alternative as yet. The time would come when they would defeat the king and supplant royal absolutism with republics or constitutional monarchies; they were not yet ready, however, to test monarchical strength, and to turn to the hated nobility was unthinkable. Such were the circumstances in which the royalist and antiroyalist theories were developed. The latter preceded the former since monarchs felt no need for a philosophy to justify their position until that position was assailed. Thus a logical approach requires a consideration first of the ideas of the monarchomachs.

A detailed description of the theories of all or even of the most important of those who resisted royal power is unnecessary here. The arguments generally fell into two categories, historical and philosophical, and they were often combined by the same writer. It is important to note that even though the theories advanced by the monarchomachs have a strongly democratic sound, they were not intended to be democratic by their advocates. The Huguenot monarchomachs were either nobles themselves or spokesmen for the nobility. But they wrote in the name of the people, believing that the nobility and the institutions which represented that class spoke for the people. A later generation could easily adapt the arguments to a much more democratic use. The student who has even a modest knowledge of the philosophical justifications of the English revolutions of the seventeenth century and the American and French revolutions of the eighteenth century will find much that is familiar in the Huguenot and the Jesuit attacks upon royal tyranny.

The historical argument was ably and typically presented by Francis Hotman (1524–1590), a Huguenot writer whose *Franco-Gallia*, published in 1573, contained the essence of this point of view. Hotman was not a radical. His contention was that royal absolutism, far from being justified by history or precedent, was, instead, a dangerous innovation. Hotman said that the king does not receive his authority from God; he is elected by the people. The people are historically sovereign, and the fact that they have let the power slip away from them or have been deprived of it by unscrupulous monarchs does not justify the ambitions of royalty. The sovereign people have the right to remove a tyrant, and they have created specific institutions for that purpose. These institutions are the King's Council and the Estates-General.[1] The latter is particularly important, for it represents the whole people and historically shares power with and places limits upon the king. Hotman's view that royal absolutism was of recent development was accurate, but the constitutional history of France did not substantiate his claim that the Estates-General had traditionally shared authority with the monarchy. Moreover, in the light of circumstances it was impracticable to assume that it could do so at the time. Hotman was proposing, essentially, a return to the medieval past rather than a step forward, and his arguments, although provocative, were unrealistic.[2]

The philosophical argument found expression in the writings of Theodore Beza (1519–1605), the teacher, friend, disciple, and biographer of Calvin. Beza was impelled by the persecution of the French Calvinists to reject Calvin's doctrine of passive obedience and to support resistance against a monarch who commanded anything contrary to God's law. The people, Beza contended, are endowed with natural rights which are protected by an implicit but unbreakable contract between ruler and

---

[1] The national, as distinguished from provincial, assembly. It is roughly the equivalent of the English Parliament.

[2] George H. Sabine, *A History of Political Theory*, 3d ed., Holt, Rinehart and Winston, Inc., New York, 1961, p. 376.

subjects. The people are obliged to obey a monarch who rules justly and does not contravene God's law, but if the king is guilty of a breach of contract, the people have a right to resist him, since God's law, as interpreted by the conscience of the people, is superior to the secular power of the ruler. Beza's revolutionary fervor, however, stops short of advocating a popular uprising. The conscience and judgment of the common people, he said, are not sufficiently reliable to provide a basis for insurrection. The magistrates must make such decisions. The people then may follow the magistrates, but they must not take this dangerous step on their own volition.[3]

By far the most renowned, at the time and subsequently, of the anti-royalist pamphlets was the great *Vindiciae contra Tyrannos (A Defense of Liberty against Tyrants)*. The work appeared in 1579 under the pseudonym Stephen Junius Brutus. The authorship is uncertain; scholarly opinion generally credits Hubert Languet or Philippe Duplessis-Mornay, although both Beza and Hotman have had their supporters. The author went more deeply into the philosophical problems underlying the anti-royalist argument than did any of his compatriots. The *Vindiciae* is mainly concerned with the rights of a subject to resist a ruler over a matter of religious differences, but the arguments proposed apply to wholly secular situations, and in this lies the lasting significance of the work.

Four questions are considered in the *Vindiciae*. They are: (1) whether subjects are required to obey a prince who commands anything against God; (2) whether it is lawful to resist a prince in such circumstances; (3) whether it is proper to resist a prince who is destroying the state; (4) whether princes should give assistance to the subjects of other princes who attack the true religion or are otherwise tyrannous. It is in the development of an answer to the third question that the political significance of the *Vindiciae* is evidenced. A number of ideas throughout the work have an important bearing on the future growth of political thought, but the central issue is that of obedience. Upon what basis does the relationship of ruler and subject depend? Why and under what conditions do subjects obey a prince? What, if any, obligations does a ruler have toward his subjects and why? May subjects not only refuse to obey the prince but also rebel against him, and if so, what are the governing circumstances in such a case? These questions are as old as political society and as new as the present. To answer them, the author of the *Vindiciae* begins with a consideration of the origin of government itself.

In the golden age of man's existence, the community was governed by wise men who "persuaded and dissuaded" the people as required in the public interest. Goods were held in common, and force was not necessary

[3] Thomas I. Cook, *History of Political Philosophy from Plato to Burke,* Prentice-Hall, Inc., Englewood Cliffs, N.J., 1936, pp. 353–354.

to maintain order.⁴ The subsequent institution of private property made it necessary to have a king. The words "mine" and "thine" gave rise to conflicts among citizens and between peoples of neighboring communities. It then became necessary to use some authority to mediate differences and to see that justice was done, that the poor were not oppressed by the rich.⁵

The organization of society following the golden age has involved a dual contract, on the basis of which rights and duties are defined. One contract is between God, on the one hand, and the king and people, on the other. Its purpose is to provide and maintain a true religion. The other contract is between the ruler and the people and establishes secular government. The king has a double responsibility. He is obligated to God to defend the faith, and since the people are contractually bound with him for this purpose they must hold him to his duty. If the king commands anything against God, the people are in duty bound to resist him and to restore the true faith. The king is also responsible to the people to rule justly; that, indeed, is the purpose for which he was chosen. He is not sovereign, and he is not the originator of law. He is merely an executive agent of the people, elected by their suffrages. His power is conditional, not absolute. The people are required to obey him only insofar as he governs in accordance with the law. The author of the *Vindiciae contra Tyrannos* states that in the contract between king and people, the people act as "stipulator" and the king as "promisor." The stipulator is the more important of the two. The people, as stipulator, have a right to demand the just governance of the king; the king, as promisor, must guarantee such performance. The promise of the king is absolute; that of the people is conditional. If the king does not keep his word, the people are "lawfully absolved" from their obligation to obey.⁶

It follows that the people have a right to resist a ruler who is guilty of a breach of either of the contracts to which he is committed. This right, however, should be enforced only if the provocation and necessity are deemed very significant. It must be remembered that princes are only humans and weak. Too much should not be expected of them, and subjects should "try all means before taking the sword." The way in which the right of resistance may be exercised is also dependent upon the kind of tyranny involved. If a tyrant is a usurper who is not a party to the contract and therefore has no legal right to rule, resistance against him may proceed from anyone. Such a ruler may be removed and even killed by a private citizen. But if the tyrant is one who has come to the

---

⁴ The author of the *Vindiciae* relies here upon Seneca's idea of the "golden age" of man. See Chap. 5.

⁵ *Vindiciae contra Tyrannos*, part 3, in Francis William Coker, *Readings in Political Philosophy*, rev. ed., The Macmillan Company, New York, 1938, p. 355.

⁶ *Ibid.*, p. 357.

throne according to legal process, resistance to him is a more serious matter and is out of the hands of the private citizens. In such a case, resistance must be instigated by the representatives of the whole people, by the "electors, palatines, patricians, assembly of estates, etc." If these do not take action, a citizen who regards himself as persecuted may flee, but that is all. The *Vindiciae* concludes its answers to the four questions it has posed by asserting the right of a neighboring prince to give assistance to subjects of a tyrannous ruler who is guilty of a breach of either of the contracts to which he is a party.

The democratic implications of the *Vindiciae* are apparent. It proposes that the people are sovereign; that public office is a public trust and that the king is a servant of the people; that the people are the source of the law and that the king is restricted by and is not above the law; that the people have a right of revolution against the ruler who betrays his trust. Still the *Vindiciae* is closer to medieval than to modern political thought. The political theory of the Middle Ages also supported the principle that government has a responsibility to the community and that the authority of rulers is conditional. Certainly the *Vindiciae* does not present a theory of popular and individual rights. It states that the people are sovereign but insists that except in the case of the usurper tyrant, they should act as a corporate body, that is to say through their traditional representatives. The *Vindiciae* does associate the contract with the right of revolution, and this association performed yeoman service in the democratic cause during the course of the next two centuries. But the *Vindiciae* was essentially an aristocratic, not a democratic, document, asserting as it did the rights and privileges of the towns, provinces, and classes rather than of the multitude of people.[7]

In their assault upon the doctrine of absolute royal authority, the Huguenot writers received assistance from an unexpected quarter. Conscientious Catholics everywhere were appalled by the mass defections of their fellows to Protestantism. Correctly attributing the Church disintegration to the long-standing abuses of their authority by Pope and clergy, those who were deeply concerned launched a program of reform which, in the last part of the sixteenth and the beginning of the seventeenth century, achieved a remarkable success. The leading force in what came to be known as the Counter Reformation was the Society of Jesus, a militant order founded by Ignatius Loyola in 1534. Pressed by the Jesuits, who were joined by the Dominicans, the Catholic Church corrected the worst of the abuses which had brought about the Reformation. The expansion of Protestantism was halted, and reunification of the Christian community appeared for a time to be a possibility. Although this view proved to be oversanguine, the Counter Reformation restored the prestige of the Roman Church and prevented its further decline.

[7] Sabine, *op. cit.*, p. 382.

Much of the success of the Counter Reformation must be attributed to the writings and activities of the Jesuits. In their view any worthwhile reform depended upon a reestablishment of papal authority and discipline; failing this, the forces of dissension within the Church would continue to tear it apart. A single head of the Christian community must speak with the authority of God behind him; otherwise, the strength required to combat Protestantism would be dissipated through internal conflict. The Jesuits recognized the impossibility of restoring to the Pope the power over both secular and spiritual affairs that he had once enjoyed. They were willing, therefore, to acknowledge the fact of national divisions and the supremacy of national monarchs in secular affairs. They asked in return that the Pope be recognized as supreme in spiritual matters and as having an indirect secular authority in cases where spiritual discipline had to be exercised. Since the decline of the papacy, the two swords of temporal and spiritual authority had been wielded principally by the kings. The heart of the Jesuit antiroyalist doctrine was the assertion that kings cannot rightfully control spiritual affairs. Although the aims of Huguenots and Jesuits differed considerably, particularly in regard to the position of the Pope, their theories were strikingly similar insofar as they sought a limitation upon the powers of the king in spiritual matters.

Robert Bellarmine (1542–1621), one of the leading Jesuit writers, typically assigned to the Pope the leadership of the universal Church. The Pope, he said, has no true secular authority, but he must be permitted an indirect control over temporal affairs where a spiritual end is to be served. The power of the Pope is authorized by God. He is the only human ruler to be so endowed. His authority is of a higher kind than that of the king since spiritual affairs are always higher than secular. The power of the king, on the other hand, does not derive from God but from the community and should be used only for secular purposes. The king has no right to influence spiritual matters; he certainly cannot be the independent and sovereign head of a state church. Indeed the Pope has the right to depose a heretical king.[8] The king has an obligation to rule justly, and his authority is accordingly conditional. The Pope may grant the right of resistance to subjects of a tyrannical king.

The political theory of another important Jesuit writer, Juan de Mariana (1536–1623), was more purely secular than that of Bellarmine. Mariana anticipated Rousseau in asserting that man lived in a state of nature prior to establishing civil government and that such control was made necessary by the institution of private property.[9] Government does

---

[8] *Ibid.*, p. 387.

[9] This concept of course was not original with Mariana. It was the standard historical view of the ancient world; it passed into Christian thought and Mariana took it from medieval authors.

not originate in God but in nature. Its establishment and evolution are the products of human necessity. The ruler receives his authority not from God but from the people, who are represented by the Estates, which act for them. The king does not rule by divine right but by community consent expressed through representatives. The king may be resisted and even killed if his rule is oppressive and if such action is sanctioned and directed by the leaders of the people. Mariana, however, is careful to warn that revolution is a dangerous thing, not to be undertaken lightly. Moreover, while he stresses the responsibility of the monarch and the rights of the people, Mariana does not advocate democracy. The best government, he believed, would be a monarchy in which the royal power is checked both by the Pope and by secular institutions such as the Estates.

A consideration of Jesuit antiroyalist theory must include a brief discussion of one of the leading contributors to that theory, Francisco Suarez (1548–1617), whose political writings form a part of his work as a jurist. Suarez and others systematized the legal philosophy of the Middle Ages with its emphasis on natural law, thus giving the natural law the form in which it was understood in the seventeenth century. In this elucidation Suarez was a forerunner of Grotius, who developed the natural law as a foundation for a system of international law. Suarez, like Bellarmine, placed the Pope at the head of a universal Christian Church and made him the supreme arbiter of all problems which have a spiritual connotation. The Pope is thus given an indirect control over secular matters. The state arises out of human needs and is organized on the basis of an agreement among the heads of households. Its function is to regulate human affairs in the general interest. Human society has an inherent right to govern itself; this is not an authority which stems from God. The authority of government (and it need not be a monarchical government) is contingent upon the consent of the people for whose service it exists. The people therefore may alter their government as they see fit. Suarez was presumably interested in nailing down the principle of papal supremacy, but his theory conduced to an end which he and his fellows would have strongly opposed—the independence and separation of secular from spiritual power. Neither Catholics nor Calvinists wanted separation of church and state. Neither believed that a community which did not espouse the "true" religion could be a wholesome one. Both, therefore, urged secular authorities to achieve religious unity. It was a difficult lesson to learn, but it ultimately became apparent that the price of enforced conformity was too great, even assuming that it could be paid at all, and the struggles over this issue in the sixteenth century made the outcome doubtful in the extreme. Separation was the only practical answer, and the theory of the Jesuits, which contributed to the idea of the state as a representative of purely secular interests, furthered its acceptance, although the Jesuits had never intended to advocate separation or anticipated the direction their argument was to take.

The Theory of Divine Right

The theory of the divine right of kings, like that of the monarchomachs, grew out of the religious struggles of the sixteenth century. The opponents of royal authority had contended that secular power inheres in the community and that the people may delegate and withdraw it as they in their sovereign capacity see fit. The counterargument of divine right was essentially an embellishment of the traditional Christian belief that all power comes from God. The supporters of the divine-right theory modified the tradition to invest secular power in the king alone. Their contention resulted in the assertion of the autonomy of the secular realm—its complete independence from control by the church. This was an important aspect of the divine-right theory. The monarchomachs' advocacy of the right of the people to resist a tyrannous monarch was attended by the development of an elaborate theory designed to support their view. No comparable effort was made by the supporters of divine right, nor could it be, since the components necessary for such a development were largely lacking. Still, the divine-right theory was important, not because it was logical or because it had historical sanction but because a great many people believed in it and advocated it. A theory need not be logical and well balanced to gain adherents. Few political philosophies have contained more absurdities than does Nazi-Fascist theory, but no one could deny its significance in the twentieth century. A theory can be influential if it provides a rationalization of an opinion already widely held or if it supports a cause in which people are interested. In France the long, sanguinary, and inconclusive struggle over differences of religious belief made it appear that the concentration of power in a supreme ruler who could demand the obedience of all citizens, irrespective of theological inclination, was the only practicable solution. Many were willing and anxious to accept a divine-right monarch simply because they believed that his unquestioned rule offered the best chance for peace. Once this view had gained popular acceptance, learned men could formulate a philosophy to support it. We shall consider here the efforts, essentially typical, of the French lawyer, Pierre de Belloy.

Belloy was born about 1540; his major works expounding the divine-right theory, *Apologie Catholique* and *De l'autorité du roi*, were published in 1585 and 1587.[10] His main contention is that monarchs receive

[10] J. W. Allen (in *A History of Political Thought in the Sixteenth Century*, Methuen & Co., Ltd., London, 1957, p. 383) states that Belloy was the first Frenchman to develop "with any fullness" a theory of the divine right of kings.

their office from God and cannot, therefore, lawfully be deprived of it by any human agency, either the people or the Pope. Authority was not required on earth until the fall of man, but thenceforth it was indispensable. Monarchical authority is, therefore, unlimited. This last assertion is a virtual non sequitur which Belloy allows to stand without explanation. Logically, there seems to be no good reason why, if God grants power to a king, he may not also place some limits upon it. Such a reservation, however, would have impaired the usefulness of the divine-right theory in the minds of its advocates. Belloy ignores the possibility altogether. His major purpose is to reinforce the principle of passive obedience to the king. The king, Belloy says, is a lieutenant of God. He is, indeed, the image of God. He acts for God and is his defender of the faith on earth. Rebellion against a king is the same as rebellion against God and is punishable by eternal damnation.

Men could resist any authority which they themselves created. The idea that authority inheres in the community contributes to disorder and anarchy. A government that exercises a power drawn from the community rests upon force and is constantly obliged to use it. It is a dangerous doctrine to tell the people that the government is "theirs," even though they are cautioned against a too liberal use of their power. Belloy understood these things very well. He believed that the only effective guarantee of peace is the recognition of a religious duty of obedience to secular government. This guarantee is given to men if they accept the king as God's representative. The king is not irresponsible. He is responsible to God and ultimately must make his accounting to God; but this is not the business of the people.

The divine-right theory was less important in England than in France because of the relatively greater unity of the English nation at this time. In sixteenth-century France the divine-right theory was formulated as a reaction to the divisionist forces of the Huguenots. It was not so necessary that the theory be asserted in England, although its irrelevance did not prevent James I of England (James VI of Scotland) from asserting it. James's theory was in the main naturalistic. Order is a function of command. Command is a natural principle exemplified by the rule of God over the angels, Satan over the devils, and kings over men. It is the only alternative to anarchy. James used Scripture to support his position, primarily to combat Calvinist citations.[11] It was also James's view that the king's power is a "mystery" which "is not lawful to be disputed." Unquestionably such a philosophy was more palatable swallowed whole, although some of James's subjects must have considered the true mystery to have been God's use of such an unprepossessing figure

[11] Francis D. Wormuth, *The Royal Prerogative*, 1603–1649, Cornell University Press, Ithaca, N.Y., 1939, pp. 83–84.

as his lieutenant. Not even James's admirers could have viewed him as an "image of God." The divine-right theory was embraced in those places and under those conditions in which it could serve the cause of peace and national unity. Support for it waned when it was no longer useful.

The Politiques

As the religious wars dragged on, a new voice, offering a new solution, began to be heard. A new party in France, known as the Politiques, shared with the divine-right advocates the belief that peace would be achieved only through the centralization of political authority and the strengthening of kingly power. The Politiques' unique contribution was their demand for religious toleration. Although Catholics, they were more nationalist than Catholic. They were desperately afraid that the wars over religious differences would wreck the nation completely. They had no moral objection to persecution; they merely urged that experience had demonstrated its futility. There were simply too many Huguenots. Even if it were possible to kill them all, France would be ruined in the process. The only solution was an official recognition of the principle of religious freedom. Spiritual and secular interests had to be separated. National unity had to be salvaged, although religious unity was lost forever.

The Politiques were the first to recognize that a united citizenry is possible despite theological differences. They argued that in fact there were fewer ideological conflicts between Catholicism and Protestantism than was generally assumed. There were many who attacked the Politiques bitterly for their attitude. It was to them inconceivable that a good government would not use its total power to defend the true religion and to wipe out heresy wherever it existed, regardless of the cost in terms of national welfare or human life. The very name "Politiques" was created by the enemies of those who took such a heretical view. The Politiques, it was said, were more concerned with their comforts than with the salvation of men's souls. The Politiques' answer was that a common Christianity was all that could be hoped for and that it was at least preferable to national collapse.

In the beginning the Politiques, perhaps because the group was not well defined, were unable to agree on the questions of what kind and how much authority should be vested in the king and whether and under what conditions he might be resisted. After 1585 a greater meeting of minds developed. The Politiques moved in the direction of monarchical absolutism, mainly because they could see no other way to achieve their goal of peace and national unity. Dangerous times always contribute to the strengthening of governmental power; the theory of the Politiques was in line with this historical fact.

Jean Bodin

A leading figure among the Politiques, whose contributions to the cause of strengthening the central government proved to be highly significant, was Jean Bodin (1530–1596). Bodin was born at Angers, studied and taught law at Toulouse, and went to Paris to practice. He was a personable man and an excellent conversationalist, and he came to be highly regarded by the king, Henry III. He was also friendly with the Duc d'Alençon, the king's brother, and was ultimately appointed, in 1576, as king's attorney at Laon. In this capacity as well as in his position of representative of the third estate at the estates-general of Blois, Bodin was involved in the political affairs of his time. Thus as a political philosopher he could bring practical administrative and legislative experience to bear upon his task, to supplement the vast learning which he had acquired through his reading and studies.

Bodin was less a mere polemicist than he was a philosopher. He was convinced that no easy and superficial answer could be given to the multitudinous problems with which France was confronted in the sixteenth century. A solution could result only from a consideration of the basic principles pertaining to law, the state, government, and human society. As it turned out, the task of producing a philosophy to answer all these problems was beyond Bodin's capacity. Still, in the course of his attempt to perform it, he made some significant contributions which occupy an important place in the development of political theory.

Bodin's interest was more than political. His *Réponse aux paradoxes de M. Malestroit,* in which he analyzed some of the economic difficulties of Western Europe, explained the revolution in prices of the sixteenth century, advocated free trade, and pointed out the economic factors that underlay the relations among states, has been cited by some as the foundation of the study of political economy.[12] Bodin also developed a theory of history, which he regarded as a necessity for anyone interested in advocating reform of current conditions. History, he said, is not important simply as a record of past events. The significance of the past lies in what it teaches for the future. History shows the inevitability of change, and the change is in the direction of progress. Bodin repudiated the theory that man had once lived in a "golden age" and had progressively deteriorated since that time. Things are better than they ever were before, and they will be better still. A great deal depends upon man's ability to interpret past events as illustrations of general principles which, when learned, may be used to improve our present position.

These principles, however, do not apply in precisely the same manner in all situations. Such factors as climate and topography must be taken into account, since the application of general rules will produce different

---

[12] *Ibid.,* p. 395.

results depending upon circumstances. Bodin proceeds from this assumption to the formulation of a theory of climate which has a direct bearing upon his political thought. He states that there are three principal types of humanity and that the characteristics of each correspond to the three main climatic zones. The people of the southern climes are intelligent but passive and lazy and inclined to submit to autocratic rule. Northerners are active and ambitious but unintelligent and given to democratic governmental forms. The people of the central zone, including France, are superior and favor monarchy. The theory is of course absurd, but it does not require great perception to see in it the ancestor thought of some much more modern asininities.

Finally it is possible to find in Bodin some ideas that anticipate the modern school of sociological jurisprudence. For Bodin the law has a social purpose; it is not to be revered simply because it is the law but for what it does. Since change is inevitable, so too must the law change. Laws and ideologies are good insofar as they are useful to humans. Thus Bodin believed that problems must be approached with a critical spirit and a willingness to put the outdated behind us if progress so demands. Of course his attempt to substitute the new nationalism for the outmoded political and religious forms of the past required that Bodin preach what he practiced.

Bodin's greatest work was his *Six Livres de la République,* published in 1577, and intended to be part of a comprehensive work on the universe. This ambitious plan was never completed, but in his *Republic* Bodin set forth his theory of the state, including the exposition of sovereignty for which he is best known. Bodin's purpose was to provide a solution for the difficulties which beset his country. The religious wars had evoked irreconcilable views on fundamental problems of political obligation, of the relationship of ruler and subject, and of the responsibilities of each to the other. Bodin recognized that the forces which contributed to disorder could not be eliminated; some new principle had to be accepted which could bring unity *despite* diversity. Bodin found what he sought in the idea of sovereignty, although his development of this concept formed only a part of a more comprehensive political theory which began with a consideration of the origin of the state.

The natural community of mankind is the family, a man and his wife, together with their children and their property. This unit represents that stage of human development which gives evidence of reason and cooperative living. Property is as much a part of this organization as are the human components. It is indispensable to the life of the family and acts as the cement that holds the family together. The possession of property is a natural right of the family which must be recognized and safeguarded by the state. Authority, too, has its origin in the family, or rather in the father of the family, who exercises an almost complete power within the family circle. He is entitled to do so because his reason is superior to that of the other members; the children are not yet fully developed, and the wife is a mere woman, too passionate and unstable to be entrusted with any real responsibility. A man cannot sell or kill his wife, but he may enforce complete obedience upon her and divorce her if he sees fit. The authority of the father over his children includes the right of taking their lives. Bodin emphasized the absolute power of the father as head of the household. No state can be better than the family units that compose it; therefore a lack of discipline and order on the family level will result in a disorderly state.

In course of time, the families organize into a number of civil societies for a variety of purposes. Economic interests, religious proclivities, and the demand for protection against their enemies all necessitate a form of social cooperation which cannot be performed on the family level; larger associations are required for these purposes. Ultimately these associations combine to form a state. The combination is effected largely by force, that is, by war and conquest. Bodin does not adequately explain how this combination comes about. The formation of families and of the wider associations is instinctive, but the state rests instead upon force, although, as we shall see, force is not the justification for the state. At any rate, a state exists when sovereignty, complete power to make and enforce laws, is recognized.

Sovereignty is not an end in itself. It is an instrument, designed to secure and advance the purposes for which the state exists. And what are those purposes? What is the end for which the state was formed? It is not merely to secure happiness; that goal would be unworthy of such a great organization and could probably be achieved by a lower level of human organization. It is not to establish unity, for unity, although desirable, is like sovereignty, a means to an end, not an end in itself. The ultimate purpose of the state is, broadly speaking, the securing of the good of both mind and body for all persons. Bodily interests come first, not because they are more important but because they must be served in the interest of survival. Thus the state must provide defense, secure justice, and contribute to the economic welfare of the people. But the higher purpose of the state is to assist the people to realize virtue, to make it possible for them to live moral lives, to enhance intellectual values. A man may exist without virtue. A state can be created and exercise sovereign power without contributing to the realization of virtue; but a state which does not contribute to that end is not, in Bodin's term, a "well-ordered" state.

To achieve these purposes the authority of the state must be pervasive. Its sovereignty must be felt; and Bodin defines sovereignty as "supreme power over citizens and subjects, unrestrained by law." In Bodin's well-ordered state, the kind of participatory citizenship which marked the Greek city-state is impossible. The modern state is too large to permit anything but a centralized administration and control. Liberty receives a unique definition. The citizen is free in the sense that he is secure and is not a slave. He obeys the laws handed down by the sovereign, but he plays no law-making role. Nor are citizens to be considered equal, one to another. They are all subject to the sovereign power, but they hold different ranks and privileges, and the sovereign power bears upon them according to their positions. Bodin does not satisfactorily explain the origin of sovereignty. It does not come from God; rather it seems to arise out of the nature of man, since it is necessitated by human conditions. Sovereignty is inherent in the state and serves the purposes for which the state exists. If the state did not possess sovereignty it would be compelled to admit that its own existence was unwarranted. It must have unlimited power to achieve its purposes. Sovereign power is demonstrated through the enactment of laws; all laws derive from the sovereign; even customary law receives its sanction from the sovereign and may be abrogated by sovereign decree. Bodin's purpose is apparent. He is convinced that the divisive forces in France can be controlled only by the imposition of an authority, the legitimacy of which is not to be judged on the basis of religious predilection.

Within the state are three possible holders of sovereignty, that is, three possible governmental forms by which the state may exercise sovereignty. These are monarchy, aristocracy, and democracy. Sovereignty is indivisible; there can be no such thing as a mixed state in which sovereign power is shared among branches of government. Governmental functions may be divided and responsibilities allocated, but always under the direction of the sovereign, who still retains ultimate power. For Bodin no situation can exist in which the advantages of all three governmental forms may be realized and their disadvantages minimized by the division of power. Diffusion of power was, to Bodin, one of the principal causes of the troubles he was attempting to overcome, and he was convinced that only the concentration of authority in a single agency could be effective. Bodin strongly preferred a monarchy. Sovereignty might possibly be held by a numerical majority of the citizens or by a small group of nobles, but to lodge power in the hands of either a democratic or an aristocratic government would be to defeat the very purpose for which sovereignty should be employed, since the inevitable weakness of all such governments is vacillation in the use of power. Only a monarchy can have the necessary efficiency, and only a monarchy can establish that unity which is the *sine qua non* of the well-ordered state.

The placing of sovereign power in the hands of a monarch makes good government possible, but only wise administration can assure it. A good ruler will recognize that the world does not stand still, that it is impossible to maintain the status quo, and that any attempt to do so will provoke revolution. He has complete power to make the laws for the country, and he will use his authority to make the gradual alterations that are necessary to the general welfare and that will forestall revolution. A wise ruler, moreover, must know his people and anticipate their response to his direction. He should be aware of the limits beyond which he cannot go without risking serious unrest. He should avoid extremes of inequality among his people, for few things contribute more greatly to instability than injustice of this sort. Yet Bodin is not an equalitarian. He has nothing but contempt for the leveling schemes of the radical Protestant sects of the day, and he fully approves of a hierarchical society in which orders and privileges are secure and in which there are corresponding degrees of economic wealth. But he is sufficiently astute to recognize that too great a gap between rich and poor will create unrest and promote revolution. Also, though the sovereign is the source of the law and can alter it as he sees fit, he must avoid instability. The law must change to accord with changing circumstances, but the citizens must be able to depend on it, and a too great variability leads to frustration and resentment. The courts, too, must render justice. They should apply the law uniformly and fairly. They should be supervised by the sovereign, who must appoint judicial officers on the basis of merit rather than offer such positions for sale.[13] Of particular significance is Bodin's advocacy of religious toleration. His position cannot be attributed to apathy with regard to matters of faith, for he was a devout man. He believes that religion is essential to the peace and order of the community, but that the form it takes is unimportant. Men should be religious, but they need not be members of a particular faith. In any event, the employment of force to achieve religious conformity is worse than useless. The state should not ignore the matter of religious belief, and it certainly should not encourage diversity; in fact, if it can exterminate minor radical religious groups before they develop sufficient strength to cause trouble, it should do so. Bodin does not advocate religious toleration on moral grounds.

In cautioning the sovereign with respect to the use of power, Bodin offers little new counsel. Indeed he is indebted to both Aristotle and Machiavelli for much of his advice to rulers. It is in his development of the theory of sovereignty that Bodin makes his most noteworthy contribution. Although the sovereign ruler *should* observe the proper restraint in the interest of wise and effective administration, the fact remains that he does not *have* to do so. His is the perpetual, inalienable, and unlimited power, and he does not exercise it by consent of the governed. Still, Bodin's sovereign ruler is not so omnipotent as he appears to be. For although, as we have seen, Bodin defines sovereignty

---

[13] In this recommendation Bodin was attacking an abuse of long standing in the French judicial system. His advocacy of reform, however, was ineffective; the sale of judicial offices continued for some two hundred years.

as "supreme power over citizens and subjects, unrestrained by law," he also imposes certain limitations upon the sovereign power which make it less than complete and, indeed, something less than sovereign.

Sovereignty, in the first place, should be exercised by a lawful government. A monarch must have assumed his office by election, succession, or as the result of a lawful war. Sovereignty does not belong merely to anyone who exercises authority. One who takes his position illegally is a tyrant, and he not only may be disobeyed but he may also be deposed and even killed, and without formal proceedings against him. But this license is not really a limitation upon sovereign power, for the tyrant never has sovereignty. Certain things the most sovereign ruler cannot lawfully do. In the first place, he cannot deprive the family of its property. To do so would abridge a natural right inherent in the family, and would, in fact, destroy the family, which is the indispensable basic unit in the structure of the state. The state, of course, requires funds, and funds mean taxes. Bodin admits the necessity of taxes, but he holds that they can be imposed only with the consent of those taxed, unless a grave emergency forces the king to resort to confiscation to save the state. There is a serious inconsistency here in Bodin's theory. A sovereign can hardly be said to have "supreme power unrestrained by law" if he is required to have the citizen's consent in order to tax him. As if aware of the contradiction, Bodin refers only incidentally to the whole problem of property rights versus sovereignty.

Seeking popular consent to taxation is the most serious of the limitations that Bodin imposes upon the sovereign, but it is by no means the only one. He assumes, as did others of his time, that a law of nature exists which can reveal the principles of right and wrong by which all men should be governed, and he makes the sovereign subject to that law. The sovereign cannot be compelled to comply with this obligation, and the people have no right of revolution against him if he does not. The same holds true if the king violates God's law. Certain fundamental or constitutional principles also are binding upon the sovereign. Bodin cites in this regard the Salic Law which prohibits a woman from taking the throne, and the law which bans the alienation of domain. The sovereign is likewise limited by the oaths he takes. Oaths are promises and contracts, and they must not be broken; if they are, disorder follows and the safety of the state is endangered. Finally, the sovereign has no authority either to alienate the royal domain or to modify the succession to the throne.

Conclusions

Bodin set himself a considerable task. He wanted above all to provide a basis for stability, and he believed that the only way stability could be ensured was through the development of a sovereign power that could impose its will, establish order, and restore the domestic tranquility. Only an absolute authority could exercise such sovereignty, and in the beginning of the *Republic,* Bodin apparently acknowledges the fact and is willing to face it. Otherwise he would not have defined sovereignty in such unequivocal terms. In fact, however, Bodin was not willing to pay the price that his definition of sovereignty demanded. He wanted authority, but he also wanted to preserve the constitution of France as well as the customs and traditions of the people. He could not have it both ways. In explanation of the contradictions with which he has been charged, it can be said that Bodin placed upon the sovereign only those limitations that were necessary to the preservation of the state itself. That is to say, the whole purpose of creating sovereignty would be defeated if such limitations were not imposed. In Bodin's terms the argument may be a valid one. He probably believed quite sincerely that the confiscation of property, the ignoring of the natural law or God's law, or the violation of the constitution would wreck the state. It is a matter of opinion perhaps; yet tyrannies that have been guilty of flouting the warnings of Bodin concerning these matters have still been able to survive for unconscionable periods of time.

Bodin saw more clearly than most of his contemporaries that the world was changing. He regarded the change as progress, and he believed correctly that institutional adjustments would have to be made accordingly. The feudal nobility fought bitterly against reform; Bodin believed that they would have to give way before a centralized power. Religious groups insisted that no secular unity was possible without religious unity; Bodin took issue with this view and offered the sovereign ruler as a rallying point for unity for all the disparate religious sects. He demanded religious toleration, on utilitarian rather than moral grounds to be sure, but it is fortunate for the world that toleration did not have to await a universal conviction of the moral rightness of religious freedom. Bodin's greatest importance for his own time is that he separated the concept of sovereignty from God's will, making it grow instead out of man's need.[14] If in doing so he glorified the state, it is only fair to remember that this was not the end he sought. His overriding concern was with the welfare of the nation. He believed that acceptance of the theory of sovereignty would conduce to this end. And since he also feared that an abuse of sovereign power would injure the national interest, he placed limitations upon it. This concession led him into contradictions from which he could not logically escape and accounts for many of the flaws which mar his theory. Still the theory had its importance, at the time and subsequently. We shall see later how the theory of sovereignty developed in the writings of Thomas Hobbes.

[14] Allen, *op. cit.,* p. 60.

SELECTED BIBLIOGRAPHY

Allen, J. W.: *A History of Political Thought in the Sixteenth Century* (reprinted with revised bibliographical notes), Methuen & Co., Ltd., London, 1957, part 3, chap. 8.

Coker, Francis William: *Readings in Political Philosophy*, rev. ed., The Macmillan Company, New York, 1938, chaps. 14, 15.

Cook, Thomas I.: *History of Political Philosophy from Plato to Burke*, Prentice-Hall, Inc., Englewood Cliffs, N.J., 1936, chaps. 13–15.

Figgis, J. N.: *The Theory of the Divine Right of Kings*, 2d ed., Cambridge University Press, New York, 1914.

Hearnshaw, F. J. C. (ed.): *The Social and Political Ideas of Some Great Thinkers of the Sixteenth and Seventeenth Centuries*, George G. Harrap & Co., Ltd., London, 1926, chaps. 1, 2, 4.

McGovern, William Montgomery: *From Luther to Hitler: The History of Fascist-Nazi Philosophy*, Houghton Mifflin Company, Boston, 1941, chap. 2.

Sabine, George H.: *A History of Political Theory*, 3d ed., Holt, Rinehart and Winston, Inc., New York, 1961, chaps. 19, 20.

twelve

THOMAS HOBBES

The England of Thomas Hobbes

The fierce winds of religious controversy that swept over Europe in the wake of the Reformation had left England relatively unscathed. All of the fuel for a major conflagration was present in England in the sixteenth century, but the political skill of the Tudors had gone far toward preventing the dangerous spark from igniting the wood. The death of Elizabeth in 1603 and the accession to the throne of James I, the "wisest fool in Christendom," as Henry IV of France called him, presaged a long and bitter period of violence. James himself did not live to reap the whirlwind of revolution he did so much to cultivate, but his son, Charles I, who followed the teachings of his father, paid the supreme penalty for learning his lessons too well. A more personable and attractive monarch than his sire, Charles was equally insistent upon maintaining his royal prerogative. He stubbornly set a course which alienated his people and violated what a great many Englishmen assumed were traditions of long standing. The root of the trouble was both religious and economic. Like his father before him, Charles harried the Puritans and made a foolish attempt to destroy Presbyterianism in Scotland. Charles also became impatient with a Parliament which was increasingly reluctant to satisfy his insatiable demands for money. The king resorted to forced "loans" from rich men—loans that Charles had not the slightest intention of repaying. The Petition of Right of 1628, in which Parliament asserted its authority against the king, was signed by Charles but with mental reservations. The abuses continued, considerable assistance being given the king's cause by the Earl of Strafford, who policed the secular sphere, and Archbishop Laud, who regulated the spiritual. Taxation without legislative consent, arbitrary arrests and imprisonment, imposition of martial law, and the billeting of troops in private houses—these were the issues which set king and Parliament at odds. In 1638, Scotland, outraged by Charles's attempt to establish Anglicanism in that country, issued the National Covenant, a proclamation of Scottish determination to defend the Presbyterian faith, and sent an army against Charles's forces in England.

Charles had ruled without Parliament for eleven years, but the dubious financial expedients which had made his reign possible did not suffice in a war crisis. Charles was compelled, in 1640, to convene his Parliament. It did not adjourn for twenty years. The Long Parliament struck vigorously for reform. Strafford and Laud were executed; the Court of the Star Chamber was abolished; the principle of legislative control of the purse was enunciated; and for the first time the Parliament, in the Grand Remonstrance, appealed to the people for support over the head of the king. The king fought back, calling for assistance in his struggle against the rebel legislators, and the lines were drawn for civil war. Although Charles's forces enjoyed some early successes, his cause was doomed from the start. The powers arrayed against him were too many and too powerful. The king had made the fatal error of alienating the middle class; the Tudors had been more prudent in basing their own autocracy upon that class. Moreover, in persecuting Puritans and Presbyterians, Charles was attempting to stem the tide of the spirit of the Reformation itself. The king's coalition consisted mainly of rural supporters, nobles, and the Anglican clergy. It was no match for the urban middle class and the Puritans who supported the Parliamentary cause, especially when Parliament secured the help of the Scots. By 1649 the parliamentary forces, under Oliver Cromwell, had defeated the royalists and beheaded Charles.

In executing Charles I, the middle class had repudiated the doctrine of divine right, to which their support had formerly given meaning and importance. Their defection was a clear indication, in other European countries as well as in England, that the doctrine was on the way to disappearance. The Commonwealth and the Cromwellian Protectorate, in reality a military dictatorship that enforced the stringent rules of Puritan morality, brought dismal days to England. Richard Cromwell, considerably weaker than his father, was unable to maintain the power of the Protectorate. Prince Charles was recalled from exile and crowned Charles II in 1660. The new king had no love for Parliament and might have preferred the restoration of a divine-right monarchy. He was not anxious, however, to go "on his travels" again, and he was wise enough not to alienate the support of those who could destroy him. There were to be, under Charles II, a few years of relative peace before events conspired to produce the second and concluding phase of the revolutionary movement in seventeenth-century England.

This era of jealous factionalism provoked by religious and economic differences, was the world known and deplored by Thomas Hobbes (1588–1679). Gone was that unity of the medieval world which had been made possible by the acceptance of a universal religion. In its place were turmoil, confusion, and social unrest. The Reformation, with its doctrines of the priesthood of all believers and the rights of private conscience and judgment, had contributed to this new state of things in England as it had in France. The theory of Hobbes, like that of Bodin, must be considered in this context. Both men longed for peace and sought to achieve it by offering a substitute for the religious unity of the past. Each constructed a theory which he hoped would provide unity in the face of the divisive forces that tore at the social fabric. It is not surprising that Hobbes should have made fear a central force in the development of his theory, or that he, like Bodin, should have seen a solution in the establishment of an absolute sovereign.

The Man and His Work

Thomas Hobbes, the second of the three children in the family, was born prematurely at Malmesbury on April 5, 1588. The early accouchement is said to have been a result of the fright experienced by Hobbes's mother upon hearing the report of the Spanish Armada. Hobbes attributes his own timorous nature to this incident.[1] His father was a vicar, albeit an uneducated one, who was also something of a carouser. When Thomas was four, his father was compelled to depart from Malmesbury in haste following a brawl in which he struck and injured a man. A generous and kindly brother, Francis Hobbes, assumed responsibility for the family and took a particular interest in Thomas, who was sent to a church school at the age of four. This phase of young Hobbes's education was followed by instruction at a private school, and at the age of fifteen, in 1603, he enrolled at Magdalen Hall, Oxford. The Scholasticism which still formed the basis of studies at Oxford did not appeal to Hobbes, and he spent most of his time in the shops of the booksellers and stationers, where, according to his own account, he would "lye gaping on mappes." Hobbes received his B.A. degree in 1608 and took a position as tutor with the Cavendish family. His pupil was William Cavendish, the second Earl of Devonshire, with whom

---

[1] Much has been made by commentators of this reputed cowardice. It is by no means a certainty that the reputation is founded on fact.

Hobbes traveled in Europe in 1610. Here Hobbes was impressed by the intellectual revolt against Scholasticism, and when he returned to England he began a study of the classics. A direct result of this interest was his famous translation of Thucydides, published in 1629. Hobbes was convinced that the troubles of his own time had parallels in ancient history and that valuable lessons might be learned from a consideration of the past.

William Cavendish, the second earl, died in 1628, and Hobbes took a position as tutor to the son of Sir Gervase Clinton. His teaching occupied him for eighteen months, and it was presumably during this period that Hobbes was first, and accidentally, exposed to the subject of geometry and became enormously impressed by its method. The systematic approach to the solution of problems offered by this new (to Hobbes) science greatly intrigued him and profoundly influenced his efforts to construct a scientific political theory. In 1631, Hobbes returned to service with the Cavendish family, this time as tutor to the son of his former pupil, who bore the name of his father, William Cavendish, and was the third Earl of Devonshire. There followed what was for Hobbes an important trip abroad. He was still a tutor and traveling companion, but being known in European intellectual circles, he became an acquaintance and associate of some of the leaders of the rebels against Scholasticism. These included such luminaries as Mersenne, Galileo, Descartes, and Gassendi.

In 1637 Hobbes returned to England from the Continent to find Charles I struggling against an influential coalition of Puritan noblemen and country gentlemen who resented the king's ecclesiastical policies and his taxation measures. Hobbes supported the king and incorporated his views on the subject in a treatise, *The Elements of Law, Natural and Politique,* which was circulated privately, but not privately enough for Hobbes's peace of mind. In 1640 Hobbes deemed it expedient to leave England. He returned to the Continent where he spent the ensuing eleven years in exile. He did not find it, until toward the end of this period, a particularly unpleasant time. Hobbes rejoined the intellectual circle in which he was now well established. He acted for a time, 1646 to 1648, as tutor in mathematics to the young Prince of Wales, who was soon to become Charles II but who was then languishing in weary exile. He engaged Descartes and others in one of those acrimonious intellectual controversies to which Hobbes's irascible nature always seemed to lead him. Most important, a great part of Hobbes's time was employed in composing his *De Cive* and *Leviathan,* each of which constituted an elaboration of the treatise that had occasioned his hasty departure from England.

In 1651 Hobbes presented a manuscript copy of his *Leviathan* to the young Charles. The work was written to support the principle of absolute government, which Hobbes believed to be the only efficient and acceptable kind, and Hobbes had designed it to advance the royalist cause. For reasons which will later become apparent, the royalists were less than enthusiastic over Hobbes's efforts. Although Charles himself was more amused than annoyed by his curmudgeonly ex-tutor, Hobbes was banned from the court in exile and bitterly attacked by his former royalist friends. Also the strongly anti-Catholic bias of the *Leviathan* provoked attacks by the French clergy. Since his banishment from court by the exiled royalists had greatly lessened the pleasure of life in Paris, and since Hobbes could not be certain that the French clergy might not succeed in persuading the French government to take steps against him, he chose the lesser of two dangers. In the winter of 1651 he returned to England, made his peace with the Commonwealth, and he was ordered to live quietly. But Hobbes was constitutionally incapable of obeying such a command to the letter. He continued to become embroiled in a series of verbal wars, in some of which he did very badly, particularly when they concerned mathematical theories, in which, though deeply interested, he was poorly informed.

In 1660 Charles II was brought to the throne of England. The king had always enjoyed the wit and company of Hobbes and restored him to favor at court. Hobbes was now an old man of seventy-two, but he had nineteen years to live, and he employed them in precisely the same argumentative debates that had distinguished his earlier life. At the age of eighty, and after a period of bitter controversy with the officials of the Anglican Church, who were scandalized by what they regarded as his atheism, Hobbes became the subject of an official investigation to determine whether or not grounds existed to support a charge of heresy. Hobbes quickly burned any of his writings which might be suspect and wrote a treatise purporting to prove that the charges against him were unfounded. He survived the attack but paid a price. Charles warned him to abstain from the publication of controversial writings if he expected to receive royal protection. Most of Hobbes's work from this point was not published until after his death. In his last years Hobbes was not permitted even to reply to the many assaults made upon him by his enemies, although he was undoubtedly comforted by the many visitors he received from abroad who attested to the greatness of his reputation in Europe. He was productive to the end. In fact he was engaged in negotiations with his publisher when he died, at the age of ninety-one, on December 4, 1679.

Hobbes's Method

The question in Hobbes's time was whether or not a coherent community could be created by human intelligence. Hobbes evidently thought it could, and spoke of the "art" by which the Leviathan is constructed.[2] Hobbes had been influenced by the scientific revolution, which had stimulated a hope that society could be reordered in such a manner as to regenerate man and make his life better than it had ever been, and all on the basis of scientific knowledge. Hobbes was convinced that the woes of mankind resulted in large part from the inept and unscientific manner in which political communities had been fashioned in the past. He knew and accepted the view of Descartes that the mathematical method could be applied to a solution of problems in other sciences. He was probably more sanguine on this point than was Descartes, because of the inadequacy of his knowledge of mathematics. At any rate Hobbes believed that a science of society could be developed if, as in mathematics, the simplest propositions could be used as a basis upon which a more complex structure could be built in a step-by-step procedure. Hobbes repudiated the inductive method and empiricism. The lessons of history were, he thought, largely worthless. To construct a commonwealth required the ascertaining of specific rules and principles that had scientific, and thus eternal, validity. It did not demand, as did "tennis-play," merely practice. Reason was a more dependable guide than history.[3]

Hobbes adapted this view to what he conceived to be a science of motion. It occurred to him that the various forms of matter are distinguishable only by the differences of motion inherent in them. In other words, if all matter were at rest, or if all had the same rate and direction of motion, there would be no distinguishing characteristics among the forms. The diversity of motion, therefore, must be the cause of all things. On this basis Hobbes conceived and set out to develop a three-part philosophy. In one phase he was to explain physical phenomena, in another knowledge and sensation, and finally social phenomena, all in terms of motion. The work was ultimately completed in three treatises, De Corpore, De Homine, and De Cive, although they did not take the form that Hobbes had originally intended, a fact attributable both to the untenableness of the hypothesis and to Hobbes's lack of information on the subject.

Certain of Hobbes's applications, however, are pertinent to his political philosophy. Man's behavior, he argued, is determined by his response to sensation, which is a form of motion. Human beings invariably respond positively toward things that are desirable and negatively toward those that are undesirable. If this simple fact is understood we can go far toward gaining an understanding of the nature of man and the kind of political community necessitated by that nature.

[2] Sheldon S. Wolin, Politics and Vision, Little, Brown and Company, Boston, 1961, pp. 241–242.
[3] Ibid., pp. 251–252.

The Nature of Man and the State of Nature

Hobbes's theory of motion is not a theory of physical science at all, but is, instead, based upon psychology. In proposing a political theory founded upon a conception of human nature, Hobbes followed a well-trodden path. Political theorists before him, including Plato, had done the same thing. Yet Hobbes's contributions were in many respects unique. The controlling factor in human life, he thought, is that inner force which compels man to seek his own self-interests, especially to avoid injury. Men are not the masters of their own fate in the sense that they can agree upon a common set of moral ideals and live peacefully and cooperatively on the basis of such an agreement. Peace is possible only through an understanding of the forces that mold human nature and a recognition of the necessity of controlling them.[4] Good and evil are only terms used by men to identify the objects of their likes and dislikes, and they have no intrinsic meaning or importance. As Hobbes states it: "But whatsoever is the object of any man's appetite or desire; that is it, which he for his part calleth *good:* And the object of his hate, and aversion, *evil.*"[5] The two fundamental drives of human nature are, first, a striving toward whatever is deemed desirable, and, second, an avoidance of what is undesirable. Various combinations of these forces account for all human feeling and for all actions.

The chief object of man's desire is self-preservation; and what he wants most to avoid is loss of life. Thus security is the greatest good, and insecurity the greatest evil. Man wants to be sure of his life and possessions. Security is attainable, however, only through the possession of power. No man ever has enough power, since he will always seek more in order to protect that which he already has. The desire for power is thus unlimited, although the supply is limited, and herein lies the cause of conflict among men.

> I put for a general inclination of all mankind, a perpetual and restless desire of power after power, that ceaseth only in death. And the cause of this, is not always that a man hopes for a more intensive delight, than he has already attained to; or that he cannot be content with a moderate power: but because he cannot assure the power and means to live well, which he hath present, without the acquisition of more.[6]

The struggle for power among men is complicated and emphasized by their relative equality. Men seek the same ends, and they have generally the same capacity to achieve them.

[4] George H. Sabine, *A History of Political Theory,* 3d ed., Holt, Rinehart and Winston, Inc., New York, 1961, p. 460.

[5] Thomas Hobbes, *Leviathan* (introduction by A. D. Lindsay), E. P. Dutton & Co., Inc., New York, 1914, chap. 6. The spelling in quotations from the *Leviathan* is modernized here and subsequently.

[6] *Ibid.,* chap. 11.

Nature hath made men so equal in the faculties of body and mind as that though there be found one man sometimes manifestly stronger in body, or of quicker mind than another, yet when all is reckoned together, the difference between man and man is not so considerable as that one man can thereupon claim to himself any benefit to which another may not pretend as well as he.[7]

This equality is both physical and mental. Physical equality is evidenced by the fact that the weakest can kill the strongest, either by guile or by allying himself with others. Mental equality is even more apparent: "As to faculties of the mind . . . I find yet a greater equality amongst men than that of strength. For prudence is but experience, which equal time equally bestows on all men in those things they equally apply themselves unto." [8] Most men regard themselves as wiser than their fellows, although they may admit that a few are wiser than themselves. "But this proveth rather that men are in that point equal, than unequal. For there is not ordinarily a greater sign of the equal distribution of any thing than that every man is contented with his share." [9] Moreover, to Hobbes the equality of man is a source of difficulty, not of satisfaction, as it is to Jefferson and the equalitarian philosophers, for whom equality provides a foundation for a democratic theory of government. Men have an unlimited desire for power, and they are generally equal in their ability to achieve it. "From this equality of ability ariseth equality of hope in the attaining of our ends. And therefore if any two men desire the same thing . . . they become enemies; and in the way to their end (which is principally their own conservation, and sometimes their delectation only) endeavour to destroy or subdue one another." [10] Society is an aggregate of individuals, each of whom seeks his own advantage and does so at the expense of other individuals when such aggressiveness seems necessary; and Hobbes believes that it generally is. No person can afford to restrain his own drive for power; others will not do so, and he will find himself at a dangerous disadvantage.

This, then, is the true nature of man. He is individualistic, self-seeking, fearful, competitive to the point of combativeness. If he were completely at liberty to follow his own inclinations he would be inevitably caught up in "such a war as is of every man against every man." Life in a state of nature would be intolerable. It is not important to Hobbes to prove that man once actually lived in a state of nature. He is interested only in demonstrating what life would be like in the absence of government. In Hobbes's expressive words:

[7] *Ibid.*, chap. 13.
[8] *Ibid.*
[9] *Ibid.*
[10] *Ibid.*

> In such a condition, there is no place for industry; because the fruit thereof
> is uncertain; and consequently no culture of the earth, no navigation, nor
> use of the commodities that may be imported by sea; no commodious build-
> ing; no instruments of moving, and removing such things as require much
> force; no knowledge of the face of the earth; no account of time; no arts;
> no letters; no society; and which is worst of all, continual fear, and danger
> of violent death; and the life of man, solitary, poor, nasty, brutish and
> short.[11]

The fact that men are what they are is demonstration of what life
would be if men had to exist in a state of nature. Hobbes offers as
"proof" of his contention the fact that men arm themselves for protection when they go on a journey, that they lock their doors against
intruders, and that they hire public officers to keep the peace. Further
evidence is available in a survey of the international situation.

> In all times, kings, and persons of sovereign authority, because of their in-
> dependency, are in continual jealousies, and in the state and posture of
> gladiators; having their weapons pointing, and their eyes fixed on one
> another; that is, their forts, garrisons, and guns, upon the frontiers of their
> kingdoms; and continual spies upon their neighbours; which is a posture of
> war.[12]

If this is what men are when they enjoy the advantages of organized
society, how much worse would they be in the unrestrained and undisci-
plined environment of a state of nature!

Establishment of the Leviathan

Men cannot hope that a change of human nature will bring peace
and security. They are unalterably selfish. Yet there is a way out—
the only practicable way since it is based upon the inescapable fact of
man's selfish nature. The passion all men have for the gratification of
selfish desire can be employed to achieve a secure and peaceful existence.
Although men are driven by selfishness, they are also reasonable creatures. Their chief goal is preservation of life; their chief fear is that
of death. Men can understand that unless they are willing to accept the
discipline imposed upon them by a superior authority their possessions
and their very lives may be forfeit.

> The passions that incline men to peace, are fear of death; desire of such
> things as are necessary to commodious living; and a hope by their industry
> to obtain them. And reason suggesteth convenient articles of peace, upon
> which men may be drawn to agreement. These articles, are they, which
> otherwise are called the laws of nature.[13]

[11] *Ibid.*
[12] *Ibid.*
[13] *Ibid.*

There are both rights and laws in nature. In a state of nature each person has a right to do anything which in his opinion will promote his own security, including the use of "another's body." As long as this condition exists, there can be no guarantee of "living out the time, which nature ordinarily alloweth men to live." Reason, however, enables men to understand those laws of nature which, when observed, can provide salvation. In the natural state, a law of nature is not a "law" in the true sense at all. Enforcement is necessary to give it such meaning. The law of nature in a state of nature is, instead, "a precept or general rule, found out by reason, by which a man is forbidden to do that which is destructive of his life." [14] Among such precepts are the injunctions to men to "seek peace, and follow it," to defend themselves by whatever means are available, and "to be willing, when others are so too... to lay down this right to all things; and be contented with so much liberty against other men, as he would allow other men against himself." [15]

It is not enough that men understand the principle upon which the secure life must be based, nor that they promise to observe it. Men are still moved by the passion to gratify their self-interest, and "the bonds of words are too weak to bridle men's ambition, avarice, anger, and other passions without the fear of some coercive power; which in the condition of mere nature, where all men are equal, and judges of the justness of their own fears, cannot possibly be supposed." [16] A covenant must be made among men to observe the peace, but it must be attended by a coercive power which will make fear of the consequences of a breach of the covenant a greater force than the greedy desire all men will have to break it. This power can be supplied only through the establishment of a commonwealth "with the constitution of a civil power sufficient to compel men" to keep their promises. In a graphic passage of the *Leviathan* Hobbes explains how the commonwealth is to be brought into being.

> The only way to erect such a common power, as may be able to defend them from the invasion of foreigners, and the injuries of one another, and thereby to secure them in such sort, as that by their own industry, and by the fruits of the earth, they may nourish themselves and live contentedly; is, to confer all their power and strength upon one man, or upon one assembly of men, that may reduce all their wills, by plurality of voices, unto one will: which is as much as to say, to appoint one man, or assembly of men, to bear their person; and every one to own, and acknowledge himself to be author of whatsoever he that beareth their person, shall act, or cause to be acted, in those things which concern the common peace and

[14] *Ibid.*
[15] *Ibid.*, chap. 14.
[16] *Ibid.*

safety; and therein to submit their wills, every one to his will, and their judgments to his judgment. This is more than consent, or concord; it is a real unity of them all, in one and the same person, made by covenant of every man with every man, in such manner, as if every man should say to every man, *I authorize and give up my right of governing myself, to this man or to this assembly of men, on this condition, that thou give up thy right to him, and authorize all his actions in like manner.* This done, the multitude so united in one person is called a COMMONWEALTH, in Latin CIVITAS. This is the generation of that great LEVIATHAN, or rather (to speak more reverently) of that *Mortal God,* to which we owe under the *Immortal God,* our peace and defence.[17]

In explaining the origin of the state, Hobbes rejects the divine-right theory. He may have realized that the theory was on the way to extinction; and besides, Hobbes's mind was of a too practical bent to accept the aura of mysticism underlying the idea. Instead Hobbes employs the contract theory, but in a unique manner. Unlike Locke and later more democratic theorists, Hobbes has no conception of a code of natural law which sovereign authority is obligated to observe and defend. Nor is the contract he describes one between sovereign and subjects. Hobbes recognized the revolutionary implications of both of these theories. If a ruler is pledged to protect the natural liberties of his subjects, those subjects have an obvious right to remove him if he fails in the task. If there is a contract between ruler and subject, either party may repudiate it since a contract implies the equality of the contracting parties. To Hobbes the troublesome party would always be the people. Hobbes's contract, therefore, is designed to avoid any justification of revolution and takes the form of an agreement "of every man with every man" to surrender the rights which were held in a state of nature, along with the power required to protect them, to a sovereign power.

The Hobbesian Sovereign

There are, Hobbes states, two kinds of commonwealths. Commonwealth by "institution" results from an agreement wherein the people voluntarily submit to a sovereign. Commonwealth by "acquisition" is formed when the sovereign takes his position by force; the subject is given the choice between death and submission, and voluntarily accepts surrender. There is no substantial difference between the two commonwealths. Both result from fear. Either the commonwealth is instituted by men because they fear one another, or it is acquired by a conqueror because the subjects fear him. The power of the sovereign over his subjects is as great in one as in another. Neither commonwealth admits the limitations and qualifications which modify the force of Bodin's theory of

[17] *Ibid.,* chap. 17. Italics are in the original.

sovereignty. Hobbes's sovereign has far more complete power than does Bodin's. The sole right which the subject retains in Hobbes's state is that of self-defense. Man is subjected to sovereign authority in order that he may achieve security. If the sovereign cannot provide for his safety, the subject need not obey. In fact a sovereign who cannot protect his subjects is no sovereign at all. There is no divine right of kings and no divine duty of obedience.

> The obligation of subjects to the sovereign, is understood to last as long, and no longer, than the power lasteth by which he is able to protect them. For the right men have by nature to protect themselves, when none else can protect them, can by no covenant be relinquished.... The end of obedience is protection; which wheresoever a man seeth it, either in his own or another's sword, nature applieth his obedience to it, and his endeavour to maintain it.[18]

The rule, in short, is that of self-preservation. Men may resist the sovereign if their lives are at stake. They should exercise great care, however, for resistance is revolution. It results in the destruction of sovereign power and reversion to a state of nature, which is worse than anything in the social state except death. While admitting, then, a limited "right of revolution," Hobbes does not dwell upon it. He is too much a product of his times, too prudent a person, and too heartily sick of the furor which accompanies revolution to seem to condone it. His purpose is to support the absolutism that he believes will maintain the domestic tranquility, not to justify rebellion against authority.

Men must obey the law if there is to be peace in the commonwealth, and, for Hobbes, law is the command of the sovereign, who alone has the power to enforce it. The sovereign is not subject in any manner to the law, for "he that can bind, can release; and therefore he that is bound to himself only, is not bound." [19] Hobbes was cognizant of situations in the past in which the authority of the monarch had been challenged on the ground that monarchical action had contravened the requirements of some kind of law. Natural law, common law, prescriptive law, and the law of custom and tradition had all been so employed. The reasoning was invalid, Hobbes argued, and the matter could only be corrected if men understood the law for what it was, an emanation of sovereign will. As explained above, Hobbes rejected the traditional idea of natural law. There are in nature some "qualities that dispose men to peace, and to obedience," but there are no true laws outside of the commonwealth, and these "qualities" become laws only when the sovereign commands them. The judges, Hobbes said, praise the virtues of the common law, contending that it is based upon reason. They are

---

[18] *Ibid.*, chap. 21.
[19] *Ibid.*, chap. 26.

correct, but the real question is, whose reason? And the answer is, the reason of the sovereign, whose capacity exceeds that of the subordinate judges of the realm. If the judges argue, as did Coke, that they are better equipped to proclaim the law because they have the advantage of study, "it is possible long study may increase, and confirm erroneous sentences: and where men build on false grounds, the more they build, the greater is the ruin . . ." [20] As far as prescription, custom, and tradition are concerned, here too, only sovereign enforcement establishes their validity.

No power on earth transcends that of the sovereign in the making of the law. To be sure, a ruler should follow the laws of God and of nature, but in this conduct he is responsible only to God. The ruler should also follow the paths of custom and tradition and recognize the rights of prescription. Hobbes hoped, too, that the ruler would be temperate and that the laws he enforced would be just and wise. In any event the subject has nothing to say about it. The Leviathan is not government by consent, and the right of the citizen is only to defend himself, not to enter into the law-making process. The law of nature demands conformity among men, and it is a function of the sovereign to enforce this law as he does others. Those who cannot be made to conform must be put out of the community.

> There is in men's aptness to society, a diversity of nature, rising from their diversity of affections; not unlike to that we see in stones brought together for building of an edifice. For as that stone which by the asperity, and irregularity of figure, takes more room from others, than itself fills; and for the hardness, cannot easily be made plain, and thereby hindereth the building, is by the builders cast away as unprofitable, and troublesome: so also, a man that by asperity of nature, will strive to retain those things which to himself are superfluous, and to others necessary; and for the stubbornness of his passions, cannot be corrected, is to be left, or cast out of society, as cumbersome there unto.[21]

Once the people have entered into the contract, it becomes permanently binding. When the covenant is completed no subject is justified in complaining of injury committed by the sovereign. In the first place, the sovereign is not a party to the contract and is not bound by it. In the second place, the people are themselves the authors of the sovereign power and consequently are responsible for whatever is done. "It is true that they that have sovereign power, may commit iniquity; but not injustice, or injury in the proper signification." [22] Tyrannicide is forbidden, not on the ground of *lèse majesté*, but because such action would constitute punishment of the sovereign for a crime authorized by the people. Worse, men would then fall back into a state of nature.

[20] *Ibid.*
[21] *Ibid.*, chap. 15.
[22] *Ibid.*, chap. 18.

The power of the sovereign over all governmental functions is complete. In addition to his authority to make and enforce the law, that is, to exercise the legislative and executive powers, he is the chief judicial officer. He hears and decides all controversies and makes determinations of both fact and law. He controls the military and levies the taxes necessary to support it. He chooses his own ministers and counselors, who are but his agents and responsible solely to him. He has the power to punish and reward his subjects. All this authority must belong to the sovereign, for if his is the responsibility for governing and keeping the peace, which is the chief end of the state, he must control the means to that end. This responsibility also requires that the sovereign govern public opinion. From opinion proceeds action, and no action repugnant to the maintenance of peace may be countenanced. A sovereign ought not to repress truth, but the problem does not arise so long as the repression conduces to peace, for no opinion which endangers the peace can be a true opinion. "It belongeth therefore to him that hath the sovereign power, to be judge, or constitute all judges of opinions and doctrines, as a thing necessary to peace; thereby to prevent discord and civil war." [23]

The power of the sovereign cannot be divided. A mixed state cannot exist: "A kingdom divided in itself, cannot stand." Hobbes believed that the false opinion entertained in England that sovereignty could be shared among kings, Lords, and Commons had led to civil war. There are three possible governmental forms for the commonwealth—monarchy, aristocracy, and democracy. Some of the ancient writers spoke of other forms, such as tyranny, oligarchy, and anarchy, but they are different names for the above-mentioned forms and are applied by those who dislike one or the other of them. One who dislikes monarchy calls it tyranny; an unpopular aristocracy is termed oligarchy; and so forth. The fact is that government will be by one man, a few men, or by many. It cannot be a mixture or combination of all three. "For that were to erect two sovereigns; and every man to have his person represented by two actors, that by opposing one another, must needs divide that power, which (if men will live in peace) is indivisible; and thereby reduce the multitude into the condition of war. . . ." [24]

The advantage or disadvantage of any one of the three possible forms is to be determined solely by its ability to keep the peace. No ethical considerations apply. "The difference between these three kinds of commonwealths, consisteth not in the difference of power; but in the difference of convenience, or aptitude to produce the peace, and security of the people; for which end they were instituted." [25] A government in

[23] *Ibid.*
[24] *Ibid.*, chap. 19.
[25] *Ibid.*

which the public and private interests are closely united is most likely to be able to keep the peace. For this a monarchy has many advantages. A monarch knows that his own fortunes will prosper if those of his subjects do also, and thus his incentive to maintain peace and establish prosperity is strong. There may be inconveniences in a monarchical system, but there are more in other forms. Representative bodies, for example, are unwieldy and given to inconstancy and disagreement among the members. Such groups take too long to make a decision, and they may undo tomorrow what is done today. A monarch, on the other hand, cannot disagree with himself, and monarchy is ordinarily more efficient than other forms of government.

Hobbes's predilection for monarchy is apparent throughout the *Leviathan*. Yet, as we have seen, the *Leviathan* aroused resentment among the royalists who read it. The reason for this reaction, which must have been surprising to Hobbes, is not difficult to discover. In Hobbes's theory it is the performance of the monarch that makes him sovereign rather than any claim to legitimacy. He is sovereign who has the power to maintain himself against those who seek to unseat him. He will survive if he is strong and if he conducts his office so efficiently that major opposition is not likely to arise. Hobbes, the skeptic, the "father of the atheists," as he was called by members of the entourage of Charles II, scorned the traditional justifications of monarchy that saw the king as a representative of God or as heir to the throne by right of succession. For Hobbes, utility is all that counts. A monarch who cannot hold his place does not deserve it. Hobbes's refusal to distinguish between a *de jure* and a *de facto* ruler gave rise to the charge that he had written the *Leviathan* to ingratiate himself with Cromwell. The allegation was unfounded, but there is no doubt that Hobbes himself laid the ground for it in his philosophy.

Despite Hobbes's proposal to vest enormous power in the hands of the sovereign he did not advocate a totalitarian state. While he asserted the "right" of the sovereign to rule in any manner he chose, providing only that he did not deprive a subject of his life, he believed that it would be unwise and impractical for a ruler to interfere with those details of the lives of his people which have nothing to do with the peace and unity of the commonwealth. Subjects should enjoy a measure of freedom. This is not a matter of rights, for rights, such as they are, have been abandoned by the people in creating a sovereign. It is simply that a meddling and greedy ruler may defeat his own ends. Resentment against despotism may bring revolution. Liberty, to Hobbes, has a practical rather than a moral value; it is nonetheless important.

When the sovereign commands, the command is preemptive. If sovereign control is claimed over an area in which subjects formerly enjoyed freedom of action, that freedom disappears. The order must not be protested. On the other hand, the subject has liberty to do anything which is not forbidden by the sovereign. Hobbes contends that this view of law leaves to subjects a broad range of personal freedoms, including "the liberty to buy, and sell, and otherwise contract with one another; to choose their own abode, their own diet, their own trade of life, and institute their children as they themselves think fit; and the like." [26] A wise sovereign, moreover, will rule equitably, knowing that failure to do so will turn his subjects toward the state of nature. The rule of law is a practical necessity rather than a moral obligation on the part of the sovereign. Despotic and arbitrary rule unsettles the foundation of the state.

> The safety of the people, requireth further, from him, or them that have the sovereign power that justice be equally administered to all degrees of people; that is, that as well the rich, and mighty, as poor and obscure persons, may be righted of the injuries done them; so as the great, may have no greater hope of impunity, when they do violence, dishonour, or any injury to the meaner sort, than when one of these, does the like to one of them: For in this consisteth equity; to which, as being a precept of the law of nature, a sovereign is as much subject, as any of the meanest of his people. [27]

But Hobbes is more concerned with security than with freedom. Preservation of the commonwealth and of sovereign power occupy his attention. If the commonwealth fails, as it assuredly will if sovereign power fails, men will be consigned to that most horrible of all fates, life in a state of nature. Hobbes, in a manner reminiscent of Machiavelli, provides a catalog of erroneous suppositions which, unless corrected, will lead to the weakening or destruction of the commonwealth. First is the assumption that a sovereign should relax a control which he has exercised and which he is entitled to exercise. This may produce a temporarily pleasant effect, but there is great danger in the relaxation, for the people will believe that the right of control itself has been abandoned. They will, therefore, greatly resent the sovereign's reimposition of the power, particularly since they will become accustomed to the liberty which attends laxity of administration. Next is that seditious doctrine "that every private man is judge of good and evil actions." This condition prevailed in the state of nature, and nothing will contribute more to a speedy return to that state than a general acceptance of this dangerous principle. Another disease which requires purging is the belief that man should do nothing contrary to conscience. Conscience is only judgment and may be erroneous. The solution to this problem is to obey the law, "because the law is the public conscience."

[26] *Ibid.*, chap. 21.
[27] *Ibid.*, chap. 30.

And the law is not what any man believes it to be but is the will of the sovereign. An additional danger to the commonwealth results from the argument that a man has a greater obligation to his religious faith than to the civil authority. Who can say what God commands? Surely the sovereign is a more reliable source of God's word than are "unlearned Divines," whose interest in propounding such a subversive view is mainly selfish. It is also wrong to contend that the sovereign is subject to the civil laws. If he were, someone would have to be judge when he is charged with a transgression, and the judge would then be above the sovereign, which is impossible. Such confusion would result that the commonwealth would be dissolved.

Although Hobbes favors a considerable measure of economic freedom for the subjects of the commonwealth, he makes it clear that such freedom is contingent upon the will of the sovereign. There is no natural right to property. One only has to know how insecure property is in a state of nature to understand this truth. Protection of property comes with the establishment of sovereign power and consequently is based upon that power. The sovereign has the power to tax, for revenue indispensable to the safety of the state. He should also intervene to prevent too great concentration of wealth in the hands of a few, for this leads to discontent and revolution.

Hobbes considers other "diseases of the commonwealth," only one of which needs to be considered here. In every community associations arise which attempt to compete with the sovereign for power. But as Hobbes stated in considering the various governmental forms available for the commonwealth, there can be only one sovereign. Men cannot serve two masters. The same principle applies to other and nongovernmental associations in the community. They must be controlled by the sovereign; they cannot be permitted a share in the sovereign power. Hobbes rejects the theory of pluralism, which contends that the loyalty of the subject may and should be shared among various organizations of the community, rather than devoted entirely to the state. Such a view encourages the development of factions, dissolves the unity of the commonwealth, and turns the community back toward the state of nature.

In his discussion of the dangers of factions, Hobbes considers the threats posed by private individuals who achieve great popularity, by towns which develop sufficient strength to challenge the authority of the central power, and by others. His chief concern, however, is with the church, for among all the organizations that may compete with the state for power the church is the principal offender. For Hobbes, religion has primarily a political significance. He was not a religious man. His exploration of the political implications of church-state relationships was not, therefore, distracted by the demands of a personal faith, and he could view the church as merely one (although the most important) of many corporations, all of which threaten the sovereign's control of the state. Like other corporations, the church must be controlled by, and subordinated to, the will of the sovereign. If religion demands of the subject some action contrary to the command of the sovereign, a wise subject will obey his sovereign. He may be told by church authorities that the word of God is not always to be comprehended by human reason and that obedience cannot solely be based upon understanding. It is possible, however, that this advice is a mere stratagem designed to attain the end of an unscrupulous cleric and to subvert the authority of the state. Unquestionably some aspects of God's knowledge transcend human reason, but reason is a better instrument than the clergy admits.

> Nevertheless, we are not to renounce our senses, and experience; nor (that which is the undoubted word of God) our natural reason. For they are the talents which He hath put into our hands to negotiate, till the coming again of our blessed Saviour; and therefore not to be folded up in the napkin of an implicit faith, but employed in the purchase of justice, peace, and true religion. For though there be many things in God's word above reason; that is to say, which cannot by natural reason be either demonstrated, or confuted; yet there is nothing contrary to it; but when it seemeth so, the fault is either in our unskillful interpretation, or erroneous ratiocination.[28]

Hobbes clearly believes that a genuine truth will withstand the probing to which it may be subjected by the reasoning mind, and his irony is nowhere more evident than when he comments upon the clerical predilection for warning against such heresy. "For it is with the mysteries of our religion," Hobbes comments, "as with wholesome pills for the sick, which swallowed whole, have the virtue to cure; but chewed, are for the most part cast up again without effect."[29] How can one know in any event whether or not a command comes from God? If God speaks directly to a man, he cannot mistake the validity of the command. But how far is one person obligated to accept the word of another that he is speaking for God? Not only unscrupulous but well-meaning, mistaken persons sometimes make false claims concerning their relationship to God.

> When God speaketh to man, it must be either immediately; or by mediation of another man, to whom He had formerly spoken by Himself immediately. How God speaketh to a man immediately, may be understood by those well enough, to whom He hath so spoken; but how the same should be understood by another, is hard, if not impossible to know. For if a man pretend to me, that God hath spoken to him supernaturally, and immediately, and I make doubt of it, I cannot easily perceive what argument he can produce, to oblige me to believe it.[30]

[28] *Ibid.*, chap. 32.
[29] *Ibid.*
[30] *Ibid.*

If the sovereign, in commanding, says that he speaks for God, the subject will find it the better part of wisdom to obey, even though reason may be outraged. He is under no similar obligation to comply with the orders of anyone else. Hobbes tosses a crumb to the unfortunate citizen who finds himself torn between the demands of church and state. If one is convinced that obedience to the sovereign will result in his eternal damnation because of his repudiation of his faith, he may decide to refuse secular obedience and take the consequences. Hobbes undoubtedly would have regarded such a decision as asinine, but the demand of logic in his theory required that the choice be offered.

Hobbes's most bitter attacks upon organized religion were reserved for the Roman Catholic Church. The final chapters of the *Leviathan* are devoted to a scathing denunciation of that organization's doctrine and officialdom. Yet Hobbes's chief complaint was political rather than doctrinal. The Roman Church, he held, was dangerous because it regarded its claims to the loyalty of the individual as superior to those put forth by the state. This teaching constituted subversion, and was a concomitant of the factionalism to which Hobbes was opposed. The Gunpowder Plot of 1605, in which Catholic conspirators attempted to destroy king and Parliament, and the assassination of Henry IV of France by François Ravaillac, a Catholic extremist, had made a deep impression upon Hobbes and led to his conviction that the Roman Catholic Church was nothing less than an earthly manifestation of the "Kingdom of Darkness." [31] Hobbes's attitude toward the English Puritans and Presbyterians was not markedly different from his view of Catholicism. They were guilty of the same offense in denying the jurisdiction of the sovereign. They encouraged private belief and urged men to follow the dictates of conscience rather than the commands of the state. In doing so they contributed to disunity and civil war.

Hobbes admitted that citizens are entitled to believe, privately, what they will. This was not a moral issue; he believed that the control of private beliefs was beyond the realm of practicality and that it was useless to make the attempt. A man's personal belief in God and his relationship to him were not issues with which the sovereign should be concerned. [32] When a faith develops an organization, however, an entirely different problem is presented. Organizations are material things; what they do has material consequences; and here the right of the sovereign to control is unchallengeable. More, it is mandatory. The only workable solution, Hobbes believed, was the establishment of a state church. In a state church the sovereign is also head of the religious

---

[31] William Ebenstein, *Great Political Thinkers*, Holt, Rinehart and Winston, Inc., New York, 1951, p. 340.

[32] It is usually thought that Hobbes had a personal motive in insisting on the inviolability of opinion. As an atheist he was vulnerable.

community, no conflict can arise between the commands of state and church authorities, for they are one and the same. The citizen is never placed on the horns of the cruel dilemma that compels him to choose between sovereign and God. Moreover the direction of the sovereign in spiritual affairs will probably accord as well with God's word as would the clerics' direction if they had the responsibility of interpreting and handing on that word.

Conclusions

Hobbes's plan to construct a social edifice with geometrical precision was indeed consummated. His philosophy is a masterpiece of logic, with each step in the theoretical structure grounded upon the preceding step. The reader of the *Leviathan* may disagree with much of its content, but he cannot deny Hobbes's capacity to reason through to a conclusion. If there is a weakness in the discussion, it lies in the foundation of the structure, in the postulates of the theory. If the foundation is firm, the structure must stand; if flaws appear in the groundwork, the structure is weaker, although it is not necessarily destroyed. Vulnerability of the structure may also result from the method by which Hobbes erects it. That method is one of logic rather than of empiricism and observation, and a strong case can be made against a total reliance on logic in the interpretation of human affairs.

Hobbes's postulates include, among others, the assumption that men are inordinately concerned with security, that fear (especially fear of death) is the prime mover among men, and that men are insatiable in their striving to serve their own interests and in their attempts to secure the power necessary to this end. Hobbes, indeed, paints a gloomy picture of man. The real question is whether the facts support his pessimism. He was not the first to view human nature in such a light. Many men have accepted both Hobbes's premises and his conclusions, and many will continue to be attracted by them in spite of challenging argument. Still, discussion may stimulate thought on the subject.

The most common charge leveled against Hobbes is that he carries his assumptions too far. The accusation is just. Man, though of course interested in his order and security, is not so concerned as Hobbes believed him to be. He knows that too high a price may be paid for these advantages in the form of a surrender of liberty. Hobbes also believes that the only purpose of the state is to provide security, and many individualist thinkers after him have echoed that sentiment. Protection of life and property is unquestionably a valuable service, but as Aristotle and modern progressives have persuasively argued, it is equally important that the state should promote morality and the good life. As to that universal fear of death which, in Hobbes's view, is an obsession among men, Hobbes exaggerates the point. We cannot deny that death is repugnant and that men seek to avoid it as long as possible, but that anything is preferable to death for all men is not true. Men have martyred themselves for a belief, and accounts of occasions when they have risked their lives in order to defeat oppression are common in history. The degree to which men fear death must vary among men, and perhaps Hobbes judged all others on the basis of his knowledge of himself.

Similar criticism may be directed against Hobbes's conviction that men are entirely selfish, that they seek only their own ends and the power (and here their desires are unlimited) to safeguard what they have. Granting that men have a strong compulsion to do what is good for themselves, it can also be argued that they are motivated, at times at least, by altruism, that human character possesses nobility, and that the spirit of self-sacrifice is evidenced too often to be dismissed as a mere aberration. It is doubtful that infants could ever reach maturity if their parents were as thoroughly selfish as Hobbes believes all men are. Indeed all human institutions, which depend upon a reasonable spirit of cooperation, would be dissolved if man had to rely only upon the fiat of the sovereign to hold them together. Moreover, if men were as selfish as Hobbes says they are, the law itself could have no force. As Professor Lindsay has stated, the effectiveness of a law against burglary results from the fact that most men do not wish to burgle.[33]

Despite Hobbes's admission of restrictions which the sovereign may impose upon the individual, his theory still contains strong elements of individualism. The sole function of the state and of the sovereign is to provide security for the individual. They exist to serve his purposes. He does not exist merely to obey the sovereign or to advance the cause of the state. The sovereign does not define morality or force the individual to live the "good life," however it may be defined. Hobbes assumes that the individual may exercise freedom within a wide latitude, and that he is at liberty to do anything which the sovereign does not, in the interest of security, proscribe. Hobbes's government is *for*, although not *by*, the people. His individualism is a symbol of the transition from medievalism to modern times, and it sets the stage for the developments of the next two centuries. Individualism was ultimately used to justify a predatory economics which has at times more closely resembled Hobbes's conception of a state of nature than his organized political state. Nevertheless it had value in helping to free the individual from the bonds of community in which he had for so many centuries been held.

Hobbes's theory had no immediate impact upon the society in which he lived, apart from the intense and personal controversy that his writings occasioned. The long-term effects were not apparent until the

[33] In Hobbes, *op. cit.*, introduction, pp. xxii–xxiii.

essential ingredients of his philosophy were incorporated into the philosophy of Bentham and the utilitarians in the late eighteenth and the nineteenth centuries. The theory was, even then, directed to ends which Hobbes would scarcely have approved.[34] The utilitarians accepted the Hobbesian premise that men are driven by their desire to avoid pain and obtain pleasure. Hobbes's doctrine of self-interest became a postulate of utilitarianism, although Bentham believed that the interest of the individual would be of a more enlightened variety, and not so innately antagonistic to the welfare of one's fellows. The utilitarians, too, judged the value of institutions on the basis of their ability to perform their designated functions. And they had no more respect than did Hobbes for what they (and he) regarded as the claptrap concerning a system of natural rights.

SELECTED BIBLIOGRAPHY

Catlin, George: *The Story of the Political Philosophers,* McGraw-Hill Book Company, Inc., New York, 1939, chap. 8.

Ebenstein, William: *Great Political Thinkers,* Holt, Rinehart and Winston, Inc., New York, 1951, chap. 14.

Hacker, Andrew: *Political Theory: Philosophy, Ideology, Science,* The Macmillan Company, New York, 1961, chap. 6.

Hearnshaw, F. J. C. (ed.): *The Social and Political Ideas of Some Great Thinkers of the Sixteenth and Seventeenth Centuries,* George G. Harrap & Co., Ltd., London, 1926, chap. 7.

Hobbes, Thomas: *Leviathan* (introduction by A. D. Lindsay), E. P. Dutton & Co., Inc., New York, 1914, introduction.

Sabine, George H.: *A History of Political Theory,* 3d ed., Holt, Rinehart and Winston, Inc., New York, 1961, chaps. 22, 23.

Wolin, Sheldon S.: *Politics and Vision,* Little, Brown and Company, Boston, 1961, chap. 8.

[34] Sabine, *op. cit.,* p. 456.

thirteen

JOHN LOCKE

Radical and Republican Theory of Seventeenth-century England

The individualism of Hobbes's theory provided support for his advocacy of absolute government. In this Hobbes was out of step with future developments, which witnessed a quite different employment of individualist doctrine. Most political philosophy in the seventeenth century contended that the interest of the individual would best be served through the limitation of governmental authority and the consequent expansion of personal freedom. To this end political theorists advocated the principles of natural law and rights, government by consent, limited and responsible government, the right of revolution, as well as the necessary enabling mechanisms. These ideas were to dominate political speculation for two hundred years. The Civil War of the 1640s in England did much to stimulate public debate on things political and governmental. With a monarch deposed and beheaded, what (or who) was to take his place? A revolution, essentially a negative act, must be followed by positive action in order to avoid anarchy. But what action? Before the century was out the English established the constitutional monarchy which, though it has been extensively reformed, has served them since that time. But factions, even in the 1640s, advocated solutions more radical than those ultimately adopted. In doing so they were rather accurately anticipating the liberal and individualist doctrines of the eighteenth and nineteenth centuries.[1]

One such faction was called the Levellers. It comprised, essentially, a group of the lower middle class in Cromwell's army. The term "leveller" was applied by enemies who charged that the end sought by the group was the complete eradication of all political, economic, and social distinctions. The accusation was unjust. The Levellers wanted a responsible government over which they could exercise control. They presented to Cromwell's officers a document incorporating their demands when they concluded that the leadership was procrastinating unjustifiably in establishing a proper government after the defeat of Charles's forces. The Leveller document, *An Agreement of the People,* called for a more equitable system of representation in Parliament through a redrawing of legislative districts. It asserted the right of the people to elect a new legislative body every two years, demanded establishment of the principles of popular sovereignty and parliamentary supremacy (over other branches of government), and proposed that Parliament should not be permitted to interfere with religious freedom, to conscript men for military service, or to deprive any person of his equality under the law irrespective of his station in life. John Lilburne (c. 1614–1657), the fiery leader of the Levellers, stated the unequivocal commitment of his following to the principle of consent in his *The Free Man's Freedom Vindicated.* It is, he said, "unnatural" and completely wrong for any person, on the basis either of claimed temporal or of spiritual authority, to rule other men unless those others give their consent freely and voluntarily to his rulership. The Levellers sought political equality and based their claim on the law of nature, which, they contended, justified it.

Another and contemporary movement made more far-reaching demands through the use of that law. This was the Diggers, a religioeconomic group, whose members argued that the revolution should bring economic equality. The Diggers held to the venerable Christian idea that the communal state is perfect, whereas the private ownership of property is evidence of man's fall. The concept was, however, altered in Digger thought. In Christian theory, man's sinfulness necessitated private property; the Diggers held that private property is the *cause* of sin and of the inequality and degradation of mankind.[2] This interpretation closely approximates the views of the nineteenth-century socialists. Another parallel is found in the Diggers' contention that wealth is the result of community effort and that justice demands consideration of the community in its distribution. This was a view strongly argued by Gerrard Winstanley (1609?–?), leader of the Diggers, in his *The Law of*

[1] George H. Sabine, *A History of Political Theory,* 3d ed., Holt, Rinehart and Winston, Inc., New York, 1961, pp. 477–478.
[2] *Ibid.,* p. 492.

Freedom in a Platform. The Diggers constituted a very small group and their views were neither widely shared nor well received. They were really less concerned with the development of a philosophy and the organization of a social movement than they were with the achievement and justification of an immediate goal, which was to produce crops on unenclosed common land. Although some of the tracts of Winstanley contain elements suggestive of proletarian theory of the nineteenth century, the Diggers were pacifists rather than revolutionaries and would undoubtedly have been repelled by the advocacy of force that marked the development of later communist thought.

Mention must also be made of the theory of republicanism which was propounded by James Harrington (1611–1677). Harrington departed from the legalistic and moralistic grounds commonly employed to justify republicanism and based his theory upon economic determinism. He was by inclination a republican. He was also a friend of Charles I, and he avoided, until the execution of the king, involvement in the struggle between crown and Parliament. After the establishment of the Commonwealth, Harrington formulated the rules for stable government which he advocated in his *Oceana,* a political romance, published in 1656. The fundamental idea in Harrington's theory is that the stability of the political community is dependent upon the proper correlation between the governmental form and the ownership of property. Governmental power derives from property ownership. If the bulk of property is owned by the few, an oligarchy is suitable. If property ownership is widespread, democracy is the appropriate form. A variety of combinations is possible under this rule.

The proper functioning of civil society is, however, not automatically achieved through the correct correlation of political and economic power. For this statesmanship is necessary, and statesmanship is more competently exercised in a commonwealth than in other forms of government. This is so, Harrington says, because in a commonwealth laws rather than men govern and because a commonwealth permits a greater coincidence of individual and public interest. In England the shifting of the economic base of power from the nobility to the middle class made a commonwealth the appropriate governmental form. The problem as Harrington saw it was to create a situation that would consolidate middle-class control. Laws should be enacted to prevent any eventual concentration of property into fewer hands, which would make a continuation of the commonwealth impossible. To this end Harrington suggested measures that would assure a division of land so as to permit no landowner an annual income in excess of 2,000 pounds.[3] The governmental structure

---

[3] Harrington assumed land to be the only important form of wealth. Though he conceded that in such small commercial countries as Florence capital might be the basis of wealth, he did not believe it could assume such importance in England.

and methods employed to select officials and hold them responsible should also be designed to maintain the commonwealth. Legislators should be salaried, and there should be a minimal property qualification for holding legislative office; this would ensure a legislative body that would not consist only of men of great wealth. Harrington advocated short terms of office and rotation in office, as well as free elections and the use of the secret ballot by citizens, although he proposed that citizenship be held only by those who had the means to an independent livelihood. Harrington also recommended separation of powers in the government between a senate of 300 members and a representative assembly of 1,050. The former was to have the function of debating and formulating policy; the latter was to act only as a ratifying body. The *Oceana* contains, in addition, proposals for a written constitution, free public education, and a considerable degree of freedom of religion.

Harrington's theory was more influential in America than it was in England. Some Americans knew Harrington's work and were impressed by it. The Massachusetts Constitutional Convention of 1799 toyed with the idea of substituting Oceana for Massachusetts as the name of the commonwealth. There is no doubt that Harrington's proposals for the ideal commonwealth entered significantly into that and many other constitutional conventions in the United States. The American concepts of a written constitution, the principle of election, separation of powers, short terms of office, religious freedom, and others all owe something to Harrington.

Harrington was not a democrat; his were the principles of republicanism rather than democracy. Nor was he a socialist. His recommendation for the division of land had a political, rather than an economic, purpose. Moreover, he was convinced that 5,000 landowners would be sufficient to ensure the continuity of the commonwealth—hardly a proposal for an equitable distribution of wealth. Yet Harrington's ideas foreshadow democratic developments, and his theory that economic power was the basis of political power makes him a forerunner of the socialists of the nineteenth century.

John Locke: The Man and His Work

The Civil War of the 1640s in England had given rise to a great amount of political speculation ranging from the advocacy of absolutism in Hobbes's *Leviathan,* through the republicanism of Harrington and John Milton, to the liberalism and radicalism of the Levellers and Diggers. The war was followed by the Commonwealth under Cromwell. That government was so unpopular that republican theory was discredited, and Englishmen generally welcomed the Restoration. Yet the acceptance of Charles II did not signify a willingness of the people to submit to the dictates of an absolute monarch. Parliament was to play a more significant role, but precisely *how* significant was not yet determined. The twenty-five-year reign of Charles II (1660–1685) was a period of relative domestic peace. The king, made wary by the fate of his father, did not outrage the sensitivities of his people, and they, weary of civil strife, were momentarily quiescent. A more precise delineation of the powers of king and Parliament was established by the "Glorious" or "Bloodless" Revolution of 1688. The revolution resulted from the efforts of James II, successor to Charles II, to promote the cause of Catholicism in England. His enemies took advantage of the Protestant sentiment in the country to remove James from the throne. The constitutional settlement that ensued recognized the supremacy of Parliament. The principles of the settlement had been anticipated in the writings of a number of philosophers of the period. Among these John Locke is predominant.

Locke was born on August 29, 1632 at Wrington, Somersetshire.[4] His father's name was also John; his mother's maiden name was Agnes Keene. His grandfather was a clothier of means, who employed a large number of persons in the spinning of yarn and weaving of cloth. Locke's father was a lawyer and a clerk to the justices of the peace in the county. He was less well to do than his merchant father but became a landowner in his own right and was by no means poor. The family was ardently Puritan and sided with the Parliamentary forces in the Civil War. Locke's father was a captain in the Cromwellian army. He was strict, as became a Puritan father, but his relationship with his son was excellent, and his death was sincerely mourned by the younger Locke.

Through family influence John Locke was admitted, at the age of fifteen, to Westminster School. The school was headed at this time by Richard Busby, an arch Royalist, whose influence on Locke was pitted against Locke's family background. Busby, however, was no autocrat and was more concerned with developing the critical faculties of his students than with indoctrinating them. The results generally were salutary, and Locke particularly was benefited. He was helped to develop a rational approach to problems, and the foundation for his later liberalism was laid at Westminster School. In 1652, when he was nineteen, Locke was elected to a scholarship at Christ Church, Oxford. He was as critical of the curriculum as Hobbes had been. Some scholars there, however, particularly in the medical faculty, were employing the empirical approach. They exerted a great influence upon Locke, and his lifelong interest in medicine and science generally, as well as his tendency toward empiricism, was developed during this period.

Locke's father died in 1660 leaving to his son some property in land and cottages. Locke was an exacting landlord. He was, throughout his life, somewhat penurious. Management of his property was turned over

---

[4] Biographical material is based mainly on Maurice Cranston, *John Locke: A Biography*, The Macmillan Company, New York, 1957.

to an uncle, and Locke remained at Oxford, where he had been elected a tutor at Christ Church as Lecturer in Greek. Locke was experiencing difficulty at this time in choosing a career. He seriously considered joining the clergy, but his main interest was science. He continued his medical studies and also studied under the great Robert Boyle. In 1665 he left Oxford for a time to become secretary to the diplomatic mission to Brandenburg of Sir Walter Vane. The excursion was significant mainly in that Locke observed and commended the large degree of religious toleration that existed in Brandenburg. Locke's diplomatic "career" was cut short with the failure of the mission, and he returned to Oxford and the study of medicine.

It was at this point that Locke met Anthony Ashley Cooper, later first Earl of Shaftesbury, who was to figure prominently in Locke's career. The two men were immediately attracted to one another, and in 1667 Locke accepted Shaftesbury's invitation to live at his home in London as the nobleman's personal physician. Shaftesbury had worked for the restoration of the monarchy and had been rewarded by the king for his efforts. He was made a Lord and given the position of Privy Councilor. He later organized the Whig party, and the Tory party came into existence in opposition. Shaftesbury was a proponent of religious toleration, mainly because of his belief that intolerance bred divisions in society and adversely affected trade and commerce. He was, nevertheless, anti-Catholic, and urged passage of the Exclusion Act, designed to remove any Catholic from the line of succession and to legitimize the Duke of Monmouth, illegitimate son of Charles II, and make him eligible for the kingship. This, and other matters, created a breach between Shaftesbury and the king, who had his former Councilor arrested and sent to the Tower on several occasions. Shaftesbury ultimately fled to Holland, where he died in January, 1683.

It is possible that Shaftesbury's opposition to Charles gave Locke the incentive to write his famous *Two Treatises of Government*. The time was indeed opportune for the development of a theory that would justify a revolution and provide a basis for the kind of government which both Locke and Shaftesbury believed should be established. Until recently it had been commonly supposed that the *Two Treatises* were written by Locke in 1689 to justify the Glorious Revolution of 1688. Current scholarship has, however, discredited the theory and placed the composition at or before 1681.[5] At any rate, Locke's close friendship with

---

[5] Cranston (*op. cit.,* p. 207) believes that the *Two Treatises* were written in 1681. Laslett places the writing somewhat earlier, in 1679 or 1680. In either case the earlier dates make sense since they correspond to the period of Shaftesbury's greatest difficulties with Charles II. See Peter Laslett (ed.), *John Locke: Two Treatises of Government* (a Critical Edition with an Introduction and Apparatus Criticus), Cambridge University Press, New York, 1960, pp. 45–59.

Shaftesbury brought him under a cloud of suspicion, and he too went to Holland, in the autumn of 1683, after having destroyed a great many of his papers.

While Locke was in Holland, events were taking place in England which would bring to a close that country's century of revolution, unseat the monarch, and bring Locke back to his native land. Charles had died in 1685, and his brother, the Duke of York, had taken the throne as James II. This was the consummation that Shaftesbury had so strongly opposed, and after the event it was apparent that his sentiments were shared by many of his countrymen. A Catholic monarch was distinctly unpalatable; James's obvious efforts to place Catholics in many positions of authority were even more so. Still James's wife, the Catholic Princess of Modena, was childless, and many Englishmen hoped that James would be succeeded by his Protestant daughter by a previous marriage, Mary of Orange. But in June of 1688 these hopes were temporarily crushed when the Queen gave birth to a son. A powerful opposition to the court developed and sought the assistance of William of Orange, husband of Mary. William, who had long been eying the situation in England, assented. An invasion fleet was launched from Holland in October; the forces of William met scanty resistance, and the "Bloodless" Revolution was soon accomplished.

Locke delayed his own departure from Holland until the following February. When he arrived in England he found that he was strongly in the court's favor. He was offered several ambassadorial posts, but he declined, saying that he mistrusted his capacity to withstand the rigors of diplomatic drinking. He accepted, instead, the more modest post of Commissioner of Appeals, which, while it paid little, made no great demand upon his time. Locke published, anonymously, his *Two Treatises of Government* in 1689. His *Letter on Toleration,* another anonymous publication, had already appeared. *The Essay Concerning Human Understanding* had appeared over his own signature; it was, moreover, generally known that he was the author of the *Treatises* and the *Letter.* By 1692 Locke's reputation as an author was well established.

The London climate proved injurious to Locke's health, and an increasing part of his time was spent in the country at Oates with friends, Sir Francis and Lady Masham. It was still a busy time for Locke. He accepted an appointment as Commissioner of Trade, a remunerative and demanding position. He devoted much energy to replying to attacks made upon him on the ground that his *Essay* demonstrated an antireligious bias.[6] He maintained his relations with a number of friends, including Sir Isaac Newton. Locke's constitution, however, was not equal to the strain placed upon it. He resigned his commissionership in the

---

[6] The charge was unfounded. Locke was tolerant and liberal-minded on religious matters, but he was a pious man.

spring of 1700; it was his last public office. During his last few years he studied the Bible, especially the Epistles of St. Paul, and wrote *A Paraphrase and Notes on the Epistles of St. Paul, etc.*, which was published posthumously. He died peacefully at Oates on October 28, 1704.

The First Treatise

In giving his comprehensive title to the *Two Treatises* John Locke supplies the key to an understanding of his purpose. That title is: *Two Treatises of Government: In the Former, the False Principles and Foundation of Sir Robert Filmer, and His Followers, Are Detected and Overthrown. The Latter Is an Essay Concerning the True Original, Extent, and End of Civil Government.*[7] Thus the first treatise was written specifically to refute the theory developed by Filmer in his *Patriarcha*. Filmer, an ardent champion of royal absolutism, had died in 1653, but his *Patriarcha* was not published until 1680, when the supporters of Charles II used it to buttress their arguments in favor of royal prerogative against the king's opposition, which included Locke and Shaftesbury. The second treatise was a more constructive work designed by Locke to explain the origin, authority, and purpose of civil government. Locke probably began the second treatise before the first, but being diverted by the publication and rising influence of the *Patriarcha,* wrote the first treatise to cut the ground from under the opposition before offering a more positive theory of his own.[8] If the treatises were written at this time, why were they not published until after the Revolution of 1688? It may well be that such a course at such a time would have been dangerous. A more moderate view than that of Locke cost the republican Algernon Sidney his life in 1683. And Locke was a prudent man, as is demonstrated by the fact that even when the treatises were finally published, Locke did not admit his authorship.

Filmer's theory purports to be a sociological account of the conditions of social order, which he designates as hierarchy and command. Filmer's position was that man is always born into society, never into a state of nature, and that society is invariably organized by command. The theory was designed to support the principle of royal prerogative. It was vulnerable insofar as Filmer used the Bible as reliable anthropological evidence to support his theory, and Locke attacked this unsound testimony, employing a rational and commonsense interpretation of the Scriptures in a point-by-point refutation. Locke's treatment of Filmer is both superficial and unfair. He attributes to Filmer positions which the latter did not take. He charges, for example, that Filmer is proposing a theory of original donation and subsequent inheritance of power from

[7] All references are to the corrected copy of the third edition in the library of Christ's College, Cambridge, reproduced in Laslett (ed.), *op. cit.*

[8] Laslett (ed.), *op. cit.*, p. 59.

God to Adam; actually Filmer does nothing of the sort. Locke was successful in pointing out the weaknesses of Filmer's Scriptural evidence; [9] it is not certain that he was successful in meeting the real issue—the patriarchal idea itself. As Laslett has said, Locke did not recognize the strength of that idea, and his own arguments did not always meet the real issue. Moreover, if Filmer's "proofs" were often fanciful, much the same charge may be leveled against Locke, for he would be hard pressed to demonstrate the historical authenticity of the state of nature, the social compact, and other aspects of his theory. [10] It was formerly and generally thought that Hobbes, rather than Filmer, was Locke's real opponent. Recent scholarship mainly rejects this thesis and takes Locke's word for the matter; he cited Filmer as the enemy, and there is no compelling reason to doubt him. Certainly Filmer's *Patriarcha* was more an object of concern to the opponents of absolutism at the time than was Hobbes's *Leviathan*. In a sense, however, the issue is unimportant. In opposing absolutism, Locke was against both Filmer and the "sage of Malmesbury," although Hobbes would have viewed Filmer's "evidence" with even greater contempt than did Locke. In the *First Treatise* Locke states the position which he maintains in the *Second* and which places him in opposition to both Filmer and Hobbes. It is not enough, he says, to insist that all men have a duty to obey government; merely to say so "signifies nothing." It is also necessary to know that the authority imposed upon men is lawful—that he who is obeyed has a right to obedience.

The Second Treatise—the Nature of Man and the State of Nature

The heart of Locke's political theory is found in the *Second Treatise*. In it he considers the origin and proper use of political power, which he defines as the *"Right* of making Laws with Penalties of Death, and consequently all less Penalties, for the Regulating and Preserving of Property, and of employing the force of the Community, in the Execution of such Laws, and in the defense of the Common-wealth from Foreign Injury, and all this only for the Publick Good." [11]

Locke begins, as did Hobbes, with a discussion of the nature of man and of a state of nature. The state of nature has two characteristics. First, it is a "state of perfect freedom," in which men do as they choose within the limits imposed by the law of nature. Second, it is a state of equality for its inhabitants. No one has any more right, authority, or jurisdiction than does anyone else. Men are born equal in this way—

[9] Francis D. Wormuth, *The Royal Prerogative*, Cornell University Press, Ithaca, N.Y., 1939, chap. 6, parts I, III.

[10] Laslett (ed.), *op. cit.*, p. 69.

[11] *Ibid.*, II, 3.

not equal in capacity but equal in the rights they possess. Locke and Hobbes agree up to this point, but a wide gap develops immediately. For Hobbes the equality and freedom of men in a state of nature leads directly to a state of war among them. Not so for Locke. His state of nature is not a utopia; neither is it a state of war. The saving feature is the existence of the law of nature.

> The State of Nature has a Law of Nature to govern it, which obliges every-one: and Reason, which is that Law, teaches all Mankind, who will but consult it, that being all equal and independent, no one ought to harm another in his Life, Health, Liberty, or Possessions.[12]

Men, then, are governed in their natural state by the natural law. This law is capable of being understood by rational men. Though rational, however, such men are not perfect, and differences of interpretation are to be expected. We are all a little selfish, some of us more than a little. Moreover, in a state of nature, each person has a responsibility for en-forcing the law of nature. No true law can exist without enforcement, and in a state of nature the authority is in every man's hands. Although these imperfect conditions create inconveniences, they do not lead to a state of war; war results only from the imposition by force of arbitrary rule. Most men are reasonable enough to understand that observance of the natural law is necessary in their own interest.

Still, it is possible for men to improve their circumstances. Specifically three defects of the state of nature impel men to consider their situation and seek remedies. First, there is no "established, settled, known law." If all men were equal in their capacity to understand the law of nature this lack would be unimportant, but they may be influenced by self-interest, or they may not have studied the law of nature. Second, the natural state lacks "a known and indifferent judge" to settle disputes which arise under the law of nature. Since each person is judge, each is likely to see too much merit in his own case and be too little concerned with justice for others. Third, in a state of nature there is no executive power to enforce judgments. This authority too is placed in the hands of each man, and various persons are unequal in their ability to enforce the law. "Thus Mankind, notwithstanding all the privileges of the state of Nature, being but in an ill condition, while they remain in it, are quickly driven into Society." [13]

It should be stated parenthetically that this matter of the relationship of man to the law of nature was a problem that long troubled Locke. He was certain that in order to have a good society it was necessary to arrive at a consensus with regard to moral beliefs. Men cannot, he be-lieved, live together in peace unless they are in substantial agreement on

[12] *Ibid.*, II, 6.
[13] *Ibid.*, II, 127.

the question of what is and is not moral conduct. In his early writings, specifically in the *Essays on the Law of Nature,* which were completed by 1664, Locke assumed that a code of moral behavior was contained in the law of nature as a divine decree. This assumption, however, raised the question of how and by whom the principles of that law and code could be apprehended. The natural-law tradition had taught that the conscience and rationality of each man were adequate for this purpose, but Locke grew increasingly dubious on the point. It seemed to him that the mass of men were incapable of the intellectual effort required for a rational understanding of the natural law; he also held grave reservations regarding the efficacy of individual conscience. These doubts are evidenced in the *Second Treatise.*

In 1695, with the publication of an essay entitled *The Reasonableness of Christianity,* Locke presented his solution to the problem. The Christian ethic, he said, presents the necessary code of moral behavior expressed in terms which the mass of men may grasp. Moreover, it is accompanied by the concept of authority necessary to enforce it. God rewards the obedient and punishes the disobedient. The principles of moral conduct, given as God's commands, can be accepted even without the intellectual comprehension that goes with philosophical study and contemplation. Thus it is the Christian ethic, enforced by divine directive, rather than the natural law as apprehended by individual conscience, which provides mankind with the rules of moral conduct necessary to the good social life. As Locke suggested in the *Second Treatise,* conscience reflects the faultiness of individual judgment and is, consequently, unreliable; it must, in civil society, give way to a collective judgment exercised by the legislative.[14] As indicated above, however, this modification of natural-law theory was not developed by Locke until 1695, some time after the writing of the *Second Treatise.*

Establishment of Society and Government

It is important to note that for Locke the inconveniences of a state of nature do not make it intolerable. Difficult as the natural state is, life in an organized society under a tyrant is far worse. This conclusion marks a significant difference between the theories of Locke and Hobbes, a fact of which Locke is well aware. He could hardly have had anything else in mind in the following passage:

> And here we have the plain *difference between the State of Nature, and the State of War,* which however some Men have confounded, are as far distant, as a State of Peace, Good Will, Mutual Assistance and Preservation,

[14] Sheldon Wolin, *Politics and Vision: Continuity and Innovation in Western Political Thought,* Little, Brown and Company, Boston, 1960, pp. 334–338. See also Leo Strauss, "Locke's Doctrine of Natural Law," *American Political Science Review,* vol. 52, no. 2, pp. 490–501, June, 1958.

and a State of Enmity, Malice, Violence, and Mutual Destruction are from one another.[15]

Men come to understand that improvement over the natural state may result from the organization of a civil society and the creation of instruments that will correct the deficiencies indicated above. This systematizing of men's affairs is accomplished by the making of a compact in which free and equal men consent to surrender their natural liberty to interpret, judge, and enforce the law of nature and "unite into a Community, for their comfortable, safe, and peaceable living one amongst another, in a secure Enjoyment of their Properties, and a greater security against any that are not of it." [16] The compact is created by the unanimous consent of those who enter into it. No one is compelled to be a party to it; those who do not wish to form a community simply remain in the state of nature. Those who have entered into the compact, however, agree from this point to be governed by majority decision. Majority rule is necessary for two reasons: First, men have agreed to create a community that can act as a single body, and a body must "move that way whither the greater force carries it, which is the *consent of the majority*." [17] Second, the only alternative—to secure the consent of each individual to every proposition —would be impossible.[18] Locke's justification of the right of the majority to make decisions is not so compelling as we could wish. Possibly he simply regarded the right as self-evident, and thought it unnecessary to devote more attention to the subject.

Locke recognized and replied to two major objections to his argument that civil society was and should be established by the consent of its members. First, is there historical evidence for this theory? Locke says there is, and he cites examples, including the founding of Rome and Venice, to support his contention. But, Locke says, the fact is that in most instances such evidence is lacking. Government precedes written records. Men are so strongly inclined to form civil society that they do

---

[15] Laslett (ed.), *op. cit.*, II, 19. Italics are in the original.

[16] *Ibid.*, II, 95.

[17] *Ibid.*, II, 96. Italics are in the original.

[18] A great deal of commentary concerning Locke's theory of majority rule has been produced. Much is valid, but apparently some rests upon a misinterpretation of Locke's meaning. It has been objected, for example, that Locke's contention that the compact and the community are destroyed if the majority do not govern is faulty since the minority can and will govern if the majority does not. I believe that the basis for such an objection, and many others, disappears if it is borne in mind that Locke meant only that minority rule would destroy the good community. Locke was not ignorant of the realities of political life; surely he knew that minorities had governed. It was merely that he objected to this kind of government. The reader who wishes to explore Locke's theory of majority rule in considerable detail will do well to consult Willmoore Kendall, *John Locke and the Doctrine of Majority-rule*, in *Illinois Studies in the Social Sciences*, vol. 26, no. 2, University of Illinois Press, Urbana, Ill., 1941.

so as soon as a number of them are brought together. There is another and related problem. If civil societies were created by consent, and if such societies are inferior when governed by a single and arbitrary ruler, why is it that, as history proves to us, most of the societies of the past have been established under an absolute ruler? Locke's view is that the single ruler was suitable to the earliest and most simple societies. Men were accustomed to obeying a father; obedience to a king was a logical next step. Moreover, the function of the early society was elementary, confined, as it was, mainly to providing for the defense of its members. There was no need for a more elaborate government and the "multiplicity of laws" that are required by the modern and complicated society. It is a grudging but necessary concession to Filmer; but, Locke adds, these were still governments established by consent. Only when rulers violated their trust did men begin to reconsider the principles upon which society was established.

Locke had to meet a more pertinent objection. Granting that some original group gives consent to the establishment of civil society, we may wonder how the compact theory applies to those who come after them, those who are *born into* civil society? Can a man be born free and yet be under the jurisdiction of society? Locke answers that, in the first place, the consent of the newborn child is not involved, for he is born a ward of his parents, not a subject. The child gives consent only when he comes of age, and then gives generally a tacit, rather than an explicit, consent. Consent is assumed when the individual remains in the society, takes advantage of the protection and services that society offers him, and obeys the laws of the community. Consent is not, however, forced upon any member of the community. Individuals who have given only tacit consent may withdraw and return to a state of nature or establish their own community. Anyone who has given an explicit consent is bound by it and may not withdraw from the community unless the government is dissolved or he is, "by some public act," put out of the community. Locke has some difficulty with the problem. The justification of consent is difficult when the matter is considered on an abstract basis. To demonstrate its validity in practical and historical terms is an infinitely harder task. As J. W. Gough has said, Locke's efforts in this direction are significant mainly in demonstrating the difficulty of proving the point.[19]

Once a society is organized, men turn their attention to the creation of the instruments that may be used to solve the problems experienced in a state of nature. In short, they now create government, and the man-

[19] John Locke, *The Second Treatise of Government (an Essay Concerning the True Original, Extent and End of Civil Government) and a Letter Concerning Toleration* (edited with an introduction by J. W. Gough), The Macmillan Company, New York, 1956, p. xxii.

ner in which government is brought into operation is significant. Neither Locke nor Hobbes imagines that the contract was used for this purpose, but they reject the postulate for a strangely similar, yet different, reason. A contract between two parties implies their equality and stipulates various rights and obligations pertaining to each. Hobbes rejects the use of contract between people and government because he does not wish to imply that people are the equal of government or that government has duties toward people. Locke's reasoning is the reverse of this. Government is not the equal of the people; moreover it has duties to the people. It must be an agent of the people, not a partner.

How, then, is government created? The answer is, through a trust arrangement. The relationship between government and governed is analogous to that which exists between the parties in a legal trust. The government is the trustee who functions for and is responsible to the people who create the trust. Thus the trustee, or government, has no rights equal to those held by the people, but only obligations to those for whom it acts as agent. Locke does not outline this arrangement as clearly as is indicated here, but the concept of trust is recurrent throughout the *Second Treatise,* and this is clearly the idea he intended to convey.

Locke now considers the *kind* of government which is to be formed through the trust arrangement and concludes that it is determined by the deficiencies of life in a state of nature. Since there is no "established, settled, known law" there must be a law-making body. This is the "legislative," and it is "the supreme power in every commonwealth." [20] The majority may place the legislative in themselves to form a democracy. The form of government is determined by the manner in which legislative authority is exercised. The best kind of government, Locke states, is that in which "the *Legislative* Power is put into the hands of divers Persons who, duly Assembled, have by themselves, or jointly with others, a Power to make Laws." [21] Locke is, of course, asserting the desirability of a representative assembly as the legislative body.

Although Locke refers to the legislative as the "supreme power" in the commonwealth, he does not intend it to be considered as having absolute authority. There are four specific limitations upon that authority: First, it cannot be exercised in an arbitrary manner. Second, it must be directed toward the good of society. Third, it cannot deprive any man of his property without his consent. Fourth, it cannot give up its power to make laws to any other body or person, for only the people have the right to assign legislative authority. Moreover, the legislative power is supreme only in relationship to other agencies of government. It is not superior to that of the people who created it.

[20] Laslett (ed.), *op. cit.,* II, 135.
[21] *Ibid.,* II, 143.

Another problem of the state of nature is that it lacks an impartial judge; there must, therefore, be "known authorized judges." [22] Finally, the state of nature lacks the power to execute judgments. Thus an executive must be set up. The executive possesses authority subordinate to that wielded by the legislative and is, in fact, an agent of the legislative. The two powers, legislative and executive, Locke states, must not be combined in the same hands, for that situation contains in itself too great a danger that power will be abused. Also, while the legislative body is supreme, it does not need to function constantly, whereas the executive must do so. Locke mentions a final governmental authority, the "federative." This is the power to conduct external policy and includes control of foreign relations and military affairs. No special body is required to exercise this authority; it is lodged in the hands of the executive.

Locke's demand that the legislative and executive authorities be wielded by different bodies creates separation of powers. It is not, however, a separation in which the bodies or branches of government are equal. Locke proposes, instead, legislative supremacy; the executive has no authority independent of legislative control. But here Locke recognizes a problem. Between sessions of the legislature difficulties may arise which have not been anticipated by that body and which are not, therefore, covered by law. Or there may be laws on the books that are inadequate to an emergency. In such cases, Locke says, the executive must exercise his "prerogative" of taking such actions as are required in the public interest, even though his stepping into the breach may involve a direct contravention of the laws.

The Right of Revolution

The right of revolution is implicit in the trust arrangement. If government violates the trust by ignoring its purpose or by using the power granted it for a selfish purpose, the people have a right to remove the government, by force if necessary. Locke does not specifically state that force is permitted, but it seems to be so strongly implied in his theory and is so logically a part of his construction that not to infer it would constitute an error. The people, however, have no right to revolt against a government which has not violated its trust.[23] The question is, who is to determine whether the trust has been violated? And the answer is, the people. It should be noted, too, that the government which betrays its trust is itself the revolutionary party, for it has placed itself in a state

[22] Locke favors a separate, but not an independent, judiciary. In the usage of Locke's day, adjudication was regarded as an executive function and the judiciary considered as a part of the executive through the king's power to appoint judges. See Francis D. Wormuth, *The Origins of Modern Constitutionalism*, Harper & Row, Publishers, Incorporated, New York, 1949, chap. 20.

[23] This seems to be an inconsistency. If there is a trust, its creator has the right to revoke it arbitrarily. Still Locke denies the right unless there is a breach of trust.

of war with the people. In the past some private persons have been factious and have provoked trouble, but history demonstrates, Locke says, that most rebellions have been caused by the violation of trust. Men are conservative and will accept much abuse before suffering the vicissitudes of revolution. The people should be cautious in exercising their right. Even when a government is established by force, an attempt to unseat it should await a determination of how well it is performing its functions. The point is, however, that force is never properly its own justification. It must further be noted that the overthrow of a government does not destroy society. An organization still remains which may immediately set about the business of creating a new agent which will be more assiduous in doing its bidding.[24]

The right of the members of society to choose and remove their agents assumes that sovereignty rests with the people. Since sovereignty occupies an important place in the theories of Bodin and Hobbes, it is regrettable that Locke does not specifically discuss the issue. At any rate it would have been difficult for him, opposed as he was to absolutes and inclined to the application of reason and common sense to problems, to dispose of the matter. If sovereignty were to be defined in Bodin's terms as "supreme power over citizens and subjects, unrestrained by law," there was no place for it in Locke's theory since such a definition is mainly suited to a frame of government headed by an absolute monarch. If sovereignty were presumed to mean absolute power to make and enforce laws, as, again, Bodin thought of it, it could not be assigned to the people generally. If sovereignty means the ultimate authority to make and remove governments, then in Locke's theory it exists and is vested in the people. This statement is only an inference, however; Locke does not use the term or discuss the matter specifically. He prefers that the people retain final power, but that they exercise it only occasionally in the election process, or, if absolutely necessary, through revolution. The day-to-day conduct of government should be in the hands of a body of persons who have superior capacity but who are representative of the people. The legislative body wears the robes of sovereignty (as does the executive to some extent), but it is not in fact sovereign.

The Rights of Man: Property Rights

According to Locke, men in a state of nature possess certain rights which are incorporated in the law of nature. The fact that these rights are inadequately defined and protected in the state of nature impels men to contract with one another to form civil society and to establish government. Certain corollaries are evident. Rights are anterior to government, and government exists to protect them. Government and law add nothing to rights, which are complete in a state of nature. Law does not

[24] Wolin, *op. cit.*, p. 308.

create morality, but is itself judged by the morality it evidences, and this in turn is determined by comparing it, through reason, with the natural law. The principle of constitutionalism is apparent. The laws enacted by governments of men are valid only insofar as they do not contravene the higher law. In the political state natural rights become legal rights which government is obliged to enforce. Good government does this; bad government serves its own, rather than the public's, ends.

What are the natural rights which men possess and to the protection of which government is committed? Locke specifies "lives, liberties and estates," which he calls, collectively, "property." [25] The use of the term "property" to define other liberties is confusing, for we cannot determine how consistent Locke really was in employing the term. On a number of occasions in the *Second Treatise* he reiterates his intent to use it in this general sense. In other places "property" has apparently the more conventional signification of material possessions. Probably Locke had both meanings in mind, and we can best interpret him by recognizing the dual use and applying the one which seems germane. Property in the common use of the term is the only right that Locke considers in detail. We must, therefore, be concerned with it and assume that Locke thought of other natural rights in the same context. His discussion, however, standing alone, is significant as a treatise on property in the conventional sense.

Both revelation and natural reason (the law of nature) tell us, Locke says, that in a state of nature property was held in common. But God, who supplies man with the goods of the earth, also gives him reason in order that he can utilize them to the best advantage. Before commonly held property can be used, it must be appropriated by an individual—it must become "a part of him." Locke says, in short, that communally owned goods must become private property before they can be consumed. How does this change come about? First, it must be acknowledged that every man is free; he has a right to his own body and to the labor of his own body. When he applies his labor to the goods which nature provides, they become a part of himself. They become private as a result of his labor. This is Locke's labor theory of the origin of private property, which he expands into a labor theory of value. It is, he says, labor that determines the value of goods. The greater the amount of labor expended on raw materials the more valuable they are. Adam Smith and David Ricardo both followed Locke's use of the labor theory of value, and Marx elaborated it to produce the theory of surplus value which he employed to attack the foundation of capitalism. The Marxian use was never intended by Locke.

Private property, then, is a natural right, but it is not an unlimited one. No person has a right, even by the application of his labor, to more

25 Laslett (ed.), *op. cit.*, II, 123.

of the common store of goods than he and his family can use "before it spoils." Anything beyond this belongs to others. Man may not, under natural law, accumulate property "to the prejudice of others." As to property in land, a man has a right only to that amount which he can cultivate and from which he can use the produce. With land, as with the "fruits of the earth," labor justifies private ownership and gives rise to value.

Thus far what Locke has to say about property rights and limitations applies to man in a state of nature. What of property rights in the political state? Here we must bear in mind that man enters society and establishes government in order better to protect his property, broadly defined. Political power, established by consent, is used "for the *regulating and preserving* of property." Government safeguards property that is legitimately (under the natural law) accumulated; it may also act to prevent its being used against the public interest. Locke was undoubtedly sympathetic to the demands of a class which protested against taxation without representation and other assaults on private property. His theory of property cannot, however, properly be cited in support of unlimited *laissez faire*. Regulation of property by the state is not contrary to natural law, provided that the consent of the people is given.

But neither is Locke committed to the principle of equalitarianism in property ownership. Some men are more industrious than others, and they are capable of accumulating a greater amount of property. In nature strict limitations exist upon their right to do so; they may not pile up goods which they cannot use. Ingenious man, however, has circumvented this restriction, by consent, through the invention of money. This device enables him to accumulate without running the risk of spoilage, and it permits a greater degree of inequality in the holding of wealth, all without violating the law of nature.

Whatever Locke may have intended by his theory of property, its influence has been on the side of an individualistic and acquisitive economy. It was convenient to read into Locke the idea that property is a natural and inalienable right which governments are created to protect but with which they may not interfere. This is clearly an improper interpretation of Locke. Property rights, in his view, were limited in nature and were necessarily limited, therefore, in society. Any other inference would violate the general tenor of his theory. A designation of Locke as a conscious spokesman for the Whiggism that substitutes the divine right of property for the divine right of monarchs is surely erroneous.

The Letter on Toleration

As we have seen, Locke's brief sojourn in Brandenburg and his association with Lord Shaftesbury both impelled him toward a more tolerant attitude in matters of religious belief. In Brandenburg he saw a community in which religious diversity did not destroy community harmony. Shaftesbury had told him of the dangers to commerce and national unity of a policy of coerced religious conformity. In his *Letter on Toleration* Locke expands on the subject, bringing into play the reasonableness and the use of commonsense arguments which are typical of the *Two Treatises*. The ideas found in the *Letter* are indeed not unrelated to the political theory of the *Treatises*.

The functions of government as well as its powers are limited, Locke states. Government exists to protect life, liberty, and property. Civil society has a *civil* function; it does not exist to compel men to believe particular religious doctrines or to join religious groups. Churches are voluntary organizations that should be devoted to the salvation of souls. They are not entitled to support from the state in the building of membership or in the punishment of members for violation of their rules. The use of force to achieve conformity (and it could only be an outer conformity) is both impractical and contrary to Christian morality. The right of men to believe as they will is one which they cannot surrender. Civil magistrates may exercise "outward force" only; because religion is a matter of "inward persuasion," it is beyond the legitimate authority of the magistrate. On the other hand, the authority of the church is purely other-worldly. The penalties it imposes must be of this variety. It may resort to "exhortations, admonitions and advices," but it may not interfere with a civil right or deprive a person of his earthly possessions. The greatest punishment the church may properly inflict is that of excommunication, but deprivation of church membership cannot involve any civil consequences. Nor does affiliation of the civil magistrate with the church enhance the power of the church. Within it he is merely another member and cannot carry his civil authority with him into the church organization.

It is, Locke says, futile to follow any other principle. A person cannot be compelled to care for his own soul, and even if he could, how would it be done? Who is qualified to prescribe? And if such a person were found, how would others be persuaded to hear and be convinced, truly convinced, by him? The magistrate has powers which may incidentally bear on religion. The rule here is that he may forbid as religious practice some action which is normally forbidden "in the ordinary course of life"; in other words, religion may not be used as a blind for activities which the state may otherwise prevent. But the magistrate's function in such proscription is civil, not religious. Also, the church authority may not forbid some act which is lawful in civil life. In short, the inward faith of a citizen does not and should not damage either his fellow man as an individual or the community as a body.

Both the state and the church are concerned with morality and the good life. It is possible for each to entertain a different view on some aspect of the matter and to find itself at cross purposes with the other. In this case the person who is both citizen and church member finds himself in an uncomfortable dilemma. What is he to do? Shall he follow the directive of the state and risk a religious penalty, or shall he obey his church and incur secular punishment? In a fairly administered state, Locke says, this conflict of duties will not appear. If, nevertheless, it does, the individual should refrain from doing anything which he "judges unlawful," and accept the punishment "which it is not unlawful for him to bear." If the magistrate sincerely believes one thing and his people another, only God can judge between them, and each should follow the dictates of his own conscience. But the magistrate should bear in mind the practical values of a policy of toleration. His attempts to achieve conformity through force will not create the true belief which is necessary to unity. If he drives the nonconformists from the country they will strengthen the country to which they go, and their talents will be lost to their homeland; and, finally, if nonconformists are persecuted they will go underground to create conspiracies and greater dangers than would result from freedom.

Locke's plea for toleration would have been more persuasive if it had concluded at this point. Unfortunately it did not. Locke believed in a greater degree of religious freedom than that which prevailed at the time; it was, however, a qualified toleration. Certain groups, he held, should be proscribed. A church which advocates actions contrary to the prescribed moral rules of the community is not to be countenanced. The same applies to any group which, under the guise of religion, assumes some prerogative or authority that places it above or in opposition to the rest of the community. Locke included here any church which demands toleration for itself but denies it to all others. No church should be tolerated whose members are required to give their allegiance to a foreign prince. Locke cited the Mohammedans as an example of this type, but his true reference was probably to Roman Catholics. Finally, toleration need not be extended to atheists. Citizens are required to take oaths and make promises and agreements in the name of God, and since atheists can have no part in such agreements they can obtain none of the benefits.

The exceptions are regrettable. Still Locke's position was liberal at the time; and we must be careful, in assessing ideas, to view them against the background of the times in which they were produced rather than in the context of present circumstances. We must admit that Locke's view of toleration was advanced for his own period; it was also far more liberal than that held by many at the present time. And we should note that in no case does Locke advocate withholding toleration for a religious purpose, that is, because he opposed the spiritual views of those involved. In his view the only legitimate ground upon which the state may withhold or withdraw toleration is that of political security. If this is endangered the state may properly take action.[26]

Conclusions

The precise sources of Locke's theory are difficult to determine. His ideas emerged after a considerable period of study and contemplation, and, unlike many of his contemporaries, he did not attempt to make his point by compiling quotations from "authorities." At any rate, Locke's contribution does not stem from the originality of his ideas, and it is likely that he was less original than even he believed. The importance of his theory rests upon the fact that it was a compendium of earlier work,[27] that it was readable, and that it was presented at a particularly appropriate time.

That it *was* important cannot be doubted. Locke's influence, particularly upon the revolutionary eighteenth and nineteenth centuries, was enormous. Locke has often and with justification been referred to as "America's philosopher." Both in justifying the American Revolution and in supplying fundamental principles for the erection of a frame of government in the United States Locke's theory played a significant role. One need only compare the Declaration of Independence with portions of the *Second Treatise* to establish the relationship between the two. Most tenets of the constitutional system of the United States are also traceable to Locke. In Locke's conception of the higher law and his insistence that the laws of men be derived from, and be not contradictory to, the higher law is found the essence of constitutionalism. Locke's assertion that men are endowed by nature with certain rights which are not within the purview of governmental authority is incorporated in the Fifth and Fourteenth Amendment clauses which forbid national and state governments to deprive any person of his "life, liberty, or property, without due process of law." The principle is elaborated in other amendments which specify additional rights and state that there are others not yet determined. Other principles which found lodgment in the American system (and many, of course, in other free systems of government) are majority rule, legislative supremacy, the right of revolution, limited government, political equality, and the view of government as an agent and instrument of the people.

Locke's theory is deceptively simple in appearance,[28] and its apparent simplicity accounts in part for the great popular interest in it and its wide acceptance. In reality the theory is highly complex. Locke attempted to supply answers to the multitudinous political problems of his time, and analysis demonstrates that the answer to one often detracts

[26] Gough, *op. cit.*, p. xxxviii.
[27] *Ibid.*, p. xii.
[28] Sabine, *op. cit.*, pp. 537–539.

from the force of an answer to another. Numerous disagreements have arisen with regard to Locke's actual meaning in particular instances. There is, for example, a controversy concerning whether Locke was an individualist or a majority-rule democrat. His support of the rights of the individual may lead to one conclusion, and his advocacy of the rights of a majority to determine a minority to the other. The emphasis placed upon property rights also seems to obscure those references, revealed through a more careful reading, to the permission of the regulation of property in the public interest. At one point it appears that Locke's proposals dealing with executive prerogative contravene his insistence on legislative supremacy. And, although Locke has often been cited as a philosopher of and apologist for revolution, such an interpretation can only be inferred from his philosophy, for Locke, himself a moderate and prudent man, is loath to incite through the use of inflammatory phrases and does not do so.

Locke should not be too much condemned for his failure to achieve complete consistency and provide an answer to all problems. Absolute answers and solutions seem generally either to be impractical or to provide for absolute governments. Consistency was easier for Hobbes, who solved many problems by abolishing the rights of the individual and concentrating authority in the hands of the sovereign. Locke was not willing to pay this price. He recognized the need for both freedom and authority and sought to create a system in which a decent balance of the two would be possible. As to the conflict between majority rule and individual rights, the answer seems to be, for Locke, that he wanted both. This is not different from the dilemma with which democracies have always been confronted. Is democracy a system in which majorities rule absolutely or one in which individual rights are paramount? It is neither. The rights of each must be recognized, and in ordinary circumstances they can be. Few would argue that the democratic system breaks down either when a law is passed by a majority in Congress or when the Supreme Court upholds the freedom of an individual to express an opinion unpopular with the majority. Reasonable men recognize that each principle must receive its fair consideration, and Locke was careful to state that reason in man was a necessary attribute of the system he proposed. Events have always occurred, of course, in which the stakes are considered too high by both majorities and minorities to permit a peaceful and reasonable solution. In such a circumstance force is resorted to, and who is to say which side represents the democratic principle? We cannot, in fairness, censure Locke for not discovering a better solution than we have been able to find.

This is not to say that there are no defects or weaknesses in Locke's theory. The artificiality of his system, based as it is upon the premise that men are isolated individuals bound together by a compact for the purpose of protecting their lives, liberty, and property, is unrealistic. It fails to take into consideration the many ties, including race, geography, and other things, which hold together the community.[29] Also, in the interest of historical accuracy we must dismiss the idea of a social contract, for there never was such a thing, at least in the sense intended by Locke. As Sir Ernest Barker has so wisely said, however, the significant thing is not whether men ever actually entered into a contract; it is important only that they have acted "as if" they did.[30]

Another questionable aspect of Locke's theory is his assumption that the "legislative" is more likely to represent the majority will than is the executive. This was undoubtedly true for Locke's time, but it is risky to regard the assumption as an eternal verity. There is a considerable difference between the position, vis-à-vis the public, of a seventeenth-century monarch (and this was the only kind of executive considered by Locke) and that of a popularly elected executive such as the President of the United States. In a day which witnesses the susceptibility of Congress to the pressures of sectional and special interests it is at least debatable whether that body is as able to act in the public interest as is the President, who, by virtue of the manner in which he is elected, is compelled to take the majority will into careful account. Still, in a sense this is a quibbling criticism of Locke; the question was not a real one in his discussion. He was interested in governmental responsibility, and his advocacy of legislative supremacy is simply a logical corollary, applicable in his time, of that principle. Locke is generally to be commended for not detailing the means by which his principles were to be implemented, for history demonstrates that the validity of means is indeed a transitory thing—that is, means quite adequate to one period are entirely inadequate to another.

He who prefers a tidy, black-and-white approach to problems and an unequivocal solution of them is apt to find Locke's tendency to qualify annoying. Individuals have rights, but majorities should rule, and vice versa. Property is a natural right, but it may be limited in the public interest. The legislative is "the supreme power in every commonwealth," but it is controllable by the people, and even the executive has his "prerogatives." The people are sovereign, but in practice their exercise of sovereignty is limited to the establishment and disestablishment of governments. There should be freedom of religion, but Catholics and atheists should not be tolerated. The qualifications seem endless. Yet anyone who recognizes the enormous complexity of political problems knows the danger of offering hard-and-fast solutions to them. An awareness of this fact leads to a greater appreciation of Locke.

[29] R. I. Aaron, *John Locke*, Oxford University Press, Fair Lawn, N.J., 1937, p. 287.

[30] *Social Contract: Essays by Locke, Hume, and Rousseau* (with an introduction by Sir Ernest Barker), Oxford University Press, Fair Lawn, N.J., 1948, p. vii.

One concluding point remains to be made. Locke has often been regarded as a patron saint of the view that government and law are pitted against the freedom and welfare of the individual. According to this idea, government is a burden, financial and otherwise, upon men; it is necessary only in order to discipline the few who are abnormal; its function should therefore be solely one of restraint; and government and law at best limit evils but are incapable of contributing positively to the good life. In short, in this view, liberty and law (and, of course, government) are antithetical. The inaccuracy of this interpretation can best be demonstrated by permitting Locke to speak for himself.

> Could . . . [men] be happier without it, the *Law*, as an useless thing would of it self vanish; and that ill deserves the Name of Confinement which hedges us in only from Bogs and Precipices. So that, however it may be mistaken, *the end of Law* is not to abolish or restrain, but *to preserve and enlarge Freedom:* For in all the states of created beings capable of *Laws, where there is no Law, there is no Freedom.* For *Liberty* is to be free from restraint and violence from others which cannot be, where there is no Law: But Freedom is not, as we are told, *A Liberty for every Man to do what he lists:* (For who could be free, when every other Man's Humour might domineer over him?) But a *Liberty* to dispose, and order as he lists, his Person, Actions, Possessions, and his whole Property, *within the* Allowance of those Laws under which he is; and therein not to be subject to the arbitrary Will of another, but freely follow his own.[31]

SELECTED BIBLIOGRAPHY

Aaron, R. I.: *John Locke,* Oxford University Press, Fair Lawn, N.J., 1937, part III, chap. 2.

Abernethy, George L. (ed.): *The Idea of Equality: An Anthology,* John Knox Press, Richmond, Va., 1959, chaps. 25–26, 31.

Cranston, Maurice: *John Locke: A Biography,* The Macmillan Company, New York, 1957.

Hacker, Andrew: *Political Theory: Philosophy, Ideology, Science,* The Macmillan Company, New York, 1961, chap. 7.

Kendall, Willmoore: *John Locke and the Doctrine of Majority Rule,* The University of Illinois Press, Urbana, Ill., 1941.

Laslett, Peter (ed.): *John Locke: Two Treatises of Government* (a Critical Edition with an Introduction and Apparatus Criticus), Cambridge University Press, New York, 1960.

Locke, John: *The Second Treatise of Government (an Essay Concerning the True Original, Extent and End of Civil Government)* and *A Letter Concerning Toleration* (edited with an introduction by J. W. Gough), The Macmillan Company, New York, 1956, introduction and *A Letter Concerning Toleration.*

[31] Laslett (ed.), *op. cit.,* II, 57. Italics supplied in part.

McDonald, Lee Cameron: *Western Political Theory: The Modern Age,* Harcourt, Brace & World, Inc., New York, 1962, chap. 4.

O'Connor, D. J.: *John Locke,* Penguin Books, Inc., Baltimore, 1952.

Sabine, George H.: *A History of Political Theory,* 3d ed., Holt, Rinehart and Winston, Inc., New York, 1961, chaps. 24–26.

Social Contract: Essays by Locke, Hume, and Rousseau (with an introduction by Sir Ernest Barker), Oxford University Press, Fair Lawn, N.J., 1948, introduction.

Strauss, Leo: "Locke's Doctrine of Natural Law," *American Political Science Review,* vol. 52, no. 2, June, 1958.

Wolin, Sheldon: *Politics and Vision: Continuity and Innovation in Western Political Thought,* Little, Brown and Company, Boston, 1960, chap. 9.

Wormuth, Francis D.: *The Royal Prerogative,* Cornell University Press, Ithaca, N.Y., 1939, chap. 6, parts I, III.

———: *The Origins of Modern Constitutionalism,* Harper & Row, Publishers, Incorporated, New York, 1949, chap. 20.

fourteen

MONTESQUIEU

England, at the beginning of the eighteenth century, was tired of domestic upheaval and more anxious to consolidate gains already made
than to attempt further reforms. It was not that further reform would
have been undesirable. English government was, by modern standards,
corrupt and unrepresentative, but compared with other European governments it was enlightened. The English generally were content, and
because political theory arises out of conflict and not in a vacuum, nothing significant in this area of speculation appeared in England until considerably later in the century.[1]

France at the time was a more fertile field for the growth of political
theory, for Frenchmen were not so satisfied with their situation as were
their fellows across the Channel. France was under the rule of Louis
XIV, whose control over his kingdom was as absolute as he could make
it. The foundation for absolutism had been laid more than a century
before in the reign of Henry IV (1553–1610), who ruled France from
1589 until 1610. A wise and public-spirited monarch, Henry IV had
restored peace and prosperity to his country, which had been divided
by the bitter religious wars of the sixteenth century.[2] He had promulgated the Edict of Nantes of 1598, which provided toleration for

---

[1] George H. Sabine, *A History of Political Theory*, 3d ed., Holt, Rinehart and Winston,
Inc., New York, 1961, p. 542.

[2] See Chap. 11.

Protestants, but this was only a first step that facilitated further efforts to achieve national unity and tranquility. Henry IV was convinced that a solution to the problems that plagued his country could not be found except on the basis of a vastly strengthened central government. To this end and with the aid of competent advisers, he increased taxes, curbed the power of the towns and the nobility, overrode the authority of the Estates, and as his power grew, launched a program of fiscal reform, abolished useless offices, and liquidated the national debt. Commerce and agriculture were improved, and the army was reorganized and strengthened.

Henry IV ruled from 1589 until his death by assassination in 1610. He was succeeded by his son, Louis XIII, who was crowned king of France at the age of nine. Louis's mother took power as regent and dominated her son and France until 1624, when that function was taken over by Richelieu, the great French cardinal and statesman. Richelieu was an ardent admirer of Machiavelli. Had the two been contemporaries, that sentiment would have been wholeheartedly reciprocated. Richelieu was "Machiavellian" in both goal and methods. His goal was to build the greatness of France, and he believed, as had Henry IV, that the threats, both internal and external, to that goal could be overcome only through a further strengthening of the central governmental power. He persuaded the youthful Louis that the Huguenots constituted a dangerous force and proceeded to destroy the political and military power that had been guaranteed to them in the Edict of Nantes. He carried forward less successfully the policy of curbing the power of the nobility, and as a consequence facilitated the completion of the task by Louis XIV. He also inaugurated the system of *intendants*, representatives of the middle class, who gradually replaced the nobility as administrators on the provincial level. The Estates-General was ignored, and the cause of centralization was advanced.

Richelieu died in 1642, and his "master," Louis XIII, died the following year. Successor to the throne was the five-year-old Louis XIV, whose mother, Anne of Austria, was appointed regent. The real power, however, during the years of Louis's minority was Mazarin, an able Italian cardinal who had been trained by Richelieu. Under Mazarin the work of stripping the nobility of its power was carried on, but not without difficulty. Both the bourgeoisie, who resented Mazarin's fiscal policy, and the nobility opposed the government. The result was the rebellion known as the Fronde. The middle class, however, decided that it had more to fear from its traditional enemy, the nobility, than from the king, and swung its support to the latter. When Mazarin died in 1661, Louis XIV proclaimed that he would himself perform the function of first minister. His was not an idle boast. The youthful monarch possessed only average intelligence, but he was shrewd and ambitious, and he had been a careful observer of Mazarin's methods and of political developments. Moreover, he had the air of a monarch and dedicated himself to the program of the further centralization of political power that had begun under his grandfather, Henry IV.

Under Louis XIV unprecedented authority was concentrated in the kingly hands. It required considerable effort. Important policy decisions were made in four councils, all of which counted Louis as a member and all of which he controlled. The power of the *intendants* was increased. The political and judicial powers of the *parlements,* the supreme courts of justice of the provinces, were curbed. The Estates-General had convened for the last time in 1614; it was not recalled by Louis XIV. The king diluted the power of the nobility by increasing the number of nobles, stripped it of still more powers, and distracted its attention by the entertainments and ceremonials at Versailles, the luxurious new court which Louis had built near Paris. Noblemen became increasingly resigned to their status; indeed, they accepted it with comparative ease, for although they had lost their power they retained their privileges, and they were not taxed.

Colbert, Louis's minister of finance, supervised the establishment of the French mercantilist system which sought to build the self-sufficiency of the kingdom by encouraging exports, discouraging imports, planting colonies, and piling up a surplus store of gold and silver. The policy involved a detailed regulation of trade by the central government. The general prosperity would probably have been more greatly benefited by the injection of substantial doses of freedom for the enterprising bourgeoisie. Still, Colbert and his system would have functioned more successfully if Louis had not determined to extend the boundaries of France and exercise greater control over the whole of Europe. The armed forces were enlarged, and Louis began the military adventures that occupied most of his attention during the final thirty years of his reign. Early successes encouraged him and increased his popularity at home, but his enemies abroad formed coalitions against him which prevented his making any important and permanent gains. The English demonstrated their skill in playing the balance-of-power game, and whereas in the end this was to save Louis from heavy losses, it did much to frustrate his ambition to become the chief arbiter of European affairs.

The heavy tax burden which the common people of France were compelled to bear, the demands of Louis's generals for more soldiers, the conspicuous and excessive luxury of the court of Versailles, all contributed to a substantial shift in public opinion with regard to Louis and the advantages of a system directed by a powerful monarch. The king's policy demanded victories, and many of them, to distract the people's attention from domestic hardship; instead, there was a disproportionate number of defeats. Religious intolerance also contributed to the internal unrest. Louis, urged on by the Catholic clergy, conceived it his duty to restore the spiritual homogeneity of France. In 1685 he revoked the Edict of Nantes and began a program of brutal and ruthless persecution against the Huguenots. It is estimated that some 200,000 of them fled to other countries. Louis and France could ill afford their loss, since this element of France's population [3] included a high proportion of ambitious and productive citizens. Louis provoked additional resentment by his harassment of the Jansenists, an ascetic group of Catholic reformers, whose criticisms of Louis's private life probably annoyed the "Sun King" more than did their attachment to some of the more fundamentalist doctrines of St. Augustine.

The decadence of the last thirty years of the reign of Louis XIV turned French thought in the direction of political speculation. The assumption that absolute monarchy was the only alternative to anarchy was increasingly questioned. At first the opposition to absolutism sought only a return to a social system in which the authority of the monarch was modified by the power of the clergy, the nobility, the Estates-General, the *parlements,* and the local and provincial governments. But the destruction of the old system had been too thorough. Henry IV, Richelieu, Mazarin, and Louis XIV had done their work well; the institutions which had formerly shared power with the king were unable to reestablish their authority. There was in fact no constitutionalism left in France. It was understandable, therefore, that the French should adopt the theories of the English, who had already revolted against a too powerful monarch. The theories of Newton and Locke became important in French social and political theory. Newton, in describing the operation of natural laws as they applied to the physical world, had encouraged the belief that human relations could be similarly understood. Locke's emphasis on reason and common sense as methods by which axioms pertaining to human society could be understood and built upon was equally influential. And Locke's principles concerning the origin, nature, and function of government, popular sovereignty, rights of life, liberty, and property appeared ready-made to apply to the situation in France.

As Professor Sabine has pointed out,[4] the planting of Locke's political philosophy in French soil resulted in a novel kind of crop. Although in England individual rights had often been disregarded by cynical and powerful monarchs, the concept had not lost its meaning. Absolutism in England had never reached the stage it had long held in France. The tradition of constitutionalism, of restraints on the royal prerogative, had not been obliterated in England as it had been under the

[3] There were about 18,000,000 people in France at the time.

[4] Sabine, *op. cit.,* pp. 542–551.

Bourbons. The English revolutions of the seventeenth century were, in some respects, conservative; they were fought, in part, to conserve a tradition rather than to install a new one. In France, on the contrary, the doctrines of Locke were genuinely revolutionary both because they were opposed to the long-established absolutism and because the French society itself was so different from that of England. The privileges and exemptions of the nobility and clergy were greater in France; there was less religious toleration; the middle class was more restrained. In short, social schisms created a bitterness among the classes in France which was not matched in England and which was reflected in the increasingly emotional quality of French political thought. Political thought in France was generally moderate in the first part of the eighteenth century, but grew more radical as the century progressed. In this chapter we shall be concerned with this earlier development.

Montesquieu: The Man and His Work

An important part of the early criticism of the French autocracy in political writing is found in the contributions of Charles Louis de Secondat, Baron de La Brede et de Montesquieu, who was born at Chateau de La Brede, near Bordeaux, on January 18, 1689. His mother was Marie Françoise de Penel, and she brought La Brede to her husband, Montesquieu's father, Jacques de Secondat, as her dowry. The title, Montesquieu, came from an uncle, Jean Baptiste de Secondat, Baron de Montesquieu, who was president of the *Parlement* of Bordeaux. Montesquieu's decision to make a career in the law was also probably influenced by his uncle. For five years, beginning at the age of eleven, Montesquieu attended the Oratorian School of Juilly, near Meaux, where he absorbed the customary classical education. From here Montesquieu went to the University at Bordeaux, where he studied law. In 1708 he was admitted to practice and at the same time was appointed a counselor to the Bordeaux *Parlement*. In 1715 he married Jeanne de Latrique, who, it is reported, brought more money than beauty and intelligence to the union, although the marriage was apparently a success.

In 1716 Montesquieu's uncle and benefactor died, leaving to his nephew his estate, fortune, name, and position as President of the Bordeaux *Parlement*.[5] Montesquieu held the position for twelve years. A deep interest in scientific matters led him to join the Academy of Science at Bordeaux, to which he contributed a number of papers on scientific subjects. In 1721 Montesquieu published the *Lettres persanes, The Persian Letters*. Constituting as it did a rather thinly veiled satire on French society, the work was issued anonymously. Written with con-

---

[5] Judgeships at the time were private property.

siderable wit and sophistication, *The Persian Letters* has been termed the first book of the *philosophe* attack upon the old order.[6] The *Letters* was an immediate success, and when Montesquieu was revealed as its author his reputation was established, although his fame at this point rested upon his abilities as a wit and satirist rather than upon his contributions as a political philosopher.

In 1725 Montesquieu was elected to the French Academy, but the election was annulled through the invocation of a requirement that all members be residents of Paris. The following year he sold his office in the *Parlement* and moved to Paris, where he spent about half his time for the next few years, the balance being spent at La Brede. In 1728 he was again elected, and this time admitted, to the Academy. Soon afterward he began a tour of Europe, which was undertaken particularly for educational purposes. Montesquieu wanted to study men, their environments, and their governmental institutions. His travels took him to Austria, Hungary, Italy, and England. He remained a year and a half in England; this was a period of great importance to him. In England Montesquieu made the acquaintance of many influential politicians and studied English political institutions. He was greatly impressed. We shall consider later the manner in which the English constitutional structure served as a model in Montesquieu's development of a political theory. When he returned to France he made his permanent home at La Brede, and here he devoted an increasing proportion of his time to study and writing. In 1734 Montesquieu published his *Considerations on the Greatness and Decline of Rome.* For those who anticipated a continuation of the style and humor found in *The Persian Letters,* the *Considerations* was a disappointment; it was sometimes referred to as the "decadence" of Montesquieu. Serious thinkers were more impressed, for despite its inaccuracies (Montesquieu was inclined to accept without reservation the accounts of the Roman historians), *Considerations* was one of the first significant attempts at a philosophy of history. The book is also important in that it prepared the way for Montesquieu's much more valuable and better known *L'Esprit des lois, The Spirit of the Laws.*

Montesquieu had been working on his great study for more than twenty years prior to its publication in 1748. A group of friends whom Montesquieu invited to review his book prior to publication advised him not to issue it. One, Helvetius, opposed what he regarded as Montesquieu's too moderate approach to political and religious problems. Fortunately the advice was rejected. *The Spirit of the Laws* was highly successful. Both its style and content were greatly admired, and

---

[6] The term *philosophe* describes the group of French popular philosophers who enjoyed enormous success in discrediting the oppressive institutions of Bourbon France and in directing public opinion toward the eventual break with the old regime.

the book, according to Montesquieu, went through twenty-two editions. There were, however, severe criticisms from both sides of the political arena. The book was placed on the *Index* and thus proscribed by authorities of the Catholic Church; and many resented Montesquieu's admiration, evidence in the *Laws*, for a political system in which the nobility plays a prominent role. On the whole, however, the work was well received. But Montesquieu was little interested in remaining in Paris to accept the plaudits of his admirers. Most of his time was spent in the country at La Brede, where he died on February 10, 1755.

The Persian Letters *of Montesquieu*

Montesquieu's technique in writing *The Persian Letters* is ingenious and effective. The book consists of a fictitious series of letters exchanged between two prominent Persians who are traveling in Europe for the first time. Their comments on European civilization, especially that of France, comprise, in fact, the criticisms of Montesquieu and others who thought as he did about the society in which they lived. Although much of the book is, of course, no longer pertinent, its style has withstood the test of time; it is still interesting reading. The *Letters* has little to offer as a political treatise compared with the *Laws*, although it has value as a special form of social criticism applicable to an important period of history. One marvels that Montesquieu was able to survive the revelation of his authorship of the *Letters*. In a comparison of eighteenth- and twentieth-century absolutism, that of the earlier period appears far less oppressive.

Many aspects of his society are ridiculed by Montesquieu in the *Letters*. We shall consider only a few of them here. Montesquieu relates a fable concerning a band of "Troglodites" who narrowly escape self-destruction because they surrender completely to the motive of self-interest. The two surviving families soon learn that subordination of the individual to the general interest is the essence of virtue and the *sine qua non* of the good life. They handed down the lesson to their children.

> They led them to see that the interest of the individual was bound up in that of the community; that to isolate oneself was to court ruin; that the cost of virtue should never be counted, nor the practice of it counted as troublesome; and that in acting justly by others, we bestow blessings on ourselves.[7]

[7] Baron de Montesquieu, *Persian Letters* (translated and introduced by John Davidson), in *Persian and Chinese Letters* (including *The Citizen of the World*, by Oliver Goldsmith, with a special introduction by Oliver H. G. Leigh), M. Walter Dunne, Publisher, Washington, 1901, Letter 12. Subsequent quotations from and references to *The Persian Letters* are from this edition.

The meaning is clear. Virtue is self-rewarding, for in doing good to others we serve our own interest. A virtuous people need no formal authority placed over them. When the Troglodites attempt to give a crown to the man regarded as the most just among them, he upbraids them. They should know, he says, that commands cannot compel them to act more nobly than they are already constrained to act by necessity. The imposition of authority will only serve to lessen their awareness that virtue is a necessity, and the result will be degradation.

Montesquieu's criticisms of the king of France are scarcely disguised, but the letters containing them are dated so as to apply to Louis XIV, who had died six years before the *Letters* was published. It is not likely, however, that Montesquieu believed that the grounds for attack on the monarchy had disappeared with the demise of Louis XIV. Although that monarch was the specific object of Montesquieu's barbs, it was the institution and the corrupt practices of the court generally to which Montesquieu was opposed. The king of France, he said, raised more money through the sale of titles than did the king of Spain from his gold mines. Montesquieu refers, of course, to the device employed by Louis XIV of weakening the nobility by increasing its numbers and of strengthening his treasury at the same time. It is fair to say that Montesquieu, who regarded a strong nobility as a necessary check on monarchical power, more bitterly opposed this kingly practice than any other. He was also critical of the king's manipulation of the national currency, which had done great damage to the fortunes of the citizens.

> The king is a great magician, for his dominion extends to the minds of his subjects; he makes them think what he wishes. If he has only a million crowns in his exchequer, and has need of two millions, he has only to persuade them that one crown is worth two, and they believe it. If he has a costly war on hand, and is short of money, he simply suggests to his subjects that a piece of paper is coin of the realm, and they are straightway convinced of it.[8]

The most devastating sarcasm of the *Letters* is reserved for the Pope and the Catholic clergy. If the king is a magician, there is a still greater one called the Pope. He controls the mind of the king as the latter controls the minds of his subjects. He has the power to make "the king believe that three are no more than one [referring to the Trinity]; that the bread which he eats is not bread; the wine which he drinks not wine; and a thousand things of a like nature."[9] Montesquieu has his Persian traveler express wonderment at the great number of "dervishes," a term applied to clergymen, who are supported by the public.

[8] *Ibid.*, Letter 24.
[9] *Ibid.*

These dervishes take three oaths: of obedience, of poverty, and of chastity. They say that the first is the best observed of the three; as to the second, it is not observed at all; you can form your own opinion with regard to the third.[10]

The Protestant countries are more prosperous and more free. The clergy in a Catholic country hoard the wealth, strangle the commerce, and prevent the use of capital in the general interest.

The dervishes hold in their hands almost all the wealth of the state; they are a miserly crew, always getting and never giving; they are continually hoarding their income to acquire capital. All this wealth falls as it were into a palsy: it is not circulated, it is not employed in trade, in industry, or in manufactures.

There is no Protestant prince who does not levy upon his people much heavier taxes than the Pope draws from his subjects; yet the latter are poor, while the former live in affluence. Commerce puts life into all ranks among the Protestants, and celibacy lays its hand of death upon all interests among the Catholics.[11]

The Spirit of the Laws

The Montesquieu of *The Spirit of the Laws* is a far more sober genius than the author of *The Persian Letters*. The earlier work is witty, ironic, and light, although it contains more wisdom than was generally credited at the time. It was, above all, destructive in its criticism of French society. *The Spirit of the Laws* differs on all counts. It has style, despite Montesquieu's tendency to discursiveness; it is serious; and it is constructive in its attempt to discover all the rules that govern social action, especially to find out how the cause of liberty may be advanced through the establishment of particular constitutional conditions. That Montesquieu largely fails to accomplish these tasks is less important than that he makes the attempt, for he does make some contributions. He is wise in his relativism, in his concession that all the social problems of men cannot be solved by the application of a single formula of political obligation. He is not inclined to accept *a priori* principles and is willing to study facts, as he saw them. His formulation of a philosophy of law incorporating these views has led one analyst to state that the study of historical jurisprudence begins with *The Spirit of the Laws*.[12] Montesquieu opens the book with a definition of law.

[10] *Ibid.,* Letter 57.
[11] *Ibid.,* Letter 118.
[12] Kingsley Martin, *The Rise of French Liberal Thought: A Study of Political Ideas from Bayle to Condorcet* (edited by J. P. Mayer), 2d rev. ed., New York University Press, New York, 1954, p. 152.

> Laws, in their most general signification, are the necessary relations arising from the nature of things. In this sense all beings have their laws: The Deity His laws, the material world its laws, the intelligences superior to man their laws, the beasts their laws, man his laws.[13]

It is a strange definition, the meaning of which has often been disputed.[14] In view of the discussion that follows, we may conclude that Montesquieu is stating his assumption that a natural law governs all things, including men. So far as men are concerned, the natural laws provide a standard of justice "antecedent to the positive law." That is to say, imperfect man is incapable of living always in accordance with the natural law. He must be provided with rules based upon natural law and formulated in such a manner as to correct, insofar as possible, certain of his imperfections. He is apt to "forget his Creator," and God provides laws concerning his religious duty. He may "forget himself," and this necessitates the rules of morality enunciated by the philosophers. He can also "forget his fellow-creatures"; legislators, therefore, create political and civil laws to remind and restrain him.

In order to understand the laws of nature, Montesquieu says, we must know what the life of man was like in a state of nature where only the laws of nature governed. First, natural man is fearful and timid. He feels "nothing in himself at first but impotency and weakness." Each man considers himself the inferior of everyone else, and would never dare to attack anyone else. Hobbes was wrong in holding that the state of nature is a state of war, Montesquieu says, for the state of war comes only with society, when man has the means to exercise force. The first law of nature is, therefore, peace. Also, in a state of nature men have many wants, and the second law of nature is man's inclination to "seek for nourishment," to attempt to satisfy his wants. Third, although men are timid and fearful, they are naturally social. They feel pleasure in associating with their own kind, and this instinct for association is the third law of nature. A fourth law of nature stems from man's intelligence and his perception that organized social life is desirable; the law is his desire to live in organized society. There are other principles of the natural law; those we have discussed relate to the formation of civil society.

From an analysis of what they believed to be man's nature and his life in a state of nature, Hobbes and Locke proceeded to the hypothesis

---

[13] Baron de Montesquieu, *The Spirit of the Laws* (translated by Thomas Nugent, with an introduction by Franz Neumann), Hafner Publishing Company, Inc., New York, 1949, I, 1. All subsequent references to *The Spirit of the Laws* are to this volume.

[14] Not the least strange aspect of the definition is Montesquieu's reference to "intelligences superior to man." For a consideration of this and other parts of Montesquieu's theory, see David Lowenthal, "Book I of Montesquieu's *The Spirit of the Laws*," *American Political Science Review*, vol. 53, no. 2, pp. 485–498, June, 1959.

of the social contract and to a discussion of the devices by which government is established. Montesquieu does not follow this line of thought; for him political society is natural. It happens.[15] But once man enters society he loses the equality that all men had in a state of nature. He also loses "the sense of his weakness." Particular societies arise and begin to contest with one another for advantage. Individuals compete for the advantages their society offers. The state of war begins. It is a condition that gives rise to positive laws, to rules and regulations necessary to keep the peace, the first law of nature. Three kinds of law are required: international law to govern relations among nations; political law to regulate relations between governors and governed; civil law to govern relations among citizens.

To provide political and civil law within a society, government is necessary. The question is, what kind of government should it be? Some have said, Montesquieu states, that the best (most natural) form of government is that of a single authority, since that form is based upon the paternal principle; [16] but their conclusion is not sound. The best government, and that which conforms most closely to nature, is the one "which best agrees with the humor and disposition of the people in whose favor it is established." [17] It is impossible under any other rule to achieve that "conjunction of wills" among the people that makes unity possible. The conformability of a government to nature is gauged by the laws it enacts. Those laws must meet certain standards.

Positive law should be based upon natural law, as it applies to man and his reason. This does not mean that all the laws of men should everywhere and at all times be the same. Quite the contrary. People's circumstances in various societies are so different "that it should be a great chance" if the laws of one were suitable to another. Laws, to be proper and in accord with nature, must be relative to a great variety of circumstances. The "nature and principle" of government must be taken into account, as must a great number of social, economic, religious, and other factors, all of which have a bearing on the law. The laws

> ... should be in relation to the climate of each country, to the quality of its soil, to its situation and extent, to the principal occupation of the natives, whether husbandmen, huntsmen, or shepherds: they should have relation to the degree of liberty which the constitution will bear; to the religion of the inhabitants, to their inclinations, riches, numbers, commerce, manners, and customs. In fine, they have relations to each other, as also to their

[15] Thomas I. Cook, *History of Political Philosophy from Plato to Burke*, Prentice-Hall, Inc., Englewood Cliffs, N.J., 1936, p. 591.

[16] Montesquieu does not say so, but it is probable that the reference here is to Filmer, with whose ideas he was certainly acquainted, either by direct reading or through the writings of Locke.

[17] *The Spirit of the Laws*, I, 3.

origin, to the intent of the legislator, and to the order of things on which they are established; in all of which different lights they ought to be considered.[18]

It is an examination of these factors and their relationship to one another that constitutes Montesquieu's task; his purpose is to consider the spirit rather than the substance of the laws. The laws of a society will be appropriate to that society, and the laws and the government which formulates and enforces them will be in accord with nature, when the proper interrelationship prevails. The goodness of a law or government cannot be judged except in this context.

> I do not pretend to treat of laws, but of their spirit; and as this spirit consists in the various relations which the laws may bear to different objects, it is not so much my business to follow the natural order of laws as that of these relations and objects.[19]

It was a formidable task, and indeed Montesquieu was not equal to it. His knowledge of history and of contemporary conditions was grossly inadequate. In fact, no person could have compiled and analyzed the mountains of material that would have been required if he was to arrive at something like a reasonable set of conclusions. Still, three assumptions seem warranted. First, there is considerable validity in Montesquieu's premise. Experience has amply demonstrated that systems of government and codes of law cannot be successfully imposed upon a people whose circumstances make such systems and codes inapplicable. The most enlightened kind of democratic constitution will ill serve a people who have no education, no understanding of public affairs, and no experience in political participation. We have seen, in our own country, a great transition in government and laws owing to a change from a predominantly rural and agrarian to a predominantly urban and industrial society. Second, if the premise is valid we may study the problem. This study, of course, is being undertaken; it is an integral and important aspect of political science. Modern scholars are more aware than was Montesquieu of the complexity of the structure whose outlines he saw only in shadow form. They have a larger store of information upon which to draw, and far more of them are devoted to the work. Third, certain conclusions at which Montesquieu arrived have been influential in the establishment and conduct of government. We shall be particularly concerned with the last point as it relates to Montesquieu's theory of separation of powers and checks and balances. But first we must consider Montesquieu's discussion of the relationship of laws to the nature and principles of government.

[18] *Ibid.*
[19] *Ibid.*

The Nature and Principle of Government

By the "nature" of government, Montesquieu means the form of ruler-ship found in a civil society. By "principles" he means the underlying force by which that society is motivated.

> There is this difference between the nature and principles of government, that the former is that by which it is constituted, the latter that by which it is made to act. One is its particular structure, and the other the human passions which set it in motion.[20]

Certain laws are appropriate to both nature and principle, and Montesquieu devotes much attention to this problem.

There are three possible forms of government—republican, monarchical, and despotic. In a republic all or some of the people govern. If all govern it is a democratic republic; if a few govern it is an aristocratic republic. In a monarchy one rules by "fixed and established laws." In a despotism one rules but does so capriciously and arbitrarily. The laws regulating the suffrage determine the kind of republic. The matter of who is to govern, whether all or a few, should be settled and maintained if stability is to be achieved; neglect in this regard was one of the principal causes of the downfall of Rome. The people of a republic should have the capacity to choose their political authorities; they need not, and do not, have the ability to rule directly. An aristocracy ought not to exhibit too wide a gap between the elite and the people; the aristocracy ought to tend more to the democratic than to the monarchic principle.

A monarchy is a governmental form in which monarchical power flows through and is checked by other "intermediate, subordinate, and dependent powers," particularly by the nobility. If the "privileges of the lords, the clergy and cities" are abolished, either a despotic government or a democracy will result. It is important in any government to have the kind of laws that maintain the form. Montesquieu says that he is "far ... from being prejudiced in favor of the privileges of the clergy"; if, however, the form of government as it has developed affords such privileges, they cannot be curbed without danger. It is also necessary in a monarchy to have a "depositary of the laws." This authority should be vested in the "judges of the supreme courts of justice, who promulgate the new laws, and revive the obsolete." Montesquieu is here defending the rights of the *parlements,* which had deteriorated under the absolutism of French monarchs.

Despotic governments are, as we have seen, governed by a single ruler who is unrestrained by law. In practice, Montesquieu says, the despot, who is "naturally lazy, voluptuous, and ignorant," turns the conduct of

[20] *Ibid.,* III, 1.

government over to a "vizier" who is invested with the full power of the despot. The term "vizier" is misleading since it refers to a position found in the Eastern despotisms, but in all probability Montesquieu's usage is deliberate. It would have been imprudent for him to imply that France was a despotism, although he believed it to be so, and that Richelieu and Mazarin were its "viziers," although he thought they were. At any rate Montesquieu wishes to leave the impression that there is no single best form of state. A government is good if its form is justified by conditions, bad if not so validated. Montesquieu wants to be scientific, to avoid any emotional attachment to a specific governmental form, but he enjoys a very limited success. His aversion to despotism is apparent, despite his contention that circumstances may make it the only natural form. His attachment to monarchical government is equally obvious. He does not think that republics are possible because the principle underlying them has long been absent among men.

What principles support each of the different forms? In a republic the governing principle is the virtue of the people. Virtue signifies several things—love of country, equality, willingness to subordinate the individual to the general interest. The people exercise power in a democratic republic; their virtue must lead them to adopt that self-restraint which prevents them from abusing their authority. The underlying principle of an aristocratic republic is also virtue; but since only a few govern here, virtue need not be so widespread among the people as in a democracy. The governing aristocrats enact laws to restrain the people. This is not a difficult matter; the real problem in an aristocracy is for the nobles to restrain themselves.

The principle of monarchical governments is honor. The law takes the place of virtue, and law is made by those "pre-eminences and ranks" which hold authority in a monarchy. The governing classes, including the king, are ambitious. They seek to serve their own interests by enhancing their honor, but in doing so they serve the public interest. The good result is possible because the pursuit of self-interest leads, in many instances, to the accomplishment of "glorious actions," and because the ambitions of one or a class are checked by those of others.

> It is with this kind of government as with the system of the universe, in which there is a power that constantly repels all bodies from the centre, and a power of gravitation that attracts them to it. Honor sets all the parts of the body politic in motion, and by its very action connects them; thus each individual advances the public good, while he only thinks of promoting his own interest.[21]

This is a "false honor," Montesquieu admits, but it works.

The sole principle of despotic governments is fear. Men obey because

[21] *Ibid.*, III, 7.

they dare not do otherwise. Neither honor nor virtue can exist under the despot; only submission is possible. Law is replaced by the will of the despot. Moderate governments may relax their controls, secure in the knowledge that this will not bring their immediate overthrow. Despots can by no means afford such a luxury, for "when a despotic prince ceases for one single moment to uplift his arm . . . all is over." [22]

Laws and Their Relation to Nature and Principles of Government

Books IV through VII of *The Spirit of the Laws* contain a consideration of various kinds of law and the relationship they bear to each of the governmental forms and principles. If the laws are appropriate, if the proper "spirit" is observed in their formulation and application, the stability of the society will be preserved. To the degree that this rule is not observed, the government will be imperfect and in danger of collapse. No more serious task confronts the legislator than that of developing laws that correspond with and support that government of which he is a part. The laws of education are critical in this regard, Montesquieu says, although he actually emphasizes the propaganda content of an educational program. In a democracy education must teach love of country, for if the people are to be governors (even though indirectly by choosing those who govern them) they must place the welfare of their country before their self-interest. In a monarchy education should teach the paramountcy of self-interest, but it should be an enlightened self-interest, conducing to honor and the general good. In a despotism servility should be taught. In each case the law will evidence the proper spirit if it supports that principle upon which the structure of government rests.

The laws of a democracy should maintain the equality of the people, especially their economic equality. Material wealth does not exist in sufficient abundance to permit universal affluence. If some are to be rich, many will have to be poor. Such a circumstance will destroy the spirit of equality that marks a democratic society, and democracy will die. The equal distribution of wealth need not be absolute, but there should be well-defined limits for inequality imposed and maintained by law. In an aristocracy, moderation is the key to stability; if equality is carried too far the nobility are corrupted. The nobility should be compelled to pay taxes and to be generous with the common people. They should be prohibited from engaging in commerce, and the law of primogeniture should be abolished to prevent a concentration of wealth in the hands of a few. The laws of a monarchy should support the principle of honor. An hereditary nobility should be maintained, along with the privileges that pertain to it. Taxation laws should not be

[22] *Ibid.*, III, 9.

burdensome, and duties should not be heaped upon the nobility to the degree that they become weary and incapable of performing those "glorious actions" which contribute to the public good. In despotisms it is necessary to have a large army, for force is required to maintain the peace. An army will constitute a heavy burden on the people, but its support cannot be avoided. Montesquieu goes into great detail here, ostensibly to consider the kind of laws required for a despotism, but the section is less an appraisal of this problem than an attack upon despotic government.

Montesquieu next considers civil and criminal laws and judgments and punishments in the various governmental forms. Briefly, Montesquieu's point is that despotisms require little in the way of law. They operate with simple systems because it is the will of the sovereign rather than the law that governs. Monarchies and republics, on the contrary, require elaborate codes of law and judicial systems.

> In republics, it is plain that as many formalities at least are necessary as in monarchies. In both governments they increase in proportion to the value which is set on the honor, fortune, liberty, and life of the subject.[23]

It is a highly pertinent observation. A common complaint in a democratic society is that the existence of a vast and complicated structure of laws, rules, regulations, and legal and judicial procedures is at best annoying and inefficient and at worst destructive of liberty. The more simple and direct methods of the absolutist state are often regarded with envy. It should be understood, however, that a government of laws, a government based upon the rule of law, *requires* laws, and that they will increase in number and complexity as time goes on. The annoyances and frustrations, even the failures constitute the price that must be paid for this kind of system. A despotism avoids the complexities, but at the cost of individual freedom and equality, because the impersonality and impartiality of general rules are abandoned in favor of the particularized or individualized making of decisions.

Books VIII and IX of *The Spirit of the Laws* deal with Montesquieu's views on the corruption of governments and on the best ways for governments to defend themselves from both internal and external forces. The ideas expressed were to have influence upon those who framed the national and state constitutions of the United States and were to leave an indelible impression upon the American mind.

A government's corruption, Montesquieu says, "begins with that of its principles." The superstructure of government rests upon the foundation provided by its appropriate principle; when the foundation is altered, the superstructure must be changed accordingly. In a democratic republic an integral feature of virtue is equality, but it is equality of a par-

[23] *Ibid.*, VI, 2.

ticular kind. A democracy that permits an excess of equality will countenance mere license; one that does not provide sufficient equality will become autocratic. In either case the republic will be destroyed. Thus it is important to have the proper kind of equality in a democratic republic. It cannot be the equality that existed in a state of nature and was lost in civil society. Rather the "spirit of equality" must prevail—a system in which differences in human capacity are recognized, in which those with superior abilities govern but do so according to the law under which they are the equals of their fellows. Montesquieu's views are very close to those of Alexander Hamilton and John Adams: that whereas the basis of a republic must be the people, a "natural aristocracy" consisting of gentlemen of demonstrated ability should play the leading role in government, while at the same time leaders and people should be equal under the law.

Virtue is also the principle in aristocracies, and corruption occurs when the nobility rules arbitrarily rather than on the basis of established laws. The principle of honor, indispensable to a monarchy, demands a sharing of power among nobility, clergy, courts, cities, and king, among all the various established ranks of privilege in the society. Corruption ensues when the king "insensibly deprives" these other groups of their traditional authority. Montesquieu believes that this is what has happened in France, although he is too prudent to say so specifically. Corruption of a despotism is, in a sense, impossible; it is already corrupt. The only problem here is maintaining a situation warranted by circumstances. If conditions, "drawn from the climate, religion, situation, or genius of the people," remain stable, the despotism will be secure; if they change, the form of government will also.

The extent of territory occupied by members of a civil society has a vital relationship to the governmental form which may be employed. A republic requires a small territory. It demands an agreement among the citizens as to their common interest, and this cooperation cannot be secured in a large area where interests are too numerous and too diverse. People then serve their own rather than the public interest. The great advantage of a republic is that it permits and demands a coincidence of the particular and the common interest. While a large territory cannot achieve such unity of spirit, still, if the republic is too small it may be conquered by external enemies. In brief, large republics are endangered by internal factions; small republics are susceptible to invasion. Is there an escape from this dilemma? Montesquieu's solution is the establishment of a confederation, which he describes in the following words.

> This form of government is a convention by which several petty states agree to become members of a larger one, which they intend to establish. It is a kind of assemblage of societies, that constitute a new one, capable of in-

creasing by means of further associations, till they arrive at such a degree of power as to be able to provide for the security of the whole body.[24]

The principle and advantage of confederation is that it permits each constituent unit of government to resolve its own domestic problems without involvement with or interference from other units. That consensus with regard to the general interest which is indispensable to republics is thus made possible. At the same time the constituent units may unite to present a common front in matters of military and foreign policy.

The theory is ingenious, and Montesquieu extends its principle to cover other kinds of government. A monarchy, he says, requires a moderate territory. A too small monarchy will become a republic; in an excessively large area the nobility cannot be controlled. The monarchical form will be destroyed in either case. A large territory, unless governed on the basis of republican and confederate principles, will become a despotism, for the subjects must be made to fear the central authority so greatly that they will not revolt against it. Montesquieu's ideas concerning the relationship between extent of territory and governmental form were well known and had considerable influence with the men who framed the Constitution of the United States.[25] Those ideas form an integral part of the theories of federalism found in the series of essays by Madison, Hamilton, and Jay, known as *The Federalist*. We shall consider later the validity of the federal principle, especially as it applies to the modern republic.

Liberty and the Separation of Powers

The part of Montesquieu's theory which is best known and has exerted the greatest influence upon Americans is that which deals with separation of powers; the subject is discussed in Book XI of *The Spirit of the Laws*. The title of the book is "Of the Laws Which Establish Political Liberty with Regard to the Constitution," and it is an apt description of the contents. Montesquieu's concern is with the constitutional arrangements necessary in a government to secure an adequate degree of liberty for the individual and at the same time assure that government has the necessary authority. Book XI was written after Montesquieu's return from his sojourn in England and reflects the impression that English political institutions had made upon him. As we shall see, Montesquieu was guilty of serious errors in his analysis of the way in

[24] *Ibid.*, IX, 1.

[25] The interested reader is advised to consult Paul Merrill Spurlin, *Montesquieu in America, 1760–1801*, Louisiana State University Press, Baton Rouge, La., 1940. The influence of Montesquieu in America in the period immediately preceding and following the framing of the Federal Constitution is covered in some detail.

which those institutions contributed to the success of the English system. But that a theory can be influential despite its inaccuracies is assuredly illustrated by Montesquieu's thesis of separation of powers.

The exposition begins with a brief discussion of liberty, which Montesquieu carefully distinguishes from license. The freedom to do anything one can get away with is not true liberty. The only valuable liberty is that which we enjoy under the law. It consists in being permitted to do those things we ought to do and in being prohibited from doing what we ought not to do. Stated somewhat differently, "Liberty is a right of doing what the laws permit, and if a citizen could do what they forbid he would be no longer possessed of liberty, because all his fellow citizens would have the same power." [26] Liberty is not anarchy; there must be laws. But laws too can deprive a people of their liberty. Laws must be of the right kind, forbidding only actions which ought to be forbidden and leaving wide areas of freedom for the individual. Only a moderate government will enact such laws, and moderation in government is a rare quality. Anticipating Lord Acton's famous dictum, Montesquieu says: "Constant experience shows us that every man invested with power is apt to abuse it, and to carry his authority as far as it will go." [27] In order to establish and maintain moderate government, power must be checked with power. One government, which has political liberty as its "particular end," has succeeded in doing this. That is the government of England, and in his description of that government Montesquieu develops his theory of separation of powers.

In all governments three kinds of power exist: a legislative power by which the laws are made; an executive power which controls external policy (diplomacy and military affairs) and internal policy, or the protection of the public security; and finally an executive power by which criminals are punished and disagreements among individuals are reconciled or settled. This last is the judicial power, which, although Montesquieu classes it as a type of executive power, is to be exercised by a body separate from that which controls other matters under executive jurisdiction. Each power should be wielded by a different body or person. A concentration of all of them in the same body will result in the lack of the governmental moderation necessary to the framing and execution of laws favorable to political liberty.

> When the legislative and executive powers are united in the same person, or in the same body of magistrates, there can be no liberty; because apprehensions may arise, lest the same monarch or senate should enact tyrannical laws, to execute them in a tyrannical manner.
>
> Again, there is no liberty, if the judiciary power be not separated from

[26] *The Spirit of the Laws*, XI, 3.
[27] *Ibid.*, XI, 4.

the legislative and executive. Were it joined with the legislative, the life and liberty of the subject would be exposed to arbitrary control; for the judge might behave with violence and oppression.

There would be an end of everything, were the same man or the same body, whether of the nobles or of the people, to exercise those three powers, that of enacting laws, that of executing the public resolutions, and of trying the causes of individuals.[28]

Some aspects of Montesquieu's discussion of the judicial power are confusing, and a determination of his precise meaning is difficult if not impossible. Certain conclusions, however, appear warranted. As compared with the executive and legislative power, that of the judiciary "is in a sense nothing." The sense of this statement seems to be that the power to judge in disputes at law is less significant than the powers of making and of enforcing the law. Still, it is important enough to justify its separation from the other agencies of government. It has been suggested that Montesquieu's separation of the judicial from the executive power is in line with English thinking of the time, which opposed the king's control over a judiciary charged with the responsibility of judging disputes between himself and Parliament.[29] Montesquieu sees potential danger of a special nature in the judiciary stemming from the fact that it alone among the agencies of government acts directly on the individual. Of the other two powers, legislative and executive, the first is "no more than the general will of the state, and the other the execution of that general will." This being the case, the composition of the judiciary should differ from that of the other agencies. It ought not to be a standing body but should instead consist of "persons taken from the body of the people." It should be temporary, meeting only at designated times and always in a manner prescribed by law. This kind of body will relieve the fear of the people; they will "fear the office, but not the magistrate."

Montesquieu proposes three exceptions to the rule that judicial powers should not be exercised by a separate branch of government. The first is prompted by his conviction that ordinary courts drawn from the people will not give justice to members of the nobility in cases at law. The nobility, therefore, should be tried only by their peers in that branch of the legislature which represents them. That same body should also act as a supreme judicial tribunal to modify judgments, coming from the ordinary courts, which have wrongly applied the law. Finally, the noble branch of the legislature should act as a court and render judgments in impeachment cases tried before it by the lower house.

Despite his extensive consideration of judicial power, however, Mon-

[28] *Ibid.*, XI, 6.
[29] Francis D. Wormuth, *The Origins of Modern Constitutionalism*, Harper & Row, Publishers, Incorporated, New York, 1949, pp. 196–197.

tesquieu is less concerned with it than he is with the legislative and executive authorities. Legislative power "should reside in the whole body of people," but since this is impossible in large states and inconvenient in small ones, representatives must be used. Because the people of particular areas are better acquainted with their own problems than are strangers, representatives should be elected by the people of those areas. Once representatives are elected they should be left free to discuss and make decisions without interference from their constituents. All persons, "except such as are in so mean a situation as to be deemed to have no will of their own," should be permitted to vote.[30] The people generally lack the capacity to play an active part in the governing process, but they are fully capable of choosing those who do. "For though few can tell the exact degree of men's capacities, yet there are none but are capable of knowing in general whether the person they choose is better qualified than most of his neighbors." [31]

The elective principle applies only to one part of the legislative body —to the house that represents the commonalty. In all states some people, on the basis of "their birth, riches, or honors," are entitled to a greater recognition than is accorded the lower classes. Moreover, the commoners would enact laws detrimental to the interests of the upper class. The nobility, therefore, must be represented separately in a legislative body of their own, a body which "has the right to check the licentiousness of the people, as the people have a right to oppose any encroachment of theirs." The nobility ought to be hereditary. This principle is not only "natural" but it is also practically essential to the class in order to "preserve its privileges" against the people who envy and resent them. Nevertheless, a nobility may also pursue their own welfare to the detriment of the people. To guard against this encroachment, their authority in matters where their own interest is concerned should be limited to the rejection of laws proposed by the lower house.

The legislative and executive branches must each possess the ability to check the other. Executive power is most efficiently exercised by a monarch; to place such authority in the hands of the legislative is to contravene the rule of separation; this in turn would destroy moderation in government and lead to the loss of political liberty. The legislature should be convened and prorogued by the executive. If the legislature were to use its own judgment with regard to the length and time of its sessions, it might meet at inconvenient times and remain in session too long. Montesquieu knows that the legislative body can be as tyrannical as the executive. He wants no "long parliaments." There should be regular and frequent elections for members of the lower house; otherwise vacancies may be filled by appointment, and the right of

[30] Montesquieu favors a modest property qualification for voting.
[31] *The Spirit of the Laws,* XI, 6.

election be thus withdrawn from the people. The legislature should not have the power to arraign and remove the executive, for such authority would transcend the power of checking and place the legislative above and in control of the executive. The legislature may, however, investigate the manner in which laws are executed, and it may punish those ministers of the king who have improperly enforced the law. Finally, the executive should have the power to veto legislative proposals, although it is not to participate in "public debates," nor is it to have the power itself to propose measures for the legislature's consideration.

> Here, then, is the fundamental constitution of the government we are treating of. The legislative body being composed of two parts, they check one another by the mutual privilege of rejecting. They are both restrained by the executive power, as the executive is by the legislative.[32]

The constitution provided by the laws of England exactly illustrates the system proposed; yet Montesquieu, strangely, says that he does not assert that the English enjoy political liberty. It is enough, he says, to say that their laws provide for it.

Political Liberty and the Individual

Montesquieu fully understands that the constitution is only one of many factors that affect the lives, the status, and the freedom of citizens. A constitution may contribute greatly to the establishment and protection of political liberty for the individual by providing the proper structure of government and other fundamental laws which support liberty. Even under such a constitution the people may not be free, just as they may enjoy freedom under a constitution that has been designed to curb liberty. This is the meaning of Montesquieu's concluding observation on the English constitution. That constitution provides, in the form of a structure of government, everything necessary to political liberty. Liberty is still not assured. The reason is that a great number of things bear upon this matter, "manners, customs, or received examples," as well as civil laws. A perfect constitution may be rendered worthless by opposition from these forces; freedom, on the other hand, may be secured with support from them in the face of a tyrannically oriented constitution. Montesquieu discusses these factors at great length. We shall consider only a few of the more important.

The criminal laws of a country have a direct bearing upon personal liberty. If they are not good, liberty vanishes. An acceptable code of criminal law will provide that no death penalty shall be assessed on the evidence of a single witness. It will establish punishments that accord with the nature of the crime and will impose them fairly and not arbitrarily. In cases where an individual is charged with an offense

[32] *Ibid.*

against religion there should be no secular punishment unless others have somehow been injured by the act of the accused; otherwise it is a matter between the offender and God. Special precautions should be taken to safeguard the rights of a defendant in cases involving witchcraft and heresy; the people are ignorant and likely to be swayed by emotion where these matters are concerned. Treason cases also warrant special attention. Treason should be carefully and narrowly defined, or governments will employ charges of treason to suppress and remove those who are merely critical or at most are guilty of some act far removed from treason. No criminal laws should be designed to control freedom of thought or of speech. Only those words against a government which are coupled with, and lead immediately to, overt action should be proscribed.

The tax laws of a country also relate to the political liberty of the individual. Good tax laws will take into account both the "necessities of the state" and "real wants of the people." States often have "imaginary wants" stemming from vanity, ambitions, and desire for luxury on the part of the rulers, and these should not be satisfied. Montesquieu well understands the sensitivity of the people where taxes are concerned and the difficulty of enacting tax laws which meet the needs of the state and are fair to all. "Nothing requires more wisdom and prudence than the regulation of that portion of which the subject is deprived, and that which he is suffered to retain." [33] Some of the principles of taxation proposed by Montesquieu would, however, be rejected by modern economists. For example, he says that taxes should not be assessed on the basis of ability to pay. He recommends the use of excise taxes, for when the taxes are added to the price of goods they are hidden, and the purchaser does not realize that he is paying them. The more freedom a people have, Montesquieu says, the higher their taxes may be, for liberty is their compensation. Taxes may be raised to the point, however, where men will be reduced to slavery, and the revenue of the state will then decline. Another of Montesquieu's strictures on taxes has a modern ring.

> A new distemper has spread itself over Europe, infecting our princes, and inducing them to keep up an exorbitant number of troops. It has its redoublings, and of necessity becomes contagious, For as soon as one prince augments his forces, the rest, of course, do the same; so that nothing is gained thereby but the public ruin. Each monarch keeps as many armies on foot as if his people were in danger of being exterminated; and they give the name of peace to this general effort of all against all.[34]

There is a great variety of laws in every society—natural, divine, ecclesiastical, international, general political (dealing with the origin of

---

[33] *Ibid.*, XIII, 1.
[34] *Ibid.*, XIII, 17.

all societies) and particular political (relating to individual societies) laws, the law of conquest, and civil law. Each should apply to the subject to which it properly relates. To the degree that this ideal is not realized the society will suffer. Canon or ecclesiastical laws, for example, should not govern those matters which are rightly under the jurisdiction of civil laws, and vice versa.

Montesquieu also warns against laws that infringe upon property rights. A "natural community of goods," he says, was abandoned by men when they entered civil society. Civil laws are designed, in part, to protect property. It is wrong for people to support a law that limits the property rights of an individual on the ground that the limitation is in the interest of the community. The community interest, he contends, is never served by the curbing of the individual's property rights. Montesquieu differs from Locke and others in associating property with civil, rather than with natural law. But he and they are on common ground in their insistence upon a great degree of governmental respect for property rights.

The laws bearing upon political liberty must take into account a great many circumstances that affect the citizens and subjects of the various societies. Climate, soil, economics, religion, customs, and traditions —to name but a few—must all be considered. They influence the physiology and psychology of a people, determining their character and, consequently, the nature of the laws and institutions suited to them. Montesquieu says that the people of hot climates are more effeminate, weaker, less brave, more slavish, more given to pleasure than are their fellows in the cold climates. As a result they have lost their liberties to despotic governments, whereas northerners have retained their freedom. Fertility of soil also gives rise to despotism, for where great prosperity is possible people devote themselves to its pursuit rather than to an interest in public affairs. Where the soil is not so productive the people develop greater virtue and are more likely to possess liberty.

> The barrenness of the earth renders men industrious, sober, inured to hardship, courageous and fit for war; they are obliged to procure by labor what the earth refuses to bestow spontaneously. The fertility of a country gives ease, effeminacy, and a certain fondness for the preservation of life.[35]

Republics are more often found in barren countries, monarchies more generally in "fruitful countries." In like manner Montesquieu correlates religion with political forms. Mohammedanism is associated with despotism, Catholicism with monarchy, and Protestantism with republicanism. With regard to economics, Montesquieu states that a republic is the appropriate governmental form for a country heavily engaged in commercial pursuits.

[35] *Ibid.,* XIII, 4.

Although we can find absurdities in the examples produced by Montesquieu to support his environmental or sociological theory of politics, the theory itself is not absurd. Religion *does* affect political theory and institutions. There *is* a compelling relationship between economics and politics. And soil quality gives rise to occupational activities which, in turn, influence governmental structure, modes of representation, and laws. Climatic conditions are directly related to economics, occupation, customs, and traditions, and thus indirectly to constitutions. It would be a serious mistake to judge the substance of Montesquieu's idea by the examples with which he supports it. Of course, too, that idea was not original with Montesquieu; both Aristotle and Bodin anticipated him here, although the scope of Montesquieu's study was greater than theirs.

In summary Montesquieu says that all the factors considered influence man and mold a "general spirit" within a nation which must be taken into account by legislators and leaders. Constitutions and laws will be successful only if they are based upon this spirit; to the degree that they do not conform they will fail. Little can be done to alter the general spirit, and extreme caution should be observed if the attempt is made. Generally the function of legislators is to discover and understand the spirit, not to change it. If changes are to be made, they must be made properly. Law should be reformed by law, customs by the introduction of new customs, "for it is very bad policy to change by law what ought to be changed by custom." [36] It is unwise, as a rule, to tinker with things through legislation.

> Should there happen to be a country whose inhabitants were of a social temper, open-hearted, cheerful, endowed with taste and a facility in communicating their thoughts; who were sprightly and agreeable; sometimes imprudent, often indiscreet; and besides had courage, generosity, frankness, and a certain notion of honor, no one ought to endeavor to restrain their manners by law, unless he would lay a constraint on their virtues. If in general the character be good, the little foibles that are found in it are of small importance.[37]

Conclusions

Montesquieu was sincerely attached to the principle of political liberty, and it was this stalwart quality in his writings that attracted the support given to *The Spirit of the Laws*. Being, however, a deeply conservative writer, he provoked the antagonism of liberals such as Helvetius. Montesquieu was not a reformer who advocated wiping the slate clean and creating new institutions designed to place power in the hands of the people. His opposition was to what he considered to be the innovation

[36] *Ibid.*, XIX, 14.
[37] *Ibid.*, XIX, 5.

of absolute monarchy; his solution was a return to the old system of mixed or moderate monarchy, in which all the ancient privileges and rights of the classes were preserved. The English constitution appealed to him because it appeared to offer the advantages which his own country had lost. But Montesquieu was deceived by appearances. For though the structure of the English government, with its distinct institutions of king, Lords, Commons, and courts, seemed to lend support to the theories of separation of powers and checks and balances which Montesquieu was certain made political liberty possible, in fact the principle of parliamentary supremacy had already been established. Ministers were more responsible to the House of Commons than to the king. In short, political authority was less divided and subject to fewer checks than Montesquieu knew. It is understandable that he should have misinterpreted a situation which few Englishmen understood, but he erred in asserting that political liberty would be lost if ever "the legislative and executive powers are united in the same person, or in the same body of magistrates." Whatever may be the merits of a system based upon separation of powers and checks and balances, it cannot, in view of the history and status of political liberty in England, validly be argued that the system is essential to the preservation of such liberty. In fairness to Montesquieu it must be stated that one of the reasons for separating the executive power from the legislative was that the executive power was assumed to be in a king, and he considered the separation, therefore, essential to the preservation of liberty. When the executive power was transferred to the House of Commons, this reason disappeared. But Montesquieu was not considering the institutional relation.

Montesquieu thought of the society of his time as a welter of conflicting interests represented by classes and by privileged ranks and offices. As long as each of these had a voice in the conduct of affairs and the power at least to compel the others to consider its circumstances, government could be exercised with the moderation that Montesquieu so greatly admired. As we have seen, he thought highly of republics, for in them particular interests and the general interest coincided. But since the virtue of the people which made good republics possible had been lost, the only practicable governmental system that could be established would have to recognize the existence of conflicting interests and somehow control them without a too great deprivation of liberty. Montesquieu's objection to despotism was that in this form order was established at the cost of liberty, and his regard for the English constitution was based upon his belief that it secured order without paying such a price, by giving each of the three major interests, monarchy, aristocracy, and commonalty, a share of power and the means whereby each could check the others. Action of almost any kind would therefore require a concert of interest which could be achieved only if the action was satisfactory to each interest. Montesquieu saw clearly enough that such a system could produce stalemate, but this did not concern him. He assumed that when things had to be done, they would be. "These three powers should naturally form a state of repose or inaction. But as there is a necessity for movement in the course of human affairs, they are forced to move, but still in concert." [38]

Considering that the system of separation of powers was designed by Montesquieu to maintain order in a society of conflicting class interests and that Montesquieu believed that in a republic there was no such conflict, we may find it remarkable that he should propose that republics, too, may benefit from separation of powers and checks and balances.[39] Nevertheless he does so, and it is in the American republic that Montesquieu's doctrines have had their greatest influence. There are so many parallels between provisions of the Constitution of the United States and *The Spirit of the Laws* that we can consider only a few of them here.

The framers of the American Constitution, like Montesquieu, sought a governmental system which could reconcile conflicting interests without an unwarranted restriction on freedom. It was logical that they should have considered the problem in Montesquieu's terms, for *The Spirit of the Laws* was well known in America. The danger of "factions" is a problem to which considerable attention is given in *The Federalist*, and Montesquieu's devices of separation of powers, checks and balances, and a federal system are mainly employed to solve that problem. It was in America that Montesquieu's theories were subjected to the acid test. How successful they have been has long been debated. Separation of powers has, some argue, saved the nation from tyranny. Others say that this is not so, that many other factors are involved, and that separation has had little if anything to do with the matter. Moreover, it is said, separation of powers so restricts the ability of government to act that tyranny is likely to follow the collapse of a system which cannot or will not solve its problems. Regardless of the merits of the arguments on either side, we may admit that to the extent that separation of powers functions, government does not. One of the most prominent features of the political system of the United States is the constant struggle to overcome the

---

[38] *Ibid.,* XI, 6.

[39] A possible explanation is that Montesquieu distinguished between republics in which the necessary principle of virtue was present and in which, logically, separation of powers would be unnecessary, on the one hand, and corrupted republics where virtue was missing and which could benefit from separation, on the other. The fact that he states at one point that republics are no longer possible because of the lack of virtue, but in other places proceeds to discuss existing republics, perhaps makes this conjecture plausible.

barriers to governmental action imposed by the system of separation of powers. The most valuable device yet conceived to accomplish this purpose has been the political party. This solution most of the framers of the Constitution would have rejected, for parties are, after all, "factions," and the framers were interested in curbing factions.

Montesquieu's advocacy of confederation is reproduced in *The Federalist*.[40] It will be recalled that Montesquieu's argument was that a consensus is impossible except in small political units and that such units are incapable of defending themselves militarily. The problem could be solved by creation of a confederation which would permit a consensus with regard to the domestic affairs of each constituent polity but provide for unified action of all units for their common defense. The American system is more complex and confers upon the central authority more power than Montesquieu's brief and simple proposal contemplated, but the underlying idea is the same. As on the subject of separation of powers, considerable disagreement has been voiced over whether or to what degree federalism has succeeded. The power of the central government has greatly overshadowed that of the "sovereign" states. Chief Justice John Marshall spoke prophetically when he stated that the question as to the proper scope of national authority "is perpetually arising, and will probably continue to arise, as long as our system shall exist." [41] Indeed the system barely survived a struggle over a problem of federalism in the Civil War, and today few political disagreements provoke more violent emotions than those that arise over the charge that the national government is usurping power which rightfully belongs to the states. The federal principle implies, among other things, that interests are largely identifiable geographically, that local governments can solve their own problems better than can a central government, that such governments are more responsive and responsible to their constituents, and that personal liberty is more adequately safeguarded on the local level. None of these assumptions has gone unchallenged. The federal system of the United States has undergone substantial changes since 1789. It is likely that Montesquieu, a relativist who insisted that governmental forms were influenced by time and circumstances, would have acknowledged the necessity of the transition.

SELECTED BIBLIOGRAPHY

Cook, Thomas I.: *History of Political Philosophy from Plato to Burke*, Prentice-Hall, Inc., Englewood Cliffs, N.J., 1936, chap. 21.

Hearnshaw, F. J. C. (ed.): *The Social and Political Ideas of Some Great French*

[40] See especially Number 10.
[41] *McCulloch v. Maryland*, 4 Wheaton 316 (1819).

Thinkers of the Age of Reason, Barnes & Noble, Inc., New York, 1950, chap. 5.

Lowenthal, David: "Book 1 of Montesquieu's *The Spirit of the Laws,*" *American Political Science Review,* vol. 53, no. 2, June, 1959.

McDonald, Lee Cameron: *Western Political Theory: The Modern Age,* Harcourt, Brace & World, Inc., New York, 1962, chap. 6.

Martin, Kingsley: *The Rise of French Liberal Thought: A Study of Political Ideas from Bayle to Condorcet,* 2d rev. ed., New York University Press, New York, 1954.

Merriam, Charles Edward: *A History of American Political Theories,* The Macmillan Company, New York, 1924, chap. 3.

Montesquieu, Baron de: *The Persian Letters* (translated and introduced by John Davidson), in *Persian and Chinese Letters* (including *The Citizen of the World,* by Oliver Goldsmith, with a special introduction by Oliver H. G. Leigh), M. Walter Dunne, Publisher, Washington, 1901.

————: *The Spirit of the Laws* (translated by Thomas Nugent, with an introduction by Franz Neumann), Hafner Publishing Company, Inc., New York, 1949.

Sabine, George H.: *A History of Political Theory,* 3d ed., Holt, Rinehart and Winston, Inc., New York, 1961, chap. 27.

Spurlin, Paul Merrill: *Montesquieu in America, 1760–1801,* Louisiana State University Press, Baton Rouge, La., 1940.

Wormuth, Francis D.: *The Origins of Modern Constitutionalism,* Harper & Row, Publishers, Incorporated, New York, 1949, chaps. 18, 20.

fifteen

ROUSSEAU

Louis XIV of France died in 1715 and was succeeded by his great-grandson. Louis XV (1710–1774) came to the throne at the age of five, and the affairs of state were for a time directed by a Regent, the Duke of Orleans. Without the iron hand of the "Sun King" at the helm, the long-frustrated nobility began to reestablish a measure of control. Intendancies were taken by nobles, and the *Parlement* of Paris reassumed its right to review and enforce legislation. This did nothing to improve the general situation in France. The middle and lower classes detested the aristocracy more than they did the king, and the nobles, governing selfishly and irresponsibly, increased the prevailing discontent.

Louis's appointment of the able Cardinal Fleury to the first minister-ship in 1726 stemmed the tide of governmental degeneration for a time. Fleury was able to stabilize the currency, stimulate trade, patch up the system of taxation, although without genuinely reforming it, and establish a brief period of peace. It was a mere holding operation. In 1743 Fleury died, and Louis XV announced that he would henceforth act as his own first minister, in the manner of his illustrious predecessor, Louis XIV. But Louis XV had neither the interest nor the capacity of his great-grandfather. He was too involved with a succession of mistresses (Madame du Barry and Madame de Pompadour are the best known), whose intrigues damaged the national interest. The economic situation worsened, and there was a progressive deterioration of the French state until the Revolution of 1789. Louis XV's statement, "After me, the deluge," was truly prophetic.

The increasing unrest of the people, especially of the middle class, was reflected in the intellectual ferment of the times. This was the period of the Enlightenment, a movement which drew to its ranks the most able thinkers in a great many fields; nearly all of them were dedicated to a reform of French institutions. Their heroes were the skeptic Bayle,[1] the philosopher Locke, and the scientist Newton. The scientific discoveries of the seventeenth century had led to the belief that the universe was governed by orderly and discoverable laws and that men could understand them and improve their world through the use of reason. As we have seen, this view carried over into the area of social relationships and gave rise to an increasing emphasis upon the venerable idea of a law of nature which sets the standard for moral behavior. The seventeenth century also produced a revival of empiricism, the theory that knowledge stems from sense experience. The two, rationalism and empiricism, were often antagonistic, and both were to play important roles in the eighteenth-century Enlightenment.

Political ideas in the eighteenth century were not as original as they had been in the seventeenth. They were, in fact, applications of the earlier thought, but in the France of Louis XV, and given the quality of the dissenters of that period, they were more stimulating. The leaders of the Enlightenment were angry, intelligent, informed, and they knew how to write. Their appeal was mainly to the bourgeoisie, and, since the crown and the clergy bitterly opposed any criticism of the old regime, the writings were often circuitous and satirical. Hardly anyone, however, missed the point.

Of the *philosophes*, who were agents of the Enlightenment, the most influential was Voltaire (1694–1778). Voltaire was not democratic; he had nothing but contempt for the masses. He was, nonetheless, profoundly rational, humane, freedom-loving, and witty. On a visit to England (1726–1729) he studied the works of Locke and Newton. Upon his return to France he dissected the old regime with his pen, using the ideas of the two great Englishmen as the basis for his attack. His bitterest assaults were reserved for the Church, and he followed Bayle and Locke in his demands for religious toleration. Although he was imprisoned for a short time for his views, his wit and his skill at writing satire kept him free during the balance of his life. He attracted a tremendous following in France and throughout Europe, and—a novelty for radical intellectuals of the time—he made a great deal of money.

There were many others. Helvetius developed a new way of consider-

---

[1] Pierre Bayle (1647–1706), a scholar of the late seventeenth century and a convert to Catholicism, renounced his faith and devoted his life to an attack upon religious superstition and intolerance. He strongly argued that faith and reason were incompatible.

ing ethics and passed it on to Bentham, in whose hands it became the important theory of utilitarianism. Holbach, the atheist and materialist, said that all phenomena are explainable in terms of natural laws and that governments exist only to exploit, thus anticipating a later and similar philosophy by Karl Marx. Diderot, the editor of the *Encyclopedia*, directed that great compendium toward the molding of opinion rather than toward the provision of information; most of the *philosophes* contributed to the *Encyclopedia*.[2] Quesnay and his group, the "physiocrats," eighteen years before the publication of Adam Smith's *Wealth of Nations* were arguing for free enterprise in economic life.

All these men were stimulating (or irritating to a supporter of the old regime), but none were democrats. Some merely sought a little less despotism, or at best an enlightened despot, who might govern according to the laws of nature as they were perceived by the *philosophes*. Others, such as Montesquieu, wanted a constitutional monarchy. They were unanimous in their conviction that government ought to improve the condition of the people; they were equally united in their opinion that anarchy would result from any system in which the people themselves governed. Still there was one who hated the society in which he lived more than did all the rest, but who was also critical of the Enlightenment and its spokesmen. He was Jean Jacques Rousseau, and in the development of political theory he was a more significant figure than any of his contemporaries.

The Man and His Work

The views of all men are shaped by their experiences; Rousseau illustrates the oft-stated rule. The relationship of his life to his ideas is clear and compelling and has been thoroughly considered by students of his philosophy. Fortunately, Rousseau himself has provided, in his *Confessions*, a wealth of biographical material, all written in a manner which leaves little to the imagination. The life he describes was not a happy one, nor is the personality that emerges from the pages of the *Confessions* particularly attractive. It is at least unconventional. We must, however, resist the temptation to judge Rousseau's philosophy by his character.

Rousseau was born in Geneva in 1712 and lived there until 1728. This fact has considerable importance. Geneva was a self-governing city-state, and its inhabitants took pride in its independence. It was also the chief stronghold of Calvinism. Rousseau never lost his admiration for the Genevan form of government, and despite his subsequent freedom of living he retained a puritanical streak probably acquired from the stringent set of moral rules that prevailed in the city of his birth. Whatever moral instruction the young Rousseau received came from the community and not from his home. His mother died when Rousseau was born;

---

[2] Those who did were known as "Encyclopedists."

his father, Issac Rousseau, was completely unsuited to the task of rearing a son. He was a watchmaker, but he preferred being a dancing master, a profession disapproved by the stern city fathers of Geneva. The father read to his son on occasion, an admirable pastime except that the literature was generally more erotic than instructive. There was little cause for remorse when Issac Rousseau, following an altercation with a "M. G_____," accepted voluntary banishment from Geneva rather than risk a prison term. Rousseau was taken in charge by an uncle, who sent him to school for two unprofitable years at Bossey. In 1725 he was apprenticed to an engraver, a harsh and brutal man named Abel Ducommun, in whose employ Rousseau learned mainly to steal and lie.

Rousseau ran away from Ducommun and Geneva in 1728 and began, at the age of sixteen, fourteen years of semivagabondage. During this period he was dependent for varying lengths of time upon a number of people. The most important was a Madame de Warens, with whom Rousseau stayed on several occasions and in whose library and company he acquired a degree of sophistication and some further learning. Here Rousseau read Plato's *Republic,* a work that strongly influenced his later political writings. Rousseau also demonstrated a natural talent for music, which Madame de Warens encouraged, and his gift helped him to gain admission to artistic circles in Paris.

Rousseau arrived in Paris in 1742, following a quarrel with his benefactress, Madame de Warens, of whom he was inordinately jealous. He was energetic, and his forceful personality attracted a considerable number of acquaintances, who were both fascinated and repelled by him. Rousseau was now thirty and optimistically certain that a new system of musical notation which he had developed would bring him immediately to prominence. The rejection of his system was the first of many disappointments he was to suffer in Paris. After a time Rousseau took employment in a minor position in the French embassy at Venice. He resigned a year later and returned to Paris, uttering scathing denunciations of the French ambassador and, in the process, alienating many who might otherwise have helped him. For the next several years Rousseau tried to break into French society. He had hoped that his musical talent would gain him social acceptance, but he was not good enough. He wrote an opera; it was a failure. What little employment he was able to obtain was clerical and routine, and Rousseau hated it. Rejected by sophisticated society, Rousseau went to the opposite extreme in search of consolation. He sought companionship in the lowest classes. Here he met Thérèse Levasseur. She was illiterate and coarse, but Rousseau was attracted to her in his loneliness, and so began a liaison that lasted throughout Rousseau's life. The union produced five children, all of whom Rousseau placed in a foundling home. His acquaintances were appalled by his association with Thérèse. Rousseau detested her mother, who was a frightful shrew; nevertheless, he found some happiness with Thérèse. Toward the close of his life he married her, although there is some doubt as to the legality of the ceremony.

The turning point in Rousseau's career occurred in October, 1749, when he saw an announcement of an essay contest sponsored by the Academy of Dijon. The essay sought an answer to the question, "Has the progress of sciences and arts contributed to corrupt or purify morals?" The question, framed in the spirit of the Enlightenment, was obviously intended to elicit an answer extolling the march of science. Because he was astute enough to recognize that a negative answer would stand out in the competition and because such a view would permit him to vent his wrath on a society that had rejected him, Rousseau took the unconventional approach. His success was spectacular. He not only won the contest but achieved, almost overnight, a considerable reputation. His essay, entitled *A Discourse on the Moral Effects of the Arts and Sciences,* argued that morals had deteriorated as the arts and sciences had carried man away from his natural state of goodness. Rousseau's arguments were more passionate than logical, and he took positions that were largely untenable. He was surprised by the furor his essay provoked and by the quality of the opposition. Once stated, the views had to be defended, and Rousseau defended them brilliantly. He developed his style as a writer and his talents as a controversialist. Moreover, he adopted the simple manners and the way of life consonant with the position he had taken in the essay. A society which had shunned him when he had sought it now pursued him as he repudiated it.

In 1754 Rousseau wrote another essay, again in a competition announced by the Academy of Dijon. Rousseau's second discourse, *The Origin of Inequality,* was better than the first, although he did not, this time, win the prize. In it he praised the state of man's innocence and attacked the decadent society which, he said, resulted from the institution of private property. The following year Rousseau contributed an essay on "Political Economy" to the *Encyclopedia.* In it he took a different position; he accepted society and private property and attempted a constructive approach to the problems of the community. This discourse is significant primarily because it contains views later developed in his great political work, the *Social Contract.*

In 1756 Rousseau was provided by friends with a home in the country. Here he lived and wrote in semiseclusion for six years. To the extent that he had relations with others, personal or by correspondence, he antagonized them. He quarreled with Madame d'Epinay, who had helped to establish him in his rustic retreat. He quarreled with Diderot and with Voltaire. It is remarkable that Rousseau, with his pathological perversity, never lacked patrons who would provide him with help even at the cost of serious inconvenience to themselves. Despite his persistent embroilments, Rousseau found time to write. His three most important works, *la Nouvelle Héloïse* (1761), *le Contrat social* (*The Social Contract*) (1762), and *Emile* (1762), were all written toward the close of this period. The first is a sentimental novel which created a sensation in a day when cynicism and sophistication dominated exposition. *Emile,* part novel, part treatise, attacked conventional education, then dominated by the Church, and proposed a naturalistic approach.

Emile provoked a vigorous counterattack from Church and state alike. Rousseau was advised by his friends to flee, and he took their advice. Denied asylum in Geneva, whose rulers were as outraged by Rousseau's deism and his unconventional approach to education as were the Catholic clergy, Rousseau found a temporary home in Neuchâtel under the protection of Frederick II of Prussia in 1762. In January, 1766, he went to England, where he remained for a little more than a year. In May, 1767, he returned to France where he spent the rest of his life, mainly in Paris. Rousseau continued to write, despite the fact that he was by now mentally unstable and occasionally actually insane. His *Confessions* and his *Dialogues* were both written at this time, and he began his *Rêveries d'un promeneur solitaire,* a work intended to complete his autobiography. In addition he designed model constitutions for Poland and Corsica. In May, 1778, Rousseau accepted an invitation from a wealthy financier, M. de Girardin, to occupy a cottage in the country at Ermenonville. Here he died of a stroke on July 2, 1778.

The Pattern and Purpose of Rousseau's Theory

There are almost as many interpretations of Rousseau's political philosophy as interpreters of it. Like the man himself, his philosophy is extraordinarily complex. His writings are often abstract and not always clear. And finally, his ideas are not entirely consistent, although a final review of his work shows more consistency than appears at first glance. At least a logical pattern may be followed and understood in the light of Rousseau's experience. He detested the society in which he lived because of the wrongs, real or imagined, it had inflicted upon him, and his disillusionment led him to praise the merits of natural man and the primitive society which he imagined might have existed before men were corrupted by civilization. But, hating society, he nevertheless needed it, and to this end he constructed a plan that he believed would regenerate the community and enable mankind to enjoy its blessings without suffering its current disadvantages. A recognition of these conflicting experiences goes far toward explaining the apparent ambivalence of Rousseau's theory.[3]

F. J. C. Hearnshaw employs a Biblical analogy to illustrate the various

[3] *Rousseau, Political Writings* (translated and edited by Frederick Watkins), Thomas Nelson & Sons, New York, 1953, p. xiii.

steps in the development of Rousseau's theory. Christianity begins with the state of man's innocence. Then follow the fall of man, the evil conditions that result, the plan for man's redemption and, finally the promise of the perfect state for those who are redeemed.[4] Rousseau also, in his first two discourses (and he touches upon the same subject in *Emile* and *la Nouvelle Héloïse*) believes man has lost his former innocence and has fallen into a corrupt existence. The discourse on *Political Economy* and the *Social Contract* represent his plan for salvation, as well as for the ideal community that will emerge if the plan is adopted. It is this total approach to the problem, this root-and-branch solution, which sets Rousseau apart from other critics of French society. The latter considered men reasonable but selfish and incapable of governing themselves, and sought to reform society on a piecemeal basis; Rousseau undertook the task of remolding man's nature and providing an entirely different kind of society. The *philosophes* generally built upon the foundation of individualism and self-interest. Rational men, they believed, ought to be free to pursue their interests, and the institutions that had been erected to block their path should be altered so as to permit them greater liberty. Rousseau favored freedom for the individual, but he was fearful that the pursuit of self-interest would atomize the community, subject one man to another, and destroy the society which alone provides the means by which man may live a moral life. Most political philosophers, in considering the problem of liberty and authority, take their stand for a balance of the two. They see in liberty and authority two opposing forces, each of which is necessary to the good life. The task then is to designate the desirable freedoms, indicate their limits, and provide institutions designed to maintain the resulting structure. Rousseau, on the other hand, attempts to synthesize freedom and authority. He insists that, given the right kind of society, these are complementary, rather than antithetical, principles.

The First and Second Discourses

Rousseau himself regarded his first *Discourse* as the poorest of his writings. It is polemical, highly charged with emotion, and appears to have been hastily written. It is an attack upon the central principles of the Enlightenment: that man has employed his reason to discover rules of nature by which human life has been vastly improved and can be further improved; that progress is assured if only reason and intelligence are brought to bear on problems; that the advances already made in the sciences and arts constitute only a beginning; much more can and will be done.

Rousseau takes the opposite view. The arts and sciences, he says, have

[4] Hearnshaw, F. J. C. (ed.), *The Social and Political Ideas of Some Great French Thinkers of the Age of Reason,* Barnes & Noble, Inc., New York, 1950, pp. 186–187.

corrupted men and weakened society. They have provided "conveniences" and luxuries and created a materialistic outlook which has undermined virtue and morals.

> As the conveniences of life increase, as the arts are brought to perfection, and luxury spreads, true courage flags, the virtues disappear; and all this is the effect of the sciences and of those arts which are exercised in the privacy of men's dwellings.[5]

Truth is not discovered by reason and intelligence. The role of science is limited; it can explain the outward manifestation of things, but "truth" must be found in some other manner. What manner? By a reliance upon instinct, feeling, faith, emotion. One should ignore the preachments of the philosophers and rely upon his own conscience.

> Why should we build our happiness on the opinions of others, when we can find it in our own hearts? Let us leave to others the task of instructing mankind in their duty, and confine ourselves to the discharge of our own. We have no occasion for greater knowledge than this.
> Virtue! sublime science of simple minds, are such industry and preparation needed if we are to know you? Are not your principles graven on every heart? Need we do more, to learn your laws, than examine ourselves and listen to the voice of conscience, when the passions are silent? [6]

The proper standard, Rousseau says, is that of the natural man, uncorrupted by the vices and luxuries of civilized living. The appeal in the first *Discourse* is not dissimilar from the modern plea to return to the "faith of our fathers," to beware of a too great preoccupation with material values, and to reassert the values of faith, patriotism, and good citizenship. Many of Rousseau's statements along this line have a modern ring.

> We have physicists, geometricians, chemists, astronomers, poets, musicians, and painters in plenty; but we have no longer a citizen among us; or if there be found a few scattered over our abandoned countryside, they are left to perish there unnoticed and neglected.[7]

In his second *Discourse* Rousseau attempts to provide an explanation of the origin of inequality among men. It is equally an essay on the origin of civil society and may be better understood in this light. Rousseau begins, as did Locke and Hobbes, with a consideration of man's life in a state of nature. To understand the reasons for man's inequality in civil society, he says, we must first know what his situation was before

---

[5] Jean Jacques Rousseau, *A Discourse on the Moral Effects of the Arts and Sciences,* in *The Social Contract and Discourses by Jean Jacques Rousseau* (translated with introduction by G. D. H. Cole), E. P. Dutton & Co., Inc., New York, 1913. Subsequent references to and quotations from the *Discourses* are from this edition.
[6] *Ibid.*
[7] *Ibid.*

civil society existed. Rousseau admits that this is mere hypothesizing, for the state of nature "no longer exists, perhaps never did exist, and probably never will exist." [8] The first man was ruled by the laws of God, and there is no evidence that he ever returned to a state of nature. Like Hobbes, Rousseau employs the state of nature as a device whereby the nature of man may be determined. Man naturally is what he would be if there were no civil society.

There are two kinds of inequality among men. The first is natural; it is the only kind which exists in a state of nature and consists of those differences "of age, health, bodily strength, and the qualities of the mind or of the soul." The other is "moral or political inequality"; it is established by man in society. It comprises such privileges as "that of being more rich, more honored, more powerful," or of being "in a position to exact obedience." In the natural state one man may be stronger than another and abuse him, but this does not create a relationship of master and slave. This is a distinction found only in civil society. In a state of nature, he who is abused can simply run away; there are no laws or organizations to restrain him. The chief error of Hobbes, Rousseau says, is in assuming that the inequalities of civil society are carried over from a state of nature and that without the authority of the civil state there would be a war of all against all. The fact is, Rousseau asserts, that the state of war is a concomitant of civil, not natural, society. We see about us the distinctions between rich and poor, strong and weak, with all their attendant sufferings, and we are prone to regard such universal phenomena as the very foundations of human nature. But these are only the sands which obscure the true foundations. They must be removed before we can clearly see what the essence of human nature really is.

Because men in a state of nature are isolated and thus have no "moral relations or determinate obligations one with another," they are neither good nor bad. Such terms as "moral," "virtuous," "good," and "bad" have meaning only insofar as they apply to human relations. Natural man is not the aggressive brute that Hobbes made him out to be. He is, rather, timid and fearful and more likely to try to avoid combat than to seek it. Men wish to preserve themselves, but they do not, in nature, try to injure one another in the process. There are, Rousseau says, two motivations in natural man. These are self-love, or the instinct for self-preservation, and compassion for one's fellows. The latter modifies the force of the former and makes society possible. "It is then certain that compassion is a natural feeling, which, by moderating the violence of love of self in each individual, contributes to the preservation of the whole species." [9]

Perfection, however, rather than peace, is the main desire of human

[8] *Discourse on Inequality,* in *ibid.*
[9] *Ibid.*

kind, and this cannot be achieved in a state of nature. Association, not isolation, is a necessity if man is to advance from an animalistic, furtive, and fearful existence to that of a moral being. Man is perfectible, but his perfectibility is a potential that requires a community for its fulfillment. The question is, how did isolated natural man develop associations? Association gave rise to comparison and then to competition and inequality.

> Whoever sang or danced best, whoever was the handsomest, the strongest, the most dexterous, or the most eloquent, came to be of most consideration; and this was the first step towards inequality, and at the same time towards vice. From these first distinctions arose on the one side vanity and contempt and on the other shame and envy: and the fermentation caused by these new leavens ended by producing combinations fatal to innocence and happiness.[10]

Thus was born the earliest society, which represented a stage between the "indolence of the primitive state and the petulant activity of our egoism." There were disadvantages, for such a society brought evils and punishment. But the advantages outweighed the disadvantages, mainly because morality was possible and man could rise above the animal existence of a state of nature. Of all conditions this was the best one for man. He had lost his innocence, but he had gained a chance for moral perfection.

Where was the opportunity lost? How did this primitive but beneficent society become the modern civil society in which selfishness and greed set men at one another's throats, in which inequality breeds hatred and envy and destroys, rather than promotes, morality? This was the result of two other and related developments, of which the most important was the institution of private property.

> The first man who, having enclosed a piece of ground, bethought himself of saying *This is mine,* and found people simple enough to believe him, was the real founder of civil society. From how many crimes, wars and murders, from how many horrors and misfortunes might not anyone have saved mankind, by pulling up the stakes, or filling up the ditch, and crying to his fellows, Beware of listening to this impostor; you are undone if you once forget that the fruits of the earth belong to us all, and the earth itself to nobody.[11]

In conjunction with the establishment of private property came the use of iron and the development of agriculture. From this point a simple society in which relations among men were "mutual" but "independent" was impossible. Instead, an interdependent society was formed, a society in which one man required the help of another. It was then that "equal-

[10] *Ibid.*
[11] *Ibid.*

ity disappeared, property was introduced, work became indispensable, and vast forests became smiling fields, which man had to water with the sweat of his brow, and where slavery and misery were soon seen to germinate and grow up with the crops." [12]

The selfish part of man's nature asserted itself. His natural inclination to compassion and the developing principles of justice, which had marked the primitive society, gave way to "avarice, ambition and vice." The state of society gave rise to war. Inequality in property holdings was the underlying cause. The rich were aware that they owed what they had to force and usurpation; they also knew that they could easily lose their possessions in the same manner, and they searched for a way to protect themselves. The solution they found was the creation of civil society with laws to protect private property and the force required to implement them. The manner in which this was accomplished, Rousseau says, was ingenious. The rich man conceived a method by which he could "employ in his favor the forces of those who attacked him." The rich persuaded the poor to join in the creation of a power which would protect each in what he had, and thus restore peace. The poor succumbed gladly.

> All ran headlong to their chains, in hopes of securing their liberty; for they had just wit enough to perceive the advantages of political institutions without experience enough to enable them to foresee the dangers.
>
> Such was or may well have been, the origin of society and law, which bound new fetters on the poor, and gave new powers to the rich; which irretrievably destroyed natural liberty, eternally fixed the law of property and inequality, converted clever usurpation into unalterable right, and for the advantage of a few ambitious individuals, subjected all mankind to perpetual labor, slavery and wretchedness.[13]

What can be done to rectify this situation? Can one return to a state of nature? This would be no advantage, for man would lose his opportunity for moral perfection. Can he return to a primitive community? This would be highly desirable but impracticable. The only answer is the creation of a new society, which will retain the advantages, but eliminate the disadvantages, of the present corrupt state. This is the problem to which Rousseau directs his efforts in his subsequent political treatises.

The Social Contract

The Social Contract was intended as part of a much larger work, which was never completed and which Rousseau admitted was beyond his capacities. Many of the most important ideas in *The Social Contract* are found in abbreviated form in his *Discourse on Political Economy*, which

[12] *Ibid.*
[13] *Ibid.*

he wrote for Diderot's *Encyclopedia*. *Political Economy* represents a significant shift in some of Rousseau's views. It is constructive, rather than destructive. Rousseau no longer insists that the "thinking man is a depraved animal." Knowledge, he now says, is necessary to the good life, although it must be the right kind of knowledge, and this implies training for citizenship. Good citizenship requires that the individual subordinate his own will to that of the community. In the long run this will benefit him, but intelligence and education are necessary for an understanding of this point. A proper educational program will teach love of country. But people cannot love their country unless there is respect for the "fundamental conventions" or customs and unless there is security for all. There must be a society in which these advantages are secured. And the state must assume responsibility for the education of the people, for nothing can be done if there is lacking a body of responsible and enlightened citizens. The "root of the matter," Rousseau says, is this:

> There can be no patriotism without liberty, no liberty without virtue, no virtue without citizens; create citizens, and you have everything you need: without them, you will have nothing but debased slaves, from the rulers of the State downwards.[14]

It is in the *Discourse on Political Economy* that Rousseau lays the foundation for his organic state, upon which he constructs his political theory in *The Social Contract*. The organic theory repudiates the individualism of Locke and Hobbes, which had taken root in the political, social, and economic ideas of the *philosophes*. Rousseau does not view the community as a mere collection of singular persons each of whom is motivated by his individual interest. It is, rather, a "living body," a "public person," a "moral being," and it is governed not by "particular wills" but by a "general will." The individual is capable of morality only as a member of this body. Outside it he is a cipher. He owes every worthwhile attribute to the state. There is no good life outside the state. His rights are not natural but social, for prior to society he had no rights. His welfare is inextricably bound up with that of the group; thus it is the group, not the individual, that is important. Rousseau's view of the community must be borne in mind in order properly to understand the political theory of *The Social Contract*.

The subtitle of *The Social Contract* is *Principles of Political Right*, and it better describes the contents of the essay than does the main title. In the opening words Rousseau poses the question for which he seeks an answer.

> Man is born free, and everywhere he is in chains. Many a man believes himself to be the master of others who is, no less than they, a slave. How did

[14] *Discourse on Political Economy*, in *ibid*.

this change take place? I do not know. What can make it legitimate? To this question I hope to be able to furnish an answer.[15]

It is somewhat surprising that Rousseau should have declared himself ignorant of the cause of political subordination; he had explained the matter in great detail in his second *Discourse*. He now says that political subordination exists and that the real question is to discover how it can be made "legitimate." In short, what kind of political community is good or morally acceptable? One thing is certain; force is not a basis for legitimacy. Might is not right, for it rests upon the principle of strength, not morality. If might is right, then as "soon as we can disobey with impunity, disobedience becomes legitimate."[16] Nor do people sell themselves into slavery under a despot in order to gain civil peace. If security were all that mattered, we could solve our problems by going to jail. "One can live peacefully enough in a dungeon, but such peace will hardly, of itself, ensure one's happiness."[17] Even if one conceded that all men at a given time were imbecilic enough to make such a fatal agreement, their children would not be bound by it.

Political legitimacy, therefore, can be based neither on force nor on a contract in which freedom is exchanged for security. In order to discover the true foundation of legitimacy it is necessary to begin with the first association of men and thus discover the purpose for which that step was taken. Rousseau assumes "for the sake of argument" that men in a state of nature encountered difficulties too great for them, in their capacity as isolated individuals, to overcome. In the natural state men had freedom, but they were compelled to rely upon their individual strength to protect it. Freedom is highly desirable, but it may also be abused. Where each seeks only his own self-interest, some are bound to suffer. Still it would be a poor, and unnecessary, bargain to surrender one's freedom in return for security. Both are desirable, and the problem is to secure them through an association which synthesizes freedom and security.

> Some form of association must be found as a result of which the whole strength of the community will be enlisted for the protection of the person and property of each constituent member, in such a way that each, when united to his fellows, renders obedience to his own will, and remains as free as he was before.[18]

[15] Jean Jacques Rousseau, *The Social Contract*, in Sir Ernest Barker (ed.), *Social Contract: Essays by Locke, Hume, and Rousseau* (Rousseau's *Social Contract* translated by Gerard Hopkins), Oxford University Press, Fair Lawn, N.J., 1948, I, 1. All subsequent quotations from and references to Rousseau's *Social Contract* are from this edition.

[16] *Ibid.*, I, 3.

[17] *Ibid.*, I, 4.

[18] *Ibid.*, I, 6.

Freedom under an authority which can protect individual security can be achieved, Rousseau says, when men obey only the laws which they themselves make.

The method of establishing this form of association is the social contract, but it is a different form of contract than those envisioned by Hobbes and Locke. In Hobbes's contract, all rights are surrendered to an authority whose duty it is to provide security. This is that concept of the contract which Rousseau specifically rejects. In Locke's contract, people agree to form a society and then entrust their security to a government which is representative of and responsible to them and is charged with protecting the rights which individuals carry with them into the civil state. As we shall see, Rousseau repudiates the notion that legislative power can be delegated without a surrender of freedom. Moreover, in Rousseau's contract, since rights are social rather than natural, there can be no reserving them on an individual basis as Locke's theory demands. The Rousseau contract requires that each member surrender to the community all of his rights. The surrender must be total and unconditional, for in the legitimate political community the people as a body are sovereign. If any rights were reserved to the individual, there would be no common and superior authority to decide what they are or the extent to which they may be exercised. Each person would have to be his own judge; chaos would ensue, and man would be back in a state of nature.

Nothing of value is lost, but a great deal is gained through the contract. Man loses the freedom to follow his antisocial impulses, but this liberty is mere license, the freedom to get everything he can and the right to keep that which his strength permits; it is not true freedom at all. In return he gains civil liberty and legal title to that which rightfully belongs to him, and these are guaranteed and protected by the whole community. The contract overcomes the handicaps suffered by the weak in a state of nature. There their inequality meant constant fear, degradation, and loss of property; in civil society they are equal under the law. Each person, under the terms of the contract, gives all his rights to everyone, as they give their rights to him. This means that, in effect, no one loses anything and everyone gains security guaranteed by the power of the community.

> In short, whoso gives himself to all gives himself to none. And, since there is no member of the social group over whom we do not acquire precisely the same rights as those over ourselves which we have surrendered to him, it follows that we gain the exact equivalent of what we lose, as well as an added power to conserve what we already have.[19]

[19] *Ibid.*

This is not so much a contract as it is the avoidance of one. It is a donation by the individuals to the community which they form. No natural rights form the subject of contract, for the "social order" is itself "the basis of all other rights." The contract does not stipulate the powers of government vis-à-vis the people, for the government is merely the instrument of the people and does not possess independent power.[20] Rousseau could have constructed his theory without bringing in the idea of contract at all. At any rate, the association which is able to provide security without loss of freedom has been established. It yet remains to discover how such an association accomplishes its task.

There now exists, Rousseau says, a "public person," which, in its "passive role," is known as the state and, in its active role, as the sovereign. The people, or individual components of this body, also have a dual role. When they exercise their sovereignty through the determination of public policy they are citizens; when they obey they are subjects. Each person acts in both capacities, and the success, or legitimacy, of the community depends upon how well each function is performed. It is possible for a person to seek his selfish interest and ignore the general interest; that is, he may "enjoy his rights as a citizen without, at the same time, fulfilling his duties as a subject." To avoid such a particularism, which may destroy the community, it is necessary for the body politic to operate on the basis of the "general will." This is a central part of Rousseau's philosophy and we must understand its meaning.

In his *Discourse on Political Economy,* Rousseau says:

> The body politic... is also a moral being possessed of a will; and this general will, which tends always to the preservation and welfare of the whole and of every part, and is the source of the laws, constitutes for all the members of the State, in their relations to one another and to it, the rule of what is just or unjust.[21]

The general will is an expression of the public mind. It emanates from all (whether all know it or not) and is directed to all. Moreover it is invariably good for every member of the community (again whether or not this is universally understood). Rousseau is saying that in the welter of particular interests of a community there is a common interest which must be discovered. This common interest must form the basis for all laws.

The general will is determined by the community acting in its sovereign capacity, and it must be distinguished from the "will of all." It is possible for the people to express an opinion or make a law which is not based upon the general will. This would be the case if the opinion

[20] George H. Sabine, *A History of Political Theory,* 3d ed., Holt, Rinehart and Winston, Inc., New York, 1961, p. 587.

[21] *Discourse on Political Economy* in Cole (ed.), *op. cit.*

rendered or the policy adopted were designed to benefit only a part of the community, whether that part comprises a minority or a majority. The "will of all" is this expression of particular interest. Even if there is unanimity there is no guarantee of an expression of the general will. Nor is unanimity required to ascertain the general will. Rousseau realizes that unanimity is not a practical basis upon which to make decisions. What we must do, he says, is "take from the expression of these separate wills the pluses and minuses—which cancel out, the sum of the differences is left, and that is the general will." [22] This procedure, however, would not be reliable unless the people, in isolation, were exercising their individual wills as *citizens*. If they are stating their opinion as members of "intriguing groups and partial associations" the result will be the "will of all," not the general will. Each must deliberate as a citizen rather than as a member of an interest group. Such groups must, in fact, be eliminated.

> If, then, the general will is to be truly expressed, it is essential that there be no subsidiary groups within the State, and that each citizen voice his own opinion and nothing but his opinion.[23]

The proposal that "pluses and minuses" should offset one another and that the balance determines the general will is another way of stating that the majority voices the general will. Rousseau says that, following the contract which establishes civil society and the body politic, "a majority vote is binding on all." This raises troublesome problems for his theory. For example, if a majority makes a decision and imposes its will upon a minority in the form of a law, how can the minority be said to be free? Freedom, as we have seen, means to Rousseau that men obey only those laws they themselves make. But, Rousseau says, "the question is wrongly put." Actually the minority *does* consent. The question is not whether consent is given to the particular proposition but whether that proposition is in accord with the general will, and the general will, under the proper circumstances, may be determined by counting votes. People may be wrong in their judgments. They may be misled by their own interest and be honestly but wrongly convinced that their interest coincides with the common interest.

> When, therefore, a view which is at odds with my own wins the day, it proves only that I was deceived, and that what I took to be the general will was no such thing. Had my own opinion won, I should have done something quite other than I wished to do, and in that case I should not have been free.[24]

[22] *Social Contract*, in Barker (ed.), *op. cit.*, II, 3.
[23] *Ibid.*
[24] *Ibid.*, IV, 2.

There is a significant and somewhat ominous note in this remark. It is generally assumed that in a political society which operates on the basis of majority rule, the minority shall give way precisely because it *is* a minority; that where there is a clash of interests the lesser interest shall bow before the greater. It may be occasionally conceded that in the long run the minority is guilty of misunderstanding its true interest and that it is actually better off if it obeys the majority. This, however, would be an exception to the rule that the condition of the minority may be worsened by a majority decision, but that it must nonetheless accede to the majority's will or risk the disruption of the community. Thus it is a difficult and perennial problem in a free state to determine in any specific case just how far the "rights" of a minority need be respected as against the will of the majority, or, to state it differently, how much freedom the minority is entitled to as against the authority of the majority.

Rousseau insists that no real conflict exists. The minority is wrong. Its interest is *always* the same as that of the majority. If it gets its own way it injures itself as much as it injures the majority. This cannot be permitted. The minority must be forced into line for its own welfare; it must be forced into freedom.

> Whoever shall refuse to obey the general will must be constrained by the whole body of his fellow citizens to do so; which is no more than to say that *it may be necessary to compel a man to be free.* . . .[25]

It may be argued that the saving grace of this idea rests in the fact that submission is, after all, to one's true self, or at worst to a sovereign majority. When a dictator or a monolithic party claims to represent the general will, however, it takes on a different and obnoxious connotation.

Rousseau himself was conscious of the implications of his proposal, and he made a rather unsuccessful attempt at qualification. He does this by stating that it is, after all, "agreed that what, as a result of the social compact, each man alienates of power, property, and liberty is only so much as concerns the well-being of the community." [26] It now appears that man does not surrender "all of his rights" when he enters the community, as Rousseau had clearly stated previously. But even if the qualification is admitted, no great gain for individual liberty is made, for the question immediately arises, what rights is the individual entitled to withhold? Rousseau's answer is that this is a determination which must be made by the sovereign, or majority. Thus we are back where we started. A further qualification is attempted with much the same result. The general will is concerned, Rousseau says, only with matters of general applicability. A decision of the people which deals with anything

[25] *Ibid.*, I, 7.
[26] *Ibid.*, II, 4.

less than this is not expressive of the general will. The implication is that there will be reserved to the individual an area in which he will be free to exercise an independent judgment. Again, however, only the sovereign majority may decide what functions or freedoms are involved. Finally, Rousseau says that the size of the majority which expresses the general will should increase in proportion to the importance of the policy being considered. It may be assumed that where matters of lesser significance are concerned a simple majority may express the general will; the more serious the issue, the larger must be the majority.

Rousseau's qualifications are neither logical nor convincing. The true meaning of Rousseau's theory of the general will is that a properly constituted and functioning majority is infallible, that what it decides is beneficial to everyone, and that a force is moral which compels individuals to do those things which are good for them and which they would do voluntarily if they were not influenced by selfish interest. There is no place for the doctrine of individual rights in this proposition, and Rousseau should logically have ignored it. It is likely that, given the emphasis upon individualism in eighteenth-century thought, he felt he could not do so. By attempting to graft a species of individualism upon his organic theory he only impairs his own logic without gaining any real advantage for individual rights.

We may now turn to the institutional arrangements designed by Rousseau to enunciate and implement the general will. Two forces, Rousseau declares, are required to produce action—will, and the strength to execute it. It is the legislative which supplies the former, and in a legitimate political community it consists of all the people. The legislative must create a constitution and establish a body of laws. It must found a government and devise methods of electing magistrates. It must meet regularly, often, and in a manner prescribed by law. The latter requirement raises another difficult problem for Rousseau. If the legislative comprises the whole body of citizens, how can such a body meet and deliberate? Can the sovereignty of the entire people be divided into populational segments and the general will be taken in each? This is impossible, for sovereignty is indivisible; to divide it is to destroy it. Can sovereignty be given to a city, which may then express the general will for all? This cannot be done, for unless all participate, some are subordinated to others. Equality disappears and the legitimacy of the political community is lost. Nor will a representative system solve the problem. Sovereignty cannot be represented. Rousseau rejects the solution offered by admirers of the English system. The English, he says, are free only when they are electing their representatives; the balance of the time they are slaves.

Rousseau suggests two solutions to the problem, one of which largely nullifies the other. First, if it is impossible to maintain the size of the state at a point which will permit all citizens to gather and deliberate at a central location, it will be necessary to shift the "machinery of government" from one city to another and "successively assemble the Estates of the Realm in each of them." That is to say, the seat of government must be moved from one place to another in order that the general will may be ascertained in each. Rousseau recognizes that this would be enormously difficult, but he insists that it is worth the effort. After all, "Where right and liberty is everything, inconvenience matters little." [27] Upon further consideration, Rousseau changes his mind. The only solution is adoption of the city-state form such as was found in ancient Greece and existed at the time in Geneva.

> Having examined the whole question thoroughly, I do not see how, henceforth, it will be possible for the sovereign to maintain among us the exercise of its rights unless the city be a very small one.[28]

Will not such a polity be vulnerable to attack, as Montesquieu suggested? Rousseau admits the possibility but states that he will later demonstrate how a confederation may be employed to minimize such a danger. He was unquestionably influenced here, as elsewhere, by *The Spirit of the Laws.* Rousseau does not fulfill his promise; the discussion of confederation was to be part of the greater study of political institutions which Rousseau did not complete.

The agency that carries out decisions of the general will is the executive. A peculiarity in Rousseau's thought here must be noted. In his plan, the executive is the government. The legislative is the sovereign people and is not a part of the government; nor does the executive share in the sovereign power. The legislative establishes the government; the latter, in turn, is the agent of the former and is completely responsible to it. Government is created by a law, not a contract. It has only duties to perform and possesses no independent rights or powers of its own. The sovereign people, or legislative, may revoke the law by which government was established and thus remove that government at its own pleasure.

The form of government may, and should, vary. If executive (government) power is shared among all the people, the government is a democracy. If power is held by a few, government is aristocratic, and it is a monarchy if the authority is wielded by a single person. No single form is innately superior to any other. There are many circumstances—population, size of country, and others—which must be taken into account in the selection of a particular form. Rousseau again demonstrates the influence that Montesquieu exerted upon his development of a political theory. For all practical purposes, Rousseau says, a democracy is impos-

[27] *Ibid.,* III, 15.
[28] *Ibid.*

sible. The entire people cannot concern themselves with administrative tasks. Moreover, the people do not have sufficient virtue to combine and adequately employ both legislative and executive authority. Democracy would only be possible in "a nation of Gods." An elective aristocracy, by which Rousseau means a system in which executive officials are elected by the people, is generally the best form of government. A hereditary aristocracy, or executive power exercised by the nobility, is the worst. A monarchy provides vigor in the execution of the laws and could be the most desirable government, but, given the character of most kings and the fact that heredity rarely produces a monarch of quality, this is unlikely. We see in this that Rousseau's discussion of democracy, aristocracy, and monarchy in government applies only to the executive, and that any form of executive may be compatible with a legitimate political community. The same is not true with respect to the legislative. Legitimacy here is inseparable from democracy. Legislative power must always be exercised by the whole body of sovereign citizens, or the entire purpose for which men undertook the establishment of political association is subverted.

There are two ends to which legislative effort should be directed. These are liberty and equality, and the former is impossible without the latter. There should be an equalitarian state, one which establishes and secures the moral and legal equality of the citizenry. To accomplish this there must be a comparative equality of wealth—an allotment fair enough to ensure that no man has enough to buy another and that that other need not sell himself. In practice the tendency to inequality in the holding of property is so great that regulation is difficult. This, however, is only an argument for regulation. "It is just because the pressure of events tends always to the destruction of equality that the force of legislation should always be directed to maintaining it." [29] Rousseau's objection to inequality of property is that if it exists in too great a degree, moral equality is impossible. He is not particularly interested in improving the standard of living of the oppressed class; it is their subjection to the wealthy that he opposes. He does not, in short, object to austerity, but to dependence.

Rousseau has now considered the purpose for which the political community is established, the agreement by which the association is created, the kind of community which is legitimate, and the institutional arrangements best suited to the community. The constitution and the methods of implementing it are theoretically constructed. But practical problems inject themselves into the best theoretical constitutions. Rousseau anticipates and attempts to deal with some of them. First, there is a question as to the ability of the people to see through the complexities of an interdependent and civilized community and to frame legislation

[29] *Ibid.*, II, 11.

which will rectify the ills of society. If the people understand, they will, in their decisions, always express the general will. To facilitate their understanding, a "legislator" is necessary. The legislator should be possessed of "superior intelligence," which will enable him to frame legislation which, when ratified by the sovereign people, will express the general will. He must be an expert and an exhorter. He must be persuasive, for he has no power to command the people, who are themselves sovereign, and he, like the executive, is responsible to the sovereign people.

Second, it may be necessary to establish a "Tribunate," a body which stands between the people and their government and provides protection to both. This agency has no power to initiate action, but it may prevent precipitate action from being taken. There is potential danger in a Tribunate, for it will not tend to weakness. Therefore it must be closely watched and its responsibility to the people maintained. If this is done, it may perform a valuable service. Third, "laws are inflexible," and it is often difficult to adapt them to rapidly moving events. Thus the constitutional structure of the state may prove inadequate in emergencies. In such event and where the danger is grave, the executive power may be temporarily increased, or, in unusually dangerous periods, the laws may be suspended and the authority of the state placed in the hands of a dictator as was done in ancient times. This is a risky business and not to be undertaken lightly or without every precaution. Nevertheless, the security of the community may demand it. Fourth, a Censorship should be set up to help prevent the degeneration of manners and morals in society. This agency is designed to help mold proper opinions "by intervening to keep them on the right lines." Rousseau does not explain how this is to be done, nor does he detail the kind of power involved in the intervention which he advocates. Presumably it is moral suasion upon which the Censorship is to rely.

Finally, and this is a point which has always damned Rousseau in the eyes of his critics, Rousseau proposes the establishment of a "civil religion." In his view this is not a question of dogma. Dogma should be of no concern to the state. The basis of Rousseau's suggestion is that religion may make demands upon the individual which lessen his ties to and his regard for the political community. Religion is to be regarded in the same light as is any other association which "disrupts the social bond of unity." No pluralist, Rousseau states categorically that "All institutions which set a man in contradiction with himself [as part of the state] are of no worth." [30] Religion, and particularly the Christian religion, has been a disruptive force in the community, Rousseau says. The only means by which divisions may be avoided is through the formation of a state religion, the principles of which, as fixed by the sovereign, preclude the possibility of its exerting a divisive social influence. No one is to be

[30] *Ibid.,* IV, 8.

compelled to believe in these principles so long as he acts as if he does. The state is to have power to banish anyone who refuses outwardly to adhere to this religion, and if a citizen declares his attachment to it and then acts in a manner contrary to its principles, he may be executed. The punishment in such cases is civil and not theological. Rousseau does not object to a separation of church and state in the hearts of men, but he insists that there be no outward manifestations of it.

Conclusions

Rousseau's theory is a grab bag containing something to support almost any theory of the community. The "rightist" will seize upon Rousseau's organicism to uphold his contention that the individual must be subordinated to the state. He may see in the Legislator, with his knowledge, his foresight, and his leadership abilities, an ancestor image of a "Fuehrer"; Rousseau's thoughts concerning a Censorship and "civil religion" he may view as harbingers of a society in which cohesion and discipline are the principal values. And Rousseau's dictum that a man may be "forced to be free" found sinister fulfillment in the fascist ideology of the twentieth century. Yet each of these applications is a grotesque distortion of Rousseau's meaning when considered in the context of his entire theory.

"Leftists," too, have taken aid and comfort from isolated aspects of Rousseau's writings. Here the issue of property has been of transcendent importance. Rousseau's statement, in the second *Discourse,* that inequality among men is attributable to the institution of private property, and that civil government is only a diabolical device which lends a spurious legality to that institution, became an essential ingredient of Marxist theory. The more moderate thesis of *The Social Contract,* that property is a social, not a natural, right, and is therefore subject to regulation in the general interest, and that moral equality demands a measure of economic equality, has long been accepted by advocates of the modern welfare state. The latter interpretation appears to be a logical application of Rousseau's theory. The former is considerably strained. Rousseau does not propose to abolish private property, even in the second *Discourse,* and his position in *The Social Contract* is still more temperate.

There is something, too, for the democrat—a great deal in fact. On balance, Rousseau is more democratic than anything else. In this regard we need only call to mind his advocacy of popular sovereignty (and no one goes so far in support of this principle as does Rousseau), his insistence that the whole body of citizens comprise the legislative, and his view of government as an instrument of the people to whom it is invariably responsible. Rousseau is indeed a democrat. The question here is whether he goes too far in his democracy, for his is essentially a totalitarian democracy. It is antiliberal; it reserves no rights for the individual.

Rousseau's good intentions cannot be doubted. He believes in and wants freedom for the individual, but he is overly fearful of the consequences of that freedom; authority must be exercised to restrain it. Yet authority, too, can be destructive. The answer lies in a synthesis, cleverly conceived, in which all antagonism between freedom and authority is reconciled. This is accomplished, as we have seen, through an arrangement in which the general will is ascertained and enforced, with the result that each person obeys only the law which he himself makes, if, and a large "if" it is indeed, he acts correctly, by which Rousseau means following the dictates of an enlightened self-interest, an interest which benefits the self as it does the group and is never opposed to the interest of the group.

Enough has already been said with respect to the difficulties that stand in the way of any practical application of this theory. The significant question seems not to be whether the theory is capable of implementation but whether it should be implemented if it were possible to do so. If, by some process of political alchemy, we could discover the general will, should we enforce it on all persons simply because they would be helped in the process and whether they understand it or not? Is a person truly forced into freedom when he is improved against his will, even if his will is selfish and wrong? Such a view assumes a relationship between freedom and welfare which is unusual to say the least. Nor need we consider this a purely hypothetical problem; its implications are intensely practical. The ill-fated Eighteenth Amendment to the United States Constitution provides an excellent illustration of the problem. Here was a case in which the enforcement of the law was undeniably designed to improve the health and the morals of the citizens. The constitutional requirement that amendments be initiated and ratified by large majorities would also roughly meet Rousseau's demand for an expression of the general will in important cases through something more than a simple majority. Yet the law prohibiting the consumption of spirituous liquors was soon widely regarded, even by many abstemious people, as an intolerable restriction on freedom. Irrespective of the effect on the health and morals of the individual, was it not precisely that? In short, a free society is one in which a person has a right to do some things that are bad for him.

There is more room for freedom in a society that stresses the rights of the individual. The theory which supports it is not so tidily constructed as is Rousseau's. There are a great many loose ends, and in practice the citizens of a free community are constantly becoming embroiled in arguments over the extent of the rights they have. This was the vagueness to which Rousseau objected, and understandably so. It is all very well to say that a person may not exercise a right to the degree that he injures or seriously inconveniences his fellows; it is another thing to determine what this principle means in practice. Yet men of reason and good will can find a way. Probably no one will be completely satisfied with the solution. On occasion force will be required, and this is always regrettable. Still such a system is the best that has yet been devised to balance the conflicting principles of freedom and authority. We do not mean to imply that Rousseau had nothing to contribute to a free society. Many of his democratic principles have validity if they are not carried too far. Perhaps his greatest contribution was his argument that the state is not the natural enemy of the people, and that if it is responsible and democratic it may, at the same time, be strong and provide valuable services without being tyrannical. In this perception Rousseau was far ahead of his contemporaries.

Rousseau's concept of the general will is original and highly provocative. Every free society has sought to minimize the conflict between the particular and the general interest. In the United States a system of government has been erected in part on the basis of an assumption that from the clash of particular interests something like a general interest will emerge. This view is implicit in both federalism and checks and balances. There has been considerable disagreement as to how well the system has solved the problem, and no thoughtful person could argue that it has worked perfectly. In relatively normal times perfect efficiency and harmony are not indispensable; a great deal of internal conflict can be tolerated and its ill effects charged off as a price of freedom. In periods of danger the problem becomes more acute. Internal dissension may weaken the structure of the community and imperil the very existence of the polity. Yet to purchase unity at the cost of liberty is to pay a terrible price. It is in such circumstances that we turn again to Rousseau, hoping to find a way to escape from our dilemma. He may not provide us with an answer, but is there not a great deal to consider in what he says?

SELECTED BIBLIOGRAPHY

Barker, Sir Ernest (ed.): *Social Contract, Essays by Locke, Hume, and Rousseau,* Oxford University Press, Fair Lawn, N.J., 1948, introduction, Rousseau's *Social Contract* (translated by Gerard Hopkins).

Cassirer, Ernst: *The Question of Jean-Jacques Rousseau* (translated and edited with an introduction and additional notes by Peter Gay), Columbia University Press, New York, 1954.

Cook, Thomas I.: *History of Political Philosophy from Plato to Burke,* Prentice-Hall, Inc., Englewood Cliffs, N.J., 1936, chap. 22.

Green, F. C.: *Jean-Jacques Rousseau, A Critical Study of His Life and Writings,* Cambridge University Press, New York, 1955.

Hacker, Andrew: *Political Theory: Philosophy, Ideology, Science,* The Macmillan Company, New York, 1961, chap. 8.

Hearnshaw, F. J. C. (ed.): *The Social and Political Ideas of Some Great French*

Thinkers of the Age of Reason, Barnes & Noble, Inc., New York, 1950, chap. 7.

Martin, Kingsley: *The Rise of French Liberal Thought: A Study of Political Ideas from Bayle to Condorcet,* 2d. rev. ed., New York University Press, New York, 1954.

Rousseau, Jean Jacques: *The Social Contract and Discourses* (translated with introduction by G. D. H. Cole), E. P. Dutton & Co., Inc., New York, 1913.

————: *Political Writings* (edited by C. E. Vaughan), Cambridge University Press, New York, 1915.

————: *Political Writings* (translated and edited by Frederick Watkins), Thomas Nelson & Sons, New York, 1953, introduction.

Sabine, George H.: *A History of Political Theory,* 3d ed., Holt, Rinehart and Winston, Inc., New York, 1961, chaps. 27, 28.

sixteen

HUME AND BURKE

The emancipation of men's minds from the intellectual restraints of the Middle Ages progressed more rapidly in the physical than in the social sciences. In the physical sciences, empiricism—the method of observation, experimentation, and experience—could now be accepted. In human relations, the concept of natural rights remained in vogue. The old concept of the natural law had undergone considerable revision with Hobbes and Locke. It was less a series of principles through which the good of society should be secured than the assertion of the indefeasible rights of individuals from interfering with which the society was enjoined. The concept was, in short, individualistic rather than social and emphasized rights more than law. In seventeenth-century England, and in eighteenth-century France and America, the theory of natural rights was predominant. Here it was used as the basis of a demand for reform and, ultimately, as a defense of revolution.

A corollary of natural rights was rationalism. Eighteenth-century radicals (Rousseau was an exception) had great faith in the efficacy of reason. Rationalism, however, came under increasing attack. Rousseau argued that feeling, emotion, and passion, rather than rational calculation, gave rise to human association and action. Moreover, he saw and resented the individualism implicit in the natural-rights theory and propounded a theory of the community to offset it. Rousseau's theory was in no sense scientific; it was highly charged with emotion, although this did not lessen

317

—indeed it increased—its impact. But an intellectual assault upon the natural-rights theory was also developing. The revolutionary ferment of eighteenth-century France kept the theory viable there. In England the public temper was more conservative; the people felt no substantial need for a theory with revolutionary implications. English philosophy developed along empirical lines, and empiricism was carried into the study of human relations. In this development, David Hume was an important figure.

Hume: The Man and His Work

David Hume was born in Edinburgh on April 26, 1711. His father was a member of the landed gentry but was a man of modest means. The young David had a great love of learning, which was not satisfied by the schools of Scotland. In 1723 he entered the University of Edinburgh. His family urged him to study law, but after a brief encounter with legal training he abandoned it. Business in Bristol also proved dull, and in 1734 Hume left for France, where he remained for three years. He was determined to pursue a literary career, and before he left France he had completed, at the age of twenty-six, his greatest work, the *Treatise of Human Nature*. With wry humor, Hume described his disappointment at the reception accorded his work. "It fell," he said, "dead-born from the press, without reaching such distinction as even to excite a murmur among the zealots." This was an exaggeration. Those who could understand the *Treatise* were impressed by it, but it was not the kind of work that could capture the public fancy. Hume, realizing its esoteric character, designed his subsequent works to appeal to a larger audience. None of them quite matched the standard set by the *Treatise*.

Hume returned to Scotland and began work on his *Essays on Moral and Political Subjects,* one volume of which was published in 1741 and a second the following year. In 1745 Hume applied for, but failed to obtain, a professorship at the University of Edinburgh. He then became secretary and, later, judge-advocate to General St. Clair, whom he accompanied to Canada and Italy. Hume's *Inquiry concerning Human Understanding* was published in 1748, and was followed by his *Inquiry concerning the Principles of Morals* in 1751. The *Political Discourses* were completed in 1752 and enjoyed great popular acclaim in England. In the same year, after again having been denied a professorship at Edinburgh, Hume became librarian of the Advocates' Library in Edinburgh. The position was of little advantage financially, but Hume used the facilities of the library to begin his *History of England,* which was completed in 1762. The *History* is generally regarded as his poorest work. Hume was often incautious with respect to his sources, and his Toryism, as well as a measure of Anglophobia, is evident in the work. Nevertheless the *History* sold well, and as a result Hume became moderately well-to-do. His reputation also grew, and when he went to France in 1763 he created something of a sensation. Hume remained in France as secretary to the British Embassy for two years before returning to England. In 1769 he retired to Edinburgh, where he worked on his *Dialogues on Natural Religion*. He became ill in the spring of 1775 and died on August 25, 1776.

The Basis of Hume's Political Theory

The premises of Hume's assault upon natural law and natural rights are supplied by the philosophy he outlines in his *Treatise of Human Nature*. Here he challenges the validity of the concept of reason as it had been employed by natural-rights and natural-law theorists, which, he holds, results in wrongly attributing to certain ideas the qualities of immutability and naturalness. Natural-law theorists had held that the norms of moral action existed a priori, that they could be discovered by reason, and that the passions of men, which would divert them from these norms, must be subordinated to reason, which alone could show the way to proper behavior. Hume's view is that this constitutes a misunderstanding of reason. The use of reason, he says, is far more limited: It may be employed to show logical relationships; it cannot demonstrate existences (facts) or values (tenets of the natural law). Human values are determined by "passion" or feeling. Reason may be helpful in directing action toward the attainment of values, but its role is secondary. It is an instrument. As Hume put it, reason is "the slave of passions."

The passions that move men are both instinctive and "secondary." The former are with men from birth and are antecedent to experience. Only experience will demonstrate how they can be satisfied. "Secondary" passions, such as "desire," are based upon some experience involving "pain and pleasure." If an experience, for example, produces pleasure, a predilection is developed for it. Everything depends upon experience. There are no a priori truths. Men learn from their experiences the things that gratify their desires and call them "right." The things they deem harmful are called "wrong." This theory proposes that social scientists should study human behavior rather than concern themselves with the supposed immutable laws of nature. This conclusion does not imply that Hume was uninterested in values. Indeed he believed that there were universal norms of social behavior, but he insisted that they grew out of, and were discoverable by, experience—not by abstract reason. Hume attributed the quality of universality to these norms because he assumed the processes of thought to be the same for all men and believed their experiences to be similar. Since experiences were not identical, institutions could vary from one place to another while the standards of behavior remained generally the same everywhere.

The fact, as Hume sees it, that reason is an instrument of passion does not mean that passion is always wisely directed. Men are not equal in their ability to use reason in such a manner as to guide their conduct toward satisfactory fulfillment. Each person seeks his own interest; his passions direct him toward this end. The majority, unfortunately, are incapable of understanding that their welfare will be better served by the establishment of rules of behavior that may require a postponement of the immediate gratification of desire in the interest of a higher but longer-range satisfaction. Hume distinguishes "calm" from "violent" passions. Calm passions are directed by a reason capable of understanding an enlightened self-interest; violent passions demand immediate gratification. The practical political significance of this distinction is that the community must be guided by a minority of persons whose reason is improved by education and who possess sufficient wealth not to be tempted to succumb to the desire to serve a selfish and short-range interest.[1] Justice is achieved when the community functions along the lines of enlightened self-interest. Moral approval is given by the people who come to see that such a system does serve their best interest. They tend to believe that they acquiesce because the system is moral, but actually they acquiesce because the system *works,* because it has utility. The "morality" grows out of utility and depends upon it. Such principles as justice, freedom, and morality have no a priori validity. They are valid to the degree that they are utilitarian. These ideas constitute the base upon which Hume erects his theory of politics.

Hume's Political Theory

The origin of society among men, Hume states, is "necessity," "natural inclination," and "habit."

> Man, born in a family, is compelled to maintain society from necessity, from natural inclination, and from habit. The same creature, in his farther progress, is engaged to establish political society in order to administer justice; without which there can be no peace among them, nor safety, nor mutual intercourse.[2]

Political society, in other words, is necessary to justice. All men know, Hume says, that peace and order are required if society is to be maintained, yet they are so perverse that it is difficult for them to maintain it. The chief problem is that each person seeks his own interest. He is aware that this course is fraught with peril to society and thus to himself, but he takes a chance that the immediate advantage he secures will more than offset any subsequent disadvantage. This tendency is, Hume says,

---

[1] *Hume: Theory of Politics* (edited by Frederick Watkins), University of Texas Press, Austin, Tex., 1953, pp. xvi–xix.

[2] David Hume, *Of the Origin of Government,* in *Hume's Moral and Political Philosophy* (edited with an introduction by Henry D. Aiken), Hafner Publishing Company, Inc., New York, 1948. All subsequent references to Hume's work are from this source.

"incurable in human nature." The only way out of the difficulty is to appoint magistrates, who compel obedience to the law. Men must be forced to look to their long-range interest, which is the only true interest. Obedience must support justice; this is the origin of government.

But what makes government *effective*? Is it fear of punishment? Does the same principle that underlies the establishment of government support its continuance? The answer, Hume says, is "No." If men only obeyed because they feared the consequences of disobedience, there would be no stability in civil society. Obviously, men would disobey whenever they felt that they could do so without being apprehended. Men, however, do not behave this way in civil society. The great majority are good citizens, who obey the law and who do not consider disobedience. The first rulers of men undoubtedly had constantly to threaten to use force; present rulers do not have to do so. The reason for this change is that men come to obey through force of habit.

> Habit soon consolidates what other principles of human nature had imperfectly founded; and men, once accustomed to obedience, never think of departing from that path in which they and their ancestors have constantly trod, and to which they are confined by so many urgent and visible motives.[3]

A more detailed analysis of the origin of government is presented by Hume in his essay, *Of the Original Contract*. Each of the two major parties of his time, Hume says, feels it necessary to support its position by constructing a "speculative system of principles." One of these traces the authority of government to God, thereby making it so sacred that any resistance is regarded as sacrilegious. The other argues that government rests upon the consent of the people expressed through a contract. Each of these views has something to commend it, although the consequences, when carried to the extremes demanded by the advocates of either system, are unjustified. There is divine sanction for government in the sense that God must have made provision for it, since security is impossible without it. Because God's action was not accomplished, however, through "any particular or miraculous interposition," a monarch is no more warranted in pleading the principle of divine support than is a constable. In short, it is God's intent that there shall be government; he does not provide a particular structure, nor does he indicate in whose hands governmental power shall rest.

An analysis of the claim that government stems from a contract is more complex. There can be no doubt that the origin of civil society involves some kind of agreement.

> When we consider how nearly equal men are in their bodily force, and even in their mental powers and faculties, till cultivated by education, we

[3] *Ibid.*

must necessarily allow that nothing but their own consent could at first associate them together and subject them to any authority. The people, if we trace government to its first origin in the woods and deserts, are the source of all power and jurisdiction, and voluntarily, for the sake of peace and order, abandoned their native liberty and received laws from their equal and companion.[4]

The conditions under which this agreement was made may have been specifically laid down, or they "were so clear and obvious that it might well be esteemed superfluous to express them." If this is what the supporters of the contract theory mean when they state their case, Hume says, they are justified. Nor is it necessary to present some kind of written proof, for the contract antedates writing. We know it to be true simply because we can "trace it plainly in the nature of man." Nothing else could account for the origin of government. The error lies in the assertion that if contract and consent provided the basis for the original government, it follows that the same principle holds true today. The first agreement was a crude thing; the first ruler undoubtedly had to rely more on persuasion than command. His position, for a considerable time, had to be justified by the "exigencies of the case" from day to day. Man was not so far advanced at that remote time as to be capable of framing a compact to provide for a "general submission." As time passed, men began to see the utility of a system of obedience and command, and such a system became habitual. The leader no longer was compelled to justify each use of power; a stable political order began to develop.

The assumption that present governments rest on consent, Hume says, flies in the face of fact. If we look at the world about us we see everywhere monarchs who claim an authority based on "conquest" or "succession." Look further, and we see subjects obeying these monarchs and acknowledging their position. The fact is that people obey habitually; it rarely occurs to them to question either their own position or that of their rulers.

> Obedience or subjection becomes so familiar that most men never make any inquiry about its origin and cause, more than about the principles of gravity, resistance, or the most universal laws of nature.... Were you to preach, in most parts of the world, that political connexions are founded altogether on voluntary consent or a mutual promise, the magistrate would soon imprison you as seditious for loosening the ties of obedience, if your friends did not before shut you up as delirious for advancing such absurdities.[5]

The original contract is no longer in force. It has been "obliterated by a thousand changes of government and princes." There have been no con-

---

[4] Hume, *Of the Original Contract,* in *ibid.*
[5] *Ibid.*

tracts since the original. The contract theory, then, implies that an agreement made centuries ago is still binding upon the present generation; but, Hume points out, "republican writers" do not admit this. Nor is there historical support for any such thesis. Modern governments and all those of which we have any record were established by "conquest" or "usurpation," without the faintest vestige of consent.

Hume brushes aside the possibility of consent as evidenced by election. An election involves "either the combination of a few great men," who make a decision for all the people or "the fury of a multitude that follow a seditious ringleader." In neither case is a decision made by the body of the people. And the worst of all possible methods for establishing a government is by revolution, for "there is not a more terrible event than a total dissolution of government, which gives liberty to the multitude, and makes the determination or choice of a new establishment depend upon a number which nearly approaches to the whole body of them." [6] And Englishmen should not think that their own Revolution (of 1688) supports a sweeping theory of consent. The only change in rulership growing out of that Revolution involved a shift in the succession to the throne, and that was made by "the majority of seven hundred who determined that change for near ten millions." The fact that a majority of the people acquiesced in what was done does not mean that their consent was either solicited or obtained.

The absence of consent in the past does not show, Hume admits, that consent is an undesirable basis upon which to found government; it is indeed admirable as a principle. The theory of consent, however, takes for granted a degree of perfection in human nature that does not exist, and assumes without warrant a "regard to justice" and a capacity to know one's true interest. In practice consent plays no role in the establishment of government. Where there is a "settled constitution," the wishes of the people are often considered, but when governments are being created, since their institution generally comes as a result of conquest, revolution, or some kind of force, it is not consent but "military force or political craft" that determines what shall be done. As a result, the new governors are regarded with suspicion at first; the people are watchful; and the ruler must be more cautious and rely more on force than will subsequently be necessary. The passage of time brings stability. The people know that they have never consented to the new ruler, but they *do now* consent, "because they think that, from long possession, he has acquired a title independent of their choice or inclination." This is not a case of the subjects giving a "tacit consent" to government, in the sense that, since they could leave the jurisdiction of the ruler but do not do so, they are in fact tacitly accepting his rulership. They have no real alternative to membership in the state, Hume says. If we argue otherwise, "we may

[6] *Ibid.*

as well assert that a man, by remaining in a vessel, freely consents to the domination of the master, though he was carried on board while asleep, and must leap into the ocean and perish the moment he leaves her."[7] Hume thus summarily disposes of Locke's theory of tacit consent.

The theory of consent, then, is not supported either by history or common sense. Nor are the philosophical grounds any more convincing. There are, Hume says, two kinds of "moral duties." Duties of the first kind are instinctive; they exist entirely apart from political relationships. Examples are "love of children," "gratitude to benefactors," and "pity to the unfortunate." We recognize that such feelings are beneficial to society, but we are moved by them irrespective of that consideration. Moral duties of the second kind are social; they are performed because they are indispensable to the maintenance of society. Among them are "justice," which Hume defines as "a regard to the property of others," and "fidelity," or the keeping of promises. Another is the political duty of "allegiance." Social moral duties result from reflection and experience. Experience soon teaches man that if he permits himself to be governed by his "primary instincts," which often lead him to seek his own interest at the expense of others, confusion and disorder will result and his true interest will be sacrificed. He sees that he must respect the good of others and keep his word. He knows, however, that unless he grants authority to magistrates and gives allegiance to them, these things will not be done.

Allegiance and fidelity stand on the same ground. Each is a practical principle that must be followed in the interest of security. Each is necessitated by the same conditions and the same flaws of human nature. There is no justification for the assertion that the principle of allegiance grows out of fidelity. In other words, we do not obey a sovereign because we have promised to do so. Then why should we keep our promise? The correct answer is that we subscribe to both principles, allegiance and fidelity, and that of "justice" in addition, because they are necessary to our social existence. "If the reason be asked of that obedience which we are bound to pay to government, I readily answer, *because society could not otherwise subsist;* and this answer is clear and intelligible to all mankind."[8]

A final question remains to be answered: "To whom is allegiance due, and who is our lawful sovereign?" That is, if we acknowledge the necessity of allegiance, arising from its utility, we have not yet determined to whom that allegiance is owed. Hume admits the question to be "often the most difficult of any." It would be fortunate, he says, if we could point to the existing rulers as having descended "in a direct line, from ancestors that have governed us for many ages." Yet, even if this proof were possible, we should find somewhere along the line that authority was

---

[7] *Ibid.*

[8] *Ibid.* Italics are in the original.

established by conquest or violence. Hume admits a predilection for "free government," which he defines as one in which powers are divided among several agents whose combined authority is as great as, or greater than, that of the monarch, and which operates on the basis of "general and equal laws that are previously known to all the members and to all their subjects." [9] He does not argue, however, that only free governments are entitled to allegiance. Nor does he say that the people are required to obey government under any conceivable conditions. In extraordinary cases resistance may be justified, although, Hume says, "I shall always incline to their side who draw the bond of allegiance very close." Resistance means civil war, and its dangers usually more than offset the disadvantages of an abuse of authority. Hume, in fact, discusses the problem of the obligation of allegiance without arriving at an answer. There is, he believes, no single basis upon which to determine legitimacy. Such factors as consent, succession, and possession all may have relevance, but legitimacy is a matter of common sense. If the people accept the government and if it is doing its job reasonably well, it may be said to be legitimate. To isolate the grounds of legitimacy is to establish a basis for insurrection, to which Hume is strongly opposed.

This is, in part, why Hume rejects "reason" and a priori principles as bases of government, and favors, instead, "use and practice." Reason is too unreliable, and anyone can assume whatever principle he chooses; together these two constitute an unsatisfactory foundation for civil society. They merely provide pretexts that disguise the search for selfish interest.

> The only rule of government . . . is use and practice; reason is so uncertain a guide that it will always be exposed to doubt and controversy; could it ever render itself prevalent over the people, men had always retained it as their sole rule of conduct; they had still continued in the primitive, unconnected state of nature, without submitting to political government, whose sole basis is not pure reason but authority and precedent. Dissolve these ties, you break all the bonds of civil society, and leave every man at liberty to consult his private interest, by those expedients which his appetite, disguised under the appearance of reason, shall dictate to him.[10]

The inability of reason to perceive a natural order leaves it free to construct its own order, and this may be based on selfish interest.

Hume was not so conservative as Burke or Hegel. He might have been had he lived another twenty years and witnessed, as did Burke, what many Englishmen regarded as the threat to their constitution posed by the French Revolution. Such persons tended to exaggerate the necessity for political authority and to say that the preservation of all values depended upon the maintenance of a powerful and conservative state.[11]

[9] *Of the Origin of Government,* in *ibid.*
[10] *Of the Coalition of Parties,* in *ibid.*
[11] Frederick Watkins (ed.), *op. cit.,* p. xxi.

The Changing Scene

It is appropriate at this point to recapitulate those major developments in the Western world, from the middle of the seventeenth to the close of the eighteenth century, which give meaning to the political theory we are considering. This period marked the emergence of the modern community. From country to country, the growth was uneven, but even where the forces for preservation were able for a time to thwart those of change, the latter were struggling to emerge. The middle class was displacing the landed aristocracy as the dominant political power, while commerce was replacing agriculture as the principal economic force. Royal prerogative was challenged by the advocates of parliamentary supremacy. In religion there was more toleration of innovation in thought and practice and less state domination of churches. The demand almost everywhere was for governmental systems responsible to a wider electorate, for more freedom, and for the principle of equal justice for all. As we have seen in the writings of the *philosophes,* agitation for reform did not constitute a demand for democracy, although there were democratic elements in the ideas propounded. Considerable change was sought, nevertheless, and as always, those who stood to lose by change strongly opposed it.

Such a transformation of society was not to come easily; in many cases violent revolution was required to achieve it, as was demonstrated by the seventeenth- and eighteenth-century revolutions in England, America, and France. Enough has been said of the first; more will be said of the last. A word of explanation is necessary with regard to the American Revolution. It was, as students of history understand, far more than a rebellion of colonials against their mother country. It was a revolution in which Americans demanded that they be permitted to share in the benefits of the reforms achieved by the English Revolution of 1640. The political, economic, social, and religious conditions that led Americans to demand their independence were similar to those which, more than a century earlier, had moved their English forebears and would, in a little more than a decade, set off another rebellion in France. The achievement of the Americans was more apparent than that of the English had been, since the English, in their customary manner, were content to retain the long-established forms in class and government structure while substantially altering the substance, whereas Americans created a society without a king or titled nobility. The lesson was not lost on those in France who were watching the turn of events.

The ease with which the old regime in France was toppled and the completeness of the collapse of ancient French institutions in the Revolution of 1789 demonstrate how fruitless and dangerous it is to attempt completely to prevent change. The refusal of the regime to make modest concessions assured its total overthrow and a thorough overhaul of the society. The event was greeted with enthusiasm by liberals in other countries, at least in the beginning; it was deprecated by conservatives. Politics in America and England were deeply influenced by events in France. In America Jefferson and his followers, and in England most of the Whigs, initially hailed the French revolutionaries as good students of their own revolutions. American Federalists and English Tories generally opposed the Revolution; the demand of the French "mob" for "liberty, equality, and fraternity" had, for them, a radical ring. The revolution was bound to stimulate the production of a great quantity of controversial writing. Among the most noteworthy contributions was Edmund Burke's *Reflections on the Revolution in France,* which represented an attempt to consider the French Revolution, and all revolutionary movements, on a philosophic basis. The effort dismayed many of Burke's Whig compatriots and comforted his Tory enemies. Since Burke had, as a member of the English Parliament, defended the American revolutionaries a few years previously, his bitter assault on the Jacobins was surprising. Still, Burke claimed with some justification that his stand was supported by the principles which he had consistently embraced.

Edmund Burke: The Man and His Work

Edmund Burke, whose lasting reputation was made as an English statesman, was born in Dublin, Ireland, on January 12, 1729. Burke's father, an attorney, was an Irish Protestant; his mother was a Catholic. Although Burke himself was a Protestant, he was cognizant of the oppression of Catholics by the Protestant English, and devoted considerable time and energy in later years to an attempt to rectify those oppressive practices. In 1743 Burke entered Trinity College in Dublin and was exposed to the conventional curriculum. As was the case with so many imaginative and creative young men at the time, the instruction seemed to him dull and unchallenging. Burke left Trinity with a degree in 1748 and in 1750 went to England to study law. It did not interest him; although he had great respect for the law, he was like Hume in finding literature more stimulating. His father was disappointed by his son's repudiation of the profession that meant so much to him, and he was extremely critical of his son's determination to devote himself to literature. As a result he cut off Burke's allowance. There was truth in Burke's later statement that he was not "swaddled and rocked and dandled" into a successful career.

In 1756 Burke established himself as an essayist with the publication of his *A Vindication of Natural Society,* in which he contrasted civilized society with the natural state, coming to much the same conclusion that Rousseau had reached in his first essay on the subject. Burke later said that he had intended the work to be satirical, and there is little reason to doubt his word, considering the enormous respect which he always accorded civil institutions. In the same year he published his *Philosoph-*

ical Inquiry into the Origin of Our Ideas on the Sublime and Beautiful,
a treatise on esthetics. Also in 1756 Burke married the daughter of the
physician who had been treating him during an illness. This was a
period of great literary activity for Burke. He began his *Abridgment of
the History of England* and in 1758 began editing the *Annual Register,*
which reviewed history, literature, and politics of the period. He continued with this work until 1791.

In 1758 Burke became secretary to William Gerald Hamilton, an English politician, who was appointed Irish Secretary. Burke accompanied
Hamilton to Ireland, where he reacquainted himself with the plight of
his oppressed countrymen and published his *Tracts on the Popery Laws,*
in which he attacked discrimination against Irish Catholics. In 1765 he
broke with Hamilton and became secretary to Lord Rockingham. He
also became a member of Parliament. Burke opposed the efforts of George
III and his supporters to throw aside the gains of the Glorious Revolution. The king attempted to subvert the principles established in 1688 by
concentrating authority in his own hands and by forcing ministers to be
personally responsible to him. Burke's reverence for the constitution and
his ability to defend it soon made him a dominant figure among those
who resisted the king's policies. Although he never attained cabinet rank,
he was, for a quarter of a century, an influential member of the Whig
party.

Burke's major parliamentary interests were the preservation of the
constitution against the aggressive designs of the king, the defense of the
Irish, the Americans, and the Indians against the tyranny of English rule,
and, finally, the attack upon revolutionary principles which grew out of
his opposition to the French Revolution. The latter event prompted
Burke to write his *Reflections on the Revolution in France,* in 1790, and
*A Letter to a Member of the National Assembly, Thoughts on French
Affairs,* and *An Appeal from the Old to the New Whigs,* all in 1791.
These publications had a considerable effect upon the development of
English opinion about the Revolution in France; through them Burke
compelled protagonists on both sides of the controversy to consider the
principles of revolution and reform rather than merely the isolated event
of the Revolution itself. In doing so Burke established the main lines of
his own political thought.

Burke sought the formation of a European coalition to destroy Jaco-
binism. His unrelenting opposition to the French revolutionaries alienated most of the important Whig leaders, including the great Charles Fox,
one of his closest friends. Burke prevailed in the end; the Whig forces
gradually came to support the government's policy of war against the
French. Burke, feeling that his most significant work was done, resigned
from Parliament in 1794. In retirement he watched events carefully.
When it appeared that England might, because of the financial drain of

the war, negotiate a peace too favorable to France, Burke was quick to oppose such a move in his *Letters on a Regicide Peace*. The *Letters* greatly strengthened the resolution of the people and caused the government under William Pitt to alter its plans. The *Letters* was Burke's last great effort in the public interest. He died on July 8, 1797, prior to the publication of the last of the *Letters*. His own instructions forbade a public funeral; he was buried quietly in a private ceremony at Beaconsfield.

The Premises of Burke's Political Theory

The underlying principle of Burke's political theory is that of "order." He believed that the universe is orderly and intelligible and that it operates according to moral law of which God is the author. Society should be governed by this law. The general principles of the moral law are universal, but they may find expression in society in a great variety of ways. Governmental structures and positive laws may vary in time and place and yet accord with the moral law. The principles of moral law are those that exist in civil society. They have developed in history; they are not "right" in any abstract sense, but they are good because they serve as guides. Political reason leads men to accept them in the conduct of human affairs. Burke was as opposed as was Hume to the speculative reason of the *philosophes*. Speculative reason, he believed, was impractical; it failed to take into account the realities of conditions and the intricacies of human nature. It was radical and imprudent.

The adaptation of moral law to social life through political reason is not possible on a short-term basis. Political reason develops in history and is evidenced in the institutions that men establish and in the customs and traditions that operate in society. These institutions and traditions would not have been formed in the first place if men could have derived no benefits from them. The danger of the rationalism of the *philosophes,* Burke holds, lies in the fact that they judge social institutions on the basis of a priori principles without taking into account the wisdom that was generated and implanted in those institutions over the years. Out of men's experience has developed an enormously complex but beautiful social structure. Changes occur in it; change, indeed, is a part of the natural order; but it has been slow, orderly, piecemeal, and continuity with the past has been preserved. Future changes must be made on the same basis. Programs of wholesale reform or, worse, of revolution, which result from the assumption of a priori principles and the use of speculative reason can destroy the delicate balance of this structure and send it crashing to ruin. Even the smallest alterations should not be attempted without intensive study.[12]

[12] Francis P. Canavan, *The Political Reason of Edmund Burke*, The Duke University Press, Durham, N.C., 1960, part 1.

Burke's Political Theory

The moral law does not, according to Burke, operate directly upon man. Its tenets are achieved only through the institutions of a civil society. This society is infinitely superior to the primitive or presocial state.

> The state of civil society ... is a state of nature; and much more truly so than a savage and incoherent mode of life. For man is by nature reasonable; and he is never perfectly in his natural state, but when he is placed where reason may be best cultivated, and most predominates. Art is man's nature. We are as much, at least, in a state of nature in formed manhood, as in immature and helpless infancy.[13]

It should be noted here that Burke is not praising nature or the natural man exactly as Rousseau did in his first *Discourse*. Indeed his position is quite the reverse. Civil society is much better than a state of nature. Civil society, says Burke, is for the purpose of perfecting man; it is much more, therefore, than an agency charged with the protection of individual rights, as the natural-rights theorists contend. Indeed, the rights which men have in civil society are not natural at all but rather a matter of convenience. They are not a priori but arise out of society, and their meaning and extent are relative to the situation within society. Man's individual welfare depends upon that of society; his immediate wants must give way before the needs of the whole. Liberty is an excellent thing, but men must remember that it is social liberty that counts, and this cannot be had at the expense of order. Order requires restraint. If men have the capacity to restrain themselves, so much the better. If they do not, society, through government, must restrain them. "Their passions forge their fetters."

"Circumstances," not abstract principles, must determine the extent to which liberty may be exercised.

> I cannot stand forward, and give praise or blame to anything which relates to human action, and human concerns, on a simple view of the object, as it stands stripped of every relation, in all the nakedness and solitude of metaphysical abstraction. Circumstances (which with some gentlemen pass for nothing) give in reality to every political principle its distinguishing colour and discriminating effect. The circumstances are what render every civil and political scheme beneficial or noxious to mankind. ... Is it because liberty in the abstract may be classed amongst the blessings of mankind, that I am seriously to felicitate a mad-man, who has escaped from the protecting restraint and wholesome darkness of his cell, on his restoration to

---

[13] Edmund Burke, *An Appeal from the Old to the New Whigs*, in *The Works of the Right Honourable Edmund Burke* (Bohn's edition), G. Bell & Sons, Ltd., London, 1891, vol. III, p. 86. Subsequent references to Burke's work will be to this source, called *Works*.

the enjoyment of light and liberty? Am I to congratulate a highwayman and murderer, who has broke prison, upon the recovery of his natural rights? [14]

Burke refers contemptuously to the "literary caballers," the "intriguing philosophers," the "political theologians," and the "theological politicians," who have stirred up so much trouble with their metaphysics, their abstract principles of liberty. "The effect of liberty to individuals is," Burke says, "that they may do what they please." But, he adds, "we ought to see what it will please them to do, before we risk congratulations, which may be soon turned into complaints." [15] Nor should liberty be enjoyed equally by all. Each man is entitled to that liberty and those rights which accord with his station in life. This contention raises the issue of the kind of government and social order best suited to achieve the ends of society.

Burke rejects the idea that each person has a right to govern himself. This concept is one of the fallacies stemming from the doctrine of natural rights. A right of self-government may have existed in the primitive state, but it is not a civil right. Like other such abstract rights, it was abandoned when man entered civil society. There is government by consent in the sense that government is a trust, but this consent does not imply the equality of all who give it. Consent is given by the whole community in its established parts, that is, classes and ranks of man play an important role in giving consent. It is absurd, Burke says, to regard the consent of an ignorant worker as of equal weight with that of an informed and propertied gentleman. There is a social contract, too, but it is not of the kind contemplated by the natural-rights theorists.

> Society is indeed a contract. Subordinate contracts for objects of mere occasional interest may be dissolved at pleasure—but the state ought not to be considered as nothing better than a partnership agreement in a trade of pepper and coffee, calico or tobacco, or some other such low concern, to be taken up for a little temporary interest, and to be dissolved by the fancy of the parties. It is to be looked upon with other reverence; because it is not a partnership in things subservient only to the gross animal existence of a temporary and perishable nature. It is a partnership in all science; a partnership in all art; a partnership in every virtue, and in all perfection. As the ends of such a partnership cannot be obtained in many generations, it becomes a partnership not only between those who are living, but between those who are living, those who are dead, and those who are to be born.[16]

This statement preeminently demonstrates Burke's great respect for the state, his reverence for its traditions, and his repugnance toward a doc-

[14] Burke, *Reflections on the Revolution in France, Works,* vol. 2, p. 282.
[15] *Ibid.,* p. 283.
[16] *Ibid.,* p. 368.

trine which, like the social-contract doctrine of Locke, justifies a right to revolt against it.

What is the best form of government? This matter, Burke says, cannot be determined except in relation to circumstances. "I reprobate," he states, "no form of government merely upon abstract principles." It is even possible, Burke admits, that conditions may justify a democratic form, although obviously he believes such a situation improbable. Furthermore, he warns that in a democracy the oppression of the minority by the majority is worse than any tyranny which may "be apprehended from the dominion of a single sceptre." Burke is mainly concerned to show that experience is the best guide in the matter of creating and reforming governments. "The science of constructing a commonwealth," he says, "or renovating it, or reforming it, is, like every experimental science, not to be taught *a priori*." [17] It is a science that can be learned only through long experience, longer than can be achieved in a single generation. This is why the experience and wisdom of the ages must be taken into account in any plan involving a change of governmental structure, operation, or tradition. Change should not be undertaken for light and transient reasons. Revolutions, which undermine and destroy the foundation built over the centuries, should be a last resort. Only when "abused and deranged" governments make it apparent that "the prospect of the future" is as dismal "as the experience of the past" is revolution justified. Then the remedy should not be supplied by the common herd, but by those members of the society who are fitted for the task. On this basis, Burke defends the English Revolution of 1688. The action was taken, he says, to preserve the constitution, not to destroy it; moreover, the Revolution was directed by that part of the community which had the requisite knowledge.

Burke has little regard for the political wisdom and capacity of the common man. His view is not entirely undemocratic, for he believes that civil society does result from some kind of original agreement among the people. But when Burke speaks of the voice of the people, he clearly has in mind something considerably less than a majority. His "public" numbers some 400,000 and includes those with sufficient means and education to enable them to take a farsighted view of the general interest and elect their representatives accordingly.

> The occupation of a hair-dresser, or of a working tallow-chandler, cannot be a matter of honour to any person—to say nothing of a number of other more servile employments. Such description of men ought not to suffer oppression from the state; but the state suffers oppression, if such as they, either individually or collectively, are permitted to rule.[18]

[17] *Ibid.*, p. 333.
[18] *Ibid.*, p. 322.

Government should be the business of a ruling class selected on the basis of ability, property, and birth. The first is important, even indispensable, but ability "is a vigorous and active principle"; if it is not counterbalanced by an even greater consideration for property, the able but propertyless will invade and destroy property rights. It is the nature of property to be unequal, and this principle should be protected by the state. The masses of people are envious of the holdings of the rich, and unless they are restrained, they will take them by force. This, of course, must be prevented. Even if an equal distribution of property were made, it would do the masses no good. "The plunder of the few would indeed give but a share inconceivably small in the distribution to the many." [19] Representation should also take hereditary distinction into account. Burke is far too wise to argue that ability is invariably found among the nobility. Nevertheless, the noble families contribute to the stability of society, and stability is highly desirable. Furthermore, if it is true that the nobility is too greatly revered by "creeping sycophants," it is also true that ability in this class is too often overlooked by the "short-sighted coxcombs of philosophy."

When elected representatives take their offices, they should have a careful regard for the interests of the people. They should even consider the opinions of the people, but they should not be dominated by them. It is not necessary to have direct representation in which representatives are popularly elected from districts containing an equal number of people. The representative "must have some relation to the constituent," but a form of "virtual," or indirect, representation is adequate and even preferable to the direct form.

> Virtual representation is that in which there is a communion of interests, and a sympathy in feelings and desires, between those who act in the name of any description of people, and the people in whose name they act, though the trustees are not actually chosen by them. This is virtual representation. Such a representation I think to be, in many cases, even better than the actual. It possesses most of its advantages, and is free from many of its inconveniences; it corrects the irregularities in the literal representation, when the shifting current of human affairs, or the acting of public interests in different ways, carry it obliquely from its first line of direction.[20]

Representation ought not to take mere numbers of men into account. Government is not a "problem in arithmetic." Burke's ideas on representation are more medieval than modern. To him, men are important as members of the class to which they belong; representation should be based on this principle.

The major function of the ruling class, Burke says, is to maintain the

[19] *Ibid.,* p. 324.
[20] Burke, *A Letter to Sir Hercules Langrishe, M.P., Works,* vol. 3, pp. 334–335.

stability of the society it governs. In addition to the power of government it employs to secure this end, three forms of social control should also be used—property, religion, and prejudice.[21] The inequality of property holdings creates a dependency of those who have less property upon those who have more. The former defer to the latter. This dependence has become habitual, and habit has a steadying influence; the principle ought, therefore, to be maintained. Religion is also a stabilizing force. It provides answers to questions where reason is inadequate. It relieves uncertainty. It supports the established order. It provides hope for those who otherwise would have no hope in a class society and thereby lessens the possibilities of insurrection.

Burke proposes the retention and cultivation of "prejudices" in the interest of social order. By prejudice he means a widely held opinion not supported by speculative reason. There are, he says, many such opinions and sentiments, which have long existed and have served to bring unity and stability to the community. They might be impossible to justify by speculative reason, but they may also contain a wisdom which is part of the higher reason that always conduces to the preservation of established institutions.

> Instead of casting away all our old prejudices, we cherish them to a very considerable degree, and, to take more shame to ourselves, we cherish them because they are prejudices; and the longer they have lasted, and the more generally they have prevailed, the more we cherish them. We are afraid to put men to live and trade each on his own private stock of reason; because we suspect that this stock in each man is small, and that the individuals would do better to avail themselves of the general bank and capital of nations and of ages. Many of our men of speculation, instead of exploding general prejudices, employ their sagacity to discover the latent wisdom which prevails in them. If they find what they seek, and they seldom fail, they think it more wise to continue the prejudice, with the reason involved, than to cast away the coat of prejudice, and to leave nothing but the naked reason; because prejudice, with its reason, has a motive to give action to that reason, and an affection which will give it permanence. Prejudice is of ready application in the emergency; it previously engages the mind in a steady course of wisdom and virtue, and does not leave the man hesitating in the moment of decision, sceptical, puzzled, and unresolved. Prejudice renders a man's virtue his habit; and not a series of unconnected acts. Through just prejudice, his duty becomes a part of his nature.[22]

The Rights of Prescription

The central theme in Burke's theory is his admiration for long-established institutions and his search for arguments to support and maintain them.

[21] Andrew Hacker, *Political Theory: Philosophy, Ideology, Science,* The Macmillan Company, New York, 1961, pp. 368–377.

[22] Burke, *Reflections on the Revolution in France, Works,* vol. 2, p. 359.

One of these arguments, as we have seen, was based upon utility. Over the centuries have evolved governmental structures, codes of law, classes of society, powers, privileges, customs, and traditions, which would not have evolved had experience not demonstrated their usefulness, their utility. There is also a religious flavor to Burke's theory. A devout man, Burke was convinced that history is the working out of God's will. What has happened, including the growth of institutions of society, is attributable to Providence. In any case, the state is not a mere mechanism designed by men at a given time and for a given purpose. It has the authority of generations of experience and the majesty of God behind it; it ought, therefore, generally to be left alone. If changes are necessary they should be made gradually and with the proper respect for the past.

A variation on this argument is found in Burke's idea of the "prescriptive constitution." In common law, prescription refers to the claim to title to a thing based upon its long use and enjoyment. Burke applies this theory to the English constitution to justify titles to office, rank, and privilege by virtue of long-term possession. To abstract natural rights, which lead to discontent, instability, and insurrection, he opposes prescriptive rights, which produce continuity and stability and enable the present generation of men to profit from the wisdom of their predecessors.

> Our constitution is a prescriptive constitution; it is a constitution whose sole authority is that it has existed time out of mind.... Your king, your lords, your judges, your juries, grand and little, all are prescriptive.... Prescription is the most solid of all titles, not only to property, but, which is to secure that property, to government. They harmonize with each other, and give mutual aid to one another. It is accompanied with another ground of authority in the constitution of the human mind,—presumption. It is a presumption in favour of any settled scheme of government against any untried project, that a nation has long existed and flourished under it. It is a better presumption even of the *choice* of a nation, far better than any sudden and temporary arrangement by actual election. Because a nation is not an idea only of local extent, and individual monetary aggregation; but it is an idea of continuity, which extends in time as well as in numbers and in space. And this is a choice not of one day, or one set of people, not a tumultuary and giddy choice; it is a deliberate election of ages and of generations; it is a constitution made by what is ten thousand times better than choice, it is made by the peculiar circumstances, occasions, tempers, dispositions, and moral, civil, and social habitudes of the people, which disclose themselves only in a long space of time. It is a vestment, which accommodates itself to the body. Nor is prescription of government formed upon blind, unmeaning prejudices—for man is a most unwise and a most wise being. The individual is foolish; the multitude, for the moment, is foolish, when they act without deliberation; but the species is wise, and, when time is given to it, as a species it always acts right.[23]

[23] Burke, *Reform of Representation in the House of Commons, Works,* vol. 6, pp. 146–147.

The principle of inheritance, Burke says, is valuable because it conforms to the idea of prescription. It ties the present to the past and the future and makes possible the utilization of the accumulated wisdom of former generations. It does not preclude the possibility of change, but it does render difficult anything entirely new. A prudent people will never march forward without carrying with them the equipage of their forefathers. The error of the French revolutionaries, Burke states, is that they decided to destroy and replace their entire system because flaws developed in some parts of it. But if the structure was dilapidated, it was not beyond repair; the foundation remained, as well as some of the walls. These should have been employed in the construction of a commonwealth which retained the valid elements of the old society. The English have made no such mistake. Their "sullen resistance to innovation" and their "cold sluggishness" have enabled them to resist the innovative siren calls of Rousseau, Voltaire, and Helvetius and to retain the "generosity and dignity of thinking of the fourteenth century." The English, Burke boasts, understand that there are no discoveries to be made in morality, and that the "great principles of government" and of liberty were made before the present generation was born. Therefore, men should be concerned with resisting change, not with experimenting with novel ideas. They are only the "temporary possessors" of power, and they hold their position in trust from past generations for the benefit of future generations. Innovation disrupts continuity, and men "become little better than the flies of the summer."

Conclusions

There are many similarities in the theories of Burke and Hume. Both men strongly distrust a priori principles and abstract or speculative reasoning, and contend that experience, the experience of the ages, is the appropriate guide to social action. Each is vitally concerned with social stability. This concern leads both to a rejection of revolution and innovation and an extremely cautious approach to reform of any kind. Since the force of habit contributes to stability, great emphasis is placed upon it, with no question as to whether the general welfare is promoted by stability. Such a judgment is, perhaps, not entirely fair; it would be more accurate to say that both Hume and Burke assume stability and the general welfare to be coincidental. They also agree that the mass of men are incapable of self-government, that a minority must govern, and that the criteria of property and education should be employed to determine that minority. Burke adds, and emphasizes, the criterion of noble birth. Both Hume and Burke regard prescription, rather than direct consent, as a legitimate foundation of political authority.

Among the differences between the ideas of Hume and Burke, some stem from the fact that the two writers were men of different personalities; others result from Burke's greater preoccupation with political affairs, and still more from the impact upon him of the French Revolution. Burke's writings evidence a greater involvement with his subject than is shown by Hume's. Both men, in the development of their theories, ostensibly say, "This is the way things *are*." One cannot avoid feeling, with Burke, that he is saying, "This is the way things *ought to be*." Hume appears more aloof, dispassionate, and objective in his analysis; Burke is a protagonist in the struggle. Both are conservatives, but whereas Hume calmly states the problems with which conservatives are confronted, Burke, particularly in the *Reflections*, summons the troops to battle. Hume is involved in analysis and appraisal; Burke is formulating a philosophy. An example of the latter point is found in the treatment each man accords the subject of reason and sentiment. Hume separates the two while making reason an instrument of sentiment. Such a tactic does not suffice for Burke's purposes. A more effective philosophy can be constructed through a combination of reason and sentiment to produce a higher reason; this is Burke's method.

Whether because Burke played a more active role than Hume in politics, or because he wrote magnificently, or both, Burke is the better known. His *Reflections* has often been called the "Bible of conservatism," although its purpose at the time was more polemical than philosophic. The tenets of Burke's conservative theory are scattered throughout his works, and are not confined to the *Reflections*. We must review and analyze some of them with a view to fixing Burke's role as a philosopher of conservatism.

The word "conservatism," like the word "liberalism," is difficult to define. In part this is because we tend to employ both terms to define attitudes toward specific policies. A "liberal" today is often described as one who demands a considerable degree of governmental control over private property; a "conservative" is one who opposes such control and takes his stand for "free enterprise." A few decades ago, however, these positions were reversed. We tend to view Alexander Hamilton as a leading "conservative," although he took his stand for a strong national government, with considerable power over private property. Thomas Jefferson, on the other hand, one of the great patron saints of present-day "liberals," was an ardent "states-righter" and opponent of centralization of political authority—principles which today are warmly embraced by "conservatives." The term "liberal" implies an interest in *liberty*, but today's conservatives say that they are concerned with liberty, and that liberals sacrifice liberty to gain security. Liberals counter with the charge that the only liberty in which conservatives are interested is that of accumulating and keeping a disproportionate share of property and that true liberty for the individual is meaningless unless he enjoys a minimum of security. Thus the argument over the meaning of the terms often flies off into a semantic confusion from which it never emerges.

Apparently we must simply do the best we can in analyzing Burke's theory (which is, after all, almost universally conceded to be conservative), and approach the problem through the use of generalizations, employing qualifications where they seem to be necessary. We can then hope for an approximation to accuracy and perhaps understand, a little better at least, what is meant by "conservatism" and, by implication, "liberalism."

Conservatism implies the desirability of *conserving*. This is a dominant theme in Burke's thought. He had a respect akin to reverence for the established government, laws, religion, classes, customs, and traditions. They embodied the wisdom of the past, and they were not to be lightly regarded. The obvious objection to this view is that established institutions may very well contain the stupidity, even the brutality, of the past as well as its wisdom. These evils may increase as time goes on, and those who benefit by such a situation may be able to prevent any desirable reform. Revolution may thus be the only means of escape from an intolerable condition. This, indeed, is what happened in France. We may deprecate the violent turn which the revolution in that country took, but we should find it difficult to support the argument that change could have occurred in any other manner. Burke does not entirely discount the necessity of change; logic demanded that he make such a concession. The weight of his argument, however, is overwhelmingly against change. Even the possibility of reform, in Burke's theory, is so hedged about with restrictions that it appears remote, if not impossible, as a practical matter.

Another tenet of Burke's conservatism is his distrust of abstract reason. He objects to the idea that rational men can view their situation, analyze the causes of their troubles, and, through their intelligence, rearrange their institutions and improve their existence. This is the dangerous and fallacious idea that leads to innovation, revolution, and the destruction of established institutions. Burke is too much the practical politician to have faith in this violent method of solving problems. For him it is experience that counts. Over the years a people develop institutions and methods of providing for their welfare, which may not meet the test of abstract reason, but which nevertheless *work*. This being so, the institutions are not unreasonable; it is more accurate to say, Burke believes, that they result from a higher reason, one which may be better understood through sentiment or instinct than through the processes of abstract reason. Burke's view here merges with his ideas concerning the value of historical institutions. Those institutions were developed by a higher reason and should be revered. A single man, a group of men, a single generation of men are incapable of understanding the knowledge that has accumulated over the ages and has been incorporated into the society we have inherited.

A corollary of this point is found in Burke's lack of regard for the wisdom of the mass of men. If reforms are to be made, he holds that the ruling class, a minority whose position is based on ability, property, and birth, should decide what is to be done. The interest of the community should be served, but it can best be served by a system of representation in which the views of the majority are largely ignored. Representatives ought to have a careful regard for the welfare of their constituents, but they should not take instructions from them; instead, they must rely upon their own judgment, for the great majority of men are incapable of knowing how to achieve their real interest. Burke is an advocate of government *for*, but not *by*, the people. Virtual representation is sufficient to promote their interests. On this basis Burke opposed attempts to reform the system of rotten and pocket boroughs that prevailed in the England of his time.

Throughout history the forces for consolidation and conservation have been pitted against the forces for change. Many factors may influence us in the position we take in this perennial conflict. Often the struggle is between the "haves," who wish to maintain their economic position in society, and the "have-nots," who feel that they stand to gain from social change. The conflict may be between those who hold and those who do not hold political power; between those who have and those who do not have religious freedom; between those who occupy, by virtue of birth, a preferred social position, and those who, from birth, are consigned to a position of inferiority; between colonials and imperialists; between lords and serfs; between masters and slaves. In any event there is much in Burke's theory to support the stand of those who wish to keep things as they are. And his is an impressive contribution that cannot be ignored. Much depends, in any appraisal of Burke, upon the circumstances surrounding those who agree or disagree with his theory. Many would argue that Burke's respect for the past and his emphasis upon conservation are exaggerated; others would charge that liberals are far too prone to assume that all change constitutes progress. Probably there is a place for both views in the affairs of men.

SELECTED BIBLIOGRAPHY

Burke, Edmund: *Works* (Bohn's edition), G. Bell & Sons, Ltd., London, 1891.

Canavan, Francis P.: *The Political Reason of Edmund Burke,* The Duke University Press, Durham, N.C., 1960.

Cobban, Alfred: *Edmund Burke and the Revolt against the Eighteenth Century,* The Macmillan Company, New York, 1961.

Hacker, Andrew: *Political Theory: Philosophy, Ideology, Science,* The Macmillan Company, New York, 1961, chap. 9.

Hume: Theory of Politics (edited by Frederick Watkins), University of Texas Press, Austin, Tex., 1953, introduction.

Hume's Moral and Political Philosophy (edited with an introduction by Henry D. Aiken), Hafner Publishing Company, Inc., New York, 1948.

McDonald, Lee Cameron: *Western Political Theory: The Modern Age,* Harcourt, Brace & World, Inc., New York, 1962, chaps. 8, 9.

Morris, C. R.: *Locke, Berkeley, Hume,* Oxford University Press, Fair Lawn, N.J., 1931, introduction, part 3.

Sabine, George H.: *A History of Political Theory,* 3d ed., Holt, Rinehart and Winston, Inc., New York, 1961, chap. 29.

Stanlis, Peter J.: *Edmund Burke and the Natural Law,* The University of Michigan Press, Ann Arbor, Mich., 1958.

seventeen

HEGEL

The ideas of rationalism and individualism which flourished in England and France in the seventeenth and eighteenth centuries provided a philosophical basis for the French Revolution. The rationalists generally thought of the past as a period in which the free use of reason had been obstructed. Once these obstructions were removed, men could employ their reason to solve their problems and to create a new and improved environment, one in which life for individual men would be vastly better than it had ever been. History was a dismal record of oppression. Concern should be for the future, not with the past. Men have the capacity to make their own world. The old society, which had long stifled both reason and ambition, should be cast aside to grant the individual free rein to seek his own ends. The doctrine of natural rights stated that he was entitled to do so.

The initial effect of the Revolution was to enhance the prestige of the philosophies that supported it. The armies of Napoleon, carrying with them the banners of liberty, equality, and fraternity, severely damaged the feudalistic and anachronistic institutions of Western Europe and appeared to many who had suffered oppression more as armies of deliverance than as the troops of a conqueror. The view did not endure. Napoleon's plans foundered on the rocks of his own ambition and of English resistance. The war dragged on interminably, decimating the manpower of the many nations involved, creating enormous economic dislocations, and ultimately discrediting the Revolution itself and the principles upon which it had been based. By comparison with the existing situation and the prospects of the future, the past took on a rosier hue, at least to many. A new philosophical outlook, one capable of taking these developments into account, began to emerge.

The writings of Rousseau and the works of Edmund Burke, particularly his *Reflections,* laid the foundation for a new philosophical approach. Both men emphasized society rather than the individual. Rousseau's rejection of rationalism was supported by Burke and Hume and by the romantic movement in art, music, and literature. Romanticism meant many things to many persons, and it stimulated liberalism as much as it did conservatism, but it drew the line against the Enlightenment's trust in reason and contended, instead, that feeling, emotion, and faith were more reliable than rationality in creating a better world. Burke insisted upon a respect for the past and for established institutions. He warned that reform which did not carry with it the accumulated experience of past generations would be self-defeating, and he implied that men were not so completely the controllers of their own destiny as the *philosophes* had believed.

Burke's thought was not presented in the form of a systematic philosophical treatise. He wrote in response to the challenges inherent in the events he witnessed, and he would surely have regarded himself more as a statesman than a philosopher. Many of Burke's ideas, however, were reflected in the writings of contemporaries who sought a more philosophical formulation of them. In Germany, Immanuel Kant (1724–1804), although he relied mainly upon the political ideas of Montesquieu and Rousseau, argued, as did Burke, that the state is the result of historical development and maintained that no right of revolution existed. And Johann Fichte (1762–1814), whose earlier writings were in the liberal tradition but who was caught up in the reaction to Napoleon and the Revolution, stimulated the patriotism of his fellow Germans, argued for national unity, and exalted the concept of state authority. It was, however, in Hegel that these ideas found their fullest and most influential philosophical expression.

Hegel: The Man and His Work

Georg Wilhelm Friedrich Hegel was born in Stuttgart, August 27, 1770. His father was a minor civil service official in the kingdom of Württemberg. The young Hegel attended grammar school at Stuttgart until he was eighteen. In 1788 he enrolled as a theology student at the University of Tübingen, where he received the degree of doctor of philosophy in 1790 and a certificate in theology in 1793. Despite a continuing interest in theology, Hegel devoted most of his time in school to a study of the classics. He developed a great admiration for the Greek city-state and its contributions to Western civilization. The political fragmentation of Germany probably contributed to Hegel's regard for the cohesion of the *polis* of antiquity, and that circumstance has a real bearing upon the subsequent development of Hegel's political theory.

From Tübingen Hegel went to Bern, where he worked as a private tutor until 1797. His studies and writing at this time were in the field of theology. Hegel sought the true meaning of Christ in the records of Christianity, and he wrote a life of the Savior. In 1797 Hegel left Bern for Frankfurt, where he continued working as a tutor. It was at this time that Hegel first evidenced an interest in governmental and economic affairs. Still, he did not abandon theological speculation; at this stage of his development Hegel was convinced that the infinite could be apprehended only through religion and that philosophy should confine itself to the realm of the finite. This view he soon altered in favor of the assumption that philosophy provides a better method than religion for understanding the infinite.

In 1799 Hegel's father died, leaving to his son a small inheritance. Hegel left his tutorship and went to Jena to study and to prepare himself for a professorship. He received his appointment from the University of Jena in 1805, but previous to that time he was made a member of the staff and lectured on philosophy and mathematics. At Jena in 1806 Hegel saw Napoleon, the "world soul," as he called him, riding through the streets prior to the famous battle of Jena in which the Prussians were defeated by the French. Hegel was apparently undismayed by the outcome of this conflict; he attributed the defeat to the corruption of the Prussian bureaucracy. As a young man Hegel had been sympathetic toward the French revolutionaries, and later he expressed his high regard for the genius and leadership of Napoleon. Like many others, Hegel became disillusioned with the principles of the Revolution. Its ideals of liberty, equality, and fraternity contradicted his later concepts of hierarchy and class, and the rationalism that had supported the revolutionary principles was a far cry from Hegel's idea of the higher reason.

In 1808 Hegel accepted a professorship at the University of Nuremberg, where he remained until 1816. In 1811 he married Marie von Tucher, a young woman twenty-two years his junior. The marriage produced two sons. In 1816 Hegel moved to the University of Heidelberg and taught for two years until he accepted the chair of philosophy, made vacant by the death of Fichte, at the University of Berlin. Here he remained until his death in 1831.

Hegel had published his first important work, *The Phenomenology of the Spirit,* in 1807. His *The Science of Logic* appeared in three volumes from 1812 to 1816, and in 1817 Hegel produced, as texts for his lectures, the *Encyclopedia of the Philosophical Sciences.* He was well known when he went to Berlin in 1818, and his fame and influence grew rapidly from this time. *The Philosophy of Right and Law,* published in 1821, added luster to an already substantial reputation. Most of Hegel's energy was poured into the preparation of his lectures, which he embellished and polished over the years. His lectures, despite the fact that they were poorly and sometimes inaudibly delivered, were attended by persons from all the German states. In 1830 Hegel was appointed rector of the University of Berlin. The following year he was decorated by the king of Prussia. He died of cholera, after a short illness, on November 14, 1831. *The Philosophy of History,* consisting of a series of lectures given from 1822 to 1831, was published posthumously in 1838. Other posthumous publications included *Lectures on the Philosophy of Religion* and *Lectures on Aesthetics.*

The Pattern of History

Hegel's distinctive contribution to political thought lies, in large part, in his philosophy of history. With this theory he opposes the rationalist view of history, freedom, individualism, and reason, and the rationalist insistence on man's ability to control his destiny. As we have seen, the rationalists had regarded past history as largely unfortunate in the sense that it was a record of opposition to the free employment of reason, which, unobstructed, could be used to create a better world. It was thought that a study of history offered little except the negative lesson that what had been ought no longer to be, that the institutions of the past should be uprooted, and that new ones should be established on the basis of the a priori truths of natural law as interpreted by reasonable men. Freedom meant the liberty of men to go about their business of accomplishing these tasks with a minimum of interference from the state, which in the past had been altogether too assiduous in limiting the freedom of the individual. Hegel completely repudiates these views.

History, Hegel says, is not a haphazard and disconnected series of events in time. It has a pattern (which Hegel calls the Idea), and it is purposeful and intelligible. The world has a destiny toward which it has always moved. This destiny has been predetermined by the author of the Idea, God. It is God's will that the world shall progress toward the fulfillment of its destiny. The Idea is reason, but a higher reason than that in which the rationalists placed their confidence. It is God's reason and cannot be disclosed or understood in its entirety until the final stage of history has been reached. Until then, only that part of reason can be understood that has been revealed by past history. The study of history suffices only to make such an understanding possible. God's purpose and his plan for achieving it are so inscrutable that not even the wisest scholar of history can predict the future on the basis of what has been learned of the past.

> When philosophy paints its grey in grey, then has a shape of life grown old. By philosophy's grey in grey it cannot be rejuvenated but only understood. The owl of Minerva spreads its wings only with the falling of dusk.[1]

Reason is the history of man, gradually unfolded in a series of historical periods, each of which represents a higher stage than the preceding one in the advancement of reason. Each period is understood in terms of the institutions, science, art, religion, and culture which develop within it. The movement is inexorable. It can be neither delayed nor controlled by men. The best that men can do is to understand what is happening, to know that an Idea, or pattern, exists and to associate themselves with it. To the extent that they are successful in doing so they will be free. Freedom does not consist in exemption from the Idea but only in subordination to it. Full freedom is a goal of man, to be achieved when all men understand and live according to the Idea, and when, as a result, men's lives accord with reason. All through the ages men have been moving toward this stage. The sacrifices, hardships, and conflicts that have been suffered have not been meaningless; rather they have been adjuncts of historical progress.

Hegel's ideas on this point are not entirely original. Lessing,[2] the great German dramatist and critic, had asserted that each great religion in history had contributed in its time to the spiritual development of mankind.[3] For Hegel, however, a theory of history was not properly a mere exercise in abstraction. His work involved an intensive study of the past, and *The Philosophy of History* is replete with concrete historical detail designed to support his thesis. Hegel was careful to point out that an analytical approach to the study of history was, standing alone, inadequate to enable the student to distinguish the "real" from the "apparent." Analysis, he said, involved the breaking down of the community into its component parts. The analyst then saw only the parts, the individuals, rather than the organic whole, which is the true essence of the community. Such an approach leads to individualism and to the belief that men are capable of molding their institutions as they see fit. Individualism and egotism create instability, disrespect for the past, and, ultimately, revolution. Such, Hegel believed, was the error of the rationalists. A proper comprehension of the meaning of the Idea can be

---

[1] *Hegel's Philosophy of Right* (translated with notes by T. M. Knox), Oxford University Press, Fair Lawn, N.J., 1942, preface. All subsequent references to and quotations from *The Philosophy of Right* are from this edition.

[2] Gotthold Ephraim Lessing (1729–1781).

[3] George H. Sabine, *A History of Political Theory*, 3d ed., Holt, Rinehart and Winston, Inc., New York, 1961, pp. 629–630.

achieved only through an understanding of the dialectic. The dialectic combines the methods of analysis and synthesis in the study of history and makes possible a true understanding of history.[4]

The Dialectic in History

The unfolding of the Idea, of reason, of the "World Spirit," in history, Hegel says, results from the operation of the dialectic. God is the author of the Idea; he also supplies the force which moves the Idea in history, and this force is the dialectic. The force, like the progress of history, is inexorable. Men do not and cannot control it; they are controlled by it. The force of the dialectic is invariably progressive. In history it always carries man toward the ultimate realization of freedom. The course of progress is not, however, even and steady; it is a movement from one stage to another and higher stage, and the advance is the result of conflict.

At any given time in world history, the Idea is represented by an "idea" or "thesis," which is a lesser and incomplete manifestation of the totality of the ultimate truth toward which the World Spirit is moving. In time, the thesis gives rise to another and contradictory idea or "antithesis." The two may survive together for awhile, but because they stand in a relation of contradiction to one another, tensions arise that lead to conflict between them. In the conflict, neither thesis nor antithesis is wholly destroyed; nor does either one emerge unscathed. The result of the clash of contradictory ideas is a fusion of the higher, the valid elements of both and the destruction of the invalid parts. The merging of the higher elements of thesis and antithesis forms a synthesis of the two which is an improvement over both of them. The synthesis, in turn, represents a new thesis against which a new antithesis soon is pitted, and the cycle begins again. Each cycle produces a higher stage in the historical advance of reason. Each synthesis is a victory for the World Spirit, a movement of reason toward the ultimate historical goal.

Each idea or thesis contains within itself the seeds of its own modification. In practical terms, since the Idea is represented by a people's culture or civilization, this means that no culture is immune from the forces of change. Progress is inherent in history. Men may wish, above all things, to prevent change, and their actions may, in their own minds, be directed to this end. Their reason, however, is inadequate to enable them to understand the consequences of their actions. When men act to preserve the status quo they set into motion forces which attack and undermine it. Progress occurs whether it is consciously willed or not and even in the face of opposition. There may be a period of quiescence for a people, but even at such a time contradictory tensions are generating the force for change. Conflict is bound to occur, and when it does

[4] *Ibid.*, pp. 626–627.

the World Spirit will advance again. For Hegel, conflict is the key to progress. It need not be violent (although it very often is), but violent or not, it is inevitable.

In this inescapable change there is no clean break with the past— no clear line of demarcation between what was, what is, and what will be. Each new synthesis, containing the valid elements of both thesis and antithesis, carries with it the truths of the past. Each new stage of history thus incorporates all the virtues and all the wisdom of past stages. True progress consists of this synthesis, rather than of the obliteration of past institutions and the creation of new ones. History is not a series of distinct and unrelated Ideas. There is only one Idea, and history is the story of its unfolding or development in the various stages, each of which represents an advance over its predecessor while it still retains all the truths of that and all other predecessors. World history as a whole is a manifestation of the advancement of the Idea. A study of the present reveals the truths of the past, for the valid elements of the past are carried forward. No truth is ever lost. The truth of the present, with which philosophy is concerned, incorporates all the truths of the past. These truths have been unfolded, stage by stage, in the march of history.[5]

The Nation in History

Thus far we have seen that in Hegel's theory progress results from the conflict of ideas. Hegel is an idealist; for him ideas are far more important than material things. Ideas, he believes, move the material world. Ideas have an independent existence, independent, that is, from the thinking of men; they are not merely "manufactured" by men for their own purposes. Material things—forces, institutions, cultures—are merely reflections of ideas or, more properly, of the Idea at a given time. But the Idea must have a vehicle on which to ride. The conflict between ideas, between thesis and antithesis, must have some concrete manifestation if progress is to be apparent in a way significant to men.

The progress of the Idea through history, Hegel says, is carried by states. States are the material manifestations of ideas, the worldly evidences of the progress of the World Spirit through history. They are the devices employed by God to achieve the gradual fulfillment of the Idea.

> The march of God in the world, that is what the state is. The basis of the state is the power of reason actualizing itself as will. In considering the Idea of the state, we must not have our eyes on particular states, or on particular institutions. Instead we must consider the Idea, this actual God by itself.[6]

[5] From Hegel's *Philosophy of History* (translated by Robert S. Hartman, Paul W. Friedrich, and Carl J. Friedrich), in *The Philosophy of Hegel* (edited with an introduction and notes by Carl J. Friedrich), Modern Library, Inc., New York, 1953, pp. 42–43 Subsequent references to the *Philosophy of History* are to this edition.

[6] Hegel, *Philosophy of Right,* par. 258, addition.

Each state (or nation) in history carries the Idea for a time; each of a succession of states has made its contribution to the development and the advancement of the Idea. A significant phase of history is represented by the dominant nation which, at the time, is charged with this responsibility. In its culture and institutions are seen the stage of progress achieved by the Idea to that point. Each stage differs in principle from its predecessor; each stage represents an advancement of the Spirit, a development of the Idea. The various attributes of each dominant nation in history express the contribution of that nation to the advance of the Spirit. Many things are involved here—law and morals, constitutions, forms of government, arts, sciences, technology, social organizations, and many more. All these, too, must be construed according to the "special principle" of the people of the nation.[7]

The nation is at its best Hegel says, when it is engaged in war or revolution. This statement should not be understood as an indication of Hegel's bloodthirsty nature. The view grows out of Hegel's thesis that progress results from conflict. War and revolution are the material evidences of the clash of ideas, of the opposition of thesis and antithesis. War is that stage in the history of the nation when a new and higher synthesis (a new thesis) is emerging. When the process is complete the nation has made its contribution to the progress of the Idea in history. Although it may contribute further in a minor way, everything from this point in the nation's history is anticlimactic. Following the conflict, a period of quiescence, even of stagnation, ensues. A new antithesis is developing which will attack the established thesis. A new nation will replace the old as the carrier of the Idea. The cycle will repeat itself.[8] The old nation may suffer, but its suffering is the price of progress. The world as a whole will benefit. The world is indebted to the old nations that have fallen by the way; they have done their part, and the valid elements of their civilizations have been incorporated into the new nation which now carries the Idea.

This view gives meaning to one of Hegel's most famous statements, found in the preface to his *The Philosophy of Right and Law,* "The rational is actual; and the actual is rational." It has sometimes been charged that by this dictum Hegel intended to sanctify the status quo and to oppose all change. But this interpretation is a negation of the entire structure of Hegel's philosophy of history. Hegel sanctifies, literally, that which exists *insofar as it accords with the Idea.* Certainly the Idea is rational; it is the plan of reason itself. So too, however, is change. Hegel's statement may be said to justify a situation which exists only at the moment a new thesis is formed and before an antithesis has devel-

---

[7] Hegel, *Philosophy of History,* p. 26.

[8] Andrew Hacker, *Political Theory: Philosophy, Ideology, Science,* The Macmillan Company, New York, 1961, pp. 442–443.

oped. But the formation of the antithesis itself demonstrates that the thesis is no longer wholly tenable and that change is consequently necessitated. In short Hegel justifies on the same ground, both change and that which exists. And that which exists is rational because it contains elements of the Idea that have developed through the dialectical process in history. Hegel, whose country was less advantageously situated than was Burke's England, was not so enamored of the status quo as was Burke. Although he wanted the wisdom of the past to be a part of future German development, there was no doubt in Hegel's mind that changes would have to occur in Germany before that country could assume its full responsibility as a carrier of the Idea. Germany, he was convinced, had to achieve the national form, consolidated and unified, which had already been attained by England, France, and Spain.

The Individual and the State

How did Hegel's philosophical ideas concern the individual and his relationship with the state? A theory, after all, is significant only as it deals with and has an effect upon singular human beings. As we have seen in the theories of all the political philosophers, the position of the individual in the state, the degree to which he influences and is influenced by the state, are the central matters. While Hegel's writings are replete with references to the Idea, the World Spirit, the dialectic, and other such abstractions, their real significance lies in their views of man and the state.

Again, the Hegelian view can best be understood by contrasting it with the ideas of the rationalists whom Hegel opposed. The rationalists assumed that the legitimate end to be sought was the happiness of mankind. They believed that reason, individual reason, pointed the way to happiness and that existing barriers to the exercise of reason should be removed. Men, moreover, were capable of creating institutions which could achieve the end of universal happiness. Government was such an institution and should be so employed. History had demonstrated, however, that governments too often obstructed man in his search for happiness. They should, therefore, be generally limited in their functions to the protection of life, liberty, and property, thus leaving to the individual a wide scope of freedom to secure his own happiness or satisfaction.

The end and purpose of man, Hegel says, is the realization of freedom. A study of history reveals that a plan to achieve this end exists and that it is advanced through the operation of the dialectic. The beneficent workings of the dialectic are evidenced in the increasing superiority of the succeeding cultures and the gradual improvement of the institutions of the successively dominant nations which carry the Idea forward. A person can, then, know what has happened and what is happening.

When men understand that there *is* an Idea, that the state and its institutions constitute its temporal manifestation, and when they accept and subordinate themselves to the state and its institutions, then they are free. This is Hegel's definition of freedom. It consists, not in freedom from the state, but in understanding and accepting the Idea, which, in practical terms, means subordination to the state. Freedom is not exemption from authority but subjection to it. This is the ultimate realization of freedom. Not all are capable of understanding the paradox, but the progress of history shows that more people are attaining such a capability. The world has passed through three great epochs of history—the Oriental, the Greek, and the Roman. It is currently in the Germanic (a term which Hegel employs to describe the nations of the West) epoch. Each of these epochs has witnessed an advance in the development of freedom. As each epoch has succeeded its predecessor a greater number of people have achieved the capacity to understand and thus to be free. In the modern (Germanic) epoch for the first time it is possible for all men to be free. They are not free yet, but the inevitable progress of the Idea will bring universal freedom. The progress of man toward the realization of freedom has been and will continue to be costly; wars and conflicts of all kinds, being the essence of the dialectical process, create misery for mankind. But, again, happiness is not the goal of man; the goal is freedom, and this can be accomplished only through an understanding of the process and through subjection to the state, the material means by which the Idea progresses. As the state is necessary to the march of the World Spirit and is a means to that end, so the individual is a means to the end of the state which serves that purpose.

All men are instruments, but some are more active and valuable than others. The great majority of men are passive. They accept what comes and make no attempt to alter the course of things. Others are activists. They may be devoted to the status quo (thesis) or to reform or revolution (antithesis); in either case they are the agents of the dialectical process. They are the "heroes" of history, the devoted, single-minded and strong men without whom progress could not occur. They are not philosophers. They may understand no better than the average man the meaning of the Idea, and they are not interested in advancing its cause. They are essentially interested in serving their own interests. To the degree that they are instruments of the Idea, they are unwitting instruments. Those who seek change do not associate the need for it with some great historical plan. They know only that change is necessary, that a system and its institutions have outlived their usefulness and become invalid. Their greatness stems not only from their ability to achieve change but also from their instinctive knowledge that a time for change has arrived. In a Machiavellian vein, Hegel exempts the heroes of history from the moral judgments assessed against ordinary men. Codes of morals are products of an established culture, and they must be transcended if that culture is to give way to a new one. It is "irrelevant and inappropriate" to judge the great men of world history on the basis of conventional standards of morality; they are beyond such standards. Such things as modesty, charity, and love, which are deemed virtues among ordinary men, have nothing to do with the "heroes." An intelligent and realistic appraisal of world history would not deal with individuals at all. Only the actions of the "spirit of peoples" matter. Only history in the "narrow sense" pays attention to individuals. History in the grand sense, Hegel says, is indifferent to the petty strictures of individual morality.[9] It is, in fact, indifferent to individuals. Its concern is with peoples, not persons, for the civilizations of whole peoples express, at any given time in history, the meaning of the Idea at that stage of history.

Similarly, the individual is important only as a citizen. Only in his relationship to the state does his existence have meaning. The state is God's instrument for achieving his purpose; it follows that the individual must act in accordance with that purpose. His total identity is, therefore, inextricably bound up in the state. Whatever fulfillment he achieves will be found in service to it. Man may not *use* the state; the state, on the contrary, uses him. His freedom, again, does not consist in throwing off the restraint of state power but in knowingly and willingly subjecting himself to that power. Whenever the individual follows the dictates of a private and selfish will he is acting contrary to the demands imposed by the Idea. He is not free when he acts in such a manner; he is, instead, a slave. Selfish action is opposed to the Idea and thus to the real will of the individual himself. The free person always acts in accordance with the Idea as expressed by the state. The time will come when he will possess a degree of understanding that will enable him to do this voluntarily; then he will experience the full realization of freedom. But until that time it will be necessary to force him to be free. There is, in Hegel's theory, no conflict between freedom and authority. The similarity of this aspect of Hegel's theory to Rousseau's view of the general will is apparent.

Through the overgrowth of philosophical abstraction which partially obscures it, Hegel's immediate purpose may be perceived. That purpose was essentially nationalistic. Hegel was appalled by the particularism that plagued his country and prevented it from taking its place as a unified nation with other great powers of the West. The divisive forces within made Germany prey to its neighbors, and yet those forces claimed justification in the name of freedom. Hegel argued that freedom which stands in the way of national unity is a false, an anarchistic, freedom and that it must give way to the true freedom which can be found only in the discipline exerted by the national state. Hegel rejected the con-

[9] Hegel, *Philosophy of History*, pp. 29–30.

cept of freedom associated with individualism and made freedom an attribute of membership in the state. If such a concept were given actual form, a nation could be created with the strength to enforce its will domestically and with respect to other nations.[10] This could never be accomplished by securing the consent of all those involved. The democratic doctrine of consent, in Hegel's opinion, was something which would have validity only in a distant future when all men were free. For the time being a strong leader, willing to use force and unrestrained by the conventional standards of morality, was necessary.

Hegel's rejection of the individualism that had developed in the seventeenth and eighteenth centuries was thoroughgoing, but it has often been misunderstood. His theory has been misapplied when it has been used to support a totalitarian system in which the individual is subject to the unrestrained power of a government controlled by a dictator or party. Hegel's ideal was the unity of the city-state of antiquity, or rather what he believed it to have been, not the totalitarian leviathan which developed in the twentieth century. He believed that to view the individual as a separate entity, valuable in and of himself, was to see a false image. Man is what he is because of the society in which he lives, and he cannot in any legitimate fashion be viewed apart from it. Freedom, therefore, should not be thought of in terms of the individual gratification of selfish desire; the individual's debt to, and reliance on, society is too great for such self-regard. Freedom, true freedom, is being able to perform some socially useful and acceptable task. Rights and liberties are social, not individual, and they are relative to the position a person occupies in society. Hegel's view may be contrasted to the individualism of Hobbes and Locke. Their theories of the state of nature and the social contract were designed to set the individual apart from society and provide him with rights against it. For Hegel the only valuable rights are social, those which the individual enjoys as a part of society. This does not mean that Hegel believed power to be the basis of society or that society should not rest on law.

> For the hardest thing which man can experience is to be so far excluded from thought and reason, from respect for the laws, and from knowing how infinitely important and divine it is that the duties of the state and the rights of citizens, as well as the rights of the state and the duties of citizens, should be defined by law.[11]

Nor does Hegel believe that the state should absorb all the loyalties of the individual. He proposes that local communes, economic interests, and other such bodies form a barrier between the individual and the state and thus serve to modify the impact of state power upon the citizen.

---

[10] Sabine, *op. cit.*, p. 633.
[11] Hegel, *Philosophy of Right*, par. 258.

Hegel's view of the relationship of church and state was not totalitarian. The state, he says should require all citizens to belong to some religious faith, but it is not the business of the state to determine what that faith shall be. It may even countenance organizations which deny the right of members to do their whole duty as citizens.[12] The church itself, insofar as it has worldly functions, such as the ownership of property, comes under the jurisdiction of the state. The state, however, should not interfere in any spiritual matter. Hegel favors a considerable degree of separation of church and state, although he does not base this on the ground that the state deals only with material, and the church with spiritual, things. The state, the instrument of God, has a sacred duty to perform.

Hegel distinguishes between the state, which is the realm of social value, and the civil society, which is the realm of particular and selfish interest. Men in civil society organize to advance their "common *particular* interests." If doing so does not adversely affect the general interest, the state should not interfere with their actions. Nevertheless, civil society and institutions and organizations are subject to state control in any matters that affect social value, or the general interest. Hegel is fearful of the dangers of overcentralization of governmental power. This, he says, was one of the unfortunate results of the Revolution in France. He advocates some freedom in civil society, but he also recognizes the danger of particularism and maintains the superior position of the state in order to check it.

The State and Constitutionalism

Unlike the rationalists, Hegel rejects the notion that reasonable men should construct the kind of constitution that will most adequately serve their purposes and best guarantee their rights. Constitutions, he says, develop over a period of time; they cannot be built as is a house. Or, more accurately, if their manufacture is attempted, the result will be a travesty. In his *The Philosophy of Right and Law,* Hegel points out that the institutions of a state can provide no more freedom for its citizens than their degree of consciousness of the Idea will permit. Governmental institutions will always accord with that necessity. "Every nation has the constitution appropriate to it and suitable for it," Hegel says.[13] If there is a tyranny, that is because a tyranny is the only system which will work at the time.

Nevertheless Hegel did not accept the existing situation in Germany as "rational." Rationality exists only in facts that express the Idea. The only "rational" governmental form for the present stage of historical development, Hegel says, is constitutional monarchy. Germans, if they

[12] Hegel is here referring to a religious sect which forbids the taking of oaths.
[13] Hegel, *Philosophy of Right,* par. 274.

are to follow the dictates of reason, of the Idea, must develop the kind of system already existing in some other nations of Western Europe. Hegel next proceeds to a consideration of the features of a suitable constitutional monarchy. In general, England provides the model for Hegel's constitutional system. The monarch of a constitutional monarchy, he says, should be primarily a symbol rather than a possessor of power. He is a representative of the sovereignty which is found in the organic whole of the people but which, for practical reasons, cannot be exercised by them. He need not be highly intelligent or have great administrative ability; the major functions of government are safely in the hands of other agencies. The monarch's power should not be arbitrary. The well-ordered state is based upon the law, and the law is supreme. "In a well-organized monarchy, the objective aspect belongs to law alone, and the monarch's part is merely to set to the law the subjective 'I will.' " [14] If Hegel rejects monarchical absolutism and even monarchical supremacy, he also repudiates the separation of powers. He sees clearly the negative connotations of the principle—that it is designed to prevent, rather than to facilitate, the exercise of state power. *Functions,* he says, should and must be separated in the interest of efficiency; each agency, however, should "contain aspects of the others." To isolate and make independent the government *powers* is fatal. Autonomy of the legislative and executive powers leads to destruction of the state.[15]

Aside from the monarchical functions, two others are to be performed in the political state—the legislative and the governmental. The legislative should have authority to make general rules.[16] The governmental or "administrative" power is "to subsume single cases and the spheres of particularity under the universal—the executive." [17] In other words the legislative formulates the rules and the administrative (including the judiciary) applies them. Administrators should be selected on the basis of their ability, not on the basis of birth, and this profession ought to be open to all.[18] Administrators should be chosen by (and, apparently, are responsible to) the monarch, who is "the decisive sovereign power." Administrators should not regard themselves as servants; rather their personal satisfaction should stem from doing their duty. If they do not do so, and seek to use their authority for selfish ends, the sovereign must protect the public.

There are three parts to Hegel's legislative. It should consist, he says, of the monarchical power and the governmental power as well as of the

[14] *Ibid.,* par. 280, addition.
[15] *Ibid.,* par. 272.
[16] *Ibid.,* par. 273.
[17] *Ibid.*
[18] *Ibid.,* par. 291.

estates or legislative body itself. The monarchical power should be represented because it has the authority to make a "final decision." The governmental power should be a part of the legislative because of its greater knowledge of affairs and of the actual needs of the state. Hegel proposes through this fusion of authorities and agencies to avoid the negativism that accompanies a system of separation of powers. He commends the English system in which ministers are required to be members of parliament. Where there is "independence" among the branches of government, he continues, the unity of the state is lost.

The legislative assembly should consist of deputies of the people represented in their estates. It is not the function of this assembly to make laws; neither the deputies nor those whom they represent are qualified to do this. Hegel insists that the notion of the liberals that the people, as such, know what is best for themselves is totally false. The people are the least suited of any part of the state to make any such determination. The deputies serve a number of valuable purposes, but lawmaking is not among them. Deputies are close to the administration of affairs on the lower levels; they may serve as observers and critics of the executive functions, and they can encourage administrators always to act in the general interest. The deputies also serve as mediators between the government and the people. They are themselves representatives of particular interests, but they also understand their dependence on government and state. As mediators in another capacity, deputies act with the governmental power to prevent the isolation of the monarchical authority from the people. Above all, the estates serve to develop the organic unity of the society. The people must be made aware of the essential wholeness of the community. They must come to regard themselves as a part, along with the agencies of political organization, of an organic entity. Through their deputies they can be made conscious of their vital part in the whole state, and they will, consequently, reject the dangerous idea that government is always a potential, and sometimes an actual, enemy. The estates perform a valuable function by providing a method through which the state enters the "subjective consciousness" of the citizens.[19]

The great value of the constitution generally, Hegel says, is that it serves a mediating function. In a despotism nothing stands between the single ruler and his subjects. The relationship is too direct. The people have no role to play and thus no responsibility. A despot is ordinarily compelled to appease his subjects and abuse his immediate supporters. He must tax the few too heavily in order to avoid antagonizing the multitude, for he fears their collective power. Lacking a constitution and the mediating forces available in a constitutional system, the people are

[19] *Ibid.*, par. 301, addition.

prone to act as a mob in effecting their will. Constitutionalism permits the interests of the people to be served "in a lawful and orderly way" and imposes a responsibility upon them.

The people in a constitutional system must be represented. They cannot govern directly. Moreover it is a mistake to assume that deputies should directly represent the people in their individual capacity. The estates should be based upon a functional rather than a geographic and populational system of representation. The state does not consist of a mass of singular individuals but of a number of organized groups. It is through membership in these groups that the individual has meaning, that he is a member of the state, and that he is entitled to a voice in public affairs. Hegel says: "The concrete state is the whole, articulated into its particular groups. The member of a state is a member of such a group, i.e., of a social class, and it is only as characterized in this objective way that he comes under a consideration when we are dealing with the state." [20] Hegel expresses his complete scorn for the individualist view that private persons understand what ought to be done and possess the capacity to do it.

> To hold that every single person should share in deliberating and deciding on political matters of general concern on the ground that all individuals are members of the state, that its concerns are their concerns, and that it is their right that what is done should be done with their knowledge and volition, is tantamount to a proposal to put the democratic element without any rational form into the organism of the state, although it is only in virtue of the possession of such a form that the state is an organism at all.[21]

Delegates are not responsible for representing *all* the people but only those in the organized groups who have knowledge, experience, and interest. Elections, says Hegel, are "superfluous." Within the various groups certain individuals will emerge who, owing to their obviously superior capacity, ought to be chosen (in some manner which Hegel does not specify) by the members of the groups. These persons, as delegates, should represent the interest, rather than the individuals, of their group. Because they know better than their constituents what the real welfare of the groups demands, they are not obliged to consult with them. To take direction from constituents is to serve their false will. To ignore such demands when they run counter to the best judgment of the deputies is to follow the real will of the group. The parallel to Burke's views on representation is obvious.

It is a duty of delegates to instruct their constituents in what constitutes their real interest. In the debates of the assembly, in the publicity that attends the search for proper policies, the public may be informed.

[20] *Ibid.*, par. 308.
[21] *Ibid.*

Public opinion should be both "respected" and "despised." The public is never able to formulate concrete policies, but the "essential basis" of popular opinion may contain elements of validity. If delegates disregard what they know to be evidences of selfish particularism in the demands of public opinion they will find that ultimately the public will accept what has been done on the basis of the independent judgment of the delegates and "make it one of its prejudices." The great leaders of history are those who find and follow the truth in the face of public opposition. Hegel says that those who do not learn how to ignore public opinion will never achieve greatness.[22]

That Hegel deals with public opinion at all is significant. Since there can be no public opinion without some freedom of expression, Hegel considers the problems growing out of freedom of speech and press. It is, he understands, a highly complicated matter that cannot be disposed of in a simple and clear-cut fashion. The opinions of an individual are his property and are thus entitled to respect. On the other hand, the expression of an opinion which does damage to other persons, public or private, or which tends to subvert the government must be restrained by law. Caution must be exercised in imposing restrictions, however, and the rule should be that a concrete danger must be threatened before restrictions are justified. Moreover, learning and scholarship are not aspects of public opinion; rather, they deal with truth, and the standards of judgment applied to public opinion should not apply to them.

International Relations and International Law

One who insists that conflict is necessary to progress can hardly be expected to be a pacifist. Hegel's views on international relations are in harmony with his philosophy of history. Peace, internal or external, should not be a goal of the state. Those who insist that the purpose of the state is to protect the lives and the property of citizens err most seriously. The function of the state is to carry forward the Idea in history, and this process cannot proceed in tranquility. In peace lies stagnation. In time of peace, men become corrupt; they tend to be governed more and more by their concern for the particular interest. The body politic requires unity, however, and particularism destroys unity.[23] The bearing of this view upon individual citizens is apparent. Men should always subordinate themselves to the purposes of the state; freedom lies only in so doing. Service to the state in any capacity is highly desirable. Service involving the sacrifice of one's life in the state's interest is most valuable. Far from decrying the necessity of standing armies, Hegel insists upon it. Professional militarism has the "characteristic of courage," and when the safety of the state demands it, all citizens have a duty

[22] *Ibid.*, par. 318.
[23] *Ibid.*, par. 324, addition.

to rally to its defense. Finally, the direction of the military and the general conduct of the affairs of the state in its relations with other states should be in the hands of the monarch.

Hegel rejects the proposition that the relationships among states can be based upon a system of international law. There can be no law, he says, without an agency of enforcement.

> States are not private persons, but completely autonomous totalities in themselves. . . . Since there is no power in existence which decides in face of the state what is right in principle and actualizes this decision, it follows that so far as international relations are concerned we can never get beyond an "ought." The relation between states is a relation between autonomous entities which make mutual stipulations but which at the same time are superior to these stipulations.[24]

We must not conclude that Hegel opposes good relations among nations or that he believes that such relations cannot be honorable. States *ought* to keep their promises, but since there is no higher sovereignty than that of the state, no legitimate power can compel them to do so. Hegel says that Kant's proposal that international peace be maintained by a federation of states assumes an agreement among states based upon moral and religious grounds or similar considerations; and since such considerations rest entirely upon the wills of the sovereigns involved, they are therefore "infected with contingency." [25] Agreements must rest upon the good will of the states involved; where that fails, war is the only recourse. War, moreover, should be understood for what it is—a necessary historical event. It is a material reflection of the operation of the dialectic, of the clash of ideas in history. There is nothing personal in war, and it ought not to give rise to personal animosities between peoples. Hostility should be confined to those who perform a direct military function. War itself should be regarded as a transitory phase, and it should be conducted as humanely as possible. Ambassadors, through whose offices peace may be restored, ought to be respected, and war should not be waged against private persons, their families, and private lives. In short, Hegel is saying that although there can be no true international law, certain conventions are valuable and should be observed.

Conclusions

It is extraordinarily difficult to analyze and classify Hegel's political thought. As was pointed out at the beginning of the chapter, Hegel's ideas have been used to support the disparate theories of both communism and fascism. The fact is that Hegel belongs in neither of those camps. His theory, although he would have strongly denied it, was a

[24] *Ibid.*, par. 330, addition.
[25] *Ibid.*, par. 333.

product of his time and environment. Stripped of its abstractions and seen through the many difficult passages that mark his writings, Hegel's is essentially an appeal to Germans to unite and to adopt the constitutional form developed by the English people. Of course it is not quite that simple; there are embellishments which have themselves become important. Moreover, Hegel had an abiding interest in theology, and this interest is reflected in the religious bent of his political theory. Another important characteristic of Hegel's theory is that it is so many-faceted that an eclectic approach to it by subsequent political theorists was a natural development. From almost any vantage point there is much to criticize and condemn in Hegel; the opportunity will not be neglected here. On the other hand, there has been considerable unfounded and unwarranted censure; this too should be considered.

Hegel has often been indicted as a spokesman for excessive nationalism, and indeed he was. Again, however, the times in which he lived and the peculiar and difficult situation of Germany must be taken into account in understanding his position. The parallels between Hegel's Germany and Machiavelli's Italy should be noted. And to the extent that nationalism is an affliction, it is at least suffered by most twentieth-century citizens. We must understand, too, that Hegel's theory is not the totalitarianism that many writers have read into it. Hegel obviously favored authoritarianism, but not totalitarianism. The misunderstanding has stemmed in part from the failure to accept Hegel's definition of the state. When Hegel spoke of the state and the relationship of the citizen to it he had in mind, as we have seen, something like the kind of community he supposed to have existed in ancient Greece. He was not anticipating or advocating the Third Reich. It was his view that the community was indispensable to the welfare of the individual, that rights were social and involved reciprocal duties, and that the state itself had a right to demand and enforce actions by individuals that were in the general interest. Hegel insisted upon garnishing this thesis with theological trimmings, but his intent seems clear. The state, as he conceives it, does not swallow the individual or make itself the focal point of all interest and loyalty. The demand for a measure of separation of church and state, for free speech and a free press, for the rights of local governments, all demonstrate Hegel's antipathy toward a totalitarian government. So too do his censure of the French for their over-centralization and his praise for constitutionalism and the rule of law. Yet Hegel is far from being a democrat or a defender of individualism. Various positions can be taken in the perennial conflict between the advocates of individualism and the defenders of authority. Although it is currently popular to see things in terms of black and white and to attach labels accordingly, it is nonetheless true that a considerable gap exists between anarchism and totalitarianism; or, to state it differently, the fact that one is not a fascist does not automatically make him a communist.

But if Hegel's individual is not entirely dominated by government, neither does he have a democratic existence under it. Hegel thought in terms of an established hierarchy in which the masses were dominated by an upper class over which they exercised no real control. Hegel is as adamant as Burke in his insistence that government should be in the hands of those who *know* and that whereas governmental representatives should have a careful regard for the welfare of their constituents, the latter should not be permitted to dictate how their interest should be served. There is, also, little room for individualism in a theory, such as Hegel's, which contends that all values are state or community values. A state seen as the material manifestation of God's will on earth does not conduce to pluralism.

This subjection of the individual to governmental power is one of the aspects of Hegel's philosophy that contributed to the later development of fascist theory. Another was Hegel's equation of power with morality. If the state is the representative of God's will, surely any exertion of that will is moral; one is no more entitled to object to it than he would be to protest an act of God himself. Might *is* right. There are also seeds of fascism in Hegel's assumption that there is and can be no authority higher than the nation state. Hegel is an international anarchist; he refuses to concede the possibility of either international law or an international organization with jurisdiction over nation states. We recognize a measure of common sense in Hegel's assertion that there can be no international law without an enforcing power, but Hegel's theory bars the way to any such development. This leads to Hegel's pronouncement, in connection with a discussion of his dialectic, that peaceful solutions are neither possible nor desirable. War is thus glorified rather than deprecated. We shall see, in a consideration of Karl Marx, how Hegel's dialectical theory of conflict becomes the central concept of modern Communist dogma.

Hegel supplies a metaphysics for Burke's conservative views, but Hegel is less conservative than Burke. Hegel is like Burke in that he sees the wisdom of the past in the institutions of the present; his philosophy of history makes anything else impossible. But Hegel is not so tied to the past as is Burke. Burke's voice was influential in support of the status quo; Hegel insisted that the status quo could not be maintained and that when men acted to preserve it they were in fact contributing to its destruction. In this Hegel was wiser than Burke, for one lesson that history teaches over and over again is that change is an inescapable fact and that governments and peoples seriously err when they fail to acknowledge this and adjust their institutions accordingly. It is understandable that a people should feel that what they have created is the best that has ever been and ought to be maintained. Hegel would agree that what *is* is better than what has gone before; but the World Spirit marches on, bringing constant change and increasing perfection. A recognition of this process and its inevitability Hegel regards as absolutely necessary to the freedom of man.

Finally, we must consider Hegel's ideas as they relate to freedom. As we have seen, Hegel defines freedom as recognition of, and subordination to, the Idea. But what does this definition signify in practical terms? Since the state is the Idea as it exists on earth, subordination to the Idea is subordination to the state. The question is, for what purpose? For one thing, Hegel believes that such an attitude is necessary to the form of national development he wishes for Germany. For another, this relationship between state and individual sustains the discipline necessary to unity. It repudiates the individualism that sees each person as an independent entity going his own way and securing his own advantage without regard for the whole. Hegel, like every other political theorist, is vitally concerned with the problem of the reconciliation of the particular and the general interest. It is the function of state and government to secure this reconciliation.

To a people committed to the idea that freedom is individual, to be conceived as freedom *from* state regulation, Hegel's view may be repugnant. Yet it must be acknowledged that the issue raised is important. The values of individualism are great, but carried too far they may also be damaging. The pursuit of individual interest may wreck the community, and it is the community which, in large part, makes a good life for the individual possible. We have explored the point previously, but may profitably reiterate it. A central issue—probably *the* central issue—in political life is that of determining the proper balance of individual and community interest, of establishing the acceptable scope for individual freedom and the proper limits of the regulatory authority of the community. In this controversy Hegel clearly takes his stand for the community. The concessions to individual freedom are slight. The individualist, who is bound to resent Hegel's position, should bear in mind that his own views on the matter may be too extreme. Freedom is highly desirable, but unlimited freedom is anarchy.

SELECTED BIBLIOGRAPHY

Georg Wilhelm Friedrich Hegel: Reason in History (translated, with an introduction by Robert S. Hartman), The Liberal Arts Press, Inc., New York, 1953, introduction.

Hacker, Andrew: *Political Theory: Philosophy, Ideology, Science,* The Macmillan Company, New York, 1961, chap. 11.

Hegel's Philosophy of Right (translated with notes by T. M. Knox), Oxford University Press, Fair Lawn, N.J., 1942.

Hobhouse, L. T.: *The Metaphysical Theory of the State,* The Macmillan Company, New York, 1918.

Hook, Sidney: *From Hegel to Marx: Studies in the Intellectual Development of Karl Marx,* The Humanities Press, New York, 1958, chap. 1.

Löwith, Karl: *Meaning in History,* The University of Chicago Press, Chicago, 1949, chap. 3.

McDonald, Lee Cameron: *Western Political Theory: The Modern Age,* Harcourt, Brace & World, Inc., New York, 1962, chap. 12.

Marcuse, Herbert: *Reason and Revolution: Hegel and the Rise of Social Theory,* Oxford University Press, Fair Lawn, N.J., 1941.

The Philosophy of Hegel (edited with an introduction and notes by Carl J. Friedrich), Modern Library, Inc., New York, 1953.

Sabine, George H.: *A History of Political Theory,* 3d ed., Holt, Rinehart and Winston, Inc., New York, 1961, chap. 30.

eighteen

BENTHAM AND MILL

Of the many factors that enter into a determination of the form and functioning of political institutions, none plays a more important role than economics. Marx is wrong in making economics the sole determining factor in human affairs, but his views on the subject have some validity. Economic causes are significant in any consideration of the development of political thought, and they are particularly applicable to that period and place, England from 1775 to 1875, which we shall consider in the present chapter. It was an era of dynamic change. England was becoming an industrial nation, and the industrial middle class, the moving force behind this transition, was demanding a political role commensurate with its contribution.

The path of that class to political preferment, however, was barred by the landowning classes. Presumably England had a representative legislative system; but a restricted suffrage and a scandalous array of rotten boroughs enabled a minority of landowners to maintain a practical monopoly of governmental authority not only in the House of Lords, where there was legal justification for a grossly undemocratic representation, but also in the House of Commons, which ostensibly represented the generality. The situation was to bring England to the brink of revolution in the 1830s, but fraught with peril as their course might be, the landowning class stubbornly resisted attempts to alter it. The Revolution of 1688 and the subsequent constitutional reform had stirred the hopes of the commercial class for a political system adapted to their own requirements; a period of reaction ensued, however, in which power reverted into the hands of their landowning antagonists. The commercial middle class lacked the ability and the numbers to do more than protest feebly. They were compelled to accept the crumbs that fell their way.

The rising industrial class was more aggressive. As their economic base broadened they demanded a share of political power sufficient to protect their economic interests. They had money and energy. They lacked a cohesive and persuasive theory and the spokesmen to exploit it. Why not employ the natural-rights theory with the corollaries, supplied by Locke, of contract, property, and representative and limited government? As theory, this ostensibly offered everything necessary. But in fact, while the theory itself appeared adequate to whatever demands the industrial class might make upon it, there were sound reasons why it was incapable of providing the necessary support. The natural-rights doctrine, with its revolutionary overtones, was discredited by the excesses of the French Revolution. Moreover, a theory so incapable of demonstration was unsatisfactory. If the theory were to be accepted it would have to win approval on the ground that its principles were, as Jefferson said, "self-evident." There was no way of proving that anyone had a "right" to life, liberty, and property. The right was a mere assumption, and it might as easily be assumed that other and antagonistic principles were equally self-evident. In addition, thinkers of the time were prone to favor the scientific approach, and this meant that they would prefer empiricism to the rationalism associated with natural rights. Finally, while they were strongly committed to the political principles that had developed out of the theory of natural rights, hard-headed businessmen were more interested in institutions than in theory, and they sought a demonstrable, thus empirical, theoretical base from which they could pursue their objectives.[1]

That base was established with the doctrine of utility, which proposed that the standard by which actions, both public and private, should be judged was the greatest happiness of the greatest number of people. Among those who espoused the principle, there were differences of opinion with respect to its application, but there were also wide areas of agreement. They shared the view that pleasure is the legitimate goal of all men and that an action should be deemed good insofar as it provides happiness for the greatest possible number. They agreed that in the calculation of this effect all men should be considered equal, that the happiness of one is as important as the happiness of any other. It was also the consensus that a determination of the legitimacy of government does not rest upon a contractual relationship between governors and gov-

[1] George H. Sabine, *A History of Political Theory*, 3d ed., Holt, Rinehart and Winston, Inc., New York, 1961, pp. 670–671.

erned but only upon utility, the capacity of government to provide its citizens with the greatest possible happiness.[2]

The elaboration of the principle of utility was the work of the philosophical radicals, especially of the acknowledged leader of the school, Jeremy Bentham. They did not, however, originate it. The fundamentals of utility had been stated by Hobbes and developed by Hume. The latter, indeed, was credited by Bentham with having started him in the right direction. The philosophical radicals were not likely to credit Hobbes with assistance; the reputation of the Sage of Malmesbury was still shady in his native England. Nevertheless he contributed greatly to the development of the utilitarian principle. Hobbes had rejected both of the major moral theories prevalent in Europe in his time. The first of these was that the principle object of man's existence is to fulfill the potential which he possesses; the second was that virtue consists of acting in accordance with rules of behavior which are discoverable by reason. Hobbes scorned the notion that men are capable of and seek moral improvement; they are interested in survival. Furthermore, Hobbes said, no rules of reason are binding upon men merely because human beings are rational and associated together in a society with others of their kind. If men act properly toward others it is not because of an innate moral urge or because such behavior is dictated by a rule of reason, but because they recognize that they will be more secure as a result. The state exists for the purpose of enforcing this kind of behavior.[3]

The utilitarians, with the exception of John Stuart Mill, whose contributions we shall consider later in this chapter, were concerned with happiness rather than with individual moral development. They rejected the idea that virtue is an end in itself. Virtue was not regarded as undesirable, but its value derived from the fact that it was a way to happiness. The state exists to secure the happiness of man, not to protect their natural rights. And the utilitarians believed, as did Hobbes, that men obey a ruler not because of a legal or moral obligation but only because it is in their interest to do so. The major political difference between Hobbes and the utilitarians is that Hobbes insisted that personal interests are best served by a powerful and unrestrained sovereign, while Bentham and his followers thought a limited government would best attain this end. Hobbes, whose greatest fear was of anarchy, believed that security was about all men could hope for. The utilitarians were far more optimistic; many things could bring happiness, and it was important to permit as much individual freedom as possible in the search for them.[4]

[2] John Plamenatz, *The English Utilitarians*, Basil Blackwell & Mott, Ltd., Oxford, 1949, p. 2.

[3] *Ibid.*, p. 11.

[4] *Ibid.*, pp. 12–16.

But Hume is the real founder of utilitarianism; he is the first clearly to enunciate the principle of utility and to lay the basis upon which Bentham and his followers were to build. In his *Treatise of Human Nature* and his *Enquiry concerning the Principles of Morals,* Hume attempts empirically to deduce "general maxims" relating to moral principles "from a comparison of particular instances." [5] Hume concludes that passion, rather than reason, determines the ends that men pursue. Men seek pleasure and avoid pain. The principle applies to all men— not that all men experience pleasure and pain equally, but that the feelings are universally shared. Experience teaches men to determine which things bring pain or pleasure. Hume is not so egoistic as Hobbes. Men have a sympathy for their fellows, and sympathy gives rise to benevolence, the desire to bring happiness to others. Admittedly, Hume says, sympathy is not the strongest of sentiments, unless those toward whom it is directed are close to us in family relationship or friendship; nevertheless the sentiment exists and is important. Hume's political theory rejects natural rights, natural law, and the contract theory of government. He assumes, as does Hobbes, that men are essentially selfish and unwise. Left to their own devices they will seek their own interest, but they are not sufficiently intelligent to know what that interest really is. They will invariably seek a short-range advantage that is contrary to their long-range interest. The purpose of government is to compel men to follow a course of conduct which is advantageous in the long run. The justification of government is dependent upon how well it sets men upon such a course; in other words, the justification is determined by the utility of the government.[6] It was after reading Hume's description of this principle in the *Treatise of Human Nature* that Bentham, who was searching for an acceptable standard by which he could proceed with his plan for reforming the legal system of England, said that he felt as if the scales had fallen from his eyes. He added to Hume's principle the idea of "the greatest happiness of the greatest number." He had first seen this phrase in a pamphlet entitled *Essay on Government,* by Joseph Priestley, and been impressed by it. The combination formed the foundation of the philosophy which was the guiding principle throughout Bentham's long and fruitful life.

Jeremy Bentham: The Man and His Work

Jeremy Bentham was born in London on February 15, 1748. His father was a prosperous attorney whose generosity enabled his son to spend his life in study and contemplation. The young Jeremy was a precocious child. He is said to have been reading Latin and historical works written in English at the age of three. He wrote Latin and was reading Voltaire when he was six. In 1755 he began attendance at Westminster School

[5] David Hume, *Enquiry concerning the Principles of Morals,* I, 5. Quoted in *ibid.,* p. 24.
[6] *Ibid.,* pp. 39–40.

where he acquired a reputation for his writing of Latin verse. He found his studies repetitious and dull, however, and was little better pleased with the course of instruction at Queen's College, Oxford, where he matriculated at the age of thirteen. Nevertheless he persevered and received his degree, at the age of fifteen, in 1763. It was his father's fondest wish that Jeremy would follow in his footsteps in the legal profession. The young Bentham, without enthusiasm, began his study of law at Lincoln's Inn. He heard Blackstone lecture at Oxford and conceived a dislike for the views expressed by that eminent jurist.

Bentham detested the practice of law, and after a brief and unsatisfactory experience with it he retired to a life of study and writing, much to the disappointment of his father. In 1776 he published his *Fragment on Government.* The work constituted a thorough analysis of, and attack on, the conservative principles of Blackstone. The *Fragment* was issued anonymously and created a considerable stir in legal circles. The work was variously attributed to such legal luminaries as Camden, Mansfield, and Ashburton. The elder Bentham, who knew the secret of its authorship, was unable to restrain his pride, and revealed that his son had written the *Fragment.* As a result interest in the book declined precipitously. Bentham was generally thought to be too young to be regarded seriously. Still it established for him a modest reputation and attracted the attention of some notables, the most important of whom was Lord Shelburne, who became a lifelong friend of Bentham.

In 1785 Bentham visited his brother, a naval engineer, who was at the time in the service of the Russian government. He remained in Russia about two and a half years. Here he wrote his *Defence of Usury,* in which he defended the lending of money at interest upon what Bentham conceived to be sound Smithian principles; in fact Bentham's logic carried him somewhat beyond Adam Smith's position. The work is noteworthy for its radical laissez-faire views (to be somewhat modified later in Bentham's *Manual of Political Economy*). Bentham returned to England in 1788. In the following year he published his best-known work, *Introduction to the Principles of Morals and Legislation.* It greatly enhanced Bentham's reputation, which soon was as great on the Continent and in America as in England. He was vitally interested in the practical issues of reform; moreover, he was not inclined to undervalue his own ability to prescribe either reforms or the methods by which they could be achieved. Although seriously lacking in the kind of experience that grows out of participation in the affairs of life, Bentham freely advised his own and other governments of their duties. After the Revolution in France he wrote to instruct the new French government on the method of representation which they should adopt and proposed a widening of the suffrage and adoption of the secret ballot. The French ignored the advice, albeit politely, and made Bentham a citizen of France, an honor which he accepted as his due but without any noticeable excitement.

In the affairs of his own country Bentham was something of a gadfly. He interested himself in a multitude of reform measures and argued at length for them. His early assumption was that it was only necessary to indicate to the ruling class of England what ought to be done and they would proceed to enact the appropriate measures. As the years passed, and England's rulers indicated little eagerness for reform, Bentham was ultimately disillusioned. He was finally persuaded by his friend and disciple, James Mill, that political reform would have to precede legal reform. Bentham the Tory became Bentham the liberal reformer, the philosophical radical. In 1823 he established the *Westminster Review,* a journal through which Bentham and his associates disseminated their ideas. Although Bentham did not live to witness the success of his many proposals, he came closer to doing so than do most political theorists. A number of the measures he recommended were incorporated in the Reform Act of 1832, which became law shortly after his death. Others followed as the century progressed. The ideas of Bentham and his followers had an enormous impact upon the development of the British political system. Bentham died on June 6, 1832, at the age of eighty-five. His request that his body be dissected and his skeleton preserved in London at University College, which he was responsible for founding, was honored.

The Fragment on Government

In our consideration of Bentham's ideas we shall be mainly concerned with his two works, the *Fragment on Government* and the *Principles of Morals and Legislation.* The first is essentially critical in nature but is important because it clears the way and establishes the groundwork for the second. The *Fragment* is more than an assault upon Blackstone; it is an attack upon the system of English law in general. That system was shot through with anachronisms, injustices, and confusion. It had failed to take into account the great changes that had occurred in English life. It needed to be reformed and brought in line with the new prevailing circumstances. Blackstone's mistake, Bentham thought, lay in his complacency, his assurance that the English system of government and law was entirely adequate to the purposes it was designed to serve and that the great necessity was only to understand and preserve it.

Against this complacent acceptance Bentham argued that the legal system was inadequate and that it is the duty of men to criticize it. "This much is certain," Bentham says, "that a system that is never to be censured, will never be improved; that if nothing is ever to be found fault with, nothing will ever be mended." [7] It is a "busy age" in which we live.

---

[7] Jeremy Bentham, *A Fragment on Government* (edited with an introduction by F. C. Montague), Oxford University Press, London, 1891, preface.

one in which "knowledge is rapidly advancing towards perfection." [8] As there is "discovery" and "improvement" in the natural world (achieved by the natural sciences) so there must be "reformation in the moral." We must discontinue our proclivity to view things with a "disposition to find everything as it should be." The resistance to innovation would be lessened if we would understand that "whatever *now* is established, *once* was innovation." [9] The criticism is directed toward the conservatism of Blackstone, but Bentham also unknowingly provided a persuasive rebuttal to the later arguments proposed by Burke in his *Reflections*.

In our appraisal of the law, Bentham says, we should not base our judgment on how long the law has been established or on how well it accords with a set of a priori principles. Such a practice leads not only to inaction and atrophy of the law, but also makes the law an instrument of the judges and the legal profession. The obfuscation attending this development enables judges to usurp the legislative function and prevent the use of the law in the general interest. Bentham strongly favors codification of the law in the interest of clarity. Moreover, the law must be improved, and this can be done only if a new and acceptable standard is established by which it may be judged. The standard is utility, in the law as in all human action.

> Now then, with respect to actions in general, there is no property in them that is calculated so readily to engage, and so firmly to fix the attention of an observer, as the *tendency* they may have *to,* or *divergency* (if one may so say) *from,* that which may be styled the common *end* of all of them. The end I mean is *Happiness:* and this *tendency* in any act is what we style its *utility:* as this divergency is that to which we give the name of *mischievousness.*[10]

With such a standard, Bentham says, we may easily judge the goodness or badness of a law. It is the consequences of a law that are important. Determine what those consequences are in terms of the pleasure they bring or the pain they cause, and assess the value of the law accordingly. Furthermore, men will not need to consult a lawyer in order to make such a determination; this is something all men can understand.

Bentham agrees with Hume that the contract theory of government is useless except as a device for exploring the general subject of political obligation. Blackstone's reliance upon the contract theory is caustically repudiated. The contract is a mere fiction, and "the season of Fiction is now over." Fictions once had their uses (a bow in the direction of Locke), but they are no longer necessary. Such fictions as "original contract," "law of nature," and "right reason" constitute chimeras which have

[8] *Ibid.*
[9] *Ibid.*
[10] *Ibid.* Italics are in the original.

"been effectually demolished by Mr. Hume." [11] The fact is, Bentham says, that men obey government when and if it is in their interest to do so. Utility, not contract, is the basis of political obligation. Rulers and ruled may go through the farcical ceremony of establishing contractual obligations, but in the end men will "obey . . . *so long as the probable mischiefs of obedience are less than the probable mischiefs of resistance.*" [12]

Bentham goes on to jeer at Blackstone's unquestioning acceptance of Montesquieu's analysis of the virtues of the English constitution. Blackstone had followed without qualification the classic definition of governmental forms—monarchy, aristocracy, and democracy—and attributed to the English system the best qualities of each, "the disadvantages vanishing at the word of command, or even without it, as not being suitable to the purpose." [13] Blackstone, Bentham points out, had admitted the existence of corruptions of these ideal forms, tyranny, oligarchy, and ochlocracy ("a sort of government fit to break one's teeth"), but he had ignored the possibility that the English constitution contained elements of any of these. The error, Bentham says, stems from Blackstone's confusion of ideality and actuality. He assumes, for example, the independence of each of the legislative powers, king, Lords, and Commons, and ignores the power of the king over the Commons, the power to dissolve it and to influence it by bestowing and taking away offices and various kinds of profits. Bentham comments acidly on Blackstone's assumption that the House of Lords represents ability because of the titles attached to its members. "Seeing that some are bishops, he knows that they are pious: seeing that some are peers, he knows that they are wise, rich, valiant." [14]

To judge the adequacy of government on such grounds is asinine. A government is not good or bad because it has a given number of branches which function in a given manner. These may indeed be important matters, but they are only means to an end and should not be considered ends in themselves. The only principle by which government may be judged is that of utility. A government which does not enact laws that conduce to the greatest happiness of the greatest number will incur resentment and may provoke revolution no matter how it may be constituted. To employ utility as a guide is to decide on the basis of fact rather than on the basis of emotion or metaphysical conjectures. If disagreement ensues, as it surely will, there will at least be a common ground upon which the disputants can meet.

[11] *Ibid.*, I, 36.
[12] *Ibid.*, I, 43. Italics are in the original.
[13] *Ibid.*, II, 28.
[14] *Ibid.*, III, 7.

The Principles of Morals and Legislation

In his *Fragment,* Bentham removes the undergrowth of a priori principles. He also establishes what he regards as a sensible foundation for the construction of a scientific political theory for his *Principles of Morals and Legislation.* He takes his cue from Hobbes in making psychology the basis of that theory; indeed his psychology is essentially that of Hobbes. The assumption of both is that a realistic political theory must take human nature into account. Failing this, the foundation will crumble, and the superstructure will inevitably fall. What is the source of human action? If this can be determined and employed as the foundation, the structure which arises from it will be correspondingly firm. Bentham begins his *Principles* with an answer to this problem. The motives of pain and pleasure lead men to act as they do.

> Nature has placed mankind under the governance of two sovereign masters, *pain* and *pleasure.* It is for them alone to point out what we ought to do, as well as to determine what we shall do. On the one hand the standard of right and wrong, on the other the chain of causes and effects, are fastened to their throne. They govern us in all we do, in all we say, in all we think: every effort we can make to throw off our subjection, will serve but to demonstrate and confirm it. In words a man may pretend to abjure their empire: but in reality he will remain subject to it all the while. The *principle of utility* recognizes this subjection and assumes it for the foundation of that system, the object of which is to rear the fabric of felicity by the hands of reason and of law. Systems which attempt to question it, deal in sounds instead of sense, in caprice instead of reason, in darkness instead of light.[15]

Bentham proceeds next to a definition of the "principle of utility."

> By the principle of utility is meant that principle which approves or disapproves of every action whatsoever, according to the tendency which it appears to have to augment or diminish the happiness of the party whose interest is in question: or, what is the same thing in other words, to promote or to oppose that happiness. I say of every action whatsoever; and therefore not only of every action of a private individual, but of every measure of government.[16]

The principle of utility is the heart of Bentham's theory; all else is elaboration, explanation, and application. Bentham says that every human action is motivated by the desire to obtain as much pleasure and avoid as much pain as possible. Morality is judged by these measuring sticks. What brings pleasure is good; what produces pain is bad. Any

[15] Jeremy Bentham, *An Introduction to the Principles of Morals and Legislation* (with an introduction by Laurence J. La Fleur), Hafner Publishing Company, New York, 1948, chap. 1, sect. 1.

[16] *Ibid.,* I, 2.

system purporting to judge morality on any other basis lacks "sense" and "reason." The principle of utility recognizes this fact, and measures the acts of both private persons and governments accordingly.

Utility is what the legislator must understand. In framing legislation, he must consider only the probable effect, in terms of pain and pleasure, of a proposed legislative measure upon the community. That measure is best which brings the greatest happiness and the least pain to the greatest number. It should be understood that Bentham's theory here is individualistic rather than communitarian. Whereas he speaks of the happiness of the greatest number and is obviously concerned with the welfare of the community, he cautiously points out that there is no community as such, but only individuals. In calculating the happiness of the community, the happiness of the individual members must be taken into account. As Bentham states it: "The community is a fictitious *body*, composed of the individual persons who are considered as it were its *members*. The interest of the community then is, what?—the sum of the interests of the several members who compose it." [17] The theory is also equalitarian. In calculating the effects of pain and pleasure for the community, each member counts for one and only one. The legislator must not consider the happiness of one group as more important than that of any other.

Bentham is quite aware of the fact that an application of the principle of utility is not so simple as it may appear to be from the foregoing discussion. On the face of the matter, apparently many logical objections can be made to the idea that pain and pleasure constitute the sole motivating force among men. Bentham recognizes, for example, that some persons appear to be moved by a desire to avoid pleasure and seek pain; Bentham terms this the principle of asceticism. Such persons, he argues, merely misapply the principle of utility but do not refute it; for them, pain is happiness and pleasure is pain. Fortunately there are few such misguided souls. If only "one-tenth" followed this principle they would turn the whole earth "into a hell." [18] Some persons, also, argue that the theological principle is superior to the principle of utility; the standard of good and bad is determined by reference to the will of God. This method, however, Bentham says, does not provide a sufficiently explicit basis upon which to enact legislation.

A legislator who is charged with the responsibility of calculating the consequences for the community of a particular piece of legislation must also be aware of the complications which stem from the existence of many kinds of pain and pleasure, and he must know how to measure them. Fortunately for the legislator, Bentham provides help here. There are, he says, fourteen simple pleasures: sense, wealth, skill, amity, good

[17] *Ibid.*, I, 4.
[18] *Ibid.*, II, 10.

name, power, piety, benevolence, malevolence, memory, imagination, expectation, association, and relief. There are twelve simple pains: privation, senses, awkwardness, enmity, ill name, piety, benevolence, malevolence, memory, imagination, expectation, and association. A sensation may produce either pain or pleasure depending upon the manner in which it is experienced; thus Bentham places some sensations in both categories. All sorts of subdivisions and combinations of these are possible, and Bentham reviews the possibilities in great detail. Finally, there must be standards of measurement for the various pains and pleasures. Seven factors must be considered—intensity, duration, certainty or uncertainty, propinquity or remoteness, fecundity, purity, and extent. The meaning, with only two exceptions, is clear. In calculating the effect of any pain or pleasure, the legislator must consider among other things such matters as how intense it is, how long it lasts, and how many people are affected. The factors of fecundity and purity require a word of explanation because Bentham, as is his wont, attributes special meanings to them. Neither, he says, is a property of pain and pleasure; rather, they represent the propensities of an act to produce or not to produce consequences, in terms of pain or pleasure. Fecundity thus means the possibility of an act "being followed by sensations of the *same* kind." Purity refers to the possibility of an act "not being followed by sensations of the *opposite* kind."

Here, then, is Bentham's "felicific calculus." What can be said in appraising it? Obviously it is replete with absurdities, particularly in categorizing the kinds of pain and pleasure and providing the means of their measurement. There are more varieties of pain and pleasure and more possible combinations than Bentham knew. The problem is highly complex, and Bentham did not have the knowledge to solve it. Both social and natural science are concerned with the problem today, and yet, in spite of all that has been done, the surface is barely scratched. Still, Bentham's speculations are far from useless. His clearly stated view that it is the function of government to act in such a manner as to maximize pleasure and minimize pain for the greatest number of people could hardly be repudiated in any democratic system. Even many who rejected other aspects of Bentham's theory accepted that one. The chief argument is over the choice of standards by which such a goal is to be attained. The natural-rights school, which Bentham was determined to refute, contended that the standards which a legislator must consult were to be found through reason in the a priori principles of natural law. Bentham calls this view impractical, mere metaphysical nonsense. How is one to know what those principles are, and how may the adequacy of reason be determined? The natural-rights idea, Bentham says, leads to stagnation, decay, and revolution. Rulers take it upon themselves to define principles and employ the reason necessary to effectuate them. In practice, the result is a perversion of the utilitarian principle; the greatest happiness of the smallest number is achieved at the expense of the greatest number.

Pain and pleasure are things that can be understood by everyone. If we acknowledge that they should form the standard by which governmental action is judged, and if we further concede that the greatest happiness or pleasure of the greatest number (each person to be counted as equal to every other) should be sought, then a community can function in the best interest of all. Admittedly, Bentham says, calculation to achieve the desired result is difficult. Nevertheless calculation is more likely to gain its end than is a reliance upon a priori principles; it is at least a scientific basis upon which to proceed. Bentham would probably have been even more sanguine than he was with respect to the possibilities of his system had he been able to foresee such modern developments as the public opinion poll, the legislative committee system, and others designed to determine not only what people want but also what is good for them.

Bentham was, in large part, attracted to the principle of utility because of his antagonism to the theory of natural rights, with its a priori assumptions, which he regarded as insupportable. Yet Bentham's theory is itself not entirely free from such assumptions. Bentham contends that a policy or action is justifiable if it produces the greatest happiness of the greatest number. This should be the basis of decision rather than the mere assertion of "rights," which are generally stated only to disguise the pursuit of selfish interest. In the first place, this view may be accepted apart from all the intricacies of the "felicific calculus." More important, however, is the fact that in stating this view Bentham is assuming that the principle of the greatest happiness of the greatest number is valid. He makes no attempt to prove the point. He admits, indeed, that it is unnecessary and impossible to prove it, "for that which is used to prove every thing else, cannot itself be proved." [19] Here, it seems, is one of those self-evident truths that Bentham found so loathsome in the natural-rights theory. The same test may be applied to Bentham's assertion that, in applying the principle of utility, all persons should be counted as equal. What proof can be offered that the happiness of one is as valuable and important as the happiness of another? This is strictly a matter of belief. It is probably a highly admirable view, but it is not proved by Bentham and is quite possibly unprovable.

Bentham's Political Theory

The fact is that the principle of utility was directly in line with Bentham's own nature. He was a kindly man. He was given, on occasion, to bitter attacks on those who disagreed with his views, but his human-

[19] *Ibid.*, I, 9.

itarian sympathies are clear. He was deeply concerned with the welfare of his fellow men and even of dumb animals. He was an ardent opponent of such "sports" as bullbaiting and cockfighting. His deep and abiding interest in prison reform and in the reform of criminal law are also indicative of Bentham's benignancy. But his wide sympathy did not mean that Bentham was a democrat. One may love his fellows and be interested in their welfare without regarding them as capable of self-government. This was the stand Bentham took, particularly in his early years. He was still a Tory when he wrote his *Principles,* and the mildly elitist nature of his ideas at the time is evident in that treatise. The legislator should, he says, on the basis of the "felicific calculus," establish a system of rewards and punishments designed to move men in the proper direction. It is the principle of the carrot and the stick, with government in the driver's seat, and there is no hint in those early writings that government should be reconstituted in a democratic manner. Bentham favored, with Adam Smith and the classical economists, a large measure of individual freedom in the realm of economics. Like Smith, he thought that the general interest would best be served if men were at liberty to pursue their economic interests with little governmental restraint. But when it came to the matter of moral behavior, he was not so optimistic about the beneficial results flowing from individual liberty. Here a system of rewards and punishments must be established and invoked by government.

In supporting this view Bentham was not suggesting severe limitations on the freedom of the individual. The very principle of utility implies limits upon the power of government. Government has authority to act to produce the greatest happiness of the greatest number; it may legitimately do nothing else. Moreover, in many instances the action of individuals may voluntarily be directed to this end, and here government ought not to interfere. Also, Bentham says in the *Fragment on Government,* men should be informed by government with respect to what is being done and why. They have a right to know and a right to protest and oppose. In addition, government ought to be responsible, and the only way to see that it exercises responsibility is to have a system that facilitates the "frequent and easy" interchange of position of governors and governed. Bentham wants an intelligent and highly trained body of governmental servants, and he wants them to be responsible to the electorate. He wants them to serve the public interest, and he is quite certain that they will, on occasion, be required to ignore the pressures of public opinion, because the public is not always capable of knowing its own interest. In fact Bentham appears somewhat confused on the whole issue. It is difficult to see how the principle of popular responsibility may be reconciled with the principle that government must sometimes ignore the voice of public opinion. A legislator in a democratic system is often faced with the dismal choice of acting in accordance with the will of his constituents, even when he is convinced that their will is dangerously wrong, in order to receive their votes, or of ignoring their will at the cost of his position. Bentham would surely have preferred the latter alternative.

Bentham's earlier position may be summed up in this manner: He favors both freedom and good government, but assuming a conflict between the two on an issue where they are of generally equal weight, Bentham would cast his vote for good government. His choice assumes, of course, that good government works to achieve the greatest good for the greatest number. Bentham's earlier work seems to grant that the existing government would follow this principle once it is understood and its execution is facilitated by an appropriate methodology—thus Bentham's development of the "felicific calculus." As time passed, however, and as the British government ignored some of Bentham's most highly regarded reform measures, particularly the one dealing with prison reform, Bentham became convinced that government was more interested in securing its own happiness than that of the greatest number. It was at this point that he began to listen more attentively to the arguments of his friend James Mill, who had long been contending that it was useless to press for moral reform without first establishing a basis for it through reform of the political machinery.

The problem, as Bentham sees it, is to devise a governmental system in which the happiness of the governors coincides with that of the governed.[20] The best solution here is representative government. If people govern themselves, if the people are both governors and governed, there will be no conflict of interest. Such self-government, however, is impossible, and Bentham does not devote any time, as did Rousseau, to the development of some such concept as the general will in an attempt to make the idea acceptable. A representative system is the only practicable answer; the task of the political theorist is to make such a system as representative as possible, the electorate as wise as possible, and the administration as efficient as possible. To this end Bentham, in his later work, proposes universal suffrage, the secret ballot, annual elections to Parliament, widespread education (although not under the control of government), and a competitive system of examinations for appointive administrative offices.

To the degree that these principles are followed, Bentham believes, the conflict between freedom and authority will be lessened. This is because the more representative and responsible a government is, the more closely it approaches self-government; and in self-government no conflict of freedom and authority exists. Where such a system can be established it will be unnecessary to invoke such safeguards as separation

[20] Plamenatz, *op. cit.*, p. 82.

of powers, checks and balances, bills of rights, and all the rest of the paraphernalia associated with limited government. Bentham and the philosophical radicals generally objected to the view, derived from the theory of Locke, that the most common characteristic of government is its tendency to abuse its authority and that therefore its power must be restricted through the use of a variety of constitutional safeguards. The Benthamite was willing to grant government considerable authority, providing that it was guided by the utilitarian principle and responsible to an enlightened majority.

Bentham did not live to witness the adoption in England of many of the reforms he so strongly urged, but a great number of his followers did. In 1832 the Reform Act gave representation for the first time to new industrial towns such as Leeds, Manchester, and Birmingham and increased the franchise by 50 per cent. It was not a thoroughgoing democratization of the British political system; there were still rotten boroughs, and the extension of the franchise meant only that one citizen in thirty could vote; industrial workers were not given the franchise. Still the Act was a substantial beginning, and it was followed the next year by a law abolishing slavery in the empire. A new Poor Law was enacted in 1834. In 1835 the Municipal Corporations Act vastly improved city government; in the same year judicial reform left only three offenses, murder, treason, and piracy, subject to capital punishment. In 1846 repeal of the Corn Laws removed the tariff on corn and resulted in substantially lower food prices, a long-sought boon for the poor. As the years passed there were many other reforms, and it would be fair to say that in all cases where the hand of reform touched it was guided by the spirit of Bentham. His "felicific calculus" may contain absurdities and inconsistencies, but the principle of utility that underlies it and the humanitarian sentiment that imbues it gave the proposals significant force and direction.

John Stuart Mill: The Man and His Work

John Stuart Mill was born in 1806. Whether his birth occasioned any joy in the heart of his father is unrecorded, but the evidence is that it did not. James Mill, the dour Scot, was considerably less interested in his family than in collaborating with Bentham on developing the principles of philosophical radicalism. The Mill household more closely resembled a center for social research than a family circle. The birth of his first son was important to James Mill mainly because it presented him with an opportunity to conduct an intensive experiment to determine how much information the human brain can absorb at the earliest possible stage of development. The opportunity was exploited to the fullest, and while the results were impressive they were at the same time depressing.

The material with which James Mill had to work was unquestionably superior; nothing else could explain the boy's remarkable achievements.

John Stuart Mill began reading the Greek classics at the age of three. By the time he was eight he had mastered a substantial number of them, had begun the study of Latin, and had assumed responsibility for tutoring his younger sister. He also began the study of algebra, philosophy, chemistry, and economics. In some of these fields he soon had advanced beyond the point where his father was able to assist him, and he was compelled to rely upon his own ingenuity and intelligence in order to continue. His major interest was history, in which discipline he read omnivorously. When he was eleven he assisted his father with the galleys of James Mill's *History of British India*. By the time he was sixteen he had completed his formal education. He then went to work with his father for the East India Company, beginning as a clerk in 1823 and rising, by 1856, to the position of chief of the office, a post which commanded an excellent salary. He resigned two years later, at the age of fifty-two, primarily because of his opposition to English control of India.

Mill's life in commerce occupied only part of his time and less of his interest. When he was sixteen he organized a circle of youthful intellectuals and gave them the name "utilitarians." Before he left the East India Company he had written and published two of his most important works, *Logic* and *Principles of Political Economy*. This all added up, however, to a seriously unbalanced life. The test-tube existence of his youth, coupled with his extreme preoccupation with difficult intellectual problems, resulted in an emotional starvation that was damaging to both his physical and mental health. He became apathetic. The great social problems, which he had formerly thought to be all-important, now appeared inconsequential. Worst of all he became convinced that he had lost his ability to have any emotions. He turned to romantic literature. Wordsworth offered solace and partially satisfied his longing for emotional nourishment, but his salvation was effected when, at the age of twenty-three, he met and fell in love with the wife of another man.

Mrs. Harriet Taylor was a remarkable woman. She, like Mill, was young and was married at the time to a man whose character was undoubtedly estimable but who apparently lacked intellectual interests. Not so with his wife. She was immediately attracted to Mill, and a friendship began which endured for twenty years, until the death of Taylor made it possible for his widow to marry John Stuart Mill. Harriet Taylor's influence on Mill was considerable. She stimulated in him a more humanitarian and imaginative approach, and her compassion for the underdog in society impelled Mill to embrace such causes as the equality of women and a program of social welfare which bordered closely on, if it did not encompass, socialism. In addition to turning out a series of revisions of his *Political Economy*, each one of which carried him further from the laissez-faire faith of the Benthamite circle, Mill wrote and published a number of works, the most important of which, for our purposes, were *Utilitarianism,* the *Autobiography, On Liberty,* and *Representative Government.* Each is typical, in its own way, of Mill's interests, and each shows the influence of Harriet Taylor Mill. After only seven years of marriage, Mill's wife died of tuberculosis. He adopted her daughter, Helen Taylor, who cared for Mill in his declining years and gave him the the affection his nature required. Mill died in 1873.

John Stuart Mill and the New Liberalism

John Stuart Mill's writings reflect the problems that grew out of the rapidly developing industrialism and democracy of England in the middle years of the nineteenth century. These problems had not been so clearly defined for Bentham and the philosophical radicals, and they had placed their hopes for improvement in a political democracy which strongly emphasized middle-class control and in a laissez-faire economics. These hopes were largely fulfilled, although not in the lifetime of the early liberals. Had they been able to witness the developments they had sought so earnestly to achieve, they would probably have experienced considerable disillusionment. For one thing, it became obvious that the mysterious workings of the unseen hand of competition did not always have the beneficent results which Adam Smith had predicted. The ghastly conditions of the industrial working classes were eloquent testimony to the fact that a policy of governmental restraint with respect to the functioning of the economic system was totally inadequate. Liberal thought turned perceptively and quickly from individualism to collectivism. It also became clear that a broadening of the suffrage was not a universal solvent for the difficulties which beset a political system. An extended suffrage alleviated the oppression that was a concomitant of the control exercised by a landowning minority, but it raised other and almost equally severe problems. Under even a democratic suffrage the individual may suffer as greatly as if he were subjected to the control of a single despot.[21]

All this demonstrated the incredible complexity of the problem of governing an industrial society. Fundamentally it was the same old political problem, liberty versus authority, with which thinkers had wrestled from time immemorial. But now it was complicated by an entirely new set of circumstances that had attended the development of an industrial system. The confusion is evidenced by the fact that liberals with profoundly humanitarian instincts were simultaneously arguing for more collectivism on the one hand and more individualism on the other. Such a situation may appear contradictory in theory, but in practical terms it need not be contradictory at all. It is perfectly logical, for example, to demand a greater degree of governmental intervention to pro-

---

[21] Mill was aware of the majoritarian tyranny implicit in Bentham's formula and, as we shall see, attempted to correct it.

vide for social welfare, and at the same time to demand greater freedom of speech for the individual. While this is an oversimplification of the problems faced by liberals of the mid-nineteenth century, it is an illustration of the dilemma with which they were confronted and which modern democracies continue to face.

An appreciation of this situation is necessary to an understanding of the contributions of John Stuart Mill. Mill cannot be fitted precisely into the categories of either collectivism or individualism, for he was both individualist and collectivist. The ideas he propounded in favor of either creed were determined by the subject matter to which they were to be applied. His inclinations toward collectivism, as we have seen, are evidenced in the increasing exceptions to the laissez-faire principle which appear in successive editions of his *Political Economy*. Nevertheless, the preponderance of his interest is in the individual. That Mill is less optimistic than were Bentham and his followers with regard to the efficacy of the democratic principle is apparent in the views he expresses in his *Representative Government*. Here he embraces the democratic idea but hedges it about with modifying restrictions. His greatest fear, however, is that society itself, apart from government, is destructive of individualism; this is the point which he makes in *On Liberty*, generally conceded to be his greatest work. Throughout these and other works, Mill insists that he remains true to the utilitarian creed. Whether he does or not has been much debated. One can say, however, that utilitarianism is substantially different when Mill has finished with it.

Mill's Representative Government

In his *Representative Government*, Mill extols the virtues of democracy and warns of its dangers. Democracy, insofar as it secures the freedom of the individual, is a highly valuable concept, and as a governmental form it is the best that has ever been conceived. More than any other system it contributes to the improvement of man. We should note here that Mill, in considering the *improvement* of man, is straying from the principles of utilitarianism as expressed by Bentham. The philosophical radicals concerned themselves with man's happiness, not his improvement. They favored democracy because they thought that it, more than any other system, contributed to that end. Mill, on the other hand, preferred democracy because he thought men would be *better* under that system, even if they were not happier. In this vein he states that a bad despotism is preferable to a good one, since despotism is always degrading, and if it is benevolent people are prone to accept their degradation. This modification of the utilitarian principle is not the only instance in which Mill departs from the course set by Bentham. In his *Utilitarianism*, for example, Mill begins by accepting the premise of the "greatest happiness" and then proceeds to argue that it must be measured by both quantitative and qualitative methods. In short, Mill distinguishes among various kinds of happiness, saying that there are higher and lower varieties. This is something that Bentham, to whom "pushpin is as good as poetry," could not accept. To Mill, what men *are* is as important as what men *do;* this point he stressed in his *On Liberty*.

The danger of democracy, Mill sees, grows out of the very advantage it offers. In a democracy men are free to pursue their own interests. If they are wise, they will understand that their selfish interest is inseparable from the general interest, and this knowledge will lead them to act so as to secure individual benefits through social advantage. Unfortunately, the majority are incapable of displaying this kind of farsightedness. They must be pressed in the direction of their true interest, but this necessity does not justify elite rule. Men must be permitted a degree of participation, or their loss of freedom will be greater than any material advantage that might be gained by despotism, no matter how benevolent. The answer is a representative system, but one somewhat more complex than that devised by Bentham.

Mill's representative system comprises three levels—the people, their elected representatives, and a policy-making body. It is the function of the mass of citizens to choose their legislative agents. They are capable of making the choice, and the process of election includes also the debate, discussion, criticism, and education which mark the limits of popular participation. This level constitutes the base of a good representative system. The representatives elected by the people, it is assumed, will have knowledge and judgment superior to that possessed by the electorate; they will not, however, have the ability to frame the intricate legislation required by a complex industrial society. For this a superior body, one composed of experts professionally trained for their task and one step removed from direct responsibility to the public, is required. Such a body should not be permitted to enact legislation on its own authority, but its greater ability enables it to understand better than do either the people or their representatives what policies are in the general interest. It is their duty to submit legislative proposals to the elected representatives. The representatives or legislators in turn debate, question members of the policy body, explain the measures to their constituents, thus educating them, and finally either ratify or reject the policies offered to them for their consideration. They also possess authority to remove members of the policy body, as they may themselves be removed by their own constituents. The power of removal may, of course, be misused by the people or by their representatives, but it is necessary to retain the element of responsibility or the democratic principle is destroyed.

A representative system of this nature will go far toward lessening the dangers that stem from a too unrestricted application of the democratic principle. Two additional precautions, however, are necessary. Even with the safeguards provided, a majority may exercise a degree of control dangerous to the minority. Nothing, in other words, has been done to curb the formation of a majority party. Mill believes that any ruling group, including a majority, tends to use its power in behalf of its own interest. The best way to forestall this tendency is to prevent the formation of a majority party. This can be done through the organization of a third party, which will hold the balance of power between two larger and contending parties. It would be possible to arrange an allocation of representatives that would encourage the creation of such a third force and at the same time prevent either of the major parties from securing a majority of seats in the legislative assembly. The other precaution suggested by Mill is always to keep the way open for a minority to become a majority. The ruling group (presumably and preferably a coalition) must not take any action that will hinder its legal and peaceful replacement by the opposition. Essentially this precaution involves the guarantee of the right to criticize, and the guarantees of freedom of speech, press, and assembly that make the right meaningful.

Mill's On Liberty

Mill's *Representative Government* is his solution to the problems that concern the relationship of the individual and government. In his *On Liberty*, Mill deals with a question which has even greater pertinency in modern times—the question of the freedom of the individual in society itself. Mill's fear is that the huge and monolithic society which tends to develop in an environment of industrialism constitutes a greater threat to individuality than does government. It is fair to say that Mill's views on this subject warrant a more thoughtful consideration by men today than do any of his other writings. The sincerity, even the passion, of Mill's words in *On Liberty* indicate that he himself had a greater interest in this work than he did in any other.

On Liberty, Mill says, deals with "the nature and limits of the power which can be legitimately exercised by society over the individual." [22] In the past, the conflict between liberty and authority involved a contest between people and government. Liberty meant freedom *from* government. With the development of the democratic idea and of the representative system this issue has declined in importance. The tyranny of government may be restrained by various constitutional safeguards. But society too may be the tyrant, and it need not rely upon its governmental agents to do so. It has its own highly effective methods.

> Society can and does execute its own mandates: and if it issues wrong mandates instead of right, or any mandates at all in things with which it ought

[22] John Stuart Mill, *On Liberty*, in *Essential Works of John Stuart Mill* (edited and with an introduction by Max Lerner), Bantam Books, Inc., New York, 1961, p. 255.

not to meddle, it practices a social tyranny more formidable than many kinds of political oppression, since, though not usually upheld by such extreme penalties, it leaves fewer means of escape, penetrating much more deeply into the details of life, and enslaving the soul itself. Protection, therefore, against the tyranny of the magistrate is not enough; there needs protection also against the tyranny of the prevailing opinion and feeling; against the tendency of society to impose, by other means than civil penalties, its own ideas and practices as rules of conduct on those who dissent from them; to fetter the development, and, if possible, prevent the formation, of any individuality not in harmony with its ways, and compel all characters to fashion themselves upon the model of its own.[23]

It would be difficult to state Mill's case more clearly than he himself does in these words. Society, as well as government, issues rules, and society, while it does not assess penalties for nonconformity in the same way as does government, nonetheless heavily penalizes nonconformity. It is both more subtle and more assiduous in doing so. There are "fewer means of escape" from its jurisdiction, a jurisdiction more all-encompassing than that possessed by government. If a majority of society is agreed upon particular standards of conduct, it tends to equate morality with its own prejudices and to punish cruelly those who do not live in accordance with them.

Everyone understands, Mill says, that absolute freedom for the individual in society is impossible. The question is where the line should properly be drawn between what a person is entitled to do and what society is entitled to prevent him from doing. A criterion must be established by which conflicts between these interests may be judged. Mill supplies such a standard.

The sole end for which mankind are warranted, individually or collectively, in interfering with the liberty of action of any of their number, is self-protection. That the only purpose for which power can be rightfully exercised over any member of a civilized community, against his will, is to prevent harm to others. His own good, either physical or moral, is not a sufficient warrant.[24]

Mill here adopts the principle of the "clear and present danger." Society is justified in restraining the actions of the individual if restraint is necessary for the protection of society. There is no warrant to restrain simply to achieve conformity, or to benefit the actor himself. It is perfectly proper, Mill says, to attempt to persuade a person through argument from acting in some manner deemed wrong by the majority, but no restraint should be imposed unless the majority is actually in some way endangered.

Mill says that while some individual actions are obviously harmful

[23] *Ibid.*, p. 258.
[24] *Ibid.*, p. 263.

and must be prohibited there are also important areas of human concern in which restraint should never be imposed.

> It comprises, first, the inward domain of consciousness; demanding liberty of conscience in the most comprehensive sense; liberty of thought and feeling; absolute freedom of opinion and sentiment on all subjects, practical or speculative, scientific, moral, or theological. . . . Secondly, the principle requires liberty of tastes and pursuits; of framing the plan of our life to suit our own character; of doing as we like, subject to such consequences as may follow: without impediment from our fellow-creatures, so long as what we do does not harm them, even though they should think our conduct foolish, perverse, or wrong. Thirdly, from this liberty of each individual, follows the liberty, within the same limits, of combination among individuals; freedom to unite, for any purpose not involving harm to others.[25]

Freedom of conscience, of thought, of speech and opinion, of personal life, and of association (unless directed to the injury of others)—these are the substantive freedoms with which society should never interfere. We should not assume that all agree with this principle. All may say they do, but in fact they do not. Too often freedom is given lip service, while the pressure for conformity undermines the principle itself.

When the freedom involved is that of opinion it must be absolute. In one of his most often quoted statements, Mill says: "If all mankind minus one were of one opinion, and only one person were of the contrary opinion, mankind would be no more justified in silencing that one person, than he, if he had the power, would be justified in silencing mankind." [26] Why is this? First, to silence an opinion is to rob mankind. If the silenced opinion is right, the loss is obvious; if it is wrong, men lose the chance to gain a "clearer perception and livelier impression of the truth" which results from the conflict between right and wrong. Second, truth is a changing thing. It alters with the change of circumstances. Even if we know the truth today, we must recognize that it will not be quite true tomorrow; to maintain its validity free speech is necessary. Third, we cannot assume, as some argue, that there is really nothing to worry about since despite suppression truth always emerges triumphant in the end. The fact is, Mill says, that history is replete with examples "of truth put down by persecution." Fourth, the silencing of opinion is an "assumption of infallibility" on the part of those who silence it, but no one is infallible and no one is capable of knowing the whole of truth. Finally, truth needs constantly to be attacked in order to preserve its vigor.

Far from restricting nonconformity, society should encourage it. Progress is made possible by individuals who think freely and imaginatively.

[25] *Ibid.*, p. 265.
[26] *Ibid.*, p. 269.

Individuals must break through the frame of reference which constitutes the status quo. Restraint hinders initiative and prevents progress. Even the most radical thinkers ought not to be discouraged from expressing their opinions. They may be entirely wrong in their views, but if they are prevented from giving them, those who are less radical and more sensible may fear to offer their own opinions.

> In this age the mere example of non-conformity, the mere refusal to bend the knee to custom, is itself a service. Precisely because the tyranny of opinion is such as to make eccentricity a reproach, it is desirable, in order to break through that tyranny, that people should be eccentric. Eccentricity has always abounded when and where strength of character has abounded; and the amount of eccentricity in a society has generally been proportioned to the amount of genius, mental vigor, and moral courage which it contained. That so few now dare to be eccentric, marks the chief danger of the time.[27]

Conclusions

Is Mill's argument for freedom truly a utilitarian one? There is no doubt that he so considered it. The argument, he says, is not made on the basis of abstract rights. Men should have freedom to express their opinions, not because they have a natural right to do so but because the greater happiness of the greater number will be achieved in this manner. The benefits which accrue to society from adherence to the principle of free speech are cited throughout Mill's treatise, and we have no reason to doubt his sincerity in making the point. On the other hand, it is equally certain that Mill regarded freedom not only as a means to happiness but as an end in itself. In this he differs from the earlier advocates of utility. The Benthamites sought a happy community, Mill a moral one. The Benthamites stressed the benefits to which the greater number were entitled; Mill states his agreement, but his concern for the individual is too apparent to admit of any total preoccupation with the "greatest number." For him freedom is both an individual and a social value, and his emphasis upon the individual in *On Liberty* is so great that we can hardly escape the conclusion that individual value is more important to him than social. Mill also differs from his predecessors in his refusal to calculate moral value solely in terms of pain and pleasure,[28] or at least pain and pleasure as the Benthamites understood them. For Mill a moral community is one in which human dignity is respected, not one in which everybody is abundantly happy. The good, the moral, community, in sum, is made up of free and moral individuals. Freedom and morality go hand in hand; one is not possible without the other. We conclude by permitting Mill to state the case in his own words.

[27] *Ibid.*, p. 315.
[28] Sabine, *op. cit.*, p. 714.

The worth of a State, in the long run, is the worth of the individuals composing it; and a State which postpones the interests of *their* mental expansion and elevation, to a little more of administrative skill, or that semblance
of it which practice gives, in the details of business; a State which dwarfs
its men, in order that they may be more docile instruments in its hands
even for beneficial purposes, will find that with small men no great thing
can really be accomplished; and that the perfection of machinery to which
it has sacrificed everything, will in the end avail it nothing, for want of
the vital power which, in order that the machine might work more
smoothly, it has preferred to banish.[29]

SELECTED BIBLIOGRAPHY

Brinton, Crane: *English Political Thought in the Nineteenth Century,* 2d ed.,
Ernest Benn, Ltd., London, 1949.
Essential Works of John Stuart Mill (edited and with an introduction by Max
Lerner), Bantam Books, Inc., New York, 1961, introduction.
Hacker, Andrew: *Political Theory: Philosophy, Ideology, Science,* The Macmil-
lan Company, New York, 1961, chaps. 10, 14.
Halévy, Elie: *The Growth of Philosophic Radicalism,* new ed. (translated by
Mary Morris, with a preface by A. D. Lindsay), Faber & Faber, Ltd., London,
1934.
McDonald, Lee Cameron: *Western Political Theory: The Modern Age,* Har-
court, Brace & World, Inc., New York, 1962, chaps. 10–11.
Plamenatz, John: *The English Utilitarians,* Basil Blackwell & Mott, Ltd., Oxford,
1949.
Sabine, George H.: *A History of Political Theory,* 3d ed., Holt, Rinehart and
Winston, Inc., New York, 1961, chaps. 31–32.
Somervell, D. C.: *English Thought in the Nineteenth Century,* 6th ed., Methuen
& Co., Ltd., London, 1950.

[29] Mill, *On Liberty,* in Lerner (ed.), *op. cit.,* p. 360.

nineteen

MARX

Industrial capitalism made great strides in the early nineteenth century in Western Europe, and particularly in England. This was a time of increasing concern for those who had been so optimistic in their belief that a laissez-faire policy in economics could best solve the multitudinous problems that attended industrial development. Members of the classical school who followed Adam Smith were not likely to stray far from the Scottish philosopher's principle of the "unseen hand," but neither were they so sanguine with regard to the results of its operation. The dolorous divine, Robert Malthus (1766–1834), predicted a dismal future for the human race on the ground that, since population increases in geometrical progression and the means of subsistence in arithmetical progression, the number of people is always too great for the supply of goods available. David Ricardo (1772–1823) propounded his theory of economic rent, which held that the increase of population depletes nattural resources, thus forcing prices higher, to the detriment of workers and capitalists who rely on those resources. In addition, Ricardo developed the theory of the subsistence wage (the "iron law of wages"), which held that the worker is never paid more than enough to assure a supply of labor, and that this amount tends to be no more than enough to permit the worker and his family to subsist.

If these were pessimistic views, they appeared to be grounded on facts. Industrial capitalism had contributed to the formation of a new class in society. They were the industrial workers or proletariat, who could not afford to own their own instruments of production in a new system that utilized large and expensive aggregates of machinery, and who were forced to rely upon those who, through the accumulation of capital, could own the means of production. The rapid growth of population contributed to the deteriorating position of the proletariat. From 1815 to 1914 the population of Europe more than doubled. This was a period in which no major wars decimated the ranks of young men; it was also a time of expanding medical knowledge, of improving sanitation, and of increasing industrial and agricultural production. All these highly beneficial developments produced also some adverse effects. For one thing, there were too many people available for the work provided by the growing factory system. Then, too, those who sought employment flocked to the cities, which were woefully unprepared to receive them, and severe housing shortages resulted.

In the absence of legislation designed to solve these most pressing problems, employers demanded a great deal of effort for a pitifully inadequate compensation. Hours of work ranged from twelve to sixteen per day. And because women and children could be employed more cheaply than men, they were found in increasing numbers in the mines and factories. Technological improvement made possible the substitution of machines for men, thus aggravating the unemployment problem and provoking, in a futile attempt at retaliation, such actions as the Luddite riots in England, in which workers attacked the mechanical monsters that had displaced them. Such reactions were not without effect in the long run. Parliamentary investigations focused public attention on a situation which seemed to have developed almost overnight.

Reformers began to study the causes of the problems that plagued the new society and to agitate for measures to ameliorate some of the most deplorable conditions. In England the beginnings of reform were made by legislative fiat. A series of acts beginning in 1802 brought some relief through the regulation of hours and working conditions, especially for women and children. This approach, however, barely scratched the surface. A laissez-faire–minded middle class regarded such measures with apathy and, in many cases, with outright antagonism. Employers sought, with considerable success, to prevent a thoroughgoing approach to reform through the legislative process. Laboring people began to organize in an attempt to improve their bargaining position. An unsympathetic Parliament at first banned labor organization in the Combination Acts of 1799 and 1800. These acts were repealed a quarter of a century later, but restrictions on the right to strike were maintained. Similar conditions obtained on the Continent, and reformers there were even less successful than their counterparts in England in achieving a program of legislative improvement. The situation in England differed mainly because the industrial revolution was more advanced in that country.

As the condition of the proletariat grew more critical, reformers tended to turn from an attempt to patch up the system of *laissez faire* to a questioning of the validity of the system itself. Some, like John Stuart Mill, began to qualify their earlier views by listing a growing number of exceptions to the principle of economic freedom from governmental restraint until they had reached a position of near-socialism. Others were more thorough in their approach; they attacked the foundations of the system and proclaimed that cooperation must supplant competition as the mainspring of economic action.[1] In a sense, capitalism itself, or at least the theory that supported it, supplied the premises of the assault which was now made upon it. In their struggle for power, the capitalist class had, at various times, waved the banners of freedom, equality, and fraternity, the greatest good of the greatest number, and progress, and had espoused the cause of revolution. That class had never contended that what they wanted was good only for themselves; on the contrary, the entire society was supposed to benefit. Now some members of society demanded an accounting. They were not going to be easily put off, and they were particularly menacing because of their unwillingness even to accept the truth of the premises of the system they assaulted. We shall consider briefly a few of these critics and the essential elements of their thought.

Many English writers before Karl Marx complained of injustices in economic society. William Thompson, John Gray, Thomas Hodgskin, John Francis Bray, and others contended that working people create the wealth which is taken from them by greedy employers. In England and in France, the "Utopian Socialists," the most notable of whom were Henri de Saint-Simon, Charles Fourier, Louis Blanc, all in France, and Robert Owen, in England, said that private property was the cause of poverty. They preached the doctrine of cooperation and developed schemes for ideal communities. As peaceful men, they rejected revolution as a means to the end they sought and appealed, with notable lack of success, to the spirit of benevolence in man. Their appeals were joined by those of the "Christian Socialists," among them Felicité Robert de Lamennais in France, and Charles Kingsley, Frederick Denison Maurice, and J. M. Ludlow in England. It was the belief of this group that competition was incompatible with Christianity, which embraces the principle of cooperation and repudiates the notion that material wealth is an acceptable criterion of success. Aside from their admonitions, the Christian Socialists instructed industrial workers in the principles of a co-

---

[1] See Eric Roll, *A History of Economic Thought*, 3d ed., Prentice-Hall, Inc., Englewood Cliffs, N.J., 1959, pp. 232–233.

operative system and attempted to assist them in the creation of cooperative producers' associations. These movements had importance in the
subsequent development of socialist theory. So, too, did the system of
"scientific socialism" constructed by a scholarly and indefatigable German Jew named Karl Marx.

The Man and His Work

Karl Marx was born May 5, 1818 in Treves in Rhenish Prussia. His father
was a prosperous lawyer. Both parents were Jewish. The family, like
other Jewish families, had benefited from the establishment in Prussia
of the Napoleonic Code, which had practically eliminated discrimination
against Jews. However, a reaction under Napoleon and later under the
Prussian authorities created considerable bitterness in the mind of the
elder Marx and may well have engendered revolutionary sentiments in
the heart of his son. When Karl Marx was six, the entire Marx family
was converted to Christianity. The expedient nature of the conversion
seems apparent, and this event too could not have failed to make an impression upon the mind of a brilliant and perceptive young man.

Marx attended grammar school in Treves. He began his university
training at the University of Bonn in 1835; later he transferred to the
University of Berlin, where he came under the influence of Hegelian philosophy. Ultimately he attended the University of Jena and received his
degree as doctor of philosophy there in 1841, at the age of twenty-three.
It had been his intention to become a teacher, but his views were considered too radical by university authorities, and Marx became, by necessity rather than by choice, a journalist. His first position was with the
Rheinische Zeitung, an organ of the liberal middle class. In 1842 he was
made an editor of the paper, but the following year the paper was suppressed by government officials, an act occasioned in large part by Marx's
radical writings. In that same year Marx married Jenny von Westphalen,
the daughter of a high-ranking civil servant and member of the petty
nobility. Although she was accustomed to the high living standards of
her class, Marx's wife shared uncomplainingly the vicissitudes of his life,
including lengthy periods of near destitution.

After the suppression of the *Rheinische Zeitung,* Marx began the first
of his periods of exile. He first went to Paris, where he studied economics,
worked for a magazine, and, most important, met Friedrich Engels. Engels was the son of a wealthy German industrialist. He was, nonetheless,
appalled by the misery of the industrial working class and devoted a considerable part of his time and energy to an attack upon the system that
had built his family's fortune. By the time he met Marx, Engels had
already made an intensive study of the condition of the working class
in England. He was impressed by Marx's views and placed his information at the disposal of his colleague. There began a period of friendship

and collaboration which endured until Marx's death. Engels not only was Marx's friend, disciple, and coworker; he was also his benefactor. Marx and his family were able to exist in the darkest days of their poverty-ridden existence mainly by virtue of Engels' generosity.

In 1847 Marx and Engels joined in writing the *Communist Manifesto*, which was published in 1848. Few more portentous documents have ever been issued. Both men were active in the revolutionary movement of the time in France, and when the revolution broke out in that country, Marx returned to Germany to advance the cause there. In Cologne he again became editor of a newspaper, the *Neue Rheinische Zeitung*, a journal with avowedly revolutionary aims. He was arrested and brought to trial, but a sympathetic jury acquitted him, and the judge gravely acknowledged with thanks a lengthy speech by Marx in which some of the essentials of his revolutionary philosophy were stated. Nevertheless, Marx was finished in Germany. In May, 1849, he was expelled by the authorities. Residence in France was permitted, but under conditions which Marx rejected, and he took his family to England, where he lived, except for brief excursions to the Continent, the rest of his life. Despite the notoriety which attached to his name on the Continent, Marx was almost unnoticed in England. He was employed briefly as a correspondent for the *New York Tribune*, at the time a newspaper with socialist inclinations. His major effort, however, was directed to writing *Capital*, the work for which, aside from the *Manifesto*, he is best known. In 1864 he became involved in the organization of the International Workingmen's Association in London; he was a member of the General Council and a leader of this very important organization. His personal problems multiplied with his years. He was unwilling to take time from his research and organizational activities to make money; as a result his family went hungry and survived mainly through Engels' help. Marx himself suffered from ill health. He lived to complete only the first volume of *Capital*. Marx died on March 14, 1883 and was buried in Highgate Cemetery in London. Engels completed work on two additional volumes of *Capital* from notes and materials which Marx had left. Although the *Communist Manifesto* and *Capital* are the best-known works of Marx (and Engels), many others are both important and influential. Some of them are *Eleven Theses on Feuerbach* (1845), *The German Ideology*, with Engels (1846), *Poverty of Philosophy* (1847), *The Class Struggles in France* (1850), and *A Contribution to the Critique of Political Economy* (1859).

Dialectical Materialism

Marx's socialism stemmed from motives no different from those which impelled other socialists of his time to develop their theories. Like them, he was stirred to resentment by the plight of large numbers of industrial workers. His compassion and sense of outrage are evident in passages of

Capital, the *Manifesto*, and other of his writings. His argument with other socialists was not so much over the ends to be sought, although there were certain differences on this subject, as it was with the methods they proposed to attain those ends. Marx claimed that his was a "scientific," rather than a "utopian" or "Christian," socialism. He was convinced that any program which was to be permanently successful would have to be based upon scientifically valid principles. It was, he thought, totally useless to preach the doctrine of cooperation and to appeal to the benevolent nature of a capitalist class, which, for reasons shortly to be examined, was unable consciously to alter the system from which it benefited. Reformers, Marx believed, would need to delve more deeply into the causes of the existing situation, to investigate the forces that move history itself. Only through such a scientific investigation is it possible to understand what has happened, what is happening, and what will happen. Any other approach, no matter how altruistically motivated, is useless.

Marx, like Hegel, developed a philosophy of history. We have seen that Marx fell under the influence of Hegel's ideas at the University of Berlin. He did not, however, accept those ideas uncritically, but rather followed the lead of Ludwig Feuerbach, who rejected the idealism of Hegel and laid the basis for a materialist interpretation of the dialectic. Hegel, it will be recalled, developed a philosophy of history which saw progress as contingent upon the dialectical clash of ideas in a sequence of thesis, antithesis, and synthesis. The material manifestations of this conflict of ideas, Hegel asserted, lie in nations, but they are only reflections of the nonmaterial forces or ideas. The progress of the Idea through a succession of historical epochs is dependent upon conflict. He who understands this and associates himself with the trend by subordinating himself to the forces of change will be free. No one can halt the march of progress which is God's plan for the world.

Marx took from Hegel the dialectical method, the view that progress results from the conflict of opposing forces. However, he reversed Hegel's view that the conflict is in the realm of ideas and that material forces are only reflections. The clash, Marx said, is one of material forces, and ideas are only products of the material environment in which men live. Hegel's theory, Marx says, is "standing on its head," although he still credits Hegel with an understanding of the general manner in which the dialectic functions. A materialist interpretation, Marx suggests, makes possible a scientific study of history and society because it deals with material things, things that can be seen and understood. Hegel's idealism, on the other hand, consists of metaphysical abstractions which mean many things to many people.

Bearing in mind Marx's adaptation of Hegel's dialectical method, we may now proceed to a consideration of Marx's development of his theory of "dialectical materialism." In doing so, we shall find it helpful to review a thumbnail sketch of that theory, provided for us by Marx in the introduction to his *A Contribution to the Critique of Political Economy*. The thesis presented here is fundamental and must be understood.

> The general conclusion at which I arrived and which, once reached, continued to serve as the leading thread in my studies may be briefly summed up as follows: In the social production which men carry on they enter into definite relations that are indispensable and independent of their will; these relations of production correspond to a definite stage of development of their material powers of production. The sum total of these relations of production constitutes the economic structure of society—the real foundation, on which rise legal and political superstructures and to which correspond definite forms of social consciousness. The mode of production in material life determines the general character of the social, political, and spiritual processes of life. It is not the consciousness of men that determines their existence, but, on the contrary, their social existence determines their consciousness. At a certain stage of their development the material forces of production in society come into conflict with the existing relations of production, or—what is but a legal expression for the same thing—with the property relations within which they had been at work before. From forms of development of the forces of production these relations turn into their fetters. Then comes the period of social revolution. With the change of the economic foundation the entire immense superstructure is more or less rapidly transformed.... No social order ever disappears before all the productive forces for which there is room in it have been developed, and new, higher relations of production never appear before the material conditions of their existence have matured in the womb of the old society.... In broad outlines we can designate the Asiatic, the ancient, the feudal, and the modern bourgeois methods of production as so many epochs in the progress of the economic formation of society. The bourgeois relations of production are the last antagonistic form of the social process of production—antagonistic not in the sense of individual antagonism, but of one arising from conditions surrounding the life of individuals in society; at the same time the productive forces developing in the womb of bourgeois society create the material conditions for the solution of that antagonism. This social formation constitutes, therefore, the closing chapter of the prehistoric stage of human society.[2]

It is possible to present an account of the relations of the material forces and their social derivations in diagram form. In such form it may provide a point of reference, which may be used by the reader as an aid to understanding the subsequent discussion.

In every society, Marx says, the fundamental determinant of all other developments is the forces of production. The forces of production consist of the raw materials or natural resources and the techniques (tech-

[2] Karl Marx, *A Contribution to the Critique of Political Economy*, 2d German ed. (translated by N. I. Stone), Charles H. Kerr and Company, Chicago, 1904, pp. 11–12.

nology) by which those materials are converted into consumable goods. The forces of production give rise to particular "relations of production." These are social relationships, the most typical and significant form of which is class structure. The relationship is always determined by the property factor; thus there are those who own and those who do not own but who operate the means of production. The relationship is also invariably one of command and obedience; those who own command those who operate the instruments of production. This is always done for the primary benefit of the commanding (owning) class. The form of production relations (class structure) is always dependent upon and controlled by the kind of production forces which exist at a given time. An alteration of production forces demands a change in the production relations. As we shall see, the failure of the production relations to accommodate such changes results in tensions that arise between the classes involved in the productive process.

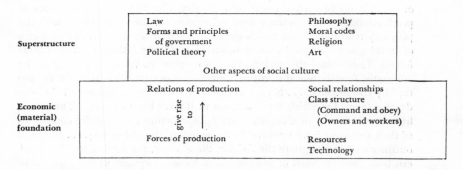

The forces of production and the relations of production combine to form the economic foundation of every society. Since these are material factors, the basis of society is itself material. On this economic foundation is erected a superstructure, which consists of the nonmaterial aspects of society. It includes such things as laws, moral codes, religion, art, governmental forms and the theories and philosophies designed to support them, and various other aspects of the culture of a society. The superstructure serves two essential purposes. First, it furnishes the commanding class of society with a justification and rationalization of its position. All the components of the superstructure support that position. This, Marx says, is strictly a matter of economic interest. A commanding class always universalizes its own position. The laws it enacts, the moral behavior it advocates, the religion it embraces, all assume the "rightness" of its place in society. Second, the superstructural components are employed as weapons of the commanding class to maintain its own superior status and the subordinate status of the obeying class. Laws are formulated to protect its property and its authority. Governments are designed to enable the commanding class to enforce its will, although in all stages of historical development except the last (which we shall consider shortly) it comprises a minority of the population as against a majority of the obeying class.

All the elements of a superstructure are dependent upon the economic foundation. A change in the foundation, which brings a new ruling class, always results in a "more or less" rapid transformation of the superstructure, since a new commanding class requires an appropriate superstructure to rationalize and defend its position. What Marx is saying is that the validity of the superstructural principles (laws, morals, philosophy, etc.), which constitute the ideology of a society, is relative. Such principles are not to be thought of as "true" or "untrue" in the ordinary sense. They are only appropriate or inappropriate, depending upon how suitably they function for the governing class. The same holds true of governmental forms. There is no single "best" form of government. There are only forms which do or do not fulfill the purposes of the class whose interests they serve.

Men do not consciously create the social environment in which they live. They are, instead, products of that environment, which has arisen in spontaneous fashion and in response to the needs of the commanding class. "It is not the consciousness of men that determines their existence, but, on the contrary, their social existence determines their consciousness." The culture, including the ideology, of a society creates a framework within which the members of society think and act. Men are generally incapable of thoughts that transcend this framework. The members of both classes think in the same terms. A member of the proletariat in a capitalist-dominated and capitalist-oriented society is so much a product of that society, so permeated with its ideas, that it is impossible, ordinarily, for him to propose or understand concepts that are antagonistic to the deeply rooted principles of the system. We have said that this is "generally" or "ordinarily" true. Marx, of course, had to leave room in his theory for such persons as himself, Engels, and a few more, who *were* able to think in terms outside of the capitalist frame of reference in which they existed. As in so many parts of his theory, Marx is here too much given to sweeping generalities, but he enunciates, nonetheless, a germ of truth. Far more than Marx believed, men are capable of thoughts outside of and opposed to the dominant ideology. But it is also true that they are to a considerable extent products of their environment, and a great many take for granted the validity of the beliefs peculiar to their society. Indeed, as we have commented many times previously, the tendency to cling to anachronistic principles is a major cause of social unrest and, sometimes, of revolution.

In the passage quoted from his *Critique of Political Economy*, **Marx** is unequivocal in his assertion that the economic factors determine the superstructural facets of society. On this basis, Marx is saying, we cannot achieve any genuine reformation of society, any real improvement of the conditions of the people, merely by tinkering with the superstructure itself. It is useless, therefore, to change laws or to reorganize the government with such an end in view. Any alterations made will be only superficial and will have no genuine impact upon the society. Only when conditions in the foundation change will any substantial transformation of society occur. In his later life, Marx apparently believed that he had gone too far and admitted that the influence of economics was not so completely determinative as he had implied previously. Both Marx and Engels, at certain points, appear to say only that economics is the *most* *important* factor in determining the form and function of society. This, it should be noted, is a far cry from saying that it is the *only* determinant. Engels and later Marxists, Stalin among them, also indicated their belief that factors in the superstructure could influence the economic foundation.[3]

The Class Struggle

There is some confusion in Marx's views on the dialectic. Is the dialectical conflict between the method of production on the one hand and the property relations on the other? Or does the dialectic involve simply a clash of one class against another? In the analysis of Marxist writings, both interpretations have been employed. Whatever Marx intended, there is no question but that class struggle is the means by which the dialectic progresses, whether that struggle constitutes the essence of the dialectic itself or is merely a reflection of other economic forces in the foundation. The concept of the class struggle is highly important in Marx's theory. We must consider both its causes and its consequences.

We have seen that in Marx's theory class structure is dependent upon the production forces of society, and that the culture of a society (the components of the superstructure) is utilized by a dominant class to hold another class in subjection. We may assume that at a very early stage of the history of a society both the class structure and the cultural aspects are perfectly suitable to the prevailing forces of production. At this juncture the foundation is firm and entirely adequate to support the superstructure. Also, there are no tensions or conflicts between the classes; one commands and the other obeys unquestioningly. What happens, then, to

[3] H. B. Mayo, *Democracy and Marxism*, Oxford University Press, Fair Lawn, N.J., 1955, pp. 52–54. Professor Mayo's book provides an excellent discussion of the vagaries, qualifications, and contradictions in Marxist theory. The interested reader is advised to consult this source.

disturb the equilibrium? The answer is, a changing technology in the method of production. The owners of the instruments of production, in seeking to maximize their advantages, alter and improve their techniques of production. In doing this they begin, without understanding that they are doing so, to destroy the foundation upon which their system rests. The "forces of production ... come into conflict with the ... relations of production." For stability it would be necessary to alter the relations of production, to adjust the class structure. But the dominant class does not, and, given the nature of the workings of the system, cannot do this. It tries with increasing desperation to maintain the status quo. It employs the factors in the superstructure to hold the subordinate class in subjection. The effort is unavailing. The tensions and contradictions in the system grow too great. Nothing can stand in the way of the inexorable movement of the dialectic. A point is ultimately reached in which the forces of production are completely incompatible with the class structure and the social superstructure. This is the "period of social revolution," in which a class realignment takes place and a new superstructure is established to meet the needs of the new situation. This dialectical process is both revolutionary and progressive. Marx states that the present is always better than the past and not so good as the future will be. Men cannot accelerate the process. It is impossible to create a class relationship and superstructure which are not justified by the existing forces of production. Every society must exploit all the potential that exists within it, and "higher relations of production never appear before the material conditions of their existence have matured in the womb of the old society."

Marx says that this phenomenon has occurred several times in history. The "Asiatic, the ancient, the feudal" and the capitalist societies succeeded one another as the forces of production in each gradually made anachronistic the class relations and superstructure of its predecessor. We are currently, Marx says, in the midst of a recurrence of the dialectical transition, one that will result in the proletariat taking control of the forces of production. This is, of course, the phase of history in which Marx is most interested and the only one he considers in detail. Indeed he would have been hard pressed to present a "scientific" analysis of the events of the past to which he refers, for the facts do not always support his theory. As Professor Mayo has said, it is absurd to hold that history is the story of class struggle. This implies that all important conflicts and wars have resulted from class antagonism, whereas struggles of this nature have in fact constituted a small minority of historical conflicts. Since this is obviously true, Marxists have defended their position by arguing that only class wars have been significant in history. The argument is absurd. The view that wars are attributable to economic causes is more easily defended but almost equally invalid. It is too apparent that noneconomic causes are involved.[4] We find also some serious errors in Marx's more complete account of the developing clash between the capitalist and proletarian classes. We must nevertheless consider his description, for it has proved highly persuasive to many and has had enormous influence—a fact that can hardly be disputed by the most implacable enemies of Marxism.

Economic Contradictions in Capitalism

The antagonism between the proletariat and the capitalist class results from contradictions which have developed in the economic foundation of the capitalist system. To understand the causes of these tension-producing contradictions, we must know something about Marx's economic theory. Marx begins with an unoriginal proposition—the labor theory of value. The "exchange value" or price of a commodity, he says, is determined by the amount of "socially useful" labor which goes into its production. In estimating what is socially useful Marx excludes any efforts of an entrepreneurial or ownership nature from a determination of the value of a commodity. Labor is the only valid measurement of value, he says, because it is the only property that goods have in common, and it is the only truly productive factor in the creation of wealth. To the labor theory of value Marx ties the theory of the subsistence wage, which, as we have seen, was developed by Ricardo, and arrives at his own distinctive position expressed in his theory of surplus value.

The theory of surplus value is itself not original with Marx. The physiocrats, Ricardo, Proudhon, and others, had all suggested that the worker produces more value than he receives in the form of wages, and that this difference constitutes the profits of the owner in industry or agriculture. Marx applies the term "surplus value" to this difference between what the worker produces and what he receives. The worker is always paid a subsistence wage, Marx says; not because of the population pressures cited by Malthus but because such a practice is essential to the operation of the capitalist system. The worker can do nothing to avoid making his contribution. His employer owns the instruments of production; the worker cannot afford to do so. He is himself a mere commodity at the mercy of the operations of the market. Since labor as a commodity is always in oversupply, the worker must sell his labor for whatever it will purchase, and this is always a mere subsistence wage.

The capitalist, too, is a victim of the system. He is compelled to extract as much surplus value as he can get. Improvements in the technology of production make possible an increasingly large-scale production. In order to take advantage of his opportunities the capitalist requires larger and larger amounts of capital. The tendency in capitalism

[4] *Ibid.*, pp. 68–71.

is toward bigger and fewer units of production and a consequent concentration of control, and the tendency is inevitable because fewer units with advanced techniques of production are capable of producing a much greater supply of commodities. The result is an enlargement of the proletariat and a decrease in the size of the capitalist class. When the capitalist system first replaced feudalism, it was characterized by the presence of a great number of capitalist owners. Units of production were small because the relatively primitive techniques of production required nothing more. A capitalist at this stage of development may have employed one or a very few workers. His relations with them (production relations) were suitable to the techniques (forces of production) employed. The concentration of ownership, however, resulting from the bitter competition among capitalists for the available surplus value, which can be converted into capital, has created an entirely different society, one marked by the existence of a handful of "industrial millionaires" who exploit an enormous majority of proletarians.

The advanced stage of capitalism is also marked by a declining rate of profit. The decline occurs because as capitalism progresses there is an increasing accumulation of capital, and since the value of anything decreases in inverse proportion to its supply, the value of capital, in terms of what can be done with it through investment, also declines. It follows, says Marx, that there is accelerated competition among capitalists for profitable capital investment, but competition merely serves to intensify the rapidity of the trend. The capitalists resort to a number of devices in an effort to stave off collapse. Labor-saving machinery is installed in an attempt to increase profits (surplus value), but this only results in unemployment and decreased demands for goods. A further effort to maximize surplus value is made by increasing hours of work for the laborer and cutting the labor force. This too leads to unemployment and decreased consumption.

Marx says that each system contains the seeds of its own destruction. Capitalism is no exception. It must follow its natural route—must accumulate capital, extract surplus value, and produce commodities. It must resort to every available tactic and utilize every improved technique that will accomplish its purposes. The capitalist is as much a captive of the system as are the members of the proletariat. A capitalist may be influenced by humanitarian sentiments to attempt to alleviate the suffering of his workers by shortening hours and increasing wages. But he will be defeated by his competitors if he does so and will himself join the ranks of the proletariat. In the long run his employees will not benefit from his action. But, meantime, the workings of the capitalist system are undermining the foundation of that system and preparing the way for a new one, for a new stage of history.

The ranks of the proletariat swell; those of the capitalists dwindle. The concentration of production and centralization of control bring members of the proletariat into close proximity in the great urban centers. Unemployment, low wages, and bad working conditions increase the misery of the workers, but at the same time their class consciousness is increased. A series of crises sweep the capitalist system, each crisis bringing it closer to the point of collapse. The extension of capitalism to underdeveloped areas in an attempt to find new markets and investment opportunities brings temporary relief, but in the end it expands the size of the proletariat, extends the struggle and makes it worldwide in scope. At the same time the proletariat is learning how to use the instruments of production and distribution in preparation for the time when it will take control. The means (forces) of production have in fact become socialized, but the class structure (production relations) is still that which was appropriate to a capitalist system. As we have seen, Marx's theory insists that production relations are determined by the forces of production. When the point is reached under capitalism that these two are no longer compatible, the revolution is inevitable.

Revolution and the Proletarian Dictatorship

The revolution in which the proletariat displaces the capitalist class differs in some respects from previous revolutions in history, Marx says. Other revolutions have involved a number of classes, including the workers. In the proletarian revolution, however, only two classes exist; the development of capitalism has produced this bipolarization of class interests. Furthermore, the revolution of the proletariat is the first in which a majority gains control and a minority becomes the oppressed class. The revolution does not immediately abolish oppression. The remnants of the capitalist class still remain, and that class must be liquidated. Still, the purpose of the revolution is to create conditions which will ultimately do away with oppression altogether.

There is a question whether, in Marx's view, the proletarian revolution need be a violent one. A consideration of the dialectical process is of little help here, for it may be construed as support either for violence or for peaceful evolution. Despite his claimed scientism, Marx himself was not clear on the matter, and his lack of clarity has resulted in considerable confusion in the ranks of his followers. Lenin and the Bolsheviks in Russia insisted upon an interpretation that sanctioned the use of revolutionary violence. Others, in Germany, England, France, and elsewhere argued that the transition from capitalist to proletarian control could be effected peacefully yet in line with Marx's pronouncements on the subject. Marx had a tendency, prior to about 1860, to stress the violent nature of dialectical progress. Certainly this is the strong impression one receives in reading the *Communist Manifesto,* an obviously revolutionary document, with its appeals to the workers to arise and shake off the chains of servitude. In his *Contribution to the Critique of Political Economy,* published in 1859, he says that the superstructure of society, following a change of productive forces, will be "more or less rapidly transformed"— an indication, perhaps, that circumstances may determine whether the change will be violent or nonviolent. Still later he suggested that in such countries as the United States and England, where the principle of majority rule was a significant political factor, a peaceful transition from capitalism to socialism might be achieved. Irrespective of his feelings on the subject—and obviously they shifted from time to time—Marx would never have opposed violence if he thought it necessary to accomplish revolutionary objectives. That is, he may have favored peaceful change where possible; but change there must be, he would have said, no matter how it is accomplished.

Whatever the revolutionary form, peaceful or violent, no immediate change can be made from a capitalist to a communist society. A transitional period must first occur, during which preparations are made for the perfect community. A few remaining elements of capitalism must be swept away. The minds of men must be purged of the remnants of capitalist mentality with which they are infected. The now small capitalist class must be liquidated. All these preparations require the use of force, which means that a state and governmental machinery must be employed. The government will be a "dictatorship of the proletariat."

The proletariat, which captures control of society, will be compelled, Marx says, to employ, in the superstructure, the conventional instruments of oppression which have been used by exploiting classes in the past. A superstructure will be established that will utilize the appropriate components of law, codes of morals, and philosophy. The governmental form will be the proletarian dictatorship. This form is not distinguished from previous forms by its dictatorial nature. All governments, Marx contends, are dictatorial. The proletarian dictatorship differs from previous dictatorships in that it provides, for the first time in history, majority control. It is, Marx says, far more democratic than other governments have been, including the bourgeois democracy of capitalism. And while the proletariat operates for a time as an exploiting class, its purpose is not to perpetuate its own power but to eliminate oppression forever.

After having established a government to supply the force required to achieve its objectives, the proletariat must inaugurate a program that will carry society toward the perfect (communist) society. The program may vary from one country to another, but it should aim immediately at substantial inroads on the institution of private property with a view to its eventual abolition. In the *Communist Manifesto,* Marx and Engels outline a series of steps which generally indicate what should be done.

1. Property in land should be abolished and rents used for public purposes.
2. A progressive income tax should be established.
3. Rights of inheritance should be abolished.
4. The property of "emigrants and rebels" should be confiscated.
5. There should be state control, centralization, and monopoly of credit.
6. The state must control and centralize transportation and communication.
7. There should be expansion of state control of production and state improvement of agriculture.
8. There should be enforcement of the obligation of all persons to work and the formation of "industrial armies," to be used especially in agriculture.
9. Agricultural and manufacturing industries ought to be combined, together with a population resettlement, with a view to the elimination of the urban-rural division.
10. Child labor must be abolished, and a system of free public education established.

The point that comes most immediately to mind in reviewing this recommended program of action is that many of its features, in greater or lesser degree, have long since been adopted by countries whose economic systems are essentially capitalistic. The changes, moreover, have come through the "bourgeois" democratic process—a development which Marx would have believed impossible.

In this transitional stage of the proletarian dictatorship, as a new society emerges from the ruins of capitalism, rewards for labor will not be equal for all. This inequality is regrettable but inevitable because the new society is marked by the ideas of the old. In this phase of development, labor remains only a "means of life." It is still something men have to do in order to subsist, rather than an activity undertaken because of the enjoyment found in it. In the capitalist society the division of labor had developed as a technique of production. In the interests of efficiency men had become automatons, each performing a single task repetitiously, and this loss of individual identity was one of the most degrading aspects of the capitalist system. The worker had no pride of accomplishment, no sense of satisfaction in viewing the product of his labor. The result was a growing "antithesis between mental and physical labor." Men, in short, hated what they did when their entire working life was concentrated on a single and meaningless task. One of the goals of the transitional stage between capitalism and communism is the establishment of a system of production which will eliminate the division of labor and will thus make possible the development of well-rounded individuals who will take pleasure in their labor. Then men will work because they want to do so, not because they have to. It will then be possible to equalize rewards, for incentives will be unnecessary. In the final stage of communist development each will contribute "according to his ability," and receive "according to his needs."

The most intensive use of coercion will necessarily occur in the early stages of the dictatorship of the proletariat. At this time the strength of the remaining elements of the capitalist class is greatest, in terms of both numbers and the influence of its ideology. The power of the proletarian dictatorship must be employed, Marx states, to liquidate the capitalist class and the influence it exercises. For the first time in history, a class does not have to be maintained for exploitative reasons. The proletariat now both owns and operates the instruments of production; the relations of production, therefore, are not based upon the need for exploitation. As Marx puts it, "The bourgeois relations of production are the last antagonistic form of the social process of production." As the capitalist class and the remnants of its superstructural elements are rooted out, the necessity for the use of force diminishes. The proletarian dictatorship is creating a society consisting of a single class. Since the state and state power are always used solely as instruments of one class over another, the need for them dwindles as capitalism wanes and the proletariat increases. Ultimately, Marx says, there will be only one class, the proletariat, living according to its own ideals. And since one class is the same as no class at all, the classless society will have been achieved. At that time, the state, which has been in the process of withering away from the time the revolution was completed, will disappear entirely. Mankind may then inaugurate the new and perfect communist society toward which the dialectical forces in history have been carrying him.

The Communist Society

Let us review briefly what Marx assumed would be the components of this "brave new world." It is, as we have seen, a classless society. A greater degree of equality will be established among men than has ever existed before, although differences of ability will be recognized in the administrative structure of the community. But men will be regarded as ends in themselves, rather than as means to the ends of others in a dominant class. It is a society without a state, for the state is the organized expression of class violence, and there are no more classes. Political problems, which have plagued men throughout history, will be irrelevant in the new society. Such troublesome issues as representation and rights will disappear. They are meaningful only in terms of class interest and obviously have no place in the classless society. There will be no private property, for private property is a feature of a system of production in which one class exploits another. Gone, too, will be the great concern with the possession and accumulation of commodities (the "fetishism of the commodity"), which was typical of a capitalist and acquisitive society. Commodities will have significance only in terms of their use; their mere possession will be of no value whatsoever.

The communist society will be highly industrialized. The old capitalist system made its contribution to historical development by creating the methods of production which make a communist society possible. Only the latter, however, knows how to employ such a system in the interest of all men. Automation, the substitution of machines for men, which created such difficulties for capitalism and indeed contributed to its collapse, will be a great advantage under communism. A society which properly distributes the commodities it produces and is unconcerned with surplus value will not have to deal with such problems as overproduction, underconsumption, unemployment, and depression. The new society will continue to develop improved techniques of production. As it does so, men will be able to work fewer hours and, instead, devote themselves to cultural pursuits. They will develop a diversity of interests and thus build the truly human personality, which was impossible under capitalism. Thus a genuinely civilized life will become a reality. Finally, the new society will be based upon the principle of cooperation, rather than competition. A true community will be formed in which freedom will be possible for all men.

This is the dialectical stage with which Marx is concerned. Its realization is close enough so that he believes he can see its outlines clearly, and he is convinced that it is a great improvement over what has gone before. But the dialectic, for Marx as for Hegel, is an unending process; even as the thesis represented by the communist society is forming, a new antithesis is preparing to attack it. But the conflict of the future is not Marx's problem. Like Hegel, he makes no pretense of being able to see beyond that phase of history upon the threshold of which he stands.

Conclusions

A careful and analytical approach to the study of Marxist theory reveals an amazing number of sweeping generalizations, inconsistencies, and contradictions. The same, however, may be said of any theory which purports, as Marx's does, to present a solution to the multitude of difficulties that beset society. The flaws in the theory do not invalidate it, particularly if we consider the impact it has had upon the world. If this be the basis of judgment, we must acknowledge its importance. Marxism is today the official ideology of millions. True, it has been imposed by force upon most of them, but many have embraced it without compulsion because they have been convinced of its essential rightness. It is a matter of controversy today whether or to what degree the Marxist theory itself constitutes a threat to free men, or whether the nationalistic policies of the nations that have espoused the doctrines constitute the real danger. Whatever the danger may be, we ought obviously to know something about the theory. This involves not only an understanding of its basic tenets, but also an appreciation of its strengths, the reasons for its appeal, and an awareness of its weaknesses. In short we should attempt to be "scientific" or objective in our attitude. We may hope, in making the attempt, to be more successful than was Marx, who, as has been said, arrived at a verdict before trying the case.

Convinced Marxists extol the "truth" of their doctrine with a zeal akin to that found in dedicated promulgators of a faith. And Marxism is in many respects greatly like a religion. Of course, no true Marxist can be religious in the conventional sense. Religion is a part of the super-structure of a capitalistic society and is used merely to rationalize the position of the ruling class and to hold the subject class in its place. By painting an appealing picture of life in the next world, the Marxist says, the capitalist can persuade the proletarian to accept his miserable lot in this one. Religion is, in Marx's words, the "opium" of the poor. Nevertheless, Marxism itself bears a resemblance to religion, and this accounts in part for its appeal. The communist utopia, which follows the proletarian dictatorship, is the communist heaven. The capitalist world represents the travail of this world, which gives way to the purga-tory of the proletarian dictatorship. The saved are those who follow the teachings of the master, and paradise may be achieved in this world—in Marx's mind, at least, a considerable improvement over Christian doc-trine. In the perfect society the essential goodness of man will permit him to live without authority. Undoubtedly many other parallels may be drawn.

Marxism also may appeal to democrats. It employs many of the slogans that have long been associated with democracy. Where could one find more liberty than is promised in the ultimate communist society? Where could there be more equality than in the classless society? Where could a greater degree of fraternity be found than in the communist world where men labor little and are able to devote a great part of their lives to cultural pursuits? [5] Even the proletarian dictatorship is a model of majority rule. And Marxism adds to these advantages a promise of se-curity. In making the promise in the nineteenth century, it was in line with other socialist movements of the time and with subsequent liberal and democratic political philosophies. As we saw at the beginning of this chapter, it had become evident that political democracy alone, particu-larly as complemented by a policy of economic *laissez faire,* could not solve the problem of society in an industrial age. The rights to vote, to have representation, to worship and to speak freely are all of consider-

[5] Marx's faith that men, freed from most toil, will utilize their free time in cultural activities, has long been a dream of utopian thinkers. It may be difficult to demonstrate, however, as we enter the age of automation, that an increased amount of leisure results in additional cultural development. The fallacy lies in the assumption that all, or at least most, men have only been restrained from extending their knowledge by the great length of time they have had to work each day. Apparently there is more to the prob-lem than establishing a six- or a four-hour day.

able value, but may mean little or nothing to an unemployed and under-nourished person. The socialist and liberal reformers of Marx's time—and later—have argued that political democracy is of little value unless supplemented by an economic system which provides a sufficient measure of security to all men. That indeed is the course that has been followed; the fact that Marxists were in the vanguard of the advocates of such a doctrine may account in part for their success. And still today, Marxism makes its appeal to the economically oppressed. Its appeal cannot be taken lightly by the opponents of communism and cannot be combatted merely by mouthing slogans, a fact understood by those who have supported such policies as economic aid for underdeveloped areas.

There is, also, a psychological appeal in Marxist thought. It offers an answer to men's problems. It tells the depressed that they are not themselves to blame for their inferior status; they are victims of a system and need only to change the system to be able to live on a plane of equality with all men. Somewhat related is the "scientific" appeal of Marxism. Marx intended his theory to be scientific, and it gives the appearance of scientific objectivity. His conclusions are fortified with statistics and historical "facts" in great abundance. To those who lack knowledge of the fields Marx deals with such a display can be convincing. Those who are attracted to the goals of Marxism take satisfaction in knowing that their cause is scientifically "proved."

Despite the strengths, or better, perhaps, the appealing qualities of Marxist doctrines, there are a great many weaknesses. The course of capitalist development has been quite unlike that foreseen by Marx, who assumed, incorrectly as it turned out, that capitalism was in his time already on the verge of collapse. True, the capitalism that has persisted has been considerably different from the system with which Marx was acquainted, but the transition from the exploitative capitalism of the early and middle nineteenth century to the moderate capitalism of the mid-twentieth century has occurred as a result of actions which Marx had deemed impossible. The regulation of hours, wages, and working conditions, the prohibition of child labor, the establishment of unemployment insurance and workmen's compensation, and many more developments have resulted from legislative enactments and have created an entirely different situation for working people. Yet Marx had specifically denied that a factor in the superstructure, in this case the law, could be utilized to improve the lot of the proletariat.

Marx also forecast the growth of the proletariat and the shrinking of the capitalist class. One would be hard pressed to demonstrate this today. In the advanced industrial countries (and the United States is surely the prime example) there has been a vast expansion of the ranks of the owners of the instruments of production through the sale and purchase of corporate stocks. It is true that the great majority of these owners play no role in the management of corporate concerns, but nevertheless, this is a development which Marx did not foresee. Also, the rapid growth of the "white-collar" class, professional people, clerical jobholders, those engaged in services of one kind or another, highly skilled workers, and others has been an outstanding social feature of a developing industrial system. The result has been a relative decline in the numbers of the proletariat and a considerable weakening of class consciousness, rather than the strengthening that Marx anticipated. In a nation in which the overwhelming majority of the people regard themselves, and rightly, as members of the middle class, it is difficult to find support for Marx's theory of class conflict.

The rise of organized labor to a position of political power has also been contrary to Marx's theory. Not that he believed workers would not or could not organize; indeed he thought their organization would be a development of the period immediately preceding the proletarian revolution. But that such a force could play a political role, that it could in fact demand and receive legislative benefits of great magnitude, was contrary to a basic tenet of Marx's theory. Marx contended that the superstructure, including government and laws, were instruments employed by the class which owned the instruments of production to achieve their own ends and to hold the working class in subjection. One who witnessed the great influence upon government of organized labor in the United States from 1932 to 1952 could hardly give credence to this fundamental aspect of Marxian theory. The same could be said of the rise of the Labor party in England; and many other examples could be cited. In short, it is not a fact that the owners of the instruments of production always monopolize government and the legislative process.

Finally, Marx believed that no society could supplant another until that other had developed fully all the potential that was in it. Capitalism was impossible until feudalism had completely run its course, and capitalism, is, Marx thought, subject to the same course of evolution. "No social order ever disappears before all the productive forces for which there is room in it have been developed." The argument seems clear-cut and unqualified. Yet if one looks at the countries which are termed communistic, Russia and China being the major examples, he sees that in neither society was there anything like a complete industrial development. They were both, in fact, primarily agrarian and nearly feudalistic societies prior to their leap into socialism. Various developments such as those we have cited meant that Marx's successors were compelled to devote themselves to adapting and interpreting Marx's theories in order to maintain their viability. This demanding task was handled with considerable competence by Nicolai Lenin.

SELECTED BIBLIOGRAPHY

Bober, M. M.: *Karl Marx's Interpretation of History,* 2d rev. ed., Harvard University Press, Cambridge, Mass., 1948.

Capital, The Communist Manifesto, and Other Writings by Karl Marx (edited with an introduction by Max Eastman), Modern Library, Inc., New York, 1932, introduction.

Chang, Sherman H. M.: *The Marxian Theory of the State,* John Spencer, Inc., Chester, Pa., 1931.

Coker, Francis W.: *Recent Political Thought,* Appleton-Century-Crofts, Inc., New York, 1934, chaps. 1–3.

Cole, G. D. H.: *What Marx Really Meant,* Alfred A. Knopf, Inc., New York, 1934.

Cornu, Auguste: *The Origins of Marxian Thought,* Charles C Thomas, Publisher, Springfield, Ill., 1957.

Ebenstein, William: *Today's Isms,* 2d ed., Prentice-Hall, Inc., Englewood Cliffs, N.J., 1958, part I.

Hacker, Andrew: *Political Theory: Philosophy, Ideology, Science,* The Macmillan Company, New York, 1961, chap. 13.

Hook, Sidney: *Marx and the Marxists, The Ambiguous Legacy,* D. Van Nostrand Company, Inc., Princeton, N.J., 1955, chaps. 1, 2.

———: *Towards the Understanding of Karl Marx: A Revolutionary Interpretation,* The John Day Company, Inc., New York, 1933.

Mayo, H. B.: *Democracy and Marxism,* Oxford University Press, Fair Lawn, N.J., 1955.

Mendel, Arthur P. (ed.): *Essential Works of Marxism,* Bantam Books, Inc., New York, 1961, introduction.

Meyer, Alfred G.: *Marxism: The Unity of Theory and Practice,* Harvard University Press, Cambridge, Mass., 1954.

Roll, Eric: *A History of Economic Thought,* 3d ed., Prentice-Hall, Inc., Englewood Cliffs, N.J., 1959, chaps. 4–6.

Sabine, George H.: *A History of Political Theory,* 3d ed., Holt, Rinehart and Winston, Inc., New York, 1961, chap. 33.

twenty

LENIN

The house of socialism has always been a commodious but quarrelsome one. Marx himself devoted a great deal of time and energy to a defense of his "scientific socialism" and to an attack upon those of his fellow socialists who disagreed with him. In 1872, following a long and bitter doctrinal dispute between Marx and the anarchist, Michael Bakunin (1814–1876), the International Association of Workingmen, which Marx had helped to found in 1864, collapsed. Marx and Bakunin agreed upon many points, but the anarchists rejected Marx's program of political action and his argument that a dictatorship of the proletariat would have to precede an anarchistic and communistic community. Bakunin's view was that man had already been prepared, by a long and arduous evolutionary development, to live a life free from governmental authority, and that it was only necessary to stage a revolution that would destroy the existing state to achieve such an idyllic existence. Marx regarded this view as arrant nonsense of the radical and utopian kind which had long damaged the socialist cause. It was, he thought, a far cry from his own scientific, practical, and hardheaded proposals.

The schismatic tendencies of socialism became even more apparent following the death of Engels in 1895. Marx's prestige, which was considerable in socialist circles during his lifetime, increased after he died. Engels, Marx's closest friend and collaborator, was widely regarded as his successor as doctrinal leader of the socialist movement and was able to maintain a degree of unity. But cohesion in the long run depended upon the ability of socialists to come to an agreement with respect to an interpretation of Marx's theory and upon the conditions prevailing within the various countries where socialist movements existed. Almost all socialist organizations claimed to base their doctrine and program on the Marxian gospel; they disagreed violently over precisely what that gospel meant. Moreover, the political, economic, and social conditions varied so greatly from one country to another that it was impossible to reach a consensus on the tactics to be employed to attain socialist goals. Marx's theory had been so sweeping and, on occasion, so vague and contradictory in nature, that it was susceptible of a multitude of differing interpretations. Socialist groups in Western Europe and in England covered a political spectrum ranging from democratic to anarchistic; they all claimed a Marxist authority for their programs.

Although many doctrinal issues divided the socialists, the most persistent division was that between the revolutionary and the evolutionary or revisionist socialists. The revolutionists insisted that violent revolution would at some stage and in some degree be necessary to displace the bourgeois state and substitute their own control. The revisionists stressed the evolutionary aspects of Marx's writings. History, they contended, is on the side of the workers, and capitalism will ultimately fall without a revolution. The revisionists, of whom the best known was Edward Bernstein (1850–1932), also rejected a number of the basic tenets of Marxism on the ground that developments had proved them invalid. Bernstein argued that capitalism was much farther from collapse than Marx had believed. For a patient supposedly on the deathbed, capitalism was demonstrating remarkable vitality. Moreover, he said, it appears that capitalism is accompanied by a growth, rather than a diminution, of the middle class. Capitalist monopoly is not following the course predicted by Marx; there are more, not fewer, enterprises than formerly. Political democracy is being employed to improve rather than to worsen the lot of the working class. Economic factors alone do not determine the nonmaterial aspects of society, although they are important. Socialism may be achieved without revolutionary violence.

A repudiation of such fundamental parts of Marxism did not constitute, as it might appear, a total departure from the theory. The revisionists claimed a tenuous connection with Marx in their attacks upon the exploitation of workers, their charge that capitalism leads to underconsumption and recurring crises, and the assertion that a system of private ownership prevents the attainment of a desirable degree of economic equality. It should be noted, however, that while these are undoubtedly principles of socialism, they are not necessarily tenets of Marxist socialism. That this tacit repudiation of Marx was ultimately recognized by the revisionists is evidenced by the fact that Bernstein and others of the school tended to move toward an independent position in their later writings. Bernstein finally rejected the dialectic completely and relied upon the empirical method. Jean Jaurès (1859–1914), the French revisionist, was even more critical of Marx than was Bernstein. An avowed democrat, Jaurès rejected the notion of class warfare, of economic determinism, and of revolution, and advocated education, reform, and the democratic process as the proper methods to achieve a socialist society.

Socialists generally embraced the principle of revolution when they were convinced that it constituted their only chance of success. Where the democratic process had been employed to achieve some reforms and improve conditions for industrial workers, socialist tactics in the main consisted of demands for more of the same. Events in Great Britain furnished the best example of this development. In 1884 the Fabian Society, comprising a group of intellectuals who had been influenced by the writings of Marx and John Stuart Mill, began its campaign for social reform. The Fabians were socialists. They proposed the eventual abolition of private property and argued for community ownership of land and industrial capital. History, they said, has demonstrated an evolutionary development of society toward economic socialism and political democracy; unlike Marx, they regarded these as complementary principles. They agreed with Marx that workers create value which is unjustifiably taken from them by owners. The Fabians, however, refused to believe that class warfare was either inevitable or desirable as a method of rectifying social evils. Instead they sought, through lectures and pamphlets, to educate the middle class, to extend the suffrage, and to make the democratic process more effective. Not revolution but legislation was the key to the establishment of a cooperative and socialist society. The influence of the Fabians was considerable, a fact attributable, perhaps, as much to the quality of the membership as to the persuasiveness of the program. The early Fabian society included such luminaries as H. G. Wells, Sidney Webb, J. Ramsey MacDonald, Keir Hardie, G. D. H. Cole, and George Bernard Shaw.

Other British socialists, believing that the Fabians placed too great an emphasis upon political solutions, without understanding the basic difficulties arising out of an industrial system, organized the Guild Socialists movement. Guild Socialists opposed, as had Marx, the dehumanizing work involved in large-scale production with its division of labor. They accepted the labor theory of value and the theory of surplus value, although in modified form, and they maintained that property is justified only when it renders a service to society. They did not object to political democracy, but they argued that a government by representatives elected on a territorial basis was incapable of understanding and solving the complex problems of an industrial society. The Guild Socialists maintained that a system of functional representation based upon industrial unions would be best suited to a modern community. They advocated the retention of the state but thought that its functions could be greatly restricted when the unions, or guilds, assumed responsibility for governing in matters primarily related to the economy. There were many disagreements among members concerning details of the program, but the Guild Socialists were as opposed to revolution as were the Fabians.

In such countries as France and Russia, where governmental opposition made unfeasible any reliance by the workers on the democratic process, socialism developed revolutionary overtones. In France this condition gave rise to the syndicalist movement. There are similarities between syndicalism and Guild Socialism; the latter, indeed, drew its initial inspiration from syndicalism. Syndicalism rejected political solutions and the Marxian idea that workers could use the state to accomplish their purposes. Like the Guild Socialists, they proposed a society organized into trade unions or *syndicats*. They suggested that most problems could be solved by local *syndicats*, and that a national system of *syndicat* affiliations could administer affairs which transcended the local level. They took from Marx the concept of the class struggle and the view that the state is an instrument of oppression and should be abolished. To this end they advocated a program of direct action, including the use of the boycott, the union label, and strike, sabotage, and the general strike. The general strike, meaning a simultaneous and concerted strike by all the workers in the nation, was never actually employed by the syndicalists, and the advisability of its use was a matter of disagreement among them. To Georges Sorel (1847–1922), one of the leaders of syndicalism, the myth value of the general strike was paramount. It served as a symbol of the power of the working class—of the extent to which society depends upon that class. It had value, too, as a threat of what could happen if the demands of workers were not met. Syndicalism developed both revolutionary and nonrevolutionary wings, but revolutionary syndicalism was the more active and important movement.

By all odds, the most significant political movement growing out of Marxism from the time of Marx's death until the Russian Revolution was social democracy. By the close of the nineteenth century the Social Democrats constituted a formidable political force in Germany and was evidencing strength in France and England. The philosophical basis of social democracy was that interpretation of Marx's theory which came to be known as "orthodox" Marxism. Its outstanding formulator and proponent, after Engels (whose later pronouncements lent support to the orthodox position), was the German, Karl Kautsky (1854–1939). Kautsky and the orthodox socialists defended Marxist doctrine against the attacks of the revisionists. They admitted that there were minor defects in

Marx's theory, but they held that the principles were fundamentally sound and that events had demonstrated the accuracy of Marx's predictions.

The most significant distinction between orthodox and revisionist socialism was the orthodox contention that revolution would at some stage and in some form be necessary to the establishment of the socialist society. Kautsky, however, after a period during which he advocated a militant program of class struggle and revolution, began to minimize the role of violence. An enlightened program, he believed, would lessen the need for violent revolution. To this end Kautsky favored agitation for universal suffrage and for social welfare legislation, the organization of cooperatives, and the use of trade unions, all of which he believed would not only improve the condition of the worker but also make for a less violent transition from capitalism to socialism. Kautsky bitterly disputed the claims of Lenin and the Bolsheviks that the proletariat must be directed by an elite party organization and charged that the undemocratic nature of Soviet government and the Communist party following the Revolution in Russia were in violation of Marxian principles. Mild as it was, the ideological bark of orthodox socialism was still more radical than its programmatic bite. In practice Kautsky and his followers were as unrevolutionary as the revisionists, the Fabians, and the Guild Socialists.

By the turn of the century it appeared that Marxism, which entered the historical scene with a militantly revolutionary explosion through the *Manifesto* and other early tracts, was evolving into little more than a combination of political democracy and social welfare. That in fact was the direction of socialist evolution in England and much of Western Europe—a demonstration of the rule that a theory, to be effective, must somehow accommodate itself to its environment. Workers in these countries were discovering that progress could be made without resort to revolution. If that progress was slow, as indeed it was in many instances, it was still preferable to a bloody conflict, the outcome of which was unpredictable. As long as governments were reasonably responsive to the demands made upon them by the working class, they had no cause for alarm. The government of one major country consistently refused to make the most modest concessions. The intransigency of the czarist regime in Russia led to the reassertion of the revolutionary qualities of Marxism and changed the course of world history.

Russia: The Setting and the Revolution

If it had been possible for any one group or leader to gather together the scattered revolutionary tendencies in nineteenth-century Russia, the Revolution would have occurred long before it did. The vastness of the country, widespread illiteracy, and the inadequacy of communications, however, enabled the rulers to concentrate their forces on one revolutionary faction at a time and thus prevent a successful uprising prior to the spring of 1917, although the regime was very nearly toppled in 1905. Adequate justification for insurrection had long existed. The base of the population was a large peasant class that was only a step removed from serfdom. Upon this base rested a landowning class, the nobility, and a czarist ruling family, all of whom exploited the peasants unmercifully. A small measure of relief was granted in the middle of the nineteenth century under the direction of Alexander II, who ruled from 1855 to 1881. A system of communal farms was established, and each peasant was granted a small plot of land for private use. The court system was reformed, education was improved, and somewhat more freedom of the press was permitted. A system of representative assemblies, the *zemstvos,* was created, although delegates were not democratically elected, and in any event they exercised little power.[1] The benefits accruing from Alexander's reforms were nominal. It became apparent to liberal-minded men that little of significance could be accomplished as long as the basic structure of society remained unchanged.

By the turn of the century three fairly well-defined movements for reform had developed. There was an attempt by the middle class to secure a constitutional system resembling those of the advanced industrial countries of Western Europe; this was represented by the Constitutional Democrats. There was an agrarian socialist movement with revolutionary proclivities which, in 1901, became the Socialist Revolutionary party. Finally, there was a Marxist group composed basically of the small but rapidly growing industrial working class, to whom the doctrine had special appeal. Marx's *Capital* had been translated into Russian in 1872 and had been strongly approved by a number of would-be Russian revolutionaries who had become convinced that the peasants lacked a revolutionary potential. The industrial workers, on the other hand, were concentrated in relatively small areas, and their working conditions, similar to those that had prevailed in the West a century before, were such as to cause them to listen to Marxian solutions with a sympathetic ear.

The reigns of Alexander III and Nicholas II in the last part of the nineteenth and the first part of the twentieth century aggravated an already dangerous situation. The Russo-Japanese War (1904–1905) weakened the regime and laid bare the corruption of the bureaucracy. Following the war, a series of strikes, rebellions, and uprisings forced the government to make a few concessions toward reform. The czar promised the establishment of a national representative assembly (the Duma) and the protection of civil rights. As soon as the government

[1] Francis W. Coker, *Recent Political Thought,* Appleton-Century-Crofts, Inc., New York, 1934, pp. 146–148.

could regroup its forces, however, it reverted to its old policy of repression. A Duma was formed, but it exercised no real authority. Civil liberties did not receive the promised protection.

The conditions growing out of World War I finally ignited the flame of revolution in Russia. As in the Russo-Japanese War, all the weaknesses of the regime were exposed by the stresses to which the governmental structure was exposed. The army suffered a number of disastrous defeats because of lack of arms and equipment. There were severe shortages of food and other necessities for the civilian population. The Revolution, when it began on February 23, 1917, grew spontaneously out of disorders among persons waiting in food lines in St. Petersburg. These were followed by strikes among the workers and a mutiny of the St. Petersburg garrison, which went over to the side of the strikers. Within five days the revolutionaries controlled St. Petersburg, and the revolution had spread over a large part of the country. On March 2, Czar Nicholas abdicated in favor of his brother, the Grand Duke Michael, but the latter refused the throne on the ground that it was too late to save the monarchy.

A provisional government was established to administer affairs until a legal government could be formed following the election of a constituent assembly. On February 27, however, a Soviet (Council) of Workers' and Soldiers' Deputies had been established in St. Petersburg. Other soviets were quickly formed in other parts of the country. These competed with the provisional government for authority. The soviets were dominated by the Menshevik, or moderate, faction of the Social Democratic party until September, at which time the radical Bolsheviks were able to establish control.[2] The provisional government and the soviets vied for favor with the people. In October the provisional government under Alexander Kerensky was overthrown, and the Bolshevik-dominated soviets became the official government of Russia.

Lenin: The Man and His Work

In carrying the Revolution to the establishment of an official government, no one played a more important role than Nicolai Lenin, the leader of the Bolsheviks. Lenin had hurried to Russia from Switzerland, where he had been living in exile, as soon as news of the uprising in St. Petersburg reached him. On his arrival he took charge of the Bolshevik faction and fought simultaneously against the provisional government and the Menshevik moderates. Lenin conceived the strategy which brought victory to the Bolsheviks. He well understood the temper of the Russian mind at the time. The provisional government assumed that the people's resentment was directed toward the inefficient conduct of the war and

[2] The term "Bolshevik" means majority. Menshevik means minority. The split in the Social Democratic party which led to the use of these terms will be discussed shortly.

promised reorganization and reform as a corrective step while promising at the same time to honor their commitments to the Allies. Lenin knew that the people were sick of war, no matter how expertly it might be conducted, and promised an immediate termination of hostilities. The provisional government stated that it favored land reform but asked the indulgence of the peasants until the convening of the Constituent Assembly could create a legal government to handle the matter. Lenin charged the provisional government with deluding the peasants, said that such promises would prove to be as chimerical as czarist promises of the past, and advocated the division of land among the peasants without delay. To the industrial workers Lenin promised the abolition of private property and the transfer of power to the proletariat. Lenin's was the well-known strategy of promising something to everyone, and while many of those promises proved in the end to be delusive, they were highly effective at the time. Of course more was involved in the rise of the Bolsheviks to power than an appealing collection of slogans and promises.

For one thing, the circumstances were favorable. The country was ripe for revolution, and the Bolsheviks were on the scene at the right time with the correct strategy. Moreover, their competitors were less ably led and were incapable of presenting a united front against the Bolsheviks, whose ability, dedication, and ruthlessness they tragically underestimated. Nonetheless, fortunate circumstances do not detract from the very considerable accomplishments of Lenin. His contributions to the cause of Marxism had, until the Revolution, been essentially polemical. But as a revolutionary strategist, as a politician, and as a statesman, he demonstrated qualities of greatness, despite possible criticisms of the ends to which his abilities were directed. The question may long be debated as to whether the Soviet Union has followed a course which Lenin would have approved. But it was he, more than any other, who established the base from which it could function. And if the ideological foundation of Soviet policy is Marxist—another point which has been questioned—it is a Marxism shaped by Leninist interpretations.

The name Lenin was a pseudonym assumed during a period of Siberian exile. Nicolai Lenin was born Vladimir Ilyich Ulyanov on April 9, 1870, at Simbirsk, now Ulyanovsk, in Russia. His parents were teachers, middle-class and respectable; they reared five children, all of whom became revolutionaries. Lenin's older brother, Alexander, was executed at the age of nineteen for having taken part in a plot to assassinate Czar Alexander III. This event stimulated the already deep hatred which Lenin had for the regime. As a boy Lenin attended school at the Simbirsk gymnasium, from which he graduated with honors in 1887. He then entered Kazan University to study law. He was expelled for a time for political activities but was later readmitted, although he devoted more attention to the works of Marx then to the study of jurisprudence. Later he went to the University of St. Petersburg, where he passed the law examinations and took his degree in 1891.

Lenin practiced law for a short time at Samara, but he had no real interest in the profession for which he had been trained. In 1894 he returned to St. Petersburg, where he began to write revolutionary pamphlets and to attack those who were, in his opinion, perverting Marxian doctrines by diluting their revolutionary principles. The following year, 1895, Lenin took a trip abroad to meet Georgi Plekhanov (1856–1918), the founder of Russian social democracy, and other revolutionaries who lived in exile from their native Russia. When he returned, Lenin organized a revolutionary group known as the "Union for the Liberation of the Working Class." In December of 1895 he was arrested by czarist police, tried and found guilty of revolutionary activities, and sentenced to prison for a term of one year. He was then sent into Siberian exile for three years. Here, in 1898, he married Nadezhda Krupskaya, also an exiled revolutionary, who loyally shared the vicissitudes of the rest of Lenin's life. While in exile in Siberia, Lenin wrote his most important economic work, *The Development of Capitalism in Russia.*

After his release, Lenin went to Switzerland to arrange for the publication of a revolutionary paper, *Iskra (The Spark)*, and to organize a revolutionary underground party to lead the proletariat against the Russian government. He soon rose to a position of leadership among the Social Democrats, although his radical approach to problems alienated many of the more moderate party elements. In 1903 he led his followers in an intraparty struggle, which resulted in the formation of the Bolshevik and Menshevik wings of the party. The issues over which the break occurred involved both organization and tactics. The Mensheviks wanted a loose and inclusive party organization on the Western model and proposed to follow an opportunist policy of cooperation with liberal elements of the bourgeoisie. Lenin and the Bolsheviks insisted upon a small, compact, militant, and disciplined party allied with the more revolutionary elements of the peasantry; they rejected any strategy which minimized the revolutionary party goal. The schism was never healed, and it plagued the Social Democratic party until the issue was finally resolved through the dissolution of the Menshevik wing following the Bolshevik assumption of power in 1917.

In 1905 Lenin took part in the abortive uprisings against the Russian government which grew out of the country's defeat in the Russo-Japanese War. In 1907 he again left Russia and did not return until 1917. These ten years were devoted to study, writing, organizational work, and the bitter struggle with the Mensheviks and others who disagreed with his ideas on organization and tactics. When World War I began, Lenin attacked its imperialist character and charged those Social Democratic leaders who supported their own governments with treason to the principles of Marxism and the working-class movement. When the Russian Revolution began in 1917, Lenin went to Russia, where he assumed leadership of the Bolsheviks. In October the soviets overthrew the provisional government, and Lenin became head of the new government. He made peace with Germany, although at the cost of a great deal of Russian territory, put down a counterrevolution, frustrated attempts of the Allies at intervention, and launched the New Economic Policy, a temporary concession to private enterprise which gave him time to consolidate his regime. Lenin demonstrated ability as a statesman and administrator in establishing a revolutionary government and setting it on its initial course. An attempt to assassinate him was made in the summer of 1918, but although he was badly wounded, he was able to return to work in the fall of that year. Exhaustion, however, accomplished what the bullets of an assassin had failed to do. Lenin became seriously ill early in 1922. He lingered on in bad health for nearly two years and died on January 21, 1924. His place was soon taken by Joseph Stalin, who had been assiduously preparing the ground for his accession long before Lenin died.

Lenin was a prolific writer. His books, pamphlets, and letters fill many volumes. We shall be primarily concerned here with his views as expressed in: *What Is To Be Done?* (1902); *Two Tactics of the Social Democracy in the Democratic Revolution* (1905); *Materialism and Empiriocriticism* (1909); *Imperialism, the Final Stage of Capitalism* (1916); *State and Revolution* (1917).

The Organization of the Proletariat

Leninism, as a body of theory, is a revision of Marxism to account for developments which Marx did not foresee or foresaw inaccurately, and an adaptation of Marxism to the necessities of the Russian Revolution of 1917 and the following period. These were difficult tasks for Lenin. Marx had evolved a doctrine applicable to an industrial country that had gone through a full period of capitalist development. Lenin had to apply this doctrine to a country, Russia, which was essentially agrarian and only entering the stage of industrial capitalism. In doing so, Lenin suggested the tactics which have subsequently been employed in the underdeveloped areas of the world where Marxism, or at least the Leninist-Stalinist adaptation of it, has been most successful. Lenin was mainly a political activist, always more interested in concrete accomplishments than in the formulation of theory. Theory was always, to him, an instrument, a justification of action. Although he accepted the "scientific" aspects of Marxism, Lenin believed that it was also useful as a faith, as something in which men could believe, with power to hold a movement together. It was also a "guide to action" rather than an inflexible dogma.[3]

[3] George H. Sabine, *A History of Political Theory*, 3d ed., Holt, Rinehart and Winston, Inc., New York, 1961, pp. 806–807.

This being so, Leninism is distinguished by its broadness, its vagueness, even by its contradictory character. Changing circumstances necessitated doctrinal shifts. And despite Lenin's skill in adjusting the ideology to meet the exigencies of the moment, those shifts are readily apparent to all whose vision is not impaired by partisan bias.

The need to adapt Marx's theory to a program of action arose early in Lenin's career as a revolutionary. Marx had stated that the course of historical development, particularly as it relates to the means of production, would create conditions which would make revolution inevitable. Competition would shrink the ranks of the capitalists and swell those of the proletariat. The lot of the workers would grow increasingly worse. At the same time they would become concentrated in urban areas, learn to operate the instruments of production, and develop a class consciousness which would ultimately lead them to revolt, destroy the bourgeois state, and create their own state, the dictatorship of the proletariat, under the rule of the vast majority. This, Marx believed, was a process which, though inevitable, could not be artificially accelerated. No system would give way to another until all the potential for development within it had been exhausted. Nevertheless, capitalism was in the twilight of its existence, and the time for the revolution of the workers was close at hand.

Conditions which had developed in several Western countries since this expression of Marx's views gave little support to his theory. Living standards had improved for the working class; contrary to what Marx had assumed, workers had enjoyed some success in influencing the legislative process; the proletariat appeared to be less inclined to violent revolution than ever before. As we have seen, the majority of socialists tended to a reinterpretation of Marx's ideas which could both explain their inherent contradictions and give greater support to a democratic application of the doctrines. Many argued that Marx had underrated the potential of political democracy and that that system was capable of lessening, if not eliminating, the socialists' need for a policy of violent revolution. Lenin scorned this explanation and offered his own, which we shall consider shortly. Mainly he was interested in retaining, or restoring, the revolutionary qualities of Marxism. His position is understandable. The socialists of England, Germany, France, and a few other countries had some reason to be optimistic with respect to the opportunities offered by democracy. Lenin's experience was with the oppressive czarist regime, and he had little cause to believe that democracy could do much to mitigate the harshness of that regime in the foreseeable future. These factors influenced Lenin's formulation of a theory of party organization and a new and different status and role for the proletariat which set him apart from the more moderate schools of socialist thought. It also brought him prestige and established him as a major leader of the revolutionary and radical wing of Marxism.

Marx had erred, Lenin said, in assuming that the proletariat would develop a revolutionary class consciousness which would carry them into conflict with the capitalists without leadership, assistance, or stimulation from any outside source. The techniques of the capitalists had been more subtle and beguiling than Marx had supposed. Moreover, the scraps thrown to the proletariat by the capitalist-dominated democratic governments had led them to believe, falsely, that the total goal of socialism could be attained in the same manner. Thus the proletariat had become captives of their environment. The limits of proletarian class consciousness in a bourgeois-conditioned society could not, without assistance, transcend trade unionism. In trade unions workers had sought, and with limited success brought about, some improvement of wages, hours, and working conditions. Such an organization, however, does not promote the revolutionary spirit that must prevail if workers are to reach their ultimate goals. Trade unions do not instruct workers in the causes of their predicament and teach them that the capitalist system itself must be destroyed.

A revolutionary class consciousness must be implanted in the minds of the proletariat by the revolutionary intellectuals of the enlightened bourgeoisie. Only this group is capable of rising above the environmental restrictions created by the capitalist class. The workers themselves are too involved with the day-to-day problems of making a living. It is too much to ask that they should develop an understanding of the intricacies of historical materialism, to know the forces acting upon them, and to form the organization which will enable them to establish their own society. Only professional revolutionaries, able and willing to devote their lives to these tasks, are capable of such accomplishments. These leaders must educate and propagandize the workers, thus creating the revolutionary spirit that characterizes the proper level of proletarian class consciousness. The revolutionary fervor of the masses may be stimulated in this manner, but even this spirit of revolt does not produce in the proletariat a sufficiently high level of socialist consciousness to permit a transition from a capitalist to a communist society. This can only be accomplished during the period of the dictatorship of the proletariat; here the final elements of bourgeois mentality will be eliminated under the guidance and supervision of the intellectual leaders of the proletariat.

To prepare the minds of the proletariat for revolution, to guide that revolution, and to direct the workers to the stage of socialism require, in Lenin's view, a kind of force greatly different from that which Marx had considered. The growth of class consciousness, the act of revolution, and the establishment and direction of a proletarian state are all developments which, in Marx's theory, involve the proletarian class as a whole. Lenin, on the other hand, believed that these things will happen only if they are anticipated and directed by a small and highly disciplined group of professional revolutionaries. The proletariat, in short, must be guided by a party which constitutes the "vanguard of the proletariat." Such a party must be capable of operating secretly. Lenin, of course, was thinking specifically of Russia, where the possibility of organizing a mass party designed to achieve control of government through the casting of ballots was practically nonexistent. Lenin's design for a party consisting of an elite corps of leaders whose function is to guide the masses was carried over into the operation of the government after the Revolution in Russia, and it became the prototype of the parties of totalitarian regimes of all kinds in the twentieth century.

Lenin's theory is more elitist and less democratic than Marx's. Marx, too, had believed that a few intellectuals were capable of grasping ideas which arose outside of the capitalist frame of reference, but he had not gone so far in his elitism as to assume the necessity of leaders to provoke and guide a revolution and the proletarian dictatorship which would follow it. To Lenin, democracy meant that the leadership should keep in touch with the masses, neither lagging too far behind nor being too far ahead of them. It did not mean ascertaining what the people wanted done and doing it, for the judgment of the masses of people was seriously defective.[4] Within the party itself an attempt was made to combine a measure of democracy with one of discipline through the formulation of the principle of "democratic centralism." This principle requires that party members elect their own officials on all levels and that officers be accountable to those who elect them. It demands, however, strict party discipline and insists upon the absolute subordination of the minority to the majority when decisions are made, and the binding quality of decisions of the higher upon the lower levels of party organization. In practice, the centralistic aspects of democratic centralism have been more in evidence than the democratic.

Lenin on Revolutions and the Revolutionary State

No part of Marx's theory had appeared more firmly established than his statement that no phase of historical development could succeed another until that other had fully exploited all its inherent possibilities for development. Accordingly a logical succession of stages—feudalism to capitalism to socialism—had to be followed; it would be impossible to eliminate any one stage since each prepared the way for its successor. Thus socialism could not succeed capitalism until the latter, through the development of industry and the enlargement of the proletariat and the development of its class consciousness, had made that succession possible.

As we have seen, Lenin rejected the idea that the operation of capital-

⁴ *Ibid.*, pp. 816–817.

ism would itself result in the development of the necessary revolutionary class consciousness of the proletariat. It was necessary, he said, to have a party, an elite leadership, to create a revolutionary sentiment and to lead the proletariat in its struggle to destroy the bourgeois state and establish its own. This view constituted a rather obvious alteration of Marx's theory, and alteration was never a matter to be taken lightly among the devotees of Marxian theory. But any tinkering with Marx's idea that history develops through a stage-by-stage process was even more hazardous, because this was the very heart of Marx's theory of historical materialism. The Mensheviks flatly refused to consider any interpretations which would modify this aspect of the theory. So far as Russia was concerned, it was essentially a feudal country. A revolution was long overdue, but it would have to be a bourgeois, not a socialist, revolution. The duty of all good followers of Marx, they held, was to support the middle class in its revolutionary struggle, overthrow feudalism, and assist in the development of a capitalist and industrial economy, upon the basis of which socialism would someday be built. No Menshevik assumed, in the beginning of the twentieth century, that he would live to see the proletarian revolution.

The relative simplicity and clarity of the theory of historical materialism created a troublesome problem for Lenin. Like other followers of Marx, he was impressed by the theory. On the other hand, a strict interpretation and application of it became increasingly difficult and, ultimately, impossible. As a Russian revolutionary Lenin was reluctant to endorse any plan that would require a lengthy period of capitalism and control by the bourgeoisie prior to a revolution and dictatorship by the proletariat. He sought a plausible interpretation of Marx's theory which would permit a more speedy assumption of power by the workers but which would not, at the same time, outrage the principle of historical materialism. His solution to the problem was outlined in his *Two Tactics of Social Democracy in the Democratic Revolution.* In this pamphlet Lenin acknowledged that the stage of economic development in Russia did not justify anything but a bourgeois revolution and stated that socialism could be reached only through the stage of capitalism and political democracy. Nonetheless, he added, the unusual circumstances in Russia necessitated a unique development of this phase of history. The Russian bourgeoisie, he said, was so "unstable," so dominated by the czarist regime, that it could not be trusted to carry through its own revolution and subsequent phase of control. There was great danger that the bourgeoisie would return power to their erstwhile masters through fear of opposition on the left. To prevent this, an alliance of workers and peasants must capture control of the bourgeois revolution and govern the subsequent bourgeois state. It would be difficult to imagine a more flagrant distortion of Marx's theory than this. Marx had insisted that the class structure and the command relationship which existed between the classes was always determined by the forces of production in the economic foundation. That workers might control productive forces in the early stage of capitalist development, he would have regarded as an impossibility. Still, Lenin accomplished what he set out to do. He had justified a premature assumption of power by the proletariat and retained Marx's idea of the logical succession of stages of development.

Lenin's strained interpretation of historical materialism was scorned by Leon Trotsky (1879–1940), the fiery Russian revolutionary in exile, who also took issue with Lenin's theory of party organization. In Trotsky's view revolutionary necessity could not be fitted into historical materialism, and therefore it had to take precedence over it. Trotsky stated flatly that the political strength of a class has no direct relationship to the productive forces of a country. The proof of this contention, he said, was much in evidence. Although the proletariat of Russia was considerably smaller than that of the United States, it was far more active and influential. It was a much more revolutionary class than the bourgeoisie, despite the fact that the stage of industrial development was far behind that which obtained in the United States. It can only be concluded, Trotsky said, that the dictatorship of the proletariat does not depend upon the level of industrial maturity. In a backward country, the workers are more likely to be revolutionary than in an advanced industrial country. The proper strategy, therefore, is for the workers themselves to destroy feudalism and immediately proceed to an attack upon capitalism. The workers should then establish their own authority and work toward socialist development. Trotsky admitted that the workers would lack power to accomplish this by themselves. They must, therefore, ally themselves with the revolutionary peasantry. But the peasantry cannot be depended upon for long-term support. Moreover, this revolution will provoke a counterrevolution by the capitalist governments of Western Europe. In order to defeat the capitalist attack and strengthen its own position, after the defection of the peasantry, the Russian workers must stir up proletarian revolution in the capitalist countries. Those countries are ready for the transition to proletarian control, and when this is achieved the proletariat of the West can render assistance to their comrades in Russia. Trotsky's doctrine of "permanent revolution" plays a significant role in the progress of events in Russia in 1917. The relationship between the Russian Revolution and the anticipated proletarian revolutions in the West described by Trotsky was widely accepted by Russian Marxists. In 1917 Bolsheviks were generally convinced that their own revolutionary efforts would be unavailing unless there was a proletarian revolution at least in Germany.[5]

Lenin continued to cling to his view of the stages of historical develop-

[5] *Ibid.*, p. 831.

ment until the beginning of the Russian Revolution. At that time he adopted, for all intents and purposes, Trotsky's theory of permanent revolution, although without acknowledging the debt. With the opportunity to take control of the Russian state now a possibility, Lenin repudiated, without admitting that he was doing so, his previous argument that democracy was a necessary antecedent to the proletarian dictatorship. The Revolution, he said, will lead directly to that dictatorship, which can then proceed to develop socialism. Democracy can benefit only the capitalists; it has nothing to offer the proletariat. Marxism, he argued, is a living thing. It must not be bound by the straitjacket of theory. A revolutionary force of workers and peasants should seize power and extend the revolution to the countries of the West. Trotsky approved Lenin's newest tactical adaptation of theory and joined forces with him to advance the Bolshevik cause. In doing so it was necessary that he, too, modify a previous position. In the past he had excoriated Lenin for the latter's views on party organization. Trotsky himself had long supported the Menshevik position, which called for a large party patterned on the Western model. He was wise enough to see in 1917, however, that the situation called for an organization such as that outlined by Lenin in his *What Is To Be Done?*

During much of the period of the struggle between the soviets and the provisional government Lenin was in hiding. For a time he left Russia and went to Finland. Here he wrote *State and Revolution,* one of his best-known works. In this pamphlet Lenin was mainly concerned to show what kind of state would emerge from the proletarian capture of power. He reviewed the ideas of Marx and Engels on the state, commented on those who had, in his opinion, distorted those ideas, and considered the relationship of the state to the Russian Revolution. Engels had said that the state results from the conflicting interests of classes. Class interests are irreconcilable, and the state is used by one class to keep the peace while it pursues its own interests. Engels refused to consider the possibility that the state might be employed to reconcile class interests, and he never bothered to explain how peace was possible in a climate of irreconcilable class interests.[6]

Lenin accepted these assumptions unquestioningly. His most bitter attacks were upon Kautsky and other "distorters" of Marxism who had sapped the revolutionary strength of the theory by contending that the state could be used to reconcile class differences. The state, he said, is always an organ of the ruling class and is used by it to secure its own interest. Class interests can never be reconciled. An oppressed class will not be free until it crushes its oppressors. This means revolution. The perverters of Marxian doctrine are wrong when they speak of the "wither-

[6] John Plamenatz, *German Marxism and Russian Communism,* David McKay Company, Inc., New York, 1954, pp. 241–242.

ing away of the state" as a prediction applicable to the bourgeois state. Only one state, the state of the dictatorship of the proletariat, will wither away. The bourgeois state must be destroyed by violent revolution. The proletarian state, like all states, however, is an instrument of a ruling class. Through it the proletariat destroys the remaining elements of bourgeois culture and mentality. This requires force, in the proletarian state as in other states. But the end sought by the proletarian state is the classless society, rather than the exploitation of one class for the benefit of another. As the bourgeois class and the remnants of its superstructural elements are rooted out and destroyed, the state declines in strength; it "withers away."

The proletarian state is not different from other states in being a dictatorship. All states are dictatorships. The bourgeois democracy was the dictatorship of the bourgeoisie. Such a democracy was for the few rich who dictated to and controlled the many. The proletarian dictatorship is the rule of the many over the few; it is nonetheless a dictatorship. It is, however, a great deal more democratic than bourgeois democracy. When the classless society has been fully established and all the elements of a bourgeois society have been extirpated, even democracy will disappear, for democracy is an expression of force made necessary by class conflict.

> And only then will democracy itself begin to *wither away* due to the simple fact that, freed from capitalist slavery, from the untold horrors, savagery, absurdities and infamies of capitalist exploitation, people will gradually *become accustomed* to the observance of the elementary rules of social life that have been known for centuries and repeated for thousands of years in all school books; they will become accustomed to observing them without force, without compulsion, without subordination, without the *special apparatus* for compulsion which is called the state.[7]

The state will disappear because there will be no need for suppression in the sense that one class suppresses and oppresses another. Individuals, of course, may still need to be suppressed. Men will not be perfect in the new society, and some will have to be restrained, but a state is not necessary for this purpose. The people will respond "as readily as any crowd of civilised people, even in modern society, parts a pair of combatants or does not allow a woman to be outraged." [8] There will be two stages of the communist society, Lenin says. The first is the phase of socialism. Here the means of production are publicly owned; classes still exist but are in the process of disappearing; so, too, is the state. A kind of equality exists in the sense that in this phase of development each contributes

[7] V. I. Lenin, *State and Revolution,* Little Lenin Library, International Publishers Company, Inc., New York, 1932, vol. 14, pp. 73–74. Italics are in the original.
[8] *Ibid.,* p. 75.

"according to his ability" and receives "according to his work," according, that is, to his productive contribution. In the second stage, classes and the state disappear. Production is vastly expanded, and human behavior achieves a degree of sociability that enables men to live without state-imposed authority. The final stage is that in which men can live according to the principle: "From each according to his ability, to each according to his needs."

Lenin's description of the state as he expects it to be under the dictatorship of the proletariat reveals a degree of fatuity not often seen in his writings. He states, for example, that capitalism has rendered the functions of government and business so simple that the transfer of their control from the bourgeoisie to the workers can be easily accomplished. Management of these enterprises will require only the most modest ability. Thus the majority can easily exercise control. A representative government will still remain, but it will be truly representative, uncorrupted by the "parliamentarism of bourgeois society." And, finally, Lenin speaks admiringly of the revolutionary Paris Commune, which governed Paris for a few weeks in the spring of 1871. This body constituted the ideal government, Lenin says, in that it combined the executive and legislative functions. It not only determined policy but also put the policy into effect. Here, presumably, was a model upon which the soviets should pattern themselves. As it turned out, the soviets became a front for the party organization which controlled them completely.

Imperialist Capitalism

To an activist such as Lenin, the apathy of the proletariat, its failure to develop an enthusiasm for revolution, and its apparent contentment with life in a bourgeois society were appalling. Marx had thought that the working class was on the brink of revolution in his time. Not only had this expectation proved to be mistaken, but also as time passed the workers apparently moved further still from revolution. The revisionists attributed this development to the success that the proletariat had enjoyed in using democracy to secure their ends, and they advocated still more democracy. Lenin, for reasons considered above, could not, or did not, accept either the explanation or the remedy proffered by the revisionists.

Equally appalling, to Lenin and his followers, was the nationalism displayed by members of the working class at the outbreak of World War I. Again Marx's theory seemed defective. The Marxian assumption had been that the growing class consciousness of the proletariat would weaken and break the bonds of nationalist sentiment that tied the workers to their country. Patriotism was merely one of the superstructural elements, employed by the bourgeoisie to control the oppressed class. The proletariat would, Marx believed, eventually come to realize the strategy of the bourgeoisie and defeat this effort by giving their loyalty to their fellow workers irrespective of national boundaries. Marxism, in this respect, was an international movement which proposed an ultimate brotherhood of men without the artificial separation that is a concomitant of the nation-state system. The majority of socialists, though they paid their respects to this view, rejected it out of hand when their patriotic fervor was stimulated by the beginning of the war. They supported their "bourgeois" governments with middle-class enthusiasm, much to the disgust of Lenin, who openly hoped for the defeat of Russia because he correctly believed that it would hasten the advent of revolution and wreck the czarist regime.

The war impelled Lenin to evolve one of his most noted adaptations of Marxist theory. In his *Imperialism, the Highest Stage of Capitalism,* he attempted an explanation of the phenomenon noted above, that the proletariat appeared to be growing less, rather than more, revolutionary. He attributed their apathy to certain operations of the capitalist system which had extended its period of growth beyond that anticipated by Marx. Marx, Lenin said, had been unable to foresee the developmental potential of capitalism. There were more things it could do, more tactics it could effect to prolong its existence and increase its strength than Marx had understood. *Imperialism* is primarily an account of the evolution of capitalism which, in Lenin's view, had taken place from the time of Marx's death to the beginning of World War I.

Competition, Lenin said, has carried capitalism to a monopolistic position which goes far beyond that which prevailed in Marx's time. Monopoly, indeed, has become the rule in the capitalist system. This has been accompanied by the increasing socialization of the means of production. Productive facilities are owned and controlled by a mere handful of capitalist monopolists, but they are operated by the masses of workers who are concentrated in the great industrial centers.

> Competition becomes transformed into monopoly. The result is immense progress in the socialisation of production. In particular, the process of technical invention and improvement becomes socialised.... Production becomes social, but appropriation remains private. The social means of production remain the private property of a few. The general framework of formally recognised free competition remains, but the yoke of a few monopolists on the rest of the population becomes a hundred times heavier, more burdensome and intolerable.[9]

Everything is socialized except the distribution of the products of labor. There is no longer any real competition between small- and large-scale industry or between technically advanced and backward enterprises. The monopolies control.

[9] V. I. Lenin, *Imperialism, the Highest Stage of Capitalism,* Little Lenin Library, International Publishers Company, Inc., New York, 1939, vol. 15, p. 25.

Up to this point, we find little new in Lenin's adaptation. He merely reiterates what Marx had said before him, but he states that the process has developed beyond the point which Marx could predict. At this stage something has occurred that Marx did not anticipate. While capitalism still appears to be based upon commodity production, in fact it is not. The growth of productive facilities under monopolistic capitalism has necessitated the use of increasingly large amounts of capital. Owners have been compelled to go to the bankers for loans, because banks are the only source from which sufficiently large amounts of capital can be secured. In order to protect their investments, the banks demand representation on the boards of directors of the enterprises to which they have supplied capital. This practice has enabled the banks, which, like industry, have moved toward monopoly, to capture control of production. In the opening years of the twentieth century, a new kind of capitalism, "finance capital," has emerged, and it now typifies the bourgeois economy.

The significant feature of "finance capital" is the export of capital. The older capitalism exported commodities. As capitalism develops, however, a surplus of capital accumulates. The greater the degree of monopoly, the larger these surpluses become. If these funds were employed to improve the lives of the proletariat, no surpluses would exist, but if this were done the system would not be capitalism.

> As long as capitalism remains what it is, surplus capital will never be utilised for the purpose of raising the standard of living in a given country, for this would mean a decline in profits for the capitalists.[10]

Instead, surplus capital is exported for investment in the backward (underdeveloped) countries of the world. New productive facilities are created here where the cost of labor and raw materials is low and profits are high. This is the policy of imperialism. It has been followed for some years now, Lenin says, and the underdeveloped areas are now mainly controlled by the imperialist powers, the advanced capitalist countries of the world.

The profits from these exploited areas are so great that part of them can be used, and are being used, to bribe and corrupt "the upper strata of the proletariat" of the imperialist countries. If it were not for imperialism, the workers of those countries would long ago have reached the revolutionary stage. As it is, the crises engendered by unemployment, underconsumption, and other features of capitalism are checked by the use of profits squeezed out of the proletariat of backward countries. A part of the workers in the imperialist countries, corrupted by their capitalist masters, join with those masters in the exploitation of their fellow workers abroad. These workers are deluded into believing that their improved status results from the beneficent workings of democracy and

[10] *Ibid.*, p. 63.

capitalism. They wrongly place their confidence in the democratic process and, for a time, lose their revolutionary will and their proletarian class consciousness.

This situation, Lenin asserts, will not endure forever. Imperialism is the highest stage of capitalism; it is also the final stage. It is no less true in this phase of economic development than in previous phases that the commanding class is digging its own grave. Investment in backward areas of the world only spreads the evils of capitalism. A proletariat is becoming established in those areas and is experiencing the problems and hardships which workers everywhere have suffered. At the same time they are learning how to operate the instruments of production and preparing themselves for the ultimate revolution. Lines of communication are being established that will enable them to act in conjunction with the proletariat in advanced capitalist countries. Imperialism expands capitalism; it also expands proletarianism and creates worldwide problems where before the problems were national in scope.

As the backward areas fall under the domination of imperialist nations, the opportunities for investment shrink. Surplus capital mounts, as the possibilities for its profitable employment dwindle. When all the underdeveloped areas are controlled by imperialist powers, the only alternative to domestic disaster for an imperialist nation is the capture of a backward area already held by a competitor nation. The productive system developed by capitalism demands a worldwide scope of operation. It requires, in order to exist, international cooperation, abolition of tariff barriers, and free world trade. Imperialist capitalism, which has substituted the competition of nations for the competition of individual enterprises, cannot adjust to these demands. The inevitable result is war. World War I, Lenin says, is "a war for the division of the world, for the partition and repartition of colonies, 'spheres of influence' of finance capital, etc." [11]

Imperialism is "parasitic" capitalism. It is the "usurer state," in which a handful live luxuriously on the labor of the masses. It is capitalism in which profits go to the financiers who contribute nothing to production. It is capitalism in which the proletariat experiences its worst degradation, not so much because of inferior living standards, for these are even improved for workers in the advanced capitalist nations, but because members of the proletariat, corrupted by their masters, willingly cooperate in the exploitation of their fellow workers in backward countries. Imperialism, for these reasons, is decaying capitalism. Lenin, however, warns against underestimating its strength on that account. Capitalism in its final stage grows more rapidly than ever and has great power. Nevertheless, Lenin believes World War I to be the beginning of the end for capitalism. It will be followed, he says, by other wars, all of which will

[11] *Ibid.*, p. 9.

be fought for the same purpose—to secure a more favorable distribution of backward areas. These wars will make the proletariat increasingly revolutionary and will speed the historical process to the final stage of world revolution.

Following the Bolsheviks' capture of the government in October, 1917, and his own rise to power, Lenin was too preoccupied with the multitude of practical and pressing problems with which he was beset to devote much time to theory. And as a matter of fact, most of these problems could not be solved within the framework of Marxian theory, even as it had been revised and interpreted by Lenin prior to the Revolution. The matter did not greatly disturb Lenin. He had always been more interested in action than in doctrine. As a Marxist he could not ignore theory completely, but he paid less attention to it than formerly. If he could not justify his policies in terms of theory, he excused them on the ground that they should be regarded as temporary expedients to be abandoned as soon as the situation permitted. The principle that the party, as "vanguard of the proletariat," should direct the masses, a principle formulated by Lenin as early as 1902, was continued in full force. It was applied after the Revolution to a solution of the problem of the relationship of the party to the government. The soviets were transformed into the formal governmental structure, but Lenin had no intention of permitting them to play the dominant role. Although membership in the soviets was not restricted to members of the Communist party, all important positions were filled by party members, and the leading role of the party in soviet affairs was openly acknowledged. The higher the level in the soviet structure, the more solidly entrenched were the party members. On the uppermost levels of the hierarchy, positions were invariably in the hands of party members, who, in most cases, were also high-ranking party officials. A kind of interlocking directorate evolved, which assured the desired degree of party control over governmental policy and administration. The same technique was applied to the relationship between the party and such organizations as trade unions, professional organizations, and youth groups. These and the soviets were nominally noncommunist; in practice they were instruments of the party and completely under its control.

In theory there was to be unrestricted debate and criticism within the ranks of the party on any policy until a decision was reached, presumably by a majority. At that point discussion was to cease, and the decision was to be absolutely binding on all. Under Lenin there was at least a degree of adherence to this principle, although whether this was attributable to Lenin's nature or to the fact that he was unable in the few years he governed to develop sufficient strength to resist its operation is open to debate. Under Stalin the extent to which criticism and free discussion were permitted was determined solely by the leader of the party, who was, in fact, the absolute despot of the nation.

Stalinism

Joseph Stalin [12] (1879–1953) was the supreme power in the Soviet Union from shortly after the death of Lenin in 1924 until his own death in 1953. He was far more a quoter of Lenin and Marx than an originator of theory, although it behooved his followers to pay lip service to his talent as a theoretician. It was as a skilled and unscrupulous politician and organizer that Stalin was able to destroy his opposition and become the first of the absolute dictators of the twentieth century. However, a conflict over a doctrinal point was useful to him in the strategy he employed to defeat Trotsky, the most formidable of the group which for a time barred the path to complete power. The issue between Stalin and Trotsky involved the feasibility of creating socialism in one country, the Soviet Union, after it became evident that the expected proletarian revolutions in the advanced capitalist countries had failed to materialize. Trotsky insisted that in the long run socialism in a single country would be doomed; only socialism on a world scale can succeed. The proper tactics, therefore, called for the greatest effort to be made to bring about revolution in other countries while making the development of industrialism and the growth of national power in the U.S.S.R. a matter of secondary emphasis. Stalin demanded a reversal of these emphases on the ground that failure to build national strength would invite capitalist intervention and certain defeat. A program of encouraging revolution in capitalist countries should, he said, be carried on, but it should be regarded as less important than the building of socialism in the Soviet Union.

Stalin's argument prevailed, less, perhaps, because of its merits than because Stalin had long since created an organization within the party on which he could rely for any necessary support. If under Lenin the party became the "vanguard of the proletariat," under Stalin the dictator became the vanguard of the party. With the party firmly under his control, Stalin destroyed those who challenged his supremacy. He also carried through, and most brutally, the liquidation of the *kulaks,* or wealthy peasants, and the collectivization of agriculture. His Five-Year Plans achieved the rapid industrialization of the country, at the cost of great hardship for the citizens. Nevertheless, it was this last accomplishment which enabled the country to withstand the onslaught of the Third Reich and ultimately to contribute heavily to the defeat of Germany.

Stalin's contributions to theory consist mainly of his interpretations of Lenin's writings and are found principally in two books, *Foundations of Leninism* and *Problems of Leninism,* both of which were published in 1924, shortly after Lenin's death. *Foundations of Leninism* reiterates and defends Lenin's theory of revolution as it was designed to support the

[12] Stalin was born Iosif Viassarionovich Dzhugashvili.

Bolshevik cause in 1917. It also describes the tactics to be employed by Communists to advance the cause of world revolution. The Soviet Union should become a base, Stalin says, from which the revolutionary cause should be advanced, bearing in mind, of course, the primary goal of building the strength of the Soviet Union. Stalin also outlines the plan for world revolution more clearly than Lenin had done. He combines Trotsky's theory of permanent revolution with Lenin's theory of imperialism and proposes that the attention of revolutionaries be directed to the colonial areas of the world rather than to the advanced capitalist countries.

> The front of capital will not necessarily be pierced where industry is most developed, and so forth; it will be broken where the chain of imperialism is weakest, for the proletarian revolution is the result of the breaking of the chain of the imperialist world front at its weakest point. It is possible therefore that the country which begins the revolution, which makes a breach in the capitalist front may prove to be less developed from the capitalist point of view than others which are more developed but have remained, nevertheless, within the framework of capitalism.[13]

As a strategy of communism this view has long prevailed, contrary though it is to the original views of Marx himself.

In his *Problems of Leninism,* Stalin warns of the dangers of imperialist capitalism in support of his argument for the building of socialism in the Soviet Union. Communism and capitalism cannot long exist side by side, he says, and the country must be prepared for the inevitable conflict. The territorial ambitions of Hitler, openly avowed less than a decade after Stalin's statement, enabled the Soviet dictator to point with pride to his capacity as a prophet and theorist. What he had not foreseen was the fact that in his struggle against the Nazi hordes his own socialist country would be allied with such "advanced" capitalist countries as Great Britain and the United States.

Conclusions

The flaws in the theory of Marxism-Leninism-Stalinism (and perhaps we should now add Khrushchevism) are so many that a comprehensive examination of them here is impractical. We shall, however, consider a few of the more apparent. As we noted in the discussion of Marx, it should be understood that a theory which contains logical and factual weaknesses may still command support. A doctrine is as strong as is the attachment of its adherents to it; and the doctrine at hand can count on great loyalty among its supporters.

The fallacies in Lenin's theories have nowhere been brought more into

---

[13] Joseph Stalin, *Foundations of Leninism,* rev. trans., International Publishers Company, Inc., New York, 1932, pp. 33–34.

evidence than in the events which followed his formulation of the theory of imperialism. These events have, for the most part, either contradicted or failed to support Lenin's prognostications. The prediction that wars in which capitalist nations would inevitably become involved would increase the revolutionary tendencies of the working class remains completely unfulfilled. That class has continued, and perhaps with increasing dedication, to support the governments under which it lives. Lenin's view on the matter was a sheer guess, unsupported by fact and logic even at the time he made it. Equally erroneous was Lenin's declaration that future conflicts would involve a struggle among the capitalist nations. Today easily the most outstanding characteristic of international tension is the antagonism between capitalist and Communist nations. In fact it would probably be fair to say that a greater rapport exists among capitalist nations than among members of the Communist bloc.

Lenin was convinced that the "final" phase of capitalism would produce a continuing conflict among imperialist nations for the redivision of colonial countries. In refuting this charge, one might point to the granting of independence by the United States to the Philippines, or to the wholesale liquidation of colonialism by the British. If it is said in rebuttal that this has been a result of necessity rather than of a softening of the capitalist heart, one can still state that what has happened is not what Lenin said would happen. Lenin also insisted that bitter competition among capitalist nations was unavoidable; cooperation among them would be impossible. But the recent development of the Common Market and associated movements negates this argument. That the capacity of capitalist (or at least semicapitalist) nations to achieve prosperity through a policy of freer trade has caused concern in the ranks of the Communist faithful is hardly a secret.

The increasing level of prosperity of the working class continues to be a bone in the throat of the dogmatic Marxist. He can do little more than reiterate the now threadbare explanations of Lenin and talk of some indefinite time in the future when the old predictions will come true. One can only say, however, that the route to the degeneration of the proletariat and its revolutionary movement, if any credence at all is to be given such predictions, must be a tortuously circuitous one. This is not to argue that capitalism, or what passes for it today, and democracy have solved all their problems. They are far from such a happy state. But who can argue that they have not enjoyed considerable success, at least as much success as have other systems, including the Marxist? Lenin, like Marx, underestimated the ability of capitalism to solve its problems. Or it would probably be more accurate to say that Lenin and Marx were wrong in contending that those problems could not be solved through the use of the democratic process. Even in the short time which has elapsed since the death of Lenin, capitalist countries have, by majority vote, imposed heavy restraints upon the aggressive exercise of property "rights," with the result that capitalism now little resembles the buccaneering force it once was. Whether the effect of the transformation has been salutary is still much argued, although if a majority had not thought so, the change would never have been made. The point is, however, that according to Leninist theory, it cannot be made at all on a permanent basis. The argument that the improvement of the condition of the working class is only transitory becomes less credible as the years pass. Such improvement can hardly be regarded, except perhaps by the most tenacious dialectician, as a fleeting phenomenon.

If the dire predictions concerning the fate of capitalism, made by Lenin and Marx, have failed to materialize, so too have their optimistic prophecies with regard to the future of the Communist state. Marx had thought that the dictatorship of the proletariat would be of brief duration and that the political power it must necessarily exercise would be greatest at the point of its inception and would begin almost immediately to decline as the classless society evolved and the state began to "wither away." Lenin was less definite in the matter. Faced with the hard facts of political life, he had to be content with vague statements which put utopia somewhere in the distant future. Under Stalin, the proletarian dictatorship became the personal rule of the despot. Far from withering away, the power of the state increased. Stalin's excuse was that it was foolish to talk about a stateless society when the only truly admirable socialist society was surrounded by the ravening wolves of capitalism. As a pragmatist, one must sympathize with Stalin's point of view. With the best will in the world, he would have been insane to attempt the liquidation of state power in a community of nations in which the principle of power politics is almost universally accepted. We need little imagination to picture what would have happened to a stateless, and therefore powerless, society in a Europe dominated by Adolf Hitler. On the other hand, given the character of Stalin, we can hardly assume that the Soviet dictator would have relaxed his iron grip on his people if all the capitalist nations had thrown their armaments into the sea and devoted full time to waving the olive branch. And since the end of World War II, developments within the Communist family of nations make it evident that an entire world of communism would be as prone to war and other kinds of conflict as the capitalist world ever was. Despite the theoretical contempt of the Communist for nationalism, patriotism continues to play a powerful role in the world, influencing socialist and capitalist nations alike.

As the state has stubbornly resisted the forces which the Marxists have long contended would destroy it, so too has a class society failed to disappear. In the Soviet Union it is acknowledged that classes exist; there are peasants, workers, and intelligentsia. But, it is argued, these are not classes in the true sense, because there is no antagonism among them. In fairness, it should be acknowledged that greater equality exists under the present system than under the regime of the czars. Moreover, the barriers between the classes are inconsiderable. Ability is rewarded, and class lines are flexible. Nevertheless, they do exist, and it is a striking fact that the class structure of the Soviet society is far more apparent than that of the United States, where an overwhelming majority of persons regard themselves as "middle-class"—and this despite the fact that Marxist theory predicts a hardening of class lines in the capitalist and an eventual elimination of them in the communist society.

The inconsistencies and inaccuracies of Marxist theory are too apparent to be ignored. It is obvious, too, that Communists do not live, and have never lived, according to the demands of their doctrine. They do not, in short, practice what they preach, although in fairness it must be acknowledged that in this deficiency they do not stand alone. How, then, is it possible for the doctrine to retain the loyalty of its adherents? Why do its supporters not abandon the doctrine and the system in view of its many shortcomings? There are many answers to this question. For one thing, as we have seen, the flaws in a theory do not particularly lessen its strength, providing that it generally justifies a desired program of action or way of life. In Marxist theory, too, there are enough elements of fact to permit a skilled dialectician to make a good case for its validity. The argument may require some agility in matters of interpretation, but the Communists have never lacked spokesmen possessing such capacity. It should also be understood that attachment to a doctrine does not always, or perhaps even often, depend upon its reasonableness. A doctrine may be supported more enthusiastically on the basis of faith than of reason.

Finally, much of what we have said here of Marxist theory can be said of other theories, including democracy and capitalism. Adam Smith's "unseen hand" did not produce the equitable society he had expected. And in societies in which the democratic principles are much praised injustice, inequality, and racial and religious discrimination still exist. Marxist doctrine has risen to prominence in the world for many reasons. Sometimes it has simply been imposed upon a people irrespective of their wishes in the matter. But those who live in democratic countries ought to understand that Marxism is often embraced freely and enthusiastically by those who are disillusioned by the failure of democratic society to live up to its avowed principles.

SELECTED BIBLIOGRAPHY

Clarkson, Jesse D.: *A History of Russia,* Random House, Inc., New York, 1961.
Coker, Francis W.: *Recent Political Thought,* Appleton-Century-Crofts, Inc., New York, 1934, chaps. 3–9.

Deutscher, Isaac: *The Prophet Armed, Trotsky: 1879–1921*, Oxford University Press, Fair Lawn, N.J., 1954.

Ebenstein, William: *Today's Isms*, 2d ed., Prentice-Hall, Inc., Englewood Cliffs, N.J., 1958, chaps. 1, 4.

Fainsod, Merle: *How Russia Is Ruled*, Harvard University Press, Cambridge, Mass., 1956, chaps. 1–10.

Hallowell, John H.: *Main Currents in Modern Political Thought*, Holt, Rinehart and Winston, Inc., New York, 1950, chaps. 11–14.

Hammond, Thomas Taylor: *Lenin on Trade Unions and Revolution*, Columbia University Press, New York, 1957.

Hook, Sidney: *Marx and the Marxists: The Ambiguous Legacy*, D. Van Nostrand Company, Inc., Princeton, N.J., 1955, chaps. 3–9.

Low, Alfred D.: *Lenin on the Question of Nationality*, Bookman Associates, Inc., New York, 1958.

Meyer, Alfred G.: *Leninism*, Harvard University Press, Cambridge, Mass., 1957.

Page, Stanley W.: *Lenin and World Revolution*, New York University Press, New York, 1959.

Plamenatz, John: *German Marxism and Russian Communism*, David McKay Company, Inc., New York, 1954.

Sabine, George H.: *A History of Political Theory*, 3d ed., Holt, Rinehart and Winston, Inc., New York, 1961, chap. 34.

Seton-Watson, Hugh: *From Lenin to Khrushchev: The History of World Communism*, Frederick A. Praeger, Inc., New York, 1960.

Towster, Julian: *Political Power in the U.S.S.R., 1917–1947*, Oxford University Press, Fair Lawn, N.J., 1948.

Wolfe, Bertram D.: *Three Who Made a Revolution*, The Dial Press, Inc., New York, 1948.

twenty-one

FASCISM AND
NATIONAL SOCIALISM

World War I created conditions in Russia which led to the toppling of the czarist regime and the ultimate establishment of the Communist dictatorship. The revolutionary impact of the war and its aftermath was not, however, concluded with that momentous event. Other countries, both the victorious and the defeated, were to suffer the consequences of the military conflagration. Industrial countries found that their productive capacity, strained to the limits by the demands of the war, exceeded the requirements of a time of peace. Farmers raised more crops than could profitably be sold. Industry fabricated more goods than purchasing power could absorb. As the years passed, many major countries moved toward an economic crisis which would pose seemingly insoluble problems. The search for solutions produced a variety of economic and political responses, but in all countries the most commonly heard demand was for a greater degree of state involvement in the national economy. In countries that had had a long and generally satisfactory experience with the democratic process, the transition from a predominantly laissez-faire economy to one in which the government played an active role was effected peacefully and with majority support, although not without strenuous protest by a minority. Other nations were not so fortunate. Changes were effected at the cost of the collapse of their constitutional systems. Whereas the nations with a democratic tradition tended to move toward what may probably best be described as the democratic social welfare state, others turned to totalitarianism. The most important developments in this direction were in Germany and Italy.

After a long and bitter internal debate, Italy in 1914 had joined in the war against the Central Powers. At the conclusion of the conflict there were great expectations in Italy that the country would benefit from a sharing of the spoils of war. Disappointment and disillusionment followed the decisions of the peace conference. Italy was denied the colonies she desired; national pride was severely damaged. In addition, she faced difficult economic problems. Italy was a country with limited natural resources and abundant poverty, and the end of the war saw growing unemployment complicated by overpopulation. Socialism was popular among the workers, who resorted to strikes, boycotts, and riots in an attempt to improve their condition. The propertied classes, uneasily recalling the events of a few years before in Russia, were in a mood to listen to the most radical proposals that promised to save them from a similar fate. Such proposals were soon forthcoming. A total solution for all the problems besetting Italian society was offered by Benito Mussolini, the leader of the fascist movement.

Mussolini was born in 1883. His father, a blacksmith, was a socialist, and the son first established a modest reputation as a socialist writer and orator. In 1912 Mussolini was made editor of *Avanti*, the most important socialist newspaper in Italy. In 1914 he broke with the paper over the question of Italian intervention in the war. Long a pacifist, Mussolini became an aggressive interventionist and urged that Italy join forces with the Allied Powers against Germany and her confederates. His stand resulted in his expulsion from the Socialist party, but he founded his own newspaper, *Popolo d'Italia*, and continued to argue for war. When Italy entered the conflict, Mussolini joined the army and served as an enlisted man.

The restoration of peace brought to Italy the confusion and difficulties described above. In this setting Mussolini sought to create an organization capable of controlling the nation. His initial strategy was to appeal to the working class for support, but in this he was unsuccessful. He then turned to the opposition. In 1919 he organized the *Fasci di Combattimento* ("combat troops"), often called the Black Shirts, with which he terrorized the working people, whose support he had formerly sought, in order to court favor with the industrialists, major landowners, and elements of the middle class. The Black Shirts' organization grew rapidly, recruiting its members from the ranks of the unemployed and the dissatisfied veterans of the war. In 1921 the Fascists tested their strength at the polls but made a dismal showing. They were able to win only 35 of 535 seats in the national parliament. Mussolini then determined to seize power by other methods. A spectacular "March on Rome" was staged, in March, 1922, at the conclusion of which Mussolini demanded that the

king turn over to him the reins of government. The Fascist forces could easily have been dispersed by the army if the king had given the word. That monarch, however, succumbed to the arguments of Mussolini and some of his powerful supporters. The king was persuaded that surrender to the Fascists was necessary to save Italy from Communist revolution. This was by no means the only alternative at the time, but the specter of Bolshevism was frightening. By October, 1922, Italian fascism, the second stage in the evolution of twentieth-century totalitarianism, was an accomplished fact. The first dictatorship of the right had been established under Benito Mussolini.

In Germany the loss of World War I had dealt a serious blow to the pride of the German people. Until the very end the German government had assured them of victory. The terms imposed upon Germany by the victorious Allies were considered excessively harsh and were bitterly resented by the Germans; and they were strongly encouraged in their attitude by nationalist rabble-rousers. The war was followed by a runaway inflation which wrecked both the economy and the confidence of the people in their government. That government was established by the Weimar Constitution, a document approved by the Allies who, as it turned out, were overly optimistic in their belief that a democratic and peace-loving Germany would be assured by the framing of a democratic constitution. Events were to preclude the possibility of a fair chance for democracy in Germany. A brief period of recovery had only begun in the late 1920s when Germany was plunged into the depths of the Great Depression. Those who had long argued that the Weimar government was incapable of defending Germany against her enemies, both external and internal, began to make increasing headway. Of those who sought power in the turbulent years from the close of the war until 1933, the most capable and, in the end, the most successful, was the Austrian expatriate, Adolf Hitler.

Hitler was born in 1889. His youth was spent, in unhappiness and frustration, in Vienna. His earliest ambition was to become an artist, but he lacked both money and talent to pursue such a career. Much of his time was occupied in listening to demagogues, from whom he derived his ideas on anti-Marxism and anti-Semitism. In 1913 he went to Munich, and the following year he joined the German army. He was an acceptable soldier and, late in the war, was wounded and was decorated for bravery. While recuperating in a military hospital he resolved to devote his life to the reestablishment of German power and to revenge against her enemies.

Hitler soon joined the National Socialist German Workers' party (Nazi party), which had only a handful of members at the time but with whose views Hitler found himself most in accord among the multitude of parties that erupted in the wake of the war. He rapidly rose to the position of leader, or *Fuehrer,* of the organization, which was closely patterned on that of the Fascist Black Shirts in Italy. The military arm of the movement was the Storm Troops, who affected brown shirts and, in the manner of their Italian counterparts, made their point by the use of force. In 1923 a *Putsch* was attempted in Munich as the first step in a projected seizure of power. It was defeated by the authorities, and Hitler was sentenced to prison for a short term. Revolution from the right was not considered a particularly serious offense. The Nazi leader devoted his time in prison to writing *Mein Kampf,* a dull and rambling document, part autobiography and part plan for German salvation and conquest. The book ultimately made Hitler a millionaire, although it did not establish any records for sales until he became dictator of Germany, when it came to be the better part of wisdom for each householder to have a copy conspicuously displayed in his home.

In 1928 the Nazi party ran candidates for seats in the Reichstag, but with little success. The party polled less than 3 per cent of the vote and had only twelve delegates. Economic depression, however, proved to be a boon to the Nazis. With no power in the government they had no responsibility. They consistently attacked the government and framed a political platform of their own in which they promised all things to all people. The strategy was effective. The Nazis gradually increased their membership in the Reichstag and by 1932 held 230 seats. In January, 1933, Hindenburg, the aging president, appointed Hitler chancellor of the German Reich. When Hindenburg died, in August, 1934, Hitler combined the presidency with the office of chancellor and became *Fuehrer* and *Reichskanzler*. He had long since taken the steps necessary to assure complete power for himself and the Nazi party. The Weimar Constitution was never formally annulled, but Hitler ruled by decree after February, 1933. The Nazi party was the only legal party after July, 1933. The Nazi totalitarian dictatorship was by that time in full force.

Fascism and national socialism were different in many respects, but both were products of their times. Not only did the problems growing out of the war help to prepare the seedbed in which the doctrines of totalitarianism grew and flourished; but conditions inherent in an advanced industrial society also played their part. Such a society is beset by problems of great complexity, and the person or party that proffers a simple and apparently logical solution can attract considerable support. Hitler and Mussolini, both astute manipulators of men and masters of the art of influencing public opinion, were quick to perceive this fact. The solutions they offered were often contradictory, but they were always couched in simple propagandistic terms that were attractive to the masses. Both dictators also salved the pride of citizens by insisting that the hardships from which their countries suffered resulted from the acts of insidious enemies (the Allies, Communists, capitalists, Jews, and others) and were by no means the result of their own inadequacies. Both offered security and the restoration of national pride to people who hungered for them. To the working classes they promised socialism, although they had no intention of keeping this promise. To the middle classes they offered salvation from the threat of proletarianization. To the industrialists they guaranteed protection from labor unions and communism.

The Philosophical Basis

The doctrines of fascism and national socialism were essentially reactionary. They were determined mainly by the nature of the doctrines of the adversaries to whom they were opposed. Since almost every other group was regarded as an enemy, both doctrines were negative and highly irrational. Because Marxism was materialistic, fascism and national socialism were idealistic. To the libertarian and the equalitarian appeals of democracy, fascism and national socialism opposed the principles of duty and hierarchy. In place of individualism, fascism and national socialism offered the homogeneity of the community. Rationalism gave way to instinct and emotion. Fascism and national socialism regarded parliamentarism as a system that gave free play to divisive forces; in its stead they offered unity and the absolute rule of dictator and party. Because many believed that the principles attacked by fascism and national socialism had been discredited, they were willing to assume the validity of their opposites. It often proved difficult, if not impossible, to defend fascist and Nazi doctrines on any rational basis. This did not, however, prove to be a major stumbling block to Nazi-fascist "philosophers." They simply argued that reason was a delusion; they insisted that faith in the leader, instinct, and blind obedience were better guides to action than was reason. It was an argument that satisfied a great many.

Unlike communism, neither fascism nor national socialism, as political and revolutionary movements, evolved out of a carefully formulated theory. Their actions were always predetermined by the nature of the immediate problems with which they were confronted, and they were not concerned, as was Lenin, with attempting to justify their acts by relating them to an established dogma. The fact that a considerable part of the program of national socialism could be tied to certain philosophical antecedents meant only that in the course of German development a number of ideas had taken root, and that collectively they seemed to corroborate and support various tenets of what came to be known as national socialism. It would be difficult, if not impossible, to determine the genesis of these ideas with any degree of precision, but they may be traced at least as far back as Luther. Although Luther's contribution to national socialism is highly controversial, some connections appear to be relevant and are worth mentioning. Luther's defection from Catholicism and his alliance with the German princes greatly strengthened the hand of the civil authority in Germany. Although there were elements of democratic ideology in Luther's doctrine of the priesthood of all believers, Luther himself was politically illiberal and intolerant. He strongly supported the efforts of the civil government to suppress peasant revolts and religious deviationism, and he was ardently anti-Semitic.

More significant, perhaps, in molding the German mind and making it receptive to national socialism were the ideas of such nineteenth-century philosophers and historians as Schopenhauer, Treitschke, and Nietzsche. These three cannot be correctly called "Nazi" philosophers. Indeed, only a carefully eclectic approach could find support in their theories for the doctrines of national socialism, but some applicable elements could be found. Schopenhauer's view that it is the will to power, rather than reason, that rules the world was readily absorbed by the national socialist movement. The same can be said for the nationalism, the pan-Germanism, the militarism, and the anti-Semitism of Treitschke. And Nietzsche's contempt for Christianity, democracy, and conventional morality, together with his distinction between the lower man and "superman," were highly praised by the National Socialists. Caution was necessary, however, in utilizing the philosophy of Nietzsche, for he was neither a nationalist nor an anti-Semite, and indeed he held a low opinion of Germans in general.

A later and more relevant philosophy for national socialism was found in the writings of Carl Schmitt, a brilliant but unstable man, whose political affiliations ran the gamut from extreme left to final lodgment in the Nazi party. In an article published in 1927, entitled "The Concept of 'The Political,'" [1] Schmitt states that the specific and unique characteristic of politics is the distinction between friend and enemy. The distinction, he says, has nothing to do with good and bad, beautiful and ugly, or with economic differences. He is the enemy who is different; his difference is what makes him the enemy. The distinction between friend and enemy is the distinction between two ways of life. A way of life different from one's own must be fought and destroyed. The struggle calls for the use of force; it is a matter of killing and being killed. This principle applies to all enemies, within or outside of the community. Thus there can be no peace, domestic or international, until the world knows only one way of life, until complete conformity exists among all men. It is not difficult to understand why Schmitt's views were praised and widely quoted in national socialist circles. The use of force to achieve conformity was an essential ingredient of national socialist thought.

The National Socialists of Germany had developed an elementary philosophy prior to their assumption of power in 1933. The Italian

[1] *Archiv für Sozialwissenschaft und Sozialpolitik*, vol. 58, September, 1927, in William Ebenstein, *Modern Political Thought: The Great Issues*, 2d ed., Holt, Rinehart and Winston, Inc., New York, 1960 (translated by William Ebenstein).

Fascists had not done so. In the earlier stages of fascist development there was, in fact, a specific repudiation of philosophy. The Fascists prided themselves in being an activist, rather than a philosophical, group. After Mussolini's advent to power, however, he decided that his movement required a philosophy to make it respectable. That philosophy, the development of which was mainly in the hands of Giovanni Gentile, took the form of a perverted Hegelianism. There are many reasons why Hegel's philosophy could not be adopted in its original form. For one thing, Hegel had insisted upon the rationality of the dialectic, and fascism was admittedly irrational. For another, he rejected the notion that the great men of history could do much to influence the course of history, a view to which Mussolini would have had to take serious exception. It was Hegel's exaltation of the state that appealed to Mussolini and the Fascists. They began at that point and proceeded to evolve a theory that suited their purposes but was a miserable caricature of Hegelianism. To this was added an element of the ideas of Georges Sorel. Sorel had suggested that the value of a social philosophy lay in the myth which enabled it to unite its adherents and rally them to action. Such a philosophy need not be "true" in the sense that it is rational. It serves its purpose by advancing the cause. For this view Hegel would have had nothing but contempt; to him philosophy was no myth. It was convenient, however, for the Fascists, who scorned rationalism; indeed their philosophy was such that they had little choice in the matter. As we shall see, the National Socialists also stressed the mythical qualities of their doctrine.

The Fascist State

If there is anything like an "official" statement of fascist theory, it is that found in an article written by Mussolini (showing the influence of Gentile) for the *Enciclopedia Italiana* in 1932. The article is entitled *The Doctrine of Fascism* and is divided into two parts, the first being a statement of "Fundamental Ideas" and the second the "Political and Social Doctrine" of fascism. In this article Mussolini attempts to refute the social theories which fascism regards as objectionable and to define the content of fascism itself, particularly as it deals with the concept of the state.

In the beginning, Mussolini says, fascism was a movement for which there was no precisely formulated doctrine. Action was its own justification. There was faith, and men were fighting and dying for it.[2] As the movement progressed the doctrine developed, its form being shaped by the responses to the pressing problems of the time. Currently, Mussolini asserts, fascism is both a regime and a doctrine.

Fascism rejects both the possibility and the desirability of peace. "War

[2] Exactly what men had faith in Mussolini does not explain.

alone brings up to their highest tension all human energies and puts the stamp of nobility upon the peoples who have the courage to meet it." [3] Fascism also rejects the materialistic interpretation of history. "Fascism believes, now and always, in holiness and in heroism, that is, in acts in which no economic motive—remote or immediate—plays a part." [4] Fascism denies that economic prosperity is a valuable goal. It is, in fact, unimportant.

As fascism repudiates the basic principles of Marxian communism, so too does it reject those of liberalism and democracy. It scorns the ideas of human equality, majority rule, and the political practices and institutions associated with and based upon them. Instead "it affirms the irremediable, fruitful and beneficent inequality of men, who cannot be levelled by such a mechanical and extrinsic fact as universal suffrage." [5] The nineteenth century was the century of "liberalism, Socialism, and Democracy." The twentieth is the century of authority and collectivism. It is "the century of the state." [6]

The individual under fascism has importance only in his relationship to the state. Individuals and groups are conceivable only as fractions of the state. The state does not exist to serve their selfish purposes, not even to protect their lives. The state serves a higher purpose.

> For Fascism, the state is not the night-watchman who is concerned only with the personal security of the citizens; nor is it an organization for purely material ends, such as that of guaranteeing a certain degree of prosperity and a relatively peaceful social order, to achieve which a council of administration would be sufficient, nor is it a creation of mere politics with no contact with the material and complex reality of the lives of individuals and the life of peoples. The State, as conceived by Fascism and as it acts, is a spiritual and moral fact because it makes concrete the political, juridical, economic organization of the nation and such an organization is, in its origin and in its development, a manifestation of the spirit. The State is the guarantor of internal and external security, but it is also the guardian and the transmitter of the spirit of the people as it has been elaborated through the centuries in language, custom, faith. The State is not only present, it is also past, and above all future. It is the State which, transcending the brief limit of individual lives, represents the immanent conscience of the nation. The forms in which States express themselves change, but the necessity of the State remains. It is the State which educates citizens for civic virtue, makes them conscious of their mission, calls them to unity; harmonizes their interests in justice; hands on the achieve-

---

[3] *The Doctrine of Fascism,* in Michael Oakeshott, *The Social and Political Doctrines of Contemporary Europe,* The Macmillan Company, New York, 1944, pp. 170–171. All subsequent quotations from this article are from this source.

[4] *Ibid.,* p. 171.

[5] *Ibid.,* p. 172.

[6] *Ibid.,* p. 175.

ments of thought in the sciences, the arts, in law, in human solidarity; it carries men from the elementary life of the tribe to the highest human expression of power which is Empire; it entrusts to the ages the names of those who died for its integrity or in obedience to its laws; it puts forward as an example and recommends to the generations that are to come the leaders who increased its territory and the men of genius who gave it glory. When the sense of the State declines and the disintegrating and centrifugal tendencies of individuals and groups prevail, national societies move to their decline.[7]

The state alone can reconcile the antagonisms that develop in society. Pluralism means division, and wrecks the fabric of society. The Marxists are wrong, Mussolini says, in assuming that the state will disappear. Quite the contrary is true. The state neither disappears nor weakens. It must, instead, grow stronger. Nor is this harmful to the individual. It is, rather, his salvation. The state enhances his importance "just as in a regiment a soldier is not weakened but multipled by the number of his comrades." [8] The state must limit "useless or harmful liberties" and maintain the essential ones.

In both democratic and socialist theory (although, admittedly, not always in practice), the state serves as an instrument of the people. There are considerable differences between the two in their respective views of the state, with respect to kind and purpose, but on this point they are in agreement. Neither views the state as sacred or as organic in the sense that it has a life and purpose of its own which transcend those of the individuals who compose it. Fascist theory, on the other hand, strongly asserts the organic nature of the state. The Fascist *Charter of Labor*, promulgated by the Fascist Grand Council in 1927, states:

> The Italian nation is an organic whole having life, purposes and means of action superior in power and duration to those of the individuals, single or associated, of which it is composed. It is a moral, political and economic unity, which is realized integrally in the Fascist State.[9]

One of the purposes for which the fascist state exists is imperialist expansion. Fascist theory called for the restoration of the Roman Empire. To this end it demanded individual sacrifice and complete subjection to the purposes of the state.

The "Folkish" State and the Theory of Race

Unlike the Fascists, the National Socialists did not exalt the state. In place of the state there was, for them, the *Volk* (folk) and the "folkish" state. The term *Volk* cannot accurately be translated into English. The

[7] *Ibid.,* p. 176.
[8] *Ibid.,* pp. 177–178.
[9] Oakeshott, *op. cit.,* p. 184.

meaning is generally given as "people" or "nation," but it is actually a more complex concept. It implies the "racial existence" of the people,[10] a community based upon ties of blood and soil which go deeper than the formal political bonds that hold a people together. The racial connotations are significant, and the race theory of national socialism cannot be separated from that of the folkish state. Although he never satisfactorily described what he meant by the folkish state, Hitler occasionally stated that he considered it the central concept of his philosophy.[11] At any rate, the state as such is not of supreme importance. It is the folkish state, the "racial existence" of man, the community of blood and soil, that is paramount. The state is merely a means to this end, to be employed to secure and protect it. The state's instrumentality does not imply that its power is limited. Indeed it may employ force of any kind and in any degree in pursuit of the end for which it exists.

Race is the principal bond that holds together the members of the folkish state. To support this contention national socialism developed a theory of race which is beneath contempt from any rational or scientific point of view. Nonetheless it was regarded as an eternal verity by a great many Germans and justified, in their minds, the most barbaric treatment ever accorded to minority groups. Nazi race theory was based mainly upon the writings of Count Arthur de Gobineau (1816–1882), a Frenchman, and Houston Stewart Chamberlain (1855–1926), a Germanicized Englishman and the son-in-law of the composer Richard Wagner. In his *Essay on the Inequality of Human Races* (1853–1854), Gobineau states that the capacity of the races is determinable mainly by their color. The white race is superior, the yellow race mediocre, and the black race inferior. The Jews, however, are "Negroid," he says, and the Latin peoples are "Semitized." Interbreeding between the races leads to national degeneration and to the decadent principles of liberalism and democracy. The white race itself is distinguished by the existence within it of various groups and subdivisions of those groups. The Aryan is the superior of the groups of the white race, and the Teutons comprise the highest level of the Aryan group. All of this was to "prove" the superiority of the French aristocracy, whose members, Gobineau contends, were descended from the Teutons.

These views were highly convincing to Chamberlain, an English expatriate and ardent German imperialist, who elaborated and altered them to support the idea of German superiority. In his *The Foundations of the Nineteenth Century* (1899), Chamberlain contends that all the great contributions of Western civilization were made by persons of Germanic origin. The great men of world history were of German extraction,

---

[10] *Ibid.,* p. 201.

[11] William L. Shirer, *The Rise and Fall of the Third Reich: A History of Nazi Germany,* Fawcett Publications, Inc., Greenwich, Conn., 1960, p. 130.

including such notable "Aryans" as Columbus, Dante, and Jesus. The greatest threat to civilization is Jewish influence. Nothing important can be achieved unless that influence is destroyed. Rome became great by doing so. The invading Germanic tribes took from Rome everything suitable to their Nordic culture and Germanized it. They constitute the highest race in the world today and are clearly entitled to rule the world. They must, however, emulate the example of the ancient Romans and wipe out all traces of Jewry. Intermarriage between Jews and Aryans should be strictly forbidden, as should all Aryan exposure to Jewish intellectual influences. Jewish influence leads inevitably to cultural degeneration. One of the manifestations of the decline is democracy, which is not a fit government for the virile Aryan.

Hitler's racism is based upon a twisted form of Darwinism. There is, he says, a continuing struggle for survival among the members of a race as well as among different races. The consequence of this struggle is the emergence of a natural elite—products of the fittest who survive the struggle. Interbreeding between races results in hybridization and cultural degeneration. The offspring of interracial breeding is always inferior to the parent who represents the superior race. This inferiority does not create a hopeless situation, because hybrids tend to die out; thus a program aimed at restoring racial purity will be successful. There are three races, Hitler says. The Aryan includes the Scandinavian, Dutch, and English peoples, in addition to the German; it is the "culture-creating" race and is superior to the others. Next is the "culture-carrying" race, an example of which is the Japanese; such peoples are unable to innovate, but the culture does not deteriorate in their hands. Finally there are the "culture destroyers," the Jews and the Negroes, who are devoted to, and responsible for, the degradation of civilization. They pursue their end of world destruction by mixing their blood with that of the culture creators. The Aryans, being the culture-creating and superior race, are justified in exploiting the members of the inferior races in order to pursue their goal of developing civilization.

The "official" Nazi race theory was provided by Alfred Rosenberg (1893–1946) in his *The Myth of the Twentieth Century* (1930). Rosenberg was among the most violent of the Nazi anti-Semites.[12] History, he said, is the story of the struggle between the culture-creating Aryans and the culture-destroying races, particularly the Jews. The Aryan race, originating somewhere in the North, had spread throughout the world and had been responsible for the development of the great cultures. The decline of those cultures was the result of interbreeding with the inferior races. The Teutons, a branch of the Aryan race, created European culture and then engaged in a struggle against the corrupting influence

[12] Rosenberg was convicted as a war criminal by the International Military Tribunal at Nuremberg in 1946 and was hanged.

of the Jews. The struggle for survival is still in progress. Aside from the attempt to degrade the Aryans by adulterating that blood with their own, the Jews have employed democracy, Marxism, and capitalism as devices to destroy the Aryan culture. Rosenberg was not concerned to support his views with scientific proof, nor of course could he do so. He provided the elements of a "myth" of "German morality" which he proposed to substitute for the corrupt and Semitized principles of the prevailing culture. If the elements of "German morality" are incomprehensible to others, Rosenberg said, this is because understanding is determined by race. Rosenberg here employs a device strikingly similar to that employed by Marxists. The Marxists say, for example, that the bourgeois arguments against socialism are products of a middle-class mentality which cannot be transcended and which shapes the mind and distorts reason in such a manner as to preclude the possibility that the bourgeoisie will ever understand true, that is, socialist, logic. Similarly Rosenberg says that the mind is structured by racial characteristics. Each race is different, and thus the logic and reason which emanate from one racial mind are different from the logic and reason formed in the mind of another race.[13]

After Hitler and the National Socialists came to power, the "scientific" ramifications of the race theory were explored and developed. The results might be regarded as ludicrous had they not had such calamitous consequences. A spurious anthropology was utilized to support the concept of Aryan supremacy. History was rewritten to accord with the new "truths." Schools throughout Germany taught the new racial "sciences." Instructors who could not bring themselves to embrace such fictions were replaced by more enthusiastic representatives of national socialism. At the University of Berlin twenty-five courses in "racial science" were added to the curriculum, under the direction of a rector who had been a storm trooper and was by profession a veterinarian.[14] The real tragedy of the race theory, of course, lay in its consequences for the Jews in Germany and throughout the German-conquered areas of Europe. Deprived of citizenship and property, segregated, scorned as subhuman, starved and beaten, the Jews were finally subjected to a policy of complete extermination, which failed only because facilities were inadequate to accomplish it before the victorious Allies could halt the slaughter.

Leadership and Hierarchy

The Nazis did not intend the claim of Aryan supremacy over other races to imply the equality of all members of the Aryan race. Just as races are unequal, they held, so are individuals within the races. According to Nazi doctrine, one of the fallacies of democracy is that it attempts to

[13] Ludwig Von Mises, *Omnipotent Government: The Rise of the Total State and Total War*, Yale University Press, New Haven, Conn., 1944, p. 145.

[14] Shirer, *op. cit.*, p. 345.

obliterate the differences among individuals and make them equal. The state should recognize the validity of the principle of inequality and provide an organizational structure to accord with it. The proper *Volk* structure is, therefore, hierarchical. Its ideal is military organization, which clearly distinguishes among the various ranks and assigns duties and power accordingly. The two main components of the *Volk* are the ruling class and the masses who follow their lead. The masses lack the capacity to reason and must rely upon the "herd instinct," which marks the limits of their ability. This instinct—the masses' substitute for intelligence—is a trustworthy guide and is sufficient for their needs. The necessary intelligence for leadership is supplied by an elite class which naturally emerges from the competitive struggle for survival.

Over both the elite group and the masses stands the Leader or *Fuehrer*. In national socialist, as in fascist, doctrine, the Leader occupies more than a functional position. Hitler disdained the titles of President and Chancellor because of their functional connotations. He preferred *Der Fuehrer* because it meant the total power of leadership. The leader, in his view, was much more than a representative of the people. In some mystic manner, the Leader incorporated into his own being all the attributes of the racial existence of the *Volk*. The Leader speaks *for* the people; he also speaks *as* the people. According to this theory, the "actual people" are to be distinguished from the "true people." The former are the people as they are, ignorant, selfish, and incapable of acting in such a manner as to serve the general interest. The "true people" are the people as they would be if they always judged and acted properly. The Leader is the incarnation of the "true people." He always represents their authentic voice. He is representative of the general will. The Leader is the master of the party and the directing force of government. He makes and judges law. His is the supreme executive, legislative, and judicial power.[15]

There was small difference between the national socialist theory of leadership and governmental practice in the Third Reich. The Enabling Act of March 24, 1933, renewed by a rubber-stamp Reichstag every four years, gave Hitler the power to rule by decree and suspended the rights guaranteed by the Weimar Constitution. Although certain individuals aside from Hitler exercised considerable authority, they were completely responsible to him. The will of the *Fuehrer* was the law of the land. The Nazis experienced brief difficulty with the judiciary, some members of which resisted the supplanting of the established law by national socialist ideology and the decrees of the dictator. Such "unreliable" elements were soon purged. In addition, the regular court system was augmented by the establishment of a number of special judicial bodies controlled by regular party members. These bodies tried most political cases and applied the

[15] William Ebenstein, *The Nazi State*, Holt, Rinehart and Winston, Inc., New York, 1943, pp. 14–20.

appropriate ideological principles. The Gestapo (Secret State Police) was a law unto itself. Its actions were not subject to review by the courts, and its responsibility was solely to Hitler and his subordinates.

Both Hitler and Mussolini shared Lenin's views on the necessity of developing an elite party consisting of dedicated professionals ready and willing to utilize force in order to gain power. Both scorned the idea that the masses had the ability to understand the intricacies of the problems that plagued the state. In his *Mein Kampf,* Hitler returned often to the subject of propaganda as a device with which the support of the masses could be secured and retained. The leader, he says, must be able to move the masses. To do this he must avoid complexities and rely upon a popular appeal that may be understood by those of the lowest intelligence.

> All propaganda must be popular and its intellectual level must be adjusted to the most limited intelligence among those it is addressed to. Consequently, the greater the mass it is intended to reach, the lower its purely intellectual level will have to be.[16]

Simplicity, repetition, and limitation are the principles to be followed for a successful propaganda program.

> The receptivity of the great masses is very limited, their intelligence is small, but their power of forgetting is enormous. In consequence of these facts, all effective propaganda must be limited to a very few points and must harp on these in slogans until the last member of the public understands what you want him to understand by your slogan. As soon as you sacrifice this slogan and try to be many-sided, the effect will piddle away, for the crowd can neither digest nor retain the material offered. In this way the result is weakened and in the end entirely cancelled out.[17]

Leadership, says Hitler, has nothing to do with the formulation of ideas. The leader is the person who understands how to *impart* ideas to the masses. He is a psychologist and an organizer. He defines goals and moves the masses toward them. Despite the obvious contempt with which Hitler and Mussolini regarded the masses, both fascism and national socialism enjoyed mass support. Many in Italy and Germany opposed the dictatorships of those countries, but until it became apparent that both of them were headed for disaster, the two regimes were popular. The undoubted fact of their appeal is disillusioning and must be accounted for by those who believe that the great majority of men are democratically inclined and are innately opposed to all forms of tyranny.

---

[16] Adolph Hitler, *Mein Kampf* (translated by Ralph Manheim), Houghton Mifflin Company, Boston, 1940, p. 180. Subsequent quotations from and references to *Mein Kampf* are from this edition.

[17] *Ibid.,* p. 234.

Expansionism in Fascism and National Socialism

One of the dreams of Mussolini was the reestablishment of the Roman Empire. Although it is unlikely that the majority of Italians accepted seriously the Duce's pronouncements that the restoration of the Empire would actually be achieved, there was a psychological appeal in the idea. The national pride, injured by the disappointments that followed World War I, could be salved by references to territorial expansion and the force required to accomplish it. In his *The Doctrine of Fascism*, Mussolini provided ideological support for a policy of imperialism.

> The Fascist State is a will to power and to government. In it the tradition of Rome is an idea that has force. In the doctrine of Fascism, Empire is not only a territorial, military, or mercantile expression, but spiritual or moral. One can think of an empire, that is to say a nation that directly or indirectly leads other nations, without needing to conquer a single square kilometre of territory. For Fascism the tendency to empire, that is to say, to the expansion of nations, is a manifestation of vitality; its opposite, staying at home, is a sign of decadence: people who rise or re-rise are imperialist, peoples who die are renunciatory. Fascism is the doctrine that is most fitted to represent the aims, the states of mind, of a people, like the Italian people, rising again after many centuries of abandonment or slavery to foreigners.[18]

The national socialist doctrine of expansionism was an amalgam of the theory of "geopolitics," [19] as developed by Karl Haushofer, and the doctrine of racial supremacy. Haushofer's work was an adaptation of the "Heartland" theory of the British geographer Sir Halford Mackinder. Mackinder, in 1905, had written that the nation which controlled the Heartland, the center of the Euro-Asian land mass, could control the world and that control of the Heartland depended, in turn, upon domination over Eastern Europe. Haushofer used the Mackinder thesis to support a resurgence of the very old Germanic idea of expansion into the East. Germany, he said, lacks living space (*Lebensraum*). It needs additional territory in order to become self-sufficient. It should take it in the East, and by force.

Haushofer did not suggest that Russia should be the victim of German expansionism. Expansion, he assumed, would stop short of Russia's borders and indeed would require an understanding with that country. Hitler was not so cautious. In his *Mein Kampf* he attacked what he regarded as the misguided policy of the Hohenzollerns in attempting to secure colonies in Africa. German expansion should be to the East, he said, and mainly at Russian expense. The fact that the territory upon

[18] Oakeshott, *op. cit.*, p. 178.
[19] The term originated with the Swedish geographer Rudolf Kjellen (1864–1922).

which Hitler cast a covetous eye was already occupied was no deterrent. The Germans were a superior people. They required more living space. They needed a subject people to serve them and greater areas from which to draw sustenance. The fertile plains of the East could provide them with the latter. The Slavs, an inferior and degenerate race, were natural slaves.

Under the Nazis the study of geopolitics became an integral part of the school curriculum. Schoolchildren were taught that since Germans had extended the blessings of culture throughout Europe, Germany had a right to extend its control to all those areas which were marked with the German cultural influence. Moreover, it was held, Germany is wherever Germans are. On the basis of these views, Hitler and the Nazis had no difficulty in justifying a policy of expansion by force, although, admittedly, in the beginning little force was required. Governmental leaders in Western Europe were not entirely unsympathetic to a German foreign policy which would, they hoped, satisfy its expansionist ambitions at the expense of the Soviet Union.

The Totalitarian State

Both Hitler and Mussolini sought and achieved absolute control of the state to prepare it for a policy of imperialist expansion. Such a goal required a high degree of national unity and cohesiveness. Both fascism and national socialism directed their energies toward the elimination of internal conflict and division. Particularism, the party leaders understood, dissipates national strength. This knowledge, of course, is not confined to dictators. Democratic leaders, too, are aware of the dangers of factionalism and strive to modify its effects. But since they know that factionalism cannot be eradicated without the loss of freedom for groups and individuals, they are compelled to weigh the advantages of unity, achieved by authority, against the disadvantages of the loss of liberty. In short liberty is, in democratic theory, a value in and of itself, and while an excess of liberty may create the dangers that are a concomitant of factionalism, liberty cannot be sacrificed merely to avoid all factionalism.

Fascism and national socialism were confronted with no such problem. Liberty, in these ideologies, has no value. Since it gives rise to particularism it must be destroyed, by increasing the power of the state and making it more pervasive. Specific areas of activity need not be reserved from state control as they are in democracies. The individual and all his activities must be totally absorbed by the state and regulated by government. All political institutions that reflect particular interests must be replaced by those that represent only the national interest. Education, religion, business, labor, entertainment, the press, all must be subjected to governmental control. Because the existence of two or more political parties implies differences of opinion on matters of public policy, all parties

except one must be eliminated. The youth of the nation must be indoc-
trinated in the "truth" and brought up to give unquestioning obedience
to the commands of leader and party. In Mussolini's time, placards in
schoolrooms conspicuously proclaimed that "Mussolini is always right."

In totalitarian dictatorship no area of individual interest or activity
is immune from the pervasive power of the state, a power which is itself
absolute. In this system the ruler is not responsible to those whom he
rules. He may, and generally will, seek their approval for what he does,
but only because he understands that as a practical matter his own position is rendered more tenable by such a policy. He knows that he can
more easily persuade than coerce, although he will not hesitate to use
coercion when he believes it necessary. Totalitarian dictatorship, however, differs from the autocracies of the past in that it seeks and obtains
mass support for its position and its policies. Totalitarian dictatorship
denies the validity of the democratic principle that ruler and ruled alike
are subject to the law. The dictator is the ultimate source of the law; he
is unrestrained by it. And he does not share his power with others in the
sense that those others can restrain him.

Friedrich and Brzezinski point to six basic features common to all
totalitarian regimes, whether they are of the right or the left. All follow
the principle of the single party, controlled by the dictator. All employ
a system of police control that relies upon the use of terror and secrecy
and utilizes modern scientific techniques in achieving its end, which is
absolute obedience to authority. All feature an ideology that gives purpose and meaning to the regime and its policies. Because of the mass
nature of totalitarianism, the authorities exercise complete control of the
various media of communications. The "means of effective armed combat" are also controlled on a monopolistic basis by the authorities.
Finally, the national economy is regarded as an arm of the state and
controlled and directed by the state.[20] The Fascists in Italy made a thinly
veiled attempt to disguise the state's control of the economy by creating
the "corporate state." This device ostensibly placed industries under the
joint control of owners and workers and presumably refuted the Marxist
dictum that there was an inherent and unavoidable conflict between
these two classes. Overtones of syndicalism and guild socialism were
evident in the plan. But the scheme was only theoretical, for the workers
in fact exercised no control over the "corporations" with which they were
associated. Owners in both Italy and Germany were permitted to profit
from the operations of their enterprises, but the state, which was always
either preparing for or waging war, directed those operations absolutely.
In the Soviet Union, a totalitarian state of the left, industry is state-
owned, and labor unions are controlled by the Communist party.

[20] Carl J. Friedrich and Zbigniew K. Brzezinski, *Totalitarian Dictatorship and Autocracy*, Harvard University Press, Cambridge, Mass., 1956, pp. 9–10.

Conclusions

The world has always been subject to the process of change. It is in the increasing tempo of change that the nineteenth and twentieth centuries differ from the past. In feudal times, things altered so slowly that men could detect no change at all. The beginning of the industrial revolution and its rapid acceleration, more apparent today than ever before, brought an entirely different condition. In a relatively brief span of time the Western world became a predominantly urban rather than a predominantly rural civilization. A new economic system was established, capable of producing large quantities of goods but subject to a dangerous instability. Education on a massive scale informed men; it also increased their tendency to criticize and led to the collapse of traditions which had helped to preserve a stable society. Technology brought a revolutionary transformation in methods of communication and facilitated the rapid spread of ideas. Whether or not change of such magnitude constitutes progress is open to debate. What is not debatable is the fact that this is the way things are and that we cannot return to the simpler existence of the past.

Life in the modern world is one of enormous complexity. Individuals are confronted with a staggering array of problems with which their ancestors were completely unacquainted. New and difficult problems arise every day. A great many of them cannot be solved by men in their capacity as individuals, and perhaps the outstanding sociopolitical phenomenon of the twentieth century is the growth of government, which has been designated as the agency through which problems are solved. This phenomenon has not been confined to authoritarian and totalitarian regimes. Even the governments of the most democratic nations have increased greatly in authority and in the scope of their activity. Still, democracies have insisted upon reserving specified areas of freedom from the pervasive authority of government, and in many things there is in fact greater liberty for the individual in a democracy today than ever before. The freedoms of religion, association, speech, and press, for example, are sometimes threatened in democracies, but on the whole they have been safeguarded and expanded. And the matter of equality has been treated with increasing concern; much has been done in recent years to assure that more than lip service is paid to that principle.

All these efforts mean that thus far democracies have been able, after a fashion, to solve their most pressing problems and remain viable as governmental systems. There is no guarantee that they can always do so. The problems remain and are constantly increased in numbers and complexity. They cannot be solved in a manner acceptable to everyone, and democratic governments, which by their nature must permit a considerable degree of factionalism in the interest of liberty, are obliged to take longer in the search for solutions than absolute governments that do not permit faction. The concern of a democracy to hear all sides of a controversial issue and to arrive at an answer that will satisfy a majority without outraging the minority is often viewed as a mark of weakness and indecision. There are always demagogues anxious to attack democracy on this ground and to offer their own solutions, which are often appealing in their deceptive simplicity. They are deceptive precisely because they are simple. The wise man understands that complex problems do not lend themselves to simple solutions. In fact, circumstances often do not permit a satisfactory solution at all, and it may well be that men must adjust themselves to living with these problems as best they can.

This answer fails to satisfy many. Men want their problems solved. If their situation is unsatisfactory or even worse, and if they are insufficiently informed with regard to the difficulties involved in finding satisfactory answers to their questions, they are likely to be susceptible to the blandishments of the demagogues who offer a world in which the terrible burden of making decisions is transferred from the individual to the leader. Such was, in part, the appeal of fascism and national socialism. There were other and important aspects of that appeal. Fascism and national socialism offered scapegoats to the troubled people. The Communists or the Jews, they alleged, were responsible for the evil conditions that prevail. Eliminate them and all others who are different, and the community will once more exist in harmony. Minority groups, particularly those of another race, should be eliminated or enslaved, and such action is justified by the fact that it serves the interest of a superior race.

The regimes of Hitler and Mussolini have been destroyed. The fundamentals of the doctrine that supported them remain. They are as old as man himself and will undoubtedly accompany him through history. The regimes of the future that utilize the principles will be known by other names, but they will be easily recognizable. Groups other than Jews or Communists may serve as scapegoats of the future. The "superior" race may be something other than Aryan. But we shall see again the simple solution, the elite party, the dictator, the restrictions upon liberty "for the good of the people," and the use of force to compel conformity. And there will be considerable support from a great many who, as in the past, will be happy to shift responsibility to the eager hands of a dictator.

SELECTED BIBLIOGRAPHY

Coker, Francis W.: *Recent Political Thought,* Appleton-Century-Crofts, Inc., New York, 1934, chaps. 16, 17.

Ebenstein, William: *Fascist Italy,* American Book Company, New York, 1939.

————: *Modern Political Thought: The Great Issues,* 2d ed., Holt, Rinehart and Winston, Inc., New York, 1960, chap. 8.

————: *The Nazi State,* Holt, Rinehart and Winston, Inc., New York, 1943.

Friedrich, Carl J., and Zbigniew K. Brzezinski: *Totalitarian Dictatorship and Autocracy,* Harvard University Press, Cambridge, Mass., 1956.

Hallowell, John H.: *Main Currents in Modern Political Thought,* Holt, Rinehart and Winston, New York, 1950, chaps. 15–17.

Hibbert, Christopher: *Il Duce: The Life of Benito Mussolini,* Little, Brown and Company, Boston, 1962.

Hitler, Adolph: *Mein Kampf* (translated by Ralph Manheim), Houghton Mifflin Company, Boston, 1940.

London, Kurt: *Backgrounds of Conflict: Ideas and Forms in World Politics,* The Macmillan Company, New York, 1945, chaps. 1–9.

Neuman, Franz: *Behemoth: The Structure and Practice of National Socialism,* Oxford University Press, Fair Lawn, N.J., 1942.

Oakeshott, Michael: *The Social and Political Doctrines of Contemporary Europe,* The Macmillan Company, New York, 1944, chaps. 4, 5.

Sabine, George H.: *A History of Political Theory,* 3d ed., Holt, Rinehart and Winston, Inc., New York, 1961, chap. 35.

Schuman, Frederick L.: *The Nazi Dictatorship: A Study in Social Pathology and the Politics of Fascism,* Alfred A. Knopf, Inc., New York, 1935.

Shirer, William L.: *The Rise and Fall of the Third Reich: A History of Nazi Germany,* Fawcett Publications, Inc., Greenwich Conn., 1960.

Von Mises, Ludwig: *Omnipotent Government: The Rise of the Total State and Total War,* Yale University Press, New Haven, Conn., 1944.

INDEX